The Devil's Final Battle

How Rejection of the Fatima Prophecies
Imminently Threatens the Church and the World
and
What You Can Do About It to
Protect Yourself and Your Family.

Compiled and Edited by

Father Paul Kramer, B.Ph., M.Div., S.T.L. (Cand.)
and the editorial staff of The Missionary Association

"In the Third Secret (of Fatima) it is foretold, among other things, that the great apostasy in the Church will begin at the top."
... *Cardinal Mario Luigi Ciappi*

The Missionary Association
Terryville, Connecticut

First Edition 2002
Second Edition 2010 (revised and updated)

Library of Congress Catalogue Card Number: 2009933148

ISBN 978-0-9787934-2-5

Please direct any correspondence expressing your concerns, questions or comments about *The Devil's Final Battle* to the publisher at one of the following addresses:

Missionary Association
Editorial Offices:
   Suite 1
   1107 William Street
   Buffalo, New York
   14206

Distributed by:
   St. Joseph's Books
   2711 Elmwood Avenue
   Kenmore, New York
   14217

Ordering information:
The Missionary Association
1-800-954-8737 • www.devilsfinalbattle.com

Visit the website for more information related to this book.

Printed in Canada

This book is respectfully dedicated to
Our Lady of Fatima
and to all Cardinals, Patriarchs, bishops, priests,
religious and lay persons
who have dedicated themselves
in humility and love to Her service.

Abbreviations:

DFB	Kramer, Father Paul, *et al.*, *The Devil's Final Battle*.
Fourth Secret	Socci, Antonio, *Il Quarto Segreto di Fatima* [*The Fourth Secret of Fatima*] (Italian edition), *The Fourth Secret of Fatima* (English edition).
Last Visionary	Bertone, Cardinal Tarcisio, *L'Ultima Veggente di Fatima* [*The Last Visionary of Fatima*] (Italian edition), *The Last Secret of Fatima* (English edition).
TMF	Joseph Cardinal Ratzinger and Archbishop Tarcisio Bertone, SDB, *The Message of Fatima* (English edition).
WTAF, Vol. I	Michel de la Sainte Trinité (Frère), *Toute la vérité sur Fatima:* Tome I, *La science et les faits* (French edition); *The Whole Truth About Fatima,* Volume I, *Science and the Facts* (English edition).
WTAF, Vol. II	Michel de la Sainte Trinité (Frère), *Toute la vérité sur Fatima:* Tome II, *Le Secret et l'Église* (French edition); *The Whole Truth About Fatima,* Volume II, *The Secret and the Church* (English edition).
WTAF, Vol. III	Michel de la Sainte Trinité (Frère), *Toute la vérité sur Fatima:* Tome III, *Le Troisième Secret* (French edition); *The Whole Truth About Fatima,* Volume III, *The Third Secret* (English edition).

"Suppose, dear friend, that Communism [one of 'the errors of Russia' mentioned in the Message of Fatima] was only the most visible of the instruments of subversion to be used against the Church and the traditions of Divine Revelation ... I am worried by the Blessed Virgin's messages to Lucy of Fatima. **This persistence of Mary about the dangers which menace the Church is a divine warning against the suicide of altering the Faith, in Her *liturgy*, Her *theology* and Her *soul*....** I hear all around me innovators who wish to dismantle the Sacred Chapel, destroy the universal flame of the Church, reject Her ornaments and make Her feel remorse for Her historical past.... A day will come when the civilized world will deny its God, when the Church will doubt as Peter doubted. She will be tempted to believe that man has become God. In our churches, Christians will search in vain for the red lamp where God awaits them, like Mary Magdalene weeping before the empty tomb, they will ask, 'where have they taken Him?' "

> ... Cardinal Eugenio Pacelli (the future Pius XII) when he was Secretary of State to Pope Pius XI. Cited in the book *Pie XII Devant L'Histoire*, pp. 52-53.

"In the Third Secret it is foretold, among other things, that the great apostasy in the Church will begin *at the top*."

> ... Cardinal Mario Luigi Ciappi, personal papal theologian to Popes Pius XII, John XXIII, Paul VI, John Paul I and John Paul II, quoted in the journal *Catholic*, March 2002.

"It [the Third Secret] has nothing to do with Gorbachev. The Blessed Virgin was alerting us against apostasy in the Church."

> ... Cardinal Oddi, quoted March 17, 1990, in the journal *Il Sabato*.

"Through some crack the smoke of satan has entered into the Church of God."

... Pope Paul VI, papal address of June 30, 1972.

"We must admit realistically and with feelings of deep pain, that Christians today in large measure feel lost, confused, perplexed and even disappointed; ideas opposed to the truth which has been revealed and always taught are being scattered abroad in abundance; heresies, in the full and proper sense of the word, have been spread in the area of dogma and morals, creating doubts, confusions and rebellion; the liturgy has been tampered with; immersed in an intellectual and moral relativism and therefore in permissiveness, Christians are tempted by atheism, agnosticism, vaguely moral enlightenment and by a sociological Christianity devoid of defined dogmas or an objective morality."

... Pope John Paul II, quoted in *L'Osservatore Romano*, February 7, 1981.

"She [the Blessed Virgin Mary] told me that the devil is in the mood for engaging in a decisive battle against the Virgin. And a decisive battle is the final battle where one side will be victorious and the other side will suffer defeat. Also from now on we must choose sides. Either we are for God or we are for the devil. There is no other possibility."

... Sister Lucy of Fatima speaking to Father Fuentes, December 26, 1957.

"Not to oppose error is to approve it; and not to defend truth is to suppress it; and indeed to neglect to confound evil men, when we can do it, is no less a sin than to encourage them."

... Pope St. Felix III (483-492 A.D.)

"The Message of Fatima is addressed to every human being."

... Pope John Paul II, May 13, 1982.

Table of Contents

Contributors

Andrew Cesanek earned a B.S. degree in Electrical Engineering from the State University of New York at Buffalo and an M.S. degree in Electrical and Computer Engineering from the University of Massachusetts. He worked as a Software Engineer at Motorola for 15 years, before retiring from the engineering profession. He is now a full time researcher and writer for the Fatima Center.

Mark Fellows is a Catholic writer known for numerous articles in various Catholic journals including *The Remnant* and *Catholic Family News*. He is author of the books *The Ninth Pius* on the life of Blessed Pope Pius IX, *A Second Coming* on the Holy Shroud of Turin, *Fatima in Twilight*, and *Sister Lucia: Apostle of Mary's Immaculate Heart*.

Christopher Ferrara earned his Baccalaureate and Juris Doctor degrees from Fordham University. He is President and Chief Counsel of the American Catholic Lawyers Association. Mr. Ferrara has written extensively on Catholic issues. His articles have appeared in *The Latin Mass* and *The Remnant*, and other publications. He authored several books, including *The Secret Still Hidden*. He has translated into English Antonio Socci's book, *Il Quarto Segreto di Fatima*.

Father Nicholas Gruner, S.T.L., S.T.D. (Cand.) heads one of the world's largest Fatima apostolates with several offices around the globe. He lectures throughout North America and overseas on the subject of Fatima, and is publisher of *The Fatima Crusader* magazine. He also produced the television program "Fatima: 'The Moment Has Come'," the radio program "Heaven's Peace Plan". He is the principal author of the book *World Enslavement or Peace ... It's Up to the Pope*.

Father Gregory Hesse, S.T.D., J.C.D. (R.I.P.) was ordained in 1981 in St. Peter's Basilica. He held doctorates in both Thomistic theology and Canon Law. From 1986-1988 he served as the Secretary to Cardinal Stickler at the Vatican. From 1991 until his death in 2006, he worked in Austria, Germany and the United States giving lectures and producing theological articles that have appeared in *Catholic Family News*, *The Fatima Crusader*, and other journals.

Father Paul Kramer, B.Ph., S.T.B., M.Div., S.T.L. (Cand.) is lecturer and author of numerous articles on the Catholic Faith and on the subject of Fatima. Father Kramer received his B.Ph., S.T.B. from the Angelicum in Rome and his Master of Divinity at Holy Apostles College in Connecticut. He authored the book *The Theological Vindication of Roman Catholic Traditionalism* and the vastly updated edition of this book entitled *The Suicide of Altering the Faith in the Liturgy*.

John Vennari is writer, researcher, catechism instructor and editor of the monthly journal *Catholic Family News*. His articles have also appeared in publications such as *Christian Order* and *The Angelus*. He is author of the books *Close-ups of the Charismatic Movement* and *The Permanent Instruction of the Alta Vendita, a Blueprint for the Subversion of the Catholic Church*.

The Heart of the Matter

Would you be surprised to learn that the terrorist attacks of September 11, 2001, the sex scandals wracking the Catholic Church and the great economic collapse of 2007-2009 are profoundly related?

This relation becomes amazingly clear when the three events are viewed through the prism of the Message of Fatima. This Message is the key to understanding our present history and how our future will be determined—a future that promises either worldwide deep and lasting peace and prosperity, or death and destruction on a scale never before seen.

We have been given a choice—two paths to follow: one prescribed at Fatima by Heaven, and the other charted by human folly and demonic intelligence. The first will lead us to salvation, here and hereafter; the second, to untold suffering for all in the near future, and, for many now living, to suffer horribly for all eternity.

This latest edition of *The Devil's Final Battle* places this choice before us in the plainest and most compelling terms.

The Mother of God warned us when She came to Fatima, Portugal, over 90 years ago, in a series of apparitions authenticated by a public miracle without precedent in world history. Since that time, the published prophetic admonitions in the Message of Fatima are either being fulfilled in an ongoing manner or have already been fulfilled—save for one: "various nations will be annihilated". Our Lady of Fatima with great sadness warned that this would be one of the most terrible consequences of ignoring or despising Her requests.

The Fatima apparitions have been deemed authentic by a series of Popes and are now commemorated in the Roman Missal (the basic book of Catholic worship) by the decree of Pope John Paul II. And yet, in what must be seen as a mystery of iniquity, the Virgin's simple requests remain unfulfilled due to conscious decisions by some of the highest-ranking prelates in the Catholic Church. The result, just as She predicted, is an ever-deepening crisis in the Church and the world, accompanied by a growing sense, even among non-Catholics, that we are witnessing the beginning of an apocalypse.

Yet, Fatima remains the Only Solution that will deliver mankind—and each one of us—from the otherwise inevitable disaster NOW overtaking us.

The Fatima solution is opposed by various people. Some are what the enemies of Fatima would call "useful idiots", some are simply ignorant or else misinformed; but there is a hard core of very intelligent, very knowledgeable people who set themselves deliberately against Our Lady of Fatima and Her Peace Plan from Heaven.

Their opposition is as REAL as it is FOOLISH. Especially foolish for those present-day powerful prelates who oppose the Fatima peace plan because they have been warned by Our Lord Jesus Christ Himself that for their opposition they will reap misfortune for themselves similar to Louis XVI, the beheaded King of France.

The vision of the bishop in white and the other bishops being killed by a band of soldiers which the Vatican released on June 26, 2000 is the prophecy of the kind of deaths awaiting the Pope and Vatican prelates who still now obstruct obedience to the Message of Fatima. Thus it is also in charity for them, to help save them, that this book continues to be published.

Some readers might be tempted to think that such type of Vatican prelates can't really exist or be so stupid. That is why this book explains the various methods and motives of the opponents of Fatima, drawn from their own published words.

This book also teaches us that we are not mere spectators in this cosmic drama. We each have an essential role to play—one assigned to us by the Queen of Heaven Herself. *The Devil's Final Battle* shows us what must be done and what we can do to avert these looming disasters before they progress beyond all human remedy.

Since the first publication of this book, and largely because of it, events have taken place that have moved us significantly closer to the end of this crisis. Almost 200,000 copies of *The Devil's Final Battle* were put into circulation and its arguments convinced people in all walks of life that Fatima is our only way out.

This latest edition incorporates crucial developments during the past 7 years that demonstrate several breakthroughs for the forces of truth.

The facts in this book incontrovertibly prove that the Vatican apparatus— starting at least with the Secretary of State—continues to hide the essential elements of the Third Secret of Fatima while claiming all has been released; continues to refuse to obey Our Lady's and Our Lord's command that the Pope and the Catholic bishops together consecrate specifically Russia to the Immaculate Heart of Mary while pretending that they have already obeyed.

This two-fold <u>disobedience</u> and <u>deception</u> is causing graces from God to be withheld—and will lead to the certain "annihilation of nations" in the near future and, if God allows it, to the Great Apostasy and the Apocalypse of One World Government with One World Religion under the Antichrist.

The Mother of God came to earth with our present circumstances clearly in view, and with the solicitude of a mother, She offered us a way out—the way chosen by God Himself for our time. That being the case, one cannot understand the state of the Church and the world today without understanding what happened at Fatima.

In the fulfillment of the Message of Fatima lies the end of the crises in the world and the Church. In the denial of that Message lies, in great measure, the origin and intensification of both.

The events at Fatima represent a heavenly focal point in the battle now raging for the Church and the world. Both the crisis in the Church and the crisis in the world center on the divine truths summed up with heavenly concision in the Fatima apparitions.

One must also understand the strange and systematic effort by certain Catholic churchmen to obstruct fulfillment of the heavenly imperatives of the Fatima Message, including: the triumph of Our Lady, which will be seen in the consecration of Russia to the Immaculate Heart of Mary; the miraculous conversion of Russia to Catholicism; and the consequent period of deep, lasting world peace.

The central importance of Fatima in the scheme of current world events is only demonstrated by the recent, almost frantic, efforts of certain Vatican officials to "deconstruct" and "demythologize" Fatima. The pages that follow present evidence against the most prominent churchmen involved in this campaign against Fatima, laying at their feet a large portion of the responsibility for the ecclesial crisis and the world crisis we must all face.

This edition answers its critics and continues to place the objective MORAL responsibility on powerful prelates in the Vatican and other influential persons.

To those who might say that our undertaking to expose their campaign against Fatima is "scandalous," we can only reply with the words of the Virgin Herself: "If My requests are heeded, Russia will be converted, and there will be peace; if not, she will spread her errors throughout the world, causing wars and persecutions against the Church. The good will be martyred; the Holy Father will have much to suffer; various nations will be annihilated."

Russia has not converted. Russia's errors, including the holocaust of "legalized" abortion, have spread throughout the world. There is no peace. And today, even non-Catholics and unbelievers live in fear of the annihilation of nations. To echo the words of Pope St. Gregory the Great, it is better that scandal arise than that the truth be hidden—especially when, as in this case, the truth can avert global disaster.

We submit this work to the judgment of the Pope and to the judgment of you, the reader. We submit this work publicly because innumerable private entreaties to high Church authorities over the past four decades have all been unavailing. Meanwhile, the Vatican bureaucracy that surrounds the Pope continues to render him effectively incapable of responding to petitions from rank-and-file clergy and laity. As the decades-long episcopal cover-up of sexual scandals among the priesthood demonstrates, in present circumstances the public forum is the *only* forum open to Catholics who seek redress of just grievances affecting the whole Church.

Our motive in presenting this book is that of loyal sons and daughters of the Church, who know and love the Faith and believe in conscience that the course still being followed by certain Church leaders is gravely mistaken, as recent events in the Catholic Church should make clear to any objective observer.

If a reader thinks we have erred or committed any injustice in what we have written, it would be the reader's duty to offer us, not invective or empty denunciations, but legitimate correction based upon *facts*, for our own sake and the sake of the Church. But if the case we present is well-founded, then the reader has a different obligation to God, himself and his fellow man, namely: the duty to *act* upon the evidence we present—now, while there is still time.

As Sister Lucy (†2005), the last surviving seer of Fatima commenting on Our Lady's message, said:

> The devil is in the mood for engaging in a decisive battle against the Virgin. And a decisive battle is the final battle where one side will be victorious and the other side will suffer defeat. Also from now on we must choose sides. Either we are for God or we are for the devil. There is no other possibility.

Father Paul Kramer and the
Editorial Team of The Missionary Association
Christmas Day 2009

Foreword to the Second Edition

For the past half-century, a bizarre story has been unfolding inside the Catholic Church that could have serious implications for the entire world.

As this book explains, the crux of the story is a message from Heaven, and hence, a matter of faith and belief. This may make it seem to be of concern only to Catholics and Church officials, but there's more to this story than that—much more.

The message was conveyed in a manner that is unique in Church history, and its form and content are also unique. This puts it in a class by itself; it can't be relegated to the broad category of "private revelations" experienced by various Catholic saints and mystics over the centuries. If it could, non-Catholics and even many otherwise devout Catholics would be free to ignore it. But ignoring this particular message is impossible for Catholics, and may also be unwise for everyone else on this troubled planet.

The message in question was delivered by the Blessed Virgin Mary to three shepherd children near the little town of Fatima, Portugal, in 1917. Far from being a private event, its delivery was accompanied by a public miracle witnessed by 70,000 people, and reported in newspaper headlines around the world. No other apparitions, not even those associated with the world-famous shrines at Lourdes in France and Guadalupe in Mexico, have been authenticated in this spectacular manner. This sets the apparitions themselves apart from all previous events of this kind, but that is only one unique aspect of Fatima.

When the content of the message received by the children was revealed, it, too, was unique in the annals of Christianity. It contained requests, as well as a warning of punishments to come if the requests were not granted. Never before has a message of this kind been reported, either in public or in private, by any witnesses to an apparition.

As it does in all cases of this kind, the Vatican subjected the Fatima events to intense scrutiny. The Church is usually reluctant to endorse such things, as they are often quite subjective, and difficult to verify. In the case of Fatima, however, the Catholic hierarchy, from the local bishops of Portugal to a series of Popes in the Vatican, has unanimously regarded the Fatima apparitions as "worthy of belief." Pope John Paul II went so far as to say that the Message of Fatima "imposes an obligation" on the Church. This uniform hierarchical approbation over the years strongly reinforced the conviction of the Catholic faithful that the Fatima apparitions had conveyed an authentic message from Heaven.

But then, on June 26, 2000, the Fatima story took a strange turn. On that day, the Cardinal in charge of Catholic doctrine at the Vatican and his immediate subordinate held a press conference which the *Los*

Angeles Times described as an attempt at "gently debunking the cult of Fatima." The theme of the conference was that the Fatima prophecies are in the category of "private revelations" and that, in any event, they "belong to the past."

What happened? How did the Fatima apparitions go from being officially declared worthy of belief to being officially "debunked" by a high-ranking Cardinal? And what about the message, with its imperative requests and its threat of punishment? These are questions any reasonable Catholic might well ask, given the strange behavior of Church leaders on this matter. But once the content of the message is considered, they are also questions every human being on earth might ask.

The content of the Fatima Message is largely concerned with matters of the Catholic religion that lie entirely within the realm of faith and belief. One part of the message, however, has wider implications that warrant wider attention. This is the part that makes requests, and then warns of punishment if the requests are not granted.

The apex of all the requests is the request that Russia be consecrated to the Immaculate Heart of Mary by the Pope, together with all the Catholic bishops of the world. To those outside the Church, this ritual may have little meaning. Inside the Church, however, such ceremonies are a well-established tradition. Consecrations have a sanctifying effect, so in the eyes of Catholics, such a ceremony would be beneficial to Russia.

Of course, performing this ceremony is something only the Catholic Church can do. However, the threat that accompanies the request extends well beyond the Catholic Church. If the consecration is done, says the message, "a period of peace will be granted to the world." But if it is not done, the message warns, then, among other things, "various nations will be annihilated."

Is this a credible threat? Should non-Catholics and non-Christians worry about such a thing? At first glance, one might think not, but the question deserves closer examination. It isn't necessary to believe this message definitely came from Heaven to give it some serious consideration. This is what gives Fatima its global dimension.

Since the Vatican judged the apparitions believable, and the annihilation of nations may be at stake, one would think the consecration would have been performed long ago. After all, what it requires is a simple, traditional ceremony that obviously can do no harm to anyone. And if the message has even the remotest chance of being authentic, the benefit of performing the ceremony as requested could be of incalculable value. Given these circumstances, even the most skeptical of outsiders might well consider the consecration "worth a try."

And yet, for reasons known only to a small group of Vatican officials, the Fatima request has not been granted, even though the Church has been aware of it for at least seven decades. Time and time again, various formal consecrations have been performed, including one that named Russia explicitly, but in all cases they have avoided fulfilling the specific requirements of the Fatima request: that the Pope and the Catholic bishops of the world consecrate Russia, by name, in a solemn public ceremony. The most recent example was a consecration of the world in Rome by Pope John Paul II and 1,500 visiting bishops on October 8, 2000. Many people thought the Pope might take that opportunity to fulfill the Fatima request, but to their disappointment, Russia was not mentioned.

To both insiders and outsiders, the Vatican's treatment of this matter seems strangely inconsistent with its own standards and traditions. It also seems to show a reckless disregard for the safety not only of the Catholic faithful, but the rest of humanity as well. If the Fatima threat is genuine, the price of the Vatican's reluctance could be very high indeed—and it would be paid by all mankind.

Under these circumstances, any reasonable person might ask why the Church persists in ignoring the message, and risking such catastrophic consequences.

How and why this is happening is the subject of this book. The story it tells involves a mixture of verifiable facts as well as facts known by faith alone. For non-believers, the facts may not prove conclusively that the message is authentic, but they go a long way in that direction—far enough to persuade many open-minded people to regard authenticity as a real possibility. And for those who share the Catholic Faith, the facts go much further, affirming authenticity and raising alarming questions about the state of the Church hierarchy today.

The story shows the Vatican undergoing a series of changes that caused it first to endorse Fatima, then to cast doubt on it, then to suppress it, and finally to discard it altogether. Tracing this process is difficult, as much of what happens in the Vatican is done in secret, and official attitudes must be decoded from pronouncements that are often cryptic.

No one can see into the hearts and minds of the Vatican officials who have treated the Fatima Message with such contempt. They can only be judged by their actions, and by the logical consequences of their avowed positions. When these are analyzed, as they are in this book, a disturbing picture emerges of a Church divided against Herself, with the rift going right to the top.

There is an ironic aspect to this story that will not be lost on unbelievers. The facts related in this book will convince many open-minded non-Catholics that the authenticity of Fatima is at least possible. If this can be said of outsiders, how much more convincing should the story be for Catholics? And yet, even as the story moves unbelievers towards belief, it seems to have the opposite effect on certain Vatican officials. Ironically, some of the people now least likely to believe in Fatima are among those who should be the most likely. Beliefs once central to the Catholic Faith are now being abandoned—not by the faithful who remain in the pews, but by some of the highest authorities in the Church.

A further irony concerns the position of the late Pope John Paul II in this matter. Like all his predecessors since the Fatima apparitions occurred, John Paul II had openly and repeatedly professed his belief in the authenticity of the apparitions. He had visited the Fatima shrine three times, and attributed his survival of an assassination attempt in 1981 to Our Lady of Fatima. And yet, even the Pope seemed powerless to prevent his own highest-ranking Cardinals from taking a very different view of Fatima. He was not present at the June 2000 press conference mentioned above, where two of the Vatican's top officials undermined the credibility of the Fatima prophecies and relegated them to the past.

As several chapters in this book explain, the Message of Fatima also has political implications that may have influenced the way Vatican officials have handled it. The message asks for the consecration of Russia specifically, in order to convert that nation to Catholicism. To perform a ceremony with that overt intention runs counter to the so-called "Ostpolitik" the Vatican adopted first with regard to international communism, and more recently to the Russian Orthodox Church. In both these areas, the Vatican apparatus has abandoned the Church's traditionally militant defense of Her teaching, agreeing to refrain from denouncing communism as evil, and to cease seeking the conversion of Russian Orthodox adherents. Hence, the Fatima Message has been and still is "politically incorrect" in the context of current Vatican policy.

One might suspect that the Vatican is refraining from consecrating Russia simply for these political reasons. But is that really credible? Given what is at stake, would the Vatican really risk the annihilation of nations just to avoid a diplomatic incident with the Russians? Would Russia really be seriously offended by a ceremony that, in effect, commends that country to the care of the Mother of God? And even if Russia were offended, what would they do about it? What could they possibly do that would be worse than the penalty for not consecrating Russia, namely, that "various nations will be annihilated"?

This book reveals and examines the political machinations that have clearly influenced attitudes towards Fatima among some high-level Vatican diplomats. There can be little doubt that the architects of the Vatican's conciliatory "Ostpolitik" find the Fatima Message inconvenient. But it still seems unlikely that these diplomatic considerations alone could persuade the Vatican to ignore a message from Heaven. For that to happen, something else must be at work, something deeper and darker than worldly politics.

That deeper and darker ailment is the ultimate subject of this book: The Catholic Church has been transformed in ways that have left many of the faithful confused, while outsiders see a church maintaining an appearance of normal function that only masks the radical transformation behind it.

Viewed from afar, the Catholic Church appears to be an institution that changes only slowly and reluctantly. The process of reform initiated by Vatican II in the 1960s led to unprecedented changes in the Church (e.g., vernacular Masses, abandonment of distinctive clerical garb, etc.) that may have seemed dramatic to insiders. But to outsiders, comparing the Church to secular trends in the latter half of the 20th Century, the Church still seemed resistant to change, maintaining Her teaching on such things as priestly celibacy, ordination of women, contraception, divorce and abortion. In all these respects, the Church still seems firmly entrenched in positions She has maintained for two thousand years.

But does this mean that Vatican leadership is resolutely traditionalist? Outsiders who rely on such things as the Pope's public utterances might well think so. But as this book explains, insiders know better. The Catholic Church today is not what She seems, and the gap between public perceptions and actual realities is at the heart of the Fatima controversy. And while traditions have been officially upheld in certain respects, they have been abandoned or undermined in others. And while the positions still being maintained have been widely publicized, those being abandoned or undermined have been barely acknowledged. Catholics who once shared a common set of beliefs around the world now find themselves drifting in different directions in different places, following contradictory and uncertain leadership at all levels.

Even John Paul II's successor, Benedict XVI (whose role in the Fatima controversy as the former Cardinal Joseph Ratzinger will be mentioned on these pages) has recognized the crisis involved in this inconsistent affirmation of Catholic Tradition, which is upheld officially in certain respects, but abandoned or undermined in others. The crisis has prompted Benedict to declare in a historic papal document of July 7, 2007 that the traditional Latin Mass of the Church was "never abrogated" and that all priests are free to offer it, and to call in general for a "hermeneutic of continuity" to address the perception of a "rupture" with the Church's own past—two astonishing prescriptions that only confirm the existence of the deeper and darker ailment diagnosed in the first edition of this book, from which the Church continues to suffer as this second edition makes its appearance. The famously monolithic Catholic Church is no longer monolithic at all; its human element is full of fractures that this book traces to their sources, revealing a fragmented Church leadership where the first fissure divides a Pope who is an ardent (if conflicted) believer from his own immediate subordinates, some of whom are anything but.

The actions of four high-ranking Vatican officials were examined closely in the first edition of this book, all of whom are no longer in the positions they once occupied: Cardinal Ratzinger, of course, who is now the Pope; Cardinal Angelo Sodano, who is no longer Vatican Secretary of State, having been retired in 2006; and Cardinal Darion Castrillón

Hoyos, who no longer serves as Prefect of the Congregation for the Clergy, having been replaced by Cardinal Claudio Hummes in 2006. Only the fourth Vatican prelate, former Archbishop Tarcisio Bertone, remains a key player on the Fatima stage, along with the Pope himself. Formerly Secretary of the Congregation for the Doctrine of the Faith under Cardinal Ratzinger, Bertone has been elevated to the rank of Cardinal and has succeeded Sodano as Vatican Secretary of State. In that capacity Bertone has become the leading protagonist in the Fatima drama, having assumed the responsibility for perpetuating what this book describes as the Secretary of State's ecumenical and diplomatic "Party Line" on the Message of Fatima and the Third Secret in particular.

The second edition of this book continues to document amply the role of all four prelates in attempting to "close the book" on Fatima as a politically incorrect expression of traditional Catholic belief. While it is impossible to be certain about their individual motivations, it is also impossible to avoid the conclusion that what they have done has contributed to the current crisis of faith and discipline in the Church. Nevertheless, major changes in the *dramatis personae* and the new pontificate of Benedict XVI have prompted, in this second edition, certain adjustments of the book's approach to the grave problem it addresses, adjustments that will be readily apparent to readers of the first edition.

This second edition also takes account of major developments in the Fatima "case" that began in November of 2006 with the publication of a book by Antonio Socci, a renowned Catholic intellectual, acquaintance and one-time collaborator of both Cardinal Bertone and the former Cardinal Ratzinger. Socci's book, *The Fourth Secret of Fatima*, recounts how he had set out to prove the "Fatimists" wrong in their contention that the Vatican apparatus (now led by Bertone and his Secretariat of State) has withheld a text of the Third Secret that explains the enigmatic vision of the "Bishop dressed in white." After studying the first edition of this book, Socci discovered that the "Fatimists" were right, and that it "is certain" that a text involving something "unspeakable" has been concealed—a text that, as Socci writes, contains "the words of the Madonna [which] preannounce an apocalyptic crisis of the faith in the Church starting at the summit" and "also an explanation of the vision... (revealed on June 26, 2000)."[1] The Fatima "case" was cracked wide open when Socci's conclusion was confirmed by the admission of a still-living eyewitness, Archbishop Loris F. Capovilla, the personal secretary of Pope John XXIII, that there are indeed two texts and two envelopes pertaining to the Third Secret, one of which ("the Capovilla envelope" as he calls it) has never been produced. Socci's publication of this testimony in his book was a bombshell dropped on the edifice of the "official account," which promptly collapsed in a series of self-defeating personal publicity

---

[1] Antonio Socci, *Il Quarto Segreto di Fatima* [*The Fourth Secret of Fatima*] (Milan: Rai and Eri Rizzoli, 2006), English ed., p. 74; popular ed., p. 55; Italian ed., p. 82.

initiatives by Cardinal Bertone, but with no official Vatican response to Socci. These developments, which have radically altered the landscape since the first edition, are fully recounted in Chapter 14.

The problem confronting the Church, however, remains the same. It is still very much the case that in the post-Vatican II epoch, beliefs once shared by virtually all Catholics have now been marginalized, and reduced *de facto* to cult status. Principal among these are beliefs in apparitions, miracles and prophecies. Over the centuries, the Catholic Church has raised to the rank of sainthood many hundreds, each of whom was canonized on the basis of miracles performed through his or her intercession. Many of these same saints experienced apparitions of Christ or the Virgin Mary. Catholic tradition affirms belief in a dialogue between earth and Heaven, mediated by visionary saints, who are called forth as prophets of their time and who authenticate their prophecies with miracles. Far from upholding this long-standing aspect of Christian belief, certain of today's Vatican officials make a point of asserting that "private apparitions" can be disregarded as "not essential" to the faith—including the apparitions at Fatima, despite Fatima's warning of global catastrophe.

In general, the post-conciliar "updating" of the Catholic Church has left Catholic beliefs reduced to a shrunken core, and even that core is challenged at high levels. Widely-published (and openly heretical) "theologian" Hans Küng has received only a slap on the wrist for questioning such basic articles of faith as the resurrection and divinity of Christ.

The plain fact is that it is no longer possible to determine clearly what some top Vatican officials actually believe.

This may seem irrelevant to outsiders, and in some respects, it is. It might be of no concern to non-Catholics or non-Christians whether Catholics attend the traditional Latin Mass or a modern vernacular Mass, or whether they pray the Rosary. What a particular Cardinal thinks about matters of Catholic doctrine generally means nothing to outsiders. But what a leader of the Church thinks about apparitions, miracles and prophecies does matter. It matters because if even some of the Church's own leaders were to disbelieve the Fatima apparitions, disregard the Miracle of the Sun, and despise the prophecies in the Fatima Message, they could be putting the whole world at risk. But this contempt for Fatima is part and parcel of the contempt for certain elements of traditional Catholicism which has moved a clearly worried Pope Benedict to call for his extraordinary "hermeneutic of continuity." For the first time in Church history a Pope is calling upon the leadership of the Church to be in continuity with the Church's own traditions, as if that continuity had somehow been placed in doubt.

The collapse of traditional belief thus emerges as the most plausible explanation for the Church's otherwise inexplicable behavior with regard to Fatima. The traditional Catholic belief in apparitions, miracles and prophecies is at the heart of the Fatima story. Abandonment of belief in these things is what has transformed Fatima from something "worthy of belief" into a "cult" that some Church leaders seem intent on discrediting.

Outsiders might wish this was entirely an internal Catholic matter, but it isn't. One doesn't have to be a Catholic to wonder about God, and how God might choose to communicate with humanity. People who lack faith in any particular religion usually don't deny the existence of God, they simply don't know whether God exists. In that state of uncertainty, how can anything be ruled out? God might well choose to communicate with the human race through the Message of Fatima, however bizarre that may seem to many people. As the Bible wisely tells us, God's ways are not our ways.

The ultimate issue is therefore not simply what the Catholic Church believes, but what this might mean for humanity as a whole. This situation invites everyone, Catholic or not, Christian or not, to consider the possibility that the Fatima Message is authentic. Improbable as it may seem on the face of it, there are some persuasive pieces of evidence to support this idea. The Vatican's own exhaustive investigation found none of the inconsistencies, contradictions or discrepancies that often invalidate events of this kind. Instead, they found everything in order. They also acknowledged the unique nature of the Miracle of the Sun, an event witnessed by tens of thousands for which there is still no adequate scientific explanation.

When the content of the message was more widely publicized in the 1940s, further support for authenticity began to accumulate. The message contained a series of prophecies, many of which have come to pass as predicted. These include the end of World War I, the election of Pope Pius XI, the start of World War II, and the expansion of communist Russia. The evidence has proved sufficient to elicit the belief of seven successive Popes since the apparitions occurred, along with millions of Catholic faithful. It had also persuaded the Vatican, under John Paul II, to beatify in the year 2000 the two deceased witnesses to the apparitions, Francisco and Jacinta Marto, and to commemorate the Fatima apparitions in the Roman Missal, the official book of Catholic worship used by the Roman Catholic Church for the celebration of Mass.

Yet another Fatima prophecy, which has only been partially revealed, is the Third Secret of Fatima. Evidence outlined in this book points strongly to a prediction of serious problems in the leadership of the Church, problems that bear an uncanny resemblance to what is actually happening in the Church today.

Most Catholics have been stunned by the recent cascade of revelations of sexual abuse of children and teenagers by members of the clergy. Such a thing is completely unprecedented in Church history, even in medieval times, when many high-ranking prelates made a mockery of celibacy. In their search for an explanation for this appalling situation, both Catholics and others might well look to the still-unrevealed Third Secret.

This book provides good reasons to believe that the Third Secret predicts exactly what is happening now. Scandals in the clergy are the beginning of the chastisement promised if the consecration is not done. While the whole world will ultimately be punished, the penalty falls first on the Church Herself. The withering of the Catholic priesthood and its moral degeneracy are just the first signs of a calamity that will ultimately engulf the whole of mankind.

The fact that the Vatican officials examined in this book have gone to great lengths to put the Fatima question to rest while still concealing the text of the Third Secret strongly supports this interpretation. Clearly, these officials still have something to hide. Otherwise, why not publish the document in question, and why did they not allow Sister Lucia dos Santos, the only surviving witness to the apparitions, to testify to its authenticity prior to her death in February 2005?

When the whole story is told, it seems obvious that the real reason the Vatican won't perform the consecration is because doing so would affirm the authenticity of the Fatima Message. And doing that, in turn, would affirm the authenticity of the prophesied apostasy reaching even into the Vatican itself. Unbelieving officials are not about to indict themselves by heeding a message that points a finger at them. Instead, they have tried to bury the message, so as to avoid giving credence to that which the Vatican itself had earlier declared *worthy* of credence.

In virtually any other era in the history of the Church, members of the top echelon in the Vatican would have been foremost among believers in a message from Heaven delivered in such convincing fashion. They would have lost no time in heeding it, and complying with its request. With the confusion that has followed the Second Vatican Council, and the rapid advance of secularism into every institution, including the Church, over the past 40 years, such a message is now being given a hostile reception even by certain Vatican officials. In ignoring the message, these prelates place themselves not only outside the ranks of believers, but even outside the ranks of non-believers possessed of common sense, because they aren't even willing to give the message the benefit of the doubt on the reasonable assumption that it could be true.

The Bible offers an enlightening example in this regard. The Fourth Book of Kings (4 Kings 5:1-15, in some Bibles it is referred to as 2 Kings 5:1-15) tells the story of Naaman, the leader of the Syrian army, whose king sent him to the prophet Eliseus in Israel to seek a miraculous cure for his leprosy. Without actually meeting him, Eliseus sent Naaman instructions to bathe seven times in the river Jordan, in order to be cured. Naaman was indignant that Eliseus didn't come to administer his cure personally. Merely bathing in the Jordan, he felt, couldn't possibly be any better than bathing in any of Syria's fine rivers. Rejecting the prophet's instructions as trivial, Naaman prepared to depart, but his advisers dissuaded him. They argued that, if the prophet had asked him to perform some arduous feat to be cured, Naaman would have done it. So why not do the very mundane thing that had been asked instead? In effect, they said to him: Why not try it, since it's such a simple thing? Naaman agreed to give it a try on this basis, and sure enough, on his seventh washing in the Jordan, his leprosy disappeared.

There is a striking parallel between this miraculous biblical event and the attitude now being taken by the Vatican regarding the consecration of Russia. Like Naaman, Vatican officials seem unable to believe that something as simple as a consecration could deliver a benefit as momentous as genuine world peace. And they are so obdurate in their position that they won't even allow the remedy to be tried, despite repeated appeals over many decades from millions of the faithful, including thousands in the Catholic clergy.

To outsiders, it may seem incredible that a tiny group of highly-placed doubters can block an action so ardently desired by huge numbers of believers. To understand this, it is necessary to understand the structure of the Church, which is very different from a democracy. Bishops of the Catholic Church are not selected by the faithful, nor even by their peers. They are chosen by the Pope and consecrated by him or (more usually) by an existing bishop, and the power conferred on them by this consecration comes directly from God. Once consecrated, each bishop is ultimately answerable to God alone and, under God, owes obedience in Church matters to the Pope alone.

Given the temper of the times and the administrative style of Pope Benedict XVI, it seems the Pope will give no direct order to all the bishops unless there is a general consensus among them first of all.

What all this means is that it is ultimately up to the bishops of the Church, who number about 4,700, to agree voluntarily to do the consecration as requested. Given their wide powers over appointments, promotions and other privileges, it is easy for the small group in charge at the Vatican to prevent such a spontaneous agreement from ever emerging.

Today, it is obvious to everyone in the Catholic clergy that speaking out on Fatima is a one-way ticket to oblivion for any priest, bishop or even Cardinal. So most bishops are silent on the matter, regardless of what they actually think or believe. The same is true for priests, who are even more vulnerable to punishment for being "politically incorrect."

This book also mentions the repressive treatment of the "Fatima Priest," Father Nicholas Gruner, whose only "crime" is to have devoted himself (as he continues to do) to the promotion of the Fatima Message at great personal cost. The Vatican's efforts to silence him, which have even included the threat of excommunication, stand in sharp contrast to the lenient treatment of hundreds of other priests, and even bishops and Archbishops, who have been embroiled in allegations of sexual molestation of minors. The sorry state of the Catholic clergy today is epitomized by this contrast between the treatment of Father Gruner and that accorded to Catholic clergy who are actually guilty of serious crimes.

The Catholic Church has in its hands a remedy that might do something no one else knows how to do—bring peace to this endlessly war-torn world. Based on the compelling case presented in this book, those who are preventing this remedy from being tried have much to answer for. They owe both the Catholic faithful and the world an explanation for their conduct. Further, given its importance to the world at large, the cover-up of the Fatima Message is even more an occasion for public outrage than the episcopal cover-ups of priestly sexual misconduct that have been exposed in the year 2002 by the press.

Chapter 18 of this book offers some suggestions as to what individuals, both believers and non-believers, might do to persuade the leaders of the Catholic Church to act in both the Church's own best interest and that of the whole human race. As this book makes clear, both Catholics and non-Catholics have much to gain if the Message of Fatima is obeyed, and a great deal to lose if the Message continues to be ignored by the very men who are charged to follow its imperatives.

Editor's Note: Among the principal sources of this book are: "Are There Two Original Manuscripts on the Third Secret?", Andrew M. Cesanek (*The Fatima Crusader*, Issue 64, Spring 2000); "Cardinal Ratzinger's Third Secret", Father Gregory Hesse (*The Fatima Crusader*, Issue 66, Winter 2001); "Chronology of a Cover-up", Father Paul Kramer (published on www.fatima.org); "Freemasonry and the Subversion of the Church (the Alta Vendita)", John Vennari (Transcript of speech from Fatima Conference in Rome, October 2001); "It Doesn't Add Up", John Vennari (*The Fatima Crusader*, Issue 70, Spring 2002); "Let us Hear the Witness, for Heaven's Sake," Christopher Ferrara (*The Fatima Crusader*, Issue 70, Spring 2002); "Lucy and the Pirates", Mark Fellows (*The Fatima Crusader*, Issue 70, Spring 2002); "The Lying Press Conference of June 26, 2000", Father Paul Kramer (Transcript of speech from Fatima Conference in Rome, October 2001); "Our Lady of Fatima vs. the Desire to Destroy our Catholic Heritage", John Vennari (Transcript of speech, Fatima Rally Against Terrorism, New York, November 2001); "The 'Party Line' and its Relationship to Fatima", Father Paul Kramer (Transcript of speech from Fatima Conference in Rome, October 2001); "Pope John Paul II Gives Us the Key to the Real Third Secret," Father Nicholas Gruner (Three-part series, *The Fatima Crusader*, Issues 67-69); "The Stalinization of the Catholic Church" (Transcript of speech from Fatima Conference in Rome, October 2001); "The Third Secret," Father Nicholas Gruner (Transcript of speech from Fatima Conference in Rome, October 2001).

Introduction

A great injustice has been committed against the Catholic Church and the world at large. The perpetrators of this injustice are men who hold high offices in the Catholic hierarchy, in particular that element of the Vatican bureaucracy known as the Vatican Secretariat of State.

The victims of this injustice include you and your loved ones. The consequences of the injustice have already been catastrophic, and if those responsible are not turned from their current course very soon, the ultimate result will be nothing short of apocalyptic in its dimensions. Indeed, even non-Catholics and unbelievers have the sense today that the world is heading toward an apocalypse. The commission of this injustice is one of the principal reasons that this is so.

The subject matter of the injustice that concerns us is commonly known as the Message of Fatima. In 1917 the Mother of God consigned to three saintly children at Fatima, Portugal a message of utmost urgency for the Church and mankind—a message authenticated by an unprecedented public miracle predicted three months in advance and witnessed by 70,000 people; a message whose prophecies of future world events have thus far been fulfilled to the letter; a message pronounced worthy of belief by the highest authorities of the Catholic Church; a message whose authenticity is attested to by a succession of Popes up to and including Pope Benedict XVI.[2] Pope John Paul II even alluded repeatedly to the apocalyptic elements of the message.

The nature of the injustice is a systematic attempt—since the year 1960—to conceal, misrepresent and deny the authenticity of this message even as its alarming prophecies are being fulfilled before our very eyes.

Without presuming that the perpetrators are conscious enemies of the Church (although some of them may well be), based on the evidence it appears that the probable reason for the injustice is this: The perpetrators recognize that the contents of the Message of Fatima, as understood in the traditional Catholic sense, cannot coexist with decisions made since the Second Vatican Council (1962-65), decisions which they unswervingly carry out, to change the entire orientation

---

[2] As we will see, Benedict XVI has made statements which indicate a "reversal," at least in his own mind, of the forty-year-old "party line" on Fatima adopted by the Secretariat of State under Cardinals Villot (1969-79), Casaroli (1979-90), Sodano (1991-2006), and now Cardinal Bertone (September 15, 2006 - present) to which he himself once adhered as Cardinal Ratzinger, head of the Congregation for the Doctrine of the Faith. Now Pope, the former Cardinal Ratzinger no longer seems willing to relegate the triumph of the Immaculate Heart to the past according to the "party line," but rather now acknowledges that the triumph of the Immaculate Heart has yet to occur. This necessarily calls into question the assertion of the "party line" that Russia was consecrated to the Immaculate Heart of Mary more than 25 years ago in a Vatican ceremony which deliberately omitted any mention of Russia, for it can hardly be the case that the world would still be awaiting the promised Triumph a quarter of a century after the consecration that was to produce it.

of the Catholic Church. This change of orientation would convert (if it were possible) the Catholic Church from a divine institution that directs its earthly activity toward the eternal salvation of souls, to a mere co-participant with human organizations in the building up of a utopian world "brotherhood" between men of all religions or no religion at all.

This new orientation of the Church pursues a vision of the world as illusory as it is contrary to the Church's divine commission to make disciples of all nations, baptizing them in the name of the Father, the Son and the Holy Ghost. This new orientation is, in fact, the cherished goal of those organized forces which have been conspiring against the Church for nearly 300 years, and whose activities stand exposed and condemned in more papal pronouncements than have been issued on any other single subject in Church history.

This is not to say that the Church Herself would ever officially renounce Her divine commission to save souls, for this is impossible according to the promise of Our Lord concerning the survival of the Catholic Church on earth until the end of time. But it is undeniable that since the Second Vatican Council much of the human element of the Church has effectively ceased to pursue that commission for the sake of a modern, more politically correct, approach to the world. This astonishing development has caused the current Pope, Benedict XVI, to call for a "hermeneutic of continuity" to avoid a "rupture" with the Church's own past and to take other measures to attempt a restoration of the Church. These include the Pope's 'liberation' of the traditional Latin Mass for the benefit of all priests and faithful with his declaration *Summorum Pontificum*, already mentioned—contrary to the false impression, maintained for nearly forty years, that Pope Paul VI had "banned" its use without special permission. Yet the problem of the "new orientation" persists, and the damage to the Church and to Her mission in the world continues.

Given the promises of Our Lord and of Our Lady of Fatima, the end of this experiment and the full and complete restoration of the Catholic Church is inevitable; but until this happens, many souls are in danger of eternal condemnation and we will continue to witness the worst crisis in the Church's history—a crisis foretold, as we will demonstrate, by the Virgin of Fatima Herself.

Both direct and circumstantial evidence of the injustice indicate that it extends to the concealment of that part of the Message of Fatima which predicts precisely this attempt to change the orientation of the Church, and the ruinous consequences of that attempt. The hidden portion of the Message, commonly known as the Third Secret of Fatima, would thus be a heavenly indictment of decisions made and actions taken by the very men who have perpetrated this injustice.

The evidence shows that the injustice also extends to tampering with the last surviving witness to the Fatima Message, Sister Lucia dos Santos, until her death in 2005. Sister Lucy had been subjected to secret "interviews" and other forms of pressure in an effort to alter her unvarying testimony on the authentic content of the Message, which stands in the way of the perpetrators' pursuit of the new orientation of the Church.

This is the injustice, and this is the motive. Now it is our burden to prove both. We will endeavor to do so in the succeeding pages, using the published statements of the very persons who are accountable, the testimony of other witnesses, and a great deal of other evidence to make the case. And when we are done presenting the evidence, we shall ask you, the reader, to render a "verdict." Not a verdict in the legal sense, for we have no right to constitute ourselves an ecclesiastical court. We mean, rather, a verdict representing the conscientious belief of members of the faithful that good grounds exist to investigate and remedy the injustice we allege here.

We shall also ask you, therefore, for your assistance in giving this information to the Pope, in keeping with the God-given right of the faithful—infallibly defined by the First Vatican Council and guaranteed by Church law—to petition the Supreme Pontiff directly and immediately for the redress of just grievances in the Church. In making these requests we have in mind as well the teaching of Saint Thomas Aquinas, and the unanimous teaching of the Doctors and theologians of the Church, that "if the faith were endangered, a subject ought to rebuke his prelate even publicly."

In considering the evidence we are about to present, we ask you to keep one overarching principle in mind: As Saint Thomas teaches, against a fact there is no argument—*contra factum non argumentum est*. If a statement is contrary to fact, then no authority on earth can expect us to believe it. Thus, for example, if a high-ranking prelate in the Vatican were to issue a decree that Catholics must believe that the Eiffel Tower is located in Saint Peter's Square, that would not make it so, and we would be obliged to reject the decree. For the *fact* is that the Eiffel Tower is located in Paris, and there is no argument against that fact. Therefore, *no man, no matter what his authority, can demand that we believe something that is manifestly contrary to fact*.

As you shall see, however, the injustice involving Fatima is largely an attempt by certain men who enjoy high offices in the Church to impose upon Catholics an understanding of the Message of Fatima that is plainly contrary to fact—as, for example, the claim that a consecration of Russia to the Immaculate Heart of Mary can be accomplished by consecrating the world, while deliberately avoiding any mention of Russia.

As the Church Herself teaches (cf. Vatican I and John Paul II's encyclical *Fides et Ratio*), the faith does not conflict with reason. Catholics are not expected to suspend the use of their reason, their common sense, in order to be Catholics. That would not be faith, but blindness—the blindness of the Pharisees. And so it is with the Message of Fatima. No matter what certain prestigious prelates may claim, *the Church* does not require us to believe nonsense when it comes to what the Message really means. On the contrary, we must love the truth to be faithful to Jesus Christ.

We ask you, then, to use your *common sense*, to keep an open mind, to consider the evidence dispassionately, and then decide. Indeed, you *must* decide. For if the charge we have made is true, then what is at stake in this case is nothing less than the salvation of millions of souls (possibly including your own), the welfare of the Church and the survival of civilization itself in this age of humanity. For no other reason did the Mother of God deliver the Message of Fatima to our increasingly endangered world.

For More Information

To request free copies of the "Petition to the Supreme Pontiff" (on pages 331-337) or of the "Chronology of the Fatima Cover-up" (Appendix II, on pages 339-371) or of John Vennari's article "A World View Based on Fatima" (referred to in footnote 222) or of *A Law for One Man* by Christopher A. Ferrara (referred to in footnote 240) or of Cathy Pearson's article "Now Is the Time: Consecrating Russia Will Help, Not Harm, Catholic-Orthodox Dialogue" (referred to in footnotes 227 and 249) or to purchase more copies of this book for your family and friends, call us at (716) 871-1763 or write to us at the address below or send us an e-mail to:

devilsfinalbattle@westelcom.com

or visit our website at:

www.devilsfinalbattle.com

To download a free copy of the index to this book, visit our website as noted above.

Missionary Association
Editorial Offices: Distributed by:
    Suite 1   St. Joseph's Books
    1107 William Street   2711 Elmwood Avenue
    Buffalo, New York   Kenmore, New York 14217
    14206   (716) 871-1763

Chapter 1

The Message
and the Miracle

God does not waste miracles. Throughout salvation history—from Joshua, to Moses, to the twelve Apostles, to the saints of the Catholic Church down through the centuries—God has granted miracles for one overriding purpose: to serve as a divine credential for a witness who invokes the miracle in His name. When God chooses a witness, and then associates an authentic miracle with the testimony of that witness, we can know for certain that the witness is worthy of belief. God does not grant miracles to vouch for unreliable witnesses; God does not *choose* unreliable witnesses.

No, God does not waste miracles. Much less does God waste a public miracle witnessed by 70,000 people, believers and unbelievers alike, which occurred at precisely the moment predicted three months earlier by three witnesses whose testimony had been doubted: Lucia dos Santos (known to the world as Lucy) and her cousins, Francisco and Jacinta Marto.[3]

It is October 13, 1917. In a humble field known as the Cova da Iria in Fatima some 70,000 people have assembled to await the happening of a miracle. This in itself is astounding. For never before in salvation history has a visionary predicted months in advance that a public miracle would occur at a precise time and place. Never before has a vast crowd assembled to witness a predicted public miracle. Yet that is exactly what was happening on this day.

Why this day? Because Lucia dos Santos and her cousins Francisco and Jacinta had been receiving apparitions from "the Lady" on the thirteenth of each month since the previous May. The Lady had been appearing to them above a holm-oak tree in the Cova, and with each apparition the crowds had grown. But doubts about the veracity of the seers had also grown, as well as mockery and persecution of the seers and their families at a time when Portugal was under the control of an atheistic and Masonic political regime.

And then, on July 13, 1917, the Lady had shown them something which would terrify them and change them forever, making them into saints who would spend their lives (in the case of Francisco and Jacinta, very brief lives) praying and making sacrifices for sinners. As Lucy

---

[3] This chapter is largely taken from Frère Michel de la Sainte Trinité, *The Whole Truth About Fatima* - Vol. I, *Science and the Facts*, (English edition, Immaculate Heart Publications, Buffalo, New York, U.S.A., 1989) Chapter 10, pp. 323-380; and from Vol. II, *The Secret and the Church*, (English edition, Immaculate Heart Publications, Buffalo, New York, U.S.A., 1990) Introduction, pp. 5-10. See also Frère François de Marie des Anges, *Fatima: Intimate Joy World Event*; Frère François is largely dependent on Frère Michel.

recounts in testimony the Catholic Church has deemed worthy of belief, the Lady showed them hell:

> She opened Her hands once more, as She had done during the two previous months. The rays of light seemed to penetrate the earth, and we saw as it were a sea of fire. Plunged in this fire were demons and souls [of the damned] in human form, like transparent burning embers, all blackened or burnished bronze, floating about in the conflagration, now raised into the air by the flames that issued from within themselves together with great clouds of smoke, now falling back on every side like sparks in huge fires, without weight or equilibrium, amid shrieks and groans of pain and despair, which horrified us and made us tremble with fear. (It must have been this sight which caused me to cry out, as people say they heard me.) The demons could be distinguished [from the souls of the damned] by their terrifying and repellent likeness to frightful and unknown animals, black and transparent like burning coals.[4] This vision lasted but an instant. How can we ever be grateful enough to our kind heavenly Mother, Who had already prepared us by promising, in the first apparition, to take us to Heaven. Otherwise, I think we would have died of fear and terror.[5]

Having shown the children the fate of the damned, which is the first part of the Great Secret of Fatima, the Lady then confided to the children the second part. Everyone, including those members of the Vatican apparatus who are the focus of this presentation, agrees that the second part of the Secret, as recorded in Sister Lucy's diaries, is as follows:

> You have seen hell where the souls of poor sinners go. To save them, God wishes to establish in the world devotion to My Immaculate Heart. If what I say to you is done, many souls will be saved and there will be peace. The war is going to end; but if people do not cease offending God, a worse one will break out during the reign of Pius XI. When you see a night illumined by an unknown light, know that this is the great sign given you by God that He is about to punish the world for its sins, by means of war, famine, and persecutions against the Church and of the Holy Father.

> To prevent this, I shall come to ask for the Consecration of Russia to My Immaculate Heart, and the Communion of Reparation on the First Saturdays. If My requests are heeded, Russia will be converted, and there will be peace; if not, she will spread her

---

[4] English translation of text in Sister Lucy, "Fourth Memoir", *Fatima in Lucia's Own Words*, (Postulation Centre, Fatima, Portugal, 1976) p. 162. See also Frère Michel de la Sainte Trinité, *The Whole Truth About Fatima* - Vol. I: *Science and the Facts*, pp. 181-182.

[5] English translation of text in Sister Lucy, "Third Memoir", *Fatima in Lucia's Own Words*, p. 104. See also *The Whole Truth About Fatima* - Vol. I, p. 182.

errors throughout the world, causing wars and persecutions of the Church. The good will be martyred, the Holy Father will have much to suffer, various nations will be annihilated.

In the end, My Immaculate Heart will triumph. The Holy Father will consecrate Russia to Me, and she will be converted, and some period of peace will be granted to the world. In Portugal the dogma of the Faith will always be preserved etc. Do not tell this to anybody. Francisco, yes, you may tell him.[6]

The basic elements of this astonishing Message are these:

- Many souls go to hell because of the sins they commit.
- To save them, God wishes to establish throughout the world the uniquely Catholic devotion to the Immaculate Heart of Mary.
- This is to be accomplished by consecrating the nation of Russia to the Immaculate Heart of Mary (in conjunction with the Communion of Reparation on the first Saturdays of each month), whereupon Russia will be converted to the Catholic Faith.
- If this is done, many souls will be saved and there will be peace.
- If it is *not* done, Russia will spread its errors throughout the world. There will be wars, famine, persecutions of the Church, and martyrdom of the good. The Holy Father will have much to suffer. And if Our Lady's requests are still not obeyed, then various nations will be annihilated.
- Nevertheless, "In the end, My Immaculate Heart will triumph. The Holy Father will consecrate Russia to Me, and she will be converted, and a period of peace will be granted to the world."

To these things, the Lady added an urgent request that Catholics include in their daily recitation of the Rosary at the end of each decade, the following prayer: "O my Jesus, forgive us our sins, save us from the fires of hell. Lead all souls to Heaven, especially those most in need." In obedience to the Lady's request, and as a testament to the authenticity of Her apparitions at Fatima, the Church included this prayer in the Rosary, and Catholics recite it to this day.

The Church has also adopted the First Saturday devotion of the Communion of Reparation, which the Lady explained thusly:

I promise to help at the hour of death, with all the graces needed for salvation, whoever on the First Saturday of five consecutive months shall: confess and receive Holy Communion, recite five decades of the Holy Rosary, and keep Me company for

---

[6] English translation of text in Sister Lucy, "Fourth Memoir", *Fatima in Lucia's Own Words*, (Postulation Centre, Fatima, Portugal, 1976) p. 162. See also Sister Lucy, *Memorias e Cartas da Irma Lucia*, (Porto, Portugal, 1973, edited by Father Antonio Maria Martins) pp. 340-341; in Sister Lucy's own handwriting there is no ellipsis after the "etc.". See also Frère Michel de la Sainte Trinité, *The Whole Truth About Fatima* - Vol. I: *Science and the Facts*, pp. 182-183.

fifteen minutes while meditating on the fifteen mysteries of the Rosary, with the intention of making reparation to Me.

We pause here to note in passing (for further discussion later) the curious phrase at the end of the first two parts of the Secret: "In Portugal the dogma of the Faith will always be preserved etc." The incomplete phrase, ending with "etc.", appears in Sister Lucy's fourth memoir of the apparitions. It clearly introduces a heavenly prediction, containing further words of Our Lady not recorded, about the state of adherence to Catholic dogma in the Church at large, distinguished from Portugal in particular, where the dogma of the Faith will always be preserved.

Standing alone, the observation about adherence to Catholic dogma in Portugal appears gratuitous and quite senseless, for the phrase does not at all follow logically from the first two parts of the Secret. Every recognized Fatima scholar concluded from this that the phrase represents the beginning of a third part of the Secret—what came to be known simply as the Third Secret of Fatima. As we shall see, Lucy was so terrified by its contents that even after she was ordered to write it down in October of 1943, she was unable to do so until the subsequent apparition on January 2, 1944 in which Our Lady assured her that she ought to write it down. And yet, to this day, the Vatican has never revealed the words of the Virgin which clearly follow "In Portugal the dogma of the Faith will always be preserved etc." The "etc." remains a secret. This ongoing concealment is a key element of the injustice that is the subject of this book.

Having received from Heaven itself a message with obviously profound importance for the Church and all humanity, Lucy knew that she and her cousins needed a divine credential if they were to be believed. During the apparition on July 13, Sister Lucy asked the Lady "to tell us who You are, and to work a miracle, so that everybody will believe that You are appearing to us." And the Lady replied: "Continue to come here every month. In October I will tell you who I am and what I want, and I will perform a miracle for all to see and believe."[7] The Lady repeated this promise in further apparitions to Lucy and the other seers on August 19 and again, at the Cova, on September 13.

And so the people assemble in a great crowd at the Cova on October 13, 1917. And at precisely the hour predicted in July—12 noon solar time, and 1:30 p.m. by the clock in Portugal—it begins. Lucy suddenly instructs the crowd of witnesses to shut their umbrellas in the midst of a drenching rain which has turned the Cova into a field of mud. Some people were standing in mud up to their ankles. She enters a state of spiritual ecstasy as the Lady, appearing again, addresses her. The Lady begins by telling Lucy who She is and what She wants, just as She had promised: "I want a chapel to be built here in My honor. I am the Lady of the Rosary." The Lady is the Mother of God, the Virgin Mary, who will

---

[7] Frère Michel de la Sainte Trinité, *The Whole Truth About Fatima* - Vol. I, pp. 180-181.

henceforth also be known under the title Our Lady of Fatima, one of many bestowed upon the Blessed Virgin by the Church. The chapel, of course, would be built, and then rebuilt after being blown up on March 6, 1922 by a bomb planted by the friends of the Tinsmith, a nickname for the Masonic Mayor of Ourem.[8]

And then the Miracle occurs. We recount here the testimony of a reporter who cannot possibly be accused of partiality in this matter and for a good reason! We refer to Avelino de Almeida, the chief editor of *O Seculo*, the large "liberal" anticlerical and Masonic daily newspaper of Lisbon. He writes:

> From the road, where the carriages were crowded together and where hundreds of persons had stayed for want of sufficient courage to advance across the muddy ground, we saw the huge crowd turn towards the sun which appeared at its zenith, clear of the clouds. It resembled a disc of silver, and it was possible to stare at it without the least discomfort. It did not burn the eyes. It did not blind. We would say that it produced an eclipse. Then a tremendous cry rang out, and the crowd nearest us were heard to shout: "Miracle! Miracle! ... Marvel! ... Marvel!" Before the dazzled eyes of the people, whose attitude transported us to biblical times, and who, dumbfounded, heads uncovered, contemplated the blue of the sky, the sun trembled, it made strange and abrupt movements, outside of all cosmic laws—"the sun danced", according to the typical expression of the peasants ...[9]

Attacked violently by all the anticlerical press, Avelino de Almeida renews his testimony, fifteen days later, in his review, *Ilustração Portuguesa*. This time he illustrates his account with a dozen photographs of the huge ecstatic crowd, and repeated as a refrain throughout his article: "I saw ... I saw ... I saw." And he concludes: "Miracle, as the people shouted? Natural phenomenon, as the experts say? For the moment, that does not concern me, I am only saying what I saw... The rest is a matter for Science and the Church."[10]

Saturday, October 13 begins for the pilgrims as a walk of penance because it had rained the whole preceding night. Now, this "almost sudden change of weather, with the dusty roads transformed into muddy quagmires by a pelting rain, causing to replace abruptly, for a day, the sweetness of autumn with the biting rigors of winter, did not succeed in moving them, to make them give up or despair."[11]

In comparing the numerous accounts of witnesses, we can distinguish the diverse aspects and the result of the astounding

---

[8] Frère Michel de la Sainte Trinité, *The Whole Truth About Fatima* - Vol. II: *The Secret and the Church*, pp. 357-358.

[9] *O Seculo* of October 15, 1917.

[10] Article of October 29, 1917. See also Frère François de Marie des Anges, *Fatima: Intimate Joy World Event*, Book One, *The Astonishing Truth*, (English edition, Immaculate Heart Publications, Buffalo, New York, U.S.A., 1993) p. 164.

[11] *Ilustração Portuguesa*, October 29, 1917.

phenomena seen by all. For each one of the phenomena, it would be possible to line up many witnesses, whose testimony would constitute in itself an impressive book.

Here is the first marvelous fact described by Dr. Almeida Garrett:

It must have been 1:30 p.m. when there arose at the exact spot where the children were, a column of smoke, thin, fine and bluish, which extended up to perhaps two meters above their heads, and evaporated at that height. This phenomenon, perfectly visible to the naked eye, lasted for a few seconds. Not having noted how long it had lasted, I cannot say whether it was more or less than a minute. The smoke dissipated abruptly, and after some time, it came back to occur a second time, then a third time ...[12]

Whereas "the low and heavy sky had a very dark color, laden with moisture, [which] released an abundant and long lasting rain," during the time of the apparition, the rain stopped totally. Abruptly the sky cleared: "The sun triumphantly pierced the thick bed of clouds hiding it until then, and shone intensely." (Dr. Almeida Garrett) This abrupt change of weather took all the eyewitnesses by surprise: "It was a day of heavy and continuous rain. But a few minutes before the miracle, it stopped raining." (Alfredo da Silva Santos)

And this testimony from a physician, a man of science, concerning the inexplicable silvering of the sun, allowing it to be viewed directly without harm to the eyes:

"Suddenly I heard the uproar of thousands of voices, and I saw the whole multitude spread out in that vast space at my feet ... turn their backs to that spot where, until then, all their expectations focused, and look at the sun on the other side ... I turned around, too, toward the point commanding their gazes, and I could see the sun, like a very clear disc, with its sharp edge, which gleamed without hurting the sight ... It could not be confused with the sun seen through a fog (there was no fog at that moment), for it was neither veiled, nor dim. At Fatima, it kept its light and heat, and stood out clearly in the sky, with a sharp edge, like a large gaming table. The most astonishing thing was to be able to stare at the solar disc for a long time, brilliant with light and heat, without hurting the eyes, or damaging the retina." (Dr. Almeida Garrett)[13]

In the same vein this testimony by the editor-in-chief of O Seculo:

"And then we witnessed a unique spectacle, an incredible spectacle, unbelievable if you did not witness it. From above the road ... We see the immense crowd turn towards the sun, which appeared at its zenith, clear of the clouds. It looked like a plate of dull silver, and it was possible to stare at it without the least discomfort. It did not burn the eyes. It did not blind. One might say

---

[12] Frère François de Marie des Anges, *Fatima: The Astonishing Truth*, pp. 171-172.
[13] Ibid., pp. 172-173.

that an eclipse had occurred." (Article of October 15, 1917)

And likewise: "The people could look at the sun as we look at the moon." (Maria do Carmo)[14]

One could multiply endlessly the testimonies about the ensuing solar phenomena, witnessed even by the secular editor-in-chief of an anticlerical newspaper. Consider these:

"It shook and trembled; it seemed like a wheel of fire." (Maria da Capelinha)[15]

"The sun turned like a fire wheel, taking on all the colors of the rainbow." (Maria do Carmo)[16]

"It appeared like a globe of snow turning on itself." (Father Lourenço)[17]

"The pearl-like disc had a giddy motion. This was not the twinkling of a star in all its brilliance. It turned on itself with impetuous speed." (Dr. Almeida Garrett)[18]

"At a certain moment, the sun stopped and then began again to dance, to spin; it stopped again, and began again to dance." (Ti Marto)[19]

"The sun took on all the colors of the rainbow. Everything assumed those same colors: our faces, our clothes, the earth itself." (Maria do Carmo)[20]

"A light, whose colors changed from one moment to the next, was reflected on the people and on things." (Dr. Pereira Gens)[21]

What happens next constitutes the most terrifying aspect of the Miracle, and one with profound implications for our era, in which man has perfected the ability to destroy the whole world with fire from the sky: the sun appears to detach itself from the sky and plunge toward the earth.

"We suddenly heard a clamor, like a cry of anguish of that entire crowd. The sun, in fact, keeping its rapid movement of rotation, seemed to free itself from the firmament and blood-red, to plunge towards the earth, threatening to crush us with its fiery mass. Those were some terrifying seconds." (Dr. Almeida Garrett)[22]

"I saw the sun turn and it seemed to descend. It was like a

---

[14] Ibid., p. 173.
[15] Frère Michel de la Sainte Trinité, *The Whole Truth About Fatima* - Vol. I, p. 337.
[16] Frère François de Marie des Anges, *Fatima: The Astonishing Truth*, p. 178.
[17] Ibid.
[18] Ibid.
[19] Ibid.
[20] Ibid.
[21] Ibid.
[22] Ibid.

bicycle wheel." (John Carreira)[23]

"The sun began to dance and, at a certain moment, it appeared to detach itself from the firmament and to rush forward on us, like a fire wheel." (Alfredo da Silva Santos)[24]

"I saw it perfectly descending as if it came to crash on the earth. It seemed to detach itself from the sky and rush toward us. It maintained itself at a short distance above our heads; but that sort of attack was of very short duration... It seemed very near the people and it continued to turn in the opposite direction." (Maria do Carmo)[25]

"Suddenly, the sun appeared with its circumference well-defined. It came down as if to the height of the clouds and began to whirl giddily upon itself like a captive ball of fire. With some interruptions, this lasted about eight minutes." (Father Pereira da Silva)[26]

"It suddenly seemed to come down in a zig-zag, menacing the earth." (Father Lourenço)[27]

"Seeing the sun falling on us ..." (Father John Gomes)[28]

"Finally, the sun stopped and everybody breathed a sigh of relief ..." (Maria da Capelinha)[29]

"From those thousands of mouths I heard shouts of joy and love to the Most Holy Virgin. And then I believed. I had the certainty of not having been the victim of a suggestion. I had seen the sun as I would never see it again." (Mario Godinho, an engineer)[30]

Another astonishing fact: all those people, who are for the most part soaked to the bone, verify with joy and amazement that they are dry. The fact is attested to in the canonical process for Jacinta and Francisco, who were ultimately beatified on May 13, 2000.

"The moment one would least expect it, our clothes were totally dry." (Maria do Carmo)[31]

"My suit dried in an instant." (John Carreira)[32]

The academician Marques da Cruz testified as follows:

This enormous multitude was drenched, for it had rained

---

[23] Ibid.
[24] Ibid., pp. 178-179.
[25] Ibid., p. 179.
[26] Frère Michel de la Sainte Trinité, *The Whole Truth About Fatima* - Vol. I, p. 337.
[27] Ibid., p. 339.
[28] Ibid., p. 340.
[29] Ibid.
[30] Frère François de Marie des Anges, *Fatima: The Astonishing Truth*, p. 179.
[31] Ibid.
[32] Ibid.

unceasingly since dawn. But—though this may appear incredible—after the great miracle everyone felt comfortable, and found his garments quite dry, a subject of general wonder ... The truth of this fact has been guaranteed with the greatest sincerity by dozens and dozens of persons of absolute trustworthiness, whom I have known intimately from childhood, and who are still alive (1937), as well as by persons from various districts of the country who were present.[33]

In one aspect, this is a most astonishing effect of the solar miracle and one of its best proofs: The amount of energy needed to accomplish this process of instantaneous drying, would have incinerated everyone present had it taken place in the natural order of things. As this aspect of the miracle contradicts the laws of nature radically, no demon could ever have achieved it.

And finally, there are also moral miracles of the conversions of many people. In his book, *Meet the Witnesses*, John Haffert writes:

> The captain of the regiment of soldiers on the mountain that day—with orders to prevent the gathering of the crowd—was converted instantly. Apparently so were hundreds of other unbelievers, as their testimony will show.[34]

> "There was an unbeliever there who had spent the morning mocking the 'simpletons' who had gone off to Fatima just to see an ordinary girl. He now seemed paralyzed, his eyes fixed on the sun. He began to tremble from head to foot, and lifting up his arms, fell on his knees in the mud, crying out to God." (Father Lourenço)[35]

> "I live eighteen miles from Fatima. And in May of 1917 we were told about the extraordinary apparitions, but the news came to us mixed up with the fantasy of the people. Naturally I did not believe. I sincerely supposed it was only [the] imagination of someone. ... At my mother's request, I went once more to the Cova da Iria in August at the time of the apparitions. Once more I came back discouraged and disappointed. But that time, something extraordinary happened. My mother, who had had a large tumor in one of her eyes for many years, was cured. The doctors who had attended her said they could not explain such a cure. Still I did not believe in the apparitions. Finally, and again at my mother's request, I went to the Cova da Iria once more on the thirteenth of October. ... In spite of what had happened to my mother, I was

---

[33] Frère Michel de la Sainte Trinité, *The Whole Truth About Fatima* - Vol. I, p. 340. See also Father John de Marchi, I.M.C., *Fatima from the Beginning*, (Missoes Consolata, Fatima, Portugal, 1981, third edition, first published in 1950) p. 141; and Joseph A. Pelletier, A.A., *The Sun Danced at Fatima*, (Doubleday, New York, 1983) pp. 129-130.

[34] John M. Haffert, *Meet the Witnesses*, (AMI International Press, Fatima, Portugal, 1961) p. 62. This book was published with an Imprimatur from the Bishop of Leiria, Portugal and provides us with credible direct testimonies of numerous witnesses to the Miracle of the Sun.

[35] Ibid., p. 65.

disappointed and did not believe in the apparitions. So I sat inside my car. Then all at once I noticed that everybody looked at the sky. Natural curiosity attracted my attention, and I got out of the car and looked at the sky, too. ... From those hundreds of mouths I heard words of belief and of love to the Blessed Virgin. And then I believed." (Mario Godinho, an engineer)[36]

Numerous other cures and conversions are documented in, among other places, the following books: *Documentação Crítica de Fátima* and *Fatima from the Beginning*.[37]

To those who would say the miracle was a product of "mass hysteria" at the scene, God Himself arranged a ready rebuttal: the phenomenon could be admired from beyond Fatima. Perfectly credible witnesses, who were very far from the Cova da Iria, related having seen the unprecedented spectacle of the dance of the sun, exactly like the 70,000 pilgrims gathered around the holm-oak where the Virgin had appeared.[38]

In the small village of Alburitel, situated about ten miles from Fatima, the whole town was able to enjoy the vision of the solar prodigy. The testimony frequently quoted is that of Father Inacio Lourenço, because it is the most detailed. But what he relates having seen, all the villagers, questioned by the investigators, confirmed seeing it exactly the same way.

The witnesses of the event were indeed innumerable, their testimonies agree and we are flooded with the documents they have left us.[39]

In the first place, numerous accounts appeared at once in the Portuguese press. It is noteworthy that the first to provide testimony were the anticlerical reporters. The three articles of Avelino de Almeida—the one of October 13, immediately before the event; the other of October 15, edited at Vila Nova de Ourem on the evening of the 13th; and a third article of October 29—merit a special mention. In spite of the jeering tone and Voltarian irony which inspire in part the first article, in spite of the expected anticlerical tones which still appear in the article of the 15th, these texts from a talented reporter, one who besides, is honest and conscientious, are historical documents of prime importance.[40] But he was not the only one to relate the facts, for other reporters were present at the Cova da Iria.

---

[36] Ibid., pp. 86-89.

[37] *Documentação Crítica de Fátima*, Vol. II, (Santuário de Fátima, 1999) 17 cases documented on pp. 277-372; and Father John de Marchi, I.M.C., *Fatima from the Beginning*.

[38] Father John de Marchi, I.M.C., *Fatima from the Beginning*, p. 136. See also *Documentação Crítica de Fátima*, Vol. I, (Santuário de Fátima, 1992) p. 408. See also Frère Michel de la Sainte Trinité, *The Whole Truth About Fatima* - Vol. I, pp. 330-331.

[39] Among the many reference works, see: Frère Michel de la Sainte Trinité, *The Whole Truth About Fatima* - Vol. I: *Science and the Facts*; John M. Haffert, *Meet the Witnesses*; Father John de Marchi, I.M.C., *Fatima from the Beginning*, pp. 135-142.

[40] We find the photographic reproduction of those three articles in *Fatima 50* of October 13, 1967, pp. 6-10 and 14-15.

Next there were the official investigations. In November 1917, at the request of Bishop de Lima Vidal, who was then administering the diocese of Lisbon, the parish priest of Fatima led his investigation and questioned several witnesses of the parish. Unfortunately, he transcribed only four depositions!

The investigations of the historians fortunately compensated for the negligence of the official investigators. The report of Father Formigao, who obtained from Dr. José Maria de Almeida Garrett, professor at the Faculty of Sciences of Coimbra, a very thorough account, is the most scientific report in our possession.[41] In addition, we have the reports of Father da Fonseca (whose work was done in order to verify the points disputed by Father Dhanis,[42] who refused to examine the evidence), Father de Marchi, Canon Barthas, Father Dias Coelho and Father Richard.

In 1977, to commemorate the sixtieth anniversary of the last apparition, it was still possible to assemble in Fatima more than thirty persons who had been present at the solar prodigy and could recount their witness. Thanks to those numerous testimonies, it is possible to reconstruct a precise running commentary, allowing us to relive, hour-by-hour and minute-by-minute, this decisive day, assuredly one of the most important in the history of the world. Indeed, the evidence of the solar miracle on October 13, 1917 is so overwhelming that in 1952 even Hollywood vouched for the authenticity of the miracle by releasing a classic film (starring Gilbert Roland) entitled "The Miracle of Our Lady of Fatima", which is marketed on video to this day.

Why was this day so important? Because it was the day on which a heavenly Message from the Mother of God was authenticated beyond any reasonable doubt; a message which, more than 90 years later, stands at the heart of the perilous situation of the Church and the world at this very moment in human history, offering us a way out.

---

[41] *Novos Documentos de Fatima*, Loyola editions, Sao Paulo, 1984, pp. 60-63.

[42] The modernist Jesuit priest, Father Dhanis, as early as the 1940s, would attempt to "debunk" the vision of hell and the prophetic elements of the Message, including the consecration and ultimate conversion of Russia. After World War II, Fatima scholars urged Dhanis to travel to Fatima to study the primary documentation and to interview Sister Lucy in order to correct his flawed thesis. Dhanis refused to go to Portugal and adhered to his erroneous opinions. (See Frère Michel de la Sainte Trinité, *The Whole Truth About Fatima* - Vol. I, pp. 499-511.) Father Dhanis will eventually be cited by key members of the Vatican apparatus in their attempt to revise the Message of Fatima according to a "commentary" published on June 26, 2000.

Chapter 2

The Long Opposition Begins

Even a cursory reading of the first two parts of the Great Secret in the Message of Fatima reveals that it is a heavenly challenge to the powers of the world, whose hold on even Catholic Portugal had been increasing since the beginning of the 20th Century.

Recalling the text of the Secret set forth in the first chapter, it is obvious that what Heaven has proposed therein would be anathema to the Masonic regime in Portugal, and indeed to all of the organized forces against the Church which, at the beginning of the last century, were plotting (by their own admission, as we shall see) a final assault upon the Catholic citadel. The basic elements of the Message constitute a veritable charter of opposition to these forces: saving souls from hell; the establishment throughout the world of a Catholic devotion to the Immaculate Heart of Mary; the consecration of Russia to that Immaculate Heart, and Russia's consequent conversion to Catholicism; and, world peace borne of the triumph of the Immaculate Heart.

The Message of Fatima is important for the salvation of souls; that much is completely obvious. But somewhat less obvious—and this is what will come to infuriate both the external and internal enemies of the Church—the Message and Our Lady's appearance are also very important for the correct ordering of human society. As Our Lord said: "But seek first the kingdom of God and His justice, and all these things shall be added unto you." (Luke 12:31)

If mankind heeds the Virgin's message, then peace among individuals, families, cities and countries, and in fact the whole world, can be achieved in the form of *Catholic social order*. (We shall see in the next chapter that this social order is not some utopian dream, but a thing which has been achieved even in the 20th Century—in Portugal, through its Consecration to the Immaculate Heart of Mary in 1931.) To be sure, Original Sin would remain, but we would see a period in human history like that prophesied by Isaias, who, under divine inspiration, envisioned a time when men would make war no more, would learn the art of war no more, but would beat their swords into plowshares.[43] The tendency of man toward sin would be vastly ameliorated and controlled by the beneficent influence of the Church and Her sacraments. And who, looking upon the world today, could seriously argue that even the worst "excesses" of men in the Catholic social order that once existed in pre-"Reformation" Europe are anything at

---

[43] "And He shall judge the Gentiles, and rebuke many people: and they shall turn their swords into plowshares, and their spears into sickles: nation shall not lift up sword against nation, neither shall they be exercised any more to war." (Is. 2:4) Also, "and they shall beat their swords into plowshares, and their spears into spades: nation shall not take sword against nation: neither shall they learn war any more." (Micheas 4:3)

all when compared with the evil and violence which have been virtually institutionalized in every nation in our time—first and foremost with the endless holocaust of "legalized" abortion.

The implications flowing from the simple text of the Great Secret of Fatima are plain enough to anyone of minimal intelligence: Such a plan for peace in the world could only be achieved if enough individuals, at every level of society, freely cooperated. (We are not speaking here of some forcibly imposed religious dictatorship, as exists in certain Islamic states, but a social order naturally arising from the common Catholic faith of the people.) The plan could succeed, even then, only if it were based on the designs of the Creator of mankind, Who has anointed Jesus Christ, the Redeemer of mankind, as King of kings and Lord of lords (Apoc. 19:16). Jesus is King, not only of individuals but also of societies and the whole world. Therefore, if this plan of the Blessed Virgin Mary, Who is Queen of Heaven and of earth, is to work, mankind must acknowledge the sovereign Kingship of Christ over all mankind as it is exercised through His Catholic Church. That men will, in fact, be moved to do so in sufficient numbers—first in Russia and then elsewhere—is the very miracle promised by the Virgin if Her requests are honored.

One can understand that the prince of this world, as Jesus Christ referred to the devil, would not accept easily the proposed destruction of his flourishing kingdom here on earth. Nor would this peace plan from Heaven be accepted by those men, associations and secret societies whose power and ill-gotten riches would be forfeited if the plan were put into effect and the conversion of Russia and the triumph of the Immaculate Heart—and thus of the Catholic Faith—were to follow.

With this background we can better appreciate why fierce opposition to the Message of Fatima arose even while the apparitions were going on, and why it continues to this day, enlisting even men within the Church as opponents of the requests of the Virgin.

At the time of the Fatima apparitions, the Mayor of Ourem, the county seat to which Fatima and Aljustrel (the village where the children who had seen Our Lady lived) belonged, was Arturo de Oliveira Santos, whom we encountered in Chapter 1. A Freemason who professed no belief in God, and a blacksmith by trade, he was popularly referred to as "the Tinsmith". His formal education had been slight, but his ambitions were large. Arturo Santos was a self-propelled and intrepid young man, who became the editor of the *Ouriense*, a local gazette in which his anti-monarchial and anti-religious opinions were expressed with bitter zeal and with some talent. At twenty-six he joined the Grand Orient Masonic Lodge at Leiria.

As the great Catholic historian, William Thomas Walsh, points out, Santos became indoctrinated with the esoteric lore of a syncretistic and naturalistic religion which had been the main opponent of the Catholic Church in modern times, and which had already boasted that, by planning and carrying out the Portuguese revolution of 1910, it had taken a long step toward the total elimination of Christianity in the Iberian Peninsula. Walsh further informs us that in 1911 the Grand Orient chief, Magalhães Lima, predicted that in a few years no young man would wish to study for the priesthood in Portugal, while the prominent Portuguese Mason Alfonso Costa assured all his brethren, and some delegates from the French lodges, that one more generation would see the finish of Catholicism, "the principal cause of the sad condition into which our country has fallen". Indeed there was much evidence to support the prediction, but not the accusation.

Professor Walsh goes on to note that in 1911 the new masters of Portugal seized Church property, scattered, imprisoned and exiled hundreds of priests and nuns, and gave the Cardinal Patriarch of Lisbon five days to leave that city, never to return. Refugee priests and religious fled to France and elsewhere. Some knelt at Lourdes and prayed to the Mother of God to help their unhappy country, once proud to call itself "The Land of Holy Mary", now a spectacle of unbelief and anarchy, with a new revolution every month.

Arturo Santos founded a new Masonic lodge in Ourem, where he had moved his blacksmith shop. By 1917 he became its president. Through friends in his brotherhood, he was able to become Mayor of Ourem. This title carried with it the corollary titles of President of the town Administration and of the Chamber, and Deputy Judge of Commerce. With all these honors and their companion authority, Senhor Santos became the most feared and influential man in his section of Portugal.

During his administration, fewer and fewer people went to Mass and the Sacraments, there were more divorces, and there were not so many children. When he arrested six priests and held them incommunicado for eight days, the leading Catholic laymen in the Council and the Chamber were too busy making profitable compromises so they did not have time to protest loudly enough to be heard. To the Tinsmith and his friends the fight for "progress and enlightenment", as they preferred to describe their conflict with the Catholic Church, was all but won.[44]

By August of 1917 all Portugal knew the story of the Apparitions at Fatima, although in a variety of versions. The journalists of the anti-religious press enjoyed writing comical versions of the story. As Father de Marchi records the attitude of the anti-religious press, they claimed that: "these children were the puppets of the Jesuits. Not the Jesuits? Well, then, the clergy in general, or the Pope, in particular—luring ignorant and unwary people to the Cova da Iria, in order to fleece them of their money. They didn't have any money? Well, then, of their political allegiance, so that the humane fabric of the enlightened Republic could be sabotaged to the advantage of Rome and Reaction. The press enjoyed its jolly excursions. The Freemasons were delighted."[45] All loyal supporters

---

[44] William Thomas Walsh, *Our Lady of Fatima*, (Image-Doubleday, New York, Imprimatur 1947) pp. 95-97.

[45] Father John de Marchi, I.M.C., *The Immaculate Heart: The True Story of Our Lady of Fatima*, (Farrar, Straus and Young, New York, 1952) p. 87.

of the reigning New Order found the situation increasingly humorous.

But Arturo Santos, the Mayor of Ourem, did not find it so humorous because the open manifestation of religion was happening in his own county. Some of his constituents already believed that Our Lady was appearing at Fatima, and he could not think what explanations he could provide his political colleagues if this Christian religious manifestation, which was contrary to the Mayor's hopes of building a Godless Republic, continued to thrive in his own county. So he decided to bring the heavy fist of "the law" down upon the three seers.

On August 11, 1917, the Mayor of Ourem ordered the parents of the three children to present them for trial at the City Hall. Ti Marto, the father of Jacinta and Francisco, said, "There's no sense in taking such young children before a court of that kind. Besides, it's three leagues, and that's too far for them to walk. And they don't know how to ride on a beast. I'm not going to do it. And I'll go over and tell the Administrator why." His wife Olimpia agreed. Lucy's father, Antonio, however was inclined to agree with his wife Maria Rosa that if Lucy was lying, it would be a good thing to have her taught a lesson, while if she was telling the truth (and they doubted she was), then Our Lady would take care of her. Antonio put his daughter on the back of a burro (she fell off three times on the way) and they set off on the journey to see the Mayor. Ti Marto left his children at home and went by himself to speak on their behalf. Before the journey, Jacinta said to Lucy, "Never mind. If they kill you, you just tell them that I am like you, and Francisco more so, and that we want to die too. And now I will go with Francisco to the well to pray very hard for you."

The Mayor asked Lucy if she had seen a Lady at the Cova da Iria, and who she thought it was. He demanded that she tell him the secret that Our Lady had confided to the children, and promise never to return to the Cova da Iria again. Lucy refused to tell him the secret and to make such a promise. (Our Lady had asked the children to return to the Cova da Iria on the 13th day of each month, and they had promised to go there at the appointed time and date for the next three visits as well.) Then the Mayor asked Antonio if the people in Fatima believed the story, and he replied, "Oh no, sir! All this is just women's tales."

"And what do you say?" the Mayor asked Ti Marto. "I am here at your command," he replied, "and my children say the same things I do." "Then you think it is true?" "Yes, sir, I believe what they say."

The bystanders laughed. The Mayor made a gesture of dismissal and one of his men told them to go. The Mayor followed them to the door and said to Lucy, "If you don't tell that secret, it will cost you your life!" Then Lucy and her father and Ti Marto returned to Aljustrel.

In the evening of August 12, three policemen summoned the children to the house of Ti Marto, where the Mayor was waiting for them in person. He told the children that death might be the penalty for not revealing the Great Secret they had learned on July 13. The children refused to tell it, on the grounds that they could not disobey Our Lady. "Never mind," whispered Jacinta to the others. "If they kill us, so much the better, for then we shall see Jesus and Our Lady." On the morning of August 13, Ti Marto was out working in the fields. He came into the house to wash the soil off his hands. There was a crowd of people around the house, who had come to be present at the apparition that was to take place that day at the Cova da Iria. His wife Olimpia was upset and she pointed towards the living room. Ti Marto went into the living room, and as we read in his own account of it to Father de Marchi: "Who should I see but the Mayor himself. Even then, I suppose, I wasn't very polite to him, because I saw a priest was there too, and I went first to shake hands with the priest. Then I said to the Mayor, 'I did not expect to see you here, sir.' "

The Mayor said he would take the children to the Cova da Iria in his wagon, to give them time to talk to the parish priest at Fatima, who, he said, wanted to question them. The children and their parents had misgivings about his suggestion of taking them in his wagon, but they complied. He took them first to see the parish priest at Fatima, and then, instead of taking them to the Cova da Iria, people saw him crack the whip and make the horse bolt off down the road in the opposite direction. He took them to Ourem, and locked them in a room in his house.

About fifteen thousand people were at the Cova da Iria, all wondering where the children were. At the time Our Lady was to appear, a number of supernatural manifestations occurred that were also noticed by the crowd at Her other apparitions at Fatima, which convinced many people, even unbelievers, that She had arrived. But the children were not there to receive Her message. Then some people arrived with the news that the Mayor of Ourem had kidnapped the children and had taken them first to the parish priest of Fatima and then to his own house at Ourem. The crowd quickly concluded that the two had conspired together in the kidnapping, which they felt had "spoiled the apparition and disappointed the Mother of God." Bitter voices were raised against the Mayor and the parish priest. But Ti Marto persuaded the crowd not to take revenge. "Boys, take it easy! Don't hurt anyone! Whoever deserves punishment will receive it. All this is (allowed) by the power of the One above!"

The next morning the Mayor of Ourem again interrogated the children, who again said they had seen a beautiful Lady, and again refused to tell him the Secret, even when he threatened them with life imprisonment, torture and death. The Mayor was resolved to obtain from the children some sort of admission that would end the religious manifestation taking place in his county. So he then had them thrown into the town jail, with its dark and bad-smelling cells with iron bars. They were put into the common room where most of the prisoners were herded together. The children were frightened and sad, especially the seven-year-old Jacinta, who thought she would never see her parents again. But they reassured one another, reminding each other of what Our Lady had told them about Heaven, and they offered their sufferings for the conversion of sinners. The children prayed the Rosary in the prison, and the convicts joined in the prayers.

Some time later, the Mayor had the children brought before him by a policeman, and he made a final demand for the Secret. Then, since they again refused to tell it, he told them they would be boiled alive in oil. He shouted a command, and a guard opened a door. He asked the guard if the oil was good and hot, and he replied it was. Then he ordered the guard to throw the youngest, Jacinta, into the boiling oil first. The guard seized the child and carried her away. A guard saw Francisco moving his lips silently, and he asked him what he was saying. "An Ave Maria", Francisco replied, "so my little sister will not be afraid." Lucy and Francisco were convinced that the guard would soon come back to kill them too. Francisco said to Lucy, "What do we care if they kill us? We'll go right to Heaven."

Later the guard came back to the room where the children were being questioned by the Mayor, and informed Lucy and Francisco that Jacinta had been boiled in oil since she would not reveal the Secret. The Mayor tried to persuade the remaining two children to reveal the Secret or the same thing would happen to them. Since they would not reveal the Secret, Francisco was taken away to the same fate. Afterwards, the guard came for Lucy. Even though she believed that Francisco and Jacinta had been killed for not revealing the Secret, she too would rather die than reveal the Secret the Blessed Virgin had entrusted to her. So she also was taken under the custody of the guard to what she thought was certain death.

It turned out that Jacinta had simply been led to another room, and Francisco and Lucy, when it was their turn to be "boiled in oil", were led to the same room, and they were all together again. It had just been a trick to frighten them into revealing the Secret. Lucy, writing in her memoirs, recalling the incident, informs us that she was certain, as were her two cousins, that they were about to be martyred at the hands of the Mayor.

The next morning, with another interrogation, the Mayor still was unable to get them to reveal the Secret. So he admitted it was no use, and ordered them sent back to Fatima. It was August 15, the Feast of the Assumption of Our Lady.

That the Masonic Mayor of Ourem would go so far as to threaten three little children with a horrible death in order to prevent people from believing and openly manifesting their faith in God, His Holy Mother and the Catholic Church, gives some indication of the extent to which the Freemasons would go in their desperation to level the Church once and for all and erect in its place their Godless Republic—not only in Portugal, but throughout the whole world.

Chapter 3

Heaven's Peace Plan in Microcosm

The "enlightened" minds of the "modern world" scoff at the notion that a simple public ceremony consecrating Russia to the Immaculate Heart of Mary could produce the conversion of that nation, and with it enormous benefits to the whole world, including peace among nations. But then, the "modern world" scoffs at miracles in general, and indeed at the divine claims of the Church whose saints have performed miracles in such abundance.

But a consecration of Russia is precisely what God had ordained in the very Message He authenticated with the solar miracle of October 13, 1917—a message which, we hasten to point out again, has received the approbation of the Catholic Church's highest authorities, including a series of Popes since the time of the apparitions at Fatima. As we saw, in 2002 Pope John Paul II even decreed that the Feast of the Virgin of Fatima be included in the Church's universal calendar of liturgical feast days, for inclusion in the *Third Typical Edition of the Roman Missal*. Thus, the Magisterium formally validates the authenticity of the apparitions.

We recall that in the Message of July 13, 1917, Our Lady had promised Lucy that "I shall come to ask for the Consecration of Russia to My Immaculate Heart and the Communion of Reparation on the first Saturdays." True to Her word, the Virgin appeared again to Lucy on June 13, 1929 in Tuy, Spain, where Lucy—now Sister Lucia dos Santos, a Dorothean nun (she would not become a Carmelite until 1948)—was in prayer in the convent chapel during the Holy Hour of Adoration and Reparation. Even among the annals of recognized heavenly apparitions to the saints of the Catholic Church, this one was extraordinary.

We will let Sister Lucy recount the apparition in her own simple but quite dramatic words—and remember that here also we are dealing with an apparition that the Church, including Pope Benedict XVI, has pronounced worthy of belief:

> I had requested and obtained permission from my superiors and confessor to make the Holy Hour from 11:00 p.m. until midnight from Thursday to Friday. Being alone one night, I knelt down before the Communion rail in the middle of the chapel to say the prayers of the Angel, lying prostrate. Feeling tired, I got up and knelt, and continued to say them with my arms in the form of a cross.
>
> The only light came from the sanctuary lamp. Suddenly a supernatural light illumined the whole chapel and on the altar appeared a cross of light which reached to the ceiling. In a brighter

part could be seen, on the upper part of the Cross, the face of a Man and His body to the waist. On His breast was an equally luminous dove, and nailed to the Cross, the body of another Man.

A little below the waist, suspended in mid-air, was to be seen a Chalice and a large Host onto Which fell some drops of Blood from the face of the Crucified and from a wound in His breast. These drops ran down over the Host and fell into the Chalice. Under the right arm of the Cross was Our Lady (Our Lady of Fatima with Her Immaculate Heart in Her hand) ... Under the left arm (of the Cross), some big letters, as it were of crystal-clear water running down over the altar, formed these words: "Grace and Mercy".

I understood that it was the mystery of the Most Holy Trinity that was shown to me ...[46]

Frère Michel has rightly called this apparition "the Trinitarian Theophany" (see picture on the inside back cover). As with the Miracle of the Sun, there is nothing else like it in the history of the world. Thus did God Himself signify the singular importance of what Our Lady was about to tell Sister Lucy:

The moment has come *when God asks* the Holy Father to make, in union with all the bishops of the world, the consecration of Russia to My Immaculate Heart, promising to save it by this means.

God Himself had requested this. Sister Lucy had been in the presence not merely of the Mother of God, but the Most Holy Trinity. Of course, Sister Lucy immediately conveyed the divine request to her confessor, Father Gonçalves, as reflected in her published correspondence with him.[47]

For at least the next seventy years Sister Lucy—the same Lucy who would not deny the truth even though threatened with a horrible death by the Masonic Mayor of Ourem—gave the same testimony: Our Lady, as God's messenger, had requested the public consecration of Russia in a ceremony to be conducted jointly by the Pope and all the world's bishops. As was noted at the beginning of this book in "The Heart of the Matter" and in the Introduction, the persistent effort by certain persons to change that testimony for the sake of human respect (to avoid offending the Russians) and to serve a new orientation of the Church, is the crux of the great Fatima controversy that persists to this day, and which has prompted this book. We shall return to this point in due course.

As if to demonstrate the efficacy of the Consecration the Virgin had requested, God saw fit to allow a demonstration project, as it were, in Portugal. On the anniversary of the first apparition at Fatima, May

---

[46] Frère Michel de la Sainte Trinité, *The Whole Truth About Fatima* - Vol. II, pp. 463-464.

[47] Sister Lucy's words cited from Frère Michel de la Sainte Trinité, *The Whole Truth About Fatima* - Vol. II, pp. 462-465. See also Sister Lucy, *Memorias e Cartas da Irma Lucia*, (Porto, Portugal, 1973, edited by Father Antonio Maria Martins) pp. 463-465.

13, 1931, and in the presence of 300,000 faithful who came to Fatima for the event, the bishops of Portugal solemnly consecrated their nation to the Immaculate Heart of Mary. These good bishops placed Portugal under the protection of Our Lady to preserve that nation from the Communist contagion that was sweeping through Europe, and especially Spain. Indeed, the Virgin's prophecy of the spread of Russia's errors throughout the world was already being fulfilled with relentless exactitude. And who, in July of 1917, could have foreseen the emergence of world communism out of Russia—months before the Bolshevik revolution and Lenin's ascent to power? Only Heaven could have foreseen it; only the Mother of God, informed by Her Divine Son.

As a result of this (1931) Consecration, Portugal experienced a three-fold miracle. Here, we will give only the barest details.

There was, first of all, a magnificent Catholic Renaissance, a great rebirth of Catholic life so striking that those who lived through it attributed it unquestionably to the work of God. During this period, Portugal enjoyed a drastic upsurge in priestly vocations. The number of religious almost quadrupled in 10 years. Religious communities rose likewise. There was a vast renewal of Christian life, which showed itself in many areas, including the development of a Catholic press, Catholic radio, pilgrimages, spiritual retreats, and a robust movement of Catholic Action that was integrated into the framework of diocesan and parish life.

This Catholic Renaissance was of such magnitude that in 1942 the bishops of Portugal declared in a Collective Pastoral Letter: "Anybody who would have closed his eyes twenty-five years ago and opened them now would no longer recognize Portugal, so vast is the transformation worked by the modest and invisible factor of the apparition of the Blessed Virgin at Fatima. Really, Our Lady wishes to save Portugal."[48]

There was also a miracle of political and social reform, in accordance with Catholic social principles. Shortly after the 1931 Consecration, a Catholic leader in Portugal ascended to power, Antonio Salazar, who inaugurated a Catholic, counter-revolutionary program. He strove to create, as much as possible, a Catholic social order wherein the laws of government and social institutions harmonize with the law of Christ, His Gospel and His Church.[49] A fierce adversary of socialism and liberalism, he was opposed to "everything which diminishes, divides or dissolves the family".[50]

---

[48] *Collective Pastoral Letter for the Jubilee of the Apparitions in 1942, Merv. XX's*, p. 338. Cited from *The Whole Truth About Fatima* - Vol. II, p. 410.

[49] Salazar's influence in the Portuguese government had been growing since 1928. He became President of the Council in 1933. Later, Salazar received for his efforts the praise and blessing of Pope Pius XII. Pius said, "I bless him with all my heart, and I cherish the most ardent desire that he be able to complete successfully his work of national restoration, both spiritual and material." Cited from *The Whole Truth About Fatima* - Vol. II, p. 412.

[50] Ibid., p. 415. (Salazar's own words).

President Salazar did not simply talk a good line; he enacted legislation to protect the family, including laws that frowned upon divorce. Article 24 read "In harmony with the essential properties of Catholic marriages: It is understood that by the very fact of the celebration of a canonical marriage, the spouses renounce the legal right to ask for a divorce."[51] The effect of this law was that Catholic marriages did not diminish in number, but increased. So that by 1960—a very critical year, as we shall see—nearly 91 percent of all marriages in the country were canonical marriages.

In addition to these astonishing religious and political changes, there was a twofold miracle of peace. Portugal was preserved from the Communist terror, especially from the Spanish Civil War which was raging next door. Portugal was also preserved from the devastations of World War II.

Regarding the Spanish Civil War, the Portuguese bishops had vowed in 1936 that if Our Lady protected Portugal, they would express their gratitude by renewing the National Consecration to the Immaculate Heart of Mary. True to their word, on May 13, 1938, they renewed the Consecration of Portugal to the Immaculate Heart in thanksgiving for Our Lady's protection. Cardinal Cerejeira acknowledged publicly: "Since Our Lady of Fatima appeared in 1917 ... A special blessing of God has descended upon the land of Portugal ... especially if we review the two years which have passed since our vow, one cannot fail to recognize that the invisible hand of God has protected Portugal, sparing it the scourge of war and the leprosy of atheistic communism."

Even Pope Pius XII expressed astonishment that Portugal was spared the horrors of the Spanish Civil War and the Communist menace. In an address to the Portuguese people, the Pope spoke of "the Red Peril, so menacing and so close to you, and yet avoided in such an unexpected manner."[52]

The Portuguese passed this first danger unscathed, but immediately there was a second staring them in the face. World War II was about to break out. In yet another fulfillment of the Virgin's prophecy of July 13, 1917, the war would begin "in the reign of Pius XI," following "a night illumined by an unknown light ..."[53]

---

[51] Ibid., p. 421.

[52] Ibid., p. 422.

[53] On January 25, 1938, the sky became a brilliant blood-red, not only over Europe, but in parts of North America and Africa. Mark Fellows writes, "The blood-red sky lasted for many hours, and was seen around half of the world at the same vivid intensity. Lucy and the Sisters watched the pulsating, violently hued inferno from Tuy. Of all the descriptions of that night, the most precise one had been prophesied over 20 years ago by the beautiful Lady at Cova da Iria. A 'night illumined by an unknown light', the Virgin told Lucy, would be 'the great sign given by God that He is about to punish the world for its crimes, by means of war, famine, and persecutions of the Church and the Holy Father...' ... Within two months of the great sign, Hitler's armies invaded Austria. As the Blessed Virgin had prophesied, the Second World War began 'in the reign of Pius XI'." Mark Fellows, *Fatima in Twilight* (Niagara Falls: Marmion Publications, 2003), pp. 101-102.

On February 6, 1939, seven months before the declaration of war, Sister Lucy wrote to her bishop, Msgr. da Silva. She told him that war was imminent, but then spoke of a miraculous promise. She said "in this horrible war, Portugal would be spared because of the national consecration to the Immaculate Heart of Mary made by the bishops."[54]

And Portugal *was* spared the horrors of war, the details of which are too numerous to recount here.[55] Even more remarkable, Sister Lucy wrote to Pope Pius XII on December 2, 1940, to tell him that Portugal was receiving special protection during the war that other nations would have received if the bishops would have consecrated their nations to the Immaculate Heart of Mary. She wrote: "Most Holy Father, Our Lord promises a special protection to our country in this war, due to the consecration of the nation, by the Portuguese prelates, to the Immaculate Heart of Mary; as proof of the graces that would have been granted to other nations, had they also consecrated themselves to Her."[56]

Likewise, Portugal's Cardinal Cerejeira did not hesitate to attribute to Our Lady of Fatima the great graces that She had obtained for Portugal during this time. On May 13, 1942 he said: "To express what has been going on here for twenty-five years, the Portuguese vocabulary has but one word: miracle. Yes, we are convinced that we owe the wonderful transformation of Portugal to the protection of the Most Holy Virgin."[57]

Cardinal Cerejeira maintained what we will maintain throughout this presentation: that the miraculous blessings Our Lady obtained for Portugal as a heavenly reward for the 1931 consecration of that nation were only a foretaste of what She will do for the entire world, once Russia is also properly consecrated to Her Immaculate Heart.[58] As the Cardinal said:

> What has taken place in Portugal proclaims the miracle. And it foreshadows what the Immaculate Heart of Mary has prepared for the world.[59]

It is not hard to understand why Portugal at this time has been called the "Showcase of Our Lady". And the triple miracle of Portugal is but a preview of how Russia and the world will look after the Collegial Consecration of Russia. The miraculous example of Portugal is also helpful to us as a gauge by which we can judge the present. If we contrast the threefold miracle of Portugal with the present condition of

---

[54] *The Whole Truth About Fatima* - Vol. II, pp. 427-428.

[55] See *The Whole Truth About Fatima* - Vol. II, pp. 369-439.

[56] Ibid., p. 428.

[57] Ibid., p. 405. Cardinal Cerejeira spoke these words during the 1942 Jubilee celebration of the Fatima apparitions.

[58] We trust the word of a Fatima believer such as Cardinal Cerejeira, rather than a Fatima debunker such as Cardinal Bertone. See later chapters.

[59] Cardinal Cerejeira, Preface to *Jacinta* (1942), *Obras Pastorais*, Vol. II, p. 333. Cf. also his homily of May 13, 1942, *Merv. XX's*, p. 339. Cited from *The Whole Truth About Fatima* - Vol. II, p. 437.

Russia and the world, it is obvious that the consecration of Russia has yet to be achieved. (We shall return to this point in a later chapter.)

For men with high offices in the Church to take actions that impede the consecration of Russia, thereby denying to the Church and the world the heavenly bounty Mary's intercession obtained for Portugal, is not only a monumental folly but also an incalculable injustice. It is this injustice that has motivated the publication of this book.

On February 6, 1939, seven months before the declaration of war, Sister Lucy (above) wrote to her bishop, Msgr. da Silva (above). She told him that war was imminent, but then spoke of a miraculous promise. She said *"in this horrible war, Portugal would be spared because of the national consecration to the Immaculate Heart of Mary made by the bishops."* And Portugal was, in fact, spared all the horrors of World War II.

Chapter 4
The Third Secret

Precisely as predicted by the Virgin in 1917, World War II had started during the reign of Pius XI. By 1943 Josef Stalin was well-practiced in liquidating Catholics and exporting world communism from Soviet Russia. In June of that same year, Sister Lucy, now age 36, had come down with pleurisy. This development greatly alarmed Bishop da Silva of Leiria-Fatima and Canon Galamba, his close friend and advisor. They both feared that Sister Lucy would die without writing down the Third Secret.

So Terrible She Could Not Write It Down

In September 1943 Bishop da Silva suggested to her that she write it down, but she declined to comply with a mere suggestion because she did not want to take responsibility for such an initiative on her own. Sister Lucy was gravely concerned that, without a formal command from her bishop, she did not yet have Our Lord's permission to reveal the Third Secret. She stated that she would, however, obey an express command from Bishop da Silva.

In mid-October 1943, during a visit to Sister Lucy at the convent in Tuy, Spain (about 250 miles from Fatima and about a 10-minute walk from the Portuguese border), Bishop da Silva gave Sister Lucy a formal order to write down the Secret. Sister Lucy then attempted every day to obey the bishop's command, but was unable to do so for the next two and a half months.

The Virgin Herself Instructs
Sister Lucy to Reveal the Secret

Finally, on January 2, 1944 the Blessed Virgin Mary appeared to Lucy again, to strengthen her and confirm that it is indeed God's will that she reveal the final part of the Secret. Only then was Sister Lucy able to overcome her trepidation and write down the Third Secret of Fatima.[60] But even so, it was not until January 9, 1944 that Sister Lucy wrote the following note to Bishop da Silva, informing him that the Secret had finally been committed to paper:

> I have written what you asked me; God willed to try me a little, but finally this was indeed His will: it [the text] is sealed in an envelope and this [the sealed envelope] is in the notebooks ...[61]

---

[60] *The Whole Truth About Fatima* - Vol. III: *The Third Secret*, (English Translation, Immaculate Heart Publications, Buffalo, New York, U.S.A., 1990, republished in 2001) p. 46.

[61] The text of this indented paragraph is a translation, not dependent on the French version of Frère Michel but rather translated from the original text of Sister Lucy in Portuguese as provided to us by Father Alonso in an article in *Fatima 50*, published on October 13,

One critic of the first edition of this book objected that this quote was an erroneous translation of Frère Michel's French text (see footnote 61—we do not depend on Frère Michel's French version). Thus, says the critic, Sister Lucy definitely refers to only a single text comprising

---

1967 in Fatima itself.

Father Alonso, in that article from *Fatima 50*, quotes twice from Sister Lucy's letter of January 9, 1944 to Bishop José da Silva, Bishop of Leiria. The first is a reference to the order given to her from Bishop da Silva, to write down the content of a part of the Secret:

> **... se eu quisesse achava bem escrever _a parte_ que me falta do segredo, que não era para ser já publicada, mas sim para ficar escrito ...**

> *... if I thought it well to write the part of the secret that I did not give before, which was, as yet, not for publication, but that, yes, could be written down ...*

In the second quote Sister Lucy tells Bishop da Silva she has accomplished the task and communicates some details about it:

> **Já escrevi o que me mandou; Deus quis provar-me um pouco (,) mas afinal era essa a sua vontade: Está _lacrada_ dentro dum _envelope_ e _este_ dentro dos cadernos...**

> *Now I wrote what Your Excellency ordered me [to write]: God wanted to try me a little (,) but finally this was His will: It [the part of the secret that I did not give before] is sealed inside an envelope and this [envelope] [is] inside the notebooks.*

One can observe that in the second quotation, when speaking of the envelope, the Portuguese adjective used is feminine: *lacrada* (sealed); whereas the local noun *envelope* is masculine, so this indicates there is a remote noun being modified by *lacrada*. If the reader refers back to the first quotation he can then understand that *lacrada* modifies the feminine noun *a parte* (the part) or more precisely *a parte que me falta do segredo* ("the part of the secret that I did not give before").

The Portuguese pronoun *este* (this), on the other hand, which follows five words after the word *lacrada*, is masculine, so it, therefore, cannot refer to *lacrada* but must instead refer to the local masculine noun *envelope* (envelope).

So Sister Lucy was explaining to Bishop da Silva that there was a missing part to the Third Secret which she did not give before, and that this missing part was sealed in an envelope that she had placed inside her notebooks.

The text of the Third Secret vision revealed by the Vatican in June 2000 was written on notebook paper. On May 31, 2007 Cardinal Bertone revealed on public television (*Porta a Porta*, RAI) in Italy that it was a broad piece of lined paper folded once in the middle and in this way comprised four connected pages. The four-page vision text is a total of 62 lines and, it is clear, was originally bound in a notebook with other pages.

In the voluminous, well-documented history of the Third Secret of Fatima, many details are recorded about a text which is obviously something different from this 62-line text. Sister Lucy mentions in her letter of January 9, 1944 to Bishop da Silva (which we quoted above) that she has sealed in an envelope "the part of the secret that I did not give before". Bishop Venancio testified that during the transfer of the Secret from Bishop da Silva's office in Leiria to the Papal Nuncio in Lisbon in 1957, in the envelope he held up to the light to observe its contents, the text was written on a single, ordinary sheet of paper, and was 20 to 25 lines in length. Cardinal Ottaviani also testified to it being written on a single sheet of paper and it was 25 lines long.

So once again, the second quote published in the magazine *Fatima 50*, which had been originally written in the letter of January 9, 1944 from Sister Lucy to Bishop da Silva, tells of how this one-page text, sealed in an envelope, was originally placed by Lucy inside her notebooks. This is because in one of those notebooks is where she had written the larger 4-page companion text, 62 lines in length, which described the vision, and placing them together like that was for the purpose that both the description of the vision and the explanation of the vision could be read together as two component parts of a unified whole. See also footnote 353 in Chapter 13.

the Secret. In response it should be noted that this book actually went beyond the French text of Frère Michel's book to his original source in the Portuguese, and our French critic needs to do the same to get to the real truth of the matter.[62]

In the meantime, this linguistic argument over the meaning of "it" has been rendered academic by the explosive developments that have occurred since the first edition appeared in 2002, which are discussed in some detail in Chapter 14. Suffice it to observe for the moment that these developments were triggered by the publication of *Il Quarto Segreto di Fatima* [*The Fourth Secret of Fatima*] in November 2006 by Antonio Socci, an Italian Catholic celebrity and public intellectual who has been a collaborator with both the currently reigning Pope (when he was Cardinal Ratzinger) and the current Vatican Secretary of State, Cardinal Bertone. In *Fourth Secret* Socci—frequently citing this very book—presents the overwhelming evidence, including the breakthrough testimony of a living eyewitness, Archbishop Loris F. Capovilla, personal secretary to Pope John XXIII, that there are two texts and two envelopes comprising the whole of the Third Secret, only one of which has been disclosed. To his own surprise, Socci reached precisely the opposite of the conclusion he intended to prove when he set out to refute what he calls "the Fatimists": in his book Socci now acknowledges that there is a text which accompanies the text of the vision of "the Bishop dressed in white" published by the Vatican on June 26, 2000, a text "not yet revealed," which contains "what follows the words of the Virgin interrupted by the 'etc.'"[63]

As attested by no less than Archbishop Capovilla, the personal secretary of John XXIII, the missing text of the Secret is evidently contained in what the Archbishop calls the "Capovilla envelope" (to distinguish it from the "Bertone envelope") on which he wrote his name, the names of those who had read its contents, and the statement by John XXIII that "I leave it to others to comment or decide." The Archbishop further revealed that the "Capovilla envelope" was kept in a desk called "Barbarigo" (named after Saint Gregory Barbarigo [† 1697], who had owned it) in the bedroom of John XXIII and not in the Holy Office archives, where the "Bertone" envelope was kept, and that Paul VI retrieved the envelope from "Barbarigo" and read its contents in 1963, not 1965, as the Vatican account claims.[64] The existence of these two envelopes finally explains why three different Popes (John XXIII, Paul VI and John Paul II) read texts of the Secret on two different dates, years apart—i.e. the text in the Holy Office archives and the text in the papal apartment. Bertone has failed and refused to produce the "Capovilla envelope" located in the papal apartment, even though the whole world

---

[62] This point is further explained in Chapter 13.

[63] Socci, *The Fourth Secret of Fatima*, English ed., p. 132; popular ed., p. 92; Italian ed., p. 142.

[64] Ibid., English ed., p. 136; popular ed., p. 94; Italian ed., p. 146; see also Appendix II in this book, *The Devil's Final Battle*.

now knows of its existence because Cardinal Bertone himself on his own television presentation in September 2007 acknowledged Archbishop Capovilla's testimony to this fact.

Furthermore, as shown by none other than Cardinal Bertone himself on national television in Italy on May 31, 2007, we have since come to learn that there are two sealed envelopes pertaining to the Third Secret prepared by Sister Lucy, on each of which she wrote the identical warning: "By express order of Our Lady, this envelope can only be opened in 1960 [only] by the Cardinal Patriarch of Lisbon or the Bishop of Leiria."[65] Sister Lucy never mentioned the existence of a second sealed envelope in any of her *published* writings (vast quantities of her writings remain under lock and key), even though we now know that the second envelope exists because Bertone showed it to the world on television.

In short, developments since 2002 have "broken the case" on the Third Secret, which is precisely why Socci's book declares: "that there is a part of the Secret not revealed and considered unspeakable *is certain* [emphasis added]. And today—having decided to deny its existence—the Vatican runs the risk of exposing itself to very heavy pressure and blackmail."[66]

A Single Sheet of Paper

Even before recent developments "broke" the case, it was already apparent that the Third Secret involved two documents: one sealed in an envelope, and the other in Lucy's notebooks. For why else would Lucy have advised the Bishop of Fatima in her letter of January 9, 1944 that a text of the Secret was in a sealed envelope and that this envelope "is in the notebooks"? Clearly, the notebooks contain something related to the Secret or there would have been no point in including them in the delivery of the envelope.

What must have happened is that sometime between the letter of January 9, 1944 and Sister Lucy's personal delivery of the Third Secret to the Bishop of Gurza on June 17, 1944 (for delivery by him to Bishop da Silva), the second text found its way into a *second* sealed envelope, appropriately bearing its own "1960 order." While Sister Lucy did not mention this other envelope in her January letter (or thereafter in any writing of which we know), we are certain it was created *because, as just noted, Cardinal Bertone revealed its existence on television* on May 31, 2007. Exactly when and how the second envelope came into the picture is probably shown somewhere in the 24 volumes of Fatima documentation, including Sister Lucy's correspondence, prepared for publication by Father Alonso but suppressed by his ecclesiastical

---

[65] Cf. Christopher A. Ferrara, *The Secret Still Hidden* (Pound Ridge, New York: Good Counsel Publications, Inc., 2008), Chapter 8, including still shots from the telecast video in which Cardinal Bertone displayed the two envelopes to the camera; see also the two photos—Figures 2 and 3—on page XV in the photo section of this book, *The Devil's Final Battle*.

[66] Socci, *The Fourth Secret of Fatima*, English ed., p. 162; popular ed., p. 111; Italian ed., p. 173.

superiors, presumably on orders from the Vatican (except for two heavily edited volumes that were eventually released for publication).

But let us focus for the time being on the contents of the lone sealed envelope mentioned by Sister Lucy on January 9, 1944, reserving for discussion in Chapter 14 the revelation of the second envelope by Cardinal Bertone in 2007. Having finally committed the Third Secret to paper and placed it in a sealed envelope, Lucy was still so filled with trepidation over the contents of the Secret that she would not entrust it (or the accompanying notebook) to anyone but a bishop for conveyance to Bishop da Silva.

On June 17, 1944, Sister Lucy left Tuy, crossed the River Minho, and arrived at Asilo Fonseca where she handed to Archbishop Manuel Maria Ferreira da Silva (the Archbishop of Gurza) the notebook in which she had inserted the envelope containing the Secret. That same day, Archbishop Manuel da Silva delivered the Secret to Bishop José Alves Correia da Silva (the Bishop of Leiria) at his country home not far from Braga. Then, the Bishop of Leiria took the Secret to the Episcopal Palace in Leiria. These details will be very important in view of what is set forth in the Vatican commentary on the Third Secret ultimately published on June 26, 2000.

From the first, the unanimous testimony was that the Third Secret is written in the form of a letter on a single sheet of paper. Father Joaquin Alonso (the official archivist of the papers on the Fatima apparitions) reports that both Sister Lucy and Cardinal Ottaviani stated that the Secret was written on a single sheet of paper:

> Lucy tells us that she wrote it on a sheet of paper. Cardinal Ottaviani, who has read it, tells us the same thing: 'She wrote it on a sheet of paper ... '.[67]

Cardinal Ottaviani, as Prefect of the Congregation for the Doctrine of the Faith in 1967, stated that he had read the Third Secret and that it was written on a single sheet of paper. He testified to this fact on February 11, 1967, during a press conference at the time of a meeting of the Pontifical Marian Academy in Rome. Cardinal Ottaviani stated:

> And then, what did she [Lucy] do to obey the Most Holy Virgin? She wrote on a sheet of paper, in Portuguese, what the Holy Virgin had asked her to tell ...[68]

Cardinal Ottaviani is a witness to this fact. In the same press conference, he states:

> I, who have had the grace and the gift to read the text of the Secret—although I too am held to secrecy because I am bound by the Secret ...[69]

We also have the testimony of Bishop Venancio, who was then the

---

[67] Father Joaquin Alonso, *La Verdad sobre el Secreto de Fatima*, (Centro Mariano, Madrid, Spain, 1976) p. 60. See also Frère Michel, *The Whole Truth About Fatima* - Vol. III, p. 651.

[68] *The Whole Truth About Fatima* - Vol. III, p. 725.

[69] Ibid., p. 727.

Auxiliary Bishop of Leiria-Fatima, that he was ordered by Bishop da Silva in mid-March 1957 to bring copies of all Sister Lucy's writings—including the original of the Third Secret—to the Apostolic Nuncio at Lisbon for transferral to Rome. Before bringing Lucy's writings to the Nuncio, Bishop Venancio looked at the envelope containing the Third Secret while holding it up to the light and saw that the Secret was "written on a small sheet of paper".[70] Frère Michel first identifies the nature of this testimony:

> However, thanks to the disclosures of Bishop Venancio, at the time Auxiliary Bishop of Leiria and intimately involved with these events, we now have many reliable facts which we will take care not to neglect. I myself received them from the mouth of Bishop Venancio on February 13, 1984, at Fatima. The former Bishop of Fatima repeated to me on this subject, almost word for word, what he had already said previously to Father Caillon, who gave a very detailed account of it in his conferences.[71]

Here now is Bishop Venancio's testimony, according to Frère Michel:

> Bishop Venancio related that once he was by himself, he took the great envelope of the Secret and tried to look through it and see the contents. In the bishop's large envelope he discerned a smaller envelope, that of Lucy, and inside this envelope *an ordinary sheet of paper* with margins on each side of three quarters of a centimeter. He took the trouble to note the size of everything. Thus the final Secret of Fatima was written on a small sheet of paper.[72] [emphasis added]

As we will see in Chapter 9, the text published by the Vatican in 2000 does not correspond to this document.

The evidence further shows that this single sheet of paper contained some 20-25 lines of text. On this point the testimonies of Sister Lucy, Cardinal Ottaviani, Bishop Venancio, Father Alonso and Frère Michel all agree:

> ... we are just as certain that the twenty or thirty lines of the third Secret ...[73]

> The final Secret of Fatima, written on a small sheet of paper, is therefore not very long. Probably twenty to twenty-five lines ...[74]

> Bishop Venancio looked "at the envelope [containing the Third Secret] while holding it up to the light. He could see inside a little sheet of which he measured the exact size. We thus know that the Third Secret is not very long, probably 20 to 25 lines ..."[75]

---

[70] Frère François de Marie des Anges, *Fatima: Tragedy and Triumph*, (Immaculate Heart Publications, Buffalo, New York, U.S.A., 1994) p. 45.

[71] *The Whole Truth About Fatima* - Vol. III, pp. 479-480.

[72] Ibid., p. 481.

[73] Ibid., p. 626.

[74] *Fatima, Tragedy and Triumph*, p. 45.

[75] Brother Michael of the Holy Trinity, *The Secret of Fatima ... Revealed*, (Immaculate Heart

As we will see in Chapter 9, the text the Vatican published comprises 62 lines.

Written in the Form of a Letter

Equally clear is that the Third Secret was written down in the form of a letter to Bishop da Silva. Sister Lucy herself tells us that the Third Secret was written as a letter. On this point we have the written testimony of Father Jongen who, on February 3-4, 1946, interrogated Sister Lucy as follows:

> "You have already made known two parts of the Secret. When will the time arrive for the third part?" "I communicated the third part in a *letter* to the Bishop of Leiria," she answered.[76] [emphasis added]

Next we have the decisive words of Canon Galamba:

> When the bishop refused to open the *letter*, Lucy made him promise that it would definitely be opened and read to the world either at her death or in 1960, whichever would come first.[77] [emphasis added]

As we will see in Chapter 9, what the Vatican published in 2000 is not a letter.

To Be Revealed to the World by 1960

Why 1960? In 1955 Cardinal Ottaviani asked her why it was not to be opened before 1960. She told him, "because then it will be clearer (*mais claro*)." Sister Lucy had made the Bishop of Leiria-Fatima promise that the Secret would be read to the world at her death, but in no event later than 1960, "because the Blessed Virgin wishes it so." And from Canon Casimir Barthas: "Moreover, it [the Third Secret] will soon be known, since Sister Lucy affirms that Our Lady wills that it can be published beginning in 1960."[78] And, sure enough, as we will see in Chapter 14, in 2007 none other than Cardinal Bertone would reveal the existence of *two* sealed envelopes, each bearing the warning in Sister Lucy's own handwriting that by order of the Blessed Virgin the envelope *was not to be opened before 1960* and not to be opened by anyone other than Bishop da Silva or the Patriarch of Lisbon.

This testimony introduces a third crucial fact concerning the Secret: that it was to be revealed by 1960. Indeed, in February 1960, the Patriarch of Lisbon would declare:

Publications, Buffalo, New York, U.S.A.) p. 7.

[76] *Revue Mediatrice et Reine*, October 1946, pp. 110-112. See also *The Whole Truth About Fatima* - Vol. III, p. 470.

[77] Father Alonso, *La Verdad sobre el Secreto de Fatima*, pp. 46-47. See also *The Whole Truth About Fatima* - Vol. III, p. 470.

[78] Barthas, *Fatima, merveille du XXe siècle*, p. 83. Fatima-editions, 1952. It must be noted that Canon Barthas published this account after having the privilege of meeting Sister Lucy again, on October 15, 1950 in the company of Msgr. Bryant, O.M.I., vicar apostolic of Athabasca-Mackenzie. See *The Whole Truth About Fatima* - Vol. III, p. 472.

Bishop da Silva enclosed (the envelope sealed by Lucy) in another envelope on which he indicated that *the letter had to be opened in 1960* by himself, Bishop José Correia da Silva, if he was still alive, or if not, by the Cardinal Patriarch of Lisbon.[79]

Father Alonso tells us:

Other bishops also spoke—and with authority—about the year 1960 as the date indicated for opening the famous letter. Thus, when the then-titular Bishop of Tiava, and Auxiliary Bishop of Lisbon asked Lucy when the Secret was to be opened, he always received the same answer: in 1960.[80]

And in 1959, Bishop Venancio, the new Bishop of Leiria, declared:

I think that the letter will not be opened before 1960. Sister Lucy had asked that it should not be opened before her death, or not before 1960. We are now in 1959 and Sister Lucy is in good health.[81]

Finally, we have the Vatican announcement of February 8, 1960 (appearing in a communiqué of the Portuguese news agency A.N.I.), concerning the decision to suppress the Secret—a document to which we shall return in Chapter 6. The Vatican announcement states:

... it is most likely that the *letter* will never be opened, in which Sister Lucy wrote down the *words which Our Lady confided* as a secret to the three shepherds of the Cova da Iria.[82] [emphasis added]

Thus far all the evidence points to the following: a secret written down in the form of a letter on a single sheet of paper, containing 20-25 lines of handwritten text, with 3/4 centimeter margins on each side; a secret to be revealed not later than 1960, and in that year, particularly, because "it will be much clearer (*mais claro*)" then.

It was this document that Bishop Venancio transferred to the Papal Nuncio, who then transferred it to the Holy Office (now known as the Congregation for the Doctrine of the Faith) in 1957:

Arriving at the Vatican on April 16, 1957, the Secret undoubtedly was placed by Pope Pius XII in his personal desk, inside a small wooden box, bearing the inscription *Secretum Sancti Officii* (Secret of the Holy Office).[83]

It is important to note that the Pope was the head of the Holy Office prior to Pope Paul VI reorganizing the Vatican in 1967. Therefore, it

---

[79] *Novidades*, February 24, 1960, quoted by *La Documentation Catholique*, June 19, 1960, col. 751. See also *The Whole Truth About Fatima* - Vol. III, p. 472.

[80] Father Alonso, *La Verdad sobre el Secreto de Fatima*, p. 46. See also *The Whole Truth About Fatima* - Vol. III, p. 475.

[81] Father Alonso, *La Verdad sobre el Secreto de Fatima*, p. 46. See also *The Whole Truth About Fatima* - Vol. III, p. 478.

[82] *The Whole Truth About Fatima* - Vol. III, p. 578.

[83] *Fatima, Tragedy and Triumph*, p. 45.

was quite appropriate for the Pope to retain the Third Secret in his possession and for the box containing it to be labeled "Secret of the Holy Office". With the Pope being the head of the Holy Office, this box became part of the Holy Office archives. Bear these crucial facts in mind for later consideration.

A Prediction of Apostasy in the Church

What about the contents of the Secret? We return now to the telltale phrase "In Portugal the dogma of the Faith will always be preserved etc." which, as noted in a previous chapter, appears at the end of the integral text of the first two parts of the Great Secret in Lucy's Fourth Memoir.

On this point we must consider the crucial testimony of Fr. Joseph Schweigl, who was entrusted by Pope Pius XII with a secret mission: to interrogate Sister Lucy about the Third Secret. This he did at the Carmel of Coimbra on September 2, 1952. Upon his return to Rome, Father Schweigl went to his residence at the Russicum and said to a colleague the following day:

> I cannot reveal anything of what I learned at Fatima concerning the Third Secret, but I can say that it has two parts: one concerns the Pope; the other logically (although I must say nothing) would have to be the continuation of the words: 'In Portugal, the dogma of the Faith will always be preserved.'[84]

Thus is confirmed the conclusion that one part of the Third Secret is indeed a continuation of the phrase whose completion the Vatican has yet to reveal: "In Portugal the dogma of the Faith will always be preserved etc." But the text the Vatican published in 2000—the text of the vision of "a Bishop dressed in white"—is in no way a continuation of that telltale phrase and does not contain even a single word uttered by the Virgin.

The conclusion that the Secret involves a continuation of Our Lady of Fatima's reference to dogma being preserved in Portugal—and by implication not preserved in other places—is corroborated by many other witnesses, including the following:

Father Fuentes

On December 26, 1957, Father Agustín Fuentes interviewed Sister Lucy. The interview was published in 1958 with an Imprimatur and the approbation of the Bishop of Fatima as well as with an Imprimatur of his Archbishop, Archbishop Sanchez of Veracruz, Mexico. Among other things, Sister Lucy told Father Fuentes the following:

> Father, the Most Holy Virgin is very sad because no one has paid any attention to Her message, neither the good nor the bad. The good continue on their way but without giving any importance

---

[84] *The Whole Truth About Fatima* - Vol. III, p. 710.

to Her message. The bad, not seeing the punishment of God falling upon them, continue their life of sin without even caring about the message. But believe me, Father, God will chastise the world and this will be in a terrible manner. The punishment from Heaven is imminent.

Father, how much time is there before 1960 arrives? It will be very sad for everyone, not one person will rejoice at all if beforehand the world does not pray and do penance. I am not able to give any other details because it is still a secret. ...

This is the Third part of the Message of Our Lady which will remain secret until 1960.

Tell them, Father, that many times, the most Holy Virgin told my cousins Francisco and Jacinta, as well as myself, that many nations will disappear from the face of the earth. She said that Russia will be the instrument of chastisement chosen by Heaven to punish the whole world if we do not beforehand obtain the conversion of that poor nation.

Father, the devil is in the mood for engaging in a decisive battle against the Blessed Virgin. And the devil knows what it is that most offends God and which in a short space of time will gain for him the greatest number of souls. *Thus, the devil does everything to overcome souls consecrated to God, because in this way, the devil will succeed in leaving souls of the faithful abandoned by their leaders, thereby the more easily will he seize them.*

That which afflicts the Immaculate Heart of Mary and the Heart of Jesus is *the fall of religious and priestly souls.* The devil knows that *religious and priests who fall away from their beautiful vocation drag numerous souls to hell. ... The devil wishes to take possession of consecrated souls.* He tries to corrupt them in order to lull to sleep the souls of laypeople and thereby lead them to final impenitence.[85]

Father Alonso

Before his death in 1981, Father Joaquin Alonso, who for sixteen years was the official archivist of Fatima, testified as follows:

It is therefore completely probable that the text makes concrete references to the crisis of faith within the Church and to the negligence of the pastors themselves [and the] internal struggles in the very bosom of the Church and of grave pastoral negligence

---

[85] English translation of Sister Lucy's interview with Father Fuentes taken from Frère Michel's *The Whole Truth About Fatima* - Vol. III, pp. 503 to 508. Frère Michel explains that the text comes from Fatima scholar Father Joaquin Alonso's *La Verdad sobre el Secreto de Fatima* (pp. 103-106), and from the text published by Father Ryan in the June 1959 issue of *Fatima Findings* and the No. 8-9 August-September 1961 issue of the Italian magazine *Messaggero del Cuore di Maria*.

of the upper hierarchy.[86]

In the period preceding the great triumph of the Immaculate Heart of Mary, terrible things are to happen. These form the content of the third part of the Secret. What are they? If 'in Portugal the dogma of the Faith will always be preserved,'... *it can be clearly deduced from this that in other parts of the Church these dogmas are going to become obscure or even lost altogether.*[87]

Does the unpublished text speak of concrete circumstances? It is very possible that it speaks not only of a real crisis of the faith in the Church during this in-between period, but like the secret of La Salette, for example, there are more concrete references to the internal struggles of Catholics or to the fall of priests and religious. *Perhaps it even refers to the failures of the upper hierarchy of the Church.* For that matter, none of this is foreign to other communications Sister Lucy has had on this subject.[88]

Cardinal Ratzinger

On November 11, 1984, Cardinal Ratzinger, then head of the Congregation for the Doctrine of the Faith, gave an interview in *Jesus* magazine, a publication of the Pauline Sisters. The interview is entitled "Here is Why the Faith is in Crisis," and was published with the Cardinal's explicit permission. In this interview Cardinal Ratzinger admits that a crisis of faith is affecting the Church around the world. In this context, he reveals that he has read the Third Secret and that the Secret refers to "dangers threatening the faith and the life of the Christian and therefore (the life) of the world."

The Cardinal thus confirms Father Alonso's thesis that the Secret pertains to widespread apostasy in the Church. Cardinal Ratzinger says in the same interview that the Secret also refers to "the importance of the *Novissimi*[89] [the Last Times/the Last Things]" and that "[i]f it is

---

[86] *The Whole Truth About Fatima* - Vol. III, p. 704.

[87] Ibid., p. 687.

[88] Ibid., p. 705.

[89] In *Il Quarto Segreto di Fatima* [*The Fourth Secret of Fatima*], the respected Italian journalist and Catholic commentator Antonio Socci reviews the evidence for the existence of a yet-to-be-disclosed text of the Third Secret, reverses his own prior opinion, and concludes that the "Fatimists" are, after all, correct in deducing its existence and its suppression by the Vatican. But he objects that no such deduction is possible on the basis of Cardinal Ratzinger's reference to the "*novissimi*" (last things), which Socci maintains (cf. *Il Quarto Segreto di Fatima*, English ed., p. 95; popular ed., p. 68; Italian ed., pp. 103-104) is merely a reference to the Last Things in the life of the individual man (death, judgment, Heaven, hell and purgatory) rather than to any apocalyptic warning concerning the world at large.

In this Socci is mistaken, since the theological term *novissimi* is the Italian rendering of the same term in Latin: *novissimis*. That term embraces *both* the "last things" as to individual men, *and* the "last things" as to the world: namely, the Second Coming of Christ, the universal judgment, and the end of the physical world as we know it. (Cf. Fathers of the Society of Jesus, *Sacrae Theologiae Summa* [La Editorial Catolica, S.A., Madrid, Spain, 1953], Biblioteca de Autores Christianos edition, Vol. IV ["*De sacramentis.*

footnote continued on next page

not made public—at least for the time being—it is in order to prevent religious prophecy from being mistaken for a quest for the sensational ..." The Cardinal further reveals that "the things contained in this 'Third Secret' correspond to what has been announced in Scripture and has been said again and again in many other Marian apparitions, first of all that of Fatima ..."[90]

Bishop Amaral

In accord with Cardinal Ratzinger regarding "dangers threatening the faith" is Bishop Amaral—the third Bishop of Fatima. In a speech in Vienna, Austria on September 10, 1984, he said the following:

> Its content concerns only our faith. To identify the [Third] Secret with catastrophic announcements or with a nuclear holocaust is to deform the meaning of the message. *The loss of faith of a continent is worse than the annihilation of a nation*; and it is true that faith is continually diminishing in Europe.[91] [Emphasis added]

Cardinal Oddi

On March 17, 1990 Cardinal Oddi gave the following testimony to Italian journalist Lucio Brunelli in the journal *Il Sabato*:

> It [the Third Secret] has nothing to do with Gorbachev. The Blessed Virgin was alerting us against apostasy in the Church.

De novissimis"], Tract VI, Book I ["*De novissimi homines*", "Of the Last Things of Men"], Chapters 1-5, pp. 874-1022; Book II ["*De novissimi mundi*", "Of the Last Things of the World"], Chapters 1-5, pp. 1023-1066; see also Father Joseph de Ste. Marie, "The Third Secret of Fatima", *The Fatima Crusader*, Issue 18, October-December 1985, pp. S-4 and S-5.) Cardinal Ratzinger's linkage of the Third Secret to "the dangers threatening the faith and the life of the Christian, and therefore *of the world*," the "absolute importance of history," *and* the "importance of the *novissimi*" in one and the same statement about the contents of the Third Secret clearly implicates the full eschatological meaning of the term as it concerns "the end" for both men and nations, which is precisely the subject of the message-warning of Our Lady of Fatima as a whole, including the second part of the Great Secret, wherein She warns that "various nations will be annihilated..."

If not a reference to the Last Day proper, "*novissimi*" in the context of the Third Secret would relate to events proximate to the Last Day, perhaps even including the appearance of the Antichrist or a forerunner. Given the enigmatic character of the Cardinal's remarks, however, clarification is needed, and that can only come with disclosure of the very text Socci agrees has been suppressed—the text in which the Virgin explains the emergence of the scenario depicted in the wordless vision of the "Bishop dressed in white" being executed by soldiers outside a devastated city littered with corpses. Indeed, the vision itself clearly points to events involving more than the "*novissimi*" as they pertain to the death of individual men in the ordinary course of earthly existence.

[90] *Jesus* magazine, November 11, 1984, p. 79; see the actual Italian text of the key part of Cardinal Ratzinger's interview in *Jesus* magazine photographically reproduced on page 352 of this book (in Appendix II), with our English translation provided in the text box on page 353. See also Frère Michel de la Sainte Trinité, *The Whole Truth About Fatima* - Vol. III, pp. 822-823; and *The Fatima Crusader*, Issue 37, Summer 1991, p. 7.

[91] *Fatima, Tragedy and Triumph*, pp. 243-244. See also Frère Michel de la Sainte Trinité, *The Whole Truth About Fatima* - Vol. III, p. 676.

Cardinal Ciappi

To these witnesses we must add the testimony of Cardinal Mario Luigi Ciappi, who was nothing less than the personal papal theologian to five popes—Pius XII, John XXIII, Paul VI, John Paul I, and John Paul II. In a personal communication to a Professor Baumgartner in Salzburg (Austria), Cardinal Ciappi revealed that:

> In the Third Secret it is foretold, among other things, that the great apostasy in the Church will begin *at the top*.[92]

Sister Lucy

All of these testimonies are consistent with the repeated remarks of Sister Lucy herself—not only to Fr. Fuentes, as quoted above, but to many other reliable witnesses. Although bound to secrecy concerning the precise contents of the Third Secret, her remarks to reliable witnesses are full of references to churchmen "being fooled by false doctrine"; to a "diabolical disorientation" afflicting "so many persons who occupy places of responsibility" in the Church; to "priests and consecrated souls" who "are so deceived and misled" because "the devil has succeeded in infiltrating evil under cover of good ... leading into error and deceiving souls having a heavy responsibility through the place which they occupy ... They are blind men guiding other blind men," and so on.[93]

Pius XII Confirms
the Secret's Prediction of Apostasy

But perhaps the most remarkable testimony of all on this score is that of Cardinal Eugenio Pacelli, before he became Pope Pius XII and while he was still serving as Vatican Secretary of State during the reign of Pope Pius XI. Speaking even before Sister Lucy had committed the Third Secret to paper, the future Pius XII made an astonishing prophecy about a coming upheaval in the Church:

> I am worried by the Blessed Virgin's messages to Lucy of Fatima. *This persistence of Mary about the dangers which menace the Church is a divine warning against the suicide of altering the Faith, in Her liturgy, Her theology and Her soul.* ... I hear all around me innovators who wish to dismantle the Sacred Chapel, destroy the universal flame of the Church, reject Her ornaments and make Her feel remorse for Her historical past.

Pope Pius XII's biographer, Msgr. Roche, noted that at this moment in the conversation, the future Pius XII then said (in answer to an objection):

---

[92] See Father Gerard Mura, "The Third Secret of Fatima: Has It Been Completely Revealed?", in the periodical *Catholic*, (published by the Transalpine Redemptorists, Orkney Isles, Scotland, Great Britain) March 2002.

[93] These quotations are condensed from numerous letters Sister Lucy wrote in the early 1970's to two of her nephews who were priests, and to other religious she knew. See *The Whole Truth About Fatima* - Vol. III, pp. 750-753.

A day will come when the civilized world will deny its God, when the Church will doubt as Peter doubted. She will be tempted to believe that man has become God. In our churches, Christians will search in vain for the red lamp where God awaits them. Like Mary Magdalene, weeping before the empty tomb, they will ask, "Where have they taken Him?"[94]

It is quite remarkable that the future Pope would relate this coming devastation in the Church specifically to "*the Blessed Virgin's messages to Lucy of Fatima*" and "*this persistence of Mary about the dangers which menace the Church.*" The prediction would be utterly senseless if it had been based on the first two parts of the Great Secret, which make no mention of such things as "the suicide of altering the Faith, in Her liturgy, Her theology and Her soul" or "innovators who wish to dismantle the Sacred Chapel, destroy the universal flame of the Church, reject Her ornaments and make Her feel remorse for Her historical past." Nor is there any indication whatsoever in the first two parts that "In our churches, Christians will search in vain for the red lamp where God awaits them."

How did the future Pope Pius XII know these things? If not by supernatural intuition, then by direct knowledge that some hitherto undisclosed portion of "the Blessed Virgin's messages to Sister Lucy of Fatima" revealed these future events in the Church.

In short, every single testimony pertaining to the contents of the Third Secret, from 1944 until at least 1984 (the date of the Ratzinger interview) confirms that it points to a catastrophic loss of faith and discipline in the Church, representing a breakthrough for the forces arrayed against Her for so long—the "innovators" that the future Pius XII heard "all around me," clamoring for the dismantling of the Sacred Chapel and changes in the liturgy and Catholic theology.

As we will show, that breakthrough began in 1960, precisely the year when (as Sister Lucy had insisted) the third part of the Secret should have been revealed. But before we return to that fateful year, when the great injustice of not revealing the Third Secret first began, we must first discuss the motive that preceded the injustice in order that we might understand why it has been perpetrated. We will now set out to uncover this motive from the known evidence as well as from the perpetrators' own words explaining their motives regarding this and related matters.

---

[94] Roche, *Pie XII Devant L'Histoire*, pp. 52-53.

Chapter 5

A Motive Emerges

As we observed in the Introduction, the injustice against the Church and the world which this book aims to expose is the systematic attempt since 1960 to conceal, misrepresent and deny part or even all of the authentic Message of Fatima even as its alarming prophecies are being fulfilled before our very eyes.

We return to the question we posed in the Introduction: Why would men in the highest positions of authority in the Church take such actions? As Aristotle observed, in order to understand an action one must look to the motive. That is what we shall do in this chapter.

To be sure, proving motive is always a difficult business, for one cannot read another man's mind, much less judge the state of his soul. In arriving at a conclusion as to motive, you the reader, much in the manner of a jury in a civil proceeding, can only base your decision on the external actions of the accused, in light of the surrounding circumstances. When a jury finds that a man has murdered his wife for the motive of obtaining insurance money, for example, it makes its finding of motive based on a reasonable inference drawn from the surrounding circumstances. Rarely would the killer in such a case openly admit "I killed her for the insurance." Instead, motive would be inferred from such things as the husband's recent purchase of a very large insurance policy on the wife.

Now, no one would accuse a jury of "rash judgment" in inferring from the circumstances that the husband in our hypothetical case harbored the intention of killing his wife for money. In the case of Fatima, too, motive can be deduced from circumstances; it is not "rash judgment" to reach a reasonable conclusion about motive based on what the identified Vatican prelates themselves have said and done. Moreover, as we will demonstrate in this case we have the equivalent of an admission as to motive. The Vatican prelates in question have been quite explicit in declaring a motive that would explain why they would conceal the posited text and militate against the Message of Fatima in general.

A New and Ruinous
Orientation of the Church

As we charged in the Introduction, the motive in this case arises from the recognition that the Message of Fatima, understood in a traditional Catholic sense, cannot be reconciled with decisions taken since the Second Vatican Council to change the entire orientation of the Catholic Church. That is, the Message stands in the way of an effort to do precisely what the future Pope Pius XII foresaw in his moment of supernatural clarity: to remake the Church into an institution oriented toward the world. The currently raging scandal in the Catholic priesthood is only one symptom of this ruinous effort to "update" the Catholic Church. Another way of putting it is that the current condition of the Catholic Church is the result of an unprecedented *invasion of the Church by liberalism*. We recall once again those prophetic words of Msgr. Pacelli (the future Pius XII), uttered in the light of the Message of Fatima:

> I am worried by the Blessed Virgin's messages to Lucy of Fatima. This persistence of Mary about the *dangers which menace the Church is a divine warning against the suicide of altering the Faith, in Her liturgy, Her theology and Her soul.* ... I hear all around me innovators who wish to dismantle the Sacred Chapel, destroy the universal flame of the Church, reject Her ornaments and make Her feel remorse for Her historical past.
>
> A day will come when the civilized world will deny its God, when the Church will doubt as Peter doubted. She will be tempted to believe that man has become God. In our churches, Christians will search in vain for the red lamp where God awaits them. Like Mary Magdalene, weeping before the empty tomb, they will ask, "Where have they taken Him?"

In the Introduction we also noted that this great change of orientation in the Church—in "Her liturgy, Her theology and Her soul", as the future Pope Pius XII put it—was the long-cherished goal of the organized forces that have been plotting against the Church for centuries; the same forces that were at work in Portugal in 1917, but were repelled by the Consecration of that nation to the Immaculate Heart of Mary in 1931. To repel those forces throughout the world was the very reason Heaven itself sent the Mother of God to Fatima to prescribe the Consecration of Russia. Those forces were soon to become the prime weapon of Satan's long war against the Church. Truly, the outcome of the war against the Church in our time hinges on the battle over fulfillment of the Fatima Message.

Our presentation of the evidence of the motive in this case—namely, a desire to impose upon the Church a new orientation to the exclusion of the Message of Fatima—requires some considerable historical background, which we will now present. This background will be of interest not only to Catholics, but also to non-Catholics who are seeking to understand what has happened to the Catholic Church since Vatican II.

The Goal of Organized Freemasonry: To Neutralize and "Instrumentalize" the Catholic Church

As we have seen with the example of Portugal in 1917, the forces of Masonry (and their Communist fellow travelers) conspired to prevent the Message of Fatima from finding its fulfillment in Portugal. The

Message was called a fraud or a childish delusion; the seers themselves were persecuted and even threatened with death. Such was the hatred of these forces for the Catholic Church and the Virgin Mother of God.

And so it is with these forces in the world at large today. One need not descend into the fever swamps of conspiracy theory to know that before 1960, the Popes issued more condemnations and warnings about the plotting of the Freemasons and the Communists against the Church than on any other single subject in Church history.

On this point, one cannot fail to consider the infamous *Permanent Instruction of the Alta Vendita*, a Masonic document that mapped out an entire plan for the infiltration and corruption of the Catholic Church in the 20th Century.[95] While it has become fashionable since the Second Vatican Council to scoff at the existence of such a conspiracy, it must be noted that the secret papers of the Alta Vendita (an Italian secret society), including the *Permanent Instruction*, fell into the hands of Pope Gregory XVI. The *Permanent Instruction* was published at the request of Blessed Pope Pius IX by Cardinal Cretineau-Joly in his work *The Roman Church and Revolution*.[96] With his brief of approbation of February 25, 1861 (addressed to the author) Pius IX guaranteed the authenticity of the *Permanent Instruction* and the other Masonic papers, but he did not allow anyone to divulge the true names of the members of the Alta Vendita implicated in the documents. Pope Leo XIII had likewise requested their publication. Both Popes acted, no doubt, in order to prevent such a tragedy from taking place. These great Pontiffs knew that such a calamity was far from impossible. (Pius XII also knew it, as we can see from his prophetic remarks while he was still Vatican Secretary of State.)

The full text of the *Permanent Instruction* is also contained in Msgr. George E. Dillon's book, *Grand Orient Freemasonry Unmasked*.[97] When Leo XIII was presented with a copy of Msgr. Dillon's book, he was so impressed that he ordered an Italian version to be completed and published at the Pope's own expense.[98]

The Alta Vendita was the highest lodge of the Carbonari, an Italian secret society with links to Freemasonry and which, along with Freemasonry, was condemned by the Catholic Church.[99] The estimable Catholic historian Father E. Cahill, SJ, who is hardly a "conspiracy nut", states in his work *Freemasonry and the Anti-Christian Movement* that the Alta Vendita was "commonly supposed to have been at the time

---

[95] For a booklet on the connection between the Alta Vendita and the new orientation of the Church since the Council, see John Vennari, *The Permanent Instruction of the Alta Vendita* (TAN Books and Publishers, Rockford, Illinois, 1999).

[96] Second volume, original edition, 1859, reprinted by Circle of the French Renaissance, Paris, 1976; Msgr. Delassus produced these documents again in his work *The Anti-Christian Conspiracy*, DDB, 1910, Tome III, pp. 1035-1092.

[97] Msgr. Dillon, *Grand Orient Freemasonry Unmasked* (Christian Book Club, Palmdale, California); see pp. 51-56 for the full text of the *Permanent Instruction*.

[98] Michael Davies, *Pope John's Council*, (Angelus Press, Kansas City, Missouri, 1992) p. 166.

[99] *The Catholic Encyclopedia*, Vol. 3, (Encyclopedia Press, New York, 1913) pp. 330-331.

the governing center of European Freemasonry."[100] The Carbonari were most active in Italy and France.

In his book *Athanasius and the Church of Our Time* (1974), Bishop Rudolph Graber, another objective and quite unimpeachable authority writing after the Second Vatican Council, quoted a prominent Freemason who declared that "the goal (of Freemasonry) is no longer the destruction of the Church, but to make use of it by infiltrating it."[101] In other words, since Freemasonry cannot completely obliterate Christ's Church, it plans not only to eradicate the influence of Catholicism in society, but to use the Church's structure and prestige as an instrument of "renewal," "progress" and "enlightenment"—that is, a means of furthering many of its own Luciferian "principles" and goals.

Discussing the Masonic vision of society and the world, Bishop Graber introduces the concept of synarchy: "What we are faced with here is the sum-total of the secret forces of all the 'orders' and schools which have joined together to set up an invisible world government. In the political sense, synarchy aims at the integration of all the financial and social forces which the world government, under socialist leadership naturally, has to support and promote. Catholicism, like all religions, would consequently be absorbed into a universal syncretism. Far from being suppressed, it would be integrated, a course which is already being steered in the principle of fellowship between clerics (of various religions)."

The strategy advanced in the *Permanent Instruction* to achieve this aim is astonishing in its audacity and cunning. From the start, the document tells of a process that will take decades to accomplish. Those who drew up the document knew that they would not see its fulfillment. They were inaugurating a work that would be carried on by succeeding generations of the initiated. The *Permanent Instruction* says, "In our ranks the soldier dies and the struggle goes on."

The *Instruction* called for the dissemination of liberal ideas and axioms throughout society and within the institutions of the Catholic Church so that laity, seminarians, clerics and prelates would, over the years, gradually be imbued with progressive principles. In time, this new mentality would be so pervasive that priests would be ordained, bishops consecrated, and Cardinals nominated whose thinking was in step with the modern thought rooted in the "Principles of 1789" (i.e. the principles of Freemasonry which caused the tremendous wars, bloodshed, and the Reign of Terror as well as the ongoing fight against God and His rights by the secular [this world only] state which inspired the French Revolution of 1789 onwards)—namely, pluralism, the equality of all religions, separation of Church and State, unbridled

---

[100] Rev. E. Cahill, S.J., *Freemasonry and the Anti-Christian Movement*, (Dublin: Gill, 1959) p. 101.

[101] Bishop Graber, *Athanasius and the Church of Our Time*, (Christian Book Club, Palmdale, California, 1974) p. 39.

freedom of speech, and so forth.

Eventually, a Pope would be elected from these ranks who would lead the Church on the path of "enlightenment and renewal". It must be stressed that it was not their aim to place a Freemason on the Chair of Peter. Their goal was to effect an environment that would eventually produce a Pope and a hierarchy won over to the ideas of liberal Catholicism, *all the while believing themselves to be faithful Catholics.*

These liberalized Catholic leaders, then, would no longer oppose the modern ideas of the revolution (as had been the consistent practice of the Popes from 1789 until 1958, who unanimously condemned these liberal principles), but would amalgamate or "baptize" them into the Church. The end result would be a Catholic clergy and laity marching under the banner of the "enlightenment", all the while thinking they are marching under the banner of the Apostolic keys.

No doubt with the *Permanent Instruction* in mind, in *Humanum Genus*, Pope Leo XIII called upon Catholic leaders to "tear off the mask from Freemasonry and make plain to all what it really is."[102] The publication of these documents of the Alta Vendita was a means of "tearing off the mask".

Lest there be any claim that we have mischaracterized the *Permanent Instruction*, we now quote from it at considerable length. What follows is not the entire *Instruction*, but the section that is most pertinent to our proof. The document reads:

> The Pope, whoever he is, will never come to the secret societies; it is up to the secret societies to take the first step toward the Church, with the aim of conquering both of them.

> The task that we are going to undertake is not the work of a day, or of a month, or of a year; it may last several years, perhaps a century; but in our ranks the soldier dies and the struggle goes on.

> We do not intend to win the Popes to our cause, to make them neophytes of our principles, propagators of our ideas. That would be a ridiculous dream; and if events turn out in some way, if Cardinals or prelates, for example, of their own free will or by surprise, should enter into a part of our secrets, this is not at all an incentive for desiring their elevation to the See of Peter. That elevation would ruin us. Ambition alone would have led them to apostasy, the requirements of power would force them to sacrifice us. What we must ask for, what we should look for and wait for, as the Jews wait for the Messiah, is a Pope according to our needs ...

> With that we shall march more securely towards the assault on the Church than with the pamphlets of our brethren in France and even the gold of England. Do you want to know the reason for this? It is that with this, in order to shatter the high rock on which

God has built His Church, we no longer need Hannibalian vinegar, or need gunpowder, or even need our arms. We have the little finger of the successor of Peter engaged in the ploy, and this little finger is as good, for this crusade, as all the Urban II's and all the Saint Bernards in Christendom.

We have no doubt that we will arrive at this supreme end of our efforts. But when? But how? The unknown is not yet revealed. Nevertheless, as nothing should turn us aside from the plan drawn up, and on the contrary everything should tend to this, as if as early as tomorrow success were going to crown the work that is barely sketched, we wish, in this instruction, which will remain secret for the mere initiates, to give the officials in charge of the supreme Vente some advice that they should instill in all the brethren, in the form of instruction or of a memorandum ...

Now then, to assure ourselves a Pope of the required dimensions, it is a question first of shaping him ... for this Pope, a generation worthy of the reign we are dreaming of. Leave old people and those of a mature age aside; go to the youth, and if it is possible, even to the children ... You will contrive for yourselves, at little cost, a reputation as good Catholics and pure patriots.

This reputation will put access to our doctrines into the midst of the young clergy, as well as deeply into the monasteries. In a few years, by the force of things, this young clergy will have overrun all the functions; they will form the sovereign's council, they will be called to choose a Pontiff who should reign. And this Pontiff, like most of his contemporaries, will be necessarily more or less imbued with the Italian and humanitarian principles that we are going to begin to put into circulation. It is a small grain of black mustard that we are entrusting to the ground; but the sunshine of justice will develop it up to the highest power, and you will see one day what a rich harvest this small seed will produce.

In the path that we are laying out for our brethren, there are found great obstacles to conquer, difficulties of more than one kind to master. They will triumph over them by experience and by clearsightedness; but the goal is so splendid that it is important to put all the sails to the wind in order to reach it. You want to revolutionize Italy, look for the Pope whose portrait we have just drawn. You wish to establish the reign of the chosen ones on the throne of the prostitute of Babylon, let the Clergy march under your standard, always believing that they are marching under the banner of the apostolic keys. You intend to make the last vestige of tyrants and the oppressors disappear; lay your snares like Simon Bar-Jona; lay them in the sacristies, the seminaries, and the monasteries rather than at the bottom of the sea: and if you do not hurry, we promise you a catch more miraculous than his. The fisher of fish became the fisher of men; you will bring friends around the apostolic Chair. You will have preached a revolution in tiara and in cope, marching with the cross and the banner, a revolution that will need to be only a little bit urged on to set fire to the four corners of the world.[103]

The Rise of Liberal Catholicism

As we have noted, the goal of Freemasonry was not to destroy the Church, which the Masons knew was impossible, but to neutralize and *instrumentalize* the Church—that is, to make the human element of the Church into an instrument for the advance of Freemasonic goals, by inducing the Church's members to embrace the Masonic worldview, which as we know is completely opposed in principle to the worldview of Our Lady of Fatima, Her message and Her promises of world peace.

The Masonic worldview regards the influence of the Catholic Church over social order as "tyranny" and seeks to free mankind from the "superstitions" of revealed religion, uniting all men in a rationalized pseudo-religion "in which all men agree"—apparently a creed of sociability and politeness—putting aside their religious differences, which are reduced to mere matters of private opinion.

Now, a liberalized hierarchy, even without a conscious association with Freemasonry, would readily lend itself to the work of establishing the Masonic ideal of a new world order (*novus ordo seclorum*) involving a false pan-religious "brotherhood" in which the Church abandons Her claim to be the sole ark of salvation and ceases Her opposition to the forces of the world. The first stage of this process was manifested in the 19th Century, by which time society had become increasingly permeated with the liberal principles of the French Revolution. Even in the mid-1800s this program was already causing great detriment to the Catholic Faith and the Catholic State. The supposedly "kinder and gentler" notions of pluralism, religious indifferentism, a democracy which believes all authority comes from the people, false notions of liberty, interfaith gatherings, separation of Church and State and other novelties were gripping the minds of post-enlightenment Europe, infecting statesmen and churchmen alike.

The Condemnation of Liberal Catholicism

The Popes of the 19th and early 20th Centuries waged war against these dangerous trends in full battle-dress. With a presence of mind rooted in the uncompromised certitude of Faith, these Popes were not taken in. They knew that evil principles, no matter how honorable they may appear, cannot bear good fruit, and that these were evil principles at their worst, since they were rooted not only in heresy, but apostasy.

---

[103] This passage is from the *Permanent Instruction of the Alta Vendita*. The full text of the *Permanent Instruction* is republished in Msgr. Dillon's *Grand Orient Freemasonry Unmasked* (Christian Book Club, Palmdale, California) on pp. 51-56.

Like commanding generals who recognize the duty to hold their ground at all cost, these Popes aimed powerful cannons at the errors of the modern world and fired incessantly. The encyclicals were their cannonballs and they never missed their target.

The most devastating blast came in the form of Blessed Pope Pius IX's monumental *Syllabus of Errors*, which he appended to his encyclical *Quanta Cura* (1864). When the smoke cleared, all involved in the battle were in no doubt as to who was on what side. The line of demarcation had been drawn clearly. In the *Syllabus*, Blessed Pius IX condemned the principal errors of the modern world, not because they were modern, but because these "new" ideas were rooted in pantheistic naturalism and, therefore, were incompatible with Catholic doctrine, as well as being destructive to society.

The teachings in the *Syllabus* were counter-liberalism, and the principles of liberalism were counter-syllabus. This was clearly recognized by all parties. Father Denis Fahey referred to this showdown as "Pius IX vs. the Pantheistic Deification of Man."[104] Speaking for the other side, the French Freemason Ferdinand Buissont declared likewise, "A school cannot remain neutral between the *Syllabus* and the *Declaration of the Rights of Man*."[105]

Yet the 19th Century saw a new breed of Catholic who sought a utopian compromise between the two. These men looked for what they believed to be "good" in the principles of 1789 and tried to introduce them into the Church. Many clergymen, infected by the spirit of the age, were caught up in a net that had been "cast into the sacristies and into the seminaries" by Freemasonry. These men came to be known as liberal Catholics. Blessed Pius IX regarded them with absolute horror. He said these "liberal Catholics" were the "worst enemies of the Church". In a letter to the French deputation headed by the Bishop of Nevers on June 18, 1871, Blessed Pius IX declared:

> That which I fear is not the Commune of Paris—no—that which I fear is Liberal Catholicism ... I have said so more than forty times, and I repeat it to you now, through the love that I bear you. The real scourge of France is Liberal Catholicism, which endeavors to unite two principles as repugnant to each other as fire and water.[106]

The Rise of Modernism

Yet in spite of this, the numbers of liberal Catholics steadily increased. The crisis reached a peak around the turn of the century when the liberalism of 1789 that had been "blowin' in the wind" swirled into the tornado of modernism. Father Vincent Miceli identified this heresy as such by describing modernism's "trinity of parents". He wrote: "Its

---

[104] Father Denis Fahey, *Mystical Body of Christ in the Modern World*, (Regina Publications, Dublin, Ireland, 1939) Chapter VII.
[105] Ibid., p. 116.
[106] Quoted from *The Catholic Doctrine*, Father Michael Muller, (Benzinger, 1888) p. 282.

religious ancestor is the Protestant Reformation ... its philosophical parent is the Enlightenment ... its political pedigree comes from the French Revolution."[107]

What is meant by "modernism"? Modernism is a synthesis or combination of all the errors of Liberal Catholicism together with a synthesis of all heresies into a comprehensive political, philosophical and theological system whose effect is to undermine the integrity of the entire Catholic Faith. While a complete examination of the vast modernist system of thought is far beyond the scope of this book,[108] it suffices for our purposes to say that, by various subtle errors, the modernist denies or undermines the divinity and divine revelation of Christ, the founding of the one true Church by Him, and the absolute immutability of Catholic doctrine (which the modernist claims can "evolve" according to changing circumstances). The modernist also embraces and promotes the liberal notions of "free speech," "freedom of conscience," and the error of religious indifferentism, which holds that all religions are more or less good and praiseworthy because they all arise from a so-called "religious sense" in man. This is an error which, of course, implicitly denies the reality of Original Sin by suggesting that all men can be truly religious and can find salvation in the various religions they invent without need of Jesus Christ and His supernatural sanctifying grace, His Redemption as well as the Catholic Church, the Catholic Faith, Baptism and the other sacraments of the Catholic Church.

Saint Pius X Puts Down the Modernist Revolt

Pope St. Pius X, who ascended to the Papal throne in 1903, recognized modernism as a most deadly plague that must be arrested. St. Pius X waged war on modernism by systematically isolating, defining and condemning its many erroneous propositions. In particular, St. Pius X issued a monumental encyclical against modernism (*Pascendi*) and a *Syllabus* of modernist errors (*Lamentabili*). In his encyclical *Pascendi* this great Pope wrote: "There is no part of Catholic truth which they leave untouched, none that they do not strive to corrupt." In the same encyclical he called modernism "the synthesis of all heresies," declaring that the most important obligation of the Pope is to insure the purity and integrity of Catholic doctrine, and that if he did nothing, then he would have failed in his essential duty.[109]

But St. Pius X did not stop there. A few years after *Pascendi*, recognizing that the Modernists had to be crushed before they rose up and caused havoc in the Church, this sainted Pope issued his letter

---

[107] Father Vincent Miceli, *The Antichrist*, (Roman Catholic Books, Harrison, New York, 1981) p. 133.

[108] For an able layman's summary of what Modernism is and how it is promoted among the laity in our time, cf. Christopher A. Ferrara, *EWTN: A Network Gone Wrong* (Pound Ridge, New York: Good Counsel Publications, 2006), pp. 19-49.

[109] Pope Pius X, *Pascendi Dominici Gregis (On the Doctrine of the Modernists)*, September 8, 1907.

Sacrorum antistitum, which mandated the *Oath Against Modernism* to be sworn by all priests and teachers. He oversaw the purging of modernists from the seminaries and universities and excommunicated the stubborn and unrepentant. St. Pius X knew that nothing less than the very nature of the Church was under attack by the modernists, who in their audacity were now acting openly for the overthrow of Catholic Dogma and Tradition:

> [T]he gravity of the evil is daily growing and must be checked at any cost. We are no longer dealing, as at the beginning, with opponents 'in sheep's clothing', but with open and bare-faced enemies in our very household, who, having made a pact with the chief foes of the Church [i.e. Freemasons, Liberals, Protestants, Jews, Muslims, etc.], are bent on overthrowing the Faith ... They want to renovate it as if it were consumed by old age, increase it and *adapt it to worldly tastes, progress and comforts*, as if it were opposed not just to the frivolity of a few, but to the good of society. ... There will never be enough vigilance and firmness on the part of those entrusted with the faithful safekeeping of the sacred deposit of evangelical doctrine and ecclesiastical tradition, in order to oppose these onslaughts against it.[110]

St. Pius X effectively halted the spread of modernism in his day. It is reported, however, that when he was congratulated for eradicating this grave error, St. Pius X immediately responded that despite all his efforts, he had not succeeded in killing this beast, but had only driven it underground. He warned that if Church leaders were not vigilant, it would return in the future more virulent than ever.[111] As we are about to see, St. Pius X's prediction has come true—with a vengeance.

Modernism Begins to Rise Again

A little-known drama that unfolded during the reign of Pope Pius XI demonstrates that the underground current of Modernist thought was alive and well in the immediate post-St. Pius X period.

Father Raymond Dulac relates that at the secret consistory of May 23, 1923, Pius XI questioned the thirty Cardinals of the Curia on the timeliness of summoning an ecumenical council. In attendance were illustrious prelates such as Merry del Val, De Lai, Gasparri, Boggiani and Billot. The Cardinals advised against it. Cardinal Billot warned, "The existence of profound differences in the midst of the episcopacy itself cannot be concealed ... [They] run the risk of giving place to discussions that will be prolonged indefinitely."

Boggiani recalled the modernist theories from which, he said, a part of the clergy and of the bishops are not exempt. "This mentality can incline certain Fathers to present motions, to introduce methods

---

[110] Pope St. Pius X, *Sacrorum antistitum*.

[111] Father Vincent Miceli, *The Antichrist*, cassette lecture, Keep the Faith, Inc. Ramsey, New Jersey.

incompatible with Catholic traditions."

Billot was even more precise. He expressed his fear of seeing the Council "maneuvered" by "the worst enemies of the Church, the Modernists, who are already getting ready, as certain indications show, to bring forth the revolution in the Church, a new 1789."[112]

Masonic Predictions of
a Modernist Breakthrough at an Ecumenical Council

In discouraging the idea of a council for such reasons, these Cardinals showed themselves more apt at recognizing the "signs of the times" than all the post-Vatican II theologians combined. Yet their caution may have been rooted in something deeper. They may also have been haunted by the writings of the infamous illuminé, the excommunicated Canon Roca (1830-1893) who preached revolution and Church "reform", and who predicted in amazingly precise detail the subversion of the Church that would be brought about by a Council.

In *Athanasius and the Church of Our Time*, Bishop Graber quotes the apostate Roca's prediction of a "newly illuminated church" which would be influenced by the "socialism of Jesus".[113] In the mid-19th Century, Roca predicted that "The new church, which might not be able to retain anything of Scholastic doctrine and the original form of the former Church, will nevertheless receive consecration and canonical jurisdiction from Rome." The anti-Catholic Roca also, amazingly enough, predicted the liturgical "reform" after Vatican II: "[T]he divine cult in the form directed by the liturgy, ceremonial, ritual and regulations of the Roman Church will shortly undergo a transformation *at an ecumenical council*, which will restore to it the venerable simplicity of the golden age of the Apostles in accordance with the dictates of conscience and modern civilization."

Roca, the forerunner of modern-day apostates, foretold that through this council will come "a perfect accord between the ideals of modern civilization and the ideal of Christ and His Gospel. This will be the consecration of the New Social Order and the solemn baptism of modern civilization." In other words, this council would usher in the triumph of the Masonic plan for subversion of the Church. Roca also spoke of the future of the papacy. He wrote "There is a sacrifice in the offing which represents a solemn act of expiation ... The papacy will fall; it will die under the hallowed knife *which the fathers of the last council will forge*. The papal caesar is a host [victim] crowned for the sacrifice." Roca enthusiastically predicted nothing short of a "new religion, new dogma, new ritual, new priesthood." He called the new priests "progressists" and speaks of the "suppression" of the soutane

---

[112] Raymond Dulac, *Episcopal Collegiality at the Second Council of the Vatican*, (Paris: Cedre, 1979) pp. 9-10.

[113] *Athanasius and the Church of Our Time*, p. 34.

[cassock] and the "marriage of priests."[114]

Pointing to the writings of the French heresiarch, Abbé Melinge (who used the pseudonym Dr. Alta), Bishop Graber warned of a revolutionary program of "the replacement of the Roman faith by a 'pluri-confessional' pontificate, able to adapt to a polyvalent ecumenism, such as we are seeing established today in the intercelebration of priests and Protestant pastors." (Melinge was referring to certain renegade priests; since then, however, Pope John Paul II himself conducted joint services, including Vespers, with Protestant "bishops.")[115]

Chilling echos of Roca, Melinge and the Alta Vendita are to be found in the words of the Rosicrucian, Dr. Rudolph Steiner who declared in 1910 "We need a council and a Pope to proclaim it."[116]

The Masonic Alliance with Communism

It must be noted that in their striving toward these goals the Masons were the kin of the Communists, who were plotting alongside them for the overthrow of both Church and State. As Pope Leo XIII observed in *Humanum Genus* (1884), his monumental encyclical on the threat posed by the Masonic societies:

> Yea, this change and overthrow is deliberately planned and put forward by many associations of communists and socialists; and to their undertakings the sect of Freemasons is not hostile, but greatly favors their designs, and holds in common with them their chief opinions.

As we have since learned from numerous independent witnesses, Communist infiltration of the Church[117] began as early as the 1930s. Lenin himself (the very founder of Russian Communism) declared in the 1920's that he would infiltrate the Catholic Church, particularly the Vatican. The historical evidence on this score was recently summarized in the venerable periodical *Christian Order*:

> Ex-Communist and celebrated convert Douglas Hyde revealed long ago that in the 1930s the Communist leadership issued a

---

[114] A full account of all of Roca's quotes printed here is found in *Athanasius and the Church of Our Time*, pp. 31-40.

[115] "Joint Catholic-Lutheran Vespers at Vatican," CWNews.com, November 13, 1999: "Archbishops G.H. Hammar and Jukka Paarma—the Lutheran primates of Sweden and Finland, respectively—and Bishops Anders Arborelius of Stockholm and Czeslaw Kozon of Copenhagen joined with the Holy Father for the Vespers service. Several other Lutheran 'bishops' from the Scandinavian countries were present for the ceremony, including two female bishops."

[116] *Athanasius and the Church of Our Time*, p. 36.

[117] See "The Secret Red Plan to Take Over the Catholic Church", published in Red China in 1959. Published in English in *The Fatima Crusader*, Issue 19, February-April, 1986, p. 6. See also "The Prophecy of Bella Dodd", a Fatima Perspective web column by Christopher Ferrara (www.fatimaperspectives.com/cs/perspective235.asp); this prediction is also found in the next paragraph. See also Chapter 8 ("The Message of Fatima versus the Party Line") on pp. 107-118 of this book and the photo caption of Lenin on page 106. See also Father Paul Kramer, "The 'Party Line' in Relation to Fatima", *The Fatima Crusader*, Issue 69, Winter 2002, pp. 10ff (on the web at www. fatimacrusader.com/cr69/cr69pg10.asp).

worldwide directive about infiltrating the Catholic Church. While in the early 1950s, Mrs. Bella Dodd was also providing detailed explanations of the Communist subversion of the Church. Speaking as a former high ranking official of the American Communist Party, Mrs. Dodd said: "*In the 1930s we put eleven hundred men into the priesthood in order to destroy the Church from within.*" The idea was for these men to be ordained and progress to positions of influence and authority as Monsignors and Bishops. A dozen years before Vatican II she stated that: "*Right now they are in the highest places in the Church*"—where they were working to bring about change in order to weaken the Church's effectiveness against Communism. She also said that these changes would be so drastic that "*you will not recognize the Catholic Church.*"[118]

As *Christian Order* points out, the existence of a Communist conspiracy to infiltrate the Church has been confirmed abundantly not only by former Communists Dodd and Hyde, but also by Soviet defectors:

> Ex-KGB officer Anatoliy Golitsyn, who defected in 1961 and in 1984 forecast with 94% accuracy all the astonishing developments in the Communist Bloc since that time, confirmed several years ago that this "penetration of the Catholic and other churches is part of the Party's 'general line' [i.e. unchanged policy] in the struggle against religion." In fact, hundreds of files smuggled into the West by former KGB archivist Vassili Mitrokhin and published in 1999 tell a similar tale, about the KGB cultivating the closest possible relationships with 'progressive' Catholics and financing their activities. One of the leftist organs identified was the small Italian Catholic press agency *Adista*, which for decades has promoted every imaginable post-conciliar cause or "reform" and whose Director was named in *The Mitrokhin Archive* as a paid KGB agent.

Mrs. Dodd, who converted to the Faith shortly before her death, was legal counsel to the Communist Party of the United States. She gave voluminous testimony on Communist infiltration of Church and State before the House Un-American Activities Committee in the 1950s. As if to atone for her role in subverting the Church, Dodd delivered a series of lectures at Fordham University and elsewhere during the years leading up to Vatican II. *Christian Order* recounts the testimony of a monk who attended one of those lectures in the early 1950s:

> I listened to that woman for four hours and she had my hair standing on end. Everything she said has been fulfilled to the letter. You would think she was the world's greatest prophet, but she was no prophet. She was merely exposing the step-by-step battle plan of Communist subversion of the Catholic Church. She explained that of all the world's religions, the Catholic Church was the only one feared by the Communists, for it was its only effective opponent.

---

[118] "The Greatest Conspiracy", *Christian Order*, November 2000.

The whole idea was to destroy, not the institution of the Church, but rather the Faith of the people, and even use the institution of the Church, if possible, to destroy the Faith through the promotion of a pseudo-religion: something that resembled Catholicism but was not the real thing. Once the Faith was destroyed, she explained that there would be a *guilt complex introduced into the Church.* ... to label the 'Church of the past' as being oppressive, authoritarian, full of prejudices, arrogant in claiming to be the sole possessor of truth, and responsible for the divisions of religious bodies throughout the centuries. This would be necessary in order to shame Church leaders into an *'openness to the world,'* and to a *more flexible attitude toward all religions and philosophies.* The Communists would then exploit this openness in order to undermine the Church.[119]

Now, if the enemies of the Church were to succeed in their plans, which we have just outlined, we would see these things happening in the Church:

- <u>First</u>, there would be, as Roca predicted, an upheaval *at an ecumenical council* of such magnitude that the entire world would realize that the Catholic Church had undergone a revolution in line with modern ideas. It would be clear to all that an "updating" of the Church had taken place.

- <u>Second</u>, a new "theology" would be introduced that would tend to contradict previous teachings.

- <u>Third</u>, the Freemasons and Communists themselves would voice their cockle-doodle of triumph, believing that the Catholic Church had finally "seen the light" on such points as pluralism, the secular state, equality of religions, and whatever other compromises had been achieved.

- <u>Fourth</u>, as the result of this subversion, the new orientation of the Church would come to take precedence over the very dogmas and traditions of the Church in Her teaching and practice—including the

---

[119] Another ex-Communist, Mr. Manning Johnson gave similar testimony. In 1953, to the House Un-American Activities Committee, Manning said: "Once the tactic of infiltration of religious organizations was set by the Kremlin ... The Communists discovered that the destruction of religion could proceed much faster through the infiltration of the Church by Communists operating within the Church itself." He then stated, "This policy of infiltrating seminaries was successful beyond even our Communist expectations." Speaking of the infiltration of religious institutions in general, Manning Johnson further explained, "... the major plot to take over religious organizations was really hatched during that particular period (1935), and the fact that the Communists, in headlines in the *Daily Worker*, can boast of 2,300 Protestant Ministers supporting them is the result of this part that began in the thirties when I was a member of the Communist party." Testimony of Manning Johnson, Investigation of Communist Activities in the New York City Area – Part 7, Hearing Before the Committee on Un-American Activities, House of Representatives, Eighty-Third Congress, First Session, July 8, 1953, (Published by the Government Printing Office, Washington, D.C., 1953) p. 2214. A collection of quotations from ex-Communists concerning the infiltration of the Church is found in John Vennari's "Heaven's Request for Reparation to the Holy Face of Jesus", Part III, *Catholic Family News*, August 2001.

Message of Fatima, which would have to be "revised" or buried to accommodate the new orientation.

It now remains for us to demonstrate the extent to which this design to promote a subversive liberalization of the Church has come to pass, and how that liberalization provides the motive for the grave offense committed: the attempt to nullify the authentic Message of Fatima in favor of a "new orientation" of the Church. We do not use the words "grave offense" lightly, for in conducting a veritable campaign against the Fatima apparitions, the identified Vatican prelates have left the Church and the world exposed to the terrible dangers of which the Message forewarns, including the annihilation of "various nations" and the loss of millions of souls. If the Message is truly from Heaven, as the Popes (especially John Paul II) have attested, then what is involved in revising, despising and even burying it can only be called a true and proper crime—not only against the Church, but against all of humanity.

Sister Lucy had corresponded with Pope John Paul II at various times, and had had several face-to-face meetings with His Holiness. Yet after all the letters and meetings, John Paul II had never claimed that Sister Lucy told him Russia had been consecrated to the Immaculate Heart of Mary as requested by Our Lady of Fatima. Sister Lucy was still under an order of silence right up to her death (see pages 344-346 and footnote 124). Sister Lucy was the only Catholic, out of one billion Catholics, who was under such a gag order. According to this order, Sister Lucy needed the permission of Cardinal Ratzinger to speak to anyone about the Consecration of Russia or the Third Secret or anything else that was not already in her pre-approved writings on Fatima. If the Consecration of Russia were truly performed and if the Third Secret were completely released, then there would have been no real purpose for such an order of silence.

Chapter 6

The Motive Takes Hold

Around 1948, Pope Pius XII, at the request of the staunchly orthodox Cardinal Ruffini, considered calling a general Council and even spent a few years making the necessary preparations. There is evidence that progressive elements in Rome eventually dissuaded Pius XII from bringing it to realization since this Council showed definite signs of being in line with *Humani Generis* and its condemnation of Modernist errors. Like this great 1950 encyclical, the proposed Council of Pius XII would combat "false opinions which threaten to undermine the foundations of Catholic doctrine."[120]

At the same time, the "errors of Russia" to which the Virgin of Fatima referred were penetrating the Church Herself. Various Catholic religious orders were being infiltrated. For example, the so-called "Catholic Priest Worker" movement was so clearly infiltrated by Communists that Pius XII called for an end to it in the 1950's.

Tragically, Pius XII became convinced that he was too advanced in years to shoulder the momentous task of a Council to combat the swelling ranks of the Church's enemies, and he resigned himself to the decision that "this will be for my successor."[121] Pope Pius XII died on October 9, 1958.

And now we have arrived very near to the critical year in our case. We have arrived at 1958, two years before 1960—the year in which the Third Secret was to be disclosed in accordance with the wishes of the Virgin of Fatima, as Sister Lucy had testified. Throughout the pontificate of Pius XII, the Holy Office, under the able leadership of Cardinal Ottaviani, maintained sound orthodoxy by keeping the wild horses of modernism firmly corralled. Many of today's Modernist theologians disdainfully recount how they and their friends had been "muzzled" during this period.

Yet even Cardinal Ottaviani could not prevent what was to happen in 1958. A new type of Pope "whom the progressives believed to favor their cause"[122] would ascend to the Pontifical Chair and would force a reluctant Ottaviani to remove the latch, open the corral and brace himself for the stampede. However, such a state of affairs was not unforeseen. At the news of the death of Pope Pius XII, the old Dom Lambert Beauduin, a friend of Roncalli's (the future Pope John XXIII) confided to Father

---

[120] A full account of this fascinating history is found in *The Whole Truth About Fatima* - Vol. III, by Frère Michel de la Sainte Trinité, pp. 257-304.

[121] Ibid., p. 297.

[122] Vicomte Leon de Poncins, *Freemasonry and the Vatican*, (Christian Book Club, Palmdale, California, 1968) p. 14.

Bouyer: "If they elect Roncalli, everything would be saved; he would be capable of calling a council and of consecrating ecumenism."[123]

At this point in our presentation it must be emphasized, especially for the non-Catholic reader, that the changes in the basic orientation of the Church we are about to discuss are totally unprecedented and represent perhaps the worst crisis in Her history. A careful study of what follows will make clear why the Message of Fatima, with its call for the consecration and *conversion* of Russia as the harbinger of world peace, has become unacceptable to the politically correct, liberalized churchmen of the last fifty years. These unprecedented changes in the Catholic Church are no boon, but a great detriment, to non-Catholics, since the result of the Church's "updating" has included not merely the clerical scandals we now see, but a failure of the human element of the Church to perform an action—the solemn consecration of Russia—that would benefit the whole of mankind.

A Council is Called as the Message of Fatima Comes Under Attack

And so it happened just as Dom Lambert foretold. Roncalli was elected and, as Pope John XXIII, called a Council and consecrated ecumenism. The "revolution in tiara and cope" predicted by the Alta Vendita was underway.

And one of the first acts of the revolution was to dispense with the Third Secret of Fatima. Contrary to the expectations of the whole world, on February 8, 1960 (just over a year after the Council had been called), the Vatican issued the following anonymous announcement through the A.N.I. press agency:

> Vatican City, February 8, 1960 (A.N.I.) – It is probable that the "Secret of Fatima" will never be made public. In Vatican circles highly worthy of belief, they have just declared to the representative of United Press International that it is most likely the letter will never be opened, in which Sister Lucy wrote down the words which the Virgin Mary addressed to the three shepherds of the Cova da Iria ... It is most probable that the "Secret of Fatima" will remain forever under absolute seal.

And in the same communiqué we find the first direct attack from Vatican sources on the credibility of the Message of Fatima as a whole:

> Although the Church recognizes the Fatima apparitions, She does not pledge Herself to guarantee the veracity of the words which the three shepherds claim to have heard from Our Lady.

Claim to have heard? Could there be any doubt about the veracity of their testimony after the Miracle of the Sun? Could there be any

---

[123] L. Bouyer, *Dom Lambert Beauduin, a Man of the Church*, Casterman, 1964, pp. 180-181, quoted by Father Didier Bonneterre in *The Liturgical Movement*, Ed. Fideliter, 1980, p. 119.

question that they had been given an authentic prophecy from Heaven in view of the complete fulfillment of every prediction in the Message thus far—from the imminent end of World War I, to the spread of Russia's errors, to World War II and the election of Pope Pius XI?

This first public attack on the Message of Fatima from within the Vatican apparatus comes in 1960, as the Vatican begins to pursue a new orientation of the Church that will arise (as we shall soon see) at the Second Vatican Council. Consider these developments surrounding the February 8, 1960 communiqué:

- The communiqué publicly questions the veracity of Lucy, Jacinta, and Francisco.

- From 1960 forward, Sister Lucy is silenced on orders of the Vatican apparatus,[124] so she could not defend herself from the implied accusation that her testimony is unreliable.

- The documents in the official Fatima archives, which Father Alonso will compile between 1965 and 1976, (more than 5,000 documents in 24 volumes) will be barred from publication, even though these documents confirm that the Fatima prophecies in the first two parts of the Secret (the election of Pope Pius XI, the coming of World War

---

[124] Jesuit Father Aparicio was Sister Lucy's confessor and spiritual director from 1926 to 1938. Then he was sent to Brazil as a missionary and corresponded with Sister Lucy over the years. In 1950 he returned to Portugal for a short while and visited Sister Lucy both in 1950 and in 1951 without difficulty. Father Aparicio testified that in August 1960, during a month-long visit to Portugal, he was not allowed to speak to Sister Lucy: "I have not been able to speak to Sister Lucy because the Archbishop could not give the permission to meet her. The *conditions of isolation in which she finds herself have been imposed by the Holy See*. Consequently, no one may speak to her without a licence from Rome. The Archbishop has only a very limited number of those licences." (*Fatima: Tragedy and Triumph*, Immaculate Heart Publications, 1994, pp. 33-34.)

The situation had not changed since then until her death on February 13, 2005. On January 16, 1983 Father Joseph de Sainte-Marie, O.C. wrote to the eminent Catholic layman Hamish Fraser to advise that: "Moreover, I remind you—she [Sister Lucy] herself reminded me recently in a request that I had addressed to her—that Sister Lucia [Lucy] cannot speak to anyone on the question of the apparitions without the express permission of the Sacred Congregation for the Doctrine of the Faith or of the Holy Father himself." (*The Fatima Crusader*, No. 13-14, p. 13.) And on March 19, 1983 Sister Lucy told the Papal Nuncio to Portugal, Most Reverend Sante Portalupi, that she had not been able to comment earlier on the inadequacy of the 1982 consecration ceremony (of the world, not Russia) because the Holy See had not given her permission to speak: "The Consecration of Russia has not been made as Our Lady demanded. I could not say so [before] because I did not have permission of the Holy See." (Ibid., p. 3; and *The Fatima Crusader*, Issue 16, September-October 1984, pp. 22ff, reprinting the article by Father Pierre Caillon in *Fidelite Catholique*, first printed in 1983.)

On February 19, 1990, Msgr. A. Duarte de Almeida, chaplain to the Coimbra Carmel, stated the following: "in order to meet Sister Lucy, it is necessary to obtain Cardinal Ratzinger's permission." (In David Boyce, "Fatima Inquest - August 1990", *The Fatima Crusader*, Issue 35, Winter 1990-1991, p. 13.)

As recently as the purported "interview" of Sister Lucy by Msgr. Bertone on November 17, 2001, Msgr. Bertone admitted (in his communiqué concerning the interview) that it had been conducted with the *consent* of Cardinal Ratzinger. Thus, as recently as 2001 even a high-ranking Vatican prelate needed the Holy See's permission to speak with Sister Lucy.

II, the spread of Communism throughout the world, etc.) had been revealed privately by Sister Lucy long before their fulfillment, and that her testimony was utterly accurate and reliable.

A veritable plot against Fatima had begun. And the motive for the plot—a desire to shift the orientation of the Church away from the Catholic certitudes of the Message of Fatima and toward an "enlightened" accommodation towards the world—would begin in earnest with the commencement of the Second Vatican Council on October 11, 1962. We recall again the words of Sister Lucy that Our Lady wished the Third Secret to be released in 1960 because it "will be clearer (*mais claro*) then." Now it would become very clear indeed.

The "Errors of Russia" Infiltrate the Church

First, just before the Council's commencement, there would be another betrayal of the Message of Fatima, a sign of many unprecedented things to come. In the spring of 1962, in Metz, France, Cardinal Eugene Tisserant had a meeting with none other than Metropolitan Nikodim of the Russian Orthodox Church—a KGB operative, as were the other Orthodox prelates. At this meeting Tisserant and Nikodim negotiated what came to be known as the Metz Pact, or more popularly, the Vatican-Moscow Agreement.[125] The existence of the Vatican-Moscow Agreement is an irrefutable historical fact attested to in all of its details by Monsignor Roche, who was Cardinal Tisserant's personal secretary. Moreover, since the first edition of this book appeared, the renowned Italian journalist Andrea Tornielli has published a biography of Pope Paul VI in which we learn that "what many considered a conspiracy theory was true: there was indeed a secret agreement, led by Cardinal Tisserant, between the Soviet Union and the papacy (under Pope John XXIII) in 1962—an agreement which Pope Paul VI ('Montini') also enforced. In a note of November 15, 1965, in fact, Paul VI (Montini) explicitly mentions among 'the commitments of the Council' also that of 'not mentioning Communism (1962).'"[126]

In substance, the agreement was as follows: Pope John XXIII, according to his fond wish, would be "favored" by the attendance of two Russian Orthodox observers at the Council. In return, the Catholic Church would agree that the Second Vatican Council would refrain from any condemnation of Soviet Communism or Soviet Russia. In essence, the Council would compromise the moral liberty of the Catholic Church by pretending that the most systematized form of human evil in human history did not exist—even though, at the very moment the Council

---

[125] See Jean Madiran, "The Vatican-Moscow Agreement", *The Fatima Crusader*, Issue 16, September-October, 1984, p. 5. Also articles on pages 4, 7, and 11 in *The Fatima Crusader*, Issue 17, February-April, 1985. See also Atila Sinke Guimarães, "The Metz Pact", *Catholic Family News*, September 2001.

[126] Giacomo Galeazzi, "Paoli VI, patto segreto con l'Urss" ("Paul VI, Secret Pact with USSR"), *La Stampa*, July 6, 2009, accessible online at http://newrassegna.camera.it/chiosco_new/pagweb/immagineFrame.asp?comeFrom=search&currentArticle=MGOJJ

opened, the Soviets were persecuting, imprisoning and murdering millions of Catholics.

Her liberty thus constrained in a bargain with Communists, the Council failed even to mention Communism. By this failure the Council departed from the teaching of Pope Leo XIII, Blessed Pius IX, Saint Pius X and also Pope Pius XI, who reminded the Church that we could not refrain from condemning this incomparable evil. As he said in *Divini Redemptoris*,

> This all too imminent danger, venerable brethren, as you have already surmised is Bolshevistic and atheistic Communism which aims at upsetting the social order and undermining the very foundations of Christian civilization. In the face of such a threat the Catholic Church *could not and does not remain silent*. This Apostolic See above all has *not refrained from raising its voice* for it knows that its proper and special mission is to defend truth, justice and all those eternal values which Communism ignores or attacks.[127]

And yet the Council would say not one word about Soviet Communism, but would instead begin a "dialogue" with the very forces the Church once opposed.

Why did this happen? It was surely no "coincidence" that the Council's silence about Communism synchronized perfectly with the Communist infiltration of the Catholic Church which, as we showed in a previous chapter, had been revealed just before Vatican II by key witnesses with no motive to lie (Dodd, Hyde, Golitsyn, Mitrokhin and others). Even without such testimonies, our common sense should tell us that the forces of Communism (working alongside those of Freemasonry) would inevitably attempt to destroy the Catholic Church from within. Satan is intelligent enough to know that the Catholic Church is the one citadel he must storm in his effort to conquer the whole world for the kingdom of darkness.

This, then, was the state of affairs in the Church at the very moment that the Second Vatican Council was wrongly constrained to observe its shameful silence on the evil of Communism. And, needless to say, under the Vatican-Moscow Agreement, the Consecration of Soviet Russia to the Immaculate Heart by the Council Fathers, in order to bring about its conversion, would be absolutely out of the question. This early shift toward a new orientation of the Church, which the Council would accelerate in a most dramatic fashion, was already in conflict with the Message of Fatima.

And so it has been ever since the meeting in Metz, which expanded the pursuit of *Ostpolitik*, the policy implemented by the Vatican Secretary of State under which the Church has ceased all condemnation and opposition to Communist regimes in favor of "dialogue" and

---

[127] Pope Pius XI, *Divini Redemptoris*, Encyclical on Atheistic Communism, March 19, 1937. See also quotation on pages 68-69 referenced by footnote 164 of this chapter.

"quiet diplomacy"—a policy which to this day has silenced the Vatican concerning the vicious persecution of the Church in Red China and other communist regimes, including Cuba, where the Vatican has also remained silent about continuing communist repression of the Church.

Thus on October 12, 1962, two representative priests of the Orthodox church debarked from a plane at Fiumicino Airport and attended the Second Vatican Council. The Council began with Orthodox observers watching its proceedings, making sure that the Vatican-Moscow Agreement was observed. The written intervention of 450 Council Fathers against Communism was mysteriously "lost" after being delivered to the Secretariat of the Council, and Council Fathers who stood up to denounce Communism were politely told to sit down and be quiet.[128]

The Church's own leaders had lowered the drawbridge to the Communists, at the same time Communists and Freemasons were attempting to destroy Her from within by (to recall the predictions of Bella Dodd):

• encouraging "the promotion of a pseudo-religion: something that resembled Catholicism but was not the real thing,"

• labelling "the 'Church of the past' as being oppressive, authoritarian, full of prejudices, arrogant in claiming to be the sole possessor of truth, and responsible for the divisions of religious bodies throughout the centuries,"

• shaming Church leaders into "an 'openness to the world,' and to a more flexible attitude toward all religions and philosophies."

And finally, as Dodd predicted, "The Communists would then exploit this openness in order to undermine the Church."

This grand effort at subversion would involve, first and foremost, the breakthrough of Modernist "theology" at an ecumenical council— just as Canon Roca and the other illumines of Freemasonry had boasted.

The Neo-Modernists Triumph at Vatican II

On October 13, 1962, the day after the two Communist observers arrived at the Council, and on the very anniversary of the Miracle of the Sun at Fatima, the history of the Church and the world was profoundly changed by the smallest of events. Cardinal Liénart of France seized the microphone in a famous incident and demanded that the candidates proposed by the Roman Curia to chair the drafting commissions at the Council be set aside and that a new slate of candidates be drawn up. The demand was acceded to and the election postponed. When the election was finally held, liberals were elected to majorities and near-majorities on the conciliar commissions—many of them from among the very "innovators" decried by Pope Pius XII. The traditionally formulated preparatory schemas for the Council were discarded and

---

[128] A more complete account of this is found in Father Ralph Wiltgen, *The Rhine flows into the Tiber*, (New York: Hawthorne, 1967; Rockford, Illinois: TAN, 1985) pp. 272-278.

the Council began literally without a written agenda, leaving the way open for entirely new documents to be written by the liberals.

It is well known and superbly documented[129] that a clique of liberal *periti* (experts) and bishops then proceeded to hijack Vatican II with an agenda to remake the Church into their own image through the implementation of a "new theology". Both critics and defenders of Vatican II are in agreement on this point. In his book *Vatican II Revisited*, Bishop Aloysius J. Wycislo (a rhapsodic advocate of the Vatican II revolution) declares with giddy enthusiasm that "theologians and biblical scholars who had been 'under a cloud' for years surfaced as *periti* (theological experts advising the bishops at the Council), and their post-Vatican II books and commentaries became popular reading."[130]

He noted that "Pope Pius XII's encyclical *Humani Generis* had ... a devastating effect on the work of a number of pre-conciliar theologians",[131] and explains that "During the early preparation of the Council, those theologians (mainly French, with some German) whose activities had been restricted by Pope Pius XII, were still under a cloud. Pope John quietly lifted the ban affecting some of the most influential ones. Yet a number remained suspect to the officials of the Holy Office."[132]

On this point, the eyewitness testimony of Msgr. Rudolf Bandas, himself a conciliar *peritus*, is of decisive importance to our case:

> No doubt good Pope John thought that these suspect theologians would rectify their ideas and perform a genuine service to the Church. But exactly the opposite happened. Supported by certain Rhine Council Fathers, and often acting in a manner positively boorish, they turned around and exclaimed: "Behold, we are named experts, our ideas stand approved." ... When I entered my tribunal at the Council, on the first day of the fourth session, the first announcement, emanating from the Secretary of State, was the following: "No more periti will be appointed." But it was too late. The great confusion was underway. It was already apparent that *neither Trent nor Vatican I nor any encyclical would be permitted to impede its advance.*[133]

Indeed, Pope John XXIII himself was happy to announce that beginning with this Council the Church would, quite inexplicably, cease condemning error and stop all Her worrying about the dire condition of the world:

> Nowadays ... the spouse of Christ prefers to make use of the

---

[129] E.g., *The Rhine flows into the Tiber* by Fr. Ralph Wiltgen; *Pope John's Council* by Michael Davies (Angelus Press, Kansas City, Missouri); and even *Vatican II Revisited*, (see next footnote) which sings praises of the reform.

[130] Most Reverend Aloysius Wycislo S.J., *Vatican II Revisited, Reflections By One Who Was There*, (Alba House, Staten Island, New York) p. x.

[131] Ibid., p. 33.

[132] Ibid., p. 27.

[133] *The Wanderer*, August 31, 1967, p. 7.

medicine of mercy rather than the arms of severity. She considers
that She meets the needs of the present day by demonstrating the
validity of Her teaching rather than by issuing condemnations. ... We
feel we must disagree with those prophets of gloom, who are always
forecasting disaster, as though the end of the world was at hand.[134]

But John XXIII's optimism was quite at odds with the profound alarm
over the state of the world to be seen in the many pronouncements of
his immediate predecessors (not to mention in the Message of Fatima
itself). Consider these few examples:

Pope St. Pius X:

> We felt a sort of terror considering the disastrous conditions
> of humanity at the present hour. Can we ignore such a profound
> and grave evil, which at this moment much more than in the past
> is working away at its very marrow and leading it to its ruin? ...
> Truly whoever ponders these things *must necessarily and firmly fear*
> whether such a perversion of minds is not the sign of announcing,
> and the beginning of the last times ... [*E Supremi*].

Pope Pius XI:

> With God and Jesus Christ excluded from political life, with
> authority derived not from God but from man, ... the chief reason
> of the distinction between ruler and subject has been eliminated.
> The result is that society is *tottering to its ruin* because it no longer
> has a secure and solid foundation [*Quas Primas*].

Pope Pius XII (*after* the end of WWII):

> We are overwhelmed with sadness and anguish, seeing that
> the wickedness of perverse men has reached a degree of impiety
> that is unbelievable and *absolutely unknown in other times* [Letter
> of February 11, 1949].

> Venerable brethren, you are well aware that almost the whole
> human race is today allowing itself to be driven into two opposing
> camps, for Christ or against Christ. *The human race is involved
> today in a supreme crisis*, which will issue in its salvation by Christ,
> or in its destruction [*Evangeli Praecones*, 1951].

To be sure, there would be countless battles at Vatican II between
the International Group of Fathers who fought to uphold the dogmas
of the Faith and Catholic Tradition, and the progressive Rhine group.
Tragically, however, it was the liberal and Modernist element that
prevailed, let loose by John XXIII's optimism that the truth would prevail
of its own force without the aid of any medicinal condemnations by
the Magisterium. Wycislo sings the praises of triumphant progressives
such as Hans Küng, Karl Rahner, John Courtney Murray, Yves Congar,
Henri de Lubac, Edward Schillebeeckx and Gregory Baum, who had

---

[134] *Council Daybook*, National Catholic Welfare Conference, Washington, D.C., Vol. 1, pp.
25, 27.

been considered suspect before the Council (for good reason) and are now the leading lights of post-Vatican II theology.[135]

In effect, those whom Pope Pius XII considered unfit to be walking the streets of Catholicism were now in control of the town. And as if to crown their achievements, the *Oath Against Modernism* and the *Index of Forbidden Books* were both quietly suppressed shortly after the close of the Council—a decision Bishop Graber called "incomprehensible."[136] St. Pius X had predicted correctly. Lack of vigilance in authority had provoked modernism to return with a vengeance.

Two Prominent Examples of "Rehabilitated" Neo-Modernists

Let us consider two examples of the "new" theologians who were let loose upon the Church to do their work of destruction: Dominique Chenu and Hans Küng.

Chenu was an advocate of the New Theology made famous by Henri de Lubac. Chenu was issued a condemnation for his progressive ideas in 1942 under Pope Pius XII.[137] His book *Une ecole de theologie* was placed on the *Index of Forbidden Books* and he lost his rectorship at the Dominican College of Le Saulchoir.[138] Father David Greenstock, writing in the 1950 *Thomist* against the New Theology of Chenu and de Lubac, explained the dangers of their system and the reason for their condemnation. Greenstock pointed out that the partisans of the New Theology reject Aristotelian-Thomistic philosophy in favor of modern philosophies. This must be done, they claim, in order to appeal to "modern man" who finds Thomistic philosophy "irrelevant". The result is that Catholic theology is knocked off of its firm, philosophical foundation and shifted onto the fluid philosophical systems of the 20th Century, most of which are founded upon atheism and agnosticism.

Chenu also rejected the unchangeableness of Catholic doctrine, claiming that the source of all theology is not immutable dogma, but rather the vital life[139] of the Church in its members, which cannot be separated from history. Thus, strictly speaking, says Greenstock, Chenu held that "theology is the life of the members of the Church, rather than a series of conclusions drawn from revealed data with the aid of reason"—a principle that is slippery, imprecise and erroneous. As a result, Chenu held that religion can change with the times, and should change with the times, according to the demands of circumstances.

---

[135] *Vatican II Revisited, Reflections By One Who Was There*, pp. 27-34.

[136] Bishop Graber, *Athanasius and the Church of Our Time*, p. 54.

[137] Atila Sinke Guimarães, *Animus Delendi (The Desire to Destroy)*, (Tradition in Action, Los Angeles, California, 2001) p. 128. The exact title is *Animus Delendi - I* (the first of two books with this title).

[138] Ibid.

[139] "Vital life" seems to be just another term for the "Vital Imminence" condemned in Pope Pius X's encyclical against Modernism, *Pascendi*. See p. 8, English translation by Newman Press.

Greenstock explained that the partisans of this New Theology are both unorthodox and deceitful. "The main contention of the partisans of this new movement," wrote Greenstock, "is that theology, to remain alive, must move with the times. At the same time, they are very careful to repeat all the fundamental propositions of traditional theology, almost as if there was no intention of any attack against it. This is very true of such writers as Fathers de Lubac, Daniélou, Rahner, ... All of whom are undoubtedly at the very center of this movement."[140]

The eminent Dominican theologian, Father Reginald Garrigou-Lagrange, writing in his famous 1946 essay "Where is the New Theology Taking Us?",[141] demonstrated that the purveyors of the New Theology (Blondel, de Lubac, Chenu) pervert entirely the concept of the immutability of Truth. Thus, he warned, the New Theology can only lead in one direction—straight back to Modernism.

While all this was going on, Father Chenu and Father de Lubac were receiving behind-the-scenes protection and encouragement from Cardinal Suhard, Archbishop of Paris. Suhard told Chenu not to worry because "In twenty years, everyone in the Church will be talking like you." As we can see, the Cardinal accurately predicted the invasion of the Church by neo-modernist thinking. Most churchmen today *do* talk like Chenu. In the early 1960s, Father Chenu was one of many radical theologians who were invited to Vatican II by Pope John XXIII. In the end, thanks to the Council's progressivist orientation, Father Chenu saw many of his formally condemned theories advanced as part of Vatican II's new teachings, especially within *Gaudium et Spes*. Chenu relates joyfully that the very points for which his work was condemned in 1942 are the same exact points now promoted by members of the hierarchy in the name of the Council.[142]

As for Hans Küng, this "leading-light" of the post-conciliar period had worked closely at the Council with other radicals such as Congar, Ratzinger, Rahner and Schillebeeckx. In the 1970s, however, because Küng had gone "too far", he was censored by the Vatican for certain heretical views, including the following: rejection of the Church's infallibility; the claim that bishops do not receive their teaching authority from Christ; the suggestion that any baptized layperson has the power to confect the Holy Eucharist; the denial that Christ is "consubstantial" with the Father; the undermining of doctrines (unspecified) concerning the Virgin Mary.[143]

It needs to be pointed out that these are only *some* of Küng's heretical views, but they were the only ones mentioned within the Vatican's

---

[140] Greenstock, David, "Thomism and the New Theology", *The Thomist* (October, 1950). The entire article is well worth reading if one wishes to grasp the erroneous nature of the "New Theology".

[141] Published in the *Angelicum* in 1946. First English translation published in *Catholic Family News*, August 1997, "Where is the New Theology Taking Us?"

[142] *Animus Delendi - I*, p. 129.

[143] Ibid., pp. 146-149.

sanctions. Thus, in effect, the Vatican left Küng's other heterodox tenets untouched. For example, in one of his most famous books entitled *On Being a Christian*, Hans Küng:

- denies the Divinity of Christ (p. 130)
- dismisses the miracles of the Gospel (p. 233)
- denies the bodily resurrection of Jesus (p. 350)
- denies that Christ founded an institutional Church (p. 109)
- denies that the Mass is the re-presentation of Calvary (p. 323).[144]

Küng has never retracted these unorthodox and heretical statements. Moreover, Küng has publicly called for a revision of Church teaching on issues such as papal infallibility, birth control, mandatory celibacy of priests, and women in the priesthood. Despite this blatant rejection of Church teaching, the only penalty that the Vatican ever inflicted against Küng was that he was "not allowed" to be considered a Catholic theologian, and as such, was not allowed to teach theology in a Catholic university. This "penalty" was circumvented when the University of Tübingen, Küng's home campus, retained Küng as a teaching professor and simply restructured part of the university so that Küng, a great celebrity, may continue teaching in that part of the university which is now chartered as a "secular" school.

Meanwhile, the Vatican has never condemned Küng as a heretic, never excommunicated him (as canon law provides), never ordered that his books be removed from libraries in Catholic seminaries and universities (where they are now found in abundance), never prevented him from being a guest-lecturer at Catholic institutions, never obstructed him from publishing articles in *Concilium* or other progressivist "Catholic" publications. Father Hans Küng is not even suspended. Rather, to this day, Küng remains a priest in good standing in the diocese of Basle, with no other canonical penalties leveled against him.

This means that a priest who continues to vomit his heretical poison upon anyone within reach is still allowed to conduct public liturgy, preach and give advice in the confessional. The Vatican's Congregation for the Clergy, under Cardinal Castrillón Hoyos, leaves him untouched. So, despite the feeble Vatican "condemnation", Küng retains access to a very wide variety of influential "pipelines" to disseminate his poisonous doctrine throughout the Church. In fact, it is said that Hans Küng's "theological breakthroughs" on the nature of the Church are what provided the "theological foundation" that made possible the 1999 "Lutheran-Catholic" Accord.

Further, in 1998, the then Vatican Secretary of State Cardinal Sodano, who at that time was the most powerful Cardinal in the

---

[144] These observations are from Msgr. Kelly's book *The Battle for the American Church*, quoted by John Vennari in "Vatican Praises Purveyor of Heresy While it Hounds Apostle of Fatima", *The Fatima Crusader*, Issue 57, Spring/Summer 1998, pp. 20-21.

Church, praised Küng in a public speech at the Lateran, in which he lauded Küng's "beautiful pages dedicated to the Christian mystery".[145] Cardinal Sodano also referred to Küng as "the German theologian" even though Küng had been supposedly stripped of that title. (This is the same Cardinal Angelo Sodano who was and is ultimately behind the on-going persecution of Father Nicholas Gruner and his Fatima apostolate, as we shall see.)

Now, the 1942 condemnation that the Vatican leveled at Chenu was much more severe than what was hurled at Küng. Yet Chenu not only survived, but became a leading light of the Conciliar Church without ever changing his erroneous views. The same is true of Rahner, Congar, de Lubac and von Balthasar, all of whom were theologically suspect before the Council but came to enjoy great prestige—even though they never abandoned a single one of their heterodox opinions. Even the likes of Küng has reason to believe that whatever mild condemnation he suffers is just a temporary inconvenience, an annoying setback, a fate meted out to all true "prophets." Just as Chenu saw his heretical views eventually win the day thanks to a revolutionary Council, so likewise Küng may fill his breast with the hope that his errors will, in the not-so-distant future, eventually emerge as "mainstream" Catholicism *de facto*, even if not by any actual teaching of the authentic Magisterium, which could never bind the Church to such errors.

The Neo-Modernists Hail the "New" Church of Vatican II

With good reason, then, have progressivists such as Cardinal Suenens, Küng, Louis Bouyer and Yves Congar celebrated Vatican II as a Revolution, as the death of one era and the beginning of a new:

• Cardinal Suenens, who wielded great influence over Pope Paul VI, and who is a darling to those in the Church who call themselves "Charismatics", rejoiced that Vatican II marked the end of the Tridentine epoch and the end of the era of Vatican I.[146]

• Hans Küng gloated, "Compared to the post-Tridentine epoch of the Counter-reformation, Vatican Council II represents in its fundamental characteristics, a 180 degree turn ... It is a new Church that has sprung up since Vatican II."[147]

• Father Bouyer, a French *peritus* at the Council, exclaimed with relish that the anti-Protestant, anti-Modernist aspect of the Catholic Church "might as well die."[148]

• Likewise, the Rome-based Jesuit magazine, *La Civiltà Cattolica*, also exclaimed joyfully, "With Vatican Council II, the Tridentine age was

[145] Ibid.
[146] Cited from Guimarães, *Animus Delendi - I*, p. 60.
[147] Ibid., p. 61.
[148] Ibid., p. 59.

brought to a close for the Church."[149]

These statements are especially audacious when we consider that the Councils of Trent and Vatican I are dogmatic Councils whose teachings can never be changed, disregarded, or reinterpreted in the name of a "deeper understanding". The First Vatican Council declared infallibly:

> The meaning of Sacred Dogmas, which must always be preserved, is that which our Holy Mother the Church has determined. Never is it permissible to depart from this in the name of a deeper understanding.[150]

Modernists, however, as Pope St. Pius X warned, do not accept anything as fixed or unchanging. Their chief principle is the "evolution of dogma". They champion the notion that religion must change for the sake of changing times. In this respect, as in many others, the prime movers of Vatican II reveal themselves as men steeped in the error of Modernism.

Masons and Communists Rejoice

Along with the neo-modernists, the Masons and Communists have rejoiced at the Council's outcome. Just as the authors of the *Permanent Instruction of the Alta Vendita* had hoped, just as the Communist infiltrators spoken of by Bella Dodd had hoped, the notions of liberal culture had finally won adherence among the major players in the Catholic hierarchy. Freemasons and Communists have celebrated the astounding turn of events wrought by the Council. They rejoice that Catholics have finally "seen the light," and that many of their Masonic "principles" have been sanctioned by the Church.

For example, Yves Marsaudon of the Scottish Rite, in his book *Ecumenism Viewed by a Traditional Freemason* praised the ecumenism nurtured at Vatican II. He said:

> Catholics ... must not forget that all roads lead to God. And they will have to accept that this courageous idea of freethinking, which we can really call a revolution, pouring forth from our Masonic lodges, has spread magnificently over the dome of St. Peter's.[151]

Yves Marsaudon was delighted to add that "One can say that ecumenism is the legitimate son of Freemasonry."[152]

The post-Vatican II spirit of doubt and revolution obviously warmed the heart of French Freemason Jacques Mitterand, who wrote approvingly:

> Something has changed within the Church, and replies given by the Pope to the most urgent questions such as priestly celibacy

[149] Ibid., p. 62.
[150] Vatican I, Session III, Chap. IV, Faith and Reason.
[151] Cited from Archbishop Marcel Lefebvre, *Open Letter to Confused Catholics*, (Kansas City, Missouri: Angelus Press, 1995) pp. 88-89.
[152] Yves Marsaudon, *Oecuménisme vu par un Maçon de Tradition* (pp. 119-120).

and birth control, are hotly debated within the Church itself; the word of the Sovereign Pontiff is questioned by bishops, by priests, by the faithful. For a Freemason, a man who questions dogma is already a Freemason without an apron.[153]

Marcel Prelot, another enemy of the Catholic Church and a senator for the Doubs region in France, describes what has taken place. He wrote:

> We had struggled for a century and a half to bring our opinions to prevail within the Church and had not succeeded. Finally, there came Vatican II and we triumphed. From then on the propositions and principles of liberal Catholicism have been definitively and officially accepted by Holy Church.[154]

The Communists were equally delighted with the results of the Council. As the Italian Communist Party declared at its 11th Party Congress in 1964: "The extraordinary 'awakening' of the Council, which is rightly compared with the Estates General of 1789, has shown the whole world that the old politico-religious Bastille is shaken to its foundations."[155] L'Unita, the official publication of the Italian Communist Party, brazenly gave advice to Pope Paul VI regarding Archbishop Marcel Lefebvre, who led traditionalist opposition to the conciliar liberals and had militated for a conciliar condemnation of Communism: "Be conscious of the danger that Lefebvre represents. And continue the magnificent movement of approach begun with the ecumenism of Vatican II."[156]

A Whole New "Orientation" for the Church

The public exclamations of delight over Vatican II from neo-modernist luminaries, Communists and Masons should not be surprising. It was obvious to anyone who had eyes to see that the Second Vatican Council appeared to embrace ideas that had been condemned by Blessed Pope Pius IX in the *Syllabus of Errors*, but were in step *with Modernist thought*. (As we will discuss further, Cardinal Ratzinger has described certain aspects of the Council's teaching as a "countersyllabus".)

Here too, events since the first edition have provided confirmation of our analysis. In 2009 Monsignor Brunero Gherardini published a major book on Vatican II entitled *Vatican Council II: We Must Talk About It*.[157] Gherardini is nothing less than a Canon of St. Peter's Basilica, a secretary for the Pontifical Academy of Theology, a professor emeritus at the Pontifical Lateran University, and the editor of *Divinitas*, a leading Roman theological journal. The book includes a foreword by

---

[153] Cited from *Open Letter to Confused Catholics*, pp. 88-89.

[154] Ibid., p. 100.

[155] Bishop Graber, *Athanasius and the Church of Our Time*, p. 64.

[156] Archbishop Marcel Lefebvre, *They Have Uncrowned Him*, (Kansas City, Missouri: Angelus Press, 1988) p. 229. Here Archbishop Lefebvre also notes that the Communist newspaper *Izvestia* demanded that Pope Paul VI condemn him and his seminary at Ecône.

[157] Brunero Gherardini, *Concilio Ecumenico Vaticano II: Un Discorso da Fare* (Casa Mariana Editrice, Frigento, 2009).

Bishop Mario Oliveri (ordinary of the Italian dioceses of Albenga and Imperia) and an introduction by Archbishop Malcolm Ranjith, former secretary of the Congregation for Divine Worship and now Archbishop of Colombo. Gherardini makes this stunning admission from within the Vatican itself:

> [M]odernistic ideas still can be found in several Council documents, notably in Gaudium et Spes, and a few prominent Council Fathers were openly sympathetic to old and new modernists. ... In short, their Church was to be a kind of research laboratory rather than a dispenser of Truths from on high.[158]

The book, about to appear in English, is reportedly on the desk of Pope Benedict XVI. It represents a breakthrough for the effort to have an honest discussion of the Council's vexatious "pastoral" pronouncements. Once again events have shown that the "Fatimists" are not "crazy" but merely willing to say openly and honestly what many believe, but have not been willing to say before.

The situation Gherardini describes did not happen by accident, but by design. The progressivists at Vatican II sought to avoid direct statements which would easily be seen as condemned Modernist errors. They also deliberately planted ambiguities in the Council texts which they intended to exploit after the Council.[159]

By utilizing deliberate ambiguities, the Council documents enabled the post-conciliar promotion of an ecumenism that had been condemned by Pope Pius XI, a religious liberty for false sects that had been condemned by the 19th Century Popes (especially Blessed Pius IX), a new liturgy along the lines of Protestantism and ecumenism that Archbishop Bugnini[160] called "a major conquest of the Catholic Church", a collegiality that strikes at the heart of the papal primacy, and a "new attitude toward the world"—especially in one of the most radical of all the Council documents, Gaudium et Spes. Even Pope Benedict XVI when he was Cardinal Ratzinger had admitted that Gaudium et Spes is permeated by the spirit of Teilhard de Chardin.[161]

The result of all this was nothing short of an entirely new orientation of the Church, or what Pope Paul VI called an "opening to the world." As Paul VI himself was forced to admit, however, the opening to the world proved to be a disastrous miscalculation.

---

[158] A. Zangrando, "Roman Landscape," Latin Mass Magazine, Summer 2009.

[159] The progressivist periti at the Council are on record stating, "We will express it in a diplomatic way, but after the Council, we shall draw the conclusions implicit in it." In Father Ralph Wiltgen's book, The Rhine flows into the Tiber, p. 242.

[160] The progressivist Archbishop Annibale Bugnini was the major architect of the liturgical revolution which culminated in the New Mass (Novus Ordo). He was eventually banished from the Vatican to Iran because Pope Paul VI was shown documents demonstrating that Bugnini was a Freemason. Michael Davies devotes an entire chapter to Archbishop Bugnini in Pope Paul's New Mass, (Angelus Press, Kansas City, 1992) Chapter 24.

[161] Cardinal Joseph Ratzinger, Principles of Catholic Theology, (Ignatius Press, San Francisco, 1987) p. 334.

Pope Paul VI Admits that the Church
Has Been Invaded by Worldly Thinking

As Paul VI himself admitted only eight years after the Council, "the opening to the world has become a veritable invasion of the Church by worldly thinking. We have perhaps been too weak and imprudent."[161a] Only three years after the Council, Paul VI had admitted that "The Church is in a disturbed period of self-criticism, or what could better be called self-demolition."[162] And in 1972, in perhaps the most astonishing remark ever made by a Roman Pontiff, Paul VI lamented that "from somewhere or other the smoke of Satan has entered the temple of God."[163]

Let us consider some of the manifest reasons for Pope Paul VI's astounding admissions.

The Church "Opens" Herself to
"Dialogue" with Communist and Masonic Enemies

With Vatican II began the large enterprise of collaboration with the forces of the world, the great opening to the world. Nowhere is this more apparent than in *Gaudium et Spes* itself, which declares: "By unremitting study they"—meaning every priest in the Catholic Church, every bishop, every member of the hierarchy—"should fit themselves to do their part in establishing dialogue with the world and with men of all shades of opinion".

Now the objection will be raised: What is wrong with peaceful collaboration and dialogue with men of all shades of opinion in those areas in which the Church can find some sort of basic agreement? Here again the pre-conciliar Popes warned us about one of the devil's snares and delusions under the appearance of good. Speaking precisely about this call to collaborate and dialogue with Communists in causes which are supposedly common to all mankind—which is really the devil's call for the Church to lay down Her arms and join the enemy—Pope Pius XI warned as follows in *Divini Redemptoris*:

> In the beginning Communism showed itself for what it was in all its perversity. But very soon it realized that it was alienating people. It has, therefore, changed its tactics and strives to entice the multitudes by trickery in various forms, hiding its real designs behind ideas that are in themselves good and attractive. ... Under various names that do not suggest Communism, they establish organizations and periodicals with the sole purpose of carrying their ideas into quarters otherwise inaccessible. They try perfidiously to worm their way even into professedly Catholic and religious organizations. Again, without receding an inch from their subversive principles, they invite Catholics to collaborate with them in the realm of so-

---

[161a] Speech of November 23, 1973; quoted in Romano Amerio, *Iota Unum*, (Kansas City: Sarto House, 1996) pp. 9-10.

[162] Speech to the Lombard College, December 7, 1968.

[163] Speech of June 30, 1972.

called humanitarianism and charity. And at times make proposals that are in perfect harmony with the Christian spirit and the doctrine of the Church.... See to it faithful brethren that the Faithful do not allow themselves to be deceived. **Communism is intrinsically evil, and no one who would save Christian civilization may collaborate with it in any undertaking whatsoever**.[164]

Pope Pius XI could not have been clearer about the duty to shun "dialogue" and collaboration with Communists. And why? The Italians have a saying: *Dimmi con chi vai, e ti diro che sei*—"Tell me who you go with and I will tell you what you are." As Pius XI recognized, if one associates with a certain class of people, one will inevitably be influenced to become as they are, in spite of oneself. If one collaborates with the forces of the world they will tend to seduce him; he will become like them. If the Church opens Herself to the world in the sense of ceasing Her opposition to the powers that She once opposed, and if She says instead that the Church will now collaborate and dialogue with Her enemies, Her members will, in time, become like those they once opposed. And the opening to the world will result in the Church becoming like the world, as Pope Paul VI himself was forced to admit in the statement quoted above.

The Church "Reconciles" Herself with Liberalism

Those "conservatives" who deny that Vatican II constitutes a break with tradition, or that it contradicts prior teaching, have failed to listen to the very movers and shakers of the Council, who shamelessly acknowledge the truth. Yves Congar, one of the Council's "experts" and chief among the artisans of the Council's reforms, remarked with quiet satisfaction that "The Church has had, peacefully, its October Revolution."[165] Congar also admitted, as if it were something to be proud of, that Vatican II's *Declaration on Religious Liberty* is contrary to the *Syllabus* of Blessed Pius IX.[166] He said:

> It cannot be denied that the affirmation of religious liberty by Vatican II says materially something other than what the *Syllabus* of 1864 said, and even just about the opposite of propositions 16,

---

[164] Pope Pius XI, *Divini Redemptoris*, Encyclical on Atheistic Communism, March 19, 1937.

[165] Yves Congar, O.P., "Le Concile au jours le jours deuxième section" ("The Council day by day, second session"), (Paris, Cerf, 1964) p. 115.

[166] In truth, there can be no such thing as a "Counter-Syllabus", since Blessed Pope Pius IX's *Syllabus* of 1864 is plainly a solemn, definitive teaching binding on all Catholics (can. 750 § 2). In Paragraph 6 of the Encyclical *Quanta Cura* which was issued with the *Syllabus* on December 8, 1864, Blessed Pope Pius IX stated solemnly: "Amid, therefore, so great perversity of depraved opinions, We, well remembering Our Apostolic Office, and very greatly solicitous for Our most holy Religion, for sound doctrine and the salvation of souls which is entrusted to Us by God, and (solicitous also) for the welfare of human society itself, have thought it right to raise up Our Apostolic voice. *Therefore, by Our Apostolic Authority, We reprobate, proscribe and condemn all the singular and evil opinions and doctrines severally mentioned in this Letter, and will and command that they be thoroughly held by all children of the Catholic Church as reprobated, proscribed and condemned.* (Our emphasis) Taken from *The Popes Against Modern Errors*, (TAN Books and Publishers, Rockford, Illinois, 1999) p. 21.

17 and 19 of this document.[167]

Congar thus blithely suggests that Vatican II has undone an infallible papal condemnation of error.

Most noteworthy are the statements of the progressivist Cardinal Suenens, one of the most liberal prelates of the Twentieth Century, himself a Council Father, who spoke glowingly of the old regimes that have come crashing down. The words he used in praise of the Council are supremely telling, perhaps the most chilling and the most damning of all. Suenens declared "Vatican II is the French Revolution of the Church."[168]

And, only a few years ago, even the then-Cardinal Ratzinger, apparently unruffled by such admissions, added that the Vatican II text *Gaudium et Spes* is nothing less than a "*counter*-Syllabus". He said:

> If it is desirable to offer a diagnosis of the text (*Gaudium et Spes*) as a whole, we might say that (in conjunction with the texts on religious liberty, and world religions) it is a revision of the *Syllabus* of Pius IX, *a kind of countersyllabus* ... Let us be content to say here that the text serves as a *countersyllabus* and, as such, represents on the part of the Church, *an attempt at an official reconciliation with the new era inaugurated in 1789*. ... the *one-sidedness* of the position adopted by the Church under Pius IX and Pius X in response to the situation created by the new phase of history inaugurated by the French Revolution was, to a large extent, *corrected via facti*, especially in Central Europe, but there was still no basic statement of the relationship that should exist between the Church and the world that had come into existence after 1789. In fact, *an attitude that was largely pre-revolutionary continued to exist in countries with strong Catholic majorities*. Hardly anyone will deny today that the Spanish and Italian Concordats strove to preserve *too much of a view of the world that no longer corresponded to the facts*. Hardly anyone will deny today that, in the field of education and with respect to the historico-critical method in modern science, anachronisms existed that corresponded closely to this adherence to *an obsolete Church-State relationship*.[169]

Consider a Cardinal calling two of the greatest Popes in Church history "one-sided" in their efforts to protect the Church from the errors of liberalism and modernism! According to the then-Cardinal Ratzinger, at Vatican II the Church made an "attempt" to "correct" and "counter" the teaching of Blessed Pius IX and Saint Pius X, and to reconcile Herself instead *with the French Revolution* and the Enlightenment.

But this was the very goal of the Permanent Instruction, *Masonry's blueprint for subversion of the Church!* That is precisely why, in his *Syllabus of Errors*, Blessed Pius IX condemned the proposition that "The Roman Pontiff can and ought to reconcile himself and come to

---

[167] Yves Congar, *La Crise d'Église et Msgr. Lefebvre*, (Paris, Cerf, 1977) p. 54.

[168] Cited from *Open Letter to Confused Catholics*, p. 100.

[169] Cardinal Joseph Ratzinger, *Principles of Catholic Theology*, pp. 381-382.

terms with progress, liberalism and modern civilization." (Condemned Proposition #80). And Saint Pius X, in his apostolic letter *Notre Charge Apostolique*, condemned the Sillon movement in France, rebuking its members because "They do not fear to make blasphemous reconciliations between the Gospel and the Revolution."

But according to Cardinal Ratzinger, *"there can be no return to the Syllabus, which may have marked the first stage in the confrontation with liberalism but cannot be the last stage."*[170] And what is this last "stage" in the "confrontation with liberalism"? Apparently, in Cardinal Ratzinger's view, it is the Church's *acceptance* of the very ideas She once condemned! Confronting liberalism by *reconciling* with it is doubletalk. The then-Cardinal Ratzinger's "confrontation" with liberalism is nothing more than an abject surrender.

Moreover, it was apparently the opinion of the then-Cardinal Ratzinger, that not only the condemnations of liberalism in the *Syllabus* of Blessed Pius IX but also the anti-modernist teaching of Saint Pius X in *Pascendi* must now be considered outdated. In 1990, the Congregation for the Doctrine of the Faith issued an "Instruction on the Theologian's Ecclesiastical Vocation." In explaining the Instruction to the press, Cardinal Ratzinger claimed that certain teachings of the Magisterium were "not considered to be the final word on the subject as such, but serve rather as a mooring in the problem, and, above all, as an expression of pastoral prudence, a kind of *temporary disposition*."[171] As examples of these "temporary dispositions," the then-Cardinal Ratzinger cited "the statements of the Popes during the last century on religious freedom, as well as the anti-modernist decisions at the beginning of this century ..."[172]—that is, the anti-modernist teaching of Saint Pius X in the early 1900s.

These comments by Cardinal Ratzinger are disturbing to a Catholic, not only because they admit that the Council embraced a cherished goal of the Church's enemies, but because they come from the then-Prefect of the Sacred Congregation for the Doctrine of the Faith (CDF), who is responsible for *guarding* the purity of Catholic doctrine. And this, as we shall soon show, is the same man who seemed to be leading us away from the traditional Catholic understanding of the Message of Fatima.[173]

---

[170] Ibid., p. 191.

[171] *L'Osservatore Romano*, English Weekly Edition, July 2, 1990, p. 5.

[172] Ibid.

[173] Since this was written in 2002, there's some good news to report on this front. First, whereas the then-Cardinal Ratzinger on June 26, 2000 seemed to state that the Immaculate Heart of Mary was no different from any other holy person's heart (see *TMF*, page 39 and the analysis of his statement provided on pages 128-130 of this book), Cardinal Ratzinger (now Pope Benedict XVI) seemed to reverse himself on June 5, 2005, less than two months after his election to the papacy, when he said the Immaculate Heart of Mary is the closest heart to the Sacred Heart of Jesus Christ.

Secondly, on June 26, 2000, Cardinal Ratzinger strongly suggested that the prophetic words of Fatima referring to "the Triumph of the Immaculate Heart of Mary" was about something 2000 years in the past. On May 13, 2009, now as Pope Benedict XVI, he reversed himself and addressed a prayer to the Blessed Virgin Mary in the most

The Teaching that the Roman Catholic Church
Is Exclusively the
One True Church of Christ Is Abandoned

As the attempt to reconcile the Church with the diabolical principles of the French Revolution would neutralize the Church's once fierce opposition to the errors of the modern age, so would the "ecumenical venture" launched at the Council soon bring about the *de facto* abandonment of all efforts to convert heretics (e.g. Protestants) and schismatics to the Catholic Faith—as in the conversion of Russia.

At the same time the Council embraced the "ecumenical movement"— only 35 years after Pope Pius XI had condemned it in his encyclical *Mortalium Animos*—the Council's document *Lumen Gentium* threw into confusion the whole doctrine of the Catholic Church as the one true Church. According to *Lumen Gentium* "the Church of Christ ... *subsists* in the Catholic Church." (Emphasis added.)

This causes bewilderment. Why doesn't the document clearly proclaim what the Catholic Church has always taught, as seen in the encyclicals of Pope Pius XII—namely, that the one true Church of Christ *is* the Catholic Church?[174] Why employ a term favorable to the progressivist error that the Church of Christ is actually *bigger* than the Catholic Church, so that schismatic and heretical (e.g. Protestant) sects are "in some mysterious way" part of (or linked with) the Church of Christ? This error, based upon Vatican II's use of the word "subsists", is trumpeted by Father Avery Dulles, who was made a Cardinal by Pope John Paul II. He said:

> **The Church of Jesus Christ is not exclusively identical to the Roman Catholic Church**. It does indeed subsist in Roman Catholicism, but it *is also present in varying modes and degrees in other Christian communities* to the extent that *they too are what God initiated in Jesus* and are obedient to the inspirations of Christ's Spirit. As a result of their common sharing in the reality of the one Church, the several Christian communities already have with one another a real but imperfect communion.[175]

The former Cardinal Ratzinger also appeared to embrace the views of the "new theology." In an interview with the German newspaper

---

significant town of Bethlehem, where the Blessed Virgin gave birth to the Son of God, and he reminded Our Lady of Her promise and prediction: "In the end, My Immaculate Heart will triumph", and prayed to Her that "May it be so."

[174] In the 1943 encyclical *Mystici Corporis*, Pope Pius XII taught that "the true Church of Jesus Christ ... is the One, Holy, Catholic, Apostolic Roman Church." This clearly means that the Church of Christ is not composed of the Catholic Church and other "Christian" denominations. Pope Pius XII reiterated this doctrine in his 1950 encyclical *Humani Generis*: "The Mystical Body of Christ and the Roman Catholic Church are one and the same thing."

[175] Taken from *Vatican II, the Work That Needs to Be Done*, edited by David Tracy with Hans Küng and Johann Metz (Concillium, Seabury Press, New York, 1978) p. 91 (emphasis added).

Frankfurter Allgemeine Zeitung, the Cardinal declared as follows:

> When the Council Fathers replaced the word "is" with the word "subsistit" [subsists], they did so for a very precise reason. The concept expressed by "is" (to be) is far broader than that expressed by "to subsist." "To subsist" is a very precise way of being, that is, to be as a subject, which exists in itself. Thus the Council Fathers meant to say that *the being of the Church as such is a broader entity than the Roman Catholic Church*, but within the latter it acquires, in an incomparable way, the character of a true and proper subject.[176]

Cardinal Ratzinger was claiming that the Council Fathers *intended* to say that the "being" of the Church is broader than the Catholic Church, but this claim is false. The generality of the Council Fathers had no intention of contradicting the teaching of Pope Pius XII that the Church of Christ *is* the Catholic Church, not some vague "entity" that is "broader" than the Catholic Church.

In truth, this ambiguity undermines the traditional teaching that the one and only Church of Christ *is* the Catholic Church—an intention he shared with his fellow partisans of the "new theology" at Vatican II. We know this because Father Ratzinger, serving as a theological *peritus* at the Council, was the *peritus* (so-called "expert") who introduced the term "subsistit" (subsists) into the drafting of the conciliar document *Lumen Gentium*. He inserted this term at the suggestion of a *Protestant minister*, Pastor Schmidt, from Germany.

The former Cardinal's explanation of the meaning of "subsistit" (subsists) in *Frankfurter Allgemeine Zeitung* was as confusing as the term itself. "Subsists" and "is" can, however, mean the very same thing, contrary to what Cardinal Ratzinger suggested at the time. For the sake of the precision that should characterize any conciliar document, the Council ought to have stated clearly that "The Church of Christ subsists *only* in the Catholic Church." But as Father Edward Schillebeeckx, another conciliar *peritus*, admitted, his liberal confreres had deliberately inserted ambiguities into the conciliar texts,[177] knowing that they would later be able to interpret them in a heterodox manner after the Council.

Objectively speaking, that truly is what Father Ratzinger did at the Council when he introduced the term "subsistit." In fact, the original German text of the above-quoted interview in *Frankfurter Allgemeine Zeitung* shows that use of the term was a *knowing departure* from the teaching of Pope Pius XII: "... die Konzilsväter das *von Pius XII gebrauchte* Wort 'ist' durch 'subsistit' ersetzten"—which translates as:

---

[176] *L'Osservatore Romano*, Italian edition, October 8, 2000, p. 4: "Quando i Padri conciliar sostituirono la parola 'è' con la parola 'subsistit' lo fecero con uno scopo ben preciso. Il concetto espresso da 'è' (essere) è piu ampio di quello espresso da 'sussistere.' 'Sussistere' un modo ben preciso di essere, ossia essere come soggeto che esiste in sé. I Padri conciliari dunque intendevano dire che l'essere della Chiesa in quanto tale è un entità piu ampia della Chiesa cattolica romana, ..."

[177] See statements by Father Schillebeeckx in the Dutch magazine *De Bauzuin*, No. 16, 1965, quoted in the French translation in *Itineraires*, No. 155, 1971, p. 40.

"... the Council Fathers replaced the word 'is,' *used by Pius XII*, with 'subsistit.'" That is, Cardinal Ratzinger admitted that Vatican II *replaced* the established terminology of papal teaching. Even worse, the original German of the interview further states: "So wollten die Väter sagen: Das Sein der Kirche als solches *reicht viel weiter* als die römisch-katholische Kirche,"—which translates as: "Thus the Fathers meant to say: the being of the Church as such *extends much further* than the Roman Catholic Church."[178] Thus, Dulles and the former Cardinal Ratzinger contradicted the perennial Catholic teaching that the Church of Christ *exists exclusively* in the Catholic Church. **Yet their view was allowed to become the common interpretation of Vatican II**. Here we see a prime example of how the "new theologians" at Vatican II passed the theological football to themselves, while pretending that it was "the Council" that had thrown the pass.

But here, yet again, events since the first edition of this book have confirmed a problem we identified. None other than the former Cardinal Ratzinger himself, now Pope Benedict, has attempted to clarify the deep confusion in the Church caused by the use of "subsists in the Catholic Church" instead of simply "*is* the Catholic Church". On June 29, 2007 the Congregation for the Doctrine of the Faith (CDF) issued a document entitled "Responses to Some Questions Regarding Certain Aspects of the Doctrine on the Church" which presented formal responses to questions about the Council's teaching in this area. The document begins with the astonishing admission that "the Congregation wishes to respond to these questions by clarifying the authentic meaning of some ecclesiological expressions used by the magisterium which are open to misunderstanding in the theological debate." In other words, it is the "ecclesiological expressions" *of the Second Vatican Council* that are "open to misunderstanding" and therefore must now be clarified—*more than forty years after the Council ended!*

Accordingly, one question addressed is: "Why was the expression 'subsists in' adopted instead of the simple word 'is'"? In response the CDF states: "The use of this expression, which indicates *the full identity of the Church of Christ with the Catholic Church*, does *not change the doctrine on the Church*. Rather, it comes from and brings out more clearly the fact that there are 'numerous elements of sanctification and of truth' which are found outside her structure, but which 'as gifts properly belonging to the Church of Christ, impel towards Catholic Unity.'"[179]

This response at least negates that interpretation of the Council—promoted by the former Cardinal Ratzinger himself—which denied that the Church of Christ and the Catholic Church are "one and the same

---

[178] *Frankfurter Allgemeine Zeitung*, September 22, 2000; Italian translation in *L'Osservatore Romano*, October 8, 2000.

[179] June 29, 2007, Congregation for the Doctrine of the Faith (CDF), "Responses to Some Questions Regarding Certain Aspects of the Doctrine on the Church," Third Question, at www.vatican.va/roman_curia/congregations/cfaith/documents/rc_con_cfaith_doc_20070629_ responsa-quaestiones_en.html.

thing." It is worth recalling here that the Catholic Church has always taught and Pius XII insisted in *Humani Generis* that the Catholic Church *is* the Church of Jesus Christ. But while the problem with "subsists in" is addressed, the related novel expression pertaining to "elements of sanctification and truth" outside the Church's "subsistence" in Her visible structure remains obscure. Does the expression connote only valid sacraments such as marriages by an Orthodox priest, or a baptism by a Protestant minister which the Church nonetheless recognizes as valid and thus as "elements of sanctification" to be found outside Her visible structure? Or does it extend even to preaching by non-Catholic ministers that happens to be true on this or that point (for whatever that truth is worth in the context of preaching also filled with objective heresies)?

Just how problematic the expression remains becomes apparent from the CDF's own comment on the interpretation of Vatican II according to which these "elements" outside the Church mean that the Church is "present" wherever these elements are. To quote the CDF directly: "It is ***possible***, according to Catholic doctrine, to affirm correctly that the Church of Christ is present and operative in the churches and ecclesial Communities not yet fully in communion with the Catholic Church, on account of the elements of sanctification and truth that are present in them. **Nevertheless, the word 'subsists' can only be attributed to the Catholic Church alone** (emphasis added)."[180]

Note well: This remarkable statement concedes that it is only *possible* to affirm this reading of the Council in accordance with Catholic doctrine, whereas the Council's Modernist proponents had insisted on a binding "development" of doctrine requiring Catholics to believe that the Church is somehow "present and operative" outside of Herself in some ill-defined way. Is it not astounding, and indeed alarming, that the CDF is reduced to saying that it is "merely *possible* to affirm" consistently with the Faith what *an ecumenical Council purportedly taught*?

So, the Council's grave ambiguity on the doctrine of the Church persists despite this clarification. Indeed, the very need to issue clarifications of the Council's teaching in the first place indicates a totally unprecedented problem with its novel and ambiguous formulations. This in itself is a disquieting "sign of the times" that must be read in the light of Fatima. One is reminded immediately of Pius XII's own reading of the signs of times in light of Fatima in 1931, which led him to warn of "innovators" who would very soon attempt the "suicide" of altering the faith, in Her liturgy, Her theology and *the very soul* of the Church.[181]

The Church No Longer Seeks the Conversion and Return of Heretics and Schismatics

Despite the recent attempt at a clarification just noted, the erroneous view persists that the Church of Christ is something much bigger

---

[180] Ibid., Response to Second Question.
[181] See Pope Pius XII on pages 36-37 of this book.

than, and therefore is not the same as, the Roman Catholic Church. Consequently, it is no wonder that after 45 years of "ecumenical activity" even Vatican prelates now openly repudiate the return of Protestants and schismatics to Rome.

One prominent example of this departure from traditional teaching is the statement of Cardinal Walter Kasper, the former secretary of the Church's most prominent post-conciliar heretic, Hans Küng. Kasper, whose Modernist views are well-known throughout the Church, was made a Cardinal by Pope John Paul II in February 2001 and now still enjoys (at the time of this writing, December 2009) the rank of Prefect of the Vatican's Pontifical Council for Promoting Christian Unity. Kasper said:

> ... today we no longer understand ecumenism in the sense of a return, by which the others would 'be converted' and return to being 'Catholics'. This was expressly abandoned at Vatican II.[182]

In fact, Kasper's statement scorns the thrice-defined infallible dogma that "outside the Church there is no salvation." (*extra ecclesia nulla salus*) The actual wording of these three solemn, infallible (and, therefore, impossible to change)[183] definitions that are binding on all Catholics[184] (of whatever rank, including Cardinals and Popes) to believe, under pain of being automatically excommunicated (expelling themselves from the Catholic Church) are as follows:

> There is but one universal Church of the faithful, outside which no one at all is saved. (Pope Innocent III, Fourth Lateran Council, 1215; Dz. 430; D.S. 802)

> We declare, say, define, and pronounce that it is absolutely necessary for the salvation of every human creature to be subject to the Roman Pontiff. (Pope Boniface VIII, the Bull *Unam Sanctam*, 1302; Dz. 469; D.S. 873)

> The most Holy Roman Church firmly believes, professes and preaches that none of those existing outside the Catholic Church, not only pagans, but also Jews and heretics and schismatics, can have a share in life eternal; but that they will go into the eternal fire which was prepared for the devil and his angels, unless before death they are joined with Her; and that so important is the unity

---

[182] *Adista*, February 26, 2001. English translation quoted from "Where Have They Hidden the Body?" by Christopher Ferrara, *The Remnant*, June 30, 2001.

[183] "We, with the approval of the sacred council, teach and define that it is a divinely revealed dogma: that the Roman Pontiff, when he speaks ex cathedra, that is, when, acting in the office of shepherd and teacher of all Christians, he defines, by virtue of his supreme apostolic authority, doctrine concerning faith or morals to be held by the universal Church, [he] possesses through the divine assistance promised to him in the person of St. Peter, the infallibility with which the divine Redeemer willed His Church to be endowed in defining doctrine concerning faith or morals; and that such definitions of the Roman Pontiff are therefore irreformable because of their nature [*ex sese*], but not because of the agreement of the Church." (D.S. 1839)

[184] "But if anyone presumes to contradict this Our definition (God forbid that he do so): let him be anathema." (D.S. 1840)

of this ecclesiastical body that only those remaining within this unity can profit by the sacraments of the Church unto salvation, and they alone can receive an eternal recompense for their fasts, their almsgivings, their other works of Christian piety and the duties of a Christian soldier. No one, let his almsgiving be as great as it may, no one, even if he pour out his blood for the Name of Christ, can be saved, unless he remain within the bosom and the unity of the Catholic Church. (Pope Eugene IV, the Bull *Cantate Domino*, 1442; Dz. 714; D.S. 1351)

Because this often misunderstood teaching is the focal point of the attack on Catholic dogma by the Church's sworn enemies, namely Masonry, it needs further explanation and defense.

The dogma means exactly what it says: if you have not received the Baptism that Jesus Christ prescribed—which is, in the normal course of Providence, the baptism of water in the name of the Father and of the Son and of the Holy Ghost—then you cannot go to Heaven.

But although Baptism and membership in the Church are necessary to salvation, they are not enough (except for infants who are baptized and who die before the age of reason). We must also live the moral law of Christ and love God with all our heart and our neighbor as ourselves. We must also receive the other Sacraments worthily.

This teaching does not deny the possibility of salvation for all souls who have not become formal members of the Catholic Church. It is possible that someone may never have had the Gospel preached to him.

If such a person were to keep all the gravely binding Commandments of God's law knowable by the light of reason alone (and in case he committed a mortal sin, he were to repent of it with a perfect act of contrition), he could be saved, but only if it were through no fault of his own that he did not know his obligation to be baptized, join the Catholic Church and practice the Catholic Faith.

For a non-Catholic to be saved in this manner would obviously be much more difficult than for a Catholic to be saved with the help of dogma, the examples of saints and the grace of the seven Sacraments.

Many are prone to self-deception, especially in these dark times, and many people who consider themselves to be of good will might easily find the truth of the Gospel if they honestly sought it. It may be that some prefer darkness to light. So we ought never to presume that a person is without fault in failing to be baptized and practice the Catholic Faith. Thus, in general, the salvation of non-Catholics is at greater risk.

In charity, we must pray and make sacrifices for the conversion of all non-Catholics.

But charity also forbids us to assign bad will or culpability to someone, or to judge him as irreformable. We must remember the examples of St. Mary Magdalen, a notorious sinner, and St. Paul, a persecutor of the Church, who both converted and drew many souls to

Christ and His Church. All things are possible with God.

But the question is raised: How could a just and merciful God give some souls the benefit of being born Catholic and deny it to others, if the Catholic Faith is essential to salvation? Should not all be given an equal chance to reach Heaven? And why should some people be denied the opportunity to have the Gospel preached to them and be put at so great a disadvantage in saving their souls? Here, we see the democratic ideology of our age at work, along with a presumption that we can judge the ways of God.

We must begin to answer these objections by establishing the authority of the Church and Her claim on our belief:

1) The Catholic Church is "the pillar and ground of the truth." (1 Tim. 3:15)

2) The Catholic Church is the one Church of God founded by Jesus Christ, who Himself is accredited by God His Father and by His many prophecies and miracles—especially His Resurrection from the dead. The Catholic Church is historically the Church He founded, and accredited as the one true Church of God. The authenticity of the Catholic Church is also guaranteed by the miracles of holiness as well as physical and moral miracles through the centuries and continuing into our own day.

3) The Catholic Church has defined infallibly that outside the Church there is no salvation. An infallible definition by its very nature is not able to be re-defined into another sense. The definition cannot fail—it is irreformable—it is the absolute truth which does not change.

The Modernist objects to such definitions. He says: "The truth is not something I know with my intellect; it is something I feel; and my feelings change, so the truth can and does change."

The Modernist who seriously professes that belief is already outside the Church since he denies Scripture: "Jesus Christ, yesterday, and today; and the same for ever." (Heb. 13:8)

But the Catholic of weak faith or of poor intellectual formation—though he might hold a Ph.D. or degree in theology—also raises the objection: the dogma "outside the Church there is no salvation" does not seem capable of being reconciled with the teachings that God is all just and God would not condemn to hell someone who through no fault of his own does not know this teaching because it has never been preached to him.

Again, we must begin with authoritative teaching, this time from the Gospel itself:

> "But without faith it is impossible to please God. For he that cometh to God, must believe that He is, and is a rewarder to them that seek Him." (Heb. 11:6)

"Neither is there salvation in any other. For there is no other Name under Heaven given to men, whereby we must be saved." (Acts 4:12)

"...unless a man be born again of water and the Holy Ghost, he cannot enter into the kingdom of God." (John 3:5)

"He that believes and is baptized, shall be saved: but he that believes not shall be condemned." (Mark 16:16)

So how do we reconcile apparently contradictory teachings of the necessity to believe in Jesus Christ and to be a member of His Church to be saved, and the Justice, Fairness and Holiness of God toward an individual who has not heard the Gospel preached to him at all; or been denied the fullness of the Gospel, such as a second-generation Protestant or Greek Orthodox or one raised in Jewish cultures? And the answer is that God is All Holy, All Just and All Good and will not condemn to the pains of hell one who is not guilty of personal mortal sin.

The personal mortal sin of unbelief condemned by Jesus more than once is the refusal to acknowledge the truth of the whole Gospel—the whole dogma of the Catholic Church—even after it has been testified to by evident signs, wonders and miracles that only God can perform.

The First Vatican Council taught most reasonably on the question of faith:

> Because man depends entirely on God as his Creator and Lord and because created reason is wholly subordinate to uncreated Truth, we are obliged to render by faith a full submission of intellect and will to God when He makes a revelation (*see canon 1*). This faith, however, which is the beginning of human salvation, the Catholic Church asserts to be a supernatural virtue. By that faith, with the inspiration and help of God's grace, we believe that what He has revealed is true—not because its intrinsic truth is seen with the natural light of reason, but because of the authority of God who reveals it, of God who can neither deceive nor be deceived (*see canon 2*). For, on the word of the Apostle: "Faith is the substance of things to be hoped for, the evidence of things that are not seen" (*Heb. 11:1*).

> Nevertheless, in order that the submission of our faith might be consonant with reason (*see Rom. 12:1*), **God has willed that external proofs of His revelation, namely divine acts and especially miracles and prophecies, should be added to the internal aids given by the Holy Spirit. Since these proofs so excellently display God's omnipotence and limitless knowledge, they constitute the surest signs of divine revelation, signs that are suitable to everyone's understanding** (*see canons 3-4*). Therefore, not only Moses and the prophets but also and preeminently Christ Our Lord performed

many evident miracles and made clear-cut prophecies. Moreover, we read of the Apostles: "But they went forth and preached everywhere, while the Lord worked with them and confirmed the preaching by the signs that followed" (*Mark 16:20*). And likewise it is written: "We have the word of prophecy, surer still, to which you do well to attend, as to a lamp shining in a dark place" (*II Pet. 1:19*).

It is clear that many people in our cities and country have been exposed to the testimony of evident miracles proving the Catholic Faith is the one true teaching of Jesus Christ. The Miracle of the Sun at Fatima is one such miracle. Thus we must remember what the Church has infallibly defined at Vatican Council I:

> (*Canon 4*) If anyone says that all miracles are impossible and, hence, that all accounts of them, even though contained in Sacred Scripture, should be classed with fables and myths; or that miracles can never be recognized with certainty and that the divine origin of the Christian religion cannot be successfully proved by them: let him be anathema.

But what about the person who never had the law of the Gospel preached to him and does not know that outside the Church there is no salvation? If such a person exists, God, the just lawgiver, would hold him bound by the Natural Law—the law written on the heart of each man who comes into the world.

That law is promulgated by the very fact that each and every man who reaches the age of reason knows there is the Natural Law to follow.

And one of the first precepts of the Natural Law is to seek the truth, obey it and follow it wherever it leads. "Seek and you shall find," said Jesus.

So if a person has diligently searched all his life and not found the Gospel or the Church through <u>no</u> fault of his own, he can be saved, in God's special providence outside the Gospel law promulgated for all men.

But that is a special exception, not the rule, and no one can know who has exercised sufficient good will and due diligence in seeking the ways of God. "Who has weighed the human heart?", asks God in Isaias, and God answers that no one except God Himself can understand fully the human heart of each individual. St. Jerome, at the end of his life, in the presence of his disciples, spoke these dreadful words: "Out of one hundred thousand people whose lives have always been bad, you will find barely one who is worthy of indulgence."

At the end of the day, the exception to the rule is only that—an exception in a particular case. The dogma "outside the Church there is no salvation" stands vindicated 100% of the time, because in that exceptional case God would have caused that exception to be joined to the Church in a special way. We must uphold the dogma—we must believe the dogma. We must defend this dogmatic teaching of the

Catholic Faith.

As Blessed Pius IX taught in *Singulari Quadem*, Catholics must not preoccupy themselves with pointless speculation about salvation for those who—through no fault of their own—are not formal members of the Church, since only God knows whom He will save (in some extraordinary manner) from among the great mass of humanity which has not exteriorly professed the Catholic religion.

Blessed Pius IX—whom Pope John Paul II himself beatified—exhorted the faithful to hold fast to the dogma "outside the Church there is no salvation" and to continue with ever greater fervor the divinely appointed work of the Church in making disciples of all nations. As for the lot of those who—through no fault of their own—remain outside the visible Church, His Holiness warned that "all further inquiry is unlawful."

Who can doubt the wisdom of Blessed Pius IX's warning? Indeed, the Church has also taught constantly and infallibly that no one in this world (absent a special private revelation) can know with absolute certainty the subjective state of any soul, much less whether a soul—even one's own—is numbered among the elect. Since it is not possible for the Church to presume (except in the case of canonized saints) that *any individual* is either saved or damned, the ministers of the Church are duty-bound to seek the conversion of every man, woman and child on the face of the earth, following Our Lord's own command: "Go forth and make disciples of all nations, baptizing them in the name of the Father, and of the Son, and of the Holy Ghost; teaching them to observe all things whatsoever I have commanded thee" (Matt. 28:19-20); "He who believes and is baptized shall be saved; he who believes not shall be condemned." (Mk. 16:16)

And in this dogma of no salvation outside the Catholic Church we have another reason in charity to promote the whole Message of Fatima—particularly the Consecration of Russia by the Pope and the Catholic bishops of the world. Because when this is finally done, Russia will be converted to the one true Church of Jesus Christ—the Catholic Church. The people of Russia will become Catholics and their salvation morally certain if they remain in the fervent practice of the Catholic Faith until their death. Millions more souls will be saved.

Not only will the Russians be saved, but billions of souls in the rest of the world will be converted to Christ and His Church—the Catholic Church. We know that because Our Lady predicted "a period of peace will be given to the world". But there can be no peace if it is not based upon the teaching and practices of the Prince of Peace—Jesus Christ. For men and women to live the teachings of Jesus Christ, they must believe the Gospel, be baptized and practice the Catholic Faith. This will happen at some time—Sacred Scripture tells us when all the nations will enter into the Catholic Church: "Come and let us go up to the mountain of the Lord, and to the house of the God of Jacob, and He will teach us His ways, and we will walk in His paths" (Isaias 2:3).

But this will only come about through the Consecration of Russia, after which the scandal of billions living in moral squalor, schism, heresy, paganism and other false religions will be ended by that obedience of the Pope to Our Lady of Fatima. We must sacrifice ourselves for this intention and pray, as Our Lady of Fatima said on June 13, 1929.

But the present-day scandal of Vatican officials in high places abandoning *de facto* the promotion of the Catholic dogma "outside the Church there is no salvation" must be examined further, so we continue with the examination of Cardinal Kasper's false teaching.

By declaring that Protestants need no longer convert to Catholicism, Cardinal Kasper brazenly defies both the infallible teaching of the Magisterium and the commands of Our Lord Himself. Kasper's view also flatly contradicts the Church's constant teaching that the only way to Christian unity is *the return of the dissidents* to the Catholic Church through their conversion. In the 1949 admonition of the Holy Office of Pope Pius XII concerning the "ecumenical movement," the bishops were warned that in any "ecumenical" discussions they might authorize, the Protestant interlocutors must be presented with "the Catholic truth" and "the teaching of the Encyclicals of the Roman Pontiffs on *the return of the dissidents* to the Church."[185] The Catholic doctrine of the return of the dissidents was stressed by Pope Pius XII on December 20, 1949: "The Catholic doctrine will have to be proposed and exposed totally and integrally: what the Catholic Church teaches about the true nature and means of justification, about the constitution of the Church, about the primacy of the jurisdiction of the Roman Pontiff, about the only true union which is accomplished with the *return of the dissidents* to the only true Church of Christ, must not be passed over in silence or covered over in ambiguous words."[186]

At least Kasper says openly what most of today's modernist prelates seem to believe, but will neither confirm nor deny. Yet Kasper's policy represents the still-prevailing "spirit of Vatican II," despite Benedict's call for a "hermeneutic of continuity" in reading the Council—in itself a devastating implied admission that the Council lent itself to a reading in *discontinuity* with prior Church teaching. That the Council lends itself to the view that the conversion of non-Catholics is no longer necessary was confirmed by the former Cardinal Ratzinger, when he was still Father Ratzinger, in his 1966 book *Theological Highlights of Vatican II*. In *Theological Highlights* the then-Father Ratzinger claimed that the Council had given the Church *a new orientation toward non-Catholics*, which dispenses with any call for their conversion:

> The Catholic Church has no right to absorb the other Churches ... [A] basic unity—of Churches that remain Churches, yet become one Church—*must replace the idea of conversion*, even though

---

[185] *Acta Apostolicae Sedis*, AAS 42, p. 142.
[186] Pius XII, Instruction of the Holy Office, *Ecclesia Catholica*, December 20, 1949 ("On the Ecumenical Movement").

conversion retains its meaningfulness for those in conscience motivated to seek it.[187]

Now, the then-Father Ratzinger wrote this book during the Council. As a co-worker with Karl Rahner, he was heavily involved with drafting the conciliar documents. He is in a position to tell us what were the actual intentions of the "architects" of Vatican II, which is not to be confused with the intention of the Council Fathers themselves. And he declares that the teaching of Vatican II, according to those who drew up the documents, was that conversion is an option.[188] That is, according to him, the non-Catholic need not convert to the true Church—either for salvation or for unity.

This view is no less radical than that of Father Edward Schillebeeckx, another progressivist Council *peritus*, who was investigated by the Vatican after the Council (but never disciplined) for his open denial of various Catholic dogmas. Schillebeeckx exulted that "At Vatican II, the Catholic Church officially abandoned its monopoly over the Christian religion."[189]

Likewise, a "Catholic" journal from the Rome-based International Jewish-Christian Documentation Service (SIDIC)[190] spoke of Vatican II's new orientation toward non-Catholics. In 1999 it spotlighted what it considers to be the "main problem" with so-called "traditional Catholics", including Archbishop Lefebvre:

> Lefebvre's refusal to accept ecumenism originates in clear teachings from the Magisterium: the encyclical *Satis Cognitum* of Leo XIII (1896); the encyclical *Mortalium Animos* of Pius XI (1928); the Dec. 20, 1949, Instruction of the Holy Office regarding ecumenism. The only ecumenism accepted by Lefebvre and his followers is that which strives for the **unconditional return** of the members of other confessions to the one Church of Christ, the Roman Catholic Church. **This hardened sectarianism is precisely the kind of logic which Vatican II**, through profound reflection on the nature of the Church, **refused to accept**. Though rooted in Tradition [sic]

---

[187] (Emphasis added) *Theological Highlights of Vatican II*, Father Joseph Ratzinger [Paulist Press, New York, 1966], pp. 65-66. This section of the book focuses on the deliberate ecumenical foundation on which is based the Council document *Lumen Gentium*. For a more complete discussion of Father Ratzinger's book, see "Vatican II vs. the Unity Willed by Christ," by J. Vennari, *Catholic Family News*, December 2000.

[188] Even if Cardinal Ratzinger completely changed his own personal views to a more orthodox position, the Council texts themselves remain ambiguous, imprecise, and appear to be oriented toward an unorthodox ecumenism which does not seek the conversion of non-Catholics to Catholicism.

[189] E. Schillebeeckx, OP, *Igreja ou igrejas?*, in V.A. *Cinco problemas que desafiam a Igreja hoje*, pp. 26f. Cited from *In the Murky Waters of Vatican II*, Atila Sinke Guimarães, (Maeta, Metairie, Louisiana, 1997) p. 243.

[190] SIDIC is an association identifying itself as Catholic that was "founded in Rome in 1965 at the request of a group of experts of the Second Vatican Council following the promulgation of *Nostra Aetate*", to promote Catholic-Jewish "dialogue". The Rome-based SIDIC has local representatives in the following countries: Australia, Belgium, Canada, England, France, Holland, Israel, Italy, United States. *Nostra Aetate* is the Council's "Declaration on the Relation of the Church to Non-Christian Religions".

the scope of the Council's reflection was without precedent in the history of Christianity. For integralists, ecumenism is one of the fundamental betrayals by Vatican II.[191]

The novel claim that non-Catholics need not convert because they are "in some mysterious way" part of the Church of Christ[192] scorns the Church's perennial teaching on the necessity of non-Catholics to abandon their errors and return to the one true Church of Jesus Christ, as the pre-conciliar Popes unanimously taught.

There are reported cases of Vatican Cardinals *actively discouraging* non-Catholics who desire to convert to Catholicism, evidently in keeping with this same false interpretation of the Council. *Catholic Family News* published the story of Father Linus Dragu Popian, who had been raised in the Romanian Orthodox religion. In 1975 he risked his life to escape Communist Romania and presented himself as a seminarian to the Vatican, expressing his wish to convert to Catholicism. The then-Secretary of State, Cardinal Villot, and other Vatican Cardinals were horrified. They told young Popian that he must not flee Communism and must not become Catholic, because this would damage the Vatican's relations with Communist Romania and the Romanian Orthodox Church.[193]

Little has changed in Rome since then. Bishop Fellay of the Society of St. Pius X related in a 2001 interview that he had met a schismatic (Orthodox) bishop who wanted to convert to the Catholic Church. Bishop Fellay advised him to deal directly with Rome. When the Orthodox bishop told the Vatican he wanted to become a Catholic, "panic ensued. The following day, Cardinal Neves, Prefect of the Congregation of Bishops said to the schismatic bishop, 'Your Excellency, it is not necessary to convert. Since the Council, things have changed! There's no need to convert any more.'"[194]

This deliberate refusal to allow a schismatic Orthodox bishop to return to Rome is completely in line with the Balamand Declaration of 1993, negotiated between certain Vatican officials and various Orthodox churches. In this document the Vatican's representative (Cardinal Cassidy of the Pontifical Council for "Christian Unity") actually agreed that, owing to "radically altered perspectives and thus attitudes"

---

[191] (Emphasis added.) *Service International de Documentation Judéo-Chrètienne* (SIDIC), Rome, [English edition from Washington, D.C.] Vol. XXXII, No. 3, 1999, p. 22.

[192] The verbal ambiguity used by Vatican II to advance this false notion is found in *Lumen Gentium* 8 wherein it says "The Church of Christ subsists in the Catholic Church" rather than Pope Pius XII's definition that the Church of Christ *is* the Catholic Church [*Mystici Corporis*, Pope Pius XII]. See previous discussion and footnotes in this chapter concerning the origin and effect of this ambiguity, as admitted by the then-Cardinal Joseph Ratzinger.

[193] For a brief account of Father Popian's story, see "Vatican says, Do Not Convert to Catholicism", John Vennari, *Catholic Family News*, December 2001. See also "Vatican says, 'You Must Not Become Catholic!'", John Vennari, *The Fatima Crusader*, Issue 69, Winter 2002. Father Popian's testimony on audio cassette entitled "Vatican's Ostpolitik and Ecumenism Tried to Prevent My Conversion to Catholicism" is also available from the Fatima Center, 17000 State Route 30, Constable, New York 12926.

[194] "We are a Sign of Contradiction", interview with Bishop Bernard Fellay, SSPX, *Latin Mass* Magazine, Fall 2001, p. 11.

engendered by Vatican II, the Catholic Church will train new priests "to pave the way for future relations between the two churches, passing beyond *the outdated ecclesiology of return to the Catholic Church.*"[195]

The claim that the Magisterium's constant teaching on the return of the dissidents (heretics and schismatics) to the one true Church as the only means of true Christian unity is now "outdated ecclesiology" is a heresy, since it flatly contradicts not only the Church's teaching on the return of the dissidents, but also the infallibly defined Catholic dogma that *outside* the Church there is no salvation.

The *de facto* abandonment of the Church's traditional teaching on this matter does not represent true charity toward the separated brethren but rather a retreat from the Church's duty to tell them the simple truth. Again, the result is no boon to non-Catholics, but rather a weakened, scandal-ridden Church which, in parts of the world, is hardly able to serve as the leaven of society it was meant to be. While the Church, being a divine as well as a human institution, will inevitably be restored to Her former vigor, as She has following other crises in Her past, the Church and the world will undergo great suffering until this crisis of faith is ended.

The Social Kingship of Christ Abandoned

As a consequence of the Church's new orientation since Vatican II, there has also been a *de facto* abandonment of the Church's constant teaching on the Social Kingship of Christ. According to this teaching, not only individual men, but all nations, are obliged to submit to Christ and conform themselves to His teaching. It is the teaching of Christ, not "dialogue" with unbelievers, that will bring peace to the world; it is His Church that must serve as the chief instrument of world peace. The constant teaching of the Church on this doctrine is summed up with admirable concision by Pope Pius XI in his encyclical *Ubi Arcano Dei*:

> Since the Church is the safe and sure guide to conscience, for to Her safekeeping alone there has been confided the doctrines and the promise of the assistance of Christ, She is able not only to bring about at the present hour a peace that is truly the peace of Christ, but can, *better than any other agency which We know of,* contribute greatly to the securing of the same peace for the future, to making war impossible in the future. For the Church teaches (*She alone has been given by God the mandate and the right to teach with authority*) that not only our acts as individuals *but also as groups and as nations* must conform to the eternal law of God. In fact, it is much more important that the acts of a nation follow God's law, since on the nation rests a much greater responsibility for the consequences of its acts than on the individual. *When, therefore, governments and nations follow in all their activities, whether they*

---

[195] Balamand Statement, nn. 13 and 30. The Balamand Statement (1993) was cited approvingly by Pope John Paul II in *Ut Unum Sint*, n. 59.

be national or international, the dictates of conscience grounded in the teachings, precepts, and example of Jesus Christ, and which are binding on each and every individual, then only can we have faith in one another's word and trust in the peaceful solution of the difficulties and controversies which may grow out of differences in point of view or from clash of interests.[196]

Speaking of efforts to obtain world peace through a League of Nations, Pope Pius XI declared:

An attempt in this direction has already and is now being made; its results, however, are almost negligible and, especially so, as far as they can be said to affect those major questions which divide seriously and serve to arouse nations one against the other. *No merely human institution of today can be as successful in devising a set of international laws which will be in harmony with world conditions as the Middle Ages were in the possession of that true League of Nations, Christianity.* It cannot be denied that in the Middle Ages this law was often violated; still it always existed as an ideal, according to which one might judge the acts of nations, and a beacon light calling those who had lost their way back to the safe road.[197]

In order to reinforce this teaching, Pope Pius XI inaugurated the Feast of Christ the King with his encyclical *Quas Primas*:

It was surely right, then, in view of the common teaching of the sacred books, that the Catholic Church, which is the kingdom of Christ on earth, destined to be spread among all men and all nations, should with every token of veneration salute Her Author and Founder in Her annual liturgy as King and Lord, and as King of kings. ... [T]he empire of our Redeemer embraces all men. To use the words of Our immortal predecessor, Pope Leo XIII: "His empire includes not only Catholic nations, not only baptized persons who, though of right belonging to the Church, have been led astray by error, or have been cut off from Her by schism, but also all those who are outside the Christian faith; so that truly the whole of mankind is subject to the power of Jesus Christ." *Nor is there any difference in this matter between the individual and the family or the State; for all men, whether collectively or individually, are under the dominion of Christ.*[198]

The "Civilization of Love" Replaces the Conversion of Pagans

After Vatican II, however, the Social Kingship of Christ was replaced by something called the "civilization of love"—a term coined by Pope Paul VI to describe the utopian notion that "dialogue with the world"

---

[196] Pope Pius XI, *Ubi Arcano Dei*, Encyclical Letter on the Peace of Christ in His Kingdom, December 23, 1922.

[197] Ibid.

[198] Pope Pius XI, *Quas Primas*, Encyclical on the Kingship of Christ, December 11, 1925.

would lead to a world brotherhood of religions that would not at all be explicitly Christian. The slogan "civilization of love" has been repeated incessantly since then. As Pope John Paul II described this novel notion in his address for the World Day of Peace in 2001:

> Dialogue leads to a recognition of diversity and opens the mind to the mutual acceptance and genuine collaboration demanded by the human family's basic vocation to unity. As such, dialogue is a privileged means for building *the civilization of love and peace* that my revered predecessor Paul VI indicated *as the ideal* to inspire cultural, social, political and economic life *in our time*. ... *The different religions too can and ought to contribute decisively to this process.* My many encounters with representatives of other religions—I recall especially the meeting in Assisi in 1986 and in Saint Peter's Square in 1999—have made me more confident that mutual openness between the followers of the various religions can greatly serve the cause of peace and *the common good of the human family*.[199]

Even John Paul II was led to think that interreligious prayer meetings such as those at Assisi in 1986 and 2002 are among the very means by which this utopian notion is supposed to be realized. Yet the mere sight of such spectacles would have horrified Pope Pius XII and every one of his predecessors. Meanwhile, the Social Kingship of Christ in a Catholic social order is *de facto* excluded from the new orientation.

Nor has the situation improved with the publication of Pope Benedict's encyclical *Caritas in Veritate* (2009), which seeks to address the crisis in Western civilization but says not one word about the Social Kingship of Jesus Christ, calling instead for "a new humanistic synthesis." Consider that Pope Pius XI's first encyclical on the Church's answer to the civilizational crisis, *Ubi Arcano*, is subtitled "On the Peace of Christ in the Kingdom of Christ," whereas Pope Benedict's encyclical on the same crisis 87 years later is subtitled "On Integral Human Development in Charity and Truth." The radical change of terminology from simple Gospel clarity to trendy jargon is as unsettling as it is revealing.

In what is clearly an effort to reconcile the novelties of Vatican II and its "opening to the world" with traditional Church teaching, *Caritas* wavers between "integral human development" as made possible only by divine grace, supernatural charity, Christian fraternity, and the Gospel as "fundamental" and "indispensable"—an indirect affirmation of the Social Kingship—and "integral human development" based on "fundamental values," "universal values" and "reason open to transcendence," all of which **seem** to be presented as available to non-Catholics and even non-believers of "good will."[200] (But if they are of good will they must therefore come to be believing Catholics at some point.) Nowhere does the encyclical state clearly (although it faintly

---

[199] (Emphasis added.) Pope John Paul II's Message for World Day of Peace, January 1, 2001, "Dialogue Between Cultures for a Civilization of Love and Peace".

[200] Cf. *Caritas*, nn. 55-57.

implies) what Pius XI and his predecessors affirmed explicitly: that *only* the Catholic Church can bring true peace, justice and charity to the world by uniting mankind in one faith and one baptism under Christ the King; that *only* Christendom, not any merely human alliance, can save a tottering civilization.

Clearly, Pope Benedict is making an effort to "turn the ship around," as is obvious with his "liberation" of the traditional Latin Mass from its bogus "prohibition" for forty years. But given the continued influence of the "new orientation" of the Church and the attendant novelties of "ecumenism," "dialogue," "interreligious dialogue," and "collegiality,"— none of which have any binding doctrinal character whatsoever—the Pope evidently feels obliged to refrain from stating the obvious: that the world simply has no hope of averting catastrophe without Christ and His Blessed Mother. Of course, the Church's new "ecumenical" and "interreligious" orientation cannot possibly be reconciled with the Message of Fatima, which explains why, beginning with Vatican II, an effort has been made to revise the Message, if not bury it completely, in keeping with the "new orientation."

Must Catholics Accept the New Orientation of the Church?

Catholics are bound to submit to the Church's dogmatic definitions on faith and morals; as well as to all the ordinary and universal teachings of the whole Church on faith and morals. These established teachings are guaranteed as true and unchangeable by God Himself. Anything that contradicts the infallible teaching of the Church must be rejected. It is clear that Catholics are *not* bound to submit to new attitudes and orientations of liberalized churchmen who are now saying and doing things unheard-of in the Church's entire history. Thus, Catholics have the right, even the duty, to resist this new orientation arising from the ambiguities of the Council and the opinions of the "new theology", which conflict with the perennial and infallible Magisterium.

For years, Catholics have labored under the misconception that they must accept the *pastoral* Council, Vatican II, with the same assent of faith that they owe to dogmatic Councils. This, however, is not the case. The Council Fathers repeatedly referred to Vatican II as a *pastoral* Council. That is, it was a Council that dealt not with *defining* the Faith, but with measures in the realm of practical and prudential judgment—such as the launching of the "ecumenical venture." The Council's own document, the Preliminary Note (in Latin, *Nota Praevia*) to *Lumen Gentium*, states this clearly: "In view of the conciliar practice and *pastoral purpose* of the present Council, the sacred Synod defines matters of faith and morals as binding on the Church only when the Synod itself openly declares so."[201] No matters of faith and morals were

---

[201] Addenda to *Lumen Gentium*, Explanatory Note of the Theological Commission, in Walter M. Abbott, S.J., ed., *The Documents of Vatican II*, (New York: America Press, 1966) pp.

defined "as binding on the Church" concerning the new "ecumenical orientation", nor as to any of the other novel "pastoral" formulations in the language of the conciliar documents.

That Vatican II was inferior in authority to a dogmatic council is confirmed by the testimony of the Council Father, Bishop Thomas Morris. At his own request, this testimony was not unsealed until after his death:

> I was relieved when we were told that this Council was not aiming at defining or giving final statements on doctrine, because a statement on doctrine has to be very carefully formulated and I would have regarded the Council documents as tentative and liable to be reformed.[202]

Then there is the important testimony from the Council's Secretary, Archbishop (later Cardinal) Pericle Felici. At the close of Vatican II, the bishops asked Archbishop Felici for that which the theologians call the "theological note" of the Council—that is, the doctrinal "weight" of its teachings. Archbishop Felici replied:

> In view of conciliar practice and the pastoral purpose of the present Council, this sacred Synod defines matters of faith or morals as binding on the Church only when the Synod itself openly declares so.[203]

He also said:

> We have to distinguish according to the *schemas* and the chapters those which have already been the subject of dogmatic definitions in the past; *as for the declarations which have a novel character, we have to make reservations*.[204]

Pope Paul VI himself observed that "Given the Council's pastoral character, it avoided pronouncing in an extraordinary manner, dogmas endowed with the note of infallibility."[205]

Thus, unlike a dogmatic Council, Vatican II does not demand an unqualified assent of faith. The Council's verbose and ambiguous documents are not on a par with the doctrinal pronouncements of past councils. Vatican II's novelties are not unconditionally binding on the faithful, nor did the Council itself ever say that they were.

And yet the ambiguous teachings of the Council, and the Church's new post-conciliar orientation, have resulted in nothing less than what, as we shall see, the then-Cardinal Ratzinger called the "demolition of bastions" in the Church. This would include demolition of the Message of Fatima. As we will now demonstrate, this destructive undertaking has

---

97-98.

[202] Bishop Morris' personal testimony reported in an article by Kieron Wood, *Catholic World News*, January 22, 1997.

[203] *The Documents of Vatican II*, Editor Walter Abbott, S.J., p. 98.

[204] Cited from *Open Letter to Confused Catholics*, p. 107.

[205] Pope Paul VI, General Audience of January 12, 1966, in *Insegnamenti di Paolo VI*, vol. 4, p. 700, cited from Atila Sinke Guimarães, *In the Murky Waters of Vatican II*, (Metairie, Louisiana: Maeta, 1997; Rockford, Illinois: TAN, 1999) pp. 111-112.

largely fulfilled the dreams of the Church's enemies, and the prophetic warnings of the Message of Fatima as reported by Pope Pius XII only 31 years before the Council.

In the late 1950s, Hans Urs von Balthasar was considered so doctrinally unsound that the Swiss bishops did not allow him to be a theological advisor at Vatican II.

Chapter 7
The Demolition of Bastions

No wonder the Church's worst enemies have been so delighted with the Council and the radical changes it introduced. They are also no doubt quite pleased with the sudden and catastrophic ecclesial collapse in every department following Vatican II. Every available statistic shows that the unprecedented changes ushered in by Vatican II have been accompanied by equally unprecedented declines in the number of priests and religious, the number of new ordinations, the number of seminarians and the number of conversions and baptisms. Immediately after Vatican II some *50,000 priests defected*, and in 2009 there remain approximately 50,000 fewer Catholic priests than there were *forty-four years ago*. In 1997 there were fewer baptisms in the United States than there were in 1970.[206]

Long before he became Pope, the former Cardinal Ratzinger spoke of "*a continuing process of decay* that has gone on largely on the basis of appeals to the Council, and thus has discredited the Council in the eyes of many people."[207] Yet Cardinal Ratzinger, along with the others who have presided over the new orientation of Vatican II, insisted that we need not less, but more of the same:

> Does this mean the Council itself must be revoked? Certainly not. It means only that the real reception of the Council has *not yet even begun*. What devastated the Church after the Council was not the Council but the refusal to accept it. ... The task, therefore, is not to suppress the Council but to *discover the real Council* and to deepen its *true intention* in the light of present experience.[208]

Going even further, and citing as his authority one of the same neo-modernist theologians who have helped produce this disaster for the Church, the then-Cardinal Ratzinger declared:

> The fact is, as Hans Urs von Balthasar pointed out as early as 1952, that ... She [the Church] must relinquish many of the things that have hitherto spelled security for Her and that She has taken for granted. *She must demolish longstanding bastions* and trust solely the shield of faith.[209]

---

[206] See, e.g., statistical analysis of the priesthood in *L'Osservatore Romano*, 13/20 August 1997, and "The Index of Leading Catholic Indicators," *The Latin Mass*, Winter 2000, presenting extensive data from the Vatican *Statistical Yearbook of the Church* and other standard reference works. See also Kenneth C. Jones, *The Index of Leading Catholic Indicators: The Church Since Vatican Council II* (Fort Collins, Colorado: Roman Catholic Publishing, 2003).

[207] Cardinal Ratzinger, *Principles of Catholic Theology*, p. 391.

[208] Ibid., p. 390.

[209] Ibid., p. 391.

The former Cardinal's call for "demolition of longstanding bastions" in the Church was and still is perhaps the most serious admission of all concerning the revolutionary new orientation of the Church brought on by the Second Vatican Council. For what could he mean by "*longstanding* bastions" if not the Church's traditional defenses against Her enemies—what the then-Cardinal himself described as "many of the things that have hitherto spelled *security* for Her and that She has taken for granted"? The Cardinal appeared to admit that he wished to *demolish* the very things that give the Church security! The Church must, in the Cardinal's apparent view of things, trust "solely in the shield of faith." But what does *that* mean? How can Catholics hold on to their faith unless it is kept secure by the very bastions that are being called to be demolished?

By citing "new theologian" Hans Urs von Balthasar as his authority for this "demolition of bastions", the then-Cardinal appeared to bless the "new theology" that tears down the Church's traditional theology, with its clear and precise definitions of the truths that Catholics must believe. In the former Cardinal's call to *demolish* the Church's "longstanding bastions", we see clearly what can only be called a "desire to destroy." That phrase is taken from a book by the Catholic writer Atila Sinke Guimarães, entitled *Animus Delendi* (Latin for "the desire to destroy"). Guimarães shows that the conciliar and post-conciliar "reformers" of the Church are motivated by a mentality that sees the destruction of the "old" Church as "tragic but necessary" for the Church's "growth and renewal" in the "modern world."

How are the "bastions" to be demolished? Our Lady says the *dogma* of Faith will be preserved in Portugal. Dogmas are in themselves bastions of the Church. Obviously, then, the demolition of bastions will involve the undermining of dogmatic definitions, even as lip-service is paid to the dogmas by the neo-modernist "new theologians" who are doing the undermining. Dogmas can be undermined in these ways: 1) simply ignore them, and they will cease to exist for all practical purposes; 2) replace clear terms with ambiguous terms—e.g. "is" with "subsist"; 3) dismiss dogma as "outdated theology", as in the Balamand Declaration and the various remarks of high-ranking churchmen cited in the preceding chapter; 4) pretend there is no such thing as infallible dogmatic definitions which every Catholic must believe, just as they are written; 5) pretend that defined Catholic dogma can and does change over time; and 6) where the dogma of no salvation outside the Church is concerned, simply refer incessantly to non-Catholics as "believers" or "Christians."

What precisely are the bastions that in the view of "reformers" must be demolished? We recall once again what Pope Pius XII accurately predicted in his inspired comments about the coming crisis in the Church:

I am worried by the Blessed Virgin's messages to Lucy of Fatima. This persistence of Mary about *the dangers which menace the Church* is a divine warning against the suicide of altering the Faith, in Her *liturgy*, Her *theology*, and Her *soul*. ... I hear all around me innovators who wish to *dismantle* the Sacred Chapel, *destroy* the universal flame of the Church, *reject* Her ornaments and make Her feel remorse for Her historical past.

Pius XII identified three elements of the Church that the "innovators" wished to alter: Her liturgy, Her theology and Her soul (i.e. Her very nature). Notice that Pope Pius XII, basing himself on the Fatima Message, as well as what he had witnessed personally in the Church at that time, spoke of a coming attempt to *dismantle*, *destroy* and *reject* these things in the Church. In other words, the "demolition of bastions."

The Demolition of the Liturgy

Before Vatican II the Popes unanimously defended the Church's ancient Latin liturgy against innovation, recognizing that the immutable Latin language was a barrier against heresy, as Pope Pius XII taught in his monumental encyclical on the liturgy, *Mediator Dei*. Indeed, the Protestant "reformers" of the 16th Century hated nothing more than the traditional Catholic Mass in Latin, the Damasian-Gregorian liturgy which was the center of the life of the Church from at least the 4th Century (and probably earlier) until the liturgical "reform" of Pope Paul VI in 1969.

Nowhere can the desire to destroy, the demolition of bastions, be seen more clearly than in Pope Paul's explanation of his decision to suppress the traditional Latin Mass of more than 1,500 years' standing and replace it with a newly concocted rite of Mass in the vernacular—a totally unprecedented action his predecessors would have regarded as shocking and unthinkable:

> It is here that the greatest newness is going to be noticed, the newness of language. No longer Latin, but the spoken language will be the principal language of the Mass. The introduction of the vernacular will certainly be a great sacrifice for those who know the beauty, the power, and the expressive sacrality of Latin. We are parting with the speech of the Christian centuries; *we are becoming like profane intruders in the literary preserve of sacred utterance*. We will lose a great part of that stupendous and incomparable artistic and spiritual thing, the Gregorian chant. We have reason for regret, reason almost for bewilderment. What can we put in the place of that language of the angels? We are giving up something of priceless worth. Why? *What is more precious than these loftiest of our Church's values*?

What indeed *is* more precious than "these loftiest of our Church's values"? According to Paul VI what was more precious was an appeal to "modern man", whom the Pope apparently viewed as so obtuse as to be unable to make heads or tails of Latin prayers in the Roman Missal, even if the same Missal included vernacular translations alongside the Latin. Paul VI continued by answering his own question:

> The answer will seem banal, almost prosaic. Yet it is a good answer because it is human, it is apostolic. Understanding of prayer is more important than the silken garments in which it is royally dressed. Participation by the people is worth more—particularly participation by *modern people*, so fond of plain language which is easily understood and converted into everyday speech.[210]

Paul VI's speech is a blueprint for what has happened to the entire Church since the Council. The conciliar and post-conciliar changes—all without precedent in Church history—are the work of *profane intruders* who labor to destroy something of *priceless worth*, to *demolish bastions* that had been standing for centuries—not only in the sacred liturgy, but in the perennial teaching of the Church. It is no accident that Vatican II caused unprecedented destruction, since the Council's prime movers were planning destruction all along.

Here, however, we can report at least the beginning of a movement toward a restoration since the appearance of the first edition of *The Devil's Final Battle*: The Pope's *motu proprio* of July 7, 2007, *Summorum Pontificum*, which declared that every priest and religious order in the Church has the right to celebrate the traditional Latin Mass, which was "never abrogated" by Paul VI. In the *motu proprio* and in his letter to the bishops of the world accompanying it, the Pope makes these stunning admissions:

> What earlier generations held as sacred, remains sacred and great for us too, and it cannot be all of a sudden entirely forbidden or even considered harmful. It behooves all of us to preserve the riches which have developed in the Church's faith and prayer, and to give them their proper place.[211]

> As for the use of the 1962 Missal as a *Forma extraordinaria* of the liturgy of the Mass, I would like to draw attention to the fact that this Missal *was never juridically abrogated* and, consequently, in principle, *was always permitted*.[212]

Never juridically abrogated. *Always* permitted. With these phrases the Pope himself vindicates what "traditionalists" have said all along—

[210] Audience Address of November 26, 1969.

[211] *Motu proprio Summorum Pontificum* (2007) at http://www.vatican.va/holy_father/benedict_xvi/motu_proprio/documents/hf_ben-xvi_motu-proprio_20070707_summorum-pontificum_lt.html (in Latin); see also http://www.vatican.va/holy_father/benedict_xvi/letters/2007/documents/hf_ben-xvi_let_20070707_lettera-vescovi_en.html

[212] Letter of His Holiness Benedict XVI to the Bishops on the Occasion of the Publication of the Apostolic Letter *"motu proprio data"* Summorum Pontificum on the Use of the Roman Liturgy Prior to the Reform of 1970, at http://www.vatican.va/holy_father/benedict_xvi/letters/2007/documents/hf_ben-xvi_let_20070707_lettera-vescovi_en.html.

that Paul VI did not, and could not, "ban" the Church's traditional rite of Mass—and has thus exposed the entire fraud of the "liturgical renewal" following Vatican II. Without any genuine legal authority whatsoever, the traditional Latin Mass was effectively outlawed and the Church's liturgy turned upside down by the very band of iconoclastic incompetents whose destructive "work" Pius XII foresaw in the light of Fatima.

On this score we have another key admission emerging from "inside the Vatican" since the time of the first edition. In a scathing interview with a pair of traditional Catholic journalists in Italy, Mons. Domenico Bartolucci, no less than the Maestro in perpetuity of the Sistine Chapel under five consecutive Popes and recently honored by Pope Benedict for his long service to the Church in that capacity, was unsparingly, even brutally, frank about the new liturgy and the fraudulent attempt to "forbid" the traditional Mass. Mons. Bartolucci—again, the Maestro of the Sistine Chapel!—revealed that *he had never celebrated the new Mass* but only the traditional Latin Mass, and that "I would on the contrary have found it difficult to celebrate the Mass of the modern rite." When asked if thoughtful and doctrinally trained people had carried out the "liturgical reform", Bartolucci gave this withering reply:

> Excuse me, but the reform was done by arid people—arid, I repeat to you. And I knew them. As far as doctrine is concerned, I recall that Cardinal Ferdinand Antonelli, of venerable memory, often said: "What are we to make of liturgists who don't know theology?"[213]

The Pope's historic *motu proprio* has to be seen as the fruit of a worldwide Rosary campaign conducted by the allegedly "schismatic" Society of Saint Pius X, which had requested "liberation" of the Latin Mass as a precondition for its discussions with the Vatican concerning the crisis in the Church and the Society's role in addressing it.

The Society's defense of Catholic Tradition was validated quite dramatically when the Pope (to howls of outrage from within and without the Church) met the Society's second precondition by lifting the purported "excommunication" of its four bishops in 1988 with a decree of the Congregation for Bishops issued January 21, 2009 (the Feast of St. Agnes, Virgin and Martyr, in the traditional Roman liturgical calendar). In a letter to the world's bishops defending his decision to take this step toward "regularizing" the Society, the Pope made perhaps the most devastating admission of all from "inside the Vatican" since this book first appeared:

> In our days, when in vast areas of *the world the faith is in danger of dying out like a flame which no longer has fuel,* the overriding priority is to make God present in this world and to show men and

---

[213] "Monsignor Bartolucci on the liturgical reform and the 'reform of the reform'," at http://disputationes-theologicae.blogspot.com/

women the way to God.[214]

What a comment on the "springtime of Vatican II" that was supposedly inaugurated by the "reforms" of Vatican II! And it is no coincidence that the Pope linked his remark about the sputtering out of faith in vast areas of the world—*for lack of fuel*—to an enumeration of what the Society has to offer the Church: "Can we be totally indifferent about a community which has 491 priests, 215 seminarians, 6 seminaries, 88 schools, 2 university-level institutes, 117 religious brothers, 164 religious sisters and thousands of lay faithful?"

Nor was this just some isolated papal remark. As recently as September 2009 the Pope reiterated the theme of a post-Vatican II disaster in the Church in an address to the Bishops of Brazil during their *ad limina* visit to the Vatican:

> Dear Brothers, in the decades following the Second Vatican Council, some have interpreted the opening to the world not as a requirement for the missionary zeal of the Heart of Christ, but as a *passage to secularization... [C]ertain fundamental truths of the faith, such as sin, grace, theological life, and the last things, were not mentioned anymore.*
>
> *Many ecclesial communities senselessly fell into self-secularization*; attempting to please those who would not come, they witnessed many members whom they had leave them, deceived and disillusioned: those of our time, when they meet us, want to see that which they do not see anywhere else, that is, the joy and hope that come from being with the risen Lord.
>
> There is today a new generation born *into this secularized ecclesial environment*. Instead of noticing an openness and consensus, they see the abyss of differences and contradictions to the Magisterium of the Church growing ever wider, especially in the field of ethics. *In this desert without God*, the new generation feels a deep thirst for transcendence.[215]

So much for "the renewal of Vatican II"! Clearly, the man who is Pope today is not the same man who spoke as Cardinal Ratzinger. He is, rather, a man who, having attained the grace of the papal office, recognizes that enemies of the Faith surround him. As he declared in his first sermon as Pope on April 24, 2005: "Pray for me, that I may not flee for fear of the wolves." But then Benedict would not be the first Pope to undergo a conservative transformation. No less than Blessed

---

[214] Letter of His Holiness Pope Benedict XVI to the Bishops of the Catholic Church Concerning the Remission of the Excommunication of the Four Bishops Consecrated by Archbishop Lefebvre, 10 March 2009, at http://www.vatican.va/holy_father/benedict_xvi/letters/2009/documents/hf_ben-xvi_let_20090310_remissione-scomunica_en.html

[215] His Holiness Pope Benedict XVI, "To Bishops of the Episcopal Conference of Brazil on their *ad Limina* visit (West 1-2 Regions)," September 7, 2009. For the complete text, see *L'Osservatore Romano*; see also translation at http://www.vatican.va/holy_father/benedict_xvi/speeches/2009/september/documents/hf_ben-xvi_spe_20090907_ad-limina-brasile_en.html.

Pius IX was a "liberalist" at the beginning of his long pontificate, only to become the archenemy of Liberalism and the "modern world" after he narrowly escaped death and had to flee the papal palace for his life, disguised as a simple priest, when Masonic "patriots" invaded Rome in the name of Liberty.

And yet despite these encouraging signs in the Benedictine pontificate, the crisis in the Church rages on. Even the Pope's *motu proprio* reduces the received and approved rite of Mass in the Church to "the extraordinary form" of the liturgy, while elevating a new rite concocted less than forty years ago by a committee to the status of "the ordinary form." This horrible inversion of man-made novelty over a perennial tradition, going back to the Apostles and forged under the influence of the Holy Ghost, is emblematic of precisely that "diabolical disorientation" in the Church of which Sister Lucy spoke again and again in her correspondence and conversations. Further, the *motu proprio*, which clearly enunciates the right of priests to offer the traditional Mass without episcopal permission, is widely ignored and even positively disobeyed by many bishops, who continue to impose ridiculous restrictions on the Church's own liturgical patrimony.

Then, too, the theological crisis (discussion of which was a third precondition raised by the Society) continues as well. The theological discussions the Society has requested with the Vatican have indeed commenced as this second edition appears. And so it is opportune to restate, in this emerging new context of ever more frank Vatican admissions, the theological concerns we expressed in the first edition.

The Demolition of Theology

In the December 19, 1946 edition of *L'Osservatore Romano*, Pope Pius XII (targeting the heterodox theories of modernists like Chenu and de Lubac) warned that what was being trumpeted as a "new theology" would end up undermining the Faith:

> There is a good deal of talk (but without the necessary clarity of concept) about a "new theology", which must be in constant transformation, following the example of all other things in the world, which are in a constant state of flux and movement, without ever reaching their term. If we were to accept such an opinion, what would become of the unchangeable dogmas of the Catholic Faith; and what would become of the unity and stability of that Faith?[216]

As we have seen, John XXIII disregarded Pope Pius XII's warning; at Vatican II Pope John rehabilitated the very proponents of the "new theology" who were under suspicion of heresy during the pontificate of Pope Pius XII. To recall the testimony of Msgr. Bandas: "No doubt good Pope John thought that these suspect theologians would rectify

---

[216] Quoted from David Greenstock, "Thomism and the New Theology", *The Thomist*, October 1950.

their ideas and perform a genuine service to the Church. But exactly the opposite happened. ... The great confusion was underway. It was already apparent that *neither Trent nor Vatican I nor any encyclical would be permitted to impede its advance.*"

Now, what have been the effects of the "new theology" upon the Church? Today, in the name of Vatican II, we are told—

- that the Church must dialogue and collaborate with Communists, Muslims, heretics, schismatics, and other real enemies (in the objective order of things) of the faith;

- that the Church's constant pre-conciliar teaching against Liberalism (as seen in the *Syllabus* of Blessed Pius IX) and against Modernism (as seen in *Pascendi* by St. Pius X) is "one-sided" and outdated;

- that the Church must "attempt" a "reconciliation" with the principles of the French Revolution;

- that the "Church of Christ" is larger than the Catholic Church;

- that heretics (e.g. Protestants) and schismatics need no longer convert and return to the Catholic Church for salvation or even for unity.

In short, the Church's enemies in the neo-modernist, Freemasonic and Communist camps have seen their anti-Catholic dreams largely come true.

But now the Vatican seems willing to discuss the resulting theological disaster with the Society of Saint Pius X. No doubt the partisans in the Vatican are intent on inducing the Society to embrace the ambiguous novelties of the Council—which, in fact, no Catholic has any duty to embrace. On the contrary, in fact, all faithful Catholics must resist and reject all errors against the Church's teaching of all time—even if those errors were promoted by a non-infallible Council such as Vatican II. That is because the Church has no power to invent new doctrines.[217] Nevertheless, some advance is being made because at least now the Vatican is willing to enter into a *discussion* regarding the Council documents instead of demanding a false "obedience" to novel and nebulous concepts that have manifestly provoked tremendous damage to the Church and the cause of the Gospel.

The Demolition of the Church's Soul

The future Pius XII was not speaking idly when, in the light of the Message of Fatima, he predicted the coming attempt to alter not only

---

[217] As the *First* Vatican Council declared in its Dogmatic Constitution on the Church of Christ, Ch. 4, § 6: "For the Holy Spirit was promised to the successors of Peter *not so that they might, by His revelation, make known some new doctrine*, but that, by His assistance, they might religiously guard and faithfully expound the revelation or deposit of faith transmitted by the apostles. Indeed, their apostolic teaching was embraced by all the venerable Fathers and reverenced and followed by all the holy orthodox Doctors..."

the Church's liturgy and theology, but *Her very soul*—what She *is*. Of course, this design can never succeed completely, because Our Lord promised that the gates of hell would not prevail against His Church. But this divine promise does not exclude the Church's human element suffering the gravest possible wounds from Her enemies, short of a final death. It was the prospect of such grave injuries to the Church that so alarmed Pope Pius XII, especially in light of the Fatima prophecies.

And indeed Pope Pius' worst fears have been realized in the post-conciliar period, in which we have witnessed an effort to change the Church from the sole ark of salvation, outside of which no one is saved, into a mere collaborator with other "churches and ecclesial communities", non-Christian religions and even atheists in building up a utopian "civilization of love." In this "civilization of love" the salvation of souls from hell—which is no longer mentioned—is replaced by a new form of "salvation": salvation through world "brotherhood" and world "peace." This is the very notion which Freemasonry has been promoting for the past three centuries.

In keeping with this Freemasonic notion of "salvation" through the "brotherhood of man" (understood in a secular, non-Christian sense), many Catholic churchmen now tell us that we must respect the various Protestant and schismatic sects as partners in "ecumenical dialogue" and the "search for Christian unity." In keeping with this new notion, there are joint ecumenical "liturgies" between Catholics, Protestants and schismatic Orthodox churches to demonstrate the supposed "partial communion" between "all Christians."

To be sure, the executors of the new orientation of the Catholic Church still allow that She is the most perfect of all churches, but the claim that the Catholic Church *is the one true Church*, to the complete exclusion of all others, has *de facto* been abandoned by all but a remnant of faithful Catholics. Today they are considered "rigid sectarians" and "pre-conciliar" for simply believing what Catholics always believed before 1965. Contrary to the unfortunate, ignorant post-conciliar "Catholics", all Catholics who know the Catholic Faith know that unchangeable Catholic dogma must always be believed in order to remain in the Catholic Church, outside of which there is no salvation.

But the Freemasons and their allies view "Christian unity" as only a step toward pan-religious unity in the world brotherhood. At the same time "Christian unity" is being promoted by pan-Christian activities which the great pre-conciliar Popes would have regarded as sacrileges, "interreligious dialogue" has made the Church more "open" to the "value" of non-Christian religions, whose followers would no longer be regarded as being in need of faith and Baptism to save their souls. Karl Rahner's "anonymous Christianity"—which holds that the sincere followers of any religion can be, and probably are, "Christians" without even knowing it—has become the *de facto* theology of the Church. Accordingly, there would be pan-religious prayer meetings in which the members of all religions gather together to pray for peace and to demonstrate their "unity" as members of the human family, without any of them being told that they are in danger of damnation without Baptism, faith in Christ and membership in His Church. In the "reformed" Good Friday liturgy, Catholics (for the first time in the Church's liturgical history) no longer pray publicly and unequivocally for the conversion of non-Catholics into the Catholic Church as a necessary step for the salvation of their souls.

As anyone can see, the replacement of the Social Kingship of Christ with the "civilization of love" has totally neutralized the Catholic Church, which no longer serves as the center of the world's moral and spiritual authority, as She was meant to be by Her divine Founder.

The progressivist theologians who advanced this new orientation of the Church have now formed almost two generations of Catholic laity and clergy. The works of Rahner, Küng, Schillebeeckx, Congar, de Lubac, von Balthasar, and their disciples now dominate the teaching-texts of Catholic seminaries and universities. For the past 40 years, the progressivist tenets of these men have served as the principal formation for priests, religious, theologians, and Catholic college students. Thus, we have now reached a stage where prelates prefer Rahner's theology to that of Saint Robert Bellarmine, for example, who is a canonized saint and Doctor of the Church, or Saint Thomas Aquinas, the great Doctor and one of the greatest saints in Church history. The teaching of Bellarmine and Aquinas—indeed, the teaching of all the Popes before Vatican II—tends to be accepted only in accordance with the spin given it by Rahner and the other "new theologians." The same is true of most professors teaching today in Catholic colleges and seminaries.

This process of attempting to change the very soul and theology of the Church, as Pope Pius XII feared, has involved not only the "ecumenical venture" and "interreligious dialogue", but also an endless series of apologies from Catholic churchmen, high and low, for the Church's past "triumphalism" in claiming to be the sole repository of divine revelation, and the supposed sins of Her deceased members against other "Christians" and other cultures. This was precisely what Pope Pius XII predicted when he spoke of the innovators who would "make Her [the Church] feel remorse for Her historical past."

The Enemy's Predictions Fulfilled

We now summarize the close correspondence between what we have seen happen in the post-conciliar Church and the goals of both Freemasonry (as revealed by Roca and various Freemasons, many quoted by Bishop Graber, and *The Permanent Instruction*) and Communism (as attested to by Bella Dodd and other ex-Communists):

• The radical revision of the Roman liturgy following an ecumenical council. (Roca)

- An accord between "the ideals of modern civilization and the ideal of Christ and His Gospel. This will be the consecration of the New Social Order and the solemn baptism of modern civilization"—that is, the overall liberalization of Catholic churchmen in accordance with the same false principles condemned in the *Syllabus* of Blessed Pius IX. (Roca, Melinge, *The Permanent Instruction of the Alta Vendita*)

- The emergence of a "pluri-confessional pontificate, able to adapt to a polyvalent ecumenism, such as we are seeing established today in the intercelebration of priests and Protestant pastors"—Pope John Paul II himself celebrated joint liturgies with Protestant clerics.[218] (Roca, Melinge)

- The introduction of a "*guilt complex into the Church* … to label the 'Church of the past' as being oppressive, authoritarian, full of prejudices, arrogant in claiming to be the sole possessor of truth, and responsible for the divisions of religious bodies throughout the centuries." (Dodd)

- The "opening up" of the Church to the world and to a more "flexible" attitude toward all religions and philosophies. (Dodd)

- The use of this new orientation to undermine the Church, without actually destroying the exterior appearance of it. (Dodd, the Soviet defectors and *The Permanent Instruction*)

And yet—we must stress once again—all of these developments were predicted by the future Pope Pius XII in remarks he related specifically to "the Blessed Virgin's messages to Lucy of Fatima" and "this persistence of Mary about the dangers which menace the Church."

The Passion of the Church

Thus, the passion that our Holy Church is presently suffering is really no great mystery. By ignoring, shunning, despising Our Lady of Fatima and Her prophetic message of warning and Her offering us the only way out of this crisis as well as by recklessly ignoring the Popes of the past, by abandoning condemnations of error, by "rehabilitating" suspect theologians and making them heroes of the Church, by abolishing the *Index of Forbidden Books* and the Holy Office, by doing away with the traditional Catholic liturgy which was a barrier against heresy, by pronouncing the anti-liberal teaching of Blessed Pius IX and the anti-

---

[218] For example see: "Joint Catholic-Lutheran Vespers at Vatican", CWNews.com, November 13, 1999: "Archbishops G.H. Hammar and Jukka Paarma—the Lutheran primates of Sweden and Finland, respectively—and Bishops Anders Arborelius of Stockholm and Czeslaw Kozon of Copenhagen joined with the Holy Father for the Vespers service. Several other Lutheran 'bishops' from the Scandinavian countries were present for the ceremony, including two female 'bishops'." Likewise, at the beginning of the Jubilee Year, Pope John Paul II opened the Holy Doors of Saint Paul Outside the Walls with Anglican Archbishop Carey and schismatic Metropolitan Athanasios. Representatives of 20 other false confessions attended the ecumenical ceremony. See "Non-Catholics Joining Pope in Rite", *Los Angeles Times*, January 19, 2000.

modernist teaching of Saint Pius X as "one-sided" and "outdated"—in short, by ruthlessly and systematically stripping the Church of almost all Her defenses—our present Church leaders have demolished nearly all the bastions that once protected the Church from infiltration and corruption, thus creating a compromised structure that we can now see collapsing in scandal, corruption, disobedience, and loss of faith.

Yet some Church leaders continue to insist that the disastrous process of change responsible for this *admitted* invasion and auto-demolition of the Church be continued full steam ahead. This is precisely why the then-Cardinal Ratzinger, many years after Vatican II, declared that the Church "must demolish longstanding bastions."[219]

As we have already demonstrated, all of this was predicted by the Church's enemies. Bishop Graber, commenting on the post-conciliar crisis in light of the Masons' own predictions of what they would soon succeed in doing, declared:

> *If* in the face of these unambiguous admissions [by Masons, etc.] *anyone still holds* to the opinion that the events in the Church [since Vatican II] are marginal phenomena or transitional difficulties which will die down of their own accord in time, *he is simply beyond hope.* **But all the greater is the responsibility of the leading men in the Church** if they do not occupy themselves with these questions and imagine that everything can be repaired by patching it up here and there.[220]

But it is these very "leading men of the Church" who are the subject of our case. Yet we hasten to say, once again, that we do not claim that every churchman who promotes novel practices, such as ecumenism, is deliberately acting as an enemy of the Church. The renowned priest of the 19th Century, Father Frederick Faber, was a true prophet when he said in a remarkable sermon preached at Pentecost, 1861 in the London Oratory:

> We must remember that if all the manifestly good men were on one side and all the manifestly bad men were on the other, there would be no danger of anyone, least of all the elect, being deceived by lying wonders. It is the good men, once good, we must hope good still, who are to do the work of anti-christ and so sadly to crucify the Lord afresh ... **Bear in mind this feature of the last days, that this deceitfulness arises from good men being on the wrong side.** [221]

As we will proceed to prove, the men who concern us *are* on the wrong side. In their "demolition of bastions" in the Catholic Church through the imposition of their new orientation—or what has been called the Council's "attempt at an official reconciliation" with "the

---

[219] Cardinal Ratzinger, *Principles of Catholic Theology*, 1987.

[220] Graber, *Athanasius and the Church of Our Time*, pp. 170-171.

[221] Quote taken from *The Mystical Body of Christ in the Modern World*, Father Denis Fahey, (Regina Publications, Dublin, first printed in 1935) p. xi.

new era" begun by the French Revolution—they have necessarily arrayed themselves against the Message of Fatima. For there is nothing more integrally Catholic, nothing more opposed to the spirit of "the new era", nothing more inimical to the conciliar ecumenism, nothing more opposed to the tearing down of Catholic bastions, than the Virgin Mary's call for the consecration of Russia to Her Immaculate Heart, Russia's consequent conversion to the Catholic Faith, and the glorious triumph of the Immaculate Heart throughout the world in a Catholic social order.

The Message of Fatima: A Final Bastion

From what we have said thus far it should be apparent that the Message of Fatima, in its sheer Catholic integrity, cannot coexist with the new vision of the Church foisted upon us by those with a "desire to destroy" through the "demolition of bastions." This destruction has happened precisely because the vast program of Vatican II's *aggiornamento* runs contrary to the Catholic truths that permeate the Fatima Message.

Our Lady did not come to Fatima to demolish bastions in the Church, but rather to exhort the members of the Church to defend Her bastions in the coming crisis. She did not preach "ecumenism" or "interreligious dialogue", but the constant and unchanging teaching of the Church: that there is no salvation outside Her. When Our Lady came to Fatima, She did not give us any "new theology"; nor did She give us any "new understanding" of doctrine that would conflict in any way with the constant teaching of the Magisterium.

What do we see in the Message of Fatima? We see the key doctrines of our Faith reinforced, the very doctrines that have come under the fiercest attack in our time.[222] When the Mother of God came to Fatima—

- She spoke of the doctrine of Heaven;

- She spoke of the doctrine of Hell;

- She showed the children Hell;

- She spoke of the doctrine of Purgatory;

- She spoke of the doctrine of the Holy Eucharist;

- She spoke of the doctrine of the Sacrament of Penance.

- And She also spoke, indirectly, of the Social Kingship of Jesus Christ when She conveyed Heaven's command that Russia be consecrated to Her Immaculate Heart and *converted* to the fervent practice of the Catholic religion, which would lead to true, lasting peace in the

---

[222] For further considerations on the fact that Our Lady of Fatima reinforced key Catholic doctrines that are denied today, see John Vennari, "A World View Based on Fatima", *The Fatima Crusader*, Spring 2000, Issue 64; also available on the web (in booklet form) at http://www.fatimacrusader.com/aworldview/tocaworldview.asp. For a free copy of this article, write to the publisher of this book (see page xxvi).

world. This peace cannot come except through Jesus Christ, the Prince of Peace. And it cannot exist unless we build upon His social doctrine for peace and justice—unless nations live the moral teaching of Jesus Christ. But they cannot do that unless they accept His grace through the Sacraments.

A Motive Clearly Exposed

In conclusion, for those who unswervingly pursue the plainly ruinous "new orientation" of the Church, the Message of Fatima can only represent another bastion that must be demolished. That is why, as Pope Pius XII revealed in his prophetic remarks, the Virgin's messages to Sister Lucy concerned "the dangers which menace the Church." Although it is not revealed in those portions of the Message of Fatima that we have thus far been allowed to see, Pius XII spoke of "a divine warning" at Fatima about the "innovators all around me" who would bring grave harm to the Church through the alteration of the faith, "in Her liturgy, Her theology and Her soul."

We now see, clearly exposed, the motive for the crime which is the subject of this book. *There is a fundamental opposition between the "new" Church ushered in by Vatican II and the Church of all time, as represented by the Message of Fatima.* The Message of Fatima is a heavenly roadblock in the path of those who are determined to bulldoze the bastions of the old Church so that they can erect a new, more "enlightened" Church on the rubble.

These two competing visions of the Church—the vision of a "new" Church and the vision of the Church of all time as seen at Fatima—cannot coexist. One vision must yield to the other. The men who are the subject of this book have (explicitly or implicitly) made their choice concerning which vision of the Church must, to their way of thinking, govern. They have chosen the new vision—the new orientation of the Church initiated at Metz and at Vatican II. *In that choice lies their motive, and in that motive lies our understanding of their otherwise inexplicable actions against the Message of Fatima.*

Putting aside for the moment the question of the subjective motives of the proponents of this new orientation—who speak for themselves in the statements we have presented—it cannot be denied that objectively their actions are scandalous, suicidal to the Church (in a relative sense, of course) and harmful to millions of souls. Thus, their actions constitute a grave injustice no matter what the perpetrators may intend subjectively, because one can commit a veritable crime against the Church through recklessness or culpable negligence without consciously intending harm. For just as a man who sincerely believes it is right to murder someone is nonetheless guilty of murder, so are those who have harmed the Church—even with the best of intentions—guilty of a crime against Her. It is the difference between what the law calls a specific intent to cause harm to another, and a general intent to do an act that one should know will cause harm, even if one does not subjectively intend harm. In other words, the law punishes deliberate acts committed by one who should have known better than to commit the act.

For some of those responsible for this disaster, it may be a misguided sense of "enlightenment"—"doing evil under the guise of good" or a "diabolical disorientation" in the leadership of the Church, to quote the words of Sister Lucy herself. With these men, it is a case of "blind men guiding other blind men" as Sister Lucy said,[223] referring to what Jesus said in the Gospel (Mt. 15:14), "the blind leading the blind." It is also a case of the blind refusing to admit that they are blind. Some of these men may, in fact, have convinced themselves that what they are doing is best for the Church, even though it is manifestly ruinous.

In any case, we will show that the identified Vatican prelates are, objectively speaking, guilty of a terrible and grave injustice against the Church and the world through their participation in what is nothing short of a conspiracy to frustrate the fulfillment of the authentic Message of Fatima. Let God be the judge of their souls. Their objective words and deeds, however, judge themselves in the external forum of history.

What is more, the actions of these men can be judged by the light of the Church's own infallible teaching. The results of this departure from infallible teachings are evil, as the current condition of the Church should demonstrate to anyone. Catholics must judge an evil to be evil when they see it, rather than pretending it is good merely because certain figures in authority insist it is good. "Woe to you that call evil good, and good evil." (Isaias 5:20).

And so now we see, fully and clearly exposed, the motive that has animated the recent efforts by the Vatican apparatus to bury the Message of Fatima once and for all. For Fatima is the sum and substance of all the bastions they seek to demolish.

---

[223] See *The Whole Truth About Fatima* - Vol. III, pp. 750-762.

Vladimir Lenin, the evil genius behind the Communist Revolution in Russia in 1917, without whom, historians agree, the Russian Revolution would not have succeeded. Two foundational principles for establishing and expanding the Communist world revolution, according to Lenin himself, are the principle of terrorism (strategically used) as well as the principle that "the lie is sacred". In other words, Lenin taught that whenever lying advances the Communist Revolution in whatever circumstances a Communist agent (or agents) finds himself in, then it is, according to Lenin, his sacred duty to lie. But because people can know when they're being lied to, if the first lie told by agent #1 does not agree with the second lie told by agent #2, Lenin came up with the need for a common lie that all agents would repeat so as to be consistent to the general public. That common lie is known as "the Party Line". This is further explained in the following chapter, where it is also explained how there is a "Party Line" used inside the Catholic Church to destroy Fatima.

Chapter 8

The Message of Fatima
versus the Party Line

What has been the overall effect of the sudden and quite dramatic changes in the Church which began in the Twentieth Century? As Catholic writers have observed, what Catholics have witnessed especially over the past 40 years represents a kind of "Stalinization of the Roman Catholic Church" that bears an eerie resemblance to what was called at the time "the Adaptation" of Russian Orthodoxy to the demands of the Stalinist regime.

The subversion of the Orthodox Church by Stalin is certainly among the developments in Russia foreseen by the Virgin of Fatima. This is precisely why She came to call for the consecration of Russia to Her Immaculate Heart: so that Russia would embrace the one true religion and the one true Church, not the schismatic Orthodox Church which was founded in human rebellion against Rome when it left the Mystical Body of Christ over 500 years ago, and thus was constitutionally incapable of avoiding its total Adaptation to Stalinism.

The Orthodox Adaptation began officially when the Metropolitan Sergius of the Russian Orthodox Church published an "Appeal" in *Isvestia* on August 19, 1927.

(We must recall that Sergius was one of a small number of Russian Orthodox priests who survived the Stalinist persecution. In 1917 there were about 50,000 Russian Orthodox priests, but by 1935 there were only 500 left.)

The Appeal of Sergius, as it came to be known, set forth a new basis for the activity of the Russian Orthodox Church. The Russian layman Boris Talantov described this as "an Adaptation to the atheistic reality of the U.S.S.R." In other words, the church had to find a way of living, so the argument goes, with the "atheistic reality" of Stalinist Russia. So Sergius proposed what came to be known in shorthand as the Adaptation.

The Adaptation consisted first and foremost of a false separation between the so-called spiritual needs of man, the purely religious needs of man, and his socio-political needs. In other words, a separation of Church and State. The church was to satisfy the purely religious needs of the citizens of the Soviet Union but without touching on the socio-political structure which had been erected by the Communist Party.

The Adaptation required a new administration of the church in Russia according to guidelines which were set forth after the appeal of Sergius was published. Basically this came down to an agreement not to criticize the official ideology or even the Party Line[224] of the Soviet Union under Stalin. And this would be reflected in all of the activities of the church. Any opposition by the Russian Orthodox Church to the Soviet regime would henceforth be considered a deviation from pure religious activity and a form of counter-revolution which was no longer to be permitted or countenanced.

In effect the Orthodox Church, through its silence, became an arm of the Soviet state. In fact, Sergius would go on to defend this betrayal and even call for the condemnation and the sentencing to concentration camps of his own fellow Orthodox for so-called counter-revolutionary activities. Talantov, who condemned the whole Adaptation, described it this way: "In actual fact all religious activity was reduced to external rites. The church preaching of those clergymen who held strictly to the Adaptation was totally remote from life and therefore had no influence whatever on hearers. As a result of this, the intellectual, social and family life of believers, and the raising of the younger generation, remained outside church influence. One cannot worship Christ and at the same time in social and family life tell lies, do what is unjust, use violence, and dream of an earthly paradise."[225]

This, then, is what the Adaptation involved: The church would be silent about the evils of the Stalinist regime. It would be silent in the presence of the Party Line being broadcast and rebroadcast again and again. It would become a purely "spiritual" community "in the abstract", would no longer voice opposition to the regime, would no longer condemn the errors and lies of Communism, and would thus become the Church of Silence, as Christianity behind the Iron Curtain was often called.

The Appeal of Sergius caused a split in the Russian Orthodox Church. The real believers who rejected the Adaptation, who denounced the Appeal and who remained attached to the Metropolitan Joseph rather than Sergius, were arrested and sent to concentration camps. Boris Talantov himself would eventually die in prison, as a political prisoner of the Stalinist regime. Meanwhile, the Church of Silence, in effect, was transformed into an organ of the KGB. Stalin decimated the Russian Orthodox Church; all of the real Orthodox believers were sent off to concentration camps or executed and replaced by KGB operatives.

Shortly before Talantov died in August of 1967, he wrote as follows about the Adaptation:

> The Adaptation to atheism implanted by Metropolitan Sergius has concluded (been completed by) the betrayal of the Orthodox Russian Church on the part of Metropolitan Nikodim and other official representatives of the Moscow Patriarch based abroad. This betrayal irrefutably proved by the documents cited must be made

---

[224] See the description of the Party Line in the photo caption (of Lenin) at the end of the previous chapter.
[225] "The Moscow Patriarchate and Sergianism" by Boris Talantov, from *Russia's Catacomb Saints*, (St. Herman of Alaska Press, Platina, California, 1982) pp. 463-486.

known to all believers in Russia and abroad because such an activity of the Patriarchate, relying on cooperation with the KGB, represents a great danger for all believers. In truth, the atheistic leaders of the Russian people and the princes of the Church have gathered together against the Lord and His Church.[226]

Here Talantov refers to the same Metropolitan Nikodim who induced the Vatican to enter into the Vatican-Moscow Agreement, under which (as we showed in Chapter 6) the Catholic Church was forced to remain silent about Communism at Vatican II. Thus, *the same Orthodox prelate who betrayed the Orthodox Church was instrumental in an agreement by which the Catholic Church was also betrayed.* At Vatican II certain Catholic churchmen, cooperating with Nikodim, agreed that *the Roman Catholic Church, too, would become a Church of Silence.*

And since the Council, the Catholic Church has almost everywhere unquestionably fallen silent not only as to the errors of Communism— which the Church has almost completely ceased condemning, even in Red China, which viciously persecutes the Church—but also as to the errors of the world at large. We recall that in his opening address to the Council, Pope John freely admitted that the Council (and most of the Church after him) would no longer condemn errors but would open Herself to the world in a "positive" presentation of Her teaching to "men of good will." What followed, as Pope Paul VI himself admitted, was not the hoped-for conversion of "men of good will" but what Paul VI himself called "a veritable invasion of the Church by worldly thinking." In other words, to the extent that this is possible in the Catholic Church (which can never completely fail in Her mission), there has been a kind of *Sergian Adaptation of Roman Catholicism.*

Now, in keeping with this Adaptation of the Catholic Church, by the year 2000 the Message of Fatima had been firmly subjugated to the demands of the new orientation. It had already been determined by certain members of the Vatican apparatus that Russia was not to be mentioned in any consecration ceremony the Pope might undertake in response to the Virgin's requests. In the November 2000 issue of *Inside the Vatican*, a leading Cardinal identified as "one of the Pope's closest advisors" (the editor confirms it was Cardinal Jozef Tomko) is quoted to the effect that "Rome fears the Russian Orthodox might regard it as an 'offense' if Rome were to make specific mention of Russia in such a prayer, as if Russia especially is in need of help when the whole world, including the post-Christian West, faces profound problems ..."[227] The

---

[226] "The Moscow Patriarchate and Sergianism: An Essay by Boris Talantov," found at www. orthodoxinfo.com/ecumenism/cat_tal.aspx.

[227] The vain fears that the Consecration of Russia by the Pope and Catholic bishops would offend the devout Orthodox is completely laid to rest by the article by Cathy Pearson, entitled "Now Is the Time: Consecrating Russia Will Help, Not Harm, Catholic-Orthodox Dialogue". First published in the magazine *Inside the Vatican*, August/September 2008; reprinted with permission in *The Fatima Crusader*, Issue 91, February 2009, pp. 3ff; also on the web at www.fatimacrusader.com/cr91/cr91pg3.pdf. A free copy of this article is

same Cardinal-advisor added: "Let us beware of becoming too literal-minded."

In other words, "Rome"—meaning a few members of the Vatican apparatus who advise the Pope—has decided not to honor the specific request of Our Lady of Fatima for fear of giving offense to the Russian Orthodox. "Rome" does not wish to give the impression that Russia should be converted to the Catholic Faith through its consecration to the Immaculate Heart of Mary, for this would be quite contrary to the new "ecumenical dialogue" launched by Vatican II. The consecration and conversion of Russia called for by the Mother of God would also be contrary to the Vatican's diplomatic agreement (in the 1993 Balamand Declaration) that the return of the Orthodox to Rome is "outdated ecclesiology"—a claim that, as we have shown, flatly contradicts the infallibly defined Catholic dogma that heretics and schismatics cannot be saved outside the Catholic Church. In keeping with this blatant departure from Catholic teaching, the Vatican's own apostolic administrator for Russia, Archbishop Tadeusz Kondrusiewicz, stated publicly in January of 1998 that "The Second Vatican Council has declared that the Orthodox Church is our Sister Church and has the same means for salvation. So there is no reason to have a policy of proselytism."[228]

Given the *de facto* abandonment of the Church's constant teaching that heretics, schismatics, Jews and pagans must be added to the Catholic flock if they are to be saved—a development we examined in the previous chapter—a consecration of Russia to the Immaculate Heart of Mary to bring about the conversion of Russia would, of course, be out of the question, so far as those who promote the new orientation of the Church are concerned.

Thus, on May 13, 1982 and again on March 25, 1984, Pope John Paul II had consecrated the *world* to the Immaculate Heart, but with no mention of Russia. In neither case had all the bishops of the world participated.[229] Thus, neither of the two requirements attested to by Sister Lucy throughout her life had been met. Clearly recognizing this, the Pope himself had made telltale remarks during and after the 1984 ceremony. During the ceremony, before 250,000 people in Saint Peter's Square, he spontaneously added to the prepared text the following: "Enlighten especially the peoples of which You Yourself *are awaiting* our consecration and confiding."[230] Hours after the ceremony, as reported in the Italian Catholic bishops' newspaper *Avvenire*, the Holy Father prayed inside St. Peter's, before 10,000 witnesses, asking Our Lady to bless "those peoples for whom You Yourself *are awaiting* our act of

---

available from the publisher of this book (see page xxvi).

[228] Remarks of January 17, 1998 at The Aid to the Church in Russia Conference, http://www.victorclaveau.com/htm_html/Around%20the%20World/Russia/catholic_church_in_russia_it.htm. Reprinted in *The Catholic Dossier*, March/April 1998, p. 4.

[229] Maybe a few bishops had done so, but not many did—thus, not fulfilling the Consecration as requested by Our Lady of Fatima that all the bishops join in.

[230] *L'Osservatore Romano*, March 26-27, 1984, Italian ed., pp. 1, 6; English ed., pp. 9-10.

consecration and entrusting."[231] Russia had not been consecrated to the Immaculate Heart, and John Paul II knew it. Evidently persuaded by his advisers, the Pope had told Bishop Cordes, head of the Pontifical Council of the Laity, that he had omitted any mention of Russia because "it would be interpreted as a provocation by the Soviet leaders."[232]

The Emergence of the "Party Line" on Fatima

But the issue of the Consecration of Russia would not go away, for it was obvious that following the 1984 ceremony Russia failed to experience the religious conversion the Virgin had promised as the fruit of a proper consecration to Her Immaculate Heart. Quite the contrary, despite certain political changes, Russia's spiritual, moral and material condition has continued to deteriorate up to the present day (2009).

As we demonstrate beyond doubt in Chapter 16, Russia has not converted in *any* sense of the word—religiously, morally, politically or even economically—much less in the sense intended by the Blessed Virgin, which would necessarily involve the reunification of the Russian people with Rome upon their embrace of the integral Catholic Faith. Russia today continues to suffer from the highest per capita abortion rate in the world (with only China exceeding Russia in the gross number of abortions), alcoholism and child pornography are rampant, and homosexual conduct has been "legalized." The nominal Russian Orthodoxy of many Russians is meaningless, as few Russians attend Mass; occultism and satanism are on the rise; and there has been no elevation of moral life among the nominally Orthodox population, but rather a steady decline fueled by a degenerate popular culture, including sexually explicit "reality TV." The Catholic Church remains a tiny minority, suffering persecution under tight legal restrictions orchestrated by Vladimir Putin, who has assembled and continues to control a neo-Stalinist dictatorship from the Kremlin through his puppet, President Medvedev. Russia's recently forged military alliance with China and her newly developed nuclear weapons evince a nation preparing for war and regional or even global domination, not peace. And the worldwide economic collapse has exposed the true nature of the so-called "capitalist explosion" in Russia: a few wealthy oligarchs bestride an economy that remains Third World in its standard of living for the overwhelming majority of the Russian people.

Clearly, 25 years after it took place the 1984 ceremony has failed to produce what Our Lady of Fatima promised, because that ceremony was not what She requested. But what She requested—the specific

---

[231] *Avvenire*, March 27, 1984, p. 11. See also *L'Osservatore Romano*, March 26-27, 1984, Italian ed., p. 4; see photo on page XVI in the photo section of this book.

[232] Father Fabrice Delestre, "Fatima: Why Isn't the Mother of God Being Obeyed as She Should Be?", *Angelus*, June 2000, Vol. 23, No. 6; on the web at http://www.fatima.org/consecrussia/notobeyed.asp. See also Frère François de Marie des Anges, *Fatima: Joie Intime Événement Mondial*, (French edition, Contre-Réforme Catholique, France, 1991) pp. 363-364; Frère François de Marie des Anges, *Fatima: Tragedy and Triumph*, pp. 168-172.

Consecration of Russia by name, so that the world would know that Russia's miraculous conversion was obtained through the intercession of Her Immaculate Heart—is absolutely unacceptable to the custodians of the Sergian Adaptation of the Church to "the modern world." Hence, from their perspective, something had to be done about Fatima.

And, in particular, something had to be done about a Canadian priest by the name of Father Nicholas Gruner, whose Fatima apostolate has become a sounding board for millions of Catholics who were convinced that the Consecration of Russia had been derailed by the plans of certain men in the Vatican. Quite simply, Fatima and "the Fatima priest" had to be buried once and for all.

The process began as early as 1988, when, Frère François recounts: "[A]n order came from the Vatican addressed to the authorities of Fatima, to Sister Lucy, to diverse ecclesiastics, including Father Messias Coelho, and a French priest [evidently Father Pierre Caillon] very much devoted to Our Lady, ordering everyone to cease pestering the Holy Father with the Consecration of Russia." Fatima devotee Father Caillon confirmed the issuance of this order: "An order came from Rome, obliging everyone to say and think: 'The Consecration is done. The Pope having done all that he can, Heaven has deigned to agree to this gesture.'"[233] It was around this time, 1988-1989, that many Fatima Apostolates who had maintained that the Consecration of Russia had not been done suddenly reversed themselves and declared that the 1984 consecration fulfilled the desires of Heaven. Sadly, even Father Caillon soon afterwards changed his testimony and began to say that the 1984 Consecration had fulfilled the Virgin's requests.

It was also at this time that typewritten and computer-generated letters, purportedly from Sister Lucy, began to circulate. Typical of the manifestly incredible letters was the one dated November 8, 1989, to a Mr. Noelker, which contains the statement by "Sister Lucy" that Pope Paul VI consecrated the world to the Immaculate Heart during his brief visit to Fatima in 1967—a consecration that never happened, as Sister Lucy certainly knew because she witnessed the entire visit.[234]

Thus emerged "the Party Line" on the Message of Fatima. What, precisely, do we mean by "the Party Line"? Vladimir Ilyich Lenin once said: "The lie is sacred and deception will be our principal weapon." Thus it was no surprise that *Pravda*, when it was the official organ of the Soviet Communist Party, was filled with lies, even though the Russian word *Pravda* means "truth." A newspaper whose name is "truth" was always filled with lies, because, as Lenin said, "the lie is sacred and deception will be our principal weapon".

Now, a liar will not convince anyone of his lies if he wears a big

---

[233] *Fatima: Tragedy and Triumph*, pp. 189-190.
[234] For a good treatment of the falsehood of the Noelker letter, see Mark Fellows, "This Present Darkness" Part II, *Catholic Family News*, September 2000. See also Mark Fellows, *Fatima in Twilight*, (Marmion Publications, Niagara Falls, 2003) Chapter 25, pp. 303-314.

placard on his chest that says "Liar!" Not even a fool would believe such a man. For the liar to convince people that his lies are truth, *the truth must be redefined*. This is what is meant by Lenin's phrase "the lie is sacred ..." The lie becomes the "truth" and is slavishly adhered to in place of the truth. As Scripture says, pronouncing the curse in the book of Isaias, "Woe to you that call evil good, and good evil: that put darkness *for* light, and light *for* darkness". (Is. 5:20) The darkness of falsehood is given the appearance of the light of truth, and this is one of the principal errors of Russia.

Since according to Lenin "the lie is sacred", he had to develop a policy for all his followers about official lies. By the phrase "the lie is sacred", Lenin taught that whenever lying advances the Communist cause then his followers must lie—to remain "true" to their "principles". But this policy could not work if Communist agent #1 told a lie that was contradicted by another lie told by Communist agent #2. So the Communist Party had to come up with a common lie for both agent #1 and agent #2 to repeat. This common lie came to be known as the Party Line.

But this trick of turning a lie into the "truth" did not originate with Russia, or with the Communists; it originated with the devil, who is the Father of Lies. St. Paul speaks of the devil under the guise of the angel of light. To be more specific, he refers to the Gospel of Our Lord Jesus Christ: "But though we, or an angel from heaven, preach a gospel to you besides that which we have preached to you, let him be anathema." (Gal. 1:8) It is the devil, appearing under the guise of an angel of light, who gives the appearance of truth in order to deceive by means of the lie. This is where the error "the lie is sacred" and "falsehood is truth" originated.

Father Paul Kramer relates a conversation he had with General Daniel Graham, a general in the US Army. "General Graham said that he had once been in Russia with a Soviet official and the Soviet official asked him, 'Don't you want peace?' And the General answered: 'No! Because I know how you define peace. I do not want that kind of peace.' As they were conversing, they drove by a huge billboard that showed soldiers with their rifles. On the billboard was the caption: 'Pobieda kommunista eta mir'. Which is, in English, 'Communist Victory is Peace.'"

According to Marxist teaching, the Communist State wages war to make revolution and uses every possible means of deception—total war—in order to subjugate the entire world to Communism. And once total war has been waged and Communism is victorious over the entire planet, then there is the Communist version of "peace". But what is peace *in reality*? It is best defined by St. Augustine: "Peace is the tranquillity of order." Which definition is correct? It is not a matter of subjective evaluation. St. Thomas Aquinas explains: *"ens et verum convertunter"*, which is a scholastic way of saying that truth is convertible with reality. That which is objectively *real* is, for that very reason, objectively *true*. In other words, truth is that which *is*, whereas a lie is that which *is not*. That which *is not* cannot be true. Therefore, if someone declares, for example, that white is black, the claim that white is black is a lie—no matter how high the authority of the one making the claim.

According to Marxist doctrine, however, *truth is that which promotes the Communist revolution*. And what is it that promotes the Communist revolution? It is whatever has been decided to be the Party Line. *What the Party dictates to be true becomes the "truth" even if, in reality, it is a lie*. Thus, if the Party Line is that black is white, then that is what all Party members must believe and say, simply because it has been decided by the Party that black is white.

Just as there has been a kind of "Stalinization" of the Church, in the sense of an Adaptation of the Church to the world, so also must there be a kind of Stalinist Party Line on Fatima—a version of Fatima dictated from on high to which all the members of the Church of the post-conciliar Adaptation must adhere. In essence, the Party Line on Fatima comes down to this: The "Consecration of Russia" is over and done with, and everyone must cease asking for it. We have "peace" as predicted by Our Lady of Fatima. Russia is undergoing the "conversion" Our Lady promised. Therefore—so the Party Line goes—nothing in the Message of Fatima remains to be accomplished, and Fatima now belongs to the past.

As we shall see, all of the terms in quotation marks—"Consecration of Russia", "peace" and "conversion"—have been redefined to accommodate the Party Line on Fatima. Where Fatima is concerned, we are now being asked to believe the equivalent of "black is white," for that is the Party Line.

The Dictatorship of the Vatican Secretary of State

Now every Party Line requires a dictator, a head of the Party, to impose it. From where, exactly, within the Vatican apparatus did the Party Line on Fatima originate? The evidence is overwhelming that it originated with the Vatican Secretary of State. On this point some brief background is in order.

First of all, in the proper state of things—what St. Augustine called "the tranquillity of order" or peace—the Church is not a dictatorship. Dictatorship is a barbaric institution. As Euripides says "among the barbarians all are slaves but one." Our Lord said "the princes of the Gentiles lord it over" their subjects. (Mt. 20:25) He said to His apostles "with you it is not to be this way." Yet the tranquillity of order—the peace of the Church—has been disturbed enormously in the post-conciliar period. What we see in the Church today is that the hierarchs of the Roman Curia (*not* the Pope, but a few of his Vatican ministers) lord it over their subjects with an oriental despotism. To be more precise, they lord it over *certain* subjects, who buck the Party Line, while the Church at large suffers from a near-collapse of faith and discipline which these same potentates ignore.

How did this come to pass? Since the restructuring of the Roman Curia, around 1967, by order of Pope Paul VI—which was actually designed and carried out by Cardinal Jean Villot—the heads of the various Roman dicasteries have been able to behave like dictators. Before the Second Vatican Council, the Roman Curia was structured as a monarchy. The Pope was the Prefect of the Holy Office, while the Cardinal in charge of the day-to-day business of the Holy Office was the second-in-command. The other dicasteries were of lower rank. And while having their own authority and jurisdiction, again in accordance with that principle of subsidiarity,[235] they were subordinate to the Holy Office, and the Holy Office was directly under the Pope. This arrangement was entirely in keeping with the Divine Constitution of the Church. The Pope, the Vicar of Jesus Christ on earth, was at the head of the chain of command.

But after Vatican II, Cardinal Villot engineered the restructuring of the Roman Curia. Long before Gorbachev announced his program of *perestroika* in the Soviet Union, the Church underwent its own *perestroika* in the Roman Curia. The Holy Office was renamed—but far more significant, the Holy Office lost its supreme position in the Curia. The Curia was restructured in such a manner that the Cardinal Secretary of State was placed over all the other dicasteries, including the former Holy Office. Renamed and restructured, it was now called the Congregation for the Doctrine of the Faith (CDF), and the Pope was no longer the Prefect. But it (the CDF) is now under a Cardinal Prefect and he is under the authority of the Secretary of State.

According to the preceding organization when the Roman Curia was directly subject to the Pope and the Holy Office, then the most important factors which determined the policy and politics of the Roman Curia were faith and morals. After the Second Vatican Council and the reorganization of the Curia, under the Cardinal Secretary of State and his dicastery, the Secretariat of State, it is *the Party Line*—that is, the policies and politics of the Secretary of State—that is the one and only determining factor in the formulation of Church policies. Even the former Holy Office, now the CDF, is subordinate to the Secretary of State. As a result of this restructuring, the Holy Father, the Supreme Pontiff, is reduced to a figurehead who gives his approval, as a rubber stamp, to rulings presented to him as a *fait accompli* by the Secretary of State. This bears repeating: *The Pope has been reduced to a figurehead in the service of the dictatorship of the Secretary of State.*[236]

In the Masonic registry required by Italian law, one did find the name of Jean Villot—the same Villot who oversaw the curial reorganization.

---

[235] The principle which requires that authority be exercised at the lowest possible level to avoid tyranny through excessive centralization of government. For example, the budget of a town should be determined by the town Fathers, not by the state or federal government.

[236] Under the old structure, before 1967, the Pope presided over the Roman Curia. Under the new structure, since 1967, it is the Vatican Secretary of State who presides over the Roman Curia. The reader is invited to check the *Annuario Pontificio* both before and after 1967 to see the change in the structure of the Roman Curia.

After Cardinal Villot died, in his private library was found a handwritten message from the Grand Master of Villot's Masonic Lodge, praising Villot for upholding Masonic traditions.[237] As a French priest living in Rome said: "At least in one area he was traditional."

The Use of False "Obedience" to Impose the Party Line

In 1917, the very year Our Lady appeared at Fatima, Saint Maximilian Kolbe was in Rome, where he saw the Masons showing their open hostility to the Catholic Church and carrying placards announcing their intention to infiltrate the Vatican so that satan would rule from the Vatican and the Pope would be his slave.[238] They also boasted at the same time that they would destroy the Church. The intention of the Masons to destroy the Church fits in perfectly with the well-known Masonic dictum, "We will destroy the Church *by means of holy obedience*." As we showed in an earlier chapter, Bishop Graber of Regensburg, Germany, collected other such testimonies of Masonic luminaries, and the *Permanent Instruction of the Alta Vendita* itself boldly declared "let the Clergy march under your standard, always believing that they are marching under the banner of the apostolic keys." That is, the demand for "obedience" would be used in dictatorial fashion to undermine true obedience and the faith itself.

And the curial reorganization of 1967 would be instrumental in accomplishing that aim by subjecting the whole Church to the Party Line of the Secretary of State—including the Party Line on Fatima—under the guise of a false "obedience" to an authority who has clearly exceeded the bounds established by God Himself. As we will demonstrate shortly, it was Cardinal Sodano who literally dictated the "interpretation" of the visional aspect of the Third Secret of Fatima, which has been published without the Virgin's own words to explain it.

The Secretary of State Targets the Message of Fatima

This brings us to the precise role of the Secretary of State in imposing the Party Line with respect to Fatima. As we have noted, this process would involve the Message of Fatima in general and, in particular, perhaps its foremost proponent in the Church: the Fatima apostolate of Father Nicholas Gruner.

As early as 1989, the Secretary of State at the time, Cardinal Casaroli (the great propagator of *Ostpolitik*) had communicated to Father Gruner's bishop at the time, His Excellency Gerardo Pierro of the Diocese of Avellino, Italy, what the bishop had called "worried signals" about Father Gruner's Fatima apostolate. Father Gruner had been ordained in Avellino in 1976

---

[237] A French priest showed the Masonic document to, among others, the American priest Father Paul Kramer, the editor of this book.

[238] Paul Fisher, *Their God is the Devil*, (American Research Foundation, Washington, D.C., 1990) p. 40.

for a Franciscan community that did not form as expected. Since 1978 he had been residing in Canada with the bishop's permission, where he had become the leader of a small Fatima apostolate that had since grown into the largest of its kind in the world. But after the Party Line concerning the "consecration" of 1984 had been imposed by the anonymous order of 1988, it was inevitable that Father Gruner's apostolate and the Secretary of State would collide—just as the traditional orientation (based on the dogmas of the Faith as defined by the popes for the past 20 centuries) and the new orientation of the Church have collided after Vatican II.

The basic technique for trying to get rid of Father Gruner had been to create a bogus canonical scenario in which, having been ordered to find some other bishop to incardinate him outside of Avellino, Father Gruner's incardination anywhere else was then blocked through unprecedented arm-twisting behind the scenes, so that Father Gruner would be forced to "return" to Avellino and abandon his apostolate. Having blocked Father Gruner's incardination by three successive benevolent bishops who were friends of Fatima, the Vatican apparatus (in a complex proceeding beyond the scope of this book[239]) had finally lowered the boom: Father Gruner must "return" to Avellino or be "suspended" for "disobedience." In essence, Father Gruner was under a threat of "suspension" for having failed to do what his very accusers had systematically prevented him from doing—namely, find another bishop to incardinate him.[240]

As Father Gruner's various canonical appeals from these unprecedented actions against him wended their way through Vatican tribunals, his Fatima apostolate continued to flourish. By the year 2000 the apostolate, particularly through its journal *The Fatima Crusader*, had become the strongest and most persistent voice in the Church for both the Consecration of Russia and disclosure of the Third Secret.

Furthermore, Pope John Paul II himself had complicated the Fatima picture with his decision to beatify Jacinta and Francisco in a ceremony at Fatima on May 13, 2000. His intention to beatify the two children was made known as early as June of 1999, and this development had clearly triggered an internal struggle within the Vatican apparatus. This is shown by the curious on-again, off-again nature of the beatification ceremony, which is most unusual for the Vatican. First, the then-Secretary of State, Cardinal Angelo Sodano, announced in October 1999 that the beatification of Jacinta and Francisco would take place on April 9, 2000 in St. Peter's Square, along with four other beatifications. The Patriarch

---

[239] See Francis Alban and Christopher A. Ferrara, *Fatima Priest*, Fourth Edition (Good Counsel Publications, Pound Ridge, New York, 2000), Chapters 12, 14, 17-22; App. I, App. II.

[240] For the details of the long and tortuous "proceedings" to silence Father Gruner, the reader may consult: *Fatima Priest* (Fourth Edition, available from The Fatima Center, 17000 State Route 30, Constable, New York 12926) or *A Law for One Man* (available free of charge from the publisher of this book, see page xxvi). Both are also available on the web at: www.fatimapriest.com/content.html and also www.fatima.org/apostolate/defense/law1man.asp

of Lisbon is quoted in the Portuguese press as having been informed by the Vatican that it was "quite impossible" for the Pope to come to Fatima for the children's beatification and that the question was "closed." The Patriarch told Portuguese journalists that he was convinced this "impossibility" of the Pope coming to Fatima was exclusively due to a decision by none other than the Vatican Secretary of State.

But the Pope had other ideas. In November of 1999 His Holiness—obviously bypassing Cardinal Sodano—informed Bishop Serafim, the Bishop of Fatima, directly that he should announce that the Pope would indeed come to Fatima on May 13 to perform the beatifications. Bishop Serafim did not make the new announcement until December 1999. And then, in March of 2000, the bishop also let it slip that "the Pope will do something special for Fatima." This prompted furious speculation in the press that the Pope was, at last, going to reveal the Third Secret. Bishop Serafim was immediately rebuked in public by the Cardinal Patriarch of Lisbon, possibly under orders from somebody in the employ of the Vatican Secretary of State, who did not wish anyone to know that the Pope was contemplating revelation of the Secret. But the proverbial cat was out of the proverbial bag. Now events would unfold rapidly, and with devastating results for the Party Line.[241]

---

[241] Regarding the on-again, off-again beatification ceremony and related matters, see: the daily newspaper *Correio da Manhã* of 14 October 1999, the article on p. 12; the weekly newspaper *Jornal de Leiria* of 14 October 1999, p. 24; the weekly newspaper *A Ordem* on 21 October 1999, p. 1; the official weekly of the Patriarchate of Lisbon *Voz da Verdade* on 31 October 1999, on p. 6, the article entitled "The Beatification of the Little Shepherds Definitely Will Be At Rome"; the official weekly of the Patriarchate of Lisbon *Voz da Verdade* on 5 December 1999, entitled "The Pope Will Return to Portugal; Fatima is the Place of the Beatification"; article in *Euronoticias* on 24 March 2000, p. 8, entitled "Bishop of Leiria-Fatima March 21 press conference"; weekly *Euronoticias* of 24 March 2000, on p. 8, "Crisis: The Bishop of Leiria-Fatima Creates A Mystery Around the Visit of the Pope Without Telling the Patriarch What It Concerns, Will the Pope Reveal the Third Secret?"; *Euronoticias* of 24 March, 2000, an article on p. 9 entitled "Analysis: Persons Who Have Studied the Apparitions Say That the Third Secret Could Concern the Destruction of the Faith. A Crisis in the Interior of the Church Would be the Third Secret".

Chapter 9

A "New" Fatima for the "New Orientation"

On May 13, 2000, John Paul II went to Fatima to beatify Jacinta and Francisco. The papal appearance was a kind of living demonstration of the conflict between the two visions of the Church we have been discussing. Evoking the Church of all time, the Pope delivered a sermon after the beatifications. In this sermon many things the Church seemed to have forgotten over the past forty years were suddenly recalled again:

> *According to the divine plan*, "a Woman clothed with the sun" (Apoc. 12:1) came down from Heaven to this earth to visit the privileged children of the Father. She speaks to them with a mother's voice and heart: She asks them to offer themselves as victims of reparation, saying that She was ready to lead them safely to God. ...

> Later Francisco, one of the three privileged children, exclaimed: "We were burning in that light which is God and we were not consumed. What is God like? It is impossible to say. In fact we will never be able to tell people". God: a light that burns without consuming. *Moses had the same experience when he saw God in the burning bush.* ...

> "Another portent appeared in Heaven; behold, a great red dragon" (Apoc. 12:3). These words from the first reading of the Mass make us think of the great struggle between good and evil, showing how, when man puts God aside, he cannot achieve happiness, but ends up destroying himself. ...

> **The Message of Fatima is a call to conversion, alerting humanity *to have nothing to do with the "dragon" whose "tail swept down a third of the stars of Heaven,*** and cast them to the earth" (Apoc. 12:4).

> Man's final goal is Heaven, his true home, where the Heavenly Father awaits everyone with His merciful love. God does not want anyone to be lost; that is why 2,000 years ago He sent His Son to earth, "to seek and to save the lost" (Lk. 19:10). ...

> In Her motherly concern, the Blessed Virgin came here to Fatima to ask men and women "to stop offending God, Our Lord, who is already too much offended". It is a mother's sorrow that compels Her to speak; *the destiny of Her children is at stake.* For this reason She asks the little shepherds: "Pray, pray much and make

sacrifices for sinners; *many souls go to hell because they have no one to pray and make sacrifices for them*".

The Pope's direct linkage of the Message of Fatima with the Book of the Apocalypse, and his likening of the Fatima seers' encounter with God to that of Moses before the burning bush, comprised a stunning papal authentication of the Fatima apparitions as divinely given prophecies for our time. All of a sudden, Fatima was squarely before the eyes of the whole Church again.

There was, first of all, the Pope's astonishing reference to the Message of Fatima as a biblical moment, the very fulfillment of Chapter 12, verse 1 of the Apocalypse, which speaks of the "Woman clothed with the sun." Here Pope John Paul II echoed Pope Paul VI, who, in his apostolic letter *Signum magnum*, delivered at Fatima on May 13, 1967, declared:

> The great sign which the Apostle John saw in Heaven, "a woman clothed with the sun," is interpreted by the sacred Liturgy, not without foundation, as referring to the Most Blessed Mary, the mother of all men by the grace of Christ the Redeemer. ... On the occasion of the religious ceremonies which are taking place at this time in honor of the Virgin Mother of God in Fatima, Portugal, where She is venerated by countless numbers of the faithful for Her motherly and compassionate heart, we wish to call the attention of all sons of the Church once more to the indissoluble link between the spiritual motherhood of Mary ... and the duties of redeemed men toward Her, the Mother of the Church.

Even more astonishing, in his sermon Pope John Paul II had explicitly linked the Message of Fatima to Apocalypse, Chapter 12, verse 4, which prophesies that the "tail of the dragon" will sweep one-third of the stars from Heaven and cast them down to the earth. As Father Gruner would later note: "In the language of the Bible, the 'stars of Heaven' are those who are set in the heavens to illumine the way for others to go to Heaven. This passage has been classically interpreted in Catholic commentaries to mean that one-third of the clergy—i.e. Cardinals, bishops, priests—fall from their consecrated state and are actually working for the devil." For example, the *Haydock Commentary* to the *Douay-Rheims Bible* notes that the image of one-third of the stars of Heaven has been interpreted to refer to "bishops and eminent persons who fell under the weight of persecution and apostatized ... The devil is always ready, as far as God permits him, to make war against the Church and the faithful servants of God."

In this connection Father Gruner and others have cited the commentary on Apoc. 12:3-4 by Father Herman B. Kramer, in *The Book of Destiny*. This work was published with an *imprimatur*, providentially enough, in 1956, only six years before the opening of Vatican II. In reference to the symbol of one-third of the stars of Heaven, Father Kramer notes: "This is one-third of the clergy" and that "'one-third' of the stars shall follow the dragon"—meaning one-third of the clergy, who are the "stars", the consecrated souls in the Church.[242] That is, one-third of the Catholic clergy will be in the service of the devil, working to destroy the Church from within. Father Herman Kramer's commentary points out that the red dragon—a sign of the devil which could also symbolize Communism because red is Communism's emblematic color—brings the Church into great distress by undermining it from within.

The commentary goes on to say that, by means of these apostate clergy, the devil will probably enforce upon the Church "the acceptance of unchristian morals, false doctrines, *compromise with error*, or obedience to the civil rulers in violation of conscience." In addition, he suggests that "The symbolic meaning of the dragon's tail may reveal that the clergy who are ripe for apostasy will hold the influential positions in the Church, having won preferment by hypocrisy, deceit and flattery." The clergy who will follow the dragon—i.e. the devil—would include those "who neglected to preach the truth or to admonish the sinner by a good example, but rather sought popularity by being lax and the slaves of human respect," as well as those "who fear for their own interests and will not remonstrate against evil practices in the Church" and bishops "who abhor upright priests who dare to tell the truth".[243] Father Kramer also observes as follows concerning the state of the Catholic Church in the times prophesied by Apoc. 12:3-4:

> "The apostolic democracy founded by Our Lord may have given way to an absolute monarchy, in which the episcopate rules with oriental despotism. The priests may be reduced to a state of servility and fawning sycophancy. The rule by reason, justice and love may have been supplanted by the absolute will of the bishop, whose every act and word are to be accepted without question, without recourse to fact, truth or justice. Conscience may have lost its right to guide the actions of the priests and may stand ignored or condemned. Diplomacy, expediency and other trickery may be upheld as the greatest virtues."[244]

But none of this is mentioned in those parts of the Message of Fatima which have thus far been revealed. Had the Pope, then, with his startling reference to Apocalypse 12:3-4, just given the world a glimpse into the contents of the Third Secret? Would he now reveal the Secret in its entirety?

But, alas, the sermon ends. It is not the Pope who will discuss the Third Secret. As quickly as it began, the Pope's momentary return to the vision of the Church of all time is over, and a chief exponent of the new vision rises to his feet. It is Cardinal Angelo Sodano, then Vatican Secretary of State—the same Cardinal Sodano who had tried, but failed, to prevent the Pope from going to Fatima to beatify Jacinta and Francisco.

---

[242] Father Herman Bernard Kramer, *The Book of Destiny*, (first published 1955, republished by TAN Books and Publishers, Inc., Rockford, Illinois, 1975) pp. 279-284.
[243] Ibid.
[244] Ibid.

For some strange reason it is Sodano, not the Pope, who will announce that the Pope has decided to reveal the Third Secret of Fatima:

> On the solemn occasion of his visit to Fatima, His Holiness has directed me to make an announcement to you. As you know, the purpose of his visit to Fatima has been to beatify the two "little shepherds". Nevertheless he also wishes his pilgrimage to be a renewed gesture of gratitude to Our Lady for Her protection during these years of his papacy. This protection seems also to be linked to the so-called "third part" of the secret of Fatima.

And then what had seemed so strange suddenly became quite explicable. Cardinal Sodano's task would be to prepare the faithful to accept the notion that the Message of Fatima, including the Third Secret, was now to be considered a thing of the past. The process would begin with the Cardinal's "interpretation" of the Third Secret:

> That text contains a prophetic vision similar to those found in Sacred Scripture, which do not describe with photographic clarity the details of future events, but rather synthesize and condense against a unified background of events spread out over time in a succession and a duration which are not specified. As a result, the text *must be interpreted in a symbolic key*. ...

> According to the interpretation of the "little shepherds", which was also recently confirmed by Sister Lucia, the "Bishop dressed in white" who prays for all the faithful is the Pope. As he makes his way with great effort towards the Cross amid the corpses of those who were martyred (bishops, priests, men and women religious and many lay persons), he too falls to the ground, *apparently* dead, under a burst of gunfire. (Emphasis added.)

As the faithful will soon learn, this is simply a lie. The "Bishop dressed in White" in the vision is not "apparently dead" but is *killed*— as the text of the vision clearly states—in the manner of a military execution, along with many bishops, priests and religious, outside a half-ruined city.

Why, then, insert the word "apparently" into the "interpretation"? Cardinal Sodano immediately tips his hand:

> After the assassination attempt of 13 May 1981, it appeared evident to His Holiness that it was "a motherly hand which guided the bullet's path", enabling the "dying Pope" to halt "at the threshold of death". ...

> The successive events of 1989 led, both in the Soviet Union and in a number of countries of Eastern Europe, to the fall of the Communist regime which promoted atheism. ...

> Even if the events to which the third part of the Secret of Fatima refers *now seem part of the past*, Our Lady's call to conversion and penance, issued at the beginning of the Twentieth Century, remains

timely and urgent today.

Quite simply, Sodano was preparing the way for an "interpretation" of the Message of Fatima that would bury it once and for all: the Message culminated with the 1981 assassination attempt and the "fall of Communism" in 1989—events which "now seem part of the past." To insure this result, a "commentary" would be prepared before the actual text of the Third Secret would be released:

> In order that the faithful may better receive the message of Our Lady of Fatima, the Pope has charged the Congregation for the Doctrine of the Faith with making public the third part of the secret, after the preparation of an appropriate commentary.

But why had this commentary not been ready in time for the May 13 ceremony? After all, news of the Third Secret's impending disclosure had been circulating since at least March of 2000. In that month, Bishop Serafim had announced that the Pope had told him during a visit to Rome that the Pope would "do something special for Fatima"[245] when he went there for the beatification ceremony in May 2000.

Curiously enough, the Pope had urged Bishop Serafim to say nothing about this while he was in Rome, but to wait until he returned to Fatima. But the subject was on the Pope's mind since the previous November, so why had no "commentary" been prepared during the period November 1999 to May 2000? Surely, such a commentary could easily have been completed in that time.

Two conclusions suggest themselves. Either the Pope had not told Cardinal Sodano of his intention concerning disclosure of the Third Secret—in which case the Pope does not trust Sodano—or the Pope did tell Sodano, whereupon Sodano assumed that he would somehow be able to prevent disclosure at the May 13, 2000 ceremony. This would explain why Sodano had not arranged for a commentary beforehand: he thought it would not be needed because he would be able to prevent any disclosure of the Third Secret. But the Pope had pressed ahead, and now the Secret had to be "managed" in such a way that the question of Fatima could be laid to rest.

A Press Conference to Announce the Sodano Party Line

We thus arrive at the fateful date of June 26, 2000. On this date the Third Secret is "disclosed" at a Vatican press conference, along with a

---

[245] On this point we refer the reader again to the following articles: in *Euronoticias* on 24 March 2000, p. 8, entitled "Bishop of Leiria-Fatima March 21 press conference"; weekly *Euronoticias* of 24 March 2000, on p. 8, "Crisis: The Bishop of Leiria-Fatima Creates A Mystery Around the Visit of the Pope Without Telling the Patriarch What It Concerns, Will the Pope Reveal the Third Secret?"; *Euronoticias* of 24 March, 2000, an article on p. 9 entitled "Analysis: Persons Who Have Studied the Apparitions Say That the Third Secret Could Concern the Destruction of the Faith. A Crisis in the Interior of the Church Would be the Third Secret".

commentary prepared by Cardinal Ratzinger and Monsignor Tarcisio Bertone, then Secretary of the CDF, entitled *The Message of Fatima* (hereafter referred to as *TMF*). In *TMF* the Party Line on Fatima would be officially promulgated—by the direct command of Cardinal Angelo Sodano.

First of all, the faithful were told that the following text of a vision seen by Sister Lucy is all there is to the Third Secret of Fatima:

> After the two parts which I have already explained, at the left of Our Lady and a little above, we saw an Angel with a flaming sword in his left hand; flashing, it gave out flames that looked as though they would set the world on fire; but they died out in contact with the splendour that Our Lady radiated towards him from her right hand: pointing to the earth with his right hand, the Angel cried out in a loud voice: 'Penance, Penance, Penance!'. And we saw in an immense light that is God: 'something similar to how people appear in a mirror when they pass in front of it' a Bishop dressed in White 'we had the impression that it was the Holy Father'. Other Bishops, Priests, men and women Religious going up a steep mountain, at the top of which there was a big Cross of rough-hewn trunks as of a cork-tree with the bark; before reaching there the Holy Father passed through a big city half in ruins and half trembling with halting step, afflicted with pain and sorrow, he prayed for the souls of the corpses he met on his way; having reached the top of the mountain, on his knees at the foot of the big Cross he was killed by a group of soldiers who fired bullets and arrows at him, and in the same way there died one after another the other Bishops, Priests, men and women Religious, and various lay people of different ranks and positions. Beneath the two arms of the Cross there were two Angels, each with a crystal aspersorium in his hand, in which they gathered up the blood of the Martyrs and with it sprinkled the souls that were making their way to God.

The immediate reaction of millions of Catholics could be summarized in two words: *That's it*? Clearly, something was amiss, since nothing in this text corresponded to what Cardinal Ratzinger himself had said about the Third Secret in 1984—a point to which we shall return shortly. Nor did it contain anything that would have explained its mysterious suppression since 1960.

Most important, this obscure vision, written down on 62 lines of notebook paper, contained no words of Our Lady. In particular, it contained nothing that would complete the famous phrase spoken by Our Lady at the conclusion of the recorded portion of the Message of Fatima as faithfully transcribed by Sister Lucy in her memoirs: "In Portugal the dogma of the faith will always be preserved etc." Sister Lucy had added this phrase, including the "etc.", to her fourth memoir as part of the integral text of the Message. This addition had led every reputable Fatima scholar to conclude that it signaled the beginning of the unrecorded Third Secret, and that the Third Secret pertained to a widespread dogmatic crisis in the Church outside of Portugal. Clearly, the Virgin had more to say that was not written down because Sister Lucy had been instructed to keep it secret—until, as we have seen, 1960.

In a curious maneuver, however, *TMF* had avoided any discussion of the telltale phrase by taking the text of the Message of Fatima from Sister Lucy's *third* memoir, where the phrase does not appear. *TMF* justifies this as follows: "For the account of the first two parts of the 'secret', which have already been published and are therefore known, we have chosen the text written by Sister Lucia in the *Third* Memoir of 31 August 1941; some *annotations* were added in the *Fourth* Memoir of 8 December 1941." Annotations? The key phrase concerning the preservation of dogma in Portugal was no "annotation" but *an integral part of the spoken words of Our Lady*, after which She had said: "Tell this to no one. Yes, you may tell Francisco."

Having deceptively mischaracterized an integral part of the Message of Fatima as an "annotation", *TMF* then buries it in a footnote that is never mentioned again: "In the 'Fourth Memoir' Sister Lucia adds: 'In Portugal, the dogma of the faith will always be preserved, etc. ...'."

Why are Sodano/Ratzinger/Bertone so leery of this key phrase that they would so obviously go out of their way to avoid it by using an earlier and *less complete* memoir of the text of the Message? If there is nothing to hide in this phrase, why not simply use the Fourth Memoir and attempt an explanation of what the phrase means? Why did the authors of *TMF* so obviously *pretend* that the phrase is a mere "annotation", when they know full well that it appears in the integral text as part of the spoken words of the Mother of God? We shall return to this suspicious behavior in a later chapter.

Another ground for suspicion was that the vision of the "Bishop dressed in White" was not at all the 25-lined, one-page "*letter* ... in which Sister Lucy wrote down the *words which Our Lady confided* as a secret to the three shepherds in the Cova da Iria"—as the Vatican itself had described it in the aforementioned 1960 press release. The text of the vision spans 62 lines and apparently *four distinct pages* of what appear to be ruled notebook paper.[246]

Yet another suspicious circumstance is that on June 26 Cardinal Sodano's falsehood of May 13 was clearly exposed: the Pope *is killed* by soldiers who fire upon him as he kneels at the foot of a large wooden Cross outside a half-ruined city. The Pope is not "apparently dead", as Sodano had falsely asserted in May; the Pope *is* dead. The vision, whatever it means, clearly has absolutely nothing to do with the 1981 assassination attempt. The faithful had already been duped in May, and now the process of duping them was clearly continuing.

The dozens of discrepancies raised by this text—prompting

---

[246] See footnote 368 for a fuller explanation of this point.

Catholics around the world to doubt that we have received the Secret in its entirety—will be addressed in a later chapter. For now, we consider the Ratzinger/Bertone "commentary" in *TMF* on the Fatima Message as a whole.

Cardinal Sodano Dictates the "Interpretation" of the Third Secret

First of all, *TMF* is a virtual admission that the "interpretation" of the Message of Fatima which Cardinal Ratzinger and Msgr. Bertone will "attempt" (to use Cardinal Ratzinger's word) has been dictated by none other than Cardinal Sodano. No fewer than four times, *TMF* states that it is following *Sodano's* "interpretation" of the Third Secret—namely, that Fatima belongs to the past:

> Before attempting an interpretation, the main lines of which can be found in the statement read by *Cardinal Sodano* on May 13 of this year ...

> For this reason the figurative language of the vision is symbolic. In this regard *Cardinal Sodano* stated ...

> As is clear from the documentation presented here, the interpretation offered by *Cardinal Sodano*, in his statement on 13 May, was first put personally to Sister Lucia. ...

> First of all *we must affirm with Cardinal Sodano*: "the events to which the third part of the 'secret' of Fatima refers now seem *part of the past*".

And just in case the reader still has not gotten the point, the basic aim of *TMF* is driven home once again:

> Insofar as individual events are described, *they belong to the past*.

Is it not curious that the interpretation of the Virgin of Fatima's vital message to the world had been given over, not to the Pope, nor even to the Congregation for the Doctrine of the Faith (which was merely aping Cardinal Sodano's opinion), but to the *Vatican Secretary of State*? What authority did Cardinal Sodano have to impose his view upon the Church? None, of course. But Cardinal Sodano had arrogated that authority to himself in keeping the overall post-conciliar ascendancy of the Vatican Secretary of State to the status of *de facto* Pope when it comes to the daily governance of Church affairs.

Here it would be opportune to provide another very telling example of this usurpation of authority by the Secretary of State. In an article entitled "The Pope, the Mass and the Politics of the Vatican Bureaucrats" (*The Latin Mass* magazine, Winter Supplement, January 2002), Italian journalist Alessandro Zangrando recounts an incident in which the Vatican Secretary of State blocked publication in *L'Osservatore*

Romano of Pope John Paul II's praise of the traditional Latin Mass. The praise had been expressed in a papal message to an assembly of the Congregation for Divine Worship and the Discipline of the Sacraments: "In the Roman Missal of St. Pius V, as in many Eastern liturgies, are very many beautiful prayers with which the priests express the most profound sense of humility and reverence before the Holy Mysteries, the prayers revealing the Substance Itself of each Liturgy."

Zangrando noted that while papal messages to Vatican congregations are routinely published soon after their release, this one was not. It was only after the Pope's praise of the traditional Mass was published in the secular Italian newspaper *Il Giornale* that the Vatican Secretary of State suddenly (within 24 hours) released the text of the Holy Father's message through the Vatican Press Office—more than a month after its issuance by the Pope. But to this day, and contrary to normal practice, the Pope's message to the Congregation has not been published in *L'Osservatore Romano*, the Pope's own newspaper. Zangrando quoted the conclusion of the renowned "Vaticanista" (specialist in Vatican affairs) Andrea Tornielli: "The very fact that 24 hours after the publication of the article [in *Il Giornale*] the Vatican Secretariat of State made public the text of the Holy Father's letter, proves that a real attempt had been made at 'censoring' the Pope's words... The operation backfired with unintended results"—that is, the Pope's praise of the traditional Mass ended up gaining even wider publicity in the secular press.

Here we see how another key element of the Church's new orientation—the abandonment of Her traditional Latin liturgy—was enforced by the Secretary of State, who tried to censor the Pope's praise for the traditional Mass. Who knows how many other papal utterances have been censored—successfully—by the Vatican Secretariat of State? This incident is only typical of the way Church governance operated, especially given Pope John Paul II's declining physical health.

Cardinal Ratzinger Executes the Sodano Party Line

Returning to the "commentary" with these facts in mind, one can see that the press conference of June 26, 2000 had one overriding purpose: to carry out Cardinal Sodano's order concerning the "correct" interpretation of the Message of Fatima. By the time the reporters left that room, the Message of Fatima—all of it—was to be buried. And once buried, the Message would no longer impede Cardinal Sodano and his collaborators in their relentless pursuit of the Church's new, post-Fatima orientation, which includes (as we shall see) the important Church business of lauding, dining and hobnobbing at the Vatican with the likes of Mikhail Gorbachev, having the Pope apologize to the Red Chinese regime, pressuring Romanian Catholics to surrender to the Orthodox church the local Catholic Church's rights to the properties stolen by Josef Stalin, supporting and even contributing money to a godless, unaccountable International Criminal Court under United Nations auspices that could try Catholics of any nation for unspecified "crimes against humanity", and other such "triumphs" of Vatican diplomacy.

In other words, every last holdout in the Church must be brought along to the Vatican's new way of thinking and speaking to the world, which does not square well with Our Lady of Fatima's prophecy of the *triumph* of Her Immaculate Heart, the spread of *devotion* to Her Immaculate Heart and the consequent *conversion* of Russia through the intervention of the Immaculate Heart. This sort of talk just won't do anymore, even if it does come from the Mother of God. So, the precise task entrusted to Cardinal Ratzinger and Msgr. Bertone on June 26 was to find a way to detach the faithful once and for all from the explicitly Catholic aspects of the Message of Fatima, which all too clearly remind us of the "triumphal" Church of the "pre-conciliar dark age". As the *Los Angeles Times* would observe in its headline of June 27, 2000: "Catholic Church Unveils Third Secret: The Vatican's Top Theologian Gently Debunks a Nun's Account of Her 1917 Vision That Fueled Decades of Speculation." The effort was so blatant that even a secular newspaper could not help but notice it. Let us provide the proof of this crime against the Virgin of Fatima and the saintly seers God chose to receive Her message.

First, there was the attempt in *TMF* to dispose of the *triumph* of the Immaculate Heart:

> I would like finally to mention another key expression of the "secret" which has become justly famous: "my Immaculate Heart will triumph". What does this mean? The Heart open to God, purified by contemplation of God, is stronger than guns and weapons of every kind. The *fiat* of Mary, the word of her heart, has changed the history of the world, because it brought the Saviour into the world—because, thanks to her *Yes*, God could become man in our world and remains so for all time.

The attentive reader will notice immediately that the first three words from the Virgin's prophecy: *In the end* have been removed. This was necessary for the revisionist "interpretation" along the lines dictated by Sodano: namely, that Fatima belongs to the past.

Thus, "*In the end*, My Immaculate Heart will triumph" is—after the expedient removal of the first three words—now to be understood as follows: "2,000 years ago My Immaculate Heart triumphed." Our Lady's prophecy of what *will* happen *in the end* is blatantly falsified into a mere acknowledgment of what had already happened 20 centuries ago at the *beginning* of Christian history. Four future events—the triumph of the Immaculate Heart, the consecration of Russia, Russia's conversion, and the resulting period of peace in the world—are cunningly converted into one event 2,000 years ago! This tampering with a message God Himself sent to earth through His Blessed Mother should cause any member of the faithful to rise up and demand justice in the name of Heaven.

But on this point it seems that Pope Benedict XVI—as if his elevation to the papacy had freed him from the dictates of the Vatican Secretary of State—has reconsidered this exercise in Fatima revisionism. In a prayer that Pope Benedict addressed to the Mother of God in the Holy Land at Bethlehem on May 13, 2009, the anniversary of the first apparition at Fatima, the Pope said: "You promised the three children of Fatima that 'in the end, My Immaculate Heart will triumph.' May it be so!"

That remark represents a stunning reversal of the Party Line that the Triumph of the Immaculate Heart is already behind us, and that it consists of the "fall of communism" following the "consecration of Russia" in 1984—during a ceremony which avoided any mention of Russia, lest the Russians be offended. We will examine the evidence that demolishes that claim more in Chapter 16. But, more to the point at issue here, the Pope's declaration is a reversal of the former Cardinal Ratzinger's truly embarrassing claim in *TMF* that the triumph of the Immaculate Heart prophesied at Fatima was Mary's "fiat" 2,000 years ago at the Annunciation of the Archangel Gabriel.

These and other words and deeds of the currently reigning Pope, Benedict XVI, some of which we have already mentioned, give reason for hope that the course of events can be altered to avert disaster for the Church and the world. But, seven years after we published the first edition of this book, the course remains essentially unaltered, with a new helmsman in the Vatican Secretariat of State—Cardinal Bertone, the successor to Cardinal Sodano—following precisely the same coordinates, even if we now have a Pope who might wish to turn the ship around. We shall explore this situation in the final chapters, especially Chapters 15 and 16.

Second, concerning Our Lady's call to establish *devotion* to Her Immaculate Heart throughout the world as "God wishes," Cardinal Ratzinger suggests:

> According to Matthew 5:8, the "immaculate heart" is a heart which, with God's grace, has come to perfect interior unity and therefore "sees God." To be "devoted" to the Immaculate Heart of Mary means therefore to embrace this attitude of heart, which makes the *fiat*—"your will be done"—the defining centre of one's whole life.

Notice, first of all, the quotation marks placed around *devoted* and *immaculate heart*, which is stripped of its upper-case I—a sure sign these words are about to acquire a new meaning.

Thus, "God wishes to establish in the world devotion to My Immaculate Heart" is now to be understood as: "God wishes everyone to do His will." In fact, everyone whose heart is open to God's will acquires an "immaculate heart" of his own. So, devotion to the Immaculate Heart of Mary means opening one's *own* heart to God, not spreading devotion to *Her* heart in order to make the world (especially Russia) Catholic.

Immaculate with a capital I becomes immaculate with a lower-case i, and Her Heart becomes everyone's heart, at least potentially. As a magician would say: "Presto, change-o!"

There is, of course, only one word to describe the demotion of the one and only Immaculate Heart—conceived without Original Sin and guilty of no personal sin whatsoever—to the level of the heart of any person who turns away from his sins and finds interior unity with God. The word is *blasphemy*.

Here too, however, we have witnessed since the first edition of this book an apparent change in the man who was Cardinal Ratzinger but is now Benedict XVI—almost as if the Pope had somehow heeded the criticism leveled in the first edition of this book against the Cardinal, even if he had never read it. In an Angelus address on June 5, 2005, less than two months after his election to the papacy, the Pope unequivocally affirmed the uniqueness of the Immaculate Heart:

> The heart that resembles that of Christ *more than any other* is without a doubt the Heart of Mary, His Immaculate Mother, and for this very reason the liturgy holds Them up together for our veneration.[247]

And then, in his homily on the Solemnity of the Sacred Heart of Jesus in 2009, the Pope offered these beautiful words of praise and tribute to the Immaculate Heart of Mary, while affirming the dogma of the Immaculate Conception:

> May the Virgin Mary, whose Immaculate Heart we shall contemplate with lively faith tomorrow, obtain this grace for us. The Curé of Ars had a filial devotion to Mary, a devotion so profound that in 1836, in anticipation of the proclamation of the dogma of the Immaculate Conception, he dedicated his parish to Mary "conceived without sin". He frequently renewed this offering of the parish to the Blessed Virgin, teaching his parishioners that "to be heard it is enough to speak to Her", for the simple reason that She "desires above all else to see us happy".[248]

Papal statements like these are an encouraging sign that perhaps this Pope will finally bring the Church to correspond to the requests of Our Lady of Fatima, if the faithful continue to pray and work for that outcome. Meanwhile, however, the Party Line as enunciated in *TMF* continues to exert its negative influence at many levels of the Church.

Third, the *conversion* of Russia had to be disposed of. This was a bit more difficult to make disappear, for there is not much one can say to obscure the Mother of God's very clear statement that "the Holy

---

[247] Benedict XVI's talk at the Angelus on June 5, 2005; on the web at http://www.vatican.va/holy_father/benedict_xvi/angelus/2005/documents/hf_ben-xvi_ang_20050605_en.html.

[248] Solemnity of the Sacred Heart of Jesus, Opening of the Year for Priests on the 150th Anniversary of the Death of Saint John Mary Vianney, Homily of His Holiness Benedict XVI, Saint Peter's Basilica, Friday, June 19, 2009.

Father will consecrate Russia to Me, which *will be converted*." But, as we have demonstrated abundantly, the conversion of Russia is no longer acceptable to the Vatican apparatus. The solution to this problem was simply to avoid any discussion of the subject in *TMF*, although Our Lady's words are quoted without comment. The conversion of Russia? What conversion?[249]

Fourth, *TMF*'s crowning insult was the citation of only one "authority" on Fatima in *TMF*: the Flemish "theologian" Edouard Dhanis, S.J., who is identified as an "eminent scholar" on Fatima. Dhanis, a modernist Jesuit, made a veritable career out of casting doubt on the Fatima apparitions. Dhanis proposed that everything in the Secret of Fatima beyond a call for prayer and penance was cobbled together in the minds of the three children from things they had seen or heard in their own lives. Dhanis thus categorized as "Fatima II" all those things which the "eminent scholar" arbitrarily rejected as fabrications—without ever once interviewing Sister Lucy or studying the official Fatima archives.

As Dhanis put it: "All things considered, it is not easy to state precisely what degree of credence is to be given to the accounts of Sister Lucy. Without questioning her sincerity, or the sound judgment she shows in daily life, one may judge it prudent to use her writings only with reservations. ... Let us observe also that a good person can be sincere and prove to have good judgment in everyday life, but have a *propensity for unconscious fabrication* in a certain area, or in any case, a tendency to relate old memories of twenty years ago with embellishments and considerable modifications."[250]

Dhanis, who refused to examine the official Fatima archives, cast doubt on every aspect of the Message of Fatima which did not accord with his neo-modernist leanings: the prayer taught by the Angel he called "inexact"; the vision of hell he called an "exaggeratedly medieval representation"; the prophecy of "a night illumined by an unknown light" heralding the advent of World War II he described as "grounds for suspicion." And as for the consecration of Russia, Dhanis flatly declared that: "Russia could not be consecrated by the Pope, without this act taking on the air of a challenge, both in regard to the separated hierarchy, as well as the Union of Soviet Socialist Republics. *This would make the consecration practically unrealizable* ..." Thus, Dhanis declared that the consecration of Russia would be "morally impossible by reason

---

[249] Following the first edition of *The Devil's Final Battle*, the respected journal *Inside the Vatican* published an article demolishing the specious objection that the Consecration of Russia by the Pope and Catholic bishops would offend the Russian Orthodox. Cf. Cathy Pearson, "Now Is the Time: Consecrating Russia Will Help, Not Harm, Catholic-Orthodox Dialogue," *Inside the Vatican*, August/September 2008; reprinted with permission in *The Fatima Crusader*, Issue 91, February 2009, pp. 3ff; also on the web at www.fatimacrusader.com/cr91/cr91pg3.pdf. A free copy of this "breakthrough" article is available from the publisher of this book (see page xxvi).

[250] Dhanis' entire thesis against Fatima is explained and critiqued in Frère Michel, *The Whole Truth About Fatima* - Vol. I, Part II, pp. 384-528. All quotations concerning his false theory are from this source.

of the reactions it would normally provoke."[251]

Dhanis' deconstruction of the Message of Fatima is a typical example of how modernists undermine Catholic truths based upon premises they themselves invent. Since (invented premise) the consecration of Russia is morally impossible, how could Our Lady of Fatima have requested it? Having thus stacked the deck against Sister Lucy, Dhanis states the "inevitable" conclusion: "But could the Most Holy Virgin have requested a consecration which, taken according to the rigor of the terms, would be practically unrealizable? ... This question indeed seems to call for a *negative response*. ... Thus, it hardly seems probable that Our Lady asked for the consecration of Russia. ..." Based entirely on the premise Dhanis invented, Sister Lucy's testimony is pronounced a fraud.

That is precisely the line adopted by Cardinal Sodano and his Vatican apparatus: the Mother of God could not possibly have requested anything as diplomatically embarrassing as a public Consecration of Russia: and so we must do away with this embarrassing notion once and for all. It is this Party Line that Cardinal Ratzinger endorsed in his "commentary" by praising Dhanis as an "eminent scholar" on Fatima. Cardinal Ratzinger, following the Party Line, suggests that the Third Secret in particular consists of "images which Lucia may have seen in devotional books and which draw their inspiration from long-standing intuitions of faith." In other words, who can really say which parts of the Third Secret are authentic and which are merely personal memories or "intuitions"? And if that were true of the Third Secret, it would also be true of the rest of the Message of Fatima.

The apparent attempt to undermine Sister Lucy's credibility, while professing great respect for the Message of Fatima, will be taken up again in the following chapter. Here it suffices to say that the former Cardinal Ratzinger's evident agreement with Dhanis that all the specifically prophetic elements of the Message are unreliable ought to have disqualified him from proposing any "interpretation" of the Third Secret, or indeed any other part of the Fatima Message. If (at least in 2000) he simply did not believe that the Mother of God called for the consecration of Russia, the conversion of Russia to the Catholic Faith, the triumph of the Immaculate Heart of Mary, and the establishment throughout the world of the specifically Catholic devotion to *the one and only* Immaculate Heart, then he had a duty to reveal that bias and abstain entirely from the matter, rather than "proposing" an "interpretation" that discredited that which he purported to "interpret."

What was left of the Message of Fatima after June 26? On this point, the then-Cardinal Ratzinger, Msgr. (now Cardinal) Bertone, and Fr. Dhanis all seemed to agree: "What remains was already evident when we began our reflections on the text of the 'secret': the exhortation to prayer as the path of 'salvation for souls' [*sic*] and, likewise, the

---

[251] Ibid.

summons to penance and conversion." On June 26, 2000 the Message of Fatima became Fatima Lite: a watered-down prescription for personal piety without any specific relevance to the future of mankind.

For *this* the Mother of God came to earth and called down the Miracle of the Sun? It is interesting to note that even in presenting this minimalist version of the Message, Cardinal Ratzinger could not write about salvation for souls without bracketing those words with the same squeamish quotation marks he used to distance himself from the words *devotion*, *triumph* and *immaculate* in his commentary. It seems even Fatima Lite is not quite light enough in Catholic content for the ecumenical palates of modern churchmen.

As for Our Lady's prophetic warning that "various nations will be annihilated" if the consecration of Russia were not done, this we are apparently supposed to forget. There will be no annihilation of nations, "Fatima is all in the past." Cardinal Sodano said as much and the then-Cardinal Ratzinger seemed to agree.

The Party Line
on the Consecration of Russia

We have mentioned Archbishop (now Cardinal) Bertone's role in *TMF*. His principal contributions to the farce were two:

First, Bertone issued the "command" (binding, of course, on no one) that the faithful must cease asking for the Consecration of Russia: "Hence any further discussion or request [of the Consecration] is without basis."

To support this claim, Bertone cited exactly one piece of evidence: the manifestly fake "letter of November 8, 1989" from "Sister Lucy" to Mr. Noelker, which we have already mentioned—the same letter in which "Sister Lucy" writes about a consecration of the world by Pope Paul VI at Fatima which she never witnessed because it never happened. Tellingly enough, Bertone fails to identify the addressee of the letter. Nor does he provide the world with a copy to examine, lest anyone notice the fatal blunder concerning Pope Paul's nonexistent "consecration of the world." Even more telling, *TMF* contains absolutely no direct testimony by Sister Lucy herself concerning the Consecration, even though Bertone himself had interviewed her about the Third Secret only two months earlier, and she was readily available to the then-Cardinal Ratzinger and the entire Vatican apparatus during the beatification ceremony in May.

Small wonder. *TMF*'s version of the "consecration of Russia"—which is to say Cardinal Sodano's version—flatly contradicts a lifetime of testimony to the contrary by Sister Lucy. We consider a few examples here.

Over 60 years ago, on July 15, 1946, the eminent author and historian, William Thomas Walsh interviewed Sister Lucy, which is recounted in his important work, *Our Lady of Fatima*, which sold over one million copies. During this interview, which appears at the book's end, Mr. Walsh asked her pointed questions about the correct procedure for the Collegial Consecration:

> Finally we came to the important subject of the second July secret, of which so many different and conflicting versions have been published. Lucia made it plain that Our Lady did not ask for the consecration of *the world* to Her Immaculate Heart. What She demanded specifically was the consecration of *Russia*. She did not comment, of course, on the fact that Pope Pius XII had consecrated the world, not Russia, to the Immaculate Heart in 1942. But she said more than once, and with deliberate emphasis: "What Our Lady wants is that the Pope and all the bishops in the world shall consecrate Russia to Her Immaculate Heart on one special day. If this is done, She will convert Russia and there will be peace. If it is not done, the errors of Russia will spread through every country in the world".[252]

Sister Lucy is clear and forthright. The collegial consecration requested by Heaven is the Consecration of *Russia*, not the *world*, which must be done by the Pope in union with the world's bishops on the same day.

Then there is the little-known revelation of Our Lady to Sister Lucy in the early 1950s, which is recounted in *Il Pellegrinaggio delle Meraviglie*, published under the auspices of the Italian episcopate. The Virgin Mary appeared to Sister Lucy in May 1952 and said: "Make it known to the Holy Father that I am always awaiting the Consecration of Russia to My Immaculate Heart. Without the Consecration, Russia will not be able to convert, nor will the world have peace."[253]

Thus, 10 years after Pope Pius XII's 1942 consecration of the world, we have the report of Our Lady reminding Sister Lucy that Russia will not be converted, nor will there be peace, unless Russia is consecrated by name.

Thirty years later, in 1982, Sister Lucy's testimony remains steadfast. On May 12, 1982, the day before the attempted 1982 consecration, the Vatican's own *L'Osservatore Romano* published an interview of Sister Lucy by Father Umberto Maria Pasquale, a Salesian priest, during which she told Father Umberto that Our Lady had never requested the consecration of the world, but *only* the Consecration of Russia:

> At a certain moment I said to her: "Sister, I should like to ask you a question. If you cannot answer me, let it be. But if you can answer it, I would be most grateful to you ... Has Our Lady ever spoken to you about the Consecration of **the world** to Her Immaculate Heart?"

---

[252] William Thomas Walsh, *Our Lady of Fatima*, (Image-Doubleday, New York, *Imprimatur* 1947) p. 221. Emphasis in the original.

[253] *Il Pellegrinaggio delle Meraviglie*, (Rome, 1960) p. 440. This same work, published under the auspices of the Italian episcopate, affirms that this message was communicated to Pope Pius XII in June. Also, Canon Casimir Barthas mentioned that apparition in his communication to the Mariological Congress of Lisbon-Fatima, in 1967; see *De Primoridiis cultus marianae, Acta congressus mariologici-mariana in Lusitania anno 1967 celebrati*, (Rome, 1970) p. 517. See *Fatima: Tragedy and Triumph*, pp. 21 and 37.

"*No,* Father Umberto! *Never!* At the Cova da Iria in 1917 Our Lady had promised: *I shall come to ask for the Consecration of Russia ...* In 1929, at Tuy, as She had promised, Our Lady came back to tell me that the moment had come to ask the Holy Father for the Consecration of *that country* [Russia]."

This testimony was confirmed by Sister Lucy in a handwritten letter to Father Umberto, which the priest also published. (See photographic reproduction below.) A translation of the letter reads:

Reverend Father Umberto, in replying to your question, I will clarify: Our Lady of Fatima, in Her request, referred only to the Consecration of Russia ... — *Coimbra 13 IV - 1980 (signed) Sister Lucia*

Again, on March 19, 1983, at the request of the Holy Father, Sister Lucy met with the Papal Nuncio, Archbishop Portalupi, Dr. Lacerda, and Father Messias Coelho. During this meeting, Sister Lucy confirmed that Pope John Paul's consecration of 1982 did not fulfill the requests of Our Lady. Sister Lucy said:

In the act of offering of May 13, 1982, Russia did not appear as being the object of the consecration. And each bishop did not organize in his own diocese a public and solemn ceremony of reparation and Consecration of Russia. Pope John Paul II simply renewed the consecration of the world executed by Pius XII on October 31, 1942. From this consecration we can expect some benefits, but not the conversion of Russia.[254]

---

[254] *Fatima: Tragedy and Triumph*, p. 165.

She concluded, "The Consecration of Russia *has not been done as Our Lady had demanded it*. I was not able to say it [before] because I did not have the permission of the Holy See."[255]

A year later, on March 25, 1984, Pope John Paul II made an act of offering wherein he again consecrated "the world", not Russia. As with the 1982 consecration, "each bishop did not organize in his own diocese a public and solemn ceremony of reparation and consecration of Russia". Concerning this ceremony Frère François writes: "In the months which followed the act of offering of March 25, 1984, which was only a renewal of the act of 1982, the principal scholars of Fatima agreed in saying that the consecration of Russia had not yet been done as Heaven wished it."[256]

Such was also the conviction of Father Antonio Maria Martins,[257] and of Father Messias Coelho who, on the eve of March 25, 1984, had announced in *Mensagem de Fátima*, of which he is the publisher-editor, "Consecration of Russia: It will not be done yet this time."[258]

These theologians based their statements not only on the bald fact that a consecration of Russia needs to mention the word "Russia", but also on the testimony of Sister Lucy herself.

On Thursday, March 22, 1984, three days before the act of offering, the Carmel of Coimbra was celebrating Sister Lucy's seventy-seventh birthday. She received on that day, as was her custom, her old friend Mrs. Eugenia Pestana. After extending good wishes to her Carmelite friend, Mrs. Pestana asked, "Then Lucy, Sunday is the Consecration?" Sister Lucy, who had already received and read the text of the Pope's consecration formula made a negative sign and declared, "That consecration cannot have a decisive character."[259]

The "decisive character" which is the stamp of the proper consecration is the miraculous conversion of Russia. Although the new "ecumenical orientation" of the Church has confused the issue, the conversion of Russia means conversion to *Catholicism*. This is not only a matter of common sense, but it is also found in the testimony of Father Joaquin Alonso, probably the foremost Fatima expert of the 20th Century. Father Alonso, who had many interviews with Sister Lucy, wrote in 1976:

> ... we should affirm that Lucia always thought that the *'conversion'* of Russia is not to be limited to the return of the Russian people to the Orthodox Christian religion, rejecting the Marxist atheism of the Soviets, but rather, it refers purely, plainly

[255] Reported within an article by Father Pierre Caillon of Centre Saint Jean, 61500, Sées, (Orne) France. This article was published by the monthly periodical *Fidelite Catholique*, B.P. 217-56402, Auray Cedex, France. English translation from *The Fatima Crusader*, Issue 13-14, (October-December, 1983) p. 3.
[256] *Fatima: Tragedy and Triumph*, p. 172.
[257] See *Fatima e o Coraçao de Maria*, pp. 101-102.
[258] *Fatima: Tragedy and Triumph*, p. 172.
[259] Ibid., pp. 167-168.

and simply to the total, integral conversion of Russia to the one true Church of Christ, the Catholic Church.[260]

In a 1985 interview in *Sol de Fatima*, Sister Lucy was asked if the Pope fulfilled the request of Our Lady when he consecrated the world in 1984. Sister Lucy replied: *"There was no participation of all the bishops, and there was no mention of Russia."* She was then asked, *"So the consecration was not done as requested by Our Lady?"* to which she replied: *"No. Many bishops attached no importance to this act."*[261]

Even Father Rene Laurentin, a comrade of the progressivists, admitted in 1986 that "Sister Lucy remains unsatisfied[262] ... Lucy seems to think that the Consecration has 'not been made' as Our Lady wanted it."[263]

Then on July 20, 1987, Sister Lucy was interviewed quickly outside her convent while voting. Here she told journalist Enrique Romero that the Consecration of Russia has not been done as requested.[264]

More of Sister Lucy's affirmations that the 1984 consecration did not fulfill Heaven's conditions could be cited,[265] but the point is made: the then-Msgr. Bertone and the former Cardinal Ratzinger, following Sodano's Party Line, relied *entirely* on a single, manifestly bogus letter to overcome more than fifty years of unwavering testimony by Sister Lucy on Heaven's requirements for an effectual consecration of Russia. They had not dared to ask Sister Lucy about the matter themselves—or, if they had, she had not provided answers consistent with the Party Line.[266]

The Party Line on Fatima and World Peace

This brings us to Msgr. Bertone's second contribution to the farce. It came in the form of this statement, which is here photographically reproduced from their June 26, 2000 statement (*TMF*), on page 9:

> The decision of His Holiness Pope John Paul II to make public the third part of the "secret" of Fatima brings to an end a period of history marked by tragic human lust for power and evil, yet pervaded by the merciful love of God and the watchful care of the Mother of Jesus and of the Church.

---

[260] *La Verdad sobre el Secreto de Fatima, Fatima sin mitos*, Father Joaquin Alonso, (2nd edition, Ejercito Azul, Madrid, 1988) p. 78. English translation by Joseph Cain. Original Spanish reads: "... podriamos decir que Lucia ha pensado siempre que la 'conversión' de Rusia no se entiende solo de un retorno de los pueblos de Rusia a la religion cristiano-ortodoxa, rechazando el ateismo marxista y ateo de los soviets, sino que se refiere pura y llanamente a la conversion total e integral de un retorno a la unica y verdadera Iglesia, la catolica-romana."

[261] *Sol de Fatima*, September 1985.

[262] *Chrètiens-Magazine*, March 1987, #8. Cited from *Fatima: Tragedy and Triumph*, p. 189.

[263] Father Laurentin, *"Multiplication des apparitions de la Vierge aujourd'hui"*, (Fayard, September, 1988), p. 45. Cited from *Fatima: Tragedy and Triumph*, p. 189.

[264] This testimony of Sister Lucy was reported in the early August (1987) edition of *Para Ti* published in Argentina. See *World Enslavement or Peace ... It's Up to the Pope*, Father Nicholas Gruner (The Fatima Crusader, Fort Erie, 1988), pp. 212-213.

[265] For more testimony, see Chapter VI of *Fatima: Tragedy and Triumph*.

[266] The reported November 17, 2001 interview between Archbishop (now Cardinal) Bertone and Sister Lucy is treated at length in Chapter 11, "Muzzling and Hiding the Witness".

It is difficult to find words to express the offensiveness of this absurd claim. Here Sodano's Party Line seriously proposes that *an entire era of human lust for power and evil has been brought to an end* with the Vatican's "disclosure" of the obscure vision of the "Bishop dressed in White." In which case, why did the Vatican wait forty years to bring on world peace, when all it had to do, according to Msgr. Bertone, was stage a press conference in 1960 to publish this vision?

Cardinal Sodano evidently recognized that he must provide the faithful with some sort of counterfeit to take the place of the triumph of the Immaculate Heart, which had never materialized following the 1984 "consecration of Russia." The press conference of June 26, 2000 was thus presented as the great culmination of the Message of Fatima!

But somehow Msgr. Bertone and Cardinal Ratzinger seemed to ignore the obvious implications of Sister Lucy's letter, entirely in her own handwriting and *purportedly* (we emphasize "purportedly" for reasons that will soon be clear) addressed to the Pope on May 12, 1982. A cropped portion of the purported letter to the Pope was photographically reproduced in *TMF*. We present that photographic reproduction here, just as it appears in *TMF*:

We also reproduce below, exactly as it appears in *TMF*, the actual typeset English translation of the Portuguese handwritten fragment reproduced above:

> *And
> if we have not yet seen the complete fulfilment of the final part of
> this prophecy, we are going towards it little by little with great strides.
> If we do not reject the path of sin, hatred, revenge, injustice, violations
> of the rights of the human person, immorality and violence, etc.*
>
> *And let us not say that it is God who is punishing us in this way;
> on the contrary it is people themselves who are preparing their own
> punishment.*[267]

This purported letter to the Pope in 1982 makes *absolutely no reference* to the 1981 assassination attempt a year before; much less does it characterize the attempt as any sort of fulfillment of the Third Secret. Clearly, a year after the attempt Sister Lucy remained worried

---

[267] The Vatican translation "we are going towards it little by little with great strides" is clearly defective. The words "little by little" do not appear in the handwritten Portuguese original published on p. 9 of *TMF* provided by the Vatican itself.

about a global chastisement in consequence of the Church's failure to heed the imperatives of the Fatima Message. She certainly was not writing to the Pope about the triumph of the Immaculate Heart, but rather the annihilation of nations.

Also very curious is that the same letter from Sister Lucy, which *TMF* represents as being addressed to Pope John Paul II, contains the phrase: "The third part of the secret that **you are so anxious to know** (*que tanto ansiais por conhecer*)". Why would the Pope be "so anxious to know" the third part of the Secret if he already had the text in his possession at the Vatican, where it has been lodged since 1957? Why would His Holiness in 1982 be "so anxious to know" what he had already read in 1981 (as Ratzinger/Bertone claim), or as early as 1978, as papal spokesman Joaquin Navarro-Valls told the Portuguese press?

It is highly suspicious that the phrase "you are so anxious to know" is deleted *from every Vatican translation of the original Portuguese letter* in the various language versions of Bertone and Ratzinger's commentary (see also pages 349-350 of this book). Even the Portuguese language version of *TMF* omits the phrase "you are so anxious to know" from the *Portuguese* typeset reproduction of the original letter. Clearly, the Vatican apparatus wanted to avoid a storm of questions about how the Pope could be anxious to know something he already knew. But by the time reporters could compare their translations with the original Portuguese letter, the press conference was over and no further questions could be asked.

Two conclusions are possible: Either the letter was not really written to the Pope, or there was something more to the Secret which the Pope really did not know as of May 12, 1982, the date of the purported letter from Sister Lucy. As Sir Walter Scott's famous aphorism goes: "Oh! What a tangled web we weave, when first we practice to deceive."[268] The first deception—that Fatima belongs to the past—leads to a tangled web of other deceptions in order to cover up the first.

Targeting Father Gruner

But there was more to be done in this campaign to bury Fatima in the past. What about "the Fatima priest", whose apostolate's publications and broadcasts were persistently and quite effectively hammering home the point that the Vatican apparatus, pursuing its new vision of the Church, had turned its back on the Virgin's requests? At the end of the June 26 press conference, the then-Cardinal Ratzinger mentioned Father Nicholas Gruner by name, stating that he is a serious man. But he then went on to imply that Father Gruner must conform himself to "the Magisterium" on the question of the Consecration of Russia, which (so the Party Line goes) was now over and done with. But the Magisterium—the authoritative teaching office of the Church—had

---

[268] "Marmion: A Tale of Flodden Field", Canto 6, stanza 17. Poem by Sir Walter Scott.

taught nothing of the kind. There was only the Sodano Interpretation of Fatima, and *TMF*'s non-binding "attempt" to explain away all of the specific prophetic content of the Fatima Message[269] (leaving only prayer and penance).

Ratcheting up this persecution, Cardinal Castrillón Hoyos had, only days before the June 26 press conference, sent Father Gruner a letter containing the astounding threat that he would be excommunicated from the Catholic Church. This letter was followed up with a communiqué to the bishops of the Philippines (where Father Gruner's apostolate is strongly supported), advising that Father Gruner would be excommunicated unless (among other things demanded) he "reconciled himself to Church authorities"—that is, according to Castrillón Hoyos, return to the Diocese of Avellino (where Father Gruner was no longer incardinated), close down his apostolate and bow to the Party Line on Fatima. For his own part, the Bishop of Avellino had never needed Father Gruner's services, never supported him financially, and had never taken any steps to secure a proper immigration visa for the "return" to Avellino. The Bishop of Avellino was nothing but a pawn in the Secretary of State's chess game. (We will have more to say about this travesty in later chapters.)

In his remarks about Father Gruner at the end of the June 26 press conference, the then-Cardinal Ratzinger had also noted that Father Gruner was no doubt suffering from *angoscia*—the Italian word for mental anguish. The Cardinal must have known of the threat of excommunication, which would indeed cause *angoscia* in any faithful priest who loves the Church. But Father Gruner's plight is only emblematic of the plight of the Church as a whole in the post-conciliar epoch: a priest who has committed no offense against faith, morals or ecclesiastical discipline is personally threatened with excommunication by the very head of the Congregation for the Clergy, while throughout the Church predators in Roman collars molest altar boys or spread heresy as their bishops move them from place to place or conceal their activities and protect them from punishment; and the Congregation for the Clergy does nothing.

What is to explain this outrageous disparity of justice? There seems to us only one sensible explanation, based on what we have shown thus far: In the Catholic Church of the post-conciliar Adaptation the one unforgivable offense—just as in Stalinist Russia—is to buck the Party Line. And Father Gruner had bucked the Party Line on Fatima.

---

[269] It should be noted that the then-Cardinal Ratzinger himself said regarding the Vatican's interpretation of the Third Secret, "The Church does not want to impose an interpretation". This quotation was reported in: "Final Secret of Fatima Published by Vatican", *Boston Herald*, June 27, 2000; "Vatican's Secret is Out", *The Express*, June 27, 2000; "Vatican Unease as it Reveals the Full Third Secret of Fatima", *Financial Times (London)*, June 27, 2000; "Fatima 'Snapshot of Martyr's Past Century'", *The Irish Times*, June 27, 2000.

Exit Our Lady, Enter Gorbachev

We have claimed that this mockery and obscuration of the Fatima Message—the Party Line on Fatima—was intended to bury it once and for all, so that Cardinal Sodano could get on with his pursuit of the Church's new orientation. Here is a particularly compelling example of what we mean:

Fatima having been "gently debunked" (to quote the *Los Angeles Times*) by Ratzinger and Bertone on June 26, the Vatican apparatus, led by Cardinal Sodano, immediately got down to what it considers the serious business of the Church. The very next day Mikhail Gorbachev was seated as a guest of honor between Cardinals Sodano and Silvestrini at a Vatican "press conference." What was the purpose of this press conference? It was called to celebrate one of the key elements of the Church's new orientation: *Ostpolitik*, the policy of "dialogue" and accommodation with Communist regimes (including Red China) that persecute the Church. The immediate occasion for the press conference was the posthumous publication of the memoirs of Cardinal Casaroli, the grand propagator of *Ostpolitik* and Cardinal Sodano's predecessor in enforcing the Party Line against Fatima.[270]

In true Stalinist fashion, no questions from the press were permitted at this curious "press conference"—a press conference with no questions from the press! Evidently the Vatican wanted to be sure that no one bucked the Party Line with any questions about Fatima, or why the Vatican was honoring the likes of Mikhail Gorbachev, a man who admits he is still a Leninist and whose tax-free foundations are promoting the use of abortion and contraception to eliminate five billion people from the world's population.[271] This is not even to mention this blood-drenched character's public defense of the Soviet invasion of Afghanistan when he was still head of the Soviet Communist Party—a genocidal campaign that included planting bombs disguised as toys, so that Afghan children would have their limbs and heads blown off.[272]

Could there be a more dramatic demonstration of the fundamental opposition between the Church of all time and the Church of the Adaptation? On June 26, 2000 Our Lady of Fatima was shown the

---

[270] News of June 27, 2000 press conference. "Gorbachev Helps Introduce Casaroli Memoirs", *Catholic World News*, June 27, 2000.

[271] In September 1995, Gorbachev held his "State of the World Forum" in San Francisco. Over 4000 of the world's "elite" paid $5,000 per person to attend the 5-day event. In a closing plenary session of the forum, a philosopher/author named Sam Keen provided a summary and concluding remarks on the conference. It reveals the Forum's anti-life, anti-Christian ethos. To the conference participants, Keen said: "there was very strong agreement that religious institutions have to take the primary responsibility for the population explosion. We must speak far more clearly about sexuality, about contraception, about abortion, about the values that control the population, because the ecological crisis, in short, is the population crisis. *Cut the population by 90 percent and there aren't enough people left to do a great deal of ecological damage.*" See "World's elite gather to talk depopulation," John Henry Western, *The Interim*, April 1996.

[272] See interview with Afghan official Abdul Shams in *Review of the News*, July 1985.

door, Her heavenly message audaciously censored and revised by men who would dare to consign it to oblivion. Then, a day later, Mikhail Gorbachev entered the Vatican to celebrate the Church's new orientation, as implemented by the late Cardinal Casaroli and by his successor, Cardinal Sodano.

Gorbachev, leader of the culture of death, was honored by the Vatican again on November 4, 2000 when he addressed the Pope and other prelates at the "Jubilee of Politicians"—a dinner gala for about 5,000 of the world's rulers of godless secular republics. The photographers captured the Pope listening very attentively to a speech by this key promoter of the abortion holocaust.[273] This grotesque mixture of a Jubilee—a spiritual tradition in the Church derived from an Old Testament custom—with speeches by pro-abortion politicians on secular matters, is only typical of the new orientation, which constantly seeks to merge the Church with the world in the great Adaptation of Roman Catholicism to "modern civilization".

Enforcing the New Orientation in a "Post-Fatima" Church

The months following the June 26 press conference witnessed an acceleration in the campaign to impose the new orientation on the Message of Fatima onto the Church at large.

For example, on June 29, 2000, only two days after the Gorbachev farce, a seemingly unrelated but actually quite relevant event took place. Cardinal Castrillón Hoyos issued a letter in his capacity as the head of the Ecclesia Dei Commission, which is supposed to insure access to the traditional Latin Mass for those who seek it. The letter announced something quite remarkable at a time of general lack of discipline in the Church: The General Chapter (meeting) of the Priestly Fraternity of St. Peter (chartered by Pope John Paul II to serve the needs of traditional Catholics who have not welcomed the changes in the Church) would be suppressed. Its election would not be held. The Fraternity's priestly members would not be allowed to re-elect as their superior Father Josef Bisig, who was expected to be nominated and re-elected by an overwhelming majority at the Chapter. Cardinal Castrillón Hoyos would simply impose upon the Fraternity a candidate more to his liking. Further, the rectors of the Fraternity's two seminaries would be removed and replaced with more liberal-minded priests.

The rationale for the Cardinal's actions is stated in his letter:

> You know quite well that your seminary is observed by many people in the Church and that it must be exemplary in all respects. In particular, it is required to avoid and combat *a certain spirit of rebellion against the present-day Church*, which spirit easily finds followers among the young students, who like all young people

---

[273] Photograph published in *Catholic Family News*, January 2001, p. 13; see also the photo on page 153 of this book.

already are inclined to extreme and rigorous positions.[274]

In a later interview in *30 Days* magazine, the Cardinal further explained that he was only helping the Fraternity "to strike a balance between their original charism and the outcome of their insertion *within the ecclesial reality of today*."[275]

Consider these two phrases together: "a certain spirit of rebellion against the present-day Church", and "their insertion within the ecclesial reality of today". Now, the seminarians of the Priestly Fraternity are baptized Catholics. They were born and raised in the "mainstream" Catholic Church. They were young men who came from the "mainstream" and joined the Fraternity's seminaries to be formed in a traditional manner and to celebrate the traditional Latin Mass.

And yet these young men, who have never gone into schism (so-called), are being told that nonetheless they must be inserted into the "present-day Church" and "the ecclesial reality of today". But if they are already Catholics, then what is this thing into which they are being "inserted"? Is it the Holy Catholic Church? Clearly, it is not. What the Cardinal is speaking of—whether he knows this explicitly or not—is *the Church of the Adaptation*; the Church of the new orientation. We know this because the priests and seminarians of the papally chartered Fraternity of Saint Peter are indubitably Catholics, so that if they are being inserted into anything it is not the Holy Catholic Church proper, but something else, something new and strange.

And that is why we speak of the Sergian Adaptation of the Church (to recall that infamous "adaptation" of the Russian Orthodox Church to the demands of Stalin and of Soviet Communism under the Metropolitan Sergius). It is not as if the Church has been completely overthrown and has ceased entirely to be what She was, for this is impossible, given the promise of Our Lord that the gates of hell would not prevail against His Church. Rather, a sort of Trojan Horse has been set up inside the Church—a church within the Church; a collection of novel practices and attitudes never before seen in Church history—that now wishes to insist that *it* is the Church. And whomever wishes to get along with this "present-day Church" must consent to be inserted into this "ecclesial reality of today" that has somehow set itself up *within* the perennial ecclesial reality of the Holy Catholic Church, alongside all the traditional beliefs and practices which have never been, and can never be, abolished, as Pope Benedict XVI confirmed so dramatically when he declared in *Summorum Pontificum* that the traditional Latin Mass was "never abrogated." But while the "ecclesial reality of today" is only a temporary phenomenon that God will surely rectify because of the untold damage it has caused the Church, Cardinal Castrillón and his collaborators, following the Party Line of the Church's new

---

[274] Letter to the General Chapter of the Priestly Fraternity of Saint Peter, June 29, 2000.
[275] *30 Days* magazine, No. 11, 2000, p. 17.

orientation—the Sergian Adaptation to the "modern world"—wished to pretend that it was to be a permanent thing.

One could not ask for a better proof of the existence of the Church's new orientation—her Stalinist Adaptation, as it were—than the Cardinal's brutal treatment of the Priestly Fraternity. Such actions would never be taken against the Jesuits or the other priestly orders that have been undermining the Church since Vatican II. Why? Because these morally and doctrinally corrupt orders *adhere to the Adaptation, to the Party Line, to the new orientation*. In the current crisis, the only thing the Vatican is willing to enforce with immediate and vigorous action is the Adaptation of the Church to the world—not sound doctrine, not sound practice, which are flouted throughout the Church with virtual impunity—but only the Adaptation. We have seen that since this book first appeared, Pope Benedict has made some effort to change this frightful situation, but the situation still dominates the ecclesial landscape.

In September of 2000 we encounter yet another dramatic example of the Church's Adaptation. From September 12-19, 2000, Cardinal Roger Etchegaray was in Red China to attend "a Symposium on Religions and Peace". While there he celebrated Mass in the presence of the schismatic bishops of the Chinese Catholic Patriotic Association (CCPA). The Mass was celebrated in the Shrine of Our Lady Help of Christians, which the Red Chinese regime has stolen from the true Catholic Church in China.[276]

The CCPA was formed in the 1950's to replace the Catholic Church after "Chairman Mao" declared the Catholic Church "illegal" in Red China. The CCPA is thus a human organization created by a Communist government and set up as a "church" which Chinese Catholics *must* join, forsaking the Roman Catholic Church, whose very existence has been declared "illegal" by the Red Chinese regime. *The CCPA constitution explicitly rejects submission to the Pope and declares the CCPA to be autonomous from Rome*. The CCPA bishops and priests, therefore, are all schismatics by definition.

Over 100 bishops have been consecrated illicitly by the CCPA without a papal mandate, in direct violation of the Code of Canon Law; worse still, those illicitly consecrated bishops publicly declared their primary allegiance to the Communist regime of China while disavowing (in the CCPA Constitution) any allegiance or submission to the Pope. As a result, these illicit bishops, and those who consecrated them, are excommunicated. In 1994 the CCPA bishops issued a so-called pastoral letter in which they endorsed China's population control policy, which includes forced abortions on all women who have one child already, calling upon Chinese Catholics to support this abomination.

In short, the CCPA is a Communist-created, Communist-controlled,

---

[276] Zenit, September 19, 2000.

blatantly schismatic, blatantly heretical, pro-abortion organization, created by the devil himself, acting through Mao Tse-tung and his successor "President" Jiang. And yet the Vatican has declared no schism, nor any excommunication of these Communist-controlled, pro-abortion clergy. On the contrary, Cardinal Etchegaray went from the Vatican to China and openly and publicly celebrated Mass in the presence of CCPA bishops in a Marian Shrine which the CCPA, with the aid of Communist goons, stole from the Catholic Church and the Catholic faithful. Cardinal Etchegaray even stated that he "recognized the fidelity to the Pope of the Catholics of the official church [i.e., the CCPA]". *Fidelity* to the Pope on the part of bishops who endorse forced abortion and whose Communist-controlled association rejects the papal primacy in its very constitution? What sort of nonsense is this?

While Cardinal Etchegaray was in China, an 82-year-old Catholic priest in the "underground" Catholic Church, which remains in union with Rome, was beaten into a coma and carted off to jail by "security" police.[277] In accordance with *Ostpolitik*, the Vatican has issued no protest over the nearly fatal beating of this priest, nor any protest over the arrest, imprisonment and torture of loyal Catholic priests, bishops and laity by the Red Chinese regime. The Vatican apparatus is still chained to the Church's new orientation—"dialogue" with the Church's enemies and silence even in the face of blatant torture and persecution of faithful Catholics. This is the fruit of the new orientation's abandonment of righteous opposition to evil. And this policy of the Adaptation of the Church will, in the long run, have the intended effect on millions more, who will lose their faith and apostatize, because the Vatican apparatus will no longer stand up and oppose evil with the righteous anger of old.

Here too we see the disparity of treatment as between traditional Catholics who in any way present an obstacle to the new orientation, and those who embrace the new orientation wholly and entirely. In contrast with the Vatican's pandering to the CCPA, Archbishop Marcel Lefebvre was publicly pronounced both excommunicated and schismatic in a *motu proprio* prepared for the Pope's signature within 48 hours of Archbishop Lefebvre's consecration of four bishops without a papal mandate[278]—an action the Archbishop took in an effort (however

---

[277] *CWN News Brief*, September 18, 2000.

[278] While it is true that in normal circumstances a bishop should not make a new bishop without explicit permission or authorization from the Pope, nevertheless it is foreseen both in law and in practice over the centuries in Church history that a bishop can and sometimes must consecrate—that is, make—another bishop without explicit permission and even to go against a specific direct order of the Pope. Canon Law recognizes the right of a subject to go against an explicit order of a higher authority—even that of a Pope—in a specific instance, after due reflection and prayer, to go directly contrary if his conscience, informed by Catholic doctrine, persuades him that he must do so. (See Canon 1323, especially Section 4; and Canon 1324, especially Section 1, subsection 8, and Section 3.) Furthermore, in law it is not *ipso facto* an act of schism for one to disobey in a specific instance while being subject to the authority of the Pope in general—but at

misguided some may think it to be) to maintain all Catholic dogmas and Tradition in a Church that appears to have gone mad.

The Red Chinese procure (through former Catholic bishops) the consecration of 100 bishops without a papal mandate for their pro-abortion "church" and the Vatican takes no punitive action. Quite the contrary, it sends a Cardinal (no less) as a representative to hobnob with some of the illicit bishops! Yet, when Archbishop Lefebvre consecrates four bishops to serve Catholic Tradition, he is immediately cast into outer darkness by the same Vatican apparatus, even though Archbishop Lefebvre and the four newly consecrated bishops consistently professed their loyalty to the Pope whom they were attempting to serve by preserving traditional Catholic practice and belief. Why this striking disparity of treatment? The answer, once again, is that Archbishop Lefebvre resisted the Adaptation; the Red Chinese bishops, on the other hand, *exemplify* it.

Of course, as we have already seen, in January 2009 Pope Benedict XVI provoked massive outrage in attempting to rectify this preposterous injustice by lifting the "excommunication" of the bishops of Lefebvre's Society of Saint Pius X. But the double standard continues. And indeed today, in a Church wracked by dissent and scandal, and a world filled with objectively heretical and schismatic sects, only the four bishops of the Society are still called "schismatic." The practitioners of the "new orientation" of the Church literally apply the word "schismatic" *to only four men in the entire world*: the traditional Catholic bishops of the Society that the Pope is accused of wrongly "rehabilitating." What better indication of the apocalyptic state of affairs that still confronts us today, seven years after this book first appeared?

But it is even worse. According to an Open Letter of protest to Cardinal Sodano and other members of the Vatican apparatus, published by the Cardinal Kung Foundation, priests of the CCPA—the Chinese Communist puppet "church", which is schismatic, Communist-controlled, and pro-abortion—have been given *canonical missions and priestly faculties in American dioceses*. Thus, these Communist priests celebrate Mass and hear confessions of Roman Catholic faithful in their local parishes where these agents of a Communist government learn the secret sins of innumerable Americans which may provide material for blackmail to the Communist masters in China.

---

most it is an act of disobedience.

But it is not even an act of disobedience, at least subjectively, nor can it be a cause for automatic excommunication if one does not feel bound to obey the Pope when one believes that the preservation of the Faith and the good of the Church demands it. The act of Archbishop Lefebvre on June 29, 1988 in consecrating four priests to the rank of bishop is beyond the scope of this book, but there are very learned articles by canonists and theologians which make a strong case for the subjective and objective defense of this act. (See articles by Patrick Valdrini, Dean of Canon Law, Institute Catholique, Paris, France and by Count Neri Caponi, Professor Emeritus of the Faculty of Canon Law, University of Florence, Italy.) Even various Cardinals in the Vatican have publicly, in various degrees, defended Archbishop Lefebvre in this act.

These CCPA "priests" are also placed in a position to poison the minds and hearts of their American penitents with Marxist advice and package it as if it were spiritual direction. This was confirmed by Archbishop Levada of San Francisco (now Cardinal Levada who has been transferred to be Prefect of the Congregation for the Doctrine of the Faith in Rome), who claims that the Vatican—and no doubt Cardinal Sodano was involved in this decision—has authorized the granting of "an apostolic mission" to these priests of the pro-abortion, Communist-controlled, schismatic CCPA.[279]

Here is a literal, visible penetration of Communist power into the body of the Church. There could not be a more dramatic demonstration of the Adaptation. But the presence of these Communist-controlled priests in American parishes is only an icon of the whole process that was propagated in Metz, France, back in 1962, when the drawbridge of the Church was let down and the forces of the world, the Church's sworn enemies, began to march into the Church, leading even Pope Paul VI to speak of the invasion of the Church by worldly thinking.

Imposing the Falsification of the Message of Fatima on the Church

Nowhere can one find a sadder example of the Adaptation of the Church (see the previous chapter, pages 107-109) than what occurred on October 8, 2000: a ceremony at the Vatican "entrusting" various things to Mary—an "entrustment" for the masses, to take their minds off the consecration of Russia. During this ceremony "all peoples", the world, the unemployed, even "youth in search of meaning"— anything and everything but Russia—were "entrusted" to Our Lady. The day before this ceremony the praying of the Rosary in Saint Peter's Square was broadcast around the world by satellite. But one thing was missing: the Fatima prayers. No one at the Vatican would pray: "O my Jesus, forgive us our sins, save us from the fires of hell. Lead all souls to Heaven, especially those most in need." One decade of the Rosary, however, was recited by Sister Lucy for the cameras in the convent in Coimbra. Looking perfectly miserable, Sister Lucy did recite the Fatima prayers—in Portuguese. She had been reduced to a prop in a publicity stunt.

Here we see the Sergianization of the Message of Fatima, the Adaptation of Fatima to the world. Our Lady of Fatima becomes Our Lady of the Unemployed, Our Lady of Youth in Search of Meaning; and the Rosary is stripped of the Fatima prayers.

And this brings us to early 2001. The year 2000 had been a busy

---

[279] Cardinal Kung Foundation's *Open Letter to the Vatican*, Sec. III, March 28, 2000 (www.cardinalkungfoundation.org/cpa/openletter.html). In reply to the Kung Foundation (quoted in the *Open Letter*), Archbishop (now Cardinal) Levada (for more information about him, see entry on page 381 of "A Glossary of Ecclesiastical Terms, Organizations and Persons") reveals that the "apostolic ministry" of CCPA priests "is being carried out according to directives received from the Holy See."

year for the Adaptation, but there was some mopping up to do. Father Gruner was still conducting his very effective Fatima apostolate. So on February 16, 2001, Cardinal Castrillón Hoyos wrote to Father Gruner to renew his threat of excommunication of the previous June. If Father Gruner did not stop what he was doing, then there would be "definitive measures that would be painful for all concerned."

In the same letter Cardinal Castrillón provided another demonstration of the new orientation at work on the Message of Fatima. According to Cardinal Castrillón "the Blessed Mother appeared to the three little visionaries in the Cova da Iria at the beginning of the century, and *marked out a program for the New Evangelization* which the whole Church finds itself engaged in, which is even more urgent at the dawn of the third millennium."[280] Our Lady of Fatima was now Our Lady of the New Evangelization—about which She had said not a single word at Fatima!

Our Lady did not come to Fatima to announce "the New Evangelization," a slogan that describes a novel and ineffectual campaign to stimulate the dying faith of those who are already Catholics and who are taken in by the ongoing Stalinization of the Catholic Church.[281] Nor did Our Lady come to announce any of the other obscure slogans that have overrun the Church in the past forty years: "ecumenical dialogue," "interreligious dialogue," "solidarity," "the civilization of love," "inculturation," and so forth. She came to announce the *Old* Evangelization, the perennial Gospel of Jesus Christ, Who is the same yesterday, today and forever—the selfsame Christ who warned the world that "He who believes and is baptized shall be saved; he who believes not shall be condemned." As a group of Father Gruner's supporters protested in their reply to the Cardinal:

> Your Eminence, where can one find *any* of these elements in your rendering of the Message of Fatima? Where is Heaven and where is hell, for you speak only vaguely of "Ultimate Realities"—a term any Mason would find acceptable? Where is the *triumph* of the Immaculate Heart? Where are the consecration and *conversion* of Russia? Where are the warnings of Our Lady? Where indeed is the Message of Fatima at all?

Our Lady of Fatima's message to the world was devoid of slogans such as "the New Evangelization." She had uttered no slogans at all but only the simple Catholic truth: that many souls are burning in hell for lack of the Catholic Faith; that to save souls God ordains it necessary to

---

[280] Letter to Father Nicholas Gruner, February 16, 2001.

[281] The New Evangelization is described as an Evangelization that is "new in its ardor, new in its method, and new in its expression". It is under the umbrella of the "New Evangelization" that has "justified" the rowdy "Charismatic Movement" and Rock and Roll Eucharistic Congresses, World Youth Days nicknamed "Catholic Woodstock", and other present-day aberrations in the Church. For a full treatment of the subject, see John Vennari, "Catholicism Dissolved, The New Evangelization" (Four-part series in *Catholic Family News*, from October 1998 to January 1999).

establish *in the world*—not just among those who are already Catholics—devotion to Her Immaculate Heart; that Her Immaculate Heart must *triumph* through the Consecration of Russia to that Heart; that only by this means can there be true peace in our time. And Our Lady of Fatima also gave us a warning about the consequences of failing to heed Her requests: wars and persecution of the Church, the martyrdom of the good, the suffering of the Holy Father, the suffering of the whole world—all of which are occurring at this very moment in history—and then, if we continue to ignore Her requests, the annihilation of various nations.

The Message of Fatima had, quite simply, been written out of existence, transformed into slogans of the Sergian Adaptation, or as some call it—the Stalinization of the Catholic Church. And in line with this Stalinist Adaptation of the Church there would be censorship of anyone who hearkened to the former understanding of the old terms. In the same letter of February 16, Cardinal Castrillón Hoyos had demanded that Father Gruner "publicly retract" certain opinions in his apostolate's magazine that the Cardinal deemed objectionable. In a Church teeming with heretical literature which has undermined the faith of millions and endangered their souls, Cardinal Castrillón Hoyos wished to censor *The Fatima Crusader* magazine! And why? Because the magazine had dared to criticize, not Catholic teaching on faith and morals, but the prudential decisions of Cardinal Sodano and his collaborators—including their press conferences and dinners with the likes of Mikhail Gorbachev, their cozy relations with the schismatic CCPA and their attempt to bury the Message of Fatima under a mountain of false interpretations.

The treatment of Father Gruner, the Priestly Fraternity of St. Peter, Archbishop Lefebvre, the Society of St. Pius X, and other perceived obstacles to the new orientation of Vatican II illustrates that the post-conciliar epoch presents a situation very much like that lamented by St. Basil at the height of the Arian heresy: "Only one offense is now vigorously punished: an accurate observance of our fathers' traditions. For this cause the pious are driven from their countries and transported into deserts."

Only one offense is now vigorously punished today: an accurate observance of the Church's constant pre-conciliar traditions—summed up in the Message of Fatima. Strange to say, the then-Cardinal Ratzinger made the following observation about the so-called "Lefebvre schism" in his 1988 address to the Bishops of Chile:

> That which previously was considered Most Holy (the form in which the Liturgy was handed down) suddenly appears to be the most forbidden of all things, the one thing that can safely be prohibited. It is intolerable to criticize decisions which have been taken since the Council. On the other hand, if men make question of ancient rules or even of the great truths of the Faith, for instance

the corporal virginity of Mary, the bodily resurrection of Jesus, the immortality of the soul, etc., nobody complains or only does so with the greatest of moderation. All this leads a great number of people to ask themselves if the Church of today is really the same as that of yesterday or if they have changed it for something else without telling people.

Stranger still, Cardinal Castrillón Hoyos has made the same admission. In the aforementioned interview in *30 Days* he said: "The great emergency of our time is to show people that the Church of today is the same as the Church has always been." But why is there such an "emergency" in the first place? When in the entire history of the Catholic Church did it ever have to be *demonstrated* that the Church was still the same as before? Why would such a demonstration even be necessary if there were not a very good reason to suspect that the Church *has* been changed?

There is indeed good reason to suspect this, as we have shown: Since Vatican II the Catholic Church has undergone an Adaptation precisely along the lines predicted, plotted and carried out by Her worst enemies. And those in charge of the Church today *refuse to recognize* what has happened, even if they are not conscious agents of destruction themselves. They are, as Our Lord said of the Pharisees: "blind, and leaders of the blind. And if the blind lead the blind, both fall into the pit." (Mt. 15:14)

As Sister Lucy herself said: "This is why the devil has waged such a war against it [the Rosary]! *And the worst is that he has succeeded in leading into error and deceiving souls having a heavy responsibility through the place which they occupy ...! They are blind men guiding other blind men ...*"[282]

And, as Saint Paul declared concerning the same type of stiff-necked person: "There are none so blind as those who will not see." It is also written in Sacred Scripture: "For the heart of this people is grown gross, and with their ears have they heard heavily, and their eyes they have shut; lest perhaps they should see with their eyes, and hear with their ears, and understand with their heart, and should be converted, and I should heal them." (Acts 28:27) They blindly and stubbornly defend the Adaptation of the Catholic Church as if it were a dogma of the Faith, while the real dogmas of the Faith are being undermined throughout the Church before their very eyes while they do very little or nothing to defend the Catholic Faith and the Catholic Church.

Summarizing the Evidence

It is now opportune for us to summarize what the evidence has shown so far concerning the "new orientation" or "Sergian Adaptation" of the Church and its intrinsic opposition to the Message of Fatima:

---

[282] See Sister Lucy's quote in *The Whole Truth About Fatima* - Vol. III, p. 758.

- The Message of Fatima is a divinely given prophecy for our time, authenticated by an unprecedented public miracle and vouched for by a series of Popes, including John Paul II and Benedict XVI.

- The prophetic warnings in the Message have mostly come to pass, save for especially the annihilation of nations that would be the consequence of failing to effect the Consecration of Russia in time.

- God has already demonstrated the benefits of a national consecration to the Immaculate Heart in the case of Portugal in 1931, whose miraculous overnight transformation from an atheistic, Masonic republic into a Catholic country was seen by the Portuguese hierarchy itself as a foretaste of what God would bestow upon the world after the Consecration of Russia.

- Instead of following the path marked out at Fatima, the leaders of the Catholic Church chose a different path—the path of a new orientation of the Church initiated at Vatican II, including an "opening to the world" and "reforms" of the Church which have fulfilled the dreams of Her worst enemies, who admitted that their goal was to bring about precisely such changes in the Church.

- In taking this path of a new orientation, the Church's leaders have disregarded the repeated warnings of the pre-conciliar Popes (including Blessed Pius IX, Leo XIII, St. Pius X, Pius XI and Pius XII) that the Church's enemies were plotting to remake Her in the very manner She has in fact been remade in the post-conciliar period.

- The changes began in 1960—the very year in which Our Lady commanded that the Third Secret be released, which had been promised by the Patriarch of Lisbon, and which Sister Lucy had insisted the Third Secret be revealed, because it would be clearer then.

- The result of these changes has been a catastrophic loss of faith and discipline in the Church which appears to be foretold in that part of the Great Secret of Fatima which begins with the words: "In Portugal the dogma of the Faith will always be preserved etc."—a phrase that remains mysteriously incomplete, despite Cardinal Bertone's claimed disclosure of the entirety of the Third Secret.

- Rather than admitting these incalculable blunders and their ruinous consequences for the Church, the current Vatican apparatus has obstinately pursued the new orientation, which is obviously inconsistent with the expressly Catholic imperatives of the Fatima Message: namely, the establishment of devotion to the Immaculate Heart of Mary in the world, the consecration of Russia to the Immaculate Heart, the conversion of Russia to the Catholic Faith, and the triumph of the Immaculate Heart, accompanied by a period of world peace according to the plans of the Most Sacred Heart of

Jesus in a Catholic social order.

- To the contrary, powerful members of the Vatican apparatus have willfully and deliberately refused to consecrate Russia by name to Mary's Immaculate Heart, but have instead conducted a systematic campaign to neutralize the Message of Fatima in order to subjugate it to the new orientation which they have imposed on much of the Church—*their* new orientation, their Adaptation of the Church to Masonic and Communist ideals—while persecuting loyal Catholics who do not follow the Party Line.

- The Vatican apparatus, led by the Secretary of State, deliberately scorns the prophecies, imperatives and warnings of the Fatima Message in favor of "enlightened" new ecclesial policies, which include not going against any of the provisions of the Vatican-Moscow Agreement (and apparently any of the errors of Russia) and avoiding any claimed "offense" to Russia by a public consecration of that nation.

- In consequence of these monumental errors of judgment, Russia has failed to convert, the Church is suffering an unprecedented crisis of faith and discipline, and the world continues to spiral downward in a cycle of violence and rebellion against God and His Holy Church—in response to which, the Vatican apparatus only redoubles its efforts to follow the utterly fruitless new orientation of the Church.

No wonder Pope Benedict has lamented, in his letter to the bishops concerning the lifting of the "excommunication" of the four bishops of the Society of Saint Pius X, that "in vast areas of the world the faith is in danger of dying out like a flame which no longer has fuel..." No wonder he has "liberated" the Latin Mass from its bogus "prohibition." No wonder he has called for a "hermeneutic of continuity" between Vatican II and the traditional teaching of the Church.

No wonder the Pope declared in September 2009 (as we noted in Chapter 7) that "in the decades following the Second Vatican Council, some interpreted the opening to the world not as a demand of the missionary ardor of the Heart of Christ, but as a passage to secularization," that "certain fundamental truths of the faith, such as sin, grace, theological life, and the last things, were not mentioned anymore," and that the result is—incredible words, coming as they do from the Pope himself—a "secularized ecclesial environment" and "desert without God." And no wonder that, as Pope, the former Cardinal Ratzinger has reconsidered, and (at least in part) disowned, his own revisionist statements nine years ago concerning Fatima, the Immaculate Heart of Mary and the Triumph of the Immaculate Heart as prophesied at Fatima, which he now admits *has yet to occur*.

Could it be that the Pope's moves in favor of Catholic Tradition, however incomplete and tentative they may seem, reflect his own knowledge of the Third Secret and the calamities of which it warns—the same calamities his predecessor, Pius XII, was able to foresee precisely in the light of Fatima? We shall consider this possibility further on.

First, however, we must consider more closely that revisionist interpretation of the Message of Fatima which, despite the new pontificate, continues to weigh upon the Church like a boulder. In particular we must examine its attempt to "neutralize" the Third Secret.

Gorbachev admits that he is still a Leninist, and he continually promotes abortion, population control and his Leninist "principles" through his State of the World Forum. Gorbachev was invited by Cardinal Sodano to sit beside him at the Vatican press conference of June 27, 2000 to promote Cardinal Casaroli's memoirs upholding the Vatican policy of *Ostpolitik*, which refuses to denounce the errors of Communism and state atheism. Pictured above is Gorbachev, invited to the Vatican in November 2000 to address the Pope and other Vatican curial officials and politicians at the "Jubilee of Politicians".

Chapter 10

The "New" Third Secret

In Chapter 8 we discussed how, in keeping with the Church's new post-conciliar "orientation," the Vatican Secretary of State has established a "Party Line" on Fatima according to which a "new" version of the Fatima Message has been substituted for the authentic Message, which is at odds with "ecumenism," "dialogue," "interreligious dialogue," the *Vatican-Moscow Agreement*, and the "updating" of the Church in general, with all the disastrous results these compromises and departures from Catholic Tradition have produced.

In this Chapter we will focus on how the Vatican "commentary" in *The Message of Fatima (TMF)*, published together with the vision of the "Bishop dressed in white" on June 26, 2000, proposes to substitute a "new" Third Secret, stripped of its admonitory and prophetic content and reduced to a mere recollection of things past. In due course we will discuss the developments in 2006-2007, which have shown beyond any doubt that the vision cannot possibly constitute the entirety of the Secret, and that a text containing precious words of the Blessed Virgin has been withheld, as Antonio Socci was forced to conclude. First, however, we must consider the "new" Third Secret advanced in *TMF* under the auspices of the Secretary of State—an office that will come to be occupied by the man who is now the principal protagonist in the Fatima controversy: Cardinal (then Archbishop) Tarcisio Bertone.[283]

The reader should bear with us if confronted with an occasional polemical comment in this more detailed theological exegesis of *TMF*, but we need not apologize for being polemical because polemics are a good thing when necessary. Today's society increasingly substitutes the Catholic Faith and replaces it with faith in the so-called "exact sciences." People of today, therefore, do not value the science and art of polemics whose purpose is to defend the Faith and the Church against the enemies of Christ, Who is the Truth. "*Ho polemos*" is the ancient Greek phrase for war. Nothing is wrong with waging war in defense of Christ and the Catholic Faith; but people who do not have the faith, or if their faith is weakened, will not understand this because they give too much faith to the so-called "exact sciences."

The "Introduction"

Already the second paragraph of the Introduction of *TMF* concerning the Third Secret, written by the future Secretary of State, Archbishop

---

[283] This chapter incorporates the original analysis by the late Father Gregory Hesse, S.T.D., J.C.D., as supplemented by a consideration of developments in the Church since the first edition.

Bertone, contains a piece of Vatican politics that seems to be oblivious of both recent history and Moral Theology:

> The Twentieth Century was one of the most crucial in human history, with its tragic and cruel events culminating in the assassination attempt on the "sweet Christ on earth."

That even an attempt to assassinate the Supreme Pontiff is a heinous crime, no person in his right mind will doubt. It is indeed under the punishment of excommunication, even in the rather liberal Code of Canon Law of 1983. However, the statement shows a tragic lack of proportion. That the "tragic and cruel events" would have been *"culminating"* in the attempt on Pope John Paul II's life, is definitely out of proportion and in grave disregard of Stalin's sixty million victims, plus the victims of all wars of the last century and the fifty-five million victims of abortion every single year! The lack of proportion is infinitely worse in its disregard of the supernatural aspect such as the real "sweet Christ on earth" in the tabernacle, Whose Real Presence is distributed in the hands and dropped on Saint Peter's Square[284] as also happens in thousands of other places. There is a purpose in this statement and it lies in *downplaying the importance of the Third Secret* in *TMF.*

The Introduction of *TMF* states on the next page that "there is only one manuscript, which is here reproduced photographically." This would be a rather misleading, but literal truth, if it is meant that only one of the manuscripts has been photographically reproduced, but in the light of Cardinal Ratzinger's statement, that the Secret has been published in its "entirety" (*TMF*, pp. 32, 39), it has to be considered false. There is a mountain of evidence[285] that there are indeed *two* parts of the Third Secret, the first one being the vision of the "Bishop dressed in White" taken from the archives of the former Holy Office and published on June 26, 2000, and the second one in the Pope's apartment. The evidence is marshaled in compelling fashion in an article by Mr. Andrew Cesanek (cf. Chapter 13 and *The Fatima Crusader*, Issue No. 64). As Mr. Cesanek points out, the published text contains no words of Our Lady. Thus, the Ratzinger/Bertone presentation of the Third Secret lacks credibility.

Without any illicit accusation of a deliberate sin against the Eighth Commandment, we are nevertheless facing the fact of a printed falsehood. As there has been no public statement to the contrary so far, it is impossible to talk about this as simply a mistake as to the number of manuscripts. Who and how many people are involved in this

---

[284] Between 1986 and 1991 several *Sanpietrini*, the uniformed guards in St. Peter's Basilica in Rome, have directly told Father Gregory Hesse (R.I.P., January 25, 2005), the principal author of this chapter (who at that time had been working in the Vatican for ten years), that after almost every single papal Mass in the Square, Sacred Hosts are found on the ground.

[285] Since this book was first published in 2002, there is even much more evidence that there are two different manuscripts which together make up the whole Third Secret. This is proven again and again in *The Secret Still Hidden* by Christopher A. Ferrara and in *The Fourth Secret of Fatima* by Antonio Socci.

falsehood is of no importance, but the published falsehood as such is of a theological importance: even if it *were* only an error, it would affect the entire theological interpretation presented in the document. If it is a falsehood, which is what we firmly believe, then it means that the theological and historical interpretations presented are leading towards a wrong conclusion or message. It affects a lot more than the theology visible in the published commentaries, as we shall see.

It is also of theological importance to see the quotation marks for both the "secret" and "Our Lady." If an "apparition" says that all religions are pleasing to God, which is heresy and blasphemy[286], we should put "Our Lady" in quotation marks, as we know the "apparition" to be someone else, most probably a demon. But to place quotation marks around Our Lady regarding an apparition that has been approved by several Popes and been proven by a definite miracle in front of 70,000 witnesses conveys a message: namely, the possibility that it was not Our Lady after all. As one piece in this jigsaw of truths, half-truths, and falsehoods, this is of great significance.

The following pages of *TMF*'s Introduction reiterate the falsehood that the Consecration has been done, especially p. 8 which cites an unsigned letter by "Sister Lucy" which, as we showed in a previous chapter, is a manifest fake, as shown also by Father Paul Kramer.[287] *The Fatima Crusader* has sufficiently dealt with this falsehood in the past and there is no need for repetitions here. In the present document the old quotations from this fake letter, however, present an explanatory context for the new lies.

Finally, we note again the incredible statement by Archbishop Bertone on p. 9 of the Introduction in *TMF*:

> The decision of His Holiness John Paul II to make public the third part of the "secret" of Fatima brings to an end a period of history marked by tragic human lust for power and evil, yet pervaded by the merciful love of God and the watchful care of the Mother of Jesus and of the Church.

Various articles already published have sufficiently explained the absurdity of this statement in the historical sense.[288] Indeed, historically seen, there can be no reasonable justification for such a statement by anyone. Clearly, this is a complete falsehood, bordering on lunacy. It is so false, so obviously wrong that who in their right mind could ever believe it or expect anyone else to believe it?

Now, the then-Archbishop Bertone, acting at the time as Secretary of the Congregation for the Doctrine of the Faith, is neither out of his mind

---

[286] Only a religion in which one can be saved can be pleasing to God, and there is only one (which is a dogma of the Faith), whence the contrary is heresy and it is also blasphemy, as God, Who is the Truth, cannot be careless about the Truth, whence to state the contrary is blasphemy.

[287] *The Fatima Crusader*, Issue 64, p. 115.

[288] Ibid., pp. 54ff.

nor a lunatic. This statement must, therefore, be of a theological nature. Father Gruner rightly suggested that according to Msgr. Bertone we are supposed to believe that "the so-called 'fall of communism' means that Fatima is no longer relevant to world politics and the conversion of Russia is no longer to be mentioned."[289] This is not only a political interpretation concerning the continuation of Cardinal Casaroli's *Ostpolitik* and Pope John Paul II's relationship to the propagator of genocide, Gorbachev, but it is a clear analysis of a changed theology which is central to the Church's new orientation, a theology called Ecumenism.

For the moment the questions resulting from these observations will have to wait, as that can be understood better in the light of the "theology" of the former Cardinal Ratzinger.

The "Secret"

As far as the authenticity of the published text is concerned, while Father Gruner seems to be convinced of its authenticity,[290] certain questions present themselves: Why did Sister Lucy—who by 1944 had surely read Holy Scripture and many "devotional books," as Cardinal Ratzinger calls them—say that the Holy Father "prayed for the souls of the *corpses* he met on his way" (*cadaveres* in Portuguese)? Throughout the history of salvation one speaks of the "souls of the dead or defunct," as one can find in the Creed (... resurrection of the dead ...). Only in the Old Testament can one find the term "corpse", and it is found in the context of apostates or lost souls.

It is equally strange in the context of the First and the Second Secret that the seer would speak about a "Bishop dressed in White," when the events of 1939 were clearly prophesied with a reference to the pope and even his name: Pius XI. A "Bishop dressed in White" could be the Abbot of Brixen in South Tyrol, any bishop in the tropics, or an impostor in Rome who pretends to be Pope—as the sedevacantists claim. We cannot and shall not venture an answer, but the phrase "Bishop dressed in White" is strangely vague in the historical context of all the events since 1917.

The Interpretation of the "Secret"

A. The Pope's Letter to Sister Lucy

In this letter, dated April 19, 2000, which is cited in *TMF* (p. 27), the Pope says:

> Since on that day [the Beatification of Francisco and Jacinta, May 13, 2000] there will be time only for a brief greeting and not a conversation, I am sending ... Archbishop Bertone ... Archbishop Bertone ... **will come in my name** [sic] to ask certain questions about the interpretation of "the third part of the secret."

---

[289] Ibid., p. 55.
[290] Ibid., p. 18.

We conclude that His Holiness had no time for a conversation with Sister Lucy. The ever-vigilant defender of the late Pope John Paul II might object to this conclusion by reminding us that it is not in our power to advise the Pope about his schedule, nor to challenge his decisions in discipline and Church government, *in rebus ... quae ad disciplinam et regimen Ecclesiae ... pertinent* (D.S. 3060).

This is certainly true. But we are allowed to ask an obvious question: How is it that the Pope's advisors and assistants scheduled His Holiness to receive the Masons of the Trilateral Commission,[291] the aforesaid Mikhail Gorbachev, the Jewish High Masons of the B'nai B'rith,[292] to preach from the pulpit of Rome's Lutheran Church,[293] to visit Rome's Synagogue,[294] to meet with the Buddhist "patriarch" Vasana Tara,[295] the Dalai Lama,[296] and Yasser Arafat,[297] and allowed the schismatic and heretical Patriarch Dimitrios I of Constantinople[298] to stand next to him on the Papal Loggia of St. Peter's Basilica in Rome (!), but they could not find the time to schedule the Pope to talk to Our Lady's personal and perhaps most important of all messengers in the past 100 years?

We do not know the answer and cannot venture to give it, but the theological connection to the Vatican's downplaying the Third Secret is obvious.

B. Cardinal Bertone's Commentary in *TMF*

This unsigned account of an alleged conversation (in April 2000) between Archbishop Bertone and Sister Lucy, commencing on p. 28 of *TMF*, is a remarkable piece of deception, probably written by Archbishop Bertone himself. As Father Paul Kramer rightly pointed out, Msgr. Bertone not only failed to ask Sister Lucy if the Consecration of Russia had been done, but he also juxtaposes two logically separate statements, namely Sister Lucy's affirmation that the figure in white was a Pope, although she *does not know the name* (!), and her agreement with Pope John Paul II's claim that it was "a mother's hand that guided the bullet's path" on May 13, 1981.[299]

There were many rather strange coincidences—or was it Providence?—in Ali Agca's assassination attempt, to consider a non-theological digression:

- Why did the gun jam after the third shot? It is not unusual for a semi-automatic pistol to jam, but it is almost impossible that Italy's best

---

[291] Daniel Le Roux, *Petrus liebst du mich?* (Stuttgart, 1990). *Peter, Lovest Thou Me?*, p. 110. The skeptic will find that I only referred to pictures which can be easily found in the English translation published by Instauratio Press, Yarra Junction, Australia, 1988.

[292] Ibid., p. 112.

[293] Ibid., p. 127.

[294] Ibid., p. 155.

[295] Ibid., p. 172.

[296] Ibid., p. 177.

[297] Ibid., p. 236.

[298] Ibid., p. 144.

[299] *The Fatima Crusader,* Issue 64, p. 31.

police force, the *Carabinieri*, would not find the cause after weeks of microscopic examination in their laboratories. Was it the Guardian Angel's interference? That would be theologically highly probable.

- Why did Ali Agca not use hollow point bullets or the readily available *Federal Hydra-Shok* ammunition which would have accomplished his purpose to assassinate the Pope? Most sources claim that some organization or secret service was behind the attack. Were they all amateurs?

- Why did he choose St. Peter's Square and a small handgun, with no chance to escape, why not a rifle (easily available back then) and one of the many elevated positions around St. Peter's Square with at least a chance to escape? Was he just a dumb fanatic?

Probably, we will not know the truth about that day in our lifetime, but we do know the truth that this attempt to assassinate the Pope has nothing to do with the Third Secret, *because he was **not** killed*. The event was tragic, but it cost the Pope in his full activities less than one year—out of more than twenty-five. It is an insult to Divine Providence and to Our Lady to claim that this *relatively* unimportant event would be at the core of a prophecy about hell, two World Wars, Communism, and the punishment still to come.

Finally, we must ask: Why would the 1981 incident be better understood after 1960, as Sister Lucy said the Third Secret would be? Anyone in the 20th Century would have understood it as we do. Would the generation that had fought in World War II and in Korea have better understood the role of soldiers in this vision only *after* 1960? Sister Lucy's insistence on disclosure in the year 1960, that "Our Lady wishes it so", can only mean that Lucy knew something was going to happen around 1960 or shortly after that would make the Secret clearly understandable as a prophecy of future events. The Secret clearly has no connection with the assassination of President Kennedy, but what about John XXIII's encyclical *Pacem in Terris*, published in 1963, or Vatican II which was opened in 1962, *but announced January 25, 1959*?

C. The "Announcement made by Cardinal Angelo Sodano ..."

The deception continues in the Secretary of State's statement that the text of the Third Secret must be interpreted "in a symbolic key". (*TMF*, p. 30) The purpose of this suggestion becomes evident when Cardinal Sodano distorts the actual vision by saying: "He [the Pope] too falls to the ground, apparently dead." As we discussed in a previous chapter, the words "apparently dead" are the exact contrary to Sister Lucy's word "killed."

This is followed by pushing the message into the past, be it by pointing at the event in 1981 or with the ridiculous declaration that 1989 ended Communism and the spreading of atheism. Gorbachev's "glasnost" and "perestroika" have been sufficiently dealt with in various issues of *The Fatima Crusader* and there is no need to repeat these analyses here. It is sad to see, however, that Cardinal Sodano, the former Secretary of State, does not shrink from using a decade-old lie to debunk a message from Our Lady.

D. Cardinal Ratzinger's "Theological Commentary"

i) Introductory Downplay

The very second line of this Commentary (*TMF*, p. 32) already contains the claim that the "so-called third 'Secret' of Fatima" has been "published here in its entirety." This falsehood is repeated later on (*TMF*, p. 39). The quoted article by Andrew Cesanek produces sufficient proof that this is false (see Chapter 13). We will deal with this deception at the conclusion of this chapter.

The next statement is cynical to say the least:

> No great mystery is revealed: nor is the future unveiled. We see the Church of the martyrs of the century which has just passed represented in a scene described in a language which is symbolic and not easy to decipher.[300]

If no great mystery is revealed, then why did Our Lady bother to make it a secret in the first place? Possibly—as we shall see later— the future is revealed in the other part of the Third Secret which has evidently been withheld from us, the part which contains the words of Our Lady following "In Portugal the dogma of the Faith will always be preserved etc." In any case, to claim that the vision of soldiers shooting the Pope dead is merely a symbol of the past, especially in the connection with the unusually clear messages of the rest of the Fatima Message, is preposterous.

In comparison to most prophecies—one thinks of the difficulties in interpreting the Apocalypse—the secrets of Fatima are indeed unusually clear and to the point; why would the Third Secret be "symbolic and not easy to decipher"? Why would the *Twentieth* Century end in nineteen hundred and ninety-nine?

In the year 1900 Kaiser Wilhelm II of Germany *decreed* this to be the beginning of the Twentieth Century, which is mathematically impossible. It would seem that the former Cardinal Ratzinger's mathematics, as well as his theology, was dependent on authority instead of the truth. To say this is not to engage in "cheap polemics" in the light of a rather remarkable change of mind between 1984 and 2000. In 1984, when discussing the content of the Third Secret, Cardinal Ratzinger spoke of "the absolute importance of history", "the last times" and "religious prophecy" and said:

> ... but the things contained in this third secret correspond to

---

[300] Joseph Cardinal Ratzinger, "Theological Commentary", *The Message of Fatima* (*TMF*), June 26, 2000, p. 32.

what is announced in Sacred Scripture and are confirmed by many other Marian apparitions themselves in their known contents.[301]

Cardinal Ratzinger's statement of 1984 is in direct contradiction to his downplaying of the Third Secret, sixteen years later, in *TMF*. Father Paul Kramer[302] collects the most important Marian messages from the other Marian apparitions on this point. They are quite frightening, and certainly—at least in a part of the prophecy—predict events yet to come.

We are once again faced with the same basic tenor of the entire publication, which trivializes the Third Secret into an insignificant prediction of a failed attempt on the Holy Father's life. May we call the failed attempt on Pope John Paul II's life an "insignificant" prediction? Yes! We have said so already and it is the truth: The attempt *failed*, and even if it had killed the Pope, this would have had nothing to do with the Third Secret. In Roman dialect we say: *"Morto un Papa, se ne fa un'altro"*: with the death of a Pope, another one is elected.

Another point arises: Why has nobody in the Vatican bothered to suggest that the Third Secret may deal with the untimely death of Pope John Paul I? Was he a completely insignificant figure? No Pope is, but God never *knew* the future—He *knows*. The failed attempt on a Pope's life is indeed "no great mystery" as the former Cardinal Ratzinger formulated it, but the actual—and quite mysterious—death of a Pope had been conveniently forgotten.

The prophecy and the three seers' comments make it abundantly clear "that the Holy Father will have much to suffer." In the context of *two* world wars and—as we shall see—much worse, it borders on idolatry to enhance one Pope's importance to the point of making a few months in the hospital *the* Third Secret. What John Paul II had to suffer in Rome's Gemelli Hospital is something that one would not even wish to contemplate. However, with today's medicine, the Pope's suffering at that time does not even compare to the average priest's fate in the Nazi concentration camps—not to mention the fate of many more priests and bishops behind the Iron Curtain.

Most telling of all, if the Third Secret predicts only that a Pope will survive an assassination attempt, then why did the then-Cardinal Ratzinger say in 1984 that the Secret had not been disclosed to avoid "confusing religious prophecy with *sensationalism*"? What would be sensational in 1984 about a prophecy concerning a *failed* assassination attempt that had taken place three years earlier? Obviously, nothing. The former Cardinal Ratzinger's June 26, 2000 version of the Third Secret is what the lawyers call a recent fabrication. The "sensational" content he had in mind in 1984 clearly could not have been the 1981 assassination attempt.

---

[301] *The Fatima Crusader*, Issue 64, pp. 34ff.
[302] Ibid., pp. 115ff.

ii) On Public and Private Revelations

Cardinal Ratzinger significantly set, at that time, the entire phenomenon of Fatima in the context of "private revelations"—one ought to call them either "fake" or "extraordinary," depending on their authenticity. Cardinal Ratzinger stated that the Message of Fatima, like all "private revelations" approved as authentic by Church authorities, "can be a genuine help in understanding the Gospel and living it better at a particular moment in time; therefore it should not be disregarded. It is a help which is offered, but *which one is not obliged to use.*" In other words, according to the then-Cardinal Ratzinger, no one in the Church is obliged to follow the Message of Fatima—not the Pope, not the bishops, not the priests, not the members of the laity. Fatima—including the consecration of Russia and the Five First Saturdays devotion—is purely optional. If we prefer, we can simply ignore it completely—as if the Miracle of the Sun had never happened; as if the requests of the Virgin of Fatima had been made by a ghost! Fatima is a mere "help" that we can take or leave at our pleasure.

One of the most erudite Popes in history, Benedict XIV, rightly says that these revelations cannot be held with the assent of Faith, but "rather an assent of human faith in keeping with the requirements of prudence which puts them before us as probable and credible to piety." But Cardinal Ratzinger's quotation of Pope Benedict seems to ignore what is so extraordinary about Fatima, and what takes it out of the category of other "private" revelations: the astounding Miracle of the Sun that proves Fatima to be a bit more than just "credible to piety."

The former Cardinal Ratzinger took this approach, it seems, with all of the extraordinary revelations of the past centuries. For example, he reduced the extraordinary revelations about the Corpus Christi Feast and the Sacred Heart to St. Margaret Mary Alacoque to an event that merely had an "*effect* even on the liturgy." This borders on blasphemy when we consider the fate of France after Louis XIV's and his two successors' impertinent and disastrous refusal to obey the request of Christ for the consecration of France to the Sacred Heart, conveyed to St. Margaret Mary in the same "private" revelations.[303]

Cardinal Ratzinger's erroneous conception of prophecy is clear in the following statement:

> ... it should be kept in mind that prophecy in the biblical sense does not mean to predict the future but to explain the will of God for the present, and therefore show the right path to take for the future. A person who foretells what is going to happen responds to the curiosity of the mind, which wants to draw back the veil on the future.

---

[303] See Bishop Emile Bougaud, *The Life of Saint Margaret Mary Alacoque* (originally published by Benzinger, 1890; republished by TAN Books and Publishers, 1990), Chapter XIV, "The Last Grand Revelation—The King of France, 1689".

This is tantamount to a denial of *all* prophecy, which is commonly called one of the highest of all freely given graces, the *gratiae gratis datae*. Prophecy often involves the correct interpretation of the past and the present, but is as such understood as a prediction of the future. Either Isaias, David, Christ, and St. Paul "responded to the curiosity of the mind" and the Church Fathers and many Doctors of the Church just wanted "to draw back the veil of the future," or Cardinal Ratzinger is wrong. May we leave the answer to you?

Perhaps Cardinal Ratzinger reduced prophecy to "the signs of the times" because (at least before he became Pope) he failed to see the real signs of the times, namely: empty churches, heresy, apostasy, blasphemy, sexual perversion and impurity, neo-paganism, and in fact, a total disagreement among many bishops and priests on anything in the Catholic Church. The only thing agreed upon among the leading powers in the Vatican is to hate traditional Catholic theology, which is scorned by them, along with the whole idea of the conversion of Russia to the Catholic Faith—again, the very conflict of ecclesial world views which gave rise to the very grave injustice we are discussing here; namely, the *de facto* suppression of the full Fatima Message from being heard and complied with, thereby imminently endangering literally billions of persons' lives and souls.

Cardinal Ratzinger seemed to think these real signs of the times have nothing to do with that event known as the Second Vatican Council, wherein it is claimed that the Holy Spirit came a second time. That is obviously false, as we can see from the Council's bitter fruits. As Our Lord said, "By their fruits you shall know them." (Matt. 7:16)

As Pope Benedict, however, the former Cardinal has come to recognize, as we noted in Chapter 7, that "in vast areas of the world the faith is in danger of dying out like a flame which no longer has fuel...", that "in the decades following the Second Vatican Council, some interpreted the opening to the world not as a demand of the missionary ardor of the Heart of Christ, but as a passage to secularization....", that "certain fundamental truths of the faith, such as sin, grace, theological life, and the last things, were not mentioned anymore [and] they were unconsciously caught up in the self-secularization of many ecclesial communities; these, hoping to please those who did not come [instead] saw the members they already had [then] leave deprived and disapppointed..." and that the result is a "secularized ecclesial environment" and—what an admission!—a "desert without God" in the very midst of the Catholic world. Stunning and bitter results of Vatican II—it is hard to imagine Our Lady of Fatima would have overlooked them and not try to warn us of them. Perhaps an explicit admission of a connection between this disaster and the Council will not be long in coming. At any rate, Pope Benedict's remarks throw cold water on the "enlightened" ones who still speak disparagingly of the "alarmism" of the "Fatimists," including those involved in the writing of this book.

To return to the unfortunate commentary in *TMF*, however, we may be accused of "polemics," but in the light of Christ's teaching and especially the Church's teaching on prophecy and the importance that St. Paul and the Church Fathers attributed to this divine gift, *TMF's* view of prophecy borders on heresy and blasphemy, to say the least. To reduce everything between the Psalms and Saint John Bosco or Fatima to a "responding to the curiosity of the mind" is tantamount to declaring Holy Scripture, the Church Fathers, Tradition, and almost all extraordinary revelation of the future as a sort of clerical Rainbow Press on the level of the lowest publication at the local supermarket's cash register. The implication that the future predictions of divine prophecies are merely objects of idle human curiosity is an insult to God and the Saints; and this cannot ever be taken lightly. On p. 38 of *TMF* Cardinal Ratzinger again refers to Cardinal Sodano's trivializing the significance of the vision:

> [they] do not describe photographically the details of future events, but synthesize and compress against a single background of events, facts which extend through time in an unspecified succession and duration.

That all of these events are in the past and no great mystery is the evident message of these eminent Cardinals.

It should be noted that Pope Benedict XVI, on May 13, 2007 in the National Marian Shrine of Aparecida in Brazil, stated that Fatima is the most prophetic message of the 20th Century. This public statement may be in reparation for his former trivializing Fatima and its prophetic message, but still the Church suffers to this day with not taking the Fatima prophecies of annihilation and many souls going to hell seriously enough.

iii) Cardinal Ratzinger's "Attempt to Interpret ..."

The first question that arises here concerns Cardinal Ratzinger's surprise. In *TMF* (p. 39) he states that the Virgin's message that devotion to Her Immaculate Heart is the way to salvation is surprising to "the Anglo-Saxon and German cultural world." Why does Cardinal Ratzinger say this? Have the English and the Germans not heard about the Sacred Heart,[304] St. Margaret Mary Alacoque, and St. Philip Benitius, let alone Pope Leo XIII, or are they too intelligent to fall for such an Italian or Spanish romanticism? Does the sober German tell his girl: "I love you with all my brain!", or would a determined Englishman communicate his passion with a dry reference to his faculty of the will? What is the purpose of such ludicrous statements? The answer may lie in the lines

---

[304] In the 13ᵗʰ Century, St. Gertrude, a German, was a "herald of the Sacred Heart". See *St. Gertrude the Great*, published by the Benedictine Convent of Clyde, Missouri, republished by TAN Books and Publishers in 1979, pp. 26ff. Thus we do not understand why the "German cultural world" would find anything strange about Devotion to the Sacred Heart or the Immaculate Heart.

that follow this incomprehensible "surprise" of the Cardinal's.

Cardinal Ratzinger's "attempt to interpret the 'secret' of Fatima" completely fails to interpret what is not the secret as such anyway, as this has not been revealed, but he ends up discrediting the Immaculate Conception Herself. This eminent prince of the Church seemed to have forgotten when Our Lady appeared at Lourdes She did not introduce Herself as "Immaculately Conceived," but rather said: "I am *the* Immaculate Conception." Only She, among all mere creatures, has ever been conceived without Original Sin *and* has never committed a sin. Only Her Heart—referring to the third faculty of the soul, not the internal organ but the heart which St. Thomas Aquinas calls the *sensus communis*—therefore, is the Immaculate Heart. Cardinal Ratzinger inflates this term, reserved to the Mother of God, to include any "heart, which, with God's grace, has come to perfect interior unity and therefore 'sees God.'" He actually abuses the Gospel with his interpretation by citing Matthew 5:8, which only says: "Blessed are the clean of heart: for they shall see God." Christ talks about the clean of heart, not "perfect interior unity" and certainly not the only Immaculate Heart. If we follow this implicit denial of the exclusiveness of the Immaculate Heart by attributing it to all who are "clean of heart," then we might as well arrive at the logical conclusion that all priests have sacred hearts, as they are consecrated an *alter Christus* (another Christ), which might account for their Latin title of *Reverendus* (to be revered). But to say all priests have sacred hearts would be blasphemous, which is exactly what one ought to think of trivializing the Immaculate Heart.

Even the 'typically Protestant' objection "that we should not place a human being between ourselves and Christ" is answered by Cardinal Ratzinger in apparent ignorance of Our Lady: he quotes St. Paul's exhortation to "imitate" him, instead of explaining that it was Our Lord Himself Who placed a mere human being between Himself and us by making His Mother the *Mediatrix* of all graces!

Sister Lucy finally was discredited as a seer when Cardinal Ratzinger said that the vision incorporates images which she "may have seen in devotional books".[305] This is tantamount to declaring the whole vision a product of fantasy, and fits snugly into the plan of dissolving Fatima "into nothing more than generic Catholic piety and platitudes, involving events that are over and done with," as Father Gruner in his article so aptly describes the Bertone/Ratzinger commentary (*TMF*).[306]

As we discussed in a previous chapter, the last page of *TMF* again declares everything in the Secret to be part of the past, including Our Lady's words: "My Immaculate Heart will triumph"—from which the Cardinal removes the words *In the end*. He reduces all of Fatima to "the *fiat* of Mary, the word of Her heart, [that] has changed the history of

---

[305] Joseph Cardinal Ratzinger, "Theological Commentary", *The Message of Fatima*, p. 42.
[306] *The Fatima Crusader*, Issue 64, p. 51.

the world".[307] This seems to be an effort to eliminate Fatima entirely from the scene.

iv) A Warning from Scripture

TMF's "liquidation" of the Message of Fatima reminds us of Our Lord's admonition to His disciples to "Take heed and beware of the leaven of the Pharisees and Sadducees." (Mt. 16:6) At first the disciples, who were eating bread at the moment, did not understand. What did this talk of leaven in bread have to do with the Pharisees? Soon, however, they grasped Our Lord's meaning: "Then they understood that He had not said that they should beware of the leaven of bread, but of the *doctrine* of the Pharisees and Sadducees." (Mt. 16:12)

As Archbishop Alban Goodier, S.J. explained in his classic commentary on this passage in Scripture, Our Lord was teaching the disciples to be on their guard against the *subtleties* of the Pharisees, which were far more dangerous than any open opposition to Christ:

> It was not so much their opposition that He feared for His own, it was their [the Pharisees'] *subtlety*. Before the Pharisees had blamed Him for His miracles and other good deeds; He knew that this would not take His friends away from Him. Now this morning they [the Pharisees] had come, with an affected simplicity, a show of desire to know the truth, an appeal to the *prophets, a zeal for tradition, a respect for law and order and obedience to the powers that be*; and all this, He knew, would be likely to affect His own *more than any open enmity*. Like leaven, unless they were careful, it would spread unconsciously among them.[308]

The Virgin of Fatima, like Our Lord Himself, was quite straightforward in Her message. But the former Cardinal's commentary obscures the simplicity of God's truth. And by the time the Cardinal had finished with his "tribute" to Fatima, nothing seems to be left of it. According to *TMF*, the matter is all very *subtle*—so subtle that it vanishes.

But the apparitions at Fatima are not so subtle. They were given to little children, who could not read, for the edification and guidance of the wise and the learned of this world, including theologians at the Vatican. Either Our Lady appeared at Fatima or She did not. Either She gave a distinct message to the children, which they could remember and repeat just as they had heard it, or She did not. Either She intended this message to be passed on to the world or She did not. Either She insured that Her message would be accurately transmitted or She did not. Either She guaranteed beyond any shadow of reasonable doubt, by the Miracle of the Sun, that it was indeed She, the Queen of Heaven and Earth, Who came, Who spoke and Who commanded, or She did not. The answer in each case is, obviously, that She did, for She is the Mother of God.

---

[307] Joseph Cardinal Ratzinger, "Theological Commentary", *The Message of Fatima*, p. 43.
[308] Archbishop Goodier, S.J., *The Public Life of Our Lord Jesus Christ*, Vol. I, (Burns Oates & Washbourne Ltd., London, England, 1932) p. 462.

Like the disciples in their encounter with the Pharisees, we must be on guard against Pharisaical subtleties which have spread like poisonous leaven through the Church over the past forty years. Now the latter day leaven of the Pharisees seeks to penetrate the Message of Fatima. The Pharisees of old were dangerous precisely because they seemed to have a genuine respect for the truth. Today a feigned respect for the Message of Fatima conceals its most determined opponents.

Conclusion

In one of the stranger events in an already very strange post-conciliar Church, we are faced with quite a few questions which arise from the unorthodox comments on the vision in the Third Secret provided by *TMF*:

- Why are the actual words of Our Lady, the real Third Secret, written down on a single sheet—and most probably still in the papal safe—withheld from the public? Why do they pretend in public that these words do not even exist?

- Why is the published vision, which obviously deals with the murder of a Pope in the future by public execution by a band of soldiers, associated with the 1981 attempt on John Paul II's life which failed?

- Why is the falsehood that the Consecration of Russia has been done repeated?

- Why the absurd statement that: "The decision of His Holiness Pope John Paul II to make public the third part of the 'secret' of Fatima *brings to an end a period of history marked by tragic human lust for power and evil*"?

- Why did the late Pope's assistants and advisors make His Holiness available for hundreds of political meetings but made available virtually no time for Sister Lucy?

- Why is the lie about the fall of Communism in 1989 repeated?[309]

- Why is the Secret, long kept secret, belittled as "no great mystery," and reduced to symbolism?

- Why is prophecy's prediction of the future denied?

- Why is the Immaculate Heart belittled and equated with the "clean of heart"?

- Why is the unchangeable future—and with it God's Providence—denied, at least implicitly?

- Why is Sister Lucy's vision belittled by mentioning "devotional books" as the possible source?

---

[309] Cardinal Sodano, on May 13, 2000 at Fatima, said in his speech: "The successive events of 1989 led, both in the Soviet Union and in a number of countries of Eastern Europe, to the fall of the Communist regimes which promoted atheism." This false statement has been disproven over and over again in *The Fatima Crusader* in the years following 1989.

- Why do the prelates fail to explain the line "In Portugal the dogma of the Faith will always be preserved *etc.*"?

- What is the purpose of publishing the vision of the Third Secret in the first place, when the words of Our Lady are withheld and the vision reduced to nothingness?

Whenever we are faced with any kind of sin, such as a lie, we have to ask the question: *Cui bono?*—to whose benefit?

The evidence points to one answer for all these questions. The Vatican's fabrications and incoherencies about the Third Secret and Fatima as such, cannot be a silly play by a few bored prelates. *There must be an important purpose to the fabrications that can be unmasked with no great difficulty. Why risk this exposure, unless for an important purpose?*

As it is evident that the Third Secret is not abused to predict some politically correct or convenient visions for the future, but—on the contrary—is reduced to the past *and* deprived of any real importance, *the only purpose of the entire act of publication must be a strategic diversion from the actual words of Our Lady: a vision and a prophecy are turned into deception or—as the intelligence communities like to call it—perception management.*

This answer is far from being a mere speculation. Every piece of evidence we have discussed so far, including the Third Secret vision itself and other approved apparitions referred to by Cardinal Ratzinger himself in 1984, points to the conclusion that the Third Secret *in its entirety* must include words of Our Lady withheld from the public.

There cannot be many reasons for withholding part of a message from Our Lady, if ever. It would be hardly conceivable that the part withheld is so terrifying as to cause panic. Possibly the message might be too symbolic to comprehend, as might be the case with a few lines in the Apocalypse. A third possibility is that the message is quite clear and explicit, but highly embarrassing for the ones who hold power over its publication.

It seems evident that the first two possibilities are out of character with Fatima and most Marian apparitions, which leads us to the third possibility as our conclusion: *The Vatican has something to hide that would be extremely embarrassing.* We recall the testimony of Father Joaquin Alonso, who for sixteen years was the official archivist of Fatima:

> It is therefore completely probable that the text makes concrete references to the crisis of faith within the Church and to the negligence of the pastors themselves [and the] internal struggles in the very bosom of the Church and of grave pastoral negligence of the upper hierarchy.[310]

This is entirely congruent with the 1846 apparition and message

---

[310] Father Joaquin Alonso, *La Verdad sobre el Secreto de Fatima,* (Centro Mariano, Madrid, Spain, 1976) p. 73. In *The Whole Truth About Fatima* - Vol. III, p. 704. See also *The Fatima Crusader*, Issue 64, p. 121.

of Our Lady at La Salette, the apparition of 1634 of Our Lady of Good Success, Quito, and a few others. And possibly we might know the actual text of the Third Secret: There is the story of some years ago of a supposedly reliable French priest who heard a supernatural message, while listening to a recording in a sort of Oratory. He claims to have heard the following lines:

> There will be a wicked council planned and prepared that will change the face of the Church. Many will lose the Faith and confusion will reign everywhere. The sheep will in vain search for their shepherds. A schism will tear apart the tunic of My Son.— This will be the end of times, announced in the Holy Scriptures and recalled to memory by Me in many places. The abomination of abominations will reach its peak and it will bring the chastisement announced in La Salette. My Son's arm, which I will not be able to hold back anymore, will punish this poor world, which has to expiate its crimes.—One will not talk but about wars and revolutions. The elements of nature will be unchained and will cause anguish, even with the best (the most courageous). The Church will bleed from all Her wounds. Blessed are they who will persevere and search for refuge in My Heart, because in the end My Immaculate Heart will triumph.

Of course, there is absolutely no proof for the authenticity of this text. We must not claim this to be the real Third Secret. However, it makes a great deal more sense than anything contained in the Vatican's "interpretation" of the visional part of the Third Secret.

The heresies and the apostasy following Vatican II are of such a tragic and widespread importance that common sense demands that we believe this to be the Third Secret, or part of it. Is it possible that Our Lady knew about the end of World War I, the beginning of World War II under Pius XI, Russia spreading her errors, Russia being the instrument of chastisement, a future Pope being shot by soldiers, but nothing about the cataclysmic developments in the Church beginning with Vatican II, an event that spiritually pales all wars into insignificance? We have already mentioned that no less than Pope Paul VI said:

> The Church finds Herself in an hour of unrest, of self-critique, one might say, even of auto-destruction! It is like an internal, acute, and complicated revolution, for which no one was prepared after the Council. (Dec. 7, 1968)

He also mentioned "the smoke of Satan" that had entered the Church. Even Paul VI, who found himself at the center of the crisis, perceived the disaster to a point. And we have already mentioned the recent and quite devastating admissions about the crisis by the former Cardinal Ratzinger, speaking now as Pope. Is it conceivable that Our Lady of Fatima had nothing to say about this unprecedented situation in the Church, when even the former Cardinal Ratzinger admitted, the Third Secret of Fatima speaks of "dangers threatening the faith and the life of the Christian, and therefore of the world"? Clearly it is impossible for Our Lady not to have mentioned the present-day apostasy and its causes!

And so while there is no proof—we say it again—for the authenticity of the above-quoted message the French priest claims to have received, there is no logical alternative to the Third Secret being *something* along these lines. This can only mean that there is a text pertaining to the Third Secret which the Vatican has yet to disclose—a text that follows the words about the dogma of the Faith being preserved in Portugal. We will discuss the contents of this text in Chapters 12 and 13; and then, in Chapter 14, we will review the explosive developments that have confirmed its existence beyond any doubt. But first we must consider in detail that famous and quite strange "interview" of Sister Lucy by a highly placed Vatican functionary—the prelate who would go on to conduct a virtual one-man public relations campaign in defense of the Secretary of State's Party Line on Fatima, including a book and a series of television and radio appearances whose aim was to control the damage caused by overwhelming evidence of a Vatican cover-up of the missing text. We mean the co-author of *TMF* and now the Cardinal Secretary of State himself: Tarcisio Bertone.

Father Caillon (left) said, "An order came from Rome, obliging everyone to say and think: 'The Consecration is done. The Pope [John Paul II] having done all that he can, Heaven has deigned to agree to this gesture.'" It was around this time, 1988-1989, that many Fatima Apostolates who had insisted that the Consecration of Russia had not been done suddenly began asserting that the 1984 consecration fulfilled the desires of Heaven (see pages 112 and 354-355).

Chapter 11

Muzzling and Hiding the Witness

Few revelations have been as unconvincing as the Vatican's version of the Third Secret of Fatima. Those who thought, or hoped, that publication of the vision of the "Bishop dressed in white" and the commentary in the CDF's *The Message of Fatima (TMF)* ended matters were probably surprised by the tumult that followed. There should be no surprise, however. For over forty years nearly every tactic—silence, intimidation, bad theology, disinformation—has been used to bury the real Message of Fatima. Among these tactics: the imposition of silence on Sister Lucy for forty-five years; the suppression of Father Alonso's 5,396 documents on Fatima; a virtual campaign by the Vatican Secretary of State to prevent public events promoting the authentic Fatima Message, including baseless threats of suspension and even excommunication directed at Father Nicholas Gruner, the most successful and determined public advocate for Fatima; and the promotion of Fatima "experts" who distort and falsify the Message in order to conform it to the Vatican Party Line that "Fatima belongs to the past."

Yet the cork keeps bobbing to the surface. On May 16, 2001, Mother Angelica of the Eternal Word Television Network made a declaration on live TV that reflected the growing skepticism of millions of Catholics the world over:

> "As for the Secret, well *I happen to be one of those individuals who thinks we didn't get the whole thing. I told ya!* I mean, you have the right to your own opinion, don't you, Father? There, you know, that's my opinion. *Because I think it's scary.*"

There could have been nothing more embarrassing to the Vatican's "official version" of the Secret than this remark by a world-renowned nun whose loyalty to Church authority was beyond question and who could not be dismissed as "one of those Fatimists." Mother Angelica had committed the unpardonable crime of going against the Party Line and so, by December 2001, "Mother Angelica Live"—that is, her regularly programmed, live, spontaneous broadcasts shown every week—were yanked off the air. Since December 2001, never again has she been on the air live!

The terrorist attacks on September 11, 2001 triggered a chain reaction of Fatima stories. The buzz in the press and on the Internet was that the attacks were part of the Third Secret of Fatima, which had still not been fully revealed. How exasperating for the drafters of *TMF*, who insist the entire secret of Fatima is contained inside its covers. They simply are not believed, in part because they are not believable, but also because of a certain collective awareness, a shared sense of our impending doom. Deep down we know that a "civilization of love" is utopian nonsense. It has never existed. The real Message of Fatima implicitly confirms this: hell is real and many souls are going there because there is no one to pray and make sacrifices for them. Heaven's remedy is *not* the well-publicized inter-religious prayer meetings, but the consecration and conversion of Russia, devotion to the Immaculate Heart of Mary, and the Rosary. The real Message of Fatima is not a request for more papal apologies. It is a plea to Jesus to "forgive us our sins," to "save us from the fires of hell". We are not experiencing the new advent of humanity. We are on the Titanic as it slides into the blackness, and the world senses the impending doom even as it continues to heap judgment on itself.

Yet not even the events of September 11, 2001 had deterred the Vatican apparatus from continuing to promote Sodano's Party Line that Fatima "belongs to the past." On the contrary, the effort to impose the Sodano Interpretation of Fatima on the Church only intensified, as if Cardinal Sodano, *et al.* had recognized that the events of September 11 might actually jolt Catholics into an awareness that—just a moment!— Fatima is *not* finished, because we are obviously not witnessing anything like the triumph of the Immaculate Heart and the promised period of peace. Some sort of bold action to reassert the Party Line was needed.

On September 12, 2001, literally within hours of the fall of the Twin Towers, the Vatican Press Office released its top bulletin for the day: a "Declaration" from the Congregation for the Clergy concerning, not the terrorist attacks, not the horrendous scandals erupting almost daily from the ranks of the priesthood, not the profusion of heresy and disobedience among the clergy over the past forty years, but Father Nicholas Gruner, "the Fatima priest." The "Declaration" stated that it had been issued "by mandate of *a* higher authority"—Vatican-speak for then Secretary of State, Cardinal Sodano, not the Pope (who is *the* highest authority).

The "Declaration" warned the entire Catholic world about a serious threat to the good of the Church; a threat of such magnitude that the Congregation for the Clergy could not even wait until the dust had settled over the former Twin Towers. The threat consisted of *a conference on world peace and Fatima* in Rome, sponsored by Father Gruner's apostolate.

Yes, the Vatican's top priority within hours of the worst terrorist attack in world history was to tell everyone to shun a conference on world peace and Fatima. Why? Because, said the "Declaration", the conference "does not enjoy the approval of legitimate ecclesiastical authority." Of course, the issuer of the "Declaration" knew quite well that no "approval" for conferences of clergy and laity is necessary under Church law. The Code of Canon Law promulgated by Pope John Paul II (Canons 212, 215, 278, 299) recognizes the natural right of the faithful to meet and discuss issues of concern in the Church today without any "approval" by anyone. Indeed, the Vatican issues no announcements about the lack of "approval" for innumerable conferences conducted by advocates of women's ordination and uncountable other heresies, even though the participants in these conferences are abusing their natural right and causing grave harm to the Church. One might as well say that the apostolate's Rome conference had not been approved by the American Medical Association. What of it?

But that was not the worst of it. The "Declaration" also stated that Father Gruner had been "suspended" by the Bishop of Avellino. Suspended for *what*? For nothing, apparently, since no grounds were stated. The reason for this curious omission was clear to anyone with a knowledge of Father Gruner's canonical proceedings: the "grounds" were so flimsy that to state them publicly would be to invite laughter.

As we have already noted, the only pretext ever given for the "suspension" was that Father Gruner must return to Avellino, Italy (where he was ordained in 1976) or be suspended. Why? Because he had "failed" to find another bishop to incardinate him. But the "Declaration" failed to mention that three successive friendly bishops had offered to incardinate Father Gruner with express permission to continue his apostolate, and that all three incardinations had been blocked (or declared "non-existent") by the same Vatican bureaucrats who had now announced the resulting "suspension". That is, Father Gruner had been "suspended" for failing to "obey" an order *his accusers themselves had prevented him from obeying*. (Not to mention that the Bishop of Avellino by September 12, 2001 had absolutely no authority over Father Gruner—since Father Gruner was now incardinated in another diocese.)

Nearly forty years after the "springtime" of Vatican II began, the Consecration of Russia—not the world, not "youth in search of meaning," not "the unemployed," but *Russia*—remains undone. The world is convulsed by regional wars, Islamic terrorism and the holocaust of abortion, as it becomes clearer by the hour that we are heading for an apocalypse. The Islamic fundamentalists, whom Vatican diplomats now like to call "our Muslim brothers", hate us and wish to subjugate or kill us in accordance with the dictates of their Koran. After forty years of utterly useless "ecumenical dialogue," the Protestant sects are even more decrepit than when they began, and the Orthodox are more adamant than ever in rejecting submission to the Vicar of Christ. The Church is gravely wounded by heresy and scandal in dioceses throughout the world, where She has lost all credibility because of the corruption of Her human members. The new orientation of Vatican II is a total debacle; a ruinous failure. Yet in the midst of all this death, chaos, heresy, scandal, and apostasy, all now reaching their respective apogees, the Vatican had considered it imperative—right *now!*—to alert the world to the "menace" of Father Nicholas Gruner.

So, one day after September 11, 2001, Father Gruner—who had committed no offense against faith and morals, who had kept his vows for the entire 25 years of his priesthood, who had not molested any altar boys or women, who had not stolen any money or preached any heresy—was publicly condemned before the entire Church in a so-called "Declaration" that gave no grounds for the condemnation, and which cited the "mandate" of an anonymous "higher authority" who did not even have the courage to name himself. In the living memory of the Church, nothing like this had ever happened to a faithful Catholic priest. The Secretary of State's obsession with destroying Father Gruner—symbol of resistance to the Party Line—had reached the level of obscenity.

Why? It could only be a deep-seated antipathy toward the Message of Fatima and all that it implies for the new orientation of the Church, which Cardinal Sodano (friend of Gorbachev) and his collaborators implement so unswervingly. Fatima, it seems, alarms them more than the current state of the Church and the world. And yet the state of the Church and the world would surely change radically for the better if only Father Gruner's persecutors would simply *do* what Our Lady requested at Fatima: "If My requests are granted, many souls will be saved and there will be peace."

But Cardinal Sodano had surely miscalculated. The issuance of this baseless condemnation of "the Fatima priest" within hours of September 11 had such a stink about it that many who might otherwise have been disposed to accept the "Declaration" at face value began to wonder about its grotesquely inappropriate timing. *In a Church being undermined and disgraced by clerical traitors in every nation, why was the Vatican apparatus so concerned about this one priest, who was not even accused of any specific wrongdoing?*

The scapegoating of Father Gruner would be no more successful than the other anti-Fatima stratagems. Contrary to what some Vatican prelates seem to be hoping, the Fatima controversy cannot be reduced to the status of one priest. In the weeks following the "Declaration" on Father Gruner, other prominent Catholics began to express serious doubts about Sodano's Party Line on the Third Secret. It was not only Mother Angelica who believed that "we didn't get the whole thing."

On October 26, 2001, the story "broke wide open", as reporters say, when *Inside the Vatican* news service (along with various Italian newspapers) ran an article entitled: "The Secret of Fatima: More to Come?" The article reported that: "News has just emerged that Sister Lucia dos Santos, the last surviving Fatima visionary, several weeks ago sent Pope John Paul II a letter reportedly warning him that his life is in danger. *According to Vatican sources*, the letter, claiming that events spoken of in the 'Third Secret' of Fatima had not yet occurred, was delivered sometime after September 11 to John Paul by the bishop emeritus [retired] of Fatima, Alberto Cosme do Amaral."

When asked about the letter, the then-Bishop of Fatima, Serafim de Sousa Ferreira e Silva, "*did not deny that Sister Lucia had sent a letter to the Pope*, but said [drawing a Jesuitical distinction] 'there are no letters from the seer that express fear for the life of the Pope.'" The *Inside the Vatican* report further revealed that "Sources have also suggested that Sister Lucia's letter encourages the Pope to fully reveal the Third Secret," and that her letter to the Pope "is said to contain this warning: 'Soon there will be great upheaval and punishment.'"

The *Inside the Vatican* article reports on yet another secret encounter with Sister Lucy behind the convent walls—only this one does not follow the Party Line. According to *Inside the Vatican*, an Italian diocesan priest, Father Luigi Bianchi, "claims to have met Sister Lucia dos Santos last week at her cloistered Carmelite convent in Coimbra, Portugal." Echoing the suspicions of Mother Angelica, Father Bianchi "speculated on the possibility that the Vatican *did not reveal the full secret* to avoid creating panic and anxiety in the population; to not scare them."

Concerning the ludicrous "interpretation" of the Secret as a prophecy of the 1981 attempt on the life of Pope John Paul II, Father Bianchi stated that "The message doesn't speak only about an attempt on the pontiff, but speaks of 'a Bishop dressed in White' who walks amongst the ruins and bodies of murdered men and women ... This means that the Pope will have to suffer greatly, that some nations will disappear, that many people will die, that we must defend the West from becoming Islamicized. That is what is happening in these days."

Inside the Vatican was careful to point out, as has *The Fatima Crusader*, that Sister Lucy "*is not allowed to speak with anyone* who has not received prior permission from the Vatican ..." Accordingly, *Inside the Vatican* hedged its bets by stating that "it is not immediately clear whether Bianchi received that approval, circumvented the need for it, or did not actually meet Sister Lucia as he maintains." But no one, including Sister Lucy herself, has ever denied that the meeting with Father Bianchi took place.

That at least some of *Inside the Vatican's* sources are within the Curia itself was suggested by Cardinal Ratzinger's response to these developments. *Inside the Vatican* quoted him as having said that the "rumors about this alleged letter are the continuation of 'an old polemic fed by certain people of dubious credibility,' for the purpose of '*destabilizing the internal equilibrium of the Roman Curia* and of troubling the people of God.'" Notice, however, that neither does Cardinal Ratzinger actually deny the existence of the letter from Sister Lucy to the Pope.

This remark by the Cardinal who became Pope was quite telling. How could people of "dubious credibility" destabilize the "internal equilibrium of the Roman Curia"? If their credibility were so dubious, the Roman Curia would hardly be destabilized by what they say. And just who are these people of "dubious credibility"? The *Inside the Vatican* piece suggested that Cardinal Ratzinger might have been referring to Father Gruner. But what about Mother Angelica? What about Father

Bianchi? What about *Inside the Vatican* itself, whose editor, Robert Moynihan, is, if anything, beholden to the Vatican apparatus, as the title of his magazine suggests? And what about the millions of other Catholics who harbor the well-founded suspicion that Msgr. (now Cardinal) Bertone and the former Cardinal Ratzinger are not being entirely forthcoming in their claim that the prophecies of the Message of Fatima, including the Third Secret, "belong to the past," and that its warning of a great chastisement of the Church and the world need no longer concern us? Indeed, what serious Catholic really believes this in his heart, given the perilous state of the world today?

Despite a determined effort to impose Sodano's Party Line (an effort that now included a Soviet-style declaration that Father Gruner is to be regarded as a "non-person" in the Church), Catholics the world over continue to wonder what has happened to the words which follow the key phrase "In Portugal the dogma of the Faith will always be preserved etc." Why had *TMF* run away from this phrase by removing it from the Message of Fatima and placing it in a footnote? *What has happened to the missing words of the Virgin? Where is the promised conversion of Russia? Why has there been no period of peace in the world, as the Virgin promised?*

In the face of these questions that would not go away, the Vatican apparatus made yet another attempt to put a lid on the rising speculation of a cover-up, before the pot boiled over and became uncontainable. Indeed, Cardinal Ratzinger's statement about a destabilized curia would indicate that the Party Line on Fatima was now meeting with resistance from within the Roman Curia itself, perhaps in view of the increasing destabilization of the world at large, which hardly squares with the notion that Fatima's warnings belong to the past.

The stratagem this time would be another secret interview of Sister Lucy in her convent in Coimbra. The interview was conducted on November 17, 2001 by Archbishop Bertone, who in five years would succeed Cardinal Sodano as Vatican Secretary of State, thus becoming the standard-bearer for the "official" account of the Secret and the one whose own revelations would (as we shall see in Chapter 14) break the Fatima "case" wide open.

For some reason the results of this secret interview were not revealed for more than a month. It was not until December 21, 2001 that *L'Osservatore Romano* (Italian edition) published Msgr. Bertone's brief communiqué about the interview, entitled "Meeting of His Excellency Mons. Tarcisio Bertone with Sister Maria Lucia of Jesus and the Immaculate Heart". This was followed by an English translation in *L'Osservatore Romano*'s English edition on January 9, 2002.

The substance of the communiqué was that, according to Msgr. Bertone, Sister Lucy said that the 1984 consecration of the world sufficed for a consecration of Russia, and that "everything has been published; there are no more secrets." As we demonstrated in Chapter

6, the former statement contradicts everything Sister Lucy has said to the contrary for the better part of seventy years. The latter statement is presented as Sister Lucy's answer to a question about the Third Secret—but the question, oddly enough, is not provided.

Now, when a newspaper or magazine publishes an interview with a person of note, the reader rightly expects a series of complete questions followed by complete answers, so that the reader can see for himself—in its full context—what the interviewee had to say in his or her own words. Not in this case. Although we are informed that Msgr. Bertone and Sister Lucy conversed for "more than two hours," Msgr. Bertone had provided only his summary of the conversation, sprinkled with a few words attributed to Sister Lucy herself. No transcript, audiotape or videotape of the two-hour session has been produced. In fact, *less than ten percent* of what Sister Lucy is quoted as saying had anything to do with the stated purpose of the interview, namely, to address continuing doubts in the minds of millions of Catholics about the Consecration of Russia and the completeness of the Vatican's disclosure of the Third Secret.

Perhaps we should have become accustomed to suspicious irregularities in the way the Vatican apparatus handled Sister Lucy, and this belatedly disclosed, elliptical "interview" was no exception. The Msgr. Bertone communiqué demonstrates that Sister Lucy was still being treated as if she were a member of the federal Witness Protection Program. Yes, of course, she was a cloistered nun. But an interview is an interview, and two hours of talk is two hours of talk. Where is the interview, and what happened to the two-hour conversation? And how can one square this curious substitute for a real interview with the claim that Sister Lucy had told us everything there was to know about the Message of Fatima? If she had told us all she knew, then there was nothing to hide. If there was nothing to hide, why not publish everything she was asked and all that she answered during those two hours? Indeed, why wouldn't they have simply allowed Sister Lucy to speak to the world herself, and lay all the questions to rest?

Yet despite publication of *TMF*, which was supposedly the last word on Fatima, revealing all that remains to be known, Sister Lucy was still being kept far away from open microphones and neutral witnesses. She was completely invisible during the process of "revealing" the Third Secret in May-June of 2000, and she remained invisible until her death, even though—so the Party Line goes—Fatima "belongs to the past."

Before addressing the particulars of the "interview" of November 2001—including the grand total of *forty-four words* attributed to Sister Lucy herself during an alleged *two hours* of conversation about the matters in controversy—it must be noted that Msgr. Bertone's communiqué undermines its own credibility immediately with the following claim: "Going on to discuss the problem of the third part of the secret of Fatima, she [Sister Lucy] says that she has read attentively and meditated upon the booklet published by the Congregation for the Doctrine of the Faith [i.e., *The Message of Fatima (TMF)*], and confirms *everything* it says."

This could not possibly be anything but a deception. To begin with, Msgr. Bertone is asking the faithful to believe all of the following:

- Sister Lucy "confirms" *TMF*'s contention that the vision contained in the Third Secret incorporates images Sister Lucy "may have seen in devotional books" and her own "intuitions of the faith". In other words, Sister Lucy "confirms" that she made it up.[311]

- Sister Lucy "confirms" Cardinal Ratzinger's praise of the modernist Jesuit Edouard Dhanis as an "eminent scholar" on Fatima, even though Dhanis dismissed as "unconscious fabrications" every prophetic aspect of the Message of Fatima—from the vision of hell, to the prediction of World War II, to the consecration and conversion of Russia. (This is discussed more fully below.)

- Sister Lucy "confirms," in essence, that she could very well be a sincere and pious fake, who only imagined that the Virgin Mary called for the consecration and conversion of Russia, so that *TMF* was quite correct in ignoring these key elements of the Message of Fatima, treating them as if they did not exist.

One must be sensible about this. When a Vatican functionary, no matter what his stature, comes out of a locked convent and declares that a 94-year-old nun inside "confirms everything" in a forty-page document he has co-authored, reasonable minds expect a bit more in the way of corroboration. All the more so when the forty-page document politely suggests that the nun in question concocted a pious fable that has held the Church in suspense, needlessly, for more than 80 years.

On these grounds alone one must conclude that the last secret Sister Lucy interview was but another attempt to manipulate and exploit a captive witness, who had yet to be allowed to come forward and speak at length to the faithful in her own unfiltered words. The last surviving Fatima visionary was still being subjected to closeted interviews during which she was surrounded by handlers, who then reported her "testimony" in little bits and pieces—an answer without the question, a question without the answer. And now the faithful were being asked to swallow the whopper that Sister Lucy, the divinely chosen seer of Fatima, agreed with "everything" in 40 pages of neo-

---

[311] On the contrary, as Father Alonso documents, Sister Lucy affirmed that "everything connected with the apparitions of the Lady was seen no longer as a simple recollection, but as a presence impressed upon her soul as though by fire. She herself points out to us these things remain impressed upon her soul in such a way that she could not possibly forget them. These reminiscences of Sister Lucia, therefore, are rather like re-reading inscriptions which are forever engraven in the deepest depths of the soul of the authoress. She appears to be 'seeing' rather than 'remembering'. The ease of her 'remembering' is indeed so great that she has only to 'read', as it were, from her soul." Father Joaquin Alonso, "Introduction", *Fatima in Lucia's Own Words*, p. 13.

modernist "commentary" which, as even the *Los Angeles Times* could see, "gently debunks the Fatima cult."

While it is clear on these grounds alone that the "interview" of November 17, 2001 is—to say the least—highly suspect, there is still an obligation to demonstrate the point more amply for the historical record.

To begin with, the Bertone interview was expressly conducted to squelch growing doubt among the faithful about the Vatican's blatant campaign to consign the Message of Fatima to the dustbin of history. As Msgr. Bertone's communiqué admits:

> In recent months, above all after the sad event of the terrorist attack of last September 11th, in foreign and Italian newspapers have appeared articles regarding presumed new revelations of Sister Lucy, announcements of warning letters to the Supreme Pontiff, apocalyptic reinterpretations of the Message of Fatima.

> Moreover, emphasis has been given to the suspicion that the Holy See has not published the integral text of the third part of the 'secret', and some 'Fatimist' movements have repeated the accusation that the Holy Father has not yet consecrated Russia to the Immaculate Heart of Mary.

> *For this reason it was considered necessary to organize a meeting with Sister Lucy ...*

We recall here that the Message of Fatima contains both promises, if the Virgin's requests are obeyed, and warnings about the consequences of a failure to obey:

The Promises:
If Russia *is* consecrated to the Immaculate Heart of Mary—

- the Immaculate Heart will triumph,

- Russia will be converted,

- many souls will be saved from hell (which the three seers were shown in a terrifying vision),

- and a period of peace will be granted to mankind.

The Warnings:
If Russia is *not* consecrated to the Immaculate Heart of Mary—

- Russia will spread its errors throughout the world,

- raising up wars and persecutions against the Church,

- the good will be martyred,

- the Holy Father will have much to suffer,

- and *various nations will be annihilated.*

While the *eventual* fulfillment of the Fatima prophecies is inevitable—"In the end, My Immaculate Heart *will* triumph. The Holy Father *will* consecrate Russia to Me, which *will* be converted, and a period of peace *will* be granted to mankind"—the question for us today is whether the world will first have to suffer the predicted chastisements in full, including the annihilation of nations, an event clearly suggested in the half-ruined city outside of which the Pope is executed in the Third Secret vision. We recall Sister Lucy's warning to the Pope (one year after the assassination attempt in St. Peter's Square) in the purported letter dated May 12, 1982, reproduced in *TMF* itself:

> And if we have not yet seen the complete fulfillment of the final part of this prophecy, *we are going towards it with great strides.*[312] If we do not reject the path of sin, hatred, revenge, injustice, violations of the rights of the human person, immorality and violence, etc. And let us not say that it is God who is punishing us in this way; on the contrary *it is people themselves who are preparing their own punishment.*

The Bertone interview, however, had failed to address continued public concern in the Church concerning the Fatima warnings. Quite the contrary, Msgr. Bertone had staked his entire position, and indeed the fate of the world, on the Party Line, to which he had adhered quite faithfully with his preposterous claim in *TMF* (his own commentary) that **"The decision of His Holiness Pope John Paul II to make public the third part of the 'secret' of Fatima brings to an end a period of history marked by tragic human lust for power and evil ..."** Thus, the Bertone interview had one aim: to persuade the world that peace is at hand, that the Fatima saga is over and can now safely be considered a part of history.

Let us examine the circumstances of the interview with reference to the standards of credibility even godless civil tribunals require for the acceptance of testimony from an important witness. We do not suggest that Sister Lucy ought to have been subjected to anything like the indignity of a civil trial, but only that the proponents of "Sister Lucy's" last "testimony" should have been held to these minimal standards in asking us to believe it.

Suspicious Circumstance #1: Although Sister Lucy was available to testify in person, she had never been produced by the party who controls access to her, at the time, Cardinal Joseph Ratzinger.

The Bertone communiqué revealed that Sister Lucy *could not even speak to Archbishop Bertone* without permission from Cardinal Ratzinger. This confirms what *The Fatima Crusader* has been reporting for years and what the aforesaid article in *Inside the Vatican* also noted: no one was allowed to speak to Sister Lucy without the Cardinal's permission.

---

[312] See footnote 267 in Chapter 9.

That is a very curious restriction on the liberty of a witness who, so we are told, had nothing to add to what she has already said.

Under the minimal standards of trustworthiness in civil proceedings, witnesses are required to testify in person if they are available, so that the parties to the case, whose rights may be affected by the testimony, will have the opportunity to pose questions to the witness. If one party has control over a witness but fails to produce him or her, civil judges instruct juries that they may draw the conclusion that *the witness' testimony would have been unfavorable to that party*. This is only common sense: a party would not fail to produce a favorable witness, but would very likely fail to produce an unfavorable one.

Sister Lucy was available to "take the stand" before the bar of history in the Fatima Case. She was not bedridden, crippled or otherwise unable to make an appearance. On the contrary, the Bertone communiqué claims that on the date of the secret interview Sister Lucy "appeared in great form, lucid and vivacious." Why was this lucid and vivacious witness, who was available to testify, never produced by the party who controls all access to her? Why was her latest "testimony" obtained behind closed doors and presented secondhand in a communiqué from Archbishop Bertone?

What would happen in a civil case if one of the parties offered a fragmentary report of a key witness' testimony when the witness herself could readily testify in person? The jury would rightly conclude that something was being hidden. In the Fatima Case, the inference can and should be drawn that Sister Lucy had been kept "off the stand" because her live, uncontrolled testimony would have contradicted Sodano's Party Line. If Sister Lucy could have been counted on to hew to the Party Line, then she would have been produced long ago to testify in person, and at length, before the Church and the world. Instead, it was *Msgr. Bertone*, not the witness herself, who testified.

But even if we assume that Sister Lucy had been bedridden or otherwise unavailable to testify, the other circumstances of the purported interview could not have failed to raise suspicion in the mind of any reasonable person. Let us proceed.

Suspicious circumstance #2: The interview of this 94-year-old nun was conducted in secret by Archbishop Bertone, an authority figure with a clear motive to manipulate the witness.

In a civil law context, undue influence is presumed when someone in a position of authority or dominance over a very elderly person extracts a statement from that person, such as a will or power of attorney. In this case, Archbishop Bertone is clearly a dominant party with the imposing authority of a Vatican title, whereas Sister Lucy was not only very elderly but has vowed to submit in holy obedience to the requests of her superiors, by whom she was surrounded during the two-hour session.

Furthermore, Msgr. Bertone was clearly intent on using the

"interview" to defend his own credibility against mounting public skepticism toward the Party Line that Fatima is finished. Given recent world events, Archbishop Bertone was obviously suffering a massive loss of face over his utterly indefensible statement in *TMF* that the *decision to publish* the Third Secret vision "brings to an end a period of history marked by tragic human lust for power and evil ..." Msgr. Bertone, being only human, would have had every motive to induce Sister Lucy to confirm his ridiculous claim of a world at peace due to the great "fulfillment" of the Third Secret in 1981, when the Pope survived the assassination attempt. (Even the secular radio commentator Paul Harvey was openly contemptuous of the Ratzinger/Bertone "interpretation" of the Third Secret as found in *TMF*.)

Under these circumstances, Msgr. Bertone conducting the "interview" and then reporting its results was akin to a prosecutor interviewing a key witness and then testifying in place of the witness, who is kept out of the courtroom. Objectively speaking, Msgr. Bertone was the last person who should have conducted the interview. The Church and the world are entitled to hear from this vital witness directly, rather than to receive reports from a partisan interrogator with an axe to grind.[313]

Suspicious Circumstance #3: The Bertone communiqué is extremely brief, occupying a mere quarter-page in *L'Osservatore Romano*. Yet the communiqué states that the interview went on "for more than two hours."

What did Bertone and Sister Lucy discuss for more than two hours, given that the entire communiqué can be read in less than two minutes? By way of comparison, a one-hour address delivered at a normal rate of speech would require roughly 14 single-spaced typewritten pages to transcribe; a two-hour address would require about 28 pages, or approximately 14,000 words.

Yet Bertone's communiqué concerning an alleged two-hour interview provides *a mere 463 words*[314] purportedly from the mouth of Sister Lucy herself. These 463 words break down as follows:

- **165 words**: A verbatim quotation of Cardinal Ratzinger's opinion in *TMF* (the June 26, 2000 Ratzinger/Bertone commentary) that the phrase "My Immaculate Heart

---

[313] Unfortunately, "a partisan interrogator with an axe to grind" was mistranslated in the Italian version of this book to read: "a partisan interrogator with an axe in his hand." In *The Fourth Secret of Fatima,* which we discuss in Chapter 14, Antonio Socci criticized the mistranslated phrase as excessively harsh. ("With some excess, Kramer writes: '... a partisan interrogator with an axe in his hand.'" *Fourth Secret,* footnote 177.) The harshness is the result of translator error, not polemical excess.

[314] When referring to or quoting the Bertone communiqué, this chapter sometimes uses the *Vatican Information Service* English translation of the December 2001 Italian original. At other times, the English translation in the *L'Osservatore Romano* English edition of January 9, 2002 is used. And very rarely, our own translation of the Italian version is used.

will triumph" (from which, as we have mentioned, the Cardinal deleted the words "In the end") does not refer to events somewhere after 1917 but rather to Mary's *fiat* in consenting to be the Mother of God 2,000 years ago.

Here we are asked to believe that Sister Lucy "confirms" that when Our Lady of Fatima predicted four future events—"In the end, My Immaculate Heart *will* triumph. The Holy Father *will* consecrate Russia to Me, which *will* be converted, and a period of peace *will* be granted to the world."—She was referring to the Annunciation in 1 B.C.! Bertone's Lucy apparently also "confirms" Cardinal Ratzinger's removal of the key words "In the end" from Our Lady's prophecy.

We note that the verbatim quotation (of 165 words) from *TMF* not only includes Cardinal Ratzinger's parenthetical citation to John 16:33 but also a summary of the rather complex theological conclusion to his 40 pages of commentary. To quote all of this verbiage word-for-word from memory is a feat very few people—if any—could perform. Either Sister Lucy had developed a photographic memory at age 94, or someone added the entire quotation to her "answer"—along with the parenthetical Scripture citation. (Or perhaps *TMF* was placed in front of Sister Lucy for her to read aloud in "obedience" to her superiors.)

- **100 words:** The significance of the heart Sister Lucy saw in the left hand of the Virgin during the apparitions at Fatima.

The Bertone communiqué informs us that this was "an unpublished particular" which Sister Lucy had added to the Message of Fatima. That is very interesting, but what does it have to do with the subject of the interview for which Bertone traveled to Portugal on such an emergency basis?

Notice also that the Bertone communiqué announces this new detail with great excitement—in italics, no less. Suddenly, Sister Lucy was the reliable visionary again, as opposed to Cardinal Ratzinger's impressionable child who made things up from what she had read in devotional books. Of course, this detail was a calculated distraction from the issue at hand.

- **69 words**: Sister Lucy denies press accounts that she is "very worried about recent events" and that she "can no longer sleep and is praying night and day."

Again, this is beside the point. But at any rate, Bertone's Lucy gives this rather flippant answer: "How could I pray during the day if I did not rest at night?" Obviously, no one had actually claimed that she never slept at all. Another distraction.

Sister Lucy is said to have added: "How many things they are putting in my mouth! How many things they make me seem to do!" Yes, but who was it that was falsely putting words in Sister Lucy's mouth and ascribed to her actions she had never taken? The objective witnesses we have previously quoted, who spoke to Sister Lucy openly and during unguarded moments, or the authority figures who surrounded Sister Lucy during Bertone's secret two-hour interrogation?

The reader will notice that Bertone's Lucy never denied that she is very worried about recent events. Who in his right mind would not be? Most tellingly, she *was never asked about her urgent letter to the Pope* (we mark this as the **First Glaring Omission** in the interview) *or her face-to-face meeting with Father Bianchi,* during which, according to Bianchi, she cast doubt on the Ratzinger/Bertone interpretation of the Third Secret (this is **Glaring Omission #2**).

- **39 words**: The effect the Fatima apparitions had on Sister Lucy's life.

What do these reminiscences have to do with the stated purpose of the emergency secret interview in the convent? Sister Lucy had covered this subject exhaustively in her voluminous memoirs. For *this* a Vatican functionary traveled to Portugal for a two-hour encounter?

- **34 words**: Sister Lucy denied that she has received any new revelations.

Oddly enough, while Bertone's Lucy denies any further revelations from Heaven, in the same communiqué she declares—contrary to all her prior testimony—that the 1984 consecration of the world "has been accepted in Heaven." (See her alleged words regarding this on a later page in this chapter under the heading **"21 words on the Consecration of Russia"**.) How would she know this, absent any new revelations?

- **12 words:** Sister Lucy said the Carmelite community had rejected the petition forms Father Gruner's apostolate is circulating for the Consecration of Russia.

What of it? What about the Consecration of Russia? Is it done or not?

Thus far we have accounted for 419 of the 463 words attributed to Sister Lucy in the communiqué's purported verbatim quotations. Only 44 words remain to deal with the questions being posed by millions of Catholics.

Yes, incredibly enough, the loudly trumpeted Bertone communiqué contains only *forty-four words* of "Sister Lucy" concerning the very matters—the Consecration of Russia and the disclosure of the Third Secret—that supposedly prompted Bertone to travel all the way to the convent in Coimbra on an emergency basis. Here is how the forty-four words break down:

- **9 words** concerning (so we are told) the Third Secret: *"Everything has been published; there are no more secrets."*

The question that elicited this answer is not provided. Instead, Bertone's communiqué declares: "To whoever imagines that some part of the secret has been hidden she replied: …"—followed by the nine quoted words.

Replied to what? What *exactly* was Sister Lucy asked about the Vatican's disclosure of the Third Secret? What was the full context of the question and the answer? And why was Sister Lucy not asked the one question millions of people around the world were asking: *Where are* the words of Our Lady which follow the phrase "In Portugal the dogma of the Faith will always be preserved etc."? We mark this as *Glaring Omission #3.*

Notice also that here, at the very crux of the matter, we are not shown that Sister Lucy was asked even one precise question, such as:

- *What are* the words of Our Lady following "In Portugal the dogma of the Faith will always be preserved etc"?

- Were any words spoken by Our Lady to explain the vision of the "Bishop dressed in White" seen in the Third Secret?

- Does the Third Secret include a separate text that explains the vision of the "Bishop dressed in White"?

- What did Sister Lucy say about the testimony of numerous witnesses (including the Bishop of Fatima and Cardinal Ottaviani) that the Third Secret was written in 25 lines of text, as opposed to the 62 lines of text in which the vision of the "Bishop dressed in White" is written?

All such particulars are studiously avoided. We are not even given the wording of the one question that *was* asked. This is *Glaring Omission #4*.

- **14 words on the Ratzinger/Bertone interpretation of the Third Secret**: "That is not true. I fully confirm the interpretation [of the Third Secret] made in the Jubilee Year."

Here Sister Lucy allegedly denied press reports that she expressed doubts to Father Luigi Bianchi and Father Jose dos Santos Valinho about *TMF*'s interpretation of the Third Secret. Yet Bertone *never asked Sister Lucy about her letter to John Paul II*, as reported by Father Bianchi, nor does she deny that she met face-to-face with Father Bianchi at the convent in Coimbra and that they discussed Sodano's interpretation of the Third Secret.

We are thus expected to believe that Lucy agrees that the Third Secret was fulfilled with the failed assassination attempt against Pope John Paul II on May 13, 1981, even though her own letter to the Pope on May 12, 1982—a year later—says nothing about the attempt but rather demolishes the Party Line by warning that "we have *not yet seen* the complete fulfillment of the final part of this prophecy." And, once again, in the same letter Sister Lucy makes no connection between the assassination attempt and the Third Secret.

- **21 words on the Consecration of Russia**: "I have already said that the consecration desired by Our Lady was made in 1984, and has been accepted in heaven."

These words were allegedly uttered by Sister Lucy in answer to the question: "What do you say to the persistent affirmations of Father Gruner who is gathering signatures in order that the Pope may finally consecrate Russia to the Immaculate Heart of Mary, which has never been done?"

First of all, that the Secretary of the CDF would travel to Coimbra to obtain comments about Father Gruner for publication to the entire Church is a dramatic demonstration that the Vatican apparatus views Father Gruner's apostolate as a prime locus of opposition to the Party Line.

Furthermore, what did "Sister Lucy" mean by the curious affirmation that a consecration of the world was "accepted" in Heaven as a consecration of Russia? Was "Sister Lucy" seriously claiming that Heaven "accepted" a compromise imposed by Vatican diplomats? Since when does Heaven accept a human substitute for a precise act that God has commanded? Further, how would "Sister Lucy" know what Heaven has "accepted" if, as Msgr. Bertone claims, she also said there have been no new revelations to her?

Now, it may be that God "accepts" our refusal to comply with His will in the sense that He will allow us the freedom to disobey Him in this life. But that does not mean that what God has "accepted" is pleasing to Him.

What is more, by saying that the act of consecration of the world in 1984 was "accepted", was not Sister Lucy saying nothing more than that it was "accepted" in the same sense as the 1942 consecration by Pius XII? Jesus said on the occasion of the 1942 consecration of the world that it would shorten World War II, but Our Lord also explains that it would not bring world peace because it did not fulfill the request of Our Lady of Fatima concerning the Consecration of Russia. Was Sister Lucy perhaps attempting to answer the question in a way that satisfied her questioner, Msgr. Bertone, yet still signaling that while what was "accepted" might confer some benefit on the world, it would not be the period of world peace that the Virgin of Fatima promised if Her precise request were honored? Indeed, where is the period of peace She promised? That we have not seen it only demonstrates that even if Heaven "accepted" the 1984 ceremony for what it was worth, Heaven has not deemed that ceremony to be the fulfillment of Our Lady of Fatima's specific request. No matter what the authority of Msgr. Bertone and his Vatican collaborators, they cannot simply declare the existence of something that our own senses tell us does not exist: the conversion of Russia and the worldwide epoch of peace that would follow a proper consecration of that nation to the Immaculate Heart of Mary.

In any case, we have already demonstrated abundantly that Sister Lucy testified repeatedly, in widely reported statements, that the consecration ceremonies of 1982 and 1984 did not suffice to honor Our Lady's request, because on neither occasion was Russia mentioned, nor did the world episcopate participate. According to the Bertone interview, however, the witness has reversed her testimony, and now testifies that the 1984 consecration ceremony "has been accepted in heaven."

What "accepted in heaven" means is anybody's guess. Did Heaven decide to "accept" something less than what Our Lady of Fatima had requested after negotiations between Heaven and Cardinal Sodano?

In any case, notice that *Sister Lucy was not questioned about her many prior statements to the contrary*, and was not asked to explain her purported change of testimony. This is **Glaring Omission #5**. We are evidently supposed to assume that nothing Sister Lucy ever said before carries any weight, and that only when she speaks *in secret* to Msgr. Bertone does she tell the truth about this matter.

It is quite significant that Bertone's Lucy does not tell us *when, where or to whom* she has "already said" that the 1984 consecration she once deemed unacceptable is now acceptable. Why such vagueness, when Msgr. Bertone had every opportunity to nail down this issue by eliciting specific testimony? Why did he not ask her, for instance, to authenticate any of the various computer-generated letters which began mysteriously to appear over her purported signature in 1989, the letters which assert the consecration had been accomplished in 1984?

And this is most suspicious: As we have noted, *TMF* relies entirely on one of these dubious letters, dated November 8, 1989, as proof that the consecration has already been accomplished. We noted also that this letter's credibility was extinguished by its false statement that Pope Paul VI consecrated the world to the Immaculate Heart during his brief visit to Fatima in 1967—a consecration that never happened. *Why did Bertone make no effort to have Sister Lucy authenticate this hotly disputed letter, when it was the only evidence cited in TMF?*

Most telling in this connection is that Father Gruner's Fatima apostolate had published proof that the letter (whose addressee, Walter Noelker, is not even revealed in *TMF*) is an obvious fake. The proof was published in Issue No. 64 of *The Fatima Crusader*, of which there were some 450,000 copies in circulation as of the date of the Bertone interview in November of 2001.

Now Msgr. Bertone was surely aware that *The Fatima Crusader* had exposed the fraudulence of the 1989 letter, yet he failed to ask Sister Lucy to authenticate the letter and thereby deliver a serious blow to the credibility of Father Gruner's apostolate. This failure could not have been an oversight, since an attempt to refute the position taken by Father Gruner and his apostolate was *the very reason* Msgr. Bertone had conducted the interview of Sister Lucy in the first place.

Why would Msgr. Bertone pass up a golden opportunity to use Sister Lucy, his "star witness", to refute Father Gruner's claim that the 1989 letter was a fake? Obviously, because Msgr. Bertone must have known that it *was* a fake, and thus he would not have dared to ask Sister Lucy to authenticate it during the interview. We must mark this is as **Glaring Omission #6.**

This, then, is the sum total—forty-four words—of what Sister Lucy was alleged to have said during a two-hour interview on one of the greatest controversies in the history of the Church. We are asked to accept these forty-four words from a closeted witness as the end of the story of Fatima. These words are supposed to allay all the doubts, questions and fears of millions of the faithful—even though Russia has manifestly failed to convert and the gathering forces of violence and rebellion against God and His law loom larger by the day.

Suspicious Circumstance #4: No tape recording or transcript of the interview has been made available.

Why has no transcript, audio tape, video tape or any other independent record of the interview been produced in order to show the precise questions Msgr. Bertone asked, the full answers Sister Lucy gave, the sequence of the questions and answers, and any comments or suggestions Msgr. Bertone and others might have made to Sister Lucy during the "more than two hours" they were in the same room together? *Where is the give and take one always sees in published interviews*?

Further, why did Msgr. Bertone require more than two hours to extract forty-four words from Sister Lucy about the matters at issue? Assuming it took Sister Lucy a full minute to utter those 44 words, what did she say, and what did Msgr. Bertone, Father Kondor and the Mother Superior say, during the remaining 119 minutes of the encounter? Was Sister Lucy reminded of her duty of "obedience"? Was it implied that the whole Church was depending on her to give the answers that would end this "divisive" controversy? Was it suggested that loyalty to "the Holy Father" required that she accept the Party Line, even though her own purported 1982 letter to the Pope contradicts it? Was she told how important it was to the Church that she assure everyone that Russia has been consecrated, despite everything she has said to the contrary throughout her life? Was she given the impression that to say otherwise would be to contradict the Pope himself?

Or did Sister Lucy perhaps give many answers that were unsatisfactory to her questioner, only to be asked the same questions repeatedly and in different ways until she got the answers "right"? To what subtle, or not-so-subtle, importuning was the witness subjected during the two hours she was surrounded by imposing authority figures in a closed room?

Surely, if there was nothing to hide Msgr. Bertone would have made certain that such a crucial interview with the only surviving witness of the Fatima apparitions, age 94 at the time, was recorded on audio or video tape, or at least transcribed *verbatim* by a stenographer so that the witness' testimony could be preserved in case of her death—which at her age was certainly very near (she died on February 13, 2005). We would wager, however, that there is no recording, no transcript, no independent record whatsoever of the Bertone interview. For it seems there had been for the last 45 years of her life a terrible fear of allowing this witness to speak at length, in her own words, in response to a series of simple and direct questions. Every one of the forty-four words from "Sister Lucy" which appear in the Bertone communiqué is carefully measured out, as if from an eyedropper.

No doubt the risk of creating such a record was too great. What if Sister Lucy consistently gave the "wrong" answers? What if the answers she did provide had to be extracted through leading questions or subtle persuasion by the interviewer or the others in attendance? What could be done with a record that revealed such things? How could it be kept from the public or only partially released? How could it be hidden or destroyed once it was created?

We would be happy to be proven wrong. Perhaps there *is* a tape or transcript of the entire two-hour session. But if there is, it will be most telling if the Vatican never produces it. (As of December 2009, the tape has never been produced.)

Suspicious Circumstance #5: The Italian communiqué purports to be signed by both Msgr. Bertone and Sister Lucy, but the English version drops her "signature."

In the first place, why would Sister Lucy have signed *Msgr. Bertone's* statement in Italian about what she allegedly told him in *Portuguese*? Why did Sister Lucy not make and sign *her own* statement in her own language? If Sister Lucy really spoke with Msgr. Bertone for more than two hours, why not simply prepare a faithful transcript of her own words in Portuguese and then have her sign that, instead of Msgr. Bertone's self-serving communiqué?

Further, why was Sister Lucy's "signature" dropped from the English translation of the communiqué? In fact, to what document was her "signature" actually affixed in the first place—the Italian communiqué or a Portuguese original of the same document that has not yet been produced?

Of what value, in any case, was Sister Lucy's "signature" on a document written in a language she does not speak, which partially quotes her testimony, but only in Italian translation (Sister Lucy did not speak Italian) and without setting forth the full questions she was asked or the full answers she gave?

The inescapable conclusion is this: *Msgr. Bertone and the Vatican apparatus had no intention of ever allowing Sister Lucy to give her own statement at length, entirely in her own words, about the major questions which remain concerning the Message of Fatima.* This is borne out by the next suspicious circumstance.

Suspicious Circumstance #6: Sister Lucy's published 303-page book on the Message of Fatima completely avoids any of the subjects supposedly covered in the secret Bertone interview.

In October 2001 the Vatican Library publishing house published a book by Sister Lucy entitled *The Appeals of the Message of Fatima.* Sister Lucy's introduction to the book, which was reviewed and approved by the Congregation for the Doctrine of the Faith, states that it is intended to be "an answer and a clarification of *doubts and questions* addressed to me." The preface, by the current Bishop of Leiria-Fatima, likewise observes that Sister Lucy had asked the Holy See's permission to write a book on Fatima in order to "answer *multiple questions* in a global manner, not being able to answer every person individually."

Yet despite the book's stated purpose, its 303 pages fail to address *any* of the prevailing "doubts and questions" about the Message of Fatima. The errors of Russia, the Triumph of the Immaculate Heart, the consecration and conversion of Russia, the period of peace promised by the Virgin as the fruit of the Consecration, and the Third Secret *are not even mentioned* in the book, let alone discussed. Not even the vision of hell is mentioned in Sister Lucy's discussion of eternal life and seeking God's pardon. In short, the book presents a thoroughly expurgated Fatima message, stripped of every one of its prophetic and admonitory elements—precisely in keeping with the Party Line. The version of Fatima presented in this book hardly required a Miracle of the Sun to confirm it.

Now this is very curious: When Sister Lucy was allowed to write a 303-page book to address "doubts and questions" concerning the Message of Fatima, she said nothing about the doubts and questions millions of people really have. Only when she was interviewed *in secret* by a self-interested questioner, who happened to be an imposing authority figure, was "Sister Lucy" allowed anywhere near these doubts and questions. But even then her answers were fragmentary and did not come from her directly, in her own language. Instead, they were conveyed by Archbishop Bertone, who provided us with forty-four relevant words out of two hours of conversation with his captive witness.

Now let us sum up the suspicious circumstances surrounding the handling of the key witness in the Fatima Case:

• No one was allowed to speak to the witness without the permission of one party to the case, who controlled all access to her, even though we are told she had nothing further to say.

- When doubts arose about official versions of the witness' testimony, she was subjected to a secret interview at the age of 94, conducted by an imposing authority figure who then presented her fragmentary answers to his questions in a communiqué to which her signature was affixed, even though the communiqué was not in her own language.

- One version of the communiqué purports to bear the witness' signature below that of her interrogator, but her signature was removed from another version, on which only the interrogator's signature appears.

- The communiqué failed to provide the full questions asked and the answers given by the witness, in their full context.

- Out of 463 words attributed to the witness in the communiqué, only 44 related to the matters in controversy—out of two hours of conversation!

- No transcript or other independent record of the witness' testimony was provided.

- The secretly elicited, fragmentary testimony contradicts many prior statements by the same witness.

- No effort was made by the witness, or by anyone else, to explain her prior inconsistent statements.

- During the secret interview of the witness, no attempt was made to have her authenticate "letters" attributed to her whose authenticity was clearly in doubt, nor was any effort made to authenticate the very "letter" *on which the interrogator himself had placed sole reliance* as proof of the witness' alleged change of testimony (regarding the Consecration of Russia).

- The secret examination of the witness avoids any specific questions about widely known major discrepancies in the case of which the witness had peculiar knowledge—including the six glaring omissions set forth here.

- When the witness was allowed to publish an entire book to address "doubts and questions" she had received regarding the Message of Fatima, the book contains no references to any of the doubts and questions that actually concern millions of people, which doubts and questions are addressed only in a secret interview for which there is *no transcript or other independent record.*

Archbishop Bertone, now Cardinal Bertone, is a man with a very high office in the Church. With all due respect to his office, however, nothing can overcome the reasonable doubts that these suspicious circumstances and glaring omissions engender in reasonable minds. No court on earth would accept the testimony of a witness fraught with so many indications of unreliability. Surely in the Church we could have expected at least that measure of openness and disclosure a civil judge would require. If there exists a video or audio tape of the interview, *let us hear the witness, for Heaven's sake*!

We must, in candor, state the conclusion that would be obvious to any neutral observer of the mysterious handling of Sister Lucia of the Immaculate Heart: There is every reason to believe that a key witness—in fact the last surviving witness—was being tampered with. This witness tampering is another element of the major injustice of *de facto* hiding the full Fatima Message and prophecies. Indeed, Antonio Socci would cite the inexplicable suspiciousness of this interview as part of the overwhelming evidence that led to his "conversion" to the "Fatimist" position. As he wrote of the interview in his bombshell of a book on the Third Secret controversy: "The few words attributed to her [Sister Lucy]… are such as to not have objective credibility."[315] As Socci concluded, with devastating effect for the "official" account:

> Let us reflect on this. Sister Lucia in November-December 2001 was a very old person, who lived in isolation from the world with a prohibition on meeting anyone, who was bound to silence and obedience and *was not able to control the account of this meeting and the words that were attributed to her*.[316]

But why would Bertone perpetrate such a manipulation of the only surviving Fatima seer and her precious testimony, less than four years before her death on February 13, 2005? Beyond the apparent motive already demonstrated—that of furthering at all costs the new orientation of the Church, which collides with the Message of Fatima—we believe a further motive exists. We base this conclusion on what we discussed in Chapter 8: the express approbation in *TMF* of the views of Edouard Dhanis, S.J.—the neo-modernist "debunker" of Fatima. With the endorsement of Dhanis as an "eminent scholar" on Fatima, Cardinal Ratzinger had made it perfectly clear that he, with Dhanis, held that the prophetic elements of the Message concerning Russia and so forth—again, what Dhanis belittled as "Fatima II"—are little more than fabrications by a simple and well-intentioned, but seriously misguided person.

As we noted earlier, *TMF* followed the line of Dhanis by stating that the Third Secret itself may be largely a concoction: "The concluding part of the 'secret' uses images which Lucia may have seen in devotional books and which draw their inspiration from long-standing intuitions of faith." If that were true of the Third Secret, it would also be true of the entire Message of Fatima. What other conclusion could the Cardinal have intended to suggest?

We recall also that the culmination of the Message of Fatima—the triumph of the Immaculate Heart—was reduced to nothing more than

---

[315] Antonio Socci, *Il Quarto Segreto di Fatima* [*The Fourth Secret of Fatima*], English ed., p. 117; popular ed., p. 82; Italian ed., p. 125.

[316] *The Fourth Secret of Fatima*, English ed., p. 116; popular ed., p. 81; Italian ed., p. 124.

the Virgin Mary's *fiat* 2,000 years ago. In like manner, *TMF* deconstructed the Virgin's prophecy that "To save them [i.e. souls from hell], God wishes to establish *in the world* devotion to My Immaculate Heart." Under Cardinal Ratzinger's interpretation (which would surely please Dhanis), devotion to the Immaculate Heart means nothing more than acquiring an "immaculate heart" of one's own. To quote *TMF* again: "According to Matthew 5:8, the 'immaculate heart' is a heart which, with God's grace, has come to perfect interior unity and therefore 'sees God'. To be 'devoted' to the Immaculate Heart of Mary *means therefore* to embrace this attitude of heart, which makes the *fiat*—'your will be done'—the defining centre of one's whole life." Cardinal Ratzinger removed the initial capitals from "Immaculate Heart" in order to reduce it to an 'immaculate heart' that anyone can have by simply conforming himself to God's will. This exercise, however, removed every bit of the Message of Fatima's explicitly Catholic prophetic content.

Here we arrive at the precisely additional motive in the former Cardinal's case: Disbelief or skepticism (at least before his elevation to the papacy) concerning the authenticity of the Message of Fatima[317]—an attitude he shared with Dhanis, the only Fatima "authority" the Cardinal cited. Thus, far from intending to perpetrate a fraud, the Cardinal may have believed that the suppression of Sister Lucy's full and unfettered testimony was actually a service to the Church. If the Cardinal *did not really believe* in the prophetic elements of the Message of Fatima concerning the need for the consecration and conversion of Russia and the triumph of the Immaculate Heart in our time, or the disastrous consequences to the Church and the world in failing to heed these elements of prophecy, he would have considered the suppression of these elements as the protection of the Church from falsehoods that are "troubling" the faithful, and "upsetting the balance of the Roman Curia", to recall his own words, however much Sister Lucy may have believed them to be true.

It is clear enough from everything the Cardinal himself said, that the then-Prefect of the Congregation for the Doctrine of the Faith, like Dhanis, placed little or no credence in the testimony of Sister Lucy that the Virgin requested the consecration and conversion of Russia in order to bring about the triumph of the Immaculate Heart of Mary in the world. The Cardinal evidently did not believe that with the Miracle of the Sun God authenticated this testimony beyond any doubt. What other conclusion can one draw from the former Cardinal's prominent endorsement of the very "theologian" who attempted to debunk the entire Fatima prophecy?

But then he owed it to the Church and mankind to be candid about his

---

[317] It should also be noted, in defense of Cardinal Ratzinger, that in writing his commentary in *TMF* he relied upon the credibility of the testimony of Msgr. (now Cardinal) Bertone as to what exactly Sister Lucy had agreed to during the meeting of April 2000. Had Cardinal Ratzinger had the benefit of the now-overwhelming evidence that Bertone's testimony is simply not reliable, and is, in fact, demonstrably false—see, in particular, Chapter 14— Cardinal Ratzinger might have commented differently.

real intentions. It seems that the Cardinal may have shared the attitude of other "enlightened" Vatican insiders who think that the "simple faithful" are too naive to appreciate what is best for them. This may explain why the Cardinal did not reveal his prejudices to the "unenlightened", but rather expected that everyone would trust his judgment.

Cardinal Ratzinger, speaking now as the Pope, has exhibited what would appear to be a change of heart concerning the veracity of the Fatima prophecies. He said in Brazil that Fatima is the most prophetic of all Our Lady's apparitions in the 20th Century. In particular he also states he hopes in the yet-to-take-place Triumph of the Immaculate Heart (as we have shown in the preceding pages). Nevertheless it seems impossible to avoid the conclusion that the Message of Fatima remains in the custody of those *who simply do not believe in it* and who wish to have done with it once and for all, as they set their sights on the Vatican's new policies of ecumenism, "interreligious dialogue", a world brotherhood of religions and a "civilization of love" under the guidance of the United Nations. This will become quite clear in Chapter 14, where we examine the leading role assumed by Cardinal Bertone, now Vatican Secretary of State, in the Fatima affair.

It remains for us, however, first to examine more closely the evidence pertaining to the actual contents of what is clearly a yet-to-be disclosed text of the Secret, a text whose existence Bertone's own words and actions have subsequently confirmed.

Sunday, March 25, 1984, 4:00 p.m.: Pope John Paul II venerates the Pilgrim Virgin Statue inside St. Peter's Basilica in Vatican City. His Holiness admitted at that time that Our Lady of Fatima was still awaiting the Consecration of Russia by the Pope in union with all the Catholic bishops. See *L'Osservatore Romano* article photographically reproduced on page XVI in the photo section for more details.

Chapter 12

The Third Secret Predicts: The Great Apostasy in the Church after Vatican II

If, as seems to be the case—and as millions of responsible Catholics believe—there is more to the Third Secret than an obscure vision of the "Bishop dressed in White" with no explanation by Our Lady of Fatima of how it is to be interpreted, then in what would the missing part of the Secret consist? We have already suggested an answer. In this chapter, we develop the answer in some detail.

Every Witness Agrees

The testimony of every single witness who has spoken on the question points to only one conclusion: the missing part of the Third Secret of Fatima foretells a catastrophic loss of faith and discipline in the human element of the Church—that is, in short, a great apostasy. Let us recall the testimonies on this point, which we first presented in Chapter 4:

The Future Pope Pius XII - 1931

I am worried by *the Blessed Virgin's messages to Lucy of Fatima.* This persistence of Mary about the dangers which menace the Church is *a divine warning against the suicide of altering the Faith, in Her liturgy, Her theology and Her soul.* ...

Fr. Joseph Schweigl - 1952

I cannot reveal anything of what I learned at Fatima concerning the Third Secret, but I can say that it has two parts: one concerns the Pope; the other logically (although I must say nothing) would have to be the continuation of the words: "In Portugal, the dogma of the Faith will always be preserved."

Father Fuentes (reporting the testimony of Sister Lucy) - 1957

On December 26, 1957, with an imprimatur and the approbation of the Bishop of Fatima, Father Agustín Fuentes published the following revelations by Sister Lucy concerning the Third Secret:

Father, the Most Holy Virgin is very sad because no one has paid any attention to Her message, neither the good nor the bad. The good continue on their way but without giving any importance to Her message. The bad, not seeing the punishment of God falling upon them, continue their life of sin without even caring about the message. But believe me, Father, God will chastise the world and this will be in a terrible manner. *The punishment from Heaven is imminent.*

Father, how much time is there before 1960 arrives? It will be very sad for everyone, not one person will rejoice at all if beforehand the world does not pray and do penance. *I am not able to give any other details because it is still a secret. ...*

This is the Third part of the Messsage of Our Lady which will remain Secret until 1960.

Tell them, Father, that many times the most Holy Virgin told my cousins Francisco and Jacinta, as well as myself, that many nations will disappear from the face of the earth. She said that Russia will be the instrument of chastisement chosen by Heaven to punish the world if we do not obtain beforehand the conversion of that poor nation.

Father, the devil is in the mood for engaging in a decisive battle against the Blessed Virgin. And the devil knows what it is that most offends God and which in a short space of time will gain for him the greatest number of souls. *Thus, the devil does everything to overcome souls consecrated to God, because in this way, the devil will succeed in leaving souls of the faithful abandoned by their leaders, thereby the more easily will he seize them.*

That which afflicts the Immaculate Heart of Mary and the Heart of Jesus is *the fall of religious and priestly souls.* The devil knows that *religious and priests who fall away from their beautiful vocation drag numerous souls to hell. ... The devil wishes to take possession of consecrated souls.* He tries to corrupt them in order to lull to sleep the souls of laypeople and thereby lead them to final impenitence.

Father Alonso - 1976

Before his death in 1981, Father Joaquin Alonso, who for sixteen years was the official archivist of Fatima and had many opportunities for speaking with Sister Lucy during those years, testified as follows:

It is therefore completely probable that the text makes concrete references to the crisis of faith within the Church and to the negligence of the pastors themselves [and the] internal struggles in the very bosom of the Church and of grave pastoral negligence of the upper hierarchy.[318]

In the period preceding the great triumph of the Immaculate Heart of Mary, terrible things are to happen. These form the content of the third part of the Secret. What are they? If "in Portugal the

---

[318] Frère Michel de la Sainte Trinité, *The Whole Truth About Fatima* - Vol. III, p. 704.

dogma of the Faith will always be preserved," ... *it can be clearly deduced from this that in other parts of the Church these dogmas are going to become obscure or even lost altogether.*[319]

Does the unpublished text speak of concrete circumstances? It is very possible that it speaks not only of a real crisis of the faith in the Church during this in-between period, but like the secret of La Salette, for example, there are more concrete references to the internal struggles of Catholics or to the fall of priests and religious. *Perhaps it even refers to the failures of the upper hierarchy of the Church.* For that matter, none of this is foreign to other communications Sister Lucy has had on this subject.[320]

Cardinal Ratzinger - 1984

[A]ccording to the judgment of the Popes, it [the Third Secret] adds nothing different to what a Christian must know concerning what derives from Revelation: i.e., a radical call for conversion; the absolute importance of history; *the dangers threatening the faith and the life of the Christian, and therefore of the world.* And then the importance of the "*novissimi*" [the last events at the end of time]. If it is not made public—at least for the time being—it is in order to prevent religious prophecy from being mistaken for a quest for the sensational [literally: "for sensationalism"]. But the things contained in this "Third Secret" correspond to what has been announced in Scripture and has been said again and again in many other Marian apparitions, first of all that of Fatima in what is already known of what its message contains. Conversion and penitence are the essential conditions for "salvation".[321] (11 November 1984)

Bishop Amaral - 1984

Its content concerns only our faith. To identify the Secret with catastrophic announcements or with a nuclear holocaust is to deform the meaning of the message. *The loss of faith of a continent is worse than the annihilation of a nation*; and it is true that faith is continually diminishing in Europe.[322]

It is important to note that, as part of the general attempt to conceal and suppress the truth about Fatima, Bishop Amaral was pressured to withdraw his remarks shortly after they were made. But then, ten years later, and then safely retired, the bishop casually *reaffirmed his*

---

[319] Ibid., p. 687.

[320] Ibid., p. 705.

[321] *Jesus* magazine, November 11, 1984, p. 79; see the actual Italian text of the key part of Cardinal Ratzinger's interview in *Jesus* magazine photographically reproduced on page 352 of this book (in Appendix II), with our English translation provided in the text box on page 353. See also Frère Michel de la Sainte Trinité, *The Whole Truth About Fatima* - Vol. III, pp. 822-823; and *The Fatima Crusader*, Issue 37, Summer 1991, p. 7.

[322] *The Whole Truth About Fatima* - Vol. III, p. 676.

testimony in a public interview in 1995, adding a crucial bit of evidence: "Before I asserted in Vienna (in 1984) that the Third Secret concerned only our Faith and the loss of Faith *I had consulted Sister Lucy and first obtained her approval.*"[323] Thus, Sister Lucy herself indirectly confirmed, yet again, that the true and complete Third Secret of Fatima predicts apostasy in the Church.

Cardinal Oddi - 1990

It [the Third Secret] has nothing to do with Gorbachev. The Blessed Virgin was alerting us against the apostasy in the Church.

Cardinal Ciappi - 1995

Cardinal Mario Luigi Ciappi, who was nothing less than Pope John Paul II's own personal papal theologian as well as the personal papal theologian of his four predecessors, in a personal communication to a Professor Baumgartner in Salzburg (Austria), revealed that:

In the Third Secret it is foretold, among other things, that the great apostasy in the Church will begin *at the top*.[324]

To this train of witnesses we must add two others who have spoken more recently: First, Father José dos Santos Valinho, who is Sister Lucy's own nephew. Second, no less than the late Pope John Paul II himself.

Father Valinho - 2000

In a book by Renzo and Roberto Allegri entitled *Reportage su Fatima* [Milan 2000], published—providentially enough—very shortly before the disclosure of the Third Secret vision and the publication of *TMF*, Father Valinho expressed the view that the Third Secret predicts apostasy in the Church.[325] Coming from the very nephew of the last surviving Fatima seer, who had spoken to his aunt innumerable times over the years, this opinion has substantial weight.

Pope John Paul II Has Twice Revealed the Essence of the Secret - 2000 and 1982

As if all this were not enough, it is apparent that John Paul II revealed the essential elements of the Secret in his sermon at Fatima on May 13, 1982, and in his sermon during the beatification ceremony for Blessed Jacinta Marto and Blessed Francisco Marto at Fatima on May 13, 2000. Indeed, in *The Fourth Secret of Fatima* Antonio Socci argues that these papal revelations represent "a compromise solution" engineered by the Vatican, according to which it was decided to reveal the missing portion of the Third Secret *indirectly* through pointed references to verses 1, 3

---

[323] *CRC*, December 1997.
[324] See Father Gerard Mura, "The Third Secret of Fatima: Has It Been Completely Revealed?", in the periodical *Catholic*, (published by the Transalpine Redemptorists, Orkney Isles, Scotland, Great Britain) March 2002.
[325] Ibid.

and 4 of Chapter 12 of the Book of the Apocalypse. The idea, writes Socci in an allusion to Scripture, was: "He who can understand, let him understand."[326] In this way, the Vatican could assert (with a mental reservation) that the Secret has been revealed in its entirety.

In 1982 John Paul II posed this question in his sermon at Fatima: "Can the Mother, Who with all the force of the love that She fosters in the Holy Spirit and Who desires everyone's salvation, can She remain silent when She sees the very bases of Her children's salvation *undermined*?" The Pope then answered his own question: "No, She cannot remain silent." Here the Pope himself tells us that the Fatima Message concerns Our Lady's warning that *the very bases of our salvation* are being undermined. Notice the striking parallel between this testimony and that of Pope Pius XII, who spoke of the suicide of altering the Faith in the Church's liturgy, theology and Her very soul.

Then, on May 13, 2000, during the beatification ceremony, the Pope issued this startling warning to the entire Catholic world:

> "Another portent appeared in Heaven; behold, a great red dragon" (Apoc. 12:3). These words from the first reading of the Mass make us think of the great struggle between good and evil, showing how, when man puts God aside, he cannot achieve happiness, but ends up destroying himself. ...
>
> The Message of Fatima is a call to conversion, alerting humanity **to have nothing to do with the "dragon" whose "tail swept down a third of the stars of Heaven**, and dragged them to the earth" (Apoc. 12:4). ...
>
> Man's final goal is Heaven, his true home, where the heavenly Father awaits everyone with His merciful love. God does not want anyone to be lost; that is why 2,000 years ago He sent His Son to earth, "to seek and to save the lost" (Lk. 19:10). ...
>
> In Her motherly concern, the Blessed Virgin came here to Fatima to ask men and women "to stop offending God, Our Lord, who is already too much offended". It is a mother's sorrow that compels Her to speak; *the destiny of Her children is at stake*. For this reason She asks the little shepherds: "Pray, pray much and make sacrifices for sinners; *many souls go to hell because they have no one to pray and make sacrifices for them*".

We have already noted that His Holiness cited Chapter 12 verses 3 and 4 of the Book of the Apocalypse, and that the reference in those verses is commonly interpreted to mean one-third of the Catholic clergy being swept down from their exalted state through loss of faith or moral corruption—and we are seeing both among possibly even one-third of the Catholic clergy today. Notice the exact coincidence of the Pope's sermon with Sister Lucy's warning to Father Fuentes about how "The

---

[326] E.g., "He who has ears to hear, let him hear!" (Matt. 11:15)

devil knows that religious and priests who *fall away* from their beautiful vocation *drag* numerous souls to hell."

Therefore, it seems perfectly clear that Pope John Paul II was trying to tell us that the Third Secret relates to the great apostasy foretold in Sacred Scripture. Why did the Pope not say these things directly and explicitly, but rather in a somewhat hidden manner, in language only the more learned would grasp? *Was the Pope trying to send a signal to the more astute about what he thought was going to be revealed very soon—namely, the whole of the Third Secret?* As it turned out, of course, we received only the vision of the "Bishop dressed in White" and the so-called "commentary" in *TMF.* Perhaps the Pope recognized the strength of the resistance posed by Cardinal Sodano and his collaborators, and hoped that he would at least be able to disclose in his sermon the essence of the Secret in the hope that sooner or later the whole truth would come out. Perhaps John Paul II did not feel that he could speak freely, precisely because he had allowed himself to be surrounded by clerics, religious, bishops and Cardinals whom he had later discovered now to be untrustworthy but whom he felt unable to replace (like King David felt regarding his general, Joab [2 Kings 3:26-39; 3 Kings 2:5]), *who were* still in office and *who were* undermining the Faith, *who were (and maybe still are)* part of that one-third of the consecrated souls swept down from their high stations by the devil. Perhaps the Pope either did not know who they were, or he did know but did not think he could speak out publicly and survive for long. (We recall here the sudden death of Pope John Paul I.) Whatever the reason, John Paul II did not speak very clearly—yet clearly enough that one can discern his meaning. As Jesus told His disciples on one occasion: "He who has ears to hear, let him hear."

In sum, a train of witnesses, from the future Pope Pius XII in the 1930s through John Paul II in 2000—and indeed the currently reigning Pope when he was Cardinal Ratzinger—is unanimous on this point: the contents of the Third Secret of Fatima pertain to a crisis of faith in the Catholic Church, an apostasy, with grave consequences for the whole world. Not a single witness has ever denied that this is what the Third Secret portends. Nor did Sister Lucy ever correct any of these testimonies before her death in 2005, even though throughout her life she had not hesitated to correct those who misrepresented the contents of the Message of Fatima.

A "Compromise Solution"?

Here we stress in particular the testimony of Pope John Paul II that the Message of Fatima foretells a widespread loss of faith, and a fall from grace among the Catholic clergy of various ranks, under the malign influence of the "tail of the dragon" to which the Pope referred at Fatima on May 13, 2000—the very date on which Cardinal Sodano announced the coming publication of the text of the vision of the "Bishop dressed in white" on June 26, 2000.

Socci tells us that while Cardinal Ratzinger and Pope John Paul II had wanted to release the full text of the Third Secret—including the 25 lines with Our Lady's own words—they were opposed by Archbishop Bertone and Cardinal Sodano.

The Pope's truly astounding reference to the dragon seen in Chapter 12 of the Book of the Apocalypse led Antonio Socci to conclude that John Paul II wished to reveal the entirety of the Third Secret, but that "a compromise solution was reached" with Cardinal Sodano and Archbishop Bertone whereby the still-unpublished portion of the Secret would be revealed *indirectly* through John Paul II's sermon at Fatima, which clearly links the Fatima prophecies to apostasy in the Church by pointed references to verses 1, 3 and 4 of Chapter 12 of the Book of the Apocalypse. The idea, writes Socci in an allusion to Scripture, was: "He who can understand, let him understand."[327]

This indirect revelation of the missing text to those "in the know," combined with publication of the wordless vision, "would permit them [the Vatican bureaucracy] to say in [good] conscience that all of the Third Secret had been revealed, but without an integral explicit publication so as to avoid (in their opinion) a great shock to the Christian people, sensationalistic broadcasts and a reaction of panic."[328]

Gateway to the Missing Text

Now, the first two parts of the Secret of Fatima say absolutely nothing about apostasy in the Church. Likewise, the visional portion of the Third Secret, concerning the "Bishop dressed in White", says absolutely nothing about an apostasy. If every witness says that the Third Secret speaks of apostasy in the Church, yet those portions of the Message of Fatima revealed to date, including the vision of "a Bishop dressed in White", say nothing about it, the inescapable conclusion is that some portion of the Third Secret has been withheld. But what precisely does this part of the Secret actually say about the coming crisis of apostasy?

The logical place to begin is with the telltale phrase from Sister Lucy's Fourth Memoir; the phrase that the Vatican apparatus has been at great pains to demote and obscure as if it were a mere footnote to the Message of Fatima: "In Portugal the dogma of the Faith will always be preserved etc." This phrase is the only evident reference to a coming apostasy in the published portions of the Message (although we hasten to add, that even without this phrase it would still be clear from all the evidence that the Third Secret relates to an apostasy in the Church). Here, *and only here*, the revealed portion of the integral Message of Fatima touches upon the question of the *dogmas* of the Faith, and how they will be *preserved* in Portugal.

And what would be the point of Our Lady mentioning the *preservation of dogma* in Portugal if not to warn us that dogma was *not* going to be

---

[327] Ibid.
[328] *The Fourth Secret of Fatima*, English ed., p. 82; popular ed., p. 60; Italian ed., p. 91.

preserved elsewhere in the Church? As we have earlier suggested, the "elsewhere" is undoubtedly described in the words comprised within Sister Lucy's "etc."

Given that the vision published on June 26, 2000 contains no further words of Our Lady, it can only be concluded that the missing words of Our Lady are found in the "sound track", as it were, of the Third Secret, in which Our Lady would explain the vision. The vision, it would seem, is the end result of this catastrophic loss of faith: The Pope and remaining hierarchy are being hunted down and killed outside the half-ruined city of Rome, perhaps (we can only speculate since the words of Our Lady are missing) after a nuclear holocaust. This, indeed, fits perfectly with Cardinal Ratzinger's admission in 1984 that the Third Secret relates to "dangers threatening the faith and the life of the Christian, and therefore (the life) *of the world*." On the figurative level, the corpses surrounding the Pope as he walks haltingly toward the hill where he is executed by soldiers would represent the victims of apostasy, and the half-ruined city the condition of the Church during this time of apostasy.

That telltale "etc" in Lucy's Fourth Memoir is, therefore, the gateway to the missing text of the Secret in which precisely the *dogmatic* crisis in the Church is foretold in connection with subsequent apostasy and calamity for the whole world.

The Greatest Threat of All:
The Loss of Catholic Dogma

When Mother Angelica stated on national television on May 16, 2001 that she believes "we didn't get the whole thing" (i.e., the whole Third Secret) because "I think it's scary," she was surely correct. There is nothing more frightening than the danger of a widespread loss of Faith in the Church, especially when the danger emanates "from the top" as Cardinal Ciappi, Pope John Paul II's own personal theologian, said concerning the Third Secret. The result of this danger, if it is not averted, will be the eternal damnation of millions of souls (maybe even billions).[329] And who knows how many have been lost already for lack of the Third Secret's salutary warnings and advice?

The vision published on June 26, however, simply does not express anything that frightening. The vision, in fact, expresses *nothing* so terrible that the Vatican would have kept it under lock and key for forty years. Indeed, Cardinal Ratzinger tells us that the Third Secret, as represented by the vision alone, contains "no great surprises". That is because the surprises follow the still-hidden conclusion of the phrase "In Portugal the dogma of the Faith will always be preserved etc"— again, the very phrase the *TMF* "commentary" has removed from the

---

[329] See the sermon of St. Leonard of Port Maurice and the introduction published in "The Little Number of Those Who Are Saved", *The Fatima Crusader*, No. 92 (May 2009), pp. 12ff; also on the web at http://www.fatimacrusader.com/cr92/cr92pg12.pdf

integral text of Our Lady's words in Sister Lucy's Fourth Memoir.

Now, when Pope John Paul II spoke of "the very bases of our salvation undermined" in his Fatima sermon in 1982, he certainly meant the undermining of the Catholic Faith. We know this from the constant teaching of the Catholic Church. For example, the Athanasian Creed says: "Whoever wishes to be saved must before all else adhere to the Catholic Faith. He must preserve this faith whole and inviolate; otherwise he shall most certainly perish in eternity." The foundation of our salvation is belonging to the Catholic Church and holding on to our Catholic Faith whole and inviolate. The loss of this foundation must be what the Third Secret concerns. Every witness said so, Pope John Paul II said so, and the telltale phrase "In Portugal the dogma of the Faith will always be preserved etc." also said so.

As Our Lord warned us: "What does it profit a man to gain the whole world if he loses his own eternal soul?" If a person loses his soul for the new orientation of the Church; the New World Order; or the Masonic, man-made One World Religion; it profits him nothing, for he will burn in hell for all eternity. For this reason alone, the Third Secret is vitally important to us. It could not be any more important, because it concerns the salvation of our own individual souls. It also concerns the salvation of the souls of the Pope, Cardinals, bishops, priests, and indeed of every living person. Thus, the Third Secret concerns every man, woman and child on the face of the earth, and particularly Catholics.

We recall again that in 1984 Cardinal Ratzinger admitted that if the Secret was not published "at least for the time being" it was to "prevent religious *prophecy* from being mistaken for a quest for the sensational"—a far cry from his claim in 2000 that, according to Sodano's Party Line, the Third Secret culminated in 1981 with the failed assassination attempt. Further, the Third Secret is a prophecy that began to be realized in 1960, which Sister Lucy said was the year by which the prophecy will be "much clearer" (*mais claro*). As Frère Michel points out, a prophecy that starts to be realized obviously becomes much clearer. The prophecy, therefore, started to be realized at least by 1960. It is, therefore, a prophecy that tells us *about our time*. It is a loving warning from Our Lady, and also advice on how to respond to the clear and present danger in the Church.

Now let us look more closely at the essence of the Third Secret. As the former Cardinal Ratzinger admitted 25 years ago (in 1984)— again, before Cardinal Sodano issued the Party Line on Fatima—the Third Secret concerns, first of all, the dangers to the Faith. St. John tells us what it is that overcomes the world: he says it is our faith. *Therefore, in order for the world to overcome the Church, it first has to overcome our faith as Catholics.*

The Third Secret's essence then concerns the world's attempt to overcome our Catholic Faith. As we have demonstrated abundantly in the previous chapters, the forces of the world have conducted a major assault on the Catholic Faith since 1960. There is simply no question about this, based on the overwhelming evidence which we have only outlined here.

Still more particularly, the Secret concerns the *dogma* of the Faith. Our Lady of Fatima spoke about the *dogma* of the Faith always being preserved in Portugal, not simply "the Faith." Why did Our Lady focus on Catholic *dogma*? Clearly, She did so because the Secret is a prophecy that Catholic dogma, *specifically*, would be the target of those who would attack the Church from within and without. As Our Lord Himself warned us in Sacred Scripture: "For false Christs and false prophets shall rise, and shall show signs and wonders, to seduce, if it were possible, even the elect" (Mk. 13:22). As the Arian crisis demonstrates, these false prophets can include even priests and bishops. We can cite here Cardinal Newman's famous description of that time in Church history: "The comparatively few who remained faithful were discredited and driven into exile; the rest were either *deceivers or deceived.*" In such times of crisis, Catholics must adhere to the dogmas of the Faith.

What is dogma? Dogma is what has been *infallibly defined by the Church*. Dogma is what Catholics must believe in order to be Catholic. The dogmas of the Faith are what is contained in the solemn, infallible definitions of the Magisterium—namely, the Pope alone, speaking in a way that clearly binds the Universal Church to believe in what he is pronouncing, or an ecumenical council of all the Catholic bishops presided over by the Pope which issues such binding pronouncements, or those things taught by the Ordinary and Universal Magisterium of the Church.

What is meant by the *infallible* definition of dogma? The word infallible means *"cannot fail"*. Therefore, the definitions of the Faith, solemnly defined by the Church, cannot fail. We know what the Faith is, what the dogmas of the Faith are, by means of the *infallible* definitions. *If we believe and hold fast to these infallible definitions, then we cannot be deceived in those matters so defined.*

How do we know that a matter has been defined infallibly as an article of the Catholic Faith? We know it from the manner in which the teaching is presented.

Four Sources of Infallible Teaching

There are four principal ways Church teaching is presented to us infallibly:

First, through the promulgation of *creeds* by the Popes and ecumenical councils, which provide a summary of what Catholics must believe in order to be Catholic.

Second, by means of solemn *definitions* containing such phrases as "We declare, pronounce and define," or some similar formula indicating that the Pope or the Pope together with an ecumenical council clearly intend to bind the Church to believe in the teaching. Such definitions are usually accompanied by *anathemas* (condemnations) of those who would in any way deny the defined teaching.

Third, the definitions of the Ordinary and Universal Magisterium, meaning the *constant* teaching of the Church in an "ordinary" manner, *always and everywhere*, even if the teaching is never solemnly defined by such words as "We declare, pronounce and define..." (One example of this is the Church's constant teaching, throughout Her history, that contraception and abortion are gravely immoral.)

Fourth, there are definitive judgments of the Pope, usually *condemned propositions*, which are those propositions a Catholic is *forbidden* to believe. When a Pope, or a Pope and Council together, solemnly condemn a proposition, we can know infallibly that it is contrary to the Catholic Faith.

An example of a *creed* is the Profession of Faith promulgated by the Council of Trent. We present it here, conveniently arranged in the form of points, with the language unaltered:

- I, N., with firm faith believe and profess each and every article contained in the Symbol of faith which the holy Roman Church uses; namely:

- I believe in one God, the Father almighty, Creator of Heaven and earth, and of all things visible and invisible; and in

- one Lord Jesus Christ, the only-begotten Son of God, born of the Father before all ages; God from God, light from light, true God from true God; begotten not made, of one substance (consubstantial) with the Father; through whom all things were made;

- who for us men and for our salvation came down from Heaven, and was made incarnate by the Holy Spirit of the Virgin Mary, and was made man.

- He was crucified also for us under Pontius Pilate, died, and was buried; and

- He rose again the third day according to the Scriptures, and ascended into Heaven;

- He sits at the right hand of the Father, and He shall come again in glory to judge the living and the dead, and of His kingdom there will be no end.

- And I believe in the Holy Spirit, the Lord, and giver of life, who proceeds from the Father and the Son; who equally with the Father and the Son is adored and glorified; who spoke through the prophets.

- And I believe that there is one, holy, Catholic, and apostolic Church.

- I confess one baptism for the remission of sins; and I hope for the resurrection of the dead, and the life of the world to come. Amen.

- I resolutely accept and embrace the apostolic and ecclesiastical traditions and the other practices and regulations of that same Church.

- In like manner I accept Sacred Scripture according to the meaning which has been held by holy Mother Church and which She now holds. It is Her prerogative to pass judgment on the true meaning and interpretation of Sacred Scripture. And I will never accept or interpret it in a manner different from the unanimous agreement of the Fathers.

- I also acknowledge that there are truly and properly seven sacraments of the New Law, instituted by Jesus Christ our Lord, and that they are necessary for the salvation of the human race, although it is not necessary for each individual to receive them all.

- I acknowledge that the seven sacraments are: Baptism, Confirmation, Eucharist, Penance, Extreme Unction, Holy Orders, and Matrimony; and that they confer grace; and that of the seven, Baptism, Confirmation, and Holy Orders cannot be repeated without committing a sacrilege.

- I also accept and acknowledge the customary and approved rites of the Catholic Church in the solemn administration of these sacraments.

- I embrace and accept each and every article on Original Sin and justification declared and defined in the most holy Council of Trent.

- I likewise profess that in the Mass a true, proper, and propitiatory sacrifice is offered to God on behalf of the living and the dead, and that the Body and Blood together with the Soul and Divinity of Our Lord Jesus Christ is truly, really, and substantially present in the most holy Sacrament of the Eucharist, and that there is a change of the whole substance of the bread into the Body, and of the whole substance of the wine into the Blood; and this change the Catholic Church calls transubstantiation.

- I also profess that the whole and entire Christ and a true Sacrament is received under each separate species.

- I firmly hold that there is a purgatory, and that the souls detained there are helped by the prayers of the faithful.

- I likewise hold that the saints reigning together with Christ should be honored and invoked, that they offer prayers to God on our behalf, and that their relics should be venerated.

- I firmly assert that images of Christ, of the Mother of God ever Virgin, and of the other saints should be owned and kept, and that due honor and veneration should be given to them.

- I affirm that the power of indulgences was left in the keeping of the

Church by Christ, and that the use of indulgences is very beneficial to Christians.

- I acknowledge the holy, Catholic, and apostolic Roman Church as the mother and teacher of all churches; and

- I promise and swear true obedience to the Roman Pontiff, vicar of Christ and successor of Blessed Peter, Prince of the Apostles.

- I unhesitatingly accept and profess all the doctrines (especially those concerning the primacy of the Roman Pontiff and his infallible teaching authority[330]) handed down, defined, and explained by the sacred canons and ecumenical councils and especially those of this most holy Council of Trent (and by the ecumenical Vatican Council I). And at the same time:

- I condemn, reject, and anathematize everything that is contrary to those propositions, and all heresies without exception that have been condemned, rejected, and anathematized by the Church.

- I, N., promise, vow, and swear that, with God's help, I shall most constantly hold and profess this true Catholic faith, outside which no one can be saved and which I now freely profess and truly hold. With the help of God, I shall profess it whole and unblemished to my dying breath; and, to the best of my ability, I shall see to it that my subjects or those entrusted to me by virtue of my office hold it, teach it, and preach it. So help me God and His holy Gospel.

As for solemn and infallible *definitions* of Catholic dogma, one recent example is the Apostolic Letter of Pope Pius IX, *Ineffabilis Deus* (1854), infallibly defining the dogma of the Immaculate Conception of Mary:

> We *declare, pronounce, and define* that the doctrine which holds that the most Blessed Virgin Mary, in the first instance of Her conception, by a singular grace and privilege granted by Almighty God, in view of the merits of Jesus Christ, the Savior of the human race, was preserved free from all stain of Original Sin, is a doctrine revealed by God and therefore to be believed firmly and constantly by all the faithful.

> Hence, if anyone shall dare—which God forbid!—to think otherwise than as has been defined by us, let him know and understand that *he is condemned by his own judgment; that he has suffered shipwreck in the faith*; that he has separated from the unity of the Church; and that, furthermore, by his own action he incurs the penalties established by law if he should dare to express in words or writing or by any other outward means the errors he

---

[330] The words in parenthesis in this paragraph are now inserted into the Tridentine profession of faith by order of Blessed Pope Pius IX in a decree issued by the Holy Office, January 20, 1877. (*Acta Sanctae Sedis*, X [1877], pp. 71ff.)

thinks in his heart.

Here we recall that in *TMF* Cardinal Ratzinger claimed that "According to Matthew 5:8, the 'immaculate heart' is *a* heart which, with God's grace, has come to perfect interior unity and therefore 'sees God.'" No, no, no! The Immaculate Heart is not "a" heart, but *the* heart—the one and only heart—of the Blessed Virgin Mary, Who is the only merely human being Who was conceived without Original Sin and Who never committed even the slightest personal sin during Her glorious life on this earth.

Finally, there is the *condemned proposition*. A prime example of this is the *Syllabus of Errors* of Blessed Pius IX, wherein this great Pope enumerated the many errors of liberalism in the form of propositions which he solemnly, definitively and infallibly condemned as errors against the Faith,[331] including proposition #80 (which we mentioned earlier): "The Roman Pontiff can and ought to reconcile himself and come to terms with progress, liberalism and modern civilization."

As we have shown, here too Cardinal Ratzinger appeared to contradict prior Church teaching, telling us that the teaching of Vatican II was a "countersyllabus", which was "an attempt at an official reconciliation with the new era inaugurated in 1789" and an effort to correct what he called "the *one-sidedness* of the position adopted by the Church under Blessed Pius IX and Saint Pius X in response to the situation created by the new phase of history inaugurated by the French Revolution ..."[332] Making his apparent rejection of the solemn, infallible teaching of Blessed Pius IX even more explicit, the Cardinal declared that at Vatican II, "the attitude of critical reserve toward the forces that have left their imprint on the modern world is to be replaced by a *coming to terms* with their movement."[333] This opinion flatly contradicts the teaching of Blessed Pius IX that the Church *must not* "come to terms" with "progress, liberalism and modern civilization."

This abuse of the dogma of the Immaculate Conception and dismissal of the *Syllabus* as "one-sided" exposes the very core of the post-conciliar crisis in the Church: an assault on *the infallible definitions* of the Magisterium.

---

[331] In Paragraph 6 of the Encyclical *Quanta Cura* which was issued with the *Syllabus* on December 8, 1864, Blessed Pope Pius IX stated solemnly: "Amid, therefore, so great perversity of depraved opinions, We, well remembering Our Apostolic Office, and very greatly solicitous for Our most holy Religion, for sound doctrine and the salvation of souls which is entrusted to Us by God, and (solicitous also) for the welfare of human society itself, have thought it right to raise up Our Apostolic voice. *Therefore, by Our Apostolic Authority, We reprobate, proscribe and condemn all the singular and evil opinions and doctrines severally mentioned in this Letter, and will and command that they be thoroughly held by all children of the Catholic Church as reprobated, proscribed and condemned.*" (Our emphasis) Taken from *The Popes Against Modern Errors*, (TAN Books and Publishers, Rockford, Illinois, 1999) p. 21.

[332] Cardinal Joseph Ratzinger, *Principles of Catholic Theology*, (Ignatius Press, San Francisco, 1987) pp. 381-382.

[333] Ibid., p. 380.

Now, for the most part, this assault has been rather indirect. The infallible definition is usually not directly denied, but rather *undermined* through criticism or "revision." The innovators in the Church are not so direct and forthright to declare that an infallible Church teaching is wrong. And, in their supposed "enlightenment" these innovators may actually think they are "deepening" or "developing" Catholic teaching for the good of the Church—again, we are not judging their subjective motivations. But the *effect* of what they do is obvious: the undermining of the infallibly defined teachings of the Magisterium.

Another example of this undermining is the attack on the dogma that outside the Catholic Church there is no salvation. The Tridentine creed, quoted in full above, states: "I shall most constantly hold and profess this true Catholic faith, outside which no one can be saved …" In Chapter 6 we show how, over and over again, the Magisterium has solemnly defined the dogma that there is no salvation outside the Catholic Church. Yet today, the dogma is denied and *undermined* by an "ecumenism" which declares that neither the Protestant heretics nor the Orthodox schismatics need return to the Catholic Church, because this is "outdated ecclesiology."[334] And in many places today, the dogma is directly denied, and in other places it is not directly denied but in practice it collapses from insidious, repeated, indirect attacks and, as a result, it is no longer believed and followed in those places.

It is undeniable that since Vatican II a host of novel notions has been passed off in the Church as "development" of Catholic doctrine, even though these novelties at least implicitly (and sometimes explicitly) contradict (or at least undermine) the infallible definitions. The idea, for example, that the Council document *Gaudium et Spes* is a "countersyllabus" that counters the solemn condemnations of Blessed Pope Pius IX[335] undermines the whole integrity of the infallible Magisterium. Such talk is an assault on the very credibility of the teaching office of the Church, and is thus, in the end, an assault on Catholic dogma itself.

There Cannot be a "New Understanding" of Catholic Dogma

This post-conciliar attack on dogma through undermining as well as implicit and explicit contradiction cannot be justified as a "development" or "new insight" into dogma. As the First Vatican Council solemnly taught: "For, the Holy Spirit was not promised to the successors of Peter that they might disclose *new doctrine*, but that by His help they might guard sacredly the revelation transmitted through the Apostles and the deposit of faith, and might faithfully set it forth."[336]

Further, as Vatican I taught, there cannot be any "new understanding"

---

[334] *The Balamand Statement*, No. 30, June 23, 1993.
[335] See footnote 331 of this chapter.
[336] Vatican Council I - 1870 A.D., see Denzinger (Dz.) 1836.

of what the Church has already infallibly defined:

> [T]hat understanding of its sacred dogmas must be *perpetually retained*, which Holy Mother Church has once declared; and there must never be a recession [moving away] from that meaning under the specious name of a deeper understanding.[337]

Thus, it is a matter of Catholic Faith that we believe that *no new doctrine has been revealed by God since the death of the last Apostle, Saint John*, and that *no new understanding of doctrine* has arisen because of Vatican II or otherwise.

Therefore, this "new" doctrine or "counter"-doctrine we have heard so much about since Vatican II can only be pseudo-doctrine. This pseudo-doctrine is being taught very subtly. When pseudo-doctrine contradicts doctrines that have been infallibly defined, then Catholics must cling to the infallible doctrines and reject the new "doctrines".

The dogma of the Faith *cannot* fail, but novelties can fail us. Men can fail; lay people can fail; priests can fail; bishops can fail; Cardinals can fail; and even the Pope can fail in matters which do not involve his charism of infallibility, as history has shown us with more than one Pope who taught or appeared to teach some novelty.

For example, Pope Honorius was posthumously condemned by the Third Council of Constantinople in 680 A.D. for aiding and abetting heresy,[338] and that condemnation was approved by Pope Leo II and repeated by later Popes. As another example, Pope John XXII, in the 14th Century (1333 A.D.), gave sermons (but not solemn definitions) in which he insisted that the blessed departed do not enjoy the Beatific Vision until the day of General Judgment. For this he was denounced and corrected by theologians, and he finally retracted his heretical opinion on his deathbed.

In the case of Pope John XXII,[339] knowledgeable Catholics (in this case theologians) knew that John XXII was wrong in his teaching about the Particular Judgment. They knew that something was wrong with John XXII's teaching because it contradicted what the Church had always believed, even if there had not yet been an infallible definition.

---

[337] Vatican Council I, see Dz. 1800.

[338] Through his negligence, Pope Honorius had been largely responsible for the spread of the Monothelite heresy by asserting that there is only one will in Christ, the divine will—an error that implicitly denies that Christ is both true God and true man—, although he understood this in a Catholic sense, namely that there could not be a conflict between the divine will and the human will of Christ. However, his formulation allowed the Monothelite heretics to assert that there was only one will in Christ and that the Pope agreed with them.

[339] John XXII (1316 – 1334) was a very erudite Pope who condemned the Waldensians, Jean Pouilly, Marsilius of Padova, and Eckhard, in 1331 and 1332. However, he preached that the blessed departed do not enjoy the Beatific Vision until the day of General Judgment. In 1333 he even wrote a booklet about it and sent it to the University of Paris. The King of France called in the Inquisition and on January 3, 1334, the Pope submitted and on his deathbed solemnly recanted, leaving the final decision to his successor, Benedict XII (D.S. 1000).

Catholics who knew their faith in the 14th Century did not simply say: "Oh, the Pope has given a sermon, therefore we must change our belief." Looking at the Church's constant teaching that the blessed departed enjoy the Beatific Vision immediately after Purgatory, the theologians knew Pope John XXII was wrong, and they told him so.

As it turned out, the immediacy of the Beatific Vision was solemnly and infallibly defined by John XXII's successor in 1336. This placed the matter beyond all further dispute—which is precisely why an infallible definition was needed. The same is true with every other matter infallibly defined by the Church. We can, and must, rely on these infallible definitions with absolute certainty, rejecting all opinions to the contrary—even if contrary opinions were to come from a Cardinal or even a Pope.

There are other examples of Popes failing. Even the first Pope, St. Peter, failed, as shown in Sacred Scripture—not by what he said but by the example he gave. Saint Peter refused to sit at table with Gentile converts, in Antioch about 50 A.D. By shunning these converts he gave the false impression that the First Council of Jerusalem was wrong in its infallible teaching that the Mosaic ceremonial law, including the prohibition against Jews eating with "unclean" Gentiles, was not binding on the Catholic Church. This was the incident for which St. Paul rebuked St. Peter to his face in public. (Gal. 2:11)

Another example is Pope Liberius in 357 A.D., who failed by signing a Creed which the Arians proposed to him, leaving out any reference to the Son being consubstantial with the Father. He did this after two years in exile and under the threat of death. And he also failed (under duress while in exile) by wrongly condemning and excommunicating—in reality, only giving the appearance of excommunicating—St. Athanasius, who was defending the Faith in this matter. Liberius, the first Pope not to be proclaimed a saint by the Church, was wrong because Athanasius was teaching the Catholic doctrine—the true doctrine, the infallible doctrine—taught infallibly by the Council of Nicea in 325 AD. It was that infallible definition, not the defective teaching of Pope Liberius, that had to be followed in that case and must be followed now and forever. Amen!

From these examples in Church history we learn that *everything* proposed to us for our belief must be judged by those definitions. And so if a Cardinal, a bishop, a priest, a layman *or even the Pope* teaches us some novelty that is contrary to any definition of the Faith, we can know that the teaching is wrong and that it must be rejected for the salvation of our immortal souls. Yes, even the Pope can fail, *and he does fail* if he expresses an opinion that is contrary to a solemn, infallible definition of the Catholic Church. This does not mean the *Church* fails when this happens, but only that the Pope has made a mistake without imposing it on the whole Church. And, of course, if even the Pope can make a mistake in teaching some novelty, then certainly Cardinals, bishops and priests can make mistakes in their teaching and opinions.

And so, when Our Lady speaks about the "dogma of the Faith", She indicates to us that "the dangers threatening the faith and the life of the Christian and therefore (the life) of the world"—to recall Cardinal Ratzinger's admission—will arise when solemn dogmatic definitions of the Catholic Faith are contradicted or undermined; for it is these definitions which are the very foundation of the Catholic Faith, and therefore the foundation of our salvation, to recall Pope John Paul II's 1982 sermon at Fatima.

To the objection that mere priests, or mere lay people, cannot disagree with high-ranking prelates, or even (in the kind of extraordinary case for which we have just given examples) the Pope, one must reply: That is why the Church has infallible definitions. It is by measuring any given teaching against solemn, infallible definitions that one can know that a teaching is true or false—not by what rank in the clergy a person has. As St. Paul taught: "But though we, or an angel from Heaven, preach a gospel to you besides that which we have preached to you, let him be anathema." (Gal. 1:8) The faithful are to regard *even an Apostle* as anathema—accursed, cut off from the Church, worthy of hellfire—if he contradicts the infallible teaching of the Church. That is why theologians were able to correct Pope John XXII (in 1333 A.D.) in his erroneous teaching from the pulpit; and it is why Catholics today can tell right from wrong teaching, even if they have a rank lower than the prelate who is committing the error.

A prime historical example of this is found in the case of a lawyer named Eusebius, who pointed out that Nestorius, a high-ranking Archbishop in Constantinople, the highest ranking prelate after the Pope, was wrong when he denied that Mary is the Mother of God. Eusebius stood up in his pew on Christmas Day, during Mass, and denounced Nestorius for preaching heresy. Yet all the "high-ranking" priests and bishops had remained silent in the face of Nestorius' heresy. Thus, a mere layman was right and all the rest of them were in error. The Council of Ephesus was called to hear the matter, and it was solemnly and infallibly defined that Mary is the Mother of God. And since Nestorius refused to recant, he was deposed and declared a heretic. Nestorius was excommunicated!

To summarize, truth is not a matter of numbers or rank; truth is a matter of what Christ and God have revealed in Sacred Scripture, dogma and Tradition, what has been solemnly defined by the Catholic Church, and what the Catholic Church has always taught—taught *always*, not just since 1965!

The Disastrous Effects of Tampering With Infallible Definitions

History likewise provides us with a prime example of what can happen to the Church when even one dogma is contradicted on a wide scale. The heresy of Arianism caused catastrophic confusion in the Church from 336 A.D. to 381 A.D. After Arianism had been formally condemned at the First Council of Nicea in 325 A.D., the Arian heretics reintroduced it to the general public of the Catholic Church around 336 A.D. The heresy eventually claimed about 90% of the bishops before it was finally defeated about forty years later. In the resulting confusion and loss of faith, even the great St. Athanasius was "excommunicated" by the Pope in 357. Arianism was still in full bloom for some time between 360 and 380. The results were utterly devastating to the Church. However, by 381 Arianism had been defeated by the First Council of Constantinople.

The Arian crisis has much to teach us about the probable contents of the missing text of the Third Secret. One reason the Arians were able to succeed for a time, was that they "successfully" attacked a *dogma* that had been solemnly and infallibly defined at the Council of Nicea in 325—that Christ is "God from God, Light from Light, true God from true God; *begotten not made, consubstantial with the Father*". This solemn and infallible definition is in the Credo of the Council of Nicea, which we say every Sunday at Mass.

The Arians overturned the definition by getting many of the "faithful" to argue for replacing it with a false definition that was not infallible. In 336 they replaced the Greek word *Homoousion* with another word *Homoiousion*. The word *Homoousion* basically means "consubstantial" with the Father. For God the Son to be consubstantial with the Father, the Son must not only be God but the *same* one God as the Father, so that the substance of the Father *is* the substance of the Son, even though the Person of the Father is not the Person of the Son. Thus, there are three Persons in one God—Father, Son and Holy Ghost—but there is only one God, with one *substance*, in three Persons. That is the mystery of the Trinity. The new word *Homoiousion*, however, means "of *similar* substance" to the Father. Thus, the critical phrase in the dogma— "consubstantial with the Father"—was changed to "of similar substance with the Father" or "like the Father."

Thus the Arians brought about mass confusion in the Church by adding *one letter* to the word *Homoousion* to create a new word with a new meaning: *Homoiousion*. They attacked a solemn definition, claiming that their new definition would be better than the solemn definition. But, of course, the new definition could not be better than the solemn definition, because the solemn definition of the Council of Nicea was infallible.

By adding *one letter to one word*, the Arians got rid of an infallible definition. This opened the way for the Arians and the semi-Arians, leading to actual warfare. People were martyred, persecuted, driven out into the desert, driven into exile over this *one* change to *one* infallible dogma. St. Athanasius was driven into exile five different times by the national conference of Egyptian bishops (and spent at least 17 years in exile as a result). But he was right and the heretical bishops of that Synod were all wrong.

Infallible Definitions Are Higher
than Any Learning or Rank in the Church

Why did Athanasius know he was right? Because he clung to the infallible definition, no matter what everyone else said. Not all the learning in the world, nor all the rank of office, can substitute for the truth of one infallibly defined Catholic teaching. Even the simplest member of the faithful, clinging to an infallible definition, will know more than the most "learned" theologian who denies or undermines the definition. *That is the whole purpose of the Church's infallibly defined teaching*—to make us independent of the mere opinions of men, however learned, however high their rank.

Now, in 325 A.D. the solemn definition of the Council of Nicea *was* infallible, but many people then did not fully realize that solemn definitions of the Faith were infallible. That is, at this time in Church history the Church had not yet issued the solemn definition teaching that the definitions of Faith are infallible. But in 1870 A.D., the First Vatican Council solemnly and infallibly defined the infallibility of the Church's solemn definitions. Now we know, infallibly, that solemn definitions are infallible. Once again: they cannot fail—*ever*.

The Infallible Definitions
Are Under Attack in Our Time

In our day, therefore, there is no excuse for being taken in by heresy and giving up the defense of solemn definitions. But that is precisely what is happening today, just as in the time of Arius. *Churchmen are judging things in light of the Second Vatican Council instead of judging the Second Vatican Council in light of the infallible definitions.* They have forgotten that the infallible definitions, not Vatican II, are the unchanging standard by which one measures every doctrine, just as a 36-inch yardstick is the unchanging standard for measuring a yard. One does not suddenly decide that the new standard for measuring a yard is a 35-inch stick. Likewise, the Church cannot suddenly decide that Vatican II is the new yardstick of the Faith.

And so we arrive again, after a more detailed examination, at the crux of the Third Secret. *This* is why it begins with Our Lady's reference to the *dogma* of the Faith. This is why Sister Lucy said the Third Secret would be "much clearer" after 1960. And here it must be noted that we are clearly living in the midst of the period of calamity the Third Secret predicts. How do we know this? We know this from four facts:

The first fact is that the Third Secret is really the third part of one secret. So we need to understand and read the Third Secret in context. The Third Secret starts with the words: "In Portugal the dogma of the Faith will always be preserved etc." We also know the end of the Third Secret which is Our Lady's words: "In the end, My Immaculate Heart will triumph. The Holy Father will consecrate Russia to Me, and she will be converted, and a period of peace will be granted to the world."

The second fact is, we know that the Third Secret is a prophecy; that is, it is a foretelling of future events. We know this from Cardinal Ottaviani who said this in 1955. We know the prophecy foretells that dogma will be preserved in Portgual, and it is implicit that it will not be preserved in other parts of Europe and possibly even the rest of the world.

The third fact is, we know that the prophecy begins on or about 1960. We know this by deducing from Lucy's comment that the Third Secret, which foretells events still in the future, will be clearer in 1960. Now why does a prophecy become clearer in 1960? Because by that year enough events have happened so that when the prophecy is heard in 1960 it would be more understandable than if it were heard before the events of 1960 took place. Thus the Third Secret will be clearer in 1960 because the prophecy begins to be realized or is about to be realized in the year 1960. We now know that the Third Secret mentions explicitly a council (see *The Fatima Crusader,* Issue 92, May 2009, pp. 7-11), as testified to by Father Döllinger, and Vatican II was announced on January 25, 1959.

The fourth fact is, we know that we are living in the period of the Third Secret because we know it started on or around 1960 (as explained above) and we also know we have not yet arrived at the consecration and conversion of Russia and the resulting period of peace predicted and promised at the end of the Third Secret. Since we are living after 1960 and we have not yet arrived at the period of peace, therefore we are still living within the period of the prophecy of the Third Secret.

The Second Vatican Council Announced in 1959 and the Council's Subtle Attack on Dogma

Now what we have seen since the Second Vatican Council is a very subtle, indirect attack on the solemn definitions of the Church. We have had a so-called *pastoral* council that refused to speak with solemn definitions and—in the view of some—actually went against certain solemn definitions. But the Council, as we have seen, wished to be "pastoral", to avoid solemn definitions, to avoid condemnations of error, as Pope John XXIII declared in his opening speech. Well, what is wrong with that? What is wrong is that by the subtle mistake of refusing to make solemn definitions, the door is opened for a Council to use language that could undermine *existing* solemn definitions— exactly this trick was used by the Arians in the Fourth Century in order to bring about confusion in the Church. And they almost succeeded in overcoming the whole Church.

This same process has been occurring again since the opening of the Second Vatican Council. But the faithful have a remedy for the problem: Vatican II is not authoritative to the extent it did not exercise its supreme Magisterium, its power to define doctrine and its power to anathematize error. Since it did not exercise this authority, everything taught by Vatican II that had not been taught infallibly *before* Vatican II has to be examined in light of the infallible dogmatic definitions and teachings of the Catholic Church.

However, that is not what is happening today. What is happening today is people are redefining "the faith" in light of Vatican II. It is surely this process that Our Lady of Fatima speaks about when, going right to the heart of the matter, She says that the *dogma* of the Faith will always be preserved in Portugal—but clearly lost in many other places—telling Sister Lucy that this warning must be made known *by 1960,* by which time the Council had been announced.

This conclusion is confirmed by Pope John Paul II's sermons at Fatima in 1982 and 2000. In 1982 the Pope said that the bases of our salvation were being *undermined.* And in 2000, in his sermon during the beatification of Blessed Jacinta and Blessed Francisco, Pope John Paul II warned us about the dangers to our salvation *today* by telling us that "The Message of Fatima is a call to conversion, alerting humanity *to have nothing to do with the 'dragon' whose 'tail swept down a third of the stars of Heaven, and dragged them to the earth'* (Apoc. 12:4)." Again, where do we find this in the revealed parts of the Fatima Message? Nowhere. It must, therefore, be in the Third Secret. The Pope is telling us that the Third Secret concerns dangers to the Faith and that one-third of the Catholic clergy in fact are working for the devil and therefore dragging many of the faithful to hell.[340]

The Attack is From Within the Church

Now we will focus on yet another particular of the Third Secret's essence. Pope John Paul II also pointed out that the attack on the Catholic Faith is coming from *within.* He said in 1982: "Can the Mother, Who with all the force of the love that She fosters in the Holy Spirit and Who desires everyone's salvation, can She remain silent when She sees the very bases of Her children's salvation *undermined*?" The word *undermine* implies a weakening of the foundation of our salvation from within. An external enemy of the Church attacks from without, an infiltrator undermines from within. In the latter case, the attack is not expected and everyone's guard is down; the attacker is viewed as a "friend."

So we have John Paul II telling us that the Catholic Faith is being undermined from within (May 13, 1982: "the very bases of Her children's salvation undermined") by the one-third of Catholic clergy (May 13, 2000: "one-third of the stars of Heaven").

We conclude this point by noting that there is another source from

---

[340] See a traditional Catholic commentary on this Scriptural passage in *The Book of Destiny* by Father Herman Bernard Kramer, (First edition 1955, republished by TAN Books and Publishers, Inc., Rockford, Illinois, 1975) pp. 280-284. See also pages 120-121 in Chapter 9 of this book, *The Devil's Final Battle.*

which we can glean this aspect of the Third Secret. In 1963 the German publication *Neues Europa* revealed what was purported to be part of the Third Secret: that Cardinal would oppose Cardinal, bishop oppose bishop. We know that when asked whether the *Neues Europa* account should be published, Cardinal Ottaviani, who also had read the Third Secret—who had a very dry personality and was pretty much opposed to most reported apparitions—exclaimed very emphatically: "Publish 10,000 copies! Publish 20,000 copies! Publish 30,000 copies!"[341]

Then we have the testimony of the late Father Malachi Martin that the message of Garabandal contains the Third Secret or parts of the Third Secret. Father Martin, who knew the Third Secret because he had read it himself, and who also read the message of Garabandal, said that because the Vatican chose not to release the Third Secret in 1960, Our Lady had appeared at Garabandal in 1961 in order to disclose the Third Secret. What is in the Garabandal message? The Garabandal message says, among other things: "many Cardinals, bishops, and priests are on the road to hell and 'dragging' many more souls with them". Notice yet again the concept of *dragging* souls down into hell. The same terminology appears in Sister Lucy's remark to Father Fuentes that "The devil knows that religious and priests who fall away from their beautiful vocation *drag* numerous souls to hell,"[342] and in John Paul II's sermon on May 13, 2000, which refers to the scene in the Book of the Apocalypse in which the tail of the dragon drags down one-third of the stars of Heaven (Cardinals, bishops and priests).

While the Garabandal apparitions are not formally approved, the Bishop with jurisdiction over Garabandal—that is, the Bishop

---

[341] Personal testimony of retired Vatican Msgr. Corrado Balducci to Father Nicholas Gruner, Christopher Ferrara and various other witnesses. This fact is also attested to by Marco Tosatti in his book *Il Segreto Non Svelato* [*The Secret Not Revealed*], (Edizioni Piemme Spa, Casale Monferrato, Italy, May 2002), p. 86.

Marco Tosatti writes: "Father Mastrocola, director of a religious newsletter 'Santa Rita', asked Cardinal Ottaviani the permission to reprint the prophecies made in 'Neues Europa'. The reply was encouraging, but in the light of the 'revealing' of the secret of June 26, 2000, embarrassing. 'Do it, do it'—replied the Cardinal custodian of the Third Secret—'publish as many copies as you want, *because the Madonna wanted it to be published already in 1960.*' And of that text Vatican Radio also spoke in 1977 on the occasion of the tenth anniversary of the trip of Pope Paul VI to Fatima. The text of 'Neues Europa' received great circulation and was republished even in the *L'Osservatore Romano* Sunday edition of October 15, 1978".

The Italian original is as follows: "Padre Mastrocola, direttore di un foglio religioso, 'Santa Rita', chiese al cardinale Ottaviani il permesso di riprendere l'anticipazione fatta da 'Neues Europa'. La risposta fu incoraggiante, ma alla luce dello 'svelamento' del segreto del 26 giugno 2000, imbarazzante. 'Fatelo, fatelo pure'—rispose il porporato custode del terzo segreto—'pubblicatene quante copie vi pare, perché la Madonna voleva che fosse reso noto già nel 1960'. E di quel testo parlò anche la Radio Vaticana nel 1977, nel decennale del viaggio di Paolo VI a Fatima. Il testo di 'Neues Europa' conobbe grande fortuna, e venne ripreso persino il 15 ottobre 1978 dall' 'Osservatore della Domenica'".

[342] See Francis Alban, *Fatima Priest*, First Edition, (Good Counsel Publications, Pound Ridge, New York, 1997) Appendix III, "A Prophetic Interview with Sister Lucy of Fatima", p. 312. See also *The Whole Truth About Fatima* - Vol. III, pp. 503-510 for the text of this interview together with further explanations by Frère Michel.

of Santander—said that nothing in the message was contrary to the Catholic Faith.

The Attack Includes Bad Practices As Well As Bad Doctrine

Here it must be noted that whether a member of the clergy (or the laity) is good or bad is not determined solely by whether he verbally upholds or does not uphold the Faith. Besides comparing the teaching (i.e. the words) of a priest, a bishop, a Cardinal or the Pope to the infallible teaching of the Magisterium, one needs to see if the person is also upholding the orthodox *practices* of the Catholic Church by his words (written and spoken), by his actions and by the Christian conduct of his life. One needs to know if the person (priest, bishop, Cardinal or Pope) is engaging in *heteropraxis*—practices contrary to the Faith— such as disrespect for the Blessed Sacrament.

The Faith can be attacked by *actions* done in either an obvious or a subtle manner. *Our actions must support our words.* We uphold the Faith by upholding the doctrines in our thoughts, words, and writings and also by upholding the pious practices of the Church that support our adherence to the Faith. By introducing novel practices into the local parish (or the local diocese or the local ecclesiastical province, or even into the Universal Church as Catholic Doctors have written is possible to happen) that give the *impression* that the defined Faith is not to be believed, one scandalizes the little ones and even some learned souls by this *heteropraxis*.

For example, we know by the solemn definitions of the Council of Trent that God guarantees to us that the consecrated Host is indeed His Real Presence—that is, really present in the Blessed Sacrament is the Body and Blood of Our Lord Jesus Christ, together with His Soul and Divinity. Now, the Protestant rebels wanted to deny this article of the Faith and they wanted to influence others to do the same. So they reintroduced the practice of Communion in the hand (it had been originally introduced as a widespread practice by the Arian heretics of the Fourth Century to deny that Jesus is God). By this symbolic action, their denial would be clear to all.

Heteropraxis has been used in our day by the enemies of the Church to scandalize many Catholics into losing their Faith in the Real Presence. That is why the abuse of Communion in the hand forbidden by the universal law of the Church for many centuries and still forbidden by the law of the Church to this day is widely promoted. The recent indult [i.e. permission] to go against the letter of the law is only allowed if this practice does not lead to the lessening of the Faith in the Real Presence and does not lead to less respect for the Real Presence. But the actual practice of Communion in the hand *always does*, as we can see from our own everyday experience with this form of heteropraxis.[343]

The practices which *uphold* orthodox doctrine, on the other hand, are referred to as *orthopraxis* (i.e. orthodox Catholic practices). These include: genuflecting in the presence of the Blessed Sacrament, distributing/receiving Communion on the tongue, maintaining the tabernacle with the Blessed Sacrament as the primary focus of attention (and worship) in the center of the sanctuary; and the solemn behavior of the clergy within the sanctuary,[344] showing due reverence to the Presence of God in the Blessed Sacrament. These examples of *orthopraxis* (orthodox actions upholding the Faith) testify to the truth of the dogma that the Blessed Sacrament *is* the Real Presence of God— the Body, Blood, Soul and Divinity of Our Lord Jesus Christ under the appearance of bread—as well as the proper respect of man to God.

Examples of *heteropraxis* against the dogma of the Real Presence include Communion in the hand. This form of *heteropraxis* conveys the erroneous message to the faithful that the Blessed Sacrament is just not that important, that It is just bread, and promotes the heresy that It is not the Real Presence of God—the Body, Blood, Soul and Divinity of Our Lord Jesus Christ under the appearance of bread. Another example of *heteropraxis* in this area is the permanent removal of the tabernacle with the Blessed Sacrament from the sanctuary to a side room or broom closet, so that the primary focus of attention (and worship) in the sanctuary becomes the chair of the "celebrant" or "Presider" over the "assembly". The message is subtly given, and received, that the person sitting in the chair is more important than the Blessed Sacrament. And since the "Presider" (or president of the "assembly") represents the people, then subtly the message is given that God is less important than the people.

These examples remind us yet again of the words of Pope Pius XII, quoted earlier:

> Suppose, dear friend, that Communism [one of "the errors of Russia" mentioned in the Message of Fatima] was only the most visible of the instruments of subversion to be used against the Church and the traditions of Divine Revelation ... I am worried by the Blessed Virgin's messages to Lucy of Fatima. This persistence of Mary about the dangers which menace the Church is a divine warning against the suicide of altering the Faith, in *Her liturgy, Her theology and Her soul.* ... I hear all around me innovators who wish to dismantle the Sacred Chapel, destroy the universal flame of the Church, reject Her ornaments and make Her feel remorse for Her historical past.... A day will come when the civilized world will deny its God, when the Church will doubt as Peter doubted. She will be tempted to believe that man has become God ... In our

---

[343] See *Fatima Priest*, Editions 1 and 2, Appendix V, "Regarding Communion in the Hand". See also *The Fatima Crusader*, Issue 28, June-July 1989, pp. 33ff, 34ff, 36ff; *The Fatima Crusader*, Issue 29, September-November 1989, p. 16; and *The Fatima Crusader*, Issue 7, Spring 1981, p. 11.

[344] See "Sanctuary", on page 379.

churches, Christians will search in vain for the red lamp where God awaits them, like Mary Magdalene weeping before the empty tomb, they will ask, "where have they taken Him?"[345]

From Pius XII's words, it seems then that these above-mentioned forms of *heteropraxis* against the Blessed Sacrament were explicitly mentioned in the Third Secret of Fatima, because while Pius XII relates them to the Fatima Message, they are not mentioned in *any* part of the Message that has been published. That is why they must be mentioned in the Third Secret—that is, the part that is not yet published. Pius XII clearly says that it is *Our Lady of Fatima* who warns us against "the suicide of altering the Faith in Her *liturgy*, Her *theology* and Her *soul*." Therefore, the Third Secret warns us about *both* false doctrine and *heteropraxis* as attacks upon "the dogma of the Faith."

The Attack Includes the Moral Corruption of the Clergy Which We Now Witness

As we have seen, with the eruption of a massive, worldwide scandal involving the sexual misconduct of members of the priesthood, there is a third line of attack on the Church during this time of great crisis: the moral corruption of many consecrated souls. The tail of the dragon sweeps souls from the heavens—down from their consecrated state—not only through heterodoxy and heteropraxis, but also through immorality. Let us recall the statements of Sister Lucy to Father Fuentes:

> The devil wishes to take possession of consecrated souls. He tries to corrupt them in order to lull to sleep the souls of lay people and thereby lead them to final impenitence. That which afflicts the Immaculate Heart of Mary and the Heart of Jesus is the fall of religious and priestly souls. The devil knows that religious and priests who fall away from their beautiful vocation drag numerous souls to hell.

Today we see widespread corruption among the Catholic clergy which is now being manifested in sexual scandals of an unspeakable nature in dioceses throughout North America, Europe and Africa. The tail of the dragon has dragged many members of the clergy down into the rankest forms of immorality.

As a result, the credibility of the many priests who do honor their vows and keep the faith is being destroyed, along with the very credibility of the Church as an institution. Even if there is good doctrine and good practice, the benefits of these often are negated when moral corruption undermines the credibility of the Church.

Who Is Responsible?

Now the question arises: But *who* is identified in the Third Secret as being responsible for the undermining of the Faith through heterodoxy,

---

[345] Pope Pius XII, quoted in the book *Pie XII Devant L'Histoire*, pp. 52-53.

heteropraxis and the moral corruption and fall of consecrated souls? First of all, it is members of the Vatican apparatus itself. We note again the revelation of Cardinal Ciappi, Pope John Paul II's official papal theologian, that "In the Third Secret it is foretold, among other things, that the great apostasy in the Church will begin *at the top.*" Thus, the responsibility lies first and foremost with men in the Vatican. In this, we see the fulfillment not only of the Third Secret, but also the warning of St. Pius X in his 1907 encyclical *Pascendi,* wherein he writes: "The partisans of error are to be sought not only among the Church's open enemies; but ... *in Her very bosom, and are the more mischievous the less they keep in the open.*" These enemies are lay people, priests and bishops "thoroughly imbued with the poisonous doctrines taught by the enemies of the Church", and who put themselves forward "*as reformers of the Church*".[346]

St. Pius X insists:

> "The Church has no greater enemies. For they put into operation their designs for Her undoing, not from without but from within. Hence, the danger is present almost in the very veins and heart of the Church, whose injury is the more certain from the very fact that their knowledge of Her is more intimate."[347]

> "They seize upon professorships in the seminaries and universities, and gradually make of them chairs of pestilence."[348]

> "It is time to tear away the mask from these people and to show them to the Church such as they are."[349]

But then it will be asked: "How do we know which of the clergy are part of the one-third of the stars alluded to by Pope John Paul II; how do we know who the partisans of error are?" The answer again lies in what has been infallibly defined. Those who uphold the Faith, who hold fast to the doctrine of Jesus, are friends. (Apoc. 12:17) Those who do not are foes. As Our Lord said, "By their fruits you shall know them." (Mt. 7:16) One can tell whom to trust by whether they are upholding the Catholic Faith as defined by the solemn definitions. Another sign is that they are living their Catholic Faith as well.

In conclusion, when Pope Paul VI lamented in 1967 that "the smoke of Satan has entered the Church" and in 1973 that "the opening to the world has become a veritable invasion of the Church by worldly thinking" he was only confirming the contents of the Third Secret; so was Pope John Paul II in his more veiled statements in 1982 and 2000. The second part of the Great Secret of Fatima warns of the spread of Russia's errors throughout the world. The Third Secret, in its full contents, is surely a warning that those errors will infiltrate the Church Herself, and especially taking hold through the "opening to the world" at Vatican II.

---

[346] Pope St. Pius X, *Pascendi Dominici Gregis,* para. no. 2.
[347] Ibid., no. 3.
[348] Ibid., no. 61.
[349] Ibid., no. 3.

The infiltration of the Catholic Church by Masonic, Communist, neo-modernist and homosexual elements is seen in the ruinous results of their activities and the loss of faith among Catholics in the pew.

To those who scoff at the claim that such a disaster has befallen the Church in our time, we can only say that they are blind, and that they have ignored the Church's own history, which shows that something very similar has happened before. We alluded earlier to Cardinal Newman's description of the state of the Church during the Arian heresy. A more extended quotation from that description, found in his book *On Consulting the Faithful in Matters of Doctrine*, suffices to prove that the state of affairs in the Church today is not without precedent:

> The body of bishops failed in their confession of the Faith. ... They spoke variously, one against another; there was nothing, after Nicea, of firm, unvarying, consistent testimony, for nearly sixty years. There were untrustworthy Councils, unfaithful bishops; there was weakness, fear of consequences, misguidance, delusion, hallucination, *endless, hopeless, extending into nearly every corner of the Catholic Church.* The comparatively few who remained faithful were discredited and driven into exile; the rest were either *deceivers or deceived.*[350]

The point of Cardinal Newman's book was that it was the laity, clinging to the defined dogma of the Faith, along with a few good priests and bishops such as Saint Athanasius, who kept the Faith alive during the Arian crisis. So it is today.

But one of the great differences between the Arian crisis and the current crisis in the Church is that the Virgin Mary not only gave us a warning many years in advance of the current crisis, but also the means to avoid it by following Her requests at Fatima. To have deprived the Church of the warning contained in the Third Secret, to have covered up the prophecy of apostasy that implicates the very men who have imposed a ruinous new orientation upon the Church and allowed Her to be invaded by the enemy, to have thus prevented the faithful from understanding the cause of it all and arming themselves against it, is another key element of the great and terrible injustice against God and all the faithful of the Catholic Church.

Yet the cover-up had not entirely succeeded. Disbelief in the completeness of the purported disclosure of the Third Secret was widespread and growing in the years following publication of the vision alone in 2000. And by the "breakthrough" year of 2006, the evidence for the existence of a second distinct text pertaining to the Secret, the "soundtrack" of the vision, had become overwhelming. Before we undertake a discussion of the "breakthrough for Fatima" that occurred in 2006, a final systematic review of the evidence for the existence of a second text is in order. That is the subject of the next chapter.

---

[350] John Henry Newman, *On Consulting the Faithful in Matters of Doctrine,* (Kansas City, Sheed and Ward, 1961) p. 77.

Chapter 13

The Third Secret Consists of
Two Distinct Texts

Even before the "breakthrough" year of 2006 and the rapid-fire series of events that have followed since, knowledgeable Catholics the world over simply did not believe that a wordless and rather obscure vision of "a Bishop dressed in White" could be all there was to a secret the Vatican had kept under lock and key for forty years. When Mother Angelica declared on live TV in 2001 that "we didn't get the whole thing," she was expressing the conviction of millions of Catholics that there had to be another text, a companion to the vision which tells us how and why a Pope comes to be executed by soldiers outside a half-ruined city filled with cadavers. For these faithful Catholics, it was inconceivable that Our Lady of Fatima could have failed to explain the vision to the Church and the world, leaving it to Vatican Cardinals to concoct a patently untenable "proposed interpretation" 83 years after the Fatima apparitions—an interpretation ludicrously suggesting that the clearly apocalyptic scene in the vision represented John Paul II *escaping* death at the hands of a would-be assassin, and then living on for another 24 years.

Let us briefly review evidence for the existence of two texts as it stood before 2006. It was indeed this body of evidence that led Antonio Socci to recognize that the "Fatimists" were right, and to change his mind completely. Later he was given the irrefutable testimony of the still-living eyewitness, Archbishop Capovilla—the personal secretary to Pope John XXIII. Armed with all this information and more, he published his "breakthrough" book in that year, declaring his conviction that the Vatican has suppressed a second text pertaining to the Secret.

We note, first of all, that even before 2006 the best witness in support of the claim that something had to be missing was, ironically enough, Cardinal Ratzinger himself, speaking in 1984 in the *Jesus* magazine interview we have already discussed in depth. From 2000 to 2006 people continued to ask: What had happened to the "religious prophecy" the Cardinal had mentioned back then, concerning "dangers threatening the faith and the life of the Christian, and therefore (the life) of the world"? What about his statement in 1984 that "the things contained in this 'Third Secret' correspond to what has been announced in Scripture and has been said *again and again in many other Marian apparitions*, beginning with that of Fatima itself in its [already] known contents"? Nothing in the vision of the "Bishop dressed in White" repeats what has been said in many other Marian apparitions, for in this vision Mary *says nothing at all*. And if, as Cardinal Ratzinger in 2000 was then claiming, the "Bishop dressed in White" was Pope John Paul II escaping death in 1981, why had Cardinal Ratzinger in 1984 not simply revealed this and declared the Third Secret to have been fulfilled?

Furthermore, as we noted in Chapter 4, the existence of two documents—one being a letter 25-lines long written on a single sheet of paper and sealed in an envelope, the other being 62-lines long written in a notebook that Sister Lucy turned over along with the envelope— was clearly suggested by the testimony of numerous credible witnesses, including Sister Lucy herself. The leading source in this regard was (and still is) Frère Michel's massive study *The Whole Truth About Fatima* - Volume III: *The Third Secret*. The 20,000 copies of the French edition of Volume III were published in 1985 and 1986 (after more than 4 years of research), and 50,000 copies of the English edition were published in 1990 and another 25,000 were printed in 2001. To our knowledge this book has never been questioned as to either the authenticity or thoroughness of its research. Volume III alone has over 1,150 footnotes, citing numerous documents, witnesses, and testimonies. Likewise, Frère Michel's sources and his own testimonies have never been questioned. Thus, Frère Michel himself must be considered a key witness.[351]

Here we must recall, as Frère Michel documents, what Sister Lucy wrote to Bishop da Silva on January 9, 1944:

> I have written what you asked me; God willed to try me a little, but finally this was indeed His will: it [the text] is sealed in an envelope and this [the sealed envelope] is in the notebooks ...[352]

Examination of the original Portuguese reveals that Sister Lucy means to say that the Secret proper is in the envelope,[353] and that the envelope is in one of her notebooks which she also consigned to Archbishop Manuel Maria Ferreira da Silva (the Archbishop of Gurza) for carrying to Bishop José Alves Correia da Silva of Fatima in June of 1944. As Frère

---

[351] In some proofs, we are dealing with circumstantial evidence. There are two reasons for this: (1) over 5,000 original documents in 24 volumes compiled by Father Alonso—the result of 11 years of research by Father Alonso, then the official archivist of Fatima—have been prevented from being published since 1976 (though two were later published in heavily-edited form) by religious authorities (i.e. the Bishop of Fatima and the Provincial of the Claretians based at Madrid, Spain), and (2) the continued imposition of a regime of silence upon Sister Lucy (in force since 1960) until her death in 2005, even though we were told in 2000 she had nothing further to reveal.

[352] Quoted by Father Alonso, *Fatima 50*, October 13, 1967, p. 11. See also Frère Michel de la Sainte Trinité, *The Whole Truth About Fatima* (hereafter, *WTAF*) - Vol. III: *The Third Secret*, (Immaculate Heart Publications, Buffalo, New York, U.S.A., 1990, republished in 2001) pp. 46-47. See also footnote 61 in this book.

[353] The text in Portuguese is as follows: "Já escrevi o que me mandou: Deus quis provar-me um pouco (,) mas afinal era essa a sua vontade: Está lacrada dentro dum envelope e este dentro dos cadernos..." Cited in Father Alonso, "O Segredo de Fatima", *Fatima 50*, October 13, 1967, p. 11. Our own translation from the above Portuguese text is as follows: "Now I wrote what Your Excellency ordered me [to write]: God wanted to try me a little (,) but finally this was His will: It [the part of the Secret that I did not give before] is sealed inside an envelope and this [envelope] [is] inside the notebooks." This translation depends on the context of Father Alonso's above-mentioned article. This is further explained in footnote 61.

Michel notes:

> The seer discreetly handed the Bishop of Gurza *the notebook* in which she had slipped the *envelope* containing the Secret. That same evening, the bishop placed the envelope into the hands of Bishop da Silva ...[354]

But what happened to the notebook? Surely it contains some text relevant to the Third Secret. Why else would Sister Lucy have entrusted both the sealed envelope *and* the notebook to the Bishop of Fatima? Even before the decisive revelations of 2006-2007 the evidence pointed unmistakably to the existence of a text from Sister Lucy's notebook as *one* of *two* texts pertaining to the Secret.

The table on the next page sets forth ten facts pointing to the existence of two manuscripts for the Third Secret of Fatima: one in the envelope, containing the words of Our Lady, and another in the notebook, probably containing the vision of the "Bishop dressed in White" which was revealed on June 26, 2000. We will examine these facts in the subsequent sections. We must emphasize at the outset, however, that one cannot discount the possibility that the text in the envelope has been lost or destroyed and that it may never be produced in its original form.

Fact #1:
Supporting Documentation for Fact #1 –
Text #1 Contains the Words of Our Lady

In Chapter 4 we noted the Vatican announcement in the February 8, 1960 communiqué of the Portuguese news agency A.N.I. (at Rome), which admits that the text of the Third Secret (i.e. Text #1 referred to in the table) contains the actual words of Our Lady:

> It has just been stated, in very reliable Vatican circles, to the representatives of United Press International, that it is most likely that the letter will never be opened, in which Sister Lucy wrote down *the words which Our Lady confided as a secret* to the three little shepherds in the Cova da Iria.[355]

We also have Sister Lucy's own testimony that the Third Secret contains Our Lady's actual words, not simply a wordless vision. Frère Michel reports:

> ... in her third Memoir, written in July-August, 1941, Sister Lucy had been content to mention the existence of a third part of the Secret, but as yet she had said nothing about it. A few months later, in her fourth Memoir, written between October-December, 1941, she decided to say more. She recopied almost word for word

---

[354] *WTAF* - Vol. III, p. 49.

[355] Quoted by Father Martins dos Reis, *O Milagre do sol e o Segredo de Fatima*, pp. 127-128. Cf. Father Joaquin Alonso, *La Verdad sobre el Secreto de Fatima*, (Centro Mariano, Madrid, Spain, 1976) pp. 55-56. See also *WTAF* - Vol. III, p. 578.

	Third Secret Text #1 Alluded to by Various Witnesses (see Chapter 4)	Third Secret Text #2 Published by the Vatican June 26, 2000
(1)	Text contains words of Our Lady.	Text does not contain any words of Our Lady.
(2)	Text transferred to Holy Office - April 16, 1957.[356]	Text transferred to Holy Office - April 4, 1957.
(3)	25 lines of text.	62 lines of text.
(4)	Text was ready on January 9, 1944.	Text was ready and dated on January 3, 1944.
(5)	Pope John Paul II read the text in October 1978, a few days after his election on October 16, 1978.[357]	Pope John Paul II read the text on July 18, 1981.
(6)	Pope John Paul II consecrated the world on June 7, 1981 after reading the text in 1978 but before reading the 62-line text which he only read on July 18, 1981.	This text was not read by Pope John Paul II prior to his act of consecrating the world on June 7, 1981.
(7)	Written in letter form (addressed and signed, possibly on letter paper).	Not written in letter form (not addressed or signed), but as an entry in Sister Lucy's notebook. Clearly written on notebook paper.
(8)	Stored by Pope Pius XII's bedside. Stored in the desk called "Barbarigo" in the papal bedroom by John XXIII.	Stored in the Holy Office building.
(9)	This text has margins on each side of three quarters of a centimeter.	This text has no margins.
(10)	Explains the vision.	Describes the vision.

---

[356] The book by Father Alonso, *The Secret of Fatima: Fact and Legend*, first published in Spanish in 1976 and republished in English in 1979, while he was still alive, affirms as a fact that the Third Secret was received by the Vatican on April 16, 1957. Frère Michel, citing Fr. Alonso, refers to the same date for the arrival of the Third Secret at the Vatican. Considering Father Alonso's impeccable credentials and his reputation as a capable and most responsible researcher, we have no reason to question his statement. Since this book was first published in 2002, however, one critic has suggested that Fr. Alonso could not have known that date as certain because he did not, according to this critic, have access to the Holy Office files. But such a criticism seems rather superficial. Surely, considering the extreme attention to detail that Bishop Venancio showed in "measuring everything," and his handling the Third Secret with such extreme care, it is reasonable to assume that he obtained a dated receipt from the Vatican confirming delivery of the text; and certainly such a receipt would have been accessible to Fr. Alonso, as Bishop Venancio was his personal friend and was also the one who had appointed Fr. Alonso official archivist of Fatima. Perhaps Father Alonso knew of the date from another source, but we will not know all of Fr. Alonso's sources until the 5,396 documents he was ready to publish in 1976 are finally released from the embargo the Vatican has imposed on them. Until those documents are published whole and entire, the critic's objection cannot be taken seriously. We would expect that if they ever publish those documents Father Alonso's positive assertion regarding April 16, 1957 to be perfectly vindicated and validated.

[357] Since the first edition of this book was published, it has come to the attention of the editors that there is more to be said about Fact #5. Not only did John Paul II read the Third Secret on two different dates years apart, it has now come to light that Pope Paul VI

the text of the third Memoir, but adding after the final words—"... and a certain period of peace will be granted to the world"—the new sentence: "*Em Portugal se conservara sempre o dogma da fe etc.*"[358]

This new sentence translates into: "In Portugal the dogma of the Faith will always be preserved etc."—directly quoting words of the Virgin of Fatima. Frère Michel also reports:

> Indeed in 1943, when Bishop da Silva had asked her to write down the text [of the Third Secret], and she was encountering insurmountable obstacles in obeying this order, she declared that it was not absolutely necessary to do so, *'since in a certain manner she had said it'*.[359] Undoubtedly Sister Lucy was alluding to the ten words she had discreetly added in December, 1941 to the text of the great Secret—but added so discreetly that almost nobody noticed them.[360]

It is very telling that these discreetly added words—"In Portugal the dogma of the Faith will always be preserved etc." are the very ones *The Message of Fatima* (*TMF*) tries to avoid by demoting them to a footnote, as if they were of no consequence, and by relying on the *Third* Memoir for the text of the Great Secret, which does not contain these added words.

We repeat the question we asked earlier: Why would Cardinal Sodano, Cardinal Ratzinger and Msgr. Bertone choose the *Third* Memoir when the Fourth Memoir offers a more complete text of the Fatima Message? The answer, clearly, is that they chose the Third Memoir in order to avoid any discussion of the momentous phrase "In Portugal the dogma of the Faith will always be preserved **etc**." By this expedient they deftly navigated around an obvious indication that the Message of Fatima includes further words of the Virgin embraced within the "etc.", and that these missing words must pertain to the Third Secret. If it were not so, then they would not have displayed such an aversion to this phrase. They would simply have used the Fourth Memoir, including that phrase, in *TMF*'s discussion of the first two parts of the Great Secret of Fatima. One can only conclude that the phrase to which they were so averse is indeed the gateway into the Third Secret of Fatima, and that they did not wish the faithful or the world at large to focus on this gateway, for it raises too many questions about what lies beyond it.

The rest of the Secret indicated by the "etc." was not recorded in

---

also read the Third Secret on two different dates years apart. It should also be noted that John XXIII read the Third Secret on August 17, 1959 and again sometime in 1960. See Chapter 14 (pages 246-249) for more details about these facts. For further evidence of the contradictory dates provided for when these Popes read the Third Secret for the first time, see the entries in Appendix II to this book, "A Chronology of the Fatima Cover-up", for the dates given here and in Chapter 14.

[358] *WTAF* - Vol. III, p. 684.

[359] Father Alonso, *La Verdad sobre el Secreto de Fatima*, p. 64. See also *WTAF* - Vol. III, p. 684.

[360] *WTAF* - Vol. III, p. 684.

the Fourth Memoir but in the later text at issue, the missing text of the Third Secret which explains the vision of the "Bishop dressed in White".

In fact, the authors of *TMF* neglect to mention that immediately after "In Portugal the dogma of the faith will always be preserved etc." we find in the Fourth Memoir: "Tell *this* to no one. Yes, you may tell Francisco." Now, if "this" referred only to the Faith always being preserved in Portugal, Our Lady would hardly have directed the seers to hide this heavenly compliment to the Portuguese people. Hence, "this" clearly involves a reference to how the dogma of the Faith would *not* always be preserved in other places—*many* other places. That is the very conclusion the authors of *TMF* have attempted to hide by demoting the key phrase to a footnote.

As we pointed out in Chapter 4, these ten words—*"Em Portugal se conservara sempre o dogma da fe etc."*—introduce a new, and incomplete, thought into the Secret of Fatima. The phrase suggests, as every reputable Fatima scholar concluded, that there is more to follow and that the "etc." is but a placeholder for the third part of the Secret. But the Vatican's June 2000 manuscript of the Third Secret (i.e. Text #2 referred to in the table on page 226), published in *TMF*, contains no words of Our Lady; it describes only the vision of the Secret seen by the three children of Fatima. This text does not explain the new sentence in the Fourth Memoir, nor does it provide the words embraced within the "etc."

Did Our Lady's actual words, spoken personally by the Mother of God, end with "etc."? Certainly, they did not. There is undoubtedly more text after the "etc." What happened to it?

What Can Be Concluded Regarding Fact #1

All this evidence demonstrates that there must be two documents: one containing the words of Our Lady, the other containing the vision seen by the three children, but with no words at all which are attributed to Our Lady.

Fact #2:
Supporting Documentation for Fact #2 – Different Dates of Transfer

Father Alonso tells us when the text of the Third Secret was transferred to the Holy Office (now known as the Congregation for the Doctrine of the Faith):

> These facts are now known: The sealed envelope containing the letter was received by Msgr. Cento, the Apostolic Nuncio in Lisbon, from Msgr. Venancio in mid-March, 1957 and forwarded to Rome. It arrived there on April 16, 1957.[361]

---

[361] Father Joaquin Alonso, *The Secret of Fatima: Fact and Legend*, (Centro Mariano, Madrid, 1976; republished by The Ravengate Press, Cambridge, 1979 and 1982) p. 50. See also Alonso, *De nuevo el Secreto de Fatima*, (Ephemerides Mariologicae, 1982) p. 86; and

It is important to recall what we noted earlier: that the Pope was the head of the Holy Office prior to Pope Paul VI reorganizing the Roman Curia in 1967. Therefore, it was quite appropriate for the Pope to retain the Third Secret in his possession and for the box containing it to be labeled as "Secret of the Holy Office." With the Pope being the head of the Holy Office, this box became part of the Holy Office archives.

The Vatican commentary, however, states that Sister Lucy's original manuscript of the Third Secret was transferred to the Holy Office on April 4, 1957. Furthermore, Archbishop Tarcisio Bertone, then Secretary of the Congregation for the Doctrine of the Faith, tells us:

> The sealed envelope was initially in the custody of the Bishop of Leiria. To ensure better protection for the 'secret' the envelope was placed in the Secret Archives of the Holy Office on 4 April 1957.[362]

What Can Be Concluded Regarding Fact #2

This difference of dates supports the conclusion that there are two documents: one document containing the vision was transferred to the Secret Archives of the Holy Office on April 4, 1957; the other document, containing the words of Our Lady of Fatima, was transferred to the Pope's apartment, which can be considered a part of the Holy Office, on April 16, 1957.

Fact #3:
Supporting Documentation for Fact #3 –
Text #1 is 25 Lines of Handwritten Text

In addition to the evidence cited so far, Frère Michel and Frère François both agree that the text of the Third Secret contains only 20 to 30 lines:

> ... we are just as certain that the twenty or thirty lines of the third Secret ...[363]

> The final Secret of Fatima, written on a small sheet of paper, is therefore not very long. Probably twenty to twenty-five lines ...[364]

> [Bishop Venancio looked] at the envelope [containing the Third Secret] while holding it up to the light. He could see inside a little sheet of which he measured the exact size. We thus know that the Third Secret is not very long, probably 20 to 25 lines ...[365]

On the other hand, the Vatican's June 2000 manuscript of the Third Secret contains 62 lines of handwritten text. Again, something is

---

WTAF - Vol. III, p. 481.

[362] Archbishop Tarcisio Bertone, SDB, "Introduction", *The Message of Fatima* (hereafter, *TMF*), June 26, 2000, p. 4.

[363] *WTAF* - Vol. III, p. 626.

[364] *Fatima: Tragedy and Triumph*, p. 45.

[365] Brother Michael of the Holy Trinity, *The Secret of Fatima ... Revealed*, (Immaculate Heart Publications, Buffalo, New York, U.S.A.,1986) p. 7.

seriously amiss.

On the *Porta a Porta* broadcast of May 31, 2007, Cardinal Bertone was asked only one pointed question concerning the Third Secret. On the live broadcast, the Vaticanista Marco Politi testified to the fact that Cardinal Ottaviani had said publicly that the Third Secret consisted of Sister Lucy writing 25 (twenty-five) lines of text. He pointed out that what Bertone published was 62 lines of text. He asked Bertone to reconcile these two facts. Cardinal Bertone never denied the fact that Ottaviani had indeed said the text was 25 lines long. Rather, he struggled for several minutes, even with the benefit of a 4-minute commercial break on the broadcast, and still with all this time he came up with only very weak excuses for why he thought Cardinal Ottaviani was mistaken in that testimony. Clearly, the text seen by Cardinal Ottaviani was only 25 lines long, and clearly the text we were given on June 26, 2000 was 62 lines long. There is obviously another text, as we know now from the direct testimony of the living witness, Archbishop Loris Capovilla. See Socci, *The Fourth Secret of Fatima*, Chapter 4 and also Ferrara, *The Secret Still Hidden*, Chapter 8.

What Can Be Concluded Regarding Fact #3

This discrepancy demonstrates that there are two documents: one with 25 lines of text, the other with 62 lines of text.

A Further Clarification

One additional note regarding the existence of two documents: As we showed in Chapter 4, Cardinal Ottaviani, as Prefect of the Congregation for the Doctrine of the Faith in 1967, stated that he had read the Third Secret and that it was written on a *single sheet* of paper. He testified to this fact on February 11, 1967, at a press conference during a meeting of the Pontifical Marian Academy in Rome:

> And then, what did she [Lucy] do to obey the Most Holy Virgin? She wrote on *a sheet of paper*, in Portuguese, what the Holy Virgin *had asked her* to tell ...[366]

Cardinal Ottaviani is a witness to this fact. In the same press conference, he states:

> I, who have had the grace and the gift to read the text of the Secret—although I too am held to secrecy because I am bound by the Secret ...[367]

Note well: Cardinal Ottaviani read the Third Secret. Cardinal Ottaviani later said it was written on *a sheet* of paper—not the four distinct pages of the vision of the "Bishop dressed in white" which the Vatican published on June 26, 2000.[368]

---

[366] *WTAF* - Vol. III, p. 725.

[367] *WTAF* - Vol. III, p. 727.

[368] The text as reproduced on June 26, 2000 in *The Message of Fatima* (*TMF*) was apparently photographically reproduced on pages 17-20 of *TMF*, giving rise to the false impression that it consisted of four different sized sheets (the first page is 6 inches and 9/16"; pages

Fact #4:
Supporting Documentation for Fact #4 –
Text #1 Was Not Ready by January 3

As we showed in Chapter 4, Lucy first attempted to write down the text of the Third Secret in October 1943. From that mid-October until early January 1944, Lucy was prevented from obeying a formal order to write down the Third Secret by an unspeakable anguish.

We noted also that the order to write down the Secret came after Sister Lucy came down with pleurisy in June of 1943, which caused Canon Galamba and Bishop da Silva to fear that she would die without having revealed the final part of the Great Secret of Fatima. Canon Galamba later convinced Bishop da Silva to suggest to Sister Lucy that she write down the Secret. However, Sister Lucy would not comply without a formal order from the Bishop, which was finally given in mid-October 1943.

Even then Sister Lucy was unable to obey for another two and a half months, until the Blessed Virgin Mary appeared to her on January 2, 1944, confirming that it was God's will that she commit the Secret to writing. Only then was Lucy able to overcome her fear and anguish and write down the Secret.[369] But it was not until January 9, 1944, that Sister Lucy wrote the following note to Bishop da Silva, informing him that the Secret was finally written down:

> I have written what you asked me; God willed to try me a little, but finally this was indeed His will: it [the text] is sealed in an envelope and this [the sealed envelope] is in the notebooks ...[370]

The Vatican's manuscript of the Third Secret, however, was completed on January 3, 1944, as shown by the date appearing at the end of Sister Lucy's 62-line handwritten document.[371] Furthermore, in 2000 Archbishop Bertone told us that:

> The third part of the "secret" was written "by order of His Excellency the Bishop of Leiria and the Most Holy Mother ..." on 3 January 1944.[372]

2, 3 and 4 are each 7 inches and 5/16"), but in one of the revelations of 2007 (the *Porta a Porta* telecast of May 31 mentioned in Chapter 4), Cardinal Bertone showed on camera that the text consists of four pages on a single folio, folded in half. It might be suggested that the single folio pertaining to the vision, folded to make four distinct pages, is the "sheet of paper" referred to by Cardinal Ottaviani. But, as we shall see, in 2007 Cardinal Bertone would admit that Cardinal Ottaviani had testified "categorically" that the Third Secret involved a *single sheet of 25 lines*, not the 62 lines of the published vision. Bertone's attempt to explain this discrepancy on television, discussed in Chapter 14, is patently *not* believable.

[369] *WTAF* - Vol. III, pp. 37-47.

[370] Quoted by Father Alonso, *Fatima 50*, p. 11. See also *WTAF* - Vol. III, pp. 46-47; and footnotes 61 and 353 in this book.

[371] Original text of Sister Lucy, "Third Part of the 'Secret'", *TMF*, p. 20.

[372] Archbishop Tarcisio Bertone, SDB, "Introduction", *TMF*, p. 4.

What Can Be Concluded Regarding Fact #4

Considering that Sister Lucy had finally written down the Secret after an apparition of the Blessed Mother, why would she not have immediately informed Bishop da Silva as soon as the document was ready, given the Mother of God's assurance that it was God's will that she deliver the document? Why would Sister Lucy, trained in obedience, wait *another* six days after obeying *Heaven's command* to write down the Third Secret—from January 3 to January 9—before informing her bishop? From this we may conclude that the text of the Third Secret was not ready until January 9, 1944 or very shortly before.

This difference of dates lends further support to the existence of two documents: one containing the vision, completed on January 3, 1944; the other containing Our Lady's words which explain that vision, completed on or very shortly before January 9, 1944.

Admittedly, this conclusion is dependent on circumstantial evidence; but Fatima scholars must rely on this kind of evidence because the anti-Fatima establishment has, since 1976, blocked publication of the works of Father Joaquin Alonso, consisting of over 5,000 documents in 24 volumes[373] which are the result of his 11 years of research up to that time. As we have noted, Fr. Alonso was official archivist of Fatima for sixteen years.

The other conclusions supported by the pre-2006 evidence (except possibly the conclusion regarding Fact #10) are not dependent on circumstantial evidence.

Fact #5:
Supporting Documentation for Fact #5 –
Different Dates for When Pope John Paul II First Read the Secret

On July 1, 2000, *The Washington Post* reported that Vatican officials recently provided contradictory dates for when Pope John Paul II read the Third Secret for the first time:

> On May 13, Vatican spokesman Joaquin Navarro-Valls said the Pope *first read the Secret within days of assuming the papacy* in 1978. On Monday, an aide to Cardinal Joseph Ratzinger, prefect of the Vatican's Congregation for the Doctrine of the Faith, said that the Pope *first saw it in the hospital* after his attack.[374]

An article in the June 26, 2000 edition of *The New York Times*

---

[373] The first two volumes of the 24-volume series were finally published in the 1990's (with approximately only one-half of the original texts prepared by Father Alonso for publication); none other have been published since, to the present day (December 2009). If everything had been revealed on June 26, 2000, why are these over 5,000 documents and 22 volumes still not published to this date?

[374] Bill Broadway and Sarah Delancy, "3rd Secret Spurs More Questions; Fatima Interpretation Departs From Vision", *The Washington Post*, July 1, 2000.

identified the aide to Cardinal Ratzinger:

> "John Paul II *read for the first time the text* of the third secret of Fatima *after the attack*," a top aide to Ratzinger, Monsignor Tarcisio Bertone, told journalists during a news conference to present the document.[375]

According to the Vatican's commentary, however, John Paul II did not read the Third Secret until July 18, 1981. Archbishop Bertone tells us:

> John Paul II, for his part, asked for the envelope containing the third part of the 'secret' following the assassination attempt on 13 May 1981. On 18 July 1981 Cardinal Franjo Seper, Prefect of the Congregation, gave two envelopes to Archbishop Eduardo Martinez Somalo, Substitute of the Secretariat of State: one white envelope, containing Sister Lucy's original text in Portuguese; the other orange, with the Italian translation of the 'secret'. On the following 11 August, Archbishop Martinez returned the two envelopes to the Archives of the Holy Office.[376]

What Can Be Concluded Regarding Fact #5

All these statements are true and can be reconciled if there are two documents: In 1978 John Paul II read the one-page, 25-line document originally sealed in the envelope, containing the words of Our Lady; and then on July 18, 1981 His Holiness read the 62-line document describing the vision of the "Bishop dressed in White." Similarly, as we shall see on pages 246-249, on June 27, 1963 Paul VI read the 25-line document and then on March 27, 1965 he read the 62-line document; and on August 17, 1959 John XXIII read the 25-line document and then in 1960 he read the 62-line document.

Fact #6:
Supporting Documentation for Fact #6 –
Text #1 Inspired Pope to Consecrate World

Immediately following the statement of Archbishop Bertone quoted in support of Fact #5, the Archbishop goes on to tell us:

> As is well known, Pope John Paul II immediately thought of consecrating the world to the Immaculate Heart of Mary and he himself composed a prayer for what he called an 'Act of Entrustment', which was to be celebrated in the Basilica of Saint Mary Major on 7 June 1981 ...[377]

What Can Be Concluded Regarding Fact #6

How could Pope John Paul II be moved by the Third Secret to consecrate the world to the Immaculate Heart of Mary on *June 7,* 1981,

---

[375] The Associated Press, "Vatican: Fatima Is No Doomsday Prophecy", *The New York Times*, June 26, 2000.

[376] Archbishop Tarcisio Bertone, SDB, "Introduction", *TMF*, p. 5.

[377] Ibid.

when, according to Archbishop Bertone, the Pope did not actually read the Third Secret until *July 18*, 1981—six weeks later?

Again, both statements can be reconciled if there are two documents: the Pope read the one-page document containing the words of Our Lady in 1978—and this is the text that moved him to consecrate the world on June 7, 1981—and then he read the four-page document describing the vision on July 18, 1981. Pope John Paul II's own statements demonstrate that he viewed this act of consecration of the world (and subsequent ones) as setting the stage for when he would finally feel free to perform the Consecration of Russia.

Fact #7:
Supporting Documentation for Fact #7 –
Text #1 is a Letter

Sister Lucy, herself, tells us that the Third Secret was written *as a letter*. We have the written testimony of Father Jongen who, on February 3-4, 1946, interrogated Sister Lucy:

> 'You have already made known two parts of the Secret. When will the time arrive for the third part?' 'I communicated the third part in a *letter* to the Bishop of Leiria,' she answered.[378]

As Canon Galamba testified:

> When the bishop refused to open the *letter*, Lucy made him promise that it would definitely be opened and read to the world either at her death or in 1960, whichever would come first.[379]

In February 1960, the Patriarch of Lisbon declared:

> Bishop da Silva enclosed (the envelope sealed by Lucy) in another envelope on which he indicated that the *letter* had to be opened in 1960 by himself, Bishop Jose Correia da Silva, if he was still alive, or if not, by the Cardinal Patriarch of Lisbon.[380]

Father Alonso tells us:

> Other bishops also spoke—and with authority—about the year 1960 as the date indicated for opening the famous *letter*. Thus, when the then-titular Bishop of Tiava, and Auxiliary Bishop of Lisbon, asked Lucy when the Secret was to be opened, he always received the same answer: in 1960.[381]

In 1959, Bishop Venancio, the new Bishop of Leiria, declared:

> I think that the *letter* will not be opened before 1960. Sister

---

[378] *Revue Mediatrice et Reine*, October 1946, pp. 110-112. See also *WTAF* - Vol. III, p. 470.

[379] Quoted by Father Alonso, *La Verdad sobre el Secreto de Fatima*, pp. 46-47. See also *WTAF* - Vol. III, p. 470.

[380] *Novidades*, February 24, 1960, quoted by *La Documentation Catholique*, June 19, 1960, col. 751. See also *WTAF* - Vol. III, p. 472.

[381] *La Verdad sobre el Secreto de Fatima*, p. 46. See also *WTAF* - Vol. III, p. 475.

Lucy had asked that it should not be opened before her death, or not before 1960. We are now in 1959 and Sister Lucy is in good health.[382]

Finally, the Vatican announcement of February 8, 1960 through the A.N.I. press agency also tells us that the text of the Third Secret was written *as a letter*:

> ... it is most likely that the *letter* will never be opened, in which Sister Lucy wrote down the *words which Our Lady confided* as a secret ...[383]

Now, the text of the vision of the Third Secret has also been identified as a letter in the Vatican's commentary. However, that text is plainly not a letter, as it:

• is not addressed to anyone; and

• is *not signed by Sister Lucy* or anyone else;

clearly, therefore, is anything but a letter.

Copies of letters written by Sister Lucy have been included in her published memoirs. These letters *all have an addressee, a date, and her signature.*

Thus, we can expect that the one-page document that was available on January 9, 1944 is a letter addressed to someone (Sister Lucy told Father Jongen in February 1946 that she sent it to the Bishop of Leiria), and is signed by Sister Lucy.

Here it is important to note that Sister Lucy was offered the option to write the Third Secret in the form of a letter or in her notebook, and that she decided to write it as a letter. According to Father Alonso, Sister Lucy wrote to Bishop da Silva on January 9, 1944:

> I have written what you asked me; God willed to try me a little, but finally this was indeed His will: it [the text] is sealed in an envelope and this [the sealed envelope] is in the notebooks ...[384]

Again, as we have noted above, Frère Michel reports that, on June 17, 1944:

> The seer discreetly handed the Bishop of Gurza the notebook in which she had slipped the envelope containing the Secret. That same evening, the bishop placed the envelope into the hands of Bishop da Silva ...[385]

---

[382] *La Verdad sobre el Secreto de Fatima*, p. 46. See also *WTAF* - Vol. III, p. 478.

[383] Quoted by Father Martins dos Reis, *O Milagre do sol e o Segredo de Fatima*, pp. 127-128. Cf. Father Alonso, *La Verdad sobre el Secreto de Fatima*, pp. 55-56. See also *WTAF* - Vol. III, p. 578.

[384] Quoted by Father Alonso, *Fatima 50*, p. 11. See also *WTAF* - Vol. III, pp. 46-47; and footnotes 61 and 353 in this book.

[385] *WTAF* - Vol. III, p. 49.

What Can Be Concluded Regarding Fact #7

The pre-2006 evidence supports this conclusion: There are two documents—the text of the Third Secret containing Our Lady's words in the form of a 25-line *letter*; and 62 lines of text *from the notebook* describing the vision.

Moreover, as we have noted, the text of the vision is dated January 3, 1944, whereas Sister Lucy's letter to the Bishop of Fatima stating "I have written what you asked me; God willed to try me a little, but finally this was indeed His will: it [the text] is sealed in an envelope and this [the sealed envelope] is in the notebooks" is dated January 9, 1944. It is entirely possible that Sister Lucy's notebooks contain a number of other things pertaining to the Third Secret which she wrote during the period January 3-9, 1944. These other things may be lesser points pertaining to the Secret, leading up to the final disclosure of the most fearsome part of the Secret on January 9—namely, the Virgin's explanation of the Secret in Her own words. We recall here Father Schweigl's testimony that there are indeed two parts to the Secret: one pertaining to the Pope and the other representing the conclusion of the *words* "In Portugal the dogma of the Faith will always be preserved etc."

In this connection it is important to remember that Sister Lucy was given the choice of writing the Third Secret in her notebooks or on a sheet of paper. Evidently, she availed herself of both options. Again, why else would she have turned over *both* a sealed envelope *and* a notebook to the Bishop of Gurza for delivery to the Bishop of Fatima?

Is it not entirely likely, then, that the obscure vision—a "safer" part of the Third Secret—was written down in the notebook, whereas the concrete explanation of the vision in the words of the Virgin Herself—whose impact was quite terrible—had to be sealed in the envelope that Sister Lucy placed *inside* the notebook? There seems to be no other sensible explanation for why Sister Lucy, in response to the Bishop of Fatima's order to write down the Third Secret, provided him with both a sealed envelope and a notebook.

In short, the vision of the "Bishop dressed in White", described in 62 lines of text, was contained in the notebook, but the explanation—in 25 lines of text that numerous witnesses have attested to—was sealed in the envelope. *That is why the notebook accompanied the sealed envelope.*[386]

---

[386] On the live *Porta a Porta* television broadcast of May 31, 2007, Cardinal Bertone displayed two envelopes sealed by Sister Lucy, each with her own handwriting regarding Our Lady's order about 1960 (see the two photos—Figures 2 and 3—on page XV in the photo section). Sister Lucy indicated in her letter of January 9, 1944 to Bishop da Silva that there was only one sealed envelope containing the Third Secret—"It [the part of the Secret that I did not give before] is sealed inside an envelope and this [envelope] [is] inside the notebooks"—and Frère Michel confirms—"The seer discreetly handed the Bishop of Gurza [in June of 1944] the notebook in which she had slipped the envelope containing the Secret. That same evening, the bishop placed the envelope into the hands of Bishop da Silva ..." Apparently, between January 9 and June 17, 1944, Our Lady

Thus, the 62 lines of text released by the Vatican on June 26, 2000 are the *visional part* of the Third Secret contained in the notebook, *certainly not* the 25-line letter that was sealed in the envelope on January 9.

Fact #8:
Supporting Documentation for Fact #8 – Text #1 Stored in Papal Apartment

Frère Michel reports the testimony of journalist Robert Serrou who, while doing a photo story at the Vatican on May 14, 1957,[387] about one month after the Third Secret had arrived at Rome on April 16, 1957, discovered that the Third Secret was being stored in the Pope's apartment by his bedside. As Frère Michel tells us:

> ... we now know that the precious envelope sent to Rome by Msgr. Cento was not placed in the archives of the Holy Office, but that Pius XII wanted to keep it in his own apartment.

> Father Caillon received this information from the mouth of journalist Robert Serrou, who himself got it from Mother Pasqualina, in this way. Robert Serrou was doing a photo story for *Paris-Match* in the apartments of Pius XII. Mother Pasqualina—this woman of great common sense who directed the handful of Sisters acting as the Pope's housekeepers, and who sometimes received his confidences—was present.

> Before a little wooden safe placed on a table and bearing the inscription "*Secretum Sancti Officii*" (Secret of the Holy Office), the journalist questioned the Mother: "Mother, what is in this little safe?" She answered: "*The third Secret of Fatima is in there ...*"

> The photograph of this safe, which we have reproduced on the following page, was published in *Paris-Match* a year and a half later ...[388]

The photograph of this safe, published in the October 18, 1958 issue of *Paris-Match* (Issue No. 497, page 82), is shown on the next page. The details of Serrou's testimony were later confirmed in a letter he wrote to Frère Michel on January 10, 1985. In this letter, Serrou states:

> It is exact that Mother Pasqualina did tell me, while showing me a little safe bearing a label with the mention, "Secret of the Holy Office": "In there is the third Secret of Fatima."[389]

---

instructed Sister Lucy to put the second text (from her notebook) in a second sealed envelope as well.

[387] *WTAF* - Vol. III, p. 486.

[388] Ibid., p. 485.

[389] Letter to Frère Michel de la Sainte Trinité of January 10, 1985. See also *WTAF* - Vol. III, p. 486.

En brisant les scellés des appartements privés, le Pape découvre les instruments du travail qui l'attend, ceux de Pie XII, et le coffre aux secrets de l'Eglise

Photo from *Paris-Match* magazine in 1958, showing the wooden safe in the papal apartment of Pius XII in which a text of the Third Secret was safeguarded. The text in this safe was *not* the text in the Holy Office archives.

The Vatican's commentary of June 26, 2000 (*TMF*), however, tells us that the Third Secret had been stored in a different building which houses the Holy Office. Again, according to Archbishop Bertone:

> The sealed envelope was initially in the custody of the Bishop of Leiria. To ensure better protection for the "secret" the envelope was placed in the Secret Archives of the Holy Office on 4 April 1957.[390]

In addition, the pre-2006 evidence also demonstrated, with Fact #3 and Fact #5, that Pope John Paul II read the text of the Third Secret (i.e. the 25-line document containing the words of Our Lady) in 1978 and then he read the 62-line document describing the vision on July 18, 1981. As discussed in Fact #5, the Holy Office records that John Paul II asked for the Third Secret in 1981, *but there is no record of the Pope asking for the Secret in 1978* because he didn't need to—it was in the papal apartments.

What Can Be Concluded Regarding Fact #8

These testimonies, all known before 2006, established that there are two documents stored in two different locations and in two different archives. In 1978 Pope John Paul II read the text of the 25-line letter containing Our Lady's words, which was stored in his apartment, a document the Pope did not need to request from the Secret Archives of the Holy Office. But in 1981 John Paul II read the 62 lines of text containing the description of the vision from Sister Lucy's notebook, which was stored in the Holy Office building. It was this text he had to request from the Secret Archives of the Holy Office.

---

[390] Archbishop Tarcisio Bertone, SDB, "Introduction", *TMF*, p. 4.

Fact #9:
Supporting Documentation for Fact #9 –
Text #1 has Margins of 3/4 Centimeter on Both Sides

Here we have the testimony of Bishop John Venancio, the second Bishop of Fatima, who examined a silhouette of the text under a strong light and noted precisely the margin outlines of the page on which it was written.

> Bishop Venancio related [to Frère Michel] that once he was alone at home, he took the great envelope of the Secret and tried to look through it and see the contents. In the bishop's large envelope he discerned a smaller envelope, that of Lucy, and inside this envelope *an ordinary sheet of paper* with margins on each side of three quarters of a centimeter. He took the trouble to note the size of everything. Thus the final Secret of Fatima was written on a small sheet of paper.[391]

Again, the text of 62 lines, which *TMF* reproduced on four separate pages of photocopies, containing the Third Secret vision, display no margins whatsoever—a small but very telling discrepancy to be added to all the other discrepancies.

What Can Be Concluded Regarding Fact #9

This discrepancy also demonstrates that the text released by Cardinal Ratzinger and Msgr. Bertone on June 26, 2000 is not the text of the Third Secret which Sister Lucy placed in the sealed envelope on January 9, 1944, and therefore we have not yet been given the complete text of the Third Secret, even though high Vatican officials claim the contrary.

Fact #10:
Supporting Documentation for Fact #10 –
Text #1 Explains the Vision

In Sister Lucy's Fourth Memoir we read that, during the apparition of Our Lady on June 13, 1917, after Sister Lucy had asked Our Lady to take the three seers to Heaven, Our Lady responded:

> Yes, I will take Jacinta and Francisco soon. But you are to stay here some time longer. Jesus wishes to make use of you to make Me known and loved. He wants to establish in the world devotion to My Immaculate Heart. To whoever embraces this devotion I promise salvation ...[392]

Sister Lucy then proceeds to give us a description of the vision that the three seers were then graced to see immediately after Our Lady spoke the above words—words which *explain* the meaning of the vision:

---

[391] *WTAF* - Vol. III, p. 481.
[392] Sister Lucy, in an account written for her confessor, Father Aparicio, at the end of 1927.

As Our Lady spoke these last words, She opened Her hands and for the second time, She communicated to us the rays of that immense light. We saw ourselves in this light, as it were, immersed in God. Jacinta and Francisco seemed to be in that part of the light which rose towards Heaven, and I in that which was poured out on the earth.[393]

Thus, we see that when Our Lady provides a vision to the children *She explains it as well*. Indeed, even in *TMF* we read Sister Lucy's description (taken from her Third Memoir) of the vision of hell given to the three little shepherds during the apparition of Our Lady on July 13, 1917:

Our Lady showed us a great sea of fire which seemed to be under the earth. Plunged in this fire were demons and souls in human form, like transparent burning embers, all blackened or burnished bronze, floating about in the conflagration, now raised into the air by the flames that issued from within themselves together with great clouds of smoke, now falling back on every side like sparks in a huge fire, without weight or equilibrium, and amid shrieks and groans of pain and despair, which horrified us and made us tremble with fear. The demons could be distinguished by their terrifying and repulsive likeness to frightful and unknown animals, all black and transparent. This vision lasted but an instant. How can we ever be grateful enough to our kind heavenly Mother, who had already prepared us by promising, in the first Apparition, to take us to heaven. Otherwise, I think we would have died of fear and terror.[394]

Following that account, Sister Lucy then proceeds to tell us Our Lady's words *explaining* what this vision means, *even though it was quite obvious* that the vision was a vision of hell:

You have seen hell where the souls of poor sinners go. To save them, God wishes to establish in the world devotion to My Immaculate Heart. If what I say to you is done, many souls will be saved and there will be peace.[395]

So, even though the children knew what they saw, nevertheless Our Lady tells them: "You have seen hell." Once again, we see that when Our Lady provides a vision to the children *She explains it as well*.

In contrast to the above-noted visions and the corresponding words

---

[393] Sister Lucy, "Fourth Memoir", December 8, 1941, p. 65. See also Frère Michel de la Sainte Trinité, *The Whole Truth About Fatima - Vol. I: Science and the Facts (WTAF - Vol. I)*, (Immaculate Heart Publications, Buffalo, New York, U.S.A., 1989) p. 159.

[394] English translation of text in Sister Lucy's "Third Memoir" quoted in "First and Second Part of the 'Secret'", *TMF*, pp. 15-16. See also Sister Lucy, "Fourth Memoir", *Fatima in Lucia's Own Words*, (Postulation Centre, Fatima, Portugal, 1976) p. 162. See also Sister Lucy, *Memorias e Cartas da Irma Lucia*, (Porto, Portugal, 1973, edited by Father Antonio Maria Martins) pp. 338-341.

[395] Sister Lucy quoted in *TMF*, p. 16. See also Sister Lucy, "Fourth Memoir", p. 162. See also Sister Lucy, *Memorias e Cartas da Irma Lucia*, pp. 340-341.

of Our Lady explaining them, *TMF* provides only the text of a vision that clearly requires an explanation, including the following:

> After the two parts which I have already explained, at the left of Our Lady and a little above, we saw an Angel with a flaming sword in his left hand ... Beneath the two arms of the Cross there were two Angels each with a crystal aspersorium in his hand, in which they gathered up the blood of the Martyrs and with it sprinkled the souls that were making their way to God.[396]

This text of the Third Secret contains no words of Our Lady. Why would Our Lady explain something as obvious as the vision of hell, but offer not one word to explain the obscure vision described by Lucy, which was presented by the Vatican?

Here it must be noted that immediately following the words "In Portugal the dogma of the Faith will always be preserved etc.", Our Lady said to Sister Lucy: "Tell this to no one, yes you may tell it to Francisco." The "this" that can be told to Francisco refers to the last thing said during the vision. If it was only a vision, without an explanation, then Francisco didn't need to be told anything, because he had just seen it himself already. But if "this" refers to additional words of the Virgin by way of explanation of the vision, then Francisco would have to be told because, as we know, he could not hear Our Lady during the Fatima apparitions. Francisco *saw* but did not *hear*, and would thus have needed to be informed about what Our Lady had *said* about the vision.

Nor can one argue plausibly that "you may tell it to Francisco" refers merely to the words Our Lady spoke during the second part of the Secret. The phrase "Tell this to no one. Yes, you may tell it to Francisco" follows immediately after "In Portugal the dogma of the Faith will always be preserved etc."[397] Clearly, then, the "etc." indicates the words, not yet written down, that Sister Lucy could *tell* Francisco orally. Those words clearly belong to the Third Secret, which was finally written down in 1944 under orders from the Bishop of Fatima.

What Can Be Concluded Regarding Fact #10

Where, then, are the words of Our Lady to *explain* this vision? If Our Lady said nothing to explain this vision, Her actions would have been inconsistent over the course of the apparitions. Given that the teaching authority of the Church—meaning a formal papal or conciliar pronouncement—is not imposing a specific interpretation on this vision, and if we have not been given any special grace to understand this vision on our own, then there is all the more reason to believe that Our Lady would explain to us the meaning of the vision of the Third Secret of Fatima. And there is obviously an absolute need for the true

---

[396] English translation of Sister Lucy, "Third Part of the 'Secret'", *TMF*, p. 21.

[397] Father Fabrice Delestre, Society of St. Pius X, "June 26, 2000: Revelation of the Third Secret of Fatima or a Curtailed Revelation", *SSPX Asia Newsletter*, July-August 2000, p. 24.

explanation by Our Lady Herself.

In fact, Cardinal Ratzinger admits in *TMF* that his own comments are merely an *attempt* at an interpretation of the vision of the Third Secret:

> In what follows, therefore, we can only *attempt* to provide a deeper foundation for *this interpretation*, on the basis of the criteria already considered.[398] [emphasis added]

Cardinal Ratzinger also confirmed that a specific interpretation is *not being imposed* on this vision. On July 1, 2000, *The Washington Post* reported:

> Ratzinger, asked to comment on the Pope's reading of the vision, said there is *"no official interpretation"* and that the text is not dogma.[399]

Now, does it seem likely that the Virgin of Fatima would have given the three children a vision so obscure that even the Prefect of the CDF can only "attempt" to interpret it, when the rest of the Message of Fatima is not only crystal clear, but fully explained by the *Virgin's own words* in *all* its visional aspects—even the obvious vision of hell?

Furthermore, the probability of Our Lady having provided a detailed explanation of the Third Secret vision rises to the level of certainty when one considers the erroneous "interpretation" offered by Sodano/ Ratzinger/Bertone—i.e. that the killing of a Pope and many other members of the hierarchy by soldiers is merely the failed assassination attempt on Pope John Paul II in 1981. Then there is Cardinal Ratzinger's "interpretation" of *devotion* to the Immaculate Heart, which he demotes to the "immaculate heart" of anyone who avoids sin, and the *triumph* of the Immaculate Heart, which he reduces to the *fiat* of the Virgin 2,000 years ago.

This, of course, is totally false. Our Lady of Fatima certainly foresaw these falsehoods and provided a definitive explanation of the vision to combat them. The Mother of God would never allow such an incorrect interpretation of Her Message to stand. This makes all the more urgent the disclosure of the true interpretation which is found, we are morally certain, in the missing words of the Virgin—most probably indicated by the "etc."[400]

Overall Conclusion from the Evidence

In conclusion, even before the revelations of 2006-2007, but beyond any reasonable doubt since then (as we shall see), the evidence overwhelmingly supports the existence of two documents:

One document consists of 62 lines of text (with no margins)

---

[398] Joseph Cardinal Ratzinger, "Theological Commentary", *TMF*, p. 39.

[399] Bill Broadway and Sarah Delancy, *The Washington Post*.

[400] This conclusion is supported by the research provided in Antonio Socci, *Il Quarto Segreto di Fatima* [*The Fourth Secret of Fatima*], published in 2006. It is also proved again by Christopher A. Ferrara in *The Secret Still Hidden*, published in 2008.

originally written in Sister Lucy's notebook (not written as a letter), which describes a vision seen by the three children of Fatima but does not contain any words of Our Lady. This text was written down by Sister Lucy on January 3, 1944, transferred to the Holy Office on April 4, 1957, read by Pope John Paul II on July 18, 1981 (but it obviously did not—and could not—move him to consecrate the world to the Immaculate Heart of Mary on June 7, 1981, 6 weeks earlier), was stored in the Holy Office, and released by the Vatican on June 26, 2000.

The other document is a 25-line letter (with 3/4 centimeter margins) containing Our Lady's own words which explain the vision, and is written in the form of a letter and is sealed in an envelope. This text was written down by Sister Lucy on or very shortly before January 9, 1944, transferred to the Holy Office on April 16, 1957, read by John Paul II in 1978 (moving him to consecrate the world to the Immaculate Heart of Mary on June 7, 1981), was stored in the Pope's apartment by his bedside, and to this day remains unreleased by the Vatican.

The 62-line document was published by the Vatican on June 26, 2000. The 25-line document is yet to be published, despite Our Lady ordering it to be revealed in 1960.

We can affirm these conclusions with moral certitude because a mountain of evidence supports them. We must, therefore, agree with Socci's conclusion, first mentioned in Chapter 4: "that there is a part of the Secret not revealed and considered unspeakable *is certain*. And today—having decided to deny its existence—the Vatican runs the risk of exposing itself to very heavy pressure and blackmail."[401] Clearly, divine providence has made it impossible for the Vatican to bury the Message of Fatima and the truth about the Third Secret in particular. In the next Chapter we discuss the truly providential events since 2006 that have placed beyond all doubt the existence of "a part of the Secret not revealed and considered unspeakable."

---

[401] Socci, *The Fourth Secret of Fatima*, English ed., p. 162; popular ed., p. 111; Italian ed., p. 173.

Chapter 14

Breakthrough for Fatima:
The Revelations of 2006-2007

On February 13, 2005 Sister Lucy of Fatima died at the age of 97 (six weeks short of her 98th birthday). On April 2, 2005 Pope John Paul II followed the last surviving Fatima seer into eternity. Seventeen days later the former Cardinal Ratzinger was elected to the papacy, taking the name of Benedict XVI. On June 22, 2006, Benedict XVI appointed Cardinal (formerly Archbishop) Tarcisio Bertone to replace Cardinal Sodano as Vatican Secretary of State, and Bertone assumed the office on September 15, 2006. Following these events the "landscape" of the Fatima affair would change dramatically, as the truth about the Third Secret broke through the surface in a veritable earthquake of new revelations.

The earthquake began with the publication of Antonio Socci's *The Fourth Secret of Fatima* on November 22, 2006, an event we have mentioned in Chapter 4 and elsewhere in the preceding chapters. As a renowned Catholic author, journalist and television personality in Italy, a prominent figure of the "mainstream" Church, and a personal acquaintance and collaborator of both the new Pope and Cardinal Bertone, Socci was certainly no friend of the "Fatimists" when he set out to write about their claims. In fact, as we have already mentioned, his intention was to refute those claims as empty "conspiracy theories."

His suspicions aroused by Cardinal Bertone's refusal to grant him a friendly interview concerning the Third Secret controversy, despite their prior acquaintance and collaboration, Socci began to suspect that something was being hidden. Examining the "Fatimist" claims with an open mind, he encountered the overwhelming evidence we have presented here. In fact, Socci's book cites the first edition of this book no fewer than 32 times, along with at least 110 other citations to the works of Frère Michel and other sources on which *The Devil's Final Battle* is based. "In the end," writes Socci, "I had to surrender…. Here I recount my voyage into the greatest mystery of the 20th century and set forth the result I honestly reached. A result that sincerely contradicts my initial convictions…"[402]

That result is Socci's conclusion that something is missing from the Vatican's disclosure: a separate text of the Third Secret containing "the words of the Madonna [which] preannounce *an apocalyptic crisis of the faith in the Church* starting at the summit." This second text is probably "also an explanation of the vision… (revealed on June 26,

---

[402] Antonio Socci, *Il Quarto Segreto di Fatima* [*The Fourth Secret of Fatima*], English ed., p. 4; popular ed., p. 11; Italian ed., p. 14.

2000).”[403] It is this text that Socci describes as “unspeakable” and whose concealment by the Vatican apparatus exposes the Vatican, as he writes, to “heavy pressure and blackmail.”[404]

Amazingly enough, Socci recounts that he received a personal letter from Pope Benedict XVI “concerning my book, thanking me for ‘the sentiments which have inspired it.’”[405] Furthermore, the Pope had not written a single word publicly (or evidently even privately) criticizing Socci’s conclusion that the Vatican apparatus, now led by Cardinal Bertone, was engaged in a veritable conspiracy to conceal precious words of the Mother of God from the Church and the world! Indeed, the Holy See has to this day observed a conspicuous official silence concerning Socci’s book, leaving Cardinal Bertone to fend for himself.

Socci’s open-minded validation of the case presented by the unjustly derided “Fatimists” was in itself an enormous breakthrough for the cause of Fatima. The promoters of the Vatican Party Line could not dismiss a man of Socci’s stature as a kook, which is why his book served as the provocation for a series of moves by Cardinal Bertone that would, as we shall see shortly, reduce the “official account” to rubble.

But perhaps Socci’s most important contribution to the search for truth in this matter was to give wide publicity to the testimony of a living eyewitness who finally and decisively confirmed the existence of “two texts” comprising the Third Secret in its totality: Archbishop Loris F. Capovilla, who was personal secretary to Pope John XXIII. Socci’s book relates how Archbishop Capovilla, now age 92 and residing in Bergamo, Italy, granted an interview to “a young Catholic intellectual,” Solideo Paolini, on July 5, 2006 in connection with Paolini’s research for a book on the Fatima controversy. During the interview Paolini asked the Archbishop whether there was an unpublished text of the Third Secret, and the Archbishop replied: “I know nothing.” That answer puzzled Paolini, who expected that “if the mysterious and never-revealed text were a fantasy, the prelate, one of the few who know the Secret, would have been able to and was obliged to reply to me that this is a completely unfounded idea and that everything had been revealed in 2000. Instead he answered: “I know nothing. (*Nulla so!*)” An expression that I imagine he wanted to invoke, ironically, a certain *omertá* [code of silence].”[406] By this sly and indirect reference to a code of silence, the Archbishop himself was trying to tell us that he was bound by a certain illicit conspiracy that required him to conceal the truth. That impression was confirmed by subsequent events.

On July 18, 2006, Paolini received from Capovilla in the mail a

---

[403] *The Fourth Secret of Fatima*, English ed., p. 74; popular ed., p. 55; Italian ed., p. 82.

[404] *The Fourth Secret of Fatima*, English ed., p. 162; popular ed., p. 111; Italian ed., p. 173.

[405] Antonio Socci, “Dear Cardinal Bertone: Who—Between You and Me—is Deliberately Lying?”, May 12, 2007, at http://www.antoniosocci.com/2007/05/caro-cardinal-bertone-chi-e’---fra-me-e-lei--che-mente-sapendo-di-mentire-e-lasciamo-stare-la-massoneria.../; English translation at http://www.fatima.org/news/newsviews/052907socci.asp. See also *The Fatima Crusader*, No. 86 (Summer 2007), pp. 35-42; see also Appendix III in this book.

[406] *The Fourth Secret of Fatima*, English ed., p. 131; popular ed., p. 91; Italian ed., p. 140.

package of papers from the Archbishop's files, along with a perplexing cover letter advising him to obtain a copy of CDF's document *The Message of Fatima* (*TMF*), which Capovilla must have known Paolini, a student of Fatima, would already have. Was this not, thought Paolini, "an invitation to read something in particular in that publication in relation to the documents sent by the same Archbishop"? That intuition was correct. Among the documents Capovilla had sent was a stamped "confidential note" by Capovilla, dated May 17, 1967, in which the Archbishop had recorded the circumstances of the reading of the Third Secret by Pope Paul VI. According to the note, Paul VI read the Secret on June 27, 1963, only six days after his election to the papacy and before he had even been officially enthroned in the Chair of St. Peter at the papal coronation Mass (which took place on June 29). But according to *TMF* and the "official account" in general, Paul VI read the Secret for the first time nearly two years later: "Paul VI read the contents with the Substitute, Archbishop Angelo Dell'Acqua, on 27 March 1965, and returned the envelope to the Archives of the Holy Office, deciding not to publish the text."[407]

The huge discrepancy between the date recorded by Capovilla and that set forth in *TMF* prompted Paolini to telephone Capovilla, at precisely 6:45 p.m. on the same day he received the documents, to ask the Archbishop to explain the discrepancy. Capovilla protested: "Ah, but I spoke the truth. Look I am still lucid!" When Paolini politely insisted that, still, there was an unexplained discrepancy, Capovilla offered explanations that suggested "eventual lapses of memory, interpretations of what a person might have intended to say," whereupon Paolini reminded Capovilla that he [Paolini] was referring to the date of the reading by Paul VI in an official Vatican document, namely *The Message of Fatima* (*TMF*), which in turn was based upon the official notes from the Vatican archive. Capovilla then gave this reply: "But I am right. Perhaps *the Bertone envelope is not the same as the Capovilla envelope*." Immediately, Paolini interrupted him and asked the question: "Therefore, both dates are true, because there are two texts of the Third Secret?" After a brief pause of silence, the Archbishop gave the explosive answer that confirmed the existence of a missing envelope and missing text of the Third Secret of Fatima: "Exactly so! (*Per l'appunto!*)."[408]

The "confidential note" completely corroborated Capovilla's testimony. According to the note recounting events on the date Pope Paul read the Secret (June 27, 1963), Monsignor Angelo Dell'Acqua— the same "Substitute" referred to in *TMF*—telephoned Capovilla to ask: "I am looking for the Fatima envelope. Do you know where it is kept?"[409] The note records that Capovilla replied: "It is in the right hand

---

[407] *The Fourth Secret of Fatima*, English ed., p. 131; popular ed., p. 91; Italian ed., p. 141; and citing *TMF*, p. 15 (English ed.).

[408] *The Fourth Secret of Fatima*, English ed., p. 132; popular ed., p. 92; Italian ed., p. 142.

[409] Notice Dell'Acqua evidently had reason to presume that the envelope was somewhere

drawer of the writing desk called Barbarigo, *in the bedroom*." That is, the envelope was in the former bedroom of John XXIII, which was now the bedroom of Paul VI; it was *not* in the Holy Office archives. The note further records that the "Fatima envelope" *was found in that desk*: "An hour later, Dell'Acqua telephoned me again. Everything is fine. The envelope has been retrieved." Finally, the note records that in an audience the next day Paul VI asked Capovilla directly: "Why is your name on the envelope?" Capovilla replied: "John XXIII asked me to inscribe a note concerning the manner of arrival of the envelope in his [Pope John's] hands and the names of all those to whom he considered it necessary to make it known."[410] Further, Pope John directed him to write on the outside of "the envelope" (*plico*) or "wrapping" (*involucro*): "I leave it to others to comment or decide."[411]

Thus, we now know for certain that a text of the Third Secret was kept in the papal bedchamber, was read by Paul VI on June 27, 1963, and was contained in an envelope on which Archbishop Capovilla had noted his name and the names of others at the instruction of Pope John XXIII and the papal dictation "I leave it to others to comment or decide." Hence not only John Paul II, but also Paul VI read two texts of the Third Secret on two different dates.

It is opportune to mention here another circumstance whose significance had been little noted before the publication of Socci's book: In 1960 Pope John read a text of the Secret he had no trouble understanding without assistance, but then, according to Archbishop Capovilla, in August 1959 the Pope read a text that contained difficult Portuguese dialect expressions requiring a translation by Monsignor Paulo José Tavares.[412] As Socci concludes: "These two opposed pieces of information can be explained by considering that the matter involves two readings of two different texts."[413] Pursuing this lead, Socci obtained the services of a Portuguese linguist, Professor Mariagrazia Russo, who analyzed the text of the vision published by the Vatican in 2000. In an appendix to Socci's book, the professor states her conclusion that the text of the vision contains *no* difficult expressions of Portuguese dialect. Ergo, the text John XXIII had difficulty reading would be the one he kept in his desk drawer.

So, it is now known that *three* Popes (John XXIII, Paul VI and John Paul II) read texts of the Third Secret on *two* different occasions—many

---

in the papal apartment, not in the Holy Office archive, of which Capovilla was not the custodian. Otherwise, Dell'Acqua would have asked the custodian of the archive, Cardinal Ottaviani, where the "Fatima envelope" was, rather than Capovilla, Pope John's former personal secretary.

[410] *The Fourth Secret of Fatima*, English ed., p. 133; popular ed., p. 93; Italian ed., p. 143.

[411] *The Fourth Secret of Fatima*, English ed., p. 133; popular ed., p. 93; Italian ed., pp. 143, 165.

[412] See the August 17, 1959 and second 1960 entries in the Appendix to this book, "A Chronology of the Fatima Cover-up". See also *WTAF* - Vol. III, pp. 555 and 568ff and *Prospettive nel mondo*, VI, 1991, cited in *The Fourth Secret of Fatima*, English ed., p. 139; popular ed., p. 96; Italian ed., p. 149.

[413] *The Fourth Secret of Fatima*, English ed., p. 139; popular ed., p. 97; Italian ed., p. 150.

months, even years apart—during their respective pontificates, whereas the "official account" in *TMF* of the history of the Secret claims only *one* reading by each Pope.[414] This can hardly be a coincidence or an error of historical record somehow repeated three times in a row. The mention of a second reading by each Pope can only have been omitted from the "official account" because *we were not meant to know of that second reading*, which points unmistakably to the existence of two different texts pertaining to one and the same Third Secret of Fatima, one of which has not been revealed.

So, on the basis of Capovilla's testimony alone, it has been established beyond doubt that there are two envelopes which hold between them the entire contents of the Third Secret of Fatima: the "Bertone envelope," kept in the Holy Office archives, whose contents were published on June 26, 2000, and the "Capovilla envelope," whose contents remain unpublished, kept in the papal bedchamber, as long ago confirmed by the photographs in *Paris-Match* magazine, the statement of Sister Pasqualina, and now, beyond any doubt, the testimony and documentation of Archbishop Capovilla.

Now, *the Vatican has never produced the "Capovilla envelope"* and the text of the Secret that it contains. Yet, as we are about to see, Cardinal Bertone has been forced to admit the Capovilla envelope's existence, *even as he fails to produce it*. This fact alone deprives the "official account" of all credibility.

Socci rightly observes that Archbishop Capovilla's testimony provides "the only possible explanation" for the many discrepancies (most of which have already been noted in the previous chapter) concerning the date of reception, format and location of the document at issue, as revealed in the accounts presented up to this point. To recapitulate:

- a document written on January 3, 1944—the date of the document published by the Vatican in 2000—and another document that was not ready until January 9, 1944, which has yet to be published;

- a document which arrived at the Holy Office on April 4, 1957, published by the Vatican in 2000, and a second document, not yet published, which arrived at the Vatican on April 16, 1957;

- a document lodged in the Holy Office archives—the published vision—and a different document lodged in the papal apartment of Pius XII;

- a document Pope John XXIII "understood completely" without need of a translation and which contains no difficult dialect expressions— the one published in 2000—and another document whose dialect expressions had to be translated for Pope John XXIII by Monsignor

---

[414] The evidentiary chart in Chapter 13 can be supplemented to reflect the reading of two different texts at two different times by both John XXIII and Paul VI as well as John Paul II, so that the chart would depict, not ten, but an even dozen facts in support of the "two texts" deduction.

Tavares;

- a document read by John XXIII and returned to the Holy Office archives, that being the vision published in 2000, and another document which never left Pope John's apartment and was still in his bedroom writing desk when Paul VI took office, as Archbishop Capovilla attests;

- a document Paul VI read on March 27, 1965 and then returned to the Holy Office archives—that is, the published vision—and a different document Pope Paul read on June 27, 1963, having retrieved it from the writing desk called "Barbarigo" in the papal bedchamber, as Archbishop Capovilla has revealed;

- a four-page[415] document containing 62 lines of text, produced by the Vatican in 2000, but also a one-page document in the form of "a letter to the Bishop of Leiria," containing 25 lines of text, as attested to by Bishop Venancio, Cardinal Ottaviani and others, which we have not yet seen;

- the description of a vision published on June 26, 2000 which records no words spoken by Our Lady, and another document containing "*the words* which Our Lady confided as a secret to the three little shepherds in the Cova da Iria," suppressed in 1960 and unpublished to this day;

- a document (per Pius XII's emissary, Father Schweigl) that "concerns the Pope," published in 2000, and another document, not yet published, that contains "the logical continuation of the *words*: 'In Portugal, the dogma of the Faith will always be preserved etc.'";

- a document in which Our Lady says nothing to Lucy, that being the published vision, and a different document which (per Cardinal Ottaviani, who read the Secret) contains "what Our Lady *told her* [Sister Lucy] to tell the Holy Father";[416]

- a document from the Holy Office archives read in July 1981 by Pope John Paul II in the hospital after the assassination attempt and then published in 2000, and another document the Pope read in 1978 within days of his election, not found in the archives.

Bertone's Campaign to Save the "Official Account"

Unlike the unjustly marginalized "Fatimists,"[417] Socci simply could

---

[415] See footnote 368.

[416] Once again, the operative words are "what Our Lady *told her*," not the Cardinal's interpolation "to tell the Holy Father."

[417] Marginalized by the illegal and immoral campaign (orchestrated by the Secretary of State) of lies, innuendoes, and half-truths which continue to this day. See, for example, Francis Alban and Christopher A. Ferrara, *Fatima Priest* (Pound Ridge, New York: Good Counsel Publications, 2001, Fourth Edition), which chronicles this vile campaign from 1981 to 2001.

not be ignored. Then again, how could he be answered without great risk to the "official account" in the form of further discrepancies, telling silences and inadvertent disclosures? In the course of Cardinal Bertone's efforts to limit the damage Socci had caused to the Party Line, there would in fact be innumerable such missteps, resulting (for those who trouble themselves to investigate the matter) in a complete demolition of the "official" version of the Third Secret.

It is impossible here to detail all of the "ins and outs" of Bertone's failed campaign to keep the lid on the Third Secret controversy, which was lifted sensationally by *Fourth Secret* and Capovilla's frank testimony. For a complete account one would need an entire book in itself, such as the one Socci himself has written or the investigation published by the Catholic attorney and commentator Christopher A. Ferrara, cited previously, which (like *Fourth Secret*) has been published in both Italy and America.[418] Or one could take an hour to watch a documentary film, *The Secret Still Silenced*, in either English or Italian to obtain a good overview of the facts spelled out in detail by Socci and Ferrara. For our purposes it suffices to touch upon the major developments in 2006-2007, the time period of Bertone's ill-fated campaign to save the "official account." Those developments support no reasonable conclusion but that a text pertaining to the Secret has been suppressed.

A Book that Answers Nothing

Cardinal Bertone's first move was to rush into print on May 10, 2007 a book of his own, *L'Ultima Veggente di Fatima* (*The Last Visionary of Fatima*), to "answer" Socci's accusation that he and the Vatican are concealing a text of the Secret. The book was in the form of an interview by Giuseppe De Carli, a "Vaticanista" (reporter on the Vatican beat) and ardent admirer of the Cardinal, whose fawning questions not only posed no real challenge to the Cardinal, but actually assisted him in promoting what Socci had called "the official reconstruction" of the Third Secret.

As Socci shows in his response to Bertone's book on May 12, 2007 in the Italian newspaper *Libero*,[419] Bertone's effort is a major embarrassment to him and to the Vatican—a disaster, in fact, because it leaves untouched the entire case in support of the thesis that the Vatican is hiding part of the Secret, while raising still more doubts about Bertone's credibility. At the same time, Bertone demeans his high office by recklessly hurling invective at Socci, pronouncing his contentions

---

[418] Cf. Christopher A. Ferrara, *The Secret Still Hidden*, which systematically presents every pertinent detail of the events following the publication of *Fourth Secret* and the Cardinal's efforts to rebut Socci's book and the "Fatimist" evidence it presents. This chapter incorporates a portion of Mr. Ferrara's text with his kind permission.

[419] Socci, "Dear Cardinal Bertone: Who—Between You and Me—is Deliberately Lying?", May 12, 2007 edition of the Italian newspaper *Libero*; at http://www.antoniosocci.com; also available photographically reproduced from the publisher of this book. English translation at http://www.fatima.org/news/newsviews/052907socci.asp; see also *The Fatima Crusader*, No. 86 (Summer 2007), pp. 35-42.

"ravings," calling him a deliberate liar ("*mendace*"), and even accusing him of the tactics of Freemasonry, which has to be one of the most ironic remarks of the post-conciliar epoch. Bertone acts like a desperate, wounded man instead of the Vatican Secretary of State.

Bertone's *Last Visionary* is essentially 140 pages of meandering "answers" in which Bertone fails to address the merits of a single one of Socci's well-supported arguments. For example, as to the key contention that the missing words of the Virgin are found within Sister Lucy's "etc.," Bertone does nothing more than restate the contention without answering it. Small wonder, for it was Bertone and his collaborators who (as Socci discusses in his own book) deliberately evaded the telltale "etc." by detaching it from the integral text of the Fatima Message and relegating it to a footnote without explanation in Bertone's *TMF*, the so-called "official commentary" on the Third Secret.

To take another example, regarding the substantial evidence (including three eyewitnesses and a photograph) that the missing 25-line, one-page text containing the Virgin's words was kept separately in the papal bedchamber rather than in the Holy Office archives, where the 62-line, four-page text of the vision was maintained, Bertone ducks the issue by stating that a one-page text was never in the archives, while saying nothing about what, if anything, was in the papal bedchamber. Having conspicuously failed to deny that a missing text was in the bedchamber, Bertone suddenly announces, for the first time ever, that some seven years ago Sister Lucy told him during an unrecorded interview that the four-page text of the vision "is the Third Secret and I have never written other."

We are asked to believe that Sister Lucy uttered this never-before-mentioned phrase during one of three interviews conducted by Bertone, totaling ten hours, which, as Socci's response notes, were "incredibly ... not taped, nor filmed, nor transcribed." Bertone claims, however, that he "took notes"—a total of four minutes' worth of phrases out of ten hours of alleged conversation. Socci rightly asks: "Why was such an important phrase not reported by Bertone in the official publication [in 2000]?" Moreover, why was it not reported until Sister Lucy was dead, and could no longer deny anything? As Socci shows with this and other examples of alleged statements by Sister Lucy during the purported interviews, Bertone's mysterious "notes" rather conveniently yield just what Bertone needs, just when he needs it—and not a moment sooner. Yet somehow not one of the same alleged statements of Sister Lucy found its way into the Vatican commentary of 2000, where they would have handily supported the Vatican's position. Indeed, Sister Lucy was kept incommunicado throughout the "revelation" of the Third Secret in that year, even though she was the only living witness to its true contents.

Socci's response poses the $64,000 question that Bertone continues to duck: "[W]hy did the prelate not ask the visionary if she had ever written the sequel to the mysterious words of the Virgin suspended by *et cetera* ('In Portugal the dogma of the faith will always be preserved') which have always been considered by the experts the beginning of the Third Secret? Very strange." Or perhaps Bertone did ask her, and got an answer he does not wish us to know. Perhaps the answer is in his "notes." But don't expect these "notes" ever to see the light of day.

As Socci further observes in his reply, Bertone's book not only fails to answer any of the points he raised in *Fourth Secret*, but also "poses further problems. I was even embarrassed to read a thing so bungled and self-wounding." For example, in order to bolster the Vatican Party Line that the Message of Fatima (and thus the Third Secret) belongs to the past because Russia has already "converted," Bertone "credits the rumor that Gorbachev, in the historic visit to Pope Wojtyla of December 1, 1989, 'made a *mea culpa*' before the Pope"—a myth that was "officially denied by the Vatican Press Office on March 2, 1998."

Another self-inflicted wound is Bertone's statement (in his book, *Last Visionary*, on page 89 of the English edition and page 101 of the Italian edition) that "Sister Lucy never worked with a computer." Here Bertone forgets that, when it was expedient for him to do so, he asserted precisely the opposite: that Sister Lucy "even used a computer" in 1989—a claim that, as Socci notes, "served to accredit certain letters that Sister Lucy had not written in her own hand and which contradicted everything she had said before on the consecration of Russia." Bertone has thus undermined all claims that Sister Lucy was the author of those letters, especially the alleged letter of November 8, 1989 to Mr. Noelker, cited in *TMF* as the sole evidence for claiming that the Consecration of Russia was done in 1984.

The damning omissions, admissions and inconsistencies in Bertone's attempt to answer Socci only reinforced Socci's conviction (and millions of others) that, as he states in his reply to *Last Visionary*, "It is evident that the 'Fourth Secret' of Fatima (or rather the hidden part of the Third) exists and in my book I think that I have demonstrated it."

But Socci is not pleased by his vindication through Bertone's flailing and ineffectual attacks. As he explains:

> For any author it would be a coup to see himself personally attacked by the Secretary of State without even a trace of argument. But for me it is a disaster, because I am first of all a Catholic before being a journalist. I would have preferred ... to be confuted. Or else I would have wanted the Holy See to reveal the whole truth about the 'Third Secret' of Fatima, publishing—as the Madonna requested—the part still hidden. Otherwise I would have preferred to be ignored, snubbed, boycotted. It is one thing to be mistaken, another to evade, and that is precisely what Bertone has done: publicly exposing himself without responding to anything and on the contrary adding disastrous findings. For him and for the Vatican. [420]

---

[420] Socci, "Dear Cardinal Bertone: Who—Between You and Me—is Deliberately Lying?", loc. cit.

It would be difficult to overestimate the importance of this development: a prominent and unimpeachable Catholic journalist and intellectual has publicly accused the Vatican of hiding a text containing a prophecy of the Virgin concerning apostasy in the Church and perhaps apocalyptic events for the world at large, and the Vatican offers no defense to the charge except a rambling collection of evasions and insults uttered by its Secretary of State.

Bertone's book boasts an introduction in the form of a letter from Pope Benedict, which tellingly avoids any details of the controversy. But, in a thickening of the plot, Socci reveals that he has received a letter from the Pope "concerning my book, thanking me for 'the sentiments which have suggested it'." Socci says that the Pope's words are "comforting before the insults and coarse accusations" Bertone has hurled at him.

While Socci is understandably comforted by the Pope's letter, however, it raises troubling questions: Why would the Pope thank Socci for a book that accuses the Vatican Cardinal Secretary of State of censoring the very words of the Mother of God and at the same time send a generic letter of apparent support to the same Secretary of State for his book which includes an attack on Socci, filled with insults and evasions that only confirm the suspicions of the faithful? If what Bertone says is true and what Socci says is false, then why did the Pope's letter to Socci apparently contain not a word of rebuke or correction? There is only one reasonable answer: *the Pope knows that Socci is onto something*, and thus the Pope cannot bring himself to condemn his book. And that is precisely why neither the Pope nor the Holy See has issued any official pronouncement against *The Fourth Secret of Fatima*. That official silence is thunderous, and in itself is confirmatory of the entire "Fatimist" position.

The Cover-Up Collapses

Recognizing that his book had failed to control the damage to the "official account" provoked by Socci's book, Bertone's next move was an utterly extraordinary television appearance to attack Socci's book. On May 31, 2007 Bertone appeared on *Porta a Porta* ["Door to Door"], Italy's most popular talk show, as the guest on a segment entitled "The Fourth Secret of Fatima Does Not Exist." While the title of the show was a direct reference to Socci's *Fourth Secret*, Socci was not invited to participate, evidently because the Cardinal would not allow himself to be subjected to any difficult questions.

Bertone appeared as a guest like any other, on a remote feed from his Vatican office and without any official mission from the Holy See, which had said absolutely nothing about Socci's book (apart from the personal letter of acknowledgment the Pope had sent Socci). His appearance was billed as a sensational on-camera display of the Third Secret documents that would supposedly end the controversy once and for all. In fact, the display of documents on live television and Bertone's own statements were utterly devastating to Bertone's version of events.

A complete account of this fateful telecast is not possible here.[421] We focus on only four of the most important revelations, which suffice to show beyond question that a text of the Secret remains, as Socci puts it, "well hidden"[422] in the Vatican:

The **first revelation**, by Cardinal Bertone on *Porta a Porta*, is that there are *two* sealed envelopes which Sister Lucy prepared for the Third Secret. Each envelope had three large wax seals on the back of the envelope, besides being glued closed in the usual way. Bertone displayed both envelopes, front and back, on camera (see the photos on page XV in the photo section).

The **second revelation** is that each of these two envelopes shown during that telecast contains the identical order in Lucy's own handwriting with the exact same words: "By express order of Our Lady, this envelope can only be opened in 1960 [only] by the Cardinal Patriarch of Lisbon or the Bishop of Leiria." We can distinguish between these two envelopes because on one envelope the words "Nossa Senhora" (Our Lady) are both on the same line, whereas on the other envelope "Nossa" and "Senhora" are on different lines (see page XV in the photo section for the photos of these two envelopes).

These first two revelations were enough to destroy the "official account." We note, first of all, that for the seven years preceding the May 31, 2007 telecast—beginning with publication of *TMF* on June 26, 2000—Bertone had represented to the world that Sister Lucy "confessed" to him that she had never received any directive from the Virgin regarding disclosure of the Secret in 1960. Bertone had made this claim both in *TMF* and in his book *Last Visionary*.[423] The claim that Lucy "confessed" that she had simply invented a connection of the Secret to the year 1960—which would make the seer a liar—was clearly intended to accomplish three purposes: (1) severing any connection between the Secret and that year, in which the Second Vatican Council had recently been announced, (2) lending support to Bertone's "interpretation" of the vision of the "Bishop dressed in white" as a depiction of the 1981 attempt on the life of John Paul II, and (3) distracting attention from the salient fact that the vision has no connection whatsoever to 1960, which would lead one to doubt that the vision standing alone is the whole of the Third Secret.

But now here was Bertone on national television blithely contradicting his own representations that Sister Lucy had never received any order from the Virgin regarding 1960. As if nothing were

---

[421] For a complete account see Christopher Ferrara, *The Secret Still Hidden*, Chapter 8.

[422] Antonio Socci, "Bertone in the 'Wasp's Nest' of the Polemics," June 2, 2007, at http://www.antoniosocci.com/2007/06/bertone-nel-"vespaio"-delle-polemiche; also available photographically reproduced from the publisher of this book. English translation at http://www.fatimacrusader.com/cr86/cr86pg43.asp; see also *The Fatima Crusader*, No. 86 (Summer 2007), pp. 43ff.

[423] *TMF*, p. 29; *Last Visionary*, English ed., p. 80; Italian ed., p. 92.

amiss, he had just displayed for the camera *two* envelopes referencing *precisely* such an order to the seer from the Mother of God! Either he was lying about the order from the Virgin or Sister Lucy was. Who was more likely to have told a lie about the "1960 order"—Lucy, who had no reason to lie about the Virgin's precise connection of the Third Secret to that year, or Bertone who had powerful motives to deny that connection? The question answers itself. And given the self-evident answer, why should anyone believe anything at all Bertone has to say about the Third Secret of Fatima?

Now, as to the revelation that there are *two* sealed envelopes pertaining to the Secret, we know that Sister Lucy, on January 9, 1944, had referred to a *single* sealed envelope in her letter to Bishop da Silva ("I have written what you asked… it is sealed in *an* envelope…"). Yet Bertone suddenly revealed for the first time that there had been *two* sealed envelopes all along, with *each* bearing its own "1960 order." What could be more obvious than that the two different envelopes were meant for two different parts of the same Secret: the vision, and the words of the Virgin explaining the vision (just as She had explained to the Fatima seers something as obvious as the vision of hell: "You have seen hell, where the souls of poor sinners go.").

The Cardinal presented the two envelopes on camera as if Lucy had placed one inside the other, even though neither the Cardinal nor Lucy herself had ever mentioned such a curiously redundant double sealed envelope (both with three wax seals) at any time. It would hardly make sense to have created *two* sealed envelopes, each thrice sealed with wax and bearing the *same* command on the outside, in order to use the resulting two "top secret" envelopes for only *one* "top secret" text.

Indeed, it would be something of a joke to write on an outer envelope "not to be opened before 1960" only to write on the inner envelope "not to be opened before 1960." Had Lucy done such an odd thing, Bertone certainly would have said so and would have had her authenticate *both* sealed envelopes during the meeting of April 2000 mentioned in the Introduction to *TMF*, rather than creating needless suspicion about a second envelope suddenly revealed for the first time on *Porta a Porta*.

Here it is crucial to note that if Sister Lucy *had* used two envelopes, both sealed, for the *same* text, then she and others would not have referred so consistently to *one* sealed envelope. For example:

"it is sealed in *an* envelope" (Lucy, 1944);

"It has been written and placed in *a* sealed envelope" (Cardinal Cerejeira, 1946);

"in the bishop's larger envelope he [Bishop Venancio] discerned *a* smaller envelope, that of Lucy, and inside *this* envelope, an ordinary sheet of paper…" (Bishop Venancio to Frère Michel).[424]

---

[424] *The Whole Truth About Fatima* – Vol. III, pp. 47, 471, 481.

Most tellingly, in his own book *Last Visionary*, ostensibly published for the very purpose of rebutting Antonio Socci's claim that the Vatican is hiding a text of the Secret, Bertone quotes Sister Lucy as referring to only *one sealed envelope* prepared by her for the text she was asked to authenticate in an April 2000 meeting with the Cardinal. Sister Lucy, reported by Cardinal Bertone, allegedly said: "This is my *envelope*, this is my writing, this is my text."[425] As Bertone states on the same page of his own book, the "authenticated" text was contained in only *one* sealed envelope of Lucy's: "An external with the note 'Third Part of the Secret,' and *an* internal *of Sister Lucy's* with the date '1960.'"[426]

These admissions leave no room for argument: Cardinal Bertone and Bishop Venancio both testified to a document ensemble consisting of an outer envelope that was *not* Sister Lucy's inside of which was only *one* envelope, sealed, that *was* Sister Lucy's. On this basis alone we can lay to rest any speculation that Lucy, for some strange reason, decided to use a redundant second envelope, with a redundant second order about 1960, to contain the text published by the Vatican on June 26, 2000.

In answer to the objection that Cardinal Bertone would not have revealed the second envelope if he had had something to hide, we can only say that its revelation may have been a mishap or else a calculated effort to smuggle into the picture, as if it had always been there, the long-suspected second envelope, whose existence could no longer be denied following Socci's publication of Archbishop Capovilla's testimony about the "Capovilla envelope" in the papal apartment. In any case, the problem is not ours to confront, but rather the problem of those whose long course of conduct has been to obviously lie to us over and over again.

Since we have learned from Bertone himself (at long last) that there *are* two sealed envelopes from Sister Lucy, each bearing its own order concerning the year 1960, and since, moreover, both Bertone and Venancio attest to having seen only *one* such sealed envelope, then we are obviously dealing with two different envelopes pertaining to *two different documents*, only one of which (the text of the vision) has been revealed.

But when was the second sealed envelope containing the second document created? As suggested in Chapter 4, it could only have been sometime before June 17, 1944 when Sister Lucy delivered the entire Secret to Bishop da Silva and sometime after she wrote to Bishop da Silva on January 9, 1944 to advise of the existence of a sealed envelope and "notebooks" that were evidently to be conveyed along with it. Only one reasonable conclusion is possible: something from Lucy's notebook ended up in one of the two envelopes.

[425] "Questa è la mia *busta*, questa è la mia scrittura, questo è il mio testo." *L'Ultima Veggente*, p. 49.
[426] Notice the rather misleading suggestion that the envelope had only the date "1960" written on the outside, when Bertone had to know, as he himself revealed only weeks later, that the outside of the envelope actually said: *"By express order of Our Lady*, this envelope only can be opened in 1960…"

Which brings us to the **third revelation** during the telecast. As Bertone showed the camera, what the Vatican published in June of 2000 is precisely *a folio of notebook paper* folded to make four sides on which there are 62 lines of writing, not the four separate pages *TMF* had appeared to present in photocopy form. This can only mean that the other sealed envelope must have been intended for the one-page document we have yet to see, the document containing only 25 lines of text famously revealed by both Bishop Venancio and Cardinal Ottaviani as discussed in Chapter 4. That one-page document was probably found in the "Capovilla envelope" in the papal apartment—in the writing desk called "Barbarigo." As we will see in the next section, during his own television presentation of September 21, 2007, Bertone publicly conceded before the whole world *that the Capovilla envelope exists*, yet he has conspicuously *failed to produce it*.

In the **fourth major revelation** of the telecast of May 31, 2007, Cardinal Bertone, backed into a corner, indirectly confirmed the truth of Cardinal Ottaviani's decisive testimony. During the broadcast the Vaticanista Marco Politi queried Bertone on the discrepancy between Cardinal Ottaviani's revelation that the Third Secret involved a text of 25 lines on a single page, and the Vatican's claim that the Secret only involved the 62 lines on four pages comprising the vision of the "Bishop dressed in white." Confronted by the discrepancy, Bertone not only did not deny that Ottaviani had so testified, but responded that "I was a little amazed that Cardinal Ottaviani had said categorically 'a folio of 25 lines'…"

And, in the ensuing moments of the broadcast, Bertone offered a most unconvincing explanation of why the late Cardinal would have said such a thing. Following a four-minute commercial break during which he had ample time to consider the problem posed for the "official" account, Bertone proposed on camera what he called "an attempt at an explanation" of Cardinal Ottaviani's testimony: that the late Cardinal had counted the first and fourth pages of the four-page vision as if it were one page consisting of 25 lines, while disregarding the second and third pages! Putting aside the utter implausibility of the claim that the very Cardinal entrusted with reading the Secret could have overlooked half its content in describing it to others, the fact is that the first and fourth pages of the text of the vision contain 32 lines in total, not 25 lines, or 30 lines if one discounts "J.M.J" on the first page and the line containing the date on the fourth page. *The "Fatimist" account of Ottaviani's revealing testimony was thus admitted by Cardinal Bertone himself.*

Certainly, Cardinal Bertone had had ample time to count the lines in question during the commercial break. Thus, he either deliberately misstated the number of lines, or never bothered to count them but only ventured a haphazard guess. In either case, Bertone had demonstrated a willingness to "fudge" the facts in order to serve the "official" account. But if this was the only explanation he could contrive for Cardinal Ottaviani's "categorical" affirmation contradicting the "official" account, then in effect Bertone had no explanation at all. Thus, Cardinal Bertone's "attempt at an explanation" only further confirms (albeit indirectly) the existence of a one-page text of the Secret containing only 25 lines.

All in all, Bertone's appearance on *Porta a Porta* was a disaster for Bertone but a triumph for the truth. As Socci wrote of the telecast, Bertone had not only failed to "give even one answer" to Socci's book, but "On the contrary, he did more: He offered the proof that I am right." Not only did Bertone fail to kick a goal into the empty net on Socci's side of the field, he

> scored the most sensational goal against himself: he demonstrated (involuntarily) that as a matter of fact the explosive part of the "Third Secret of Fatima" exists yet is well hidden.... For this service to the truth (although indirect) it is necessary to thank the Cardinal. And to encourage him now to tell everything because— as the Gospel explains—"the truth will make you free."[427]

The "Cardinal Bertone" Show

Facing disaster, Bertone's next move was to stage his own television show, broadcast on the Telepace channel on September 21, 2007. The press were invited to attend. Billed as a "presentation" of Bertone's *Last Visionary*—months after that book had already been presented to the public with great fanfare—this too was an unofficial initiative, with no backing from the Holy See, to discredit Socci and "save" the "official account." Socci, in fact, came as an invited journalist to the auditorium where the telecast was conducted in the hope of questioning Bertone, but was *thrown out of the building* by security guards.[428]

Part of this "Cardinal Bertone Show" was a heavily-edited videotaped segment of an interview of Archbishop Capovilla conducted, not by the Vatican, but by none other than Giuseppe De Carli, the same fawning "Vaticanista" who had collaborated with Bertone on *Last Visionary*. While the interview segment was clearly offered in an effort to counter Capovilla's testimony to Solideo Paolini as discussed above, Capovilla *failed to mention that testimony* or even mention Paolini's name, even once. On the contrary, he confirmed all of the following facts on camera:

- that on June 27, 1963 Paul VI contacted him, through Monsignor Dell'Acqua, to determine the location of the "Capovilla envelope" in the papal apartment,

- that the envelope was retrieved from the Barbarigo desk in the apartment,

[427] Antonio Socci, "Bertone in the 'Wasp's Nest' of the Polemics," June 2, 2007, at www.antoniosocci.com.
[428] "'Fourth Secret' of Fatima: Socci challenges Cardinal Bertone, thrown out by gendarmes," Bartolini Bruno, *Corriere della Sera*, September 22, 2007. See "Bertone's Cover-up of Third Secret Continues to Unravel" in *The Fatima Crusader*, No. 87 (Autumn 2007), pp. 16ff; at http://www.fatimacrusader.com/cr87/cr87pg16.asp

- that Paul VI read its contents on that date,
- that Paul VI *replaced the text and resealed the "Capovilla envelope,"* having left it to "others to decide," as had John XXIII.

To leave the reader with no doubt about the matter, here is the verbatim transcript of what Capovilla said on this score:

> On June 27, 1963 I was, that afternoon, with the Sisters of the Poor in Via Casilina. A worried Monsignor Dell'Acqua telephoned me. The Fatima envelope could not be found. *I replied that probably it could be found in the writing desk called "Barbarigo,"* because it belonged to Saint Gregory Barbarigo and was gifted to Pope John by Count della Torre. *Pope John held it dear, in his bedroom, like a relic.* There were on the right and on the left five or six drawers. Later, Dell'Acqua telephoned me and communicated that *the envelope had been found.*
>
> On June 28 Pope Paul called me and asked *who had dictated the lines on the envelope.* I explained that it was the Pope himself who wanted to indicate the persons who had knowledge of the text. "Pope John did not say anything else to you?," Pope Paul asked me. "No, Holy Father, he left it to others to decide." "I will also do as much", responded Pope Montini. The envelope was resealed and *I don't know if it was spoken of further.*[429]

So Bertone had finally admitted through Archbishop Capovilla, whom he had made his own witness, that there was indeed a "Capovilla envelope" located in the papal apartment and containing a text of the Secret read some two years before the date provided in the Bertone "official account." Yet, through his surrogate De Carli, Bertone proceeded brazenly to claim on live television that the never-produced Capovilla envelope was the same as the documentation he had already produced on *Porta a Porta.* As De Carli declared to the camera:

> I conclude, therefore, there is not a **Capovilla envelope** to contrast to a **Bertone envelope**. The two envelopes are the same document.

But this was utter nonsense, since we know that the Capovilla envelope bears the handwriting of Archbishop Capovilla indicating the names of all those who had read its contents, his own name, and the dictation of John XXIII that "I leave it to others to comment or decide." Bertone had never at any time over the previous seven years produced this envelope, nor did he produce it during the telecast of September 21, 2007. Nor has he done so as of the publication of this second edition of *The Devil's Final Battle* (December 2009). Yet Bertone *has* shown us the Bertone envelope, and it clearly is *not* the Capovilla envelope testified to by Archbishop Capovilla in such exacting and irrefutable

---

[429] Cf. Christopher A. Ferrara, *The Secret Still Hidden*, p. 187.

detail during *the very telecast Bertone himself had orchestrated.* Thus De Carli—and by extension Bertone himself—had the audacity to declare what he and Bertone had to know was precisely the opposite of the truth. And notice that it is *De Carli*, not Archbishop Capovilla, who "concludes" this, providing the "testimony" he clearly could not extract from the Archbishop since it was manifestly false.

There are other telling slip-ups in this telecast, but the details of these need not delay us, as significant as they are.[430] For we have already seen enough in the three moves, each disastrous, Socci's book had provoked Bertone to undertake. Bertone's book and his two telecasts had only served to confirm what was already apparent: that there are two envelopes and two texts comprising the Third Secret of Fatima in its entirety, and that we have seen only one of the texts—the text of the vision—while the text containing the words of the Virgin explaining the vision and predicting a crisis for the Church and the world remains hidden, evidently inside the "Capovilla envelope" that Bertone wishes to pretend he has produced without actually producing it.

As Scripture says, "He that diggeth a pit, shall fall into it..."[431] Despite all his efforts to the contrary, Cardinal Bertone had only further revealed that which, as Socci courageously recognizes, Cardinal Bertone and his collaborators in the Vatican apparatus wish to conceal. Five years after this book first appeared, Divine Providence had written straight with Bertone's crooked lines, shining the light of Heaven itself on the Secret still hidden.

But that is not all. Before the guards threw Socci out on the street at the location of the telecast of September 21, 2007, he was able to play for the assembled journalists an audiotape of Capovilla's statements to Paolini during a further meeting of the two on June 21, 2007. As the major Italian daily *Il Giornale* reported, on the tape Capovilla is heard to state: "Besides the four pages [of the vision of the bishop dressed in white] there was also something else, an attachment, yes." As the reporter from *Il Giornale* concluded, Capovilla's statement "would confirm the thesis of the existence of a second sheet with the interpretation of the Secret. The mystery, and above all the polemics, will continue."[432]

Thanks to the revelations of 2006-2007 the mystery and the polemics will indeed continue. Meanwhile, however, not only the Church, but the whole world, is moving inexorably toward the ultimate consequences the missing text of the Third Secret no doubt foretells and gives us the means to avoid. The next chapters of this book will focus on the ever increasing danger posed by deliberate concealment of the Heaven-sent text that completes the Third Secret of Fatima.

---

[430] Cf. *The Secret Still Hidden*, Chapter 10, for a full account.
[431] Ecclesiastes, 10:8.
[432] "Non esiste un quarto segreto di Fatima" ["The Fourth Secret of Fatima does not exist"], *Il Giornale*, September 22, 2007.

Chapter 15

Bertone versus Benedict

Throughout this book we have developed the theme of a Vatican "Party Line" on Fatima dictated by the Secretary of State, with even Pope John Paul II hewing to its requirements: that the Message of Fatima be consigned to the past, that the Third Secret be "interpreted" as merely a depiction of past events (supposedly culminating with the 1981 assassination attempt) and that its explicitly Catholic call for the consecration and conversion of Russia be "revised" in keeping with a "new orientation" of the Church. This new orientation involves "ecumenism," "dialogue," and Vatican diplomacy, including the Vatican-Moscow Agreement according to which Vatican II observed (and the Vatican apparatus continues to observe) a shameful silence in the face of Communist persecution of the Church.

We have also shown that key figures involved in implementing this Party Line have left the "scene of the crime," so to speak, since the first edition of this book appeared: the former Secretary of State, Cardinal Angelo Sodano; the former head of the Congregation for the Clergy, Cardinal Castrillón Hoyos; and, of course, the former Cardinal Ratzinger, who is now Pope Benedict XVI. But, as the preceding chapter demonstrates in considerable detail, one key figure remains very much involved in perpetuating the Party Line: the current Vatican Secretary of State, Cardinal Bertone. As should be obvious from what we recounted in Chapter 14, Cardinal Bertone perseveres in the Party Line even more vigorously than his predecessor—and this despite the devastating revelations of 2006-2007, which have exposed it as nothing less than a fraud upon the Church, as even Antonio Socci, an acquaintance and collaborator of the Cardinal, was forced to conclude.

At the same time, however, the former Cardinal Ratzinger has undergone a certain transformation of his former "revisionist" views on Fatima—views evidently dictated by the Party Line. As Pope, the former Cardinal Ratzinger—

- Has abandoned the view, expressed in his theological commentary on the Message of Fatima in June of 2000, published as part of *TMF*, that the Triumph of the Immaculate Heart occurred 2,000 years ago when Mary agreed to become the Mother of God. Today, Pope Benedict speaks of that Triumph as a future event, and declares: "May it be so!"

- Has thus implicitly abandoned the view, expressed by Cardinal Bertone in his Introduction to *TMF*, that Fatima "belongs to the past" and that publication of the vision of "the Bishop dressed in white" on June 26, 2000 "brings to an end a period of history marked by tragic human lust for power and evil"—a preposterous and reprehensible falsehood designed to lull the faithful to sleep in the face of grave danger.

- Has abandoned the view, also expressed in *TMF*, that the Immaculate Heart is like any heart that draws close to God. Today, Pope Benedict declares that the Immaculate Heart is the Heart most like that of Jesus, the Heart closest to His among all of humanity. He no longer places the words "Immaculate Heart" in the skeptical quotation marks and lower case letters we saw in *TMF*.

- Has abandoned the view implied by his citation to Edouard Dhanis as an "eminent scholar" on Fatima—Dhanis having contended that everything Sister Lucy reported about the consecration and conversion of Russia was her own invention. Today, Pope Benedict pronounces the Message of Fatima to be "the most important prophetic message of the 20th Century."

- Has admitted that the Church is in the midst of a terrible crisis of faith and discipline, which is no doubt foretold in the part of the Third Secret consisting of the 25 lines attested to by Cardinal Ottaviani, and which the Pope has read. Pope Benedict, unlike his immediate predecessors, does not speak of the "renewal" or "springtime" of Vatican II, but of a true ecclesial disaster of unprecedented proportions.

In view of these papal words and deeds, the divergence between Benedict XVI and Cardinal Bertone and his Party Line on Fatima is now so dramatic that it is fair to speak of a situation that can be described as "Bertone vs. Benedict."

Furthermore, it is evident that the former Cardinal Ratzinger, precisely because he has read the Third Secret in its entirety (giving tantalizing hints of its contents in 1984), is today as Pope attempting to implement (however partially) a program of ecclesial "course correction" that would seem to be aimed at addressing what the unpublished part of the Third Secret predicts: a truly apocalyptic collapse of faith and discipline in the Church, leading to what the Pope himself called (in September 2009) a "secularized ecclesial environment" and a "desert without God." We have seen that the Pope's attempt to change course has included his historic "liberation" of the Latin Mass, his lifting of the "excommunication" of the bishops of the Society of Saint Pius X, and his extraordinary exclusive invitation to the Society's representatives to engage in "theological discussions" with the Vatican concerning the enormously problematical Vatican II texts (which discussions commenced on October 26, 2009).

Cardinal Bertone, on the other hand, continues as before, pursuing unswervingly the worldly wisdom of a Vatican bureaucracy that wishes to be done with Fatima once and for all. In Chapter 14 we outlined how the revelations of 2006-2007 exposed the Party Line as a tissue of lies. We recall here three of the most flagrant lies the Cardinal has perpetrated over the past several years, despite conclusive evidence that he cannot possibly be telling the truth:

- That Sister Lucy "confessed" to him that Our Lady of Fatima never said anything to her about the Third Secret being connected to 1960, when Bertone himself produced on television *two* envelopes (clearly meant for two different texts pertaining to the Secret) on each of which Sister Lucy had recorded the "express order of Our Lady" that the contents were not to be revealed until that year. This falsehood alone destroys the Cardinal's credibility.

- That the "Capovilla envelope" Bertone has never produced is the same as the "Bertone envelope." It is Bertone himself who presented the testimony of Archbishop Capovilla on television that the "Capovilla envelope," containing a text pertaining to the Secret and lodged in the papal apartment, bears the Archbishop's handwriting, a list of the names of the prelates who had read its contents, and the dictation of Pope John XXIII that "I leave it to others to comment or decide." It requires unbelievable audacity for Bertone to maintain that what he has never produced is the same as what he has produced. Yet he persists in this falsehood even though it is perfectly obvious that it is false.

- That publication of the vision on June 26, 2000 "brings to an end a period of history marked by tragic human lust for power and evil." The terrorist attacks of September 11, 2001; the wars in Iraq and Afghanistan; the rise of a neo-Stalinist, abortion-ridden Russia and a new Sino-Soviet military alliance; the worldwide economic collapse of 2008-2009 (provoked precisely by greed) and the continuing descent of the entire world into ever-worsening moral depravity, make a mockery of this falsehood. And yet the Cardinal refuses to recant it.

We refer the reader to the preceding pages for the facts regarding all the falsehoods that comprise the Party Line on Fatima. All of these falsehoods, of course, have served the Big Lie that Fatima "belongs to the past" and that its prophecies need no longer concern us.

Cardinal Bertone persists in the Big Lie—and all the smaller lies that serve it—despite the very public collapse of his version of events, and the very public correction he has received from Socci and other Catholics whose legitimate objections he has utterly failed to answer, even as he pretends, with great fanfare, to have given an answer. Consider these key events recounted on the preceding pages, which remind us of the pertinacity with which the Cardinal clings to his utterly discredited testimony:

- On November 22, 2006, Antonio Socci published his devastating exposé on the Third Secret, including the testimony of Archbishop Capovilla that there are two texts and two envelopes (the "Capovilla envelope" and the "Bertone envelope") pertaining to the Secret. Pope Benedict himself sent Socci a personal note of acknowledgment and thanks for his book, even though Socci had accused Bertone of a cover-up of the second text.

- In the face of this damning indictment, Bertone not only refused to back down, but published his own book on May 10, 2007, attacking Socci while failing to address a single point he had raised.

- When Socci replied publicly (on May 12, 2007) that Bertone's book had ignored every single issue and had thus conceded Socci's entire case, Bertone's only answer was silence.

- On May 31, 2007, however, Bertone appeared on the Italian television show *Porta a Porta* to attack Socci a second time—again without answering him. In the process, Bertone not only failed to address the evidence Socci had presented, but also revealed devastating new evidence against his own position, including the existence of two different sealed envelopes pertaining to the Third Secret, each with its own order from the Virgin that it could not be opened before 1960, and Bertone's admission that Cardinal Ottaviani had testified "categorically" to the existence of a text of the Third Secret comprised of one page and 25 lines.

- When, on June 2, 2007, Antonio Socci publicly replied that Bertone's appearance on *Porta a Porta* had only confirmed that he was concealing the second text of the Third Secret, Bertone once again observed a telling silence.

- On September 21, 2007, his position now in shambles, Bertone conducted his own telecast during which he not only failed (yet again) to answer any of the questions that Socci—and now Bertone's own disclosures—had raised, but also produced a heavily-edited videotape interview of Archbishop Capovilla, during which the Archbishop *confirmed the existence of the very envelope (the "Capovilla envelope") Bertone has failed and refused to produce,* even as Bertone audaciously and falsely continued to maintain that he has produced everything.

- Before the start of the telecast of September 21, 2007, Socci was thrown out of the building in which the telecast was conducted so that he would not be able to pose any questions to Bertone, but not before he played for other journalists an audio tape in which Archbishop Capovilla is heard to admit that there is an "attachment" to the text of the vision of "the Bishop dressed in white"—an attachment that has never been published, and probably contains the explanatory words of the Virgin. When the Italian press reported on this revelation the next day, Bertone again observed a telling silence, conspicuously failing to deny that there is an unpublished "attachment" to the text of the vision.

- In June-July 2008 the Italian translation of a book by the Catholic attorney and commentator Christopher A. Ferrara was published (the original English was published a few months earlier), wherein all of the developments mentioned above and numerous others are presented in a way that systematically demonstrates that Cardinal Bertone is not telling the truth about the Third Secret. Although Ferrara's book was published in Italian and circulated throughout Italy, Bertone offered no response other than to complain privately about the book in a letter to a priest, without addressing any of the points it raises—thus repeating his suspicious silence with respect to the questions raised by Socci's book.

In sum, Cardinal Bertone is a thoroughly impeached witness who stubbornly persists in defending his testimony long after his credibility has been destroyed. He thus represents an even greater problem for the Church—by far—than his predecessor in the office of Secretary of State. For Bertone is not only committed to defending the Party Line, but also his personal reputation, which has been damaged by a public scandal in which one of Italy's most prominent Catholics, Antonio Socci, has accused him of concealing the words of the Mother of God. This is what accounts for Bertone's furious public relations campaign in defense of his discredited testimony, including a book and two television appearances that have only confirmed the incredibility of his account. And yet Bertone digs in his heels, refusing to admit the obvious implications of his own disclosures and admissions. He has thus created in himself a major obstacle to the Church's obedience to the Message of Fatima. It is literally the case that the personal pride of a lone Vatican bureaucrat has placed the Church and the world at risk.

Now, back in the year 2000 Bertone was the former Cardinal Ratzinger's subordinate as Secretary of the Congregation for the Doctrine of the Faith, and both Ratzinger and Bertone were carrying out the Party Line under former Secretary of State Sodano. Under those circumstances, it was at least arguable that Cardinal Ratzinger was able to justify to himself that the testimony of then-Archbishop Bertone—as the emissary Sodano had sent to interview Sister Lucy—was reliable in April of 2000 in connection with the impending publication of the vision of the "Bishop dressed in white." Again in November 2001 Cardinal Ratzinger still felt justified in believing the testimony of Archbishop Bertone for that infamous "interview" from which, out of an alleged two hours of unrecorded conversation with the seer, Bertone published exactly nine words he attributed to her concerning the Third Secret. Perhaps at that time Ratzinger felt he had no choice but to follow the testimony of Archbishop Bertone and the dictates of Cardinal Sodano, the then Vatican Secretary of State, as indicated by his numerous deferential references to Sodano's "interpretation" of the vision in his theological commentary in *TMF*—an "interpretation" Sodano had absolutely no authority or competence to make, but which he simply arrogated to himself.

And, as we have suggested earlier, perhaps under the "compromise solution" hypothesized by Socci, in 2000 the former Cardinal Ratzinger felt justified in adopting a mental reservation concerning the still hidden one-page text of 25 lines that undoubtedly contains the words of the Virgin explaining the vision. Pursuant to the "compromise solution," it may well have been determined that during Bertone's "interviews" of Lucy (of which, conveniently, there is no independent record of any kind) he would obtain Lucy's "agreement"—that is, the obedient cloistered nun's submissive acceptance or at least non-objection—to the proposition that the unpublished text might not be "authentic." Then Pope John Paul II could be permitted to reveal only the substance of the "disputed" text by way of his apocalyptic references to the "tail of the dragon" at Fatima on May 13, 2000, and those veiled references, together with the vision, could be presented as the "entire" Third Secret without any overt misrepresentation, exactly as Socci suggests.

But this speculation aside, the former Cardinal Ratzinger is now the Pope, and since he became Pope evidence has surfaced which makes it objectively impossible to believe Bertone's testimony. Indeed, the Pope's own dramatic changes of position since his election to the papacy indicate that he knows quite well that the Third Secret contains precisely those prophetic warnings we have not yet been allowed to see. Then too there is the Pope's telling note to Socci, thanking him for a book in which Socci accuses the Vatican Secretary of State of deliberately concealing part of the Third Secret. One can be certain that if Socci had falsely accused Bertone of such a grave misdeed, the Pope would have told him so and directed him to make reparation for the scandal.

Clearly, then, the Pope knows he cannot commit to Cardinal Bertone's version of the facts because it does not correspond to the truth. And yet the Pope, in the face of decisions made before he became Pope, finds himself in a quandary: the text which, in fact, actually is not yet published has been "revealed" in a veiled way by John Paul II at Fatima, but under the "compromise solution" which involved that veiled revelation of the missing text which itself has been conveniently deemed by the anti-Fatima Cardinals Bertone and Sodano and the anti-Fatima Party in the Vatican to be "questionable" or—even worse—"inauthentic." How can the Pope now reveal it without risking a revolution in the papal household?

And yet reveal it he must. As Socci wrote on June 2, 2007, following Bertone's appearance on *Porta a Porta*, the Pope himself "had opened the road to the truth" by stating in a letter Bertone included in his book that "the authentic words of the third part of the Secret were published," which "clearly implies that there exist words of the Secret deemed 'not authentic.' Courage, then: publish everything. 'The truth will make you free.'"[433]

The truth *will* make us free. And the Vatican Secretary of State must no longer be allowed to impede its revelation. Benedict is the Roman

---

[433] *Libero*, June 2, 2007; see also footnote 422.

Pontiff, and Bertone is merely his subordinate. It is time for the Roman Pontiff to end the Secretary of State's domination in the Fatima affair. It is incumbent on the Pope to undo the damage Bertone and Sodano, his predecessor, have caused and continue to cause by their ongoing deception. The Roman Pontiff alone is in a position to remedy this grave injustice instantly. In addition to revealing the entirety of the Third Secret and performing the Consecration of Russia so long overdue, the remedy would involve either Bertone's public recantation of the Party Line and his own demonstrable falsehoods in support of it, or else his removal from office for the good of the Church and all humanity. We are constrained to request nothing less than this in the Petition to the Holy Father with which this book concludes.

Sister Lucy, at the time of this photograph, was a Sister of the Dorothean nuns, and about three years after this picture was taken, she received a message from Our Lord Jesus Christ Himself telling her to relay to the Pope and bishops what will happen to them personally if they delay too long to do the Consecration of Russia. Jesus said:

> **Make it known to My ministers, given that they follow the example of the King of France in delaying the execution of My command, like him they will follow him into misfortune.**

The vision of the execution of the Pope and the bishops which was released by the Vatican on June 26, 2000 would be explained by the words of Our Lord Himself quoted above.

"The Big Three" in the Third Secret Cover-up

Angelo Cardinal Sodano (left), former Vatican Secretary of State, who "managed" the revelation of the vision of the "Bishop dressed in white" in 2000 and whose patently untenable "interpretation" of the vision as a depiction of the 1981 attempt on the life of John Paul II was widely rejected by the faithful. Sodano's "interpretation" was cited no fewer than four times in the Vatican commentary on the vision, *The Message of Fatima*, published together with the vision on June 26, 2000. But what business is it of the Vatican Secretary of State to "interpret" the Message conveyed to the Church and the world by the Virgin Mother of God back in 1917? Here we see how Vatican "diplomacy" has made a captive of the Message of Fatima for the sake of fallible human initiatives, including "dialogue," "ecumenism" and "Ostpolitik."

Tarcisio Cardinal Bertone (center). Successor to Cardinal Sodano as Secretary of State, and formerly Secretary of the Congregation for the Doctrine of the Faith as Archbishop Bertone (in which capacity he co-authored *The Message of Fatima*). Bertone's actions, disclosures and revelations between 2000 and 2008 concerning the cover-up of an unpublished text of the words of the Blessed Virgin, a text no doubt explaining the published vision, are central to the whole "detective story" and are extensively discussed in this book.

Giuseppe De Carli (right): The "Vaticanist" (journalist of Vatican affairs) whose fawning, "softball" questions and biased defense of Bertone have been instrumental to the cover-up. It was De Carli who, acting as Bertone's private agent, conducted a heavily edited interview of Archbishop Capovilla, eyewitness to the existence of a second text of the Third Secret kept in the papal apartment. In this interview, De Carli attempted to use leading questions to induce the Archbishop to change his testimony about the existence of an unpublished text of the Secret. The effort not only failed, but on the contrary the Archbishop confirmed that the "Capovilla envelope" containing this text exists. Yet it has never been produced by Bertone or Sodano.

Chapter 16

Counting the Cost

"In the end, My Immaculate Heart will triumph. The Holy Father will consecrate Russia to Me, and she will be converted, and a period of peace will be granted to the world." So the Mother of God promised the Church and the world at Fatima. But something has gone wrong. The Fatima prophecies, fulfilled unerringly in every other respect—except for the annihilation of nations—have not been fulfilled here. Did the Mother of God mislead us? Or is it, rather, certain men who have misled us?

As this book moves toward its conclusion, we must recall that with Our Lady's promise comes an ultimatum concerning the consequences of failing to perform the Consecration of Russia in time: "If My requests are heeded, Russia will be converted, and there will be peace; if not, she will spread her errors throughout the world, causing wars and persecutions of the Church. The good will be martyred; the Holy Father will have much to suffer; *various nations will be annihilated.*"

So, the Triumph of the Immaculate Heart *will* take place—"in the end"—for nothing mere men can do will prevent the ultimate fulfillment of the divine plan for our time as announced at Fatima. But Catholics who believe in the Message of Fatima rightly wonder how much more the Church and the world will have to suffer before the Consecration is done and we reach the glorious fulfillment that Antonio Socci describes as a victory for Our Lady more astonishing than the one over Islam at the Battle of Lepanto, "a radical and extraordinary change in the world, an overthrow of the mentality dominating modernity, *probably following dramatic events for humanity.*" Must we first witness the annihilation of nations and other "dramatic events for humanity" before the Triumph of the Immaculate Heart comes to pass? How many souls have been lost, and how many will be lost on account of human failure to follow the Blessed Virgin's simple prescription—a failure attributable to a worldly wisdom that seeks an accommodation of the Church to worldly powers?

On March 3, 2002, *Time* magazine reported that "a month after the Sept. 11 attacks, top federal officials feared a nuclear weapon obtained from the Russian arsenal was being smuggled into New York. The White House's Counterterrorism Security Group, part of the National Security Council, was alerted to the danger through a report by an agent code-named DRAGONFIRE, according to the magazine, but New York officials and senior FBI officials were not informed in an effort to avoid panic." Although the report later proved to be inaccurate, in Washington, D.C. a "shadow government" facility has been installed in underground bunkers, and nuclear detectors have been arrayed at key locations throughout the United States in anticipation of what the President and his advisors believe to be an inevitable, and far more deadly, attack by Islamic terrorists. As *The Washington Post* reported on March 3, 2002: "Alarmed by growing hints of al Qaeda's progress toward obtaining a nuclear or radiological weapon, the Bush administration has deployed hundreds of sophisticated sensors since November to U.S. borders, overseas facilities and choke points around Washington. It has placed the Delta Force, the nation's elite commando unit, on a new standby alert to seize control of nuclear materials that the sensors may detect."

Based on fallible human intelligence reports, political leaders showed sufficient prudence to prepare for the worst, which they know is coming sooner or later. But the Fatima revisionists in the Vatican apparatus, following the Party Line on Fatima, tell us that the Fatima prophecies, including the Third Secret, "belong to the past" (to recall Cardinal Sodano's and Cardinal Bertone's truly infamous words), that we may safely disregard a heavenly intelligence report from an infallible source, warning us of the annihilation of nations and the loss of countless souls. Worse, they hide from the Church a vital portion of that heavenly intelligence report—the still-missing words of the Secret—while assuring us that everything has been revealed. And it seems that as the world hurtles towards disaster, there is no short supply in the Church of what Lenin, speaking of Western liberals, called "useful idiots," people who are only too happy to parrot the Party Line while helpfully denouncing anyone who questions it.

The promises of Our Lady at Fatima entail two great gifts to all of humanity: peace in the world through the conversion of Russia, and peace and renewal in the Church also consequent to the Consecration of Russia as well as the worldwide establishment of devotion to the Immaculate Heart of Mary. And yet, as of the time the second edition of this book appears (December 2009), we manifestly have neither.

Russia Has Not Been Converted

Twenty-five years after the Vatican ceremony in which the world was consecrated to Mary, but any mention of Russia was deliberately avoided so that the Russian Orthodox would not be offended, those who preach the Party Line speak of the "fall of communism," a mere regime change, as if this were the miraculous conversion of Russia the Mother of God promised. But the facts—and as Saint Thomas teaches, against a fact there is no argument—tell us that Russia has not converted in any sense of the word, no matter how one wishes to twist "conversion" to mean something other than what the Mother of God intended: the return of the Russian people to union with Rome through their embrace of the integral Catholic Faith.

There is no argument against a fact. No argument, no matter how high the authority proposing it, can establish that the Eiffel Tower is located in Rome. And no argument, no matter how high the Churchman proposing it, can establish that Russia has been converted since the 1984 ceremony from which any mention of Russia was excluded. The *facts* destroy the Party Line, and bring to light the terrible cost of the Church's continued adherence to it. Let us summarize some of the facts here:

A. No conversion to the Catholic Faith

Father Joaquin Alonso, probably the foremost Fatima expert of the 20th Century, had many interviews with Sister Lucy. In 1976 he wrote:

> ...we should affirm that Lucia always thought that the *'conversion'* of Russia is not to be limited to the return of the Russian people to the Orthodox Christian religion, rejecting the Marxist atheism of the Soviets, but rather, it refers purely, plainly and simply to the total, integral conversion of Russia to the one true Church of Christ, the Roman Catholic Church.[434]

Why is Our Lady of Fatima so insistent on the *conversion* of Russia? The answer is that the Catholic Church has thrice defined as infallible dogma that there is no salvation outside the Church: at the Fourth Lateran Council (1215 AD) by Pope Innocent III; in the Bull *Unam Sanctam* (1302) by Boniface VIII; and at the Council of Florence, in the Bull *Cantate Domino* (1442) by Pope Eugene IV. Christ did not found His Church for nothing, or to serve as an optional "body of believers." He founded it for one purpose: to sanctify souls and save them from hell, through the grace He won for all men on the Cross.

We know Our Lady came to Fatima precisely to obtain the salvation of souls: "If My requests are granted *many souls will be saved.*" From which it obviously follows that many souls will be lost if Her requests are not granted, for otherwise the request would have been pointless. In this context the word "conversion" as used in the Message of Fatima cannot possibly mean anything other than a conversion to Catholicism and thus membership in the Catholic Church. It is nonsensical, therefore to argue, as some do, that by "conversion" the Mother of God—Who is also known by Catholics under the title Mother of the *Catholic* Church—meant that Russia would embrace the *Orthodox* religion following the "fall of communism" in 1991. The Mother of the Catholic Church did not come to Fatima to announce the "conversion" of Russia *to a state of schism from Rome.* What is more, Russian Orthodoxy was already the predominant religion in Russia when Our Lady appeared at Fatima. Therefore, according to this argument, Russia would already have been

---

[434] *La Verdad sobre el Secreto de Fatima, Fatima sin mitos,* Father Joaquin Alonso, (2nd edition, Ejercito Azul, Madrid, 1988) p. 78. English translation by Joseph Cain. Original Spanish reads: "... *podriamos decir que Lucia ha pensado siempre que la conversión de Rusia no se entiende solo de un retorno de los pueblos de Rusia a la religion cristiano-ortodoxa, rechazando el ateismo marxista y ateo de los soviets, sino que se refiere pura y llanmente a la conversion total e integral de un retorno a la unica y verdadera Iglesia, la catolica-romana.*"

"converted" in 1917 and Our Lady of Fatima's statement that Russia *"will be* converted" would have been senseless.

Now, it is simply undeniable that Russia has shown no sign whatsoever of conversion rightly understood. More than a quarter century after the ceremony of 1984, Catholics remain a tiny and benighted minority in Russia. Consider these facts:

- There are a mere ten Russian-born priests in the whole country—five in Siberia and five in Kazakhstan. Ninety-five percent of the priests and nuns in Russia are foreign born. In Archbishop Bukovsky's frank opinion the Catholic Church "is small."[435]

- According to the Vatican, there are 500,000 Catholics in Russia, and most of these are in Siberia, where Stalin had sent their grandparents in exile.[436]

- Statistics revealed by the flagship Russian Embassy in Washington, D.C. paint a grim picture for Roman Catholicism in "converted" Russia as of 2009.[437] According to the Embassy report on "Religion in Russia" today, the Russian Orthodox have nearly 5,000 approved religious associations in the country; the Muslims, 3,000; the Baptists, 450; the Old Believers, over 200; and Roman Catholics only 200—*only 132 more than the "Hari Krishna people,"* who have 68.

- All told, Russia's 2 million Protestants have 1,150 communities, or *five times more than the Catholics*.

- The number of Muslims in Russia (19 million) is about *thirty-eight times higher* than the number of Catholics.

- There were 150 Roman Catholic parishes before the Russian Revolution in 1917, but today there are only 83 parishes.

If this is a "conversion of Russia," then the word "conversion" has lost its meaning.

B. The Church is persecuted in Russia

Not only has Russia manifestly failed to embrace the Catholic Faith since 1984—the only reasonable meaning of the word "conversion"—the years since 1984 have witnessed a steady *decline* of the Church's position in Russia, to the point where the Church has been undergoing *outright persecution* under the Yeltsin regime and now today the Putin/Medeved regime. Consider these facts:

- In 1997 Russia enacted a new law on "freedom of conscience" which gave privileged status to Russian Orthodoxy, Islam, Judaism and Buddhism as Russia's "traditional religions," while forbidding

---

[435] Sarah Karush, "Foreign Priests Spark Controversy", Associated Press, February 12, 2002.
[436] *Radio Free Europe Report*, June 20, 2001. See also Catholic News Service, February 17, 2002.
[437] "Religion in Russia," at http://www.russianembassy.org/RUSSIA/religion.htm.

Catholic "proselytism" and requiring Catholic parishes to obtain approval from local bureaucrats for their very existence.

- The small percentage of Catholics who even go to Mass on Sunday (most of them in Siberia) is dependent almost entirely on a total of 165 Russian priests, nearly all of whom are foreign-born clerics not allowed into Russia without visitor's visas that require a departure from the country every three months to seek renewal, which can be denied at any time and for any reason, often for no reason at all.

- In 2002 Russian authorities began expelling non-Russian Catholic clergy from the country. As of November 2002 five priests, including the bishop for Siberia, Bishop Jerzy Mazur, had been expelled and their visas confiscated without explanation. Bishop Mazur learned that he had been added to a secret "list" of Catholic clergy who are considered "undesirables" and will no longer be allowed to enter Russian territory. After ignoring even the Pope's request for an explanation of the expulsions, Vladimir Putin sent a perfunctory letter stating nothing more than that the expulsions were in accordance with Russian law.[438]

- The Russian Orthodox hierarchy exploded in outrage when the Vatican announced in February 2002 that its "apostolic administrations" in Russia would be designated as dioceses. These would not even be dioceses in the traditional Catholic sense. There would, for example, be only an "Archdiocese of the Mother of God *at* Moscow"; and the Archbishop in charge of this structure will not be called the Archbishop of Moscow, lest the Vatican give offense to the then Russian Orthodox Partriarch of Moscow, the ex-KGB agent, Alexy II.

- On March 2, 2002, Pope John Paul II conducted a Saturday prayer service that was broadcast from the Vatican by satellite into Russia. The broadcast was totally blacked out by the same Russian television networks now under Vladimir Putin's thumb. Only by shipping special equipment into the country (that was held up at customs until the last possible moment) could a few thousand Catholics see the Pope on television screens set up at Assumption Cathedral in Moscow. The BBC reported that "Patriarch Alexy of the Russian Orthodox Church said it (the satellite broadcast) was an 'invasion of Russia' and referred to the Polish occupation of Moscow in the early 17th Century. John-Paul is of Polish origin."[439] Hence, after 40 years of *Ostpolitik* and "ecumenical dialogue", the Orthodox hierarchy will not even tolerate a video image of the Pope in even one single Catholic Church in Moscow.

- Trying to put a happy face on the debacle in Russia, Archbishop Tadeusz

---

[438] "Rebuff for the Pope: Vatican Fears New Persecution," *The Catholic World Report*, October 2002, p. 9.
[439] BBC Online, March 2, 2002.

Kondrusiewicz, the then head of the "Archdiocese of the Mother of God *at* Moscow", claimed that "It's all a misunderstanding," referring to Orthodox charges that the Catholic Church is "proselytizing" in Russia.

- An Associated Press story on Kondrusiewicz's reaction to Orthodox hostility noted that "Parishioners have come to Kondrusiewicz in tears recently, complaining that the indignant rhetoric by Orthodox leaders on national newscasts since February 11 has made them afraid to practice their faith."[440]

- Archbishop Kondrusiewicz has issued a formal protest on behalf of the Conference of Catholic Bishops of Russia, entitled "Religious Liberty in Russia is in Serious Danger." The protest declares:

  > Catholics in Russia ask themselves: What will happen next? Are the constitutional guarantees valid also for them, including liberty of conscience and of the right to have their own pastors, which comprises inviting them from abroad, not forgetting that for 81 years the Catholic Church was deprived of the right of forming and ordaining its own priests? Perhaps the State really considers Catholics second-class citizens? Are they (the State) returning to the times of persecution of the faith? ... The expulsion of a Catholic bishop who has not violated any law, surpasses all imaginable limits of civilized relations between the State and the Church. ... With grave worry, we express our decisive protest in respect to violation of the constitutional rights of Catholics.[441]

- By October 2002 Pope John Paul II's own spokesman, Joaquin Navarro-Valls, had declared that the actions against the Catholic Church by Russian authorities had reached the level of "a true persecution."[442]

The situation has not improved materially since 2002. In at least one way it has gotten worse. As the U.S. State Department reported in its 2008 International Report on Religious Freedom, in 2007 "the Russian government introduced new visa rules that allow foreigners (including religious workers) with business or humanitarian visas to spend only 90 of every 180 days in the country."[443]

In other words, the new visa rules create a preposterous situation for the Church in Russia: *nearly every Catholic priest in the country is obliged to leave Russia for what amounts to six months out of every year,* to remain in Russia for no more than 90 days at a time, and to reapply at least twice a year for readmission at the discretion of bureaucrats. As the State Department notes, the Catholic Church is "particularly hard

[440] AP News, March 1, 2002.
[441] *National Catholic Register* Online Web Edition, April 28 - May 5, 2002.
[442] *The Catholic World Report*, October 2002, p. 10.
[443] U.S. Department of State, International Religious Freedom Report (2008), at http://www.state.gov/g/drl/rls/irf/2008/108468.htm.

hit by this provision" because, given the almost total lack of Russian-born priests—a quarter-century after Russia's supposed "conversion"—the Church is forced to rely *almost exclusively on priests from outside the country…*" The new provision thus "limits their [priests serving in Russia] ability to work and significantly increases their expenses."

The aim of the 2007 law is clear: to prevent the Catholic Church from sinking any roots in Russian soil, while giving the false appearance of "religious freedom" to a marginalized and bureaucratically hounded tiny minority of priests and faithful struggling to survive.

To speak of a "conversion of Russia" to the Faith despite all these facts is, quite simply, ludicrous. No wonder Fatima "revisionists"—i.e., those who "revise" the Fatima Message to mean what they wish it to mean instead of what it really means—have tried to redefine the word "conversion" to make their false claims fit the evidence. Fatima "revisionism" is, in fact, the very essence of the Party Line on Fatima as examined thematically in the earlier chapters.

C. Russia has not even "converted" to Russian Orthodoxy

One of the revised meanings of "conversion" the Fatima revisionists have proposed is an alleged "conversion of Russia" to Russian Orthodoxy, already mentioned above. But even if this claim could be reconciled with the plain words of Our Lady of Fatima—and it cannot—it too founders on the evidence.

Here it suffices to note that more than 25 years after the supposed Consecration of Russia in 1984, nearly all of those who designate themselves Russian Orthodox do not practice their religion. *The Economist* notes that "Russia is suffering a crisis of faith" and that 94% of Russians aged 18-29 do not go to church.[444]

In fact, the aforementioned report by the Russian embassy in Washington reveals that *sixty percent of the Russian people do not identify themselves as having any religion at all*, not even the nominal Russian Orthodoxy that almost no one takes seriously.

Even the late Russian Orthodox patriarch, Alexy II (he died in December 2008), publicly admitted that Satanism, occultism and witchcraft are on the rise in Russia.[445]

No "Moral Conversion" in Russia

Twisting the meaning of "conversion" even further away from its true meaning, certain Fatima revisionists, hewing as always to the Party Line of the Vatican Secretary of State, argue that there has been some sort of "moral conversion" or "turning away from evil" in Russia since 1984. But not even this has taken place. Quite the contrary, since 1984 Russia has undergone a rapid moral decline, as if to make a mockery of

---

[444] Zenit News, December 22, 2000.
[445] "Satanism on the Rise in Russia", compiled by John Vennari. See www.fatima.org/news/newsviews/satanism2.asp.

this revisionist claim. Consider these facts:

- Today, Russia has *the highest abortion rate in the world* at 53.7 per 1,000 women between the ages of 15 and 44—a rate even higher than that in China (which has more total abortions).[446]

- Fr. Daniel Maurer, C.J.D., who spent eight years in Russia, says that statistically, the average Russian woman will have eight abortions during her childbearing years—though Fr. Maurer believes the actual number averaged out to be about 12 abortions per woman. He has spoken to women who have had as many as 25 abortions. A major reason for these dreadful figures is that other contraception methods (which are immoral anyway) have not been introduced in Russia, nor are they trusted. This leaves abortion as the "cheapest way to limit the family size."[447]

- *In Russia, abortions are free, but childbirth is not.*[448]

- The Russian birth rate is plummeting and Russia's population is dropping at the rate of 700,000 people each year—an unprecedented event in a civilized nation during "peacetime."[449]

- Russia has the highest per capita rate of alcohol consumption in the world.[450]

- Homosexuality is rampant in Moscow and throughout the country. In fact, in April 1993, nine years after the 1984 "consecration", Boris Yeltsin allowed homosexuality to be de-criminalized. Homosexuality is now "legal" in Russia.[451]

- Russia is a leading world center for the distribution of child

---

[446] CBC News, July 30, 2009, "13 million abortions a year reported in China," at http://www.cbc.ca/health/story/2009/07/30/abortions-china.html.

[447] Father Maurer's remarks appeared in an interview in *Catholic World Report*, February 2001. A synopsis and commentary on this interview was published in "The Myth of a Converted Russia Exposed", Marian Horvat, Ph.D., *Catholic Family News*, March 2001.

[448] Ibid.

[449] See Mark Fellows, "This Present Darkness", Part III, *Catholic Family News*, October 2000.

[450] Regarding alcohol in Russia, researchers concluded: "Russia's rate of alcohol consumption, traditionally among the highest in the world, and rising significantly in the 1990s, is a major contributor to the country's health crisis ... alcoholism has reached epidemic proportions, particularly among males ... A 1995 Russian study found that regular drunkenness affected between 25 and 60 percent of blue-collar workers ... In 1994 some 53,000 people died of alcohol poisoning, an increase of about 36,000 since 1991." In the ten years since the alleged consecration of Russia, there has also been a sharp increase in illegal drug use: "In 1995 an estimated 2 million Russians used narcotics, more than twenty times the total recorded ten years earlier in the entire Soviet Union, with the number of users increasing 50 percent every year in the mid-1990s." From Mark Fellows, "This Present Darkness", Part II, *Catholic Family News*, September 2000. See also Mark Fellows, *Fatima in Twilight*, (Marmion Publications, Niagara Falls, 2003) Chapter 19, p. 246.

[451] "Russia Legalizes Homosexuality", *United Press International*, May 28, 1993. To quote the beginning of the article: "Russia's homosexual activists Friday celebrated a major victory for gay rights in post-Soviet Russia following the repeal of Article 121 of the Soviet criminal code, which outlawed consensual sex between men. 'This is great news for gays and lesbians in Russia,' said Vladislav Ortanov, editor of the Moscow gay magazine *Risk*."

pornography. The Associated Press reported on a Moscow-based child pornography ring linked to another child pornography ring in Texas. To quote AP: "Russian law does not distinguish between child pornography and pornography involving adults, and treats the production and distribution of either as a minor crime, said Dmitry Chepchugov, head of the Russian Interior Ministry's department for high technology crimes. Russian police often complain about the legal chaos that has turned Russia into an international center of child pornography production. '*Unfortunately, Russia has turned into a world trash bin of child pornography*,' Chepchugov told reporters in Moscow."[452]

- Russians are addicted to grossly immoral "reality-based" TV. On the vilest of the "reality-based" shows, cameras film the intimate personal lives of Russian "couples," including their activity of breaking the 6th Commandment. Despite grumbles of disapproval from old hard-line Communists, Russian viewers "cannot get enough" of this pornography. The program "boasts an audience share of more than 50% and thousands of Russians have endured sub-zero temperatures and stood in line for more than an hour to catch a glimpse of it through a window of the apartment. Millions have logged on to the website, which has crashed frequently under the weight of the heavy traffic."[453]

A "moral conversion" of Russia? Hardly—unless one means a conversion to *immorality* leaving Russia even worse off morally than before the 1984 ceremony.

No "Political Conversion" in Russia

Another argument of the Fatima revisionists, noted already, is that "conversion of Russia" means only regime change since the "fall of communism." Of course, Our Lady did not come to Fatima to announce a Russian regime change in the 1990s. The claim is absurd. Nevertheless, here too the Fatima revisionists are confounded by the evidence.

By now the whole world knows that since he rose to power in 1999, Vladimir Putin has systematically made himself the virtual dictator of Russia: arresting and imprisoning his domestic critics on trumped up charges; shutting down all opposition media; outlawing the popular election of Russia's local governors and replacing them with Kremlin appointees.

Nor has the situation changed since 2008, with the "election" of Dmitry Anatolyevich Medvedev as "President" of Russia. Russian expert Jonathan Dimbleby's in-depth report, headlined "Russia: A totalitarian regime in thrall to a Tsar who's creating the new Fascist empire,"

---

[452] "Activist Says Child Porn Prosecutions Will be Difficult in Indonesia, Russia", Christine Brummitt, *Associated Press*, August 9, 2001 (emphasis added).

[453] "Big Brotherski goes too far for Staid Russians", Mark Franchetti, *Sunday Times* (London), November 25, 2001.

observes that Putin has arranged Russian affairs so that the country's so-called "President" Medvedev operates as nothing more than his executive assistant, and that "No decision of any significance for the Russian people or the rest of us will be made in the foreseeable future without the say-so of Medvedev's unsmiling master."[454]

A. Stifling all political opposition

In 2002, as the *London Times* reported, "Russia's last independent television station was closed yesterday, leaving the country's entire broadcast media under Kremlin control"[455]—the same broadcast media that have since been denouncing the Catholic Church over the question of Russian dioceses for the Church.

Over the past seven years the situation for the press and freedom of speech in general has continued to deteriorate under both Putin and his supposed successor, "President" Medvedev. In an editorial published on June 9, 2008, *The New York Times* protested that "Russia's national networks are routinely deleting news or opinions critical of the Kremlin. In one notable case, Mikhail Delyagin, a political analyst, criticized Vladimir Putin during the taping of a talk show. When the program aired, most of Delyagin was missing. Only his disembodied legs remained in the picture." The *Times* noted that under Stalin "Soviet news agencies grew to be experts in removing unwanted comrades from official photographs. People disappeared in the developing rooms just as they disappeared in real life," and that the same thing is happening all over again in Putin's Russia.[456]

Consider these additional facts:

- Diana Kachalova, editor-in-chief of a chain of newspapers in Russia, declared in 2008 that "United Russia is like a tank coming down on the people," and that "I feel like I'm returning to when I was young, in the 1970s"—that is, during the Soviet era.[457]

- In 2006 *The New York Times* reported "Russia is unquestionably a dangerous place for journalists," and that on average more than two a year are murdered under mysterious circumstances.[458]

- From 2000 to 2008 twenty-one journalists have been murdered in Russia, according to the World Association of Newspapers. In 2008 a student expressed the common fear that "It is dangerous to want a free press in Russia." When asked "Just to want it?", she replied: "It is

---

[454] Jonathan Dimbleby, Daily Mail Online, at http://www.dailymail.co.uk/news/article-566931/Russia-A-totalitarian-regime-thrall-Tsar-whos-creating-new-Facist-empire.html.

[455] *London Times,* online edition, January 12, 2002.

[456] Quoted in Christopher A. Ferrara, "Putin Brings Russia Back to the Good Old Days", at http://www.fatimaperspectives.com/cr/perspective567.asp

[457] "Free press under siege in Russia," *The Star*, January 12, 2008, at http://www.thestar.com/comment/article/293303.

[458] Steven Lee Myers, "In Russia, free press comes with a price," October 11, 2006 (reprinting article from *International Herald Tribune*), at http://www.nytimes.com/2006/10/11/world/europe/11iht-russia.3117121.html.

dangerous just to want it."[459]

- The situation for freedom of the press in Russia has reached the point where Russian journalists are speaking of a "last stand" against government oppression.[460] As if by a prearranged schedule, the same thing is happening in the Ukraine. "The torch of liberty has grown dimmer in the former Soviet republic of Ukraine—as *it has across most of the territory of the old USSR.*"[461]

B. Making Criticism of the Kremlin a Crime

The Kremlin's campaign against a free press and indeed any form of political opposition to the Putin regime reached a new height at the end of 2008. On December 17, 2008 Associated Press reported that "New legislation backed by Prime Minister Vladimir Putin would allow Russian authorities to label any government critic a traitor—a move that rights activists said Wednesday was a chilling throwback to times of Soviet dictator Josef Stalin."

Quoting Russian rights activists, AP notes that this new law "would essentially let authorities interpret *any* act against the state as treason—a crime punishable by up to 20 years in prison."[462]

C. Reviving the Soviet era and "rehabilitating" Stalin

In conjunction with his systematic takeover of the mass media, Putin has been coordinating a campaign to bring back the "glory days" of the "former Soviet Union." He has restored the Soviet (i.e. Communist) national anthem and ordered the production of a commemorative calendar glorifying the Soviet-era Lubyanka Prison (capstone of the Soviet gulag) and the Soviet-era butcher Felix Dzerzhinsky (who gloried in torturing humans before killing them).

It was none other than Dzerzhinsky who founded the KGB, authorized the torture and execution of Catholic priests, and presided over Lenin's liquidation of the Russian middle class. The calendar commemorating this criminal against humanity is for use in the offices of the KGB, which has been strategically renamed the FSB. This development is in keeping with the situation observed by British historian Orlando Figes, who has conducted extensive research on Stalin's crimes: "What we have now [in Russia] effectively is the KGB in power."[463]

Egged on by Putin's Kremlin, the Russian people are even "rediscovering" the "virtues" of Josef Stalin, the very incarnation of the evil of Communism and the errors of Russia. On December 27, 2008,

---

[459] Kelly Toughill, "Free press under siege in Russia," *The Star*, January 12, 2008, at http://www.thestar.com/comment/columnists/article/293303.

[460] Ibid.

[461] *WorldNetDaily*, December 21, 2001.

[462] "Russian Bill Could Hit Kremlin Critics," AP report at http://www.breitbart.com/print.php?id=D954K4Q80&show_article=1.

[463] Richard Galpin, "Stalin's new status in Russia," BBC Online, December 27, 2008, at http://news.bbc.co.uk/2/hi/europe/7798497.stm.

the Russian expert Richard Galpin of the BBC's Moscow bureau reported that during a nationwide TV poll on the question of who is "the greatest Russian of all time," none other than Stalin, the butcher of millions of Catholics, led the pack with more than 3.5 million votes. Stalin dropped from first place only after the show's producer "appealed to viewers to vote for someone else." The other poll leaders included Ivan the Terrible and Lenin.[464]

Sergei Malinkovich, leader of the St. Petersburg Communist Party, has stated that: "In all opinion polls he [Stalin] comes out on top as the most popular figure. Nobody else comes close. So for his service to this country we can forgive his mistakes."[465] Forgive his "mistakes"? What about the conservatively estimated 20-30 million people Stalin murdered, including some five million Catholic peasants in the Ukraine?

Nor is this just nostalgia on the part of older Russians for their "great leader." In a July 2007 poll, 54 percent of Russian youth agreed with the statement "Stalin did more good than bad" and half agreed with the statement that Stalin was "a wise leader."[466]

What does it tell us about the spiritual state of the Russian people that a substantial number of them, both young and old, would revere a satanic madman, perhaps the worst persecutor of Catholics in human history, who all but exterminated the Church in Russia?

This development reflects what Galpin describes as "a much broader campaign to rehabilitate Stalin" that "seems to be coming from the highest levels of government." Historian Alexander Danilov told Galpin that "I believe it was the idea of former President, now Prime Minister, Vladimir Putin. It fits completely with the political course we have had for the last eight years…"[467]

Galpin identifies the source of this "unity" as "Putinism"—a "strident form of nationalism" according to which "Russians are to be proud of their history, not ashamed, and so those investigating and cataloguing the atrocities of the past are no longer welcome."

By mysterious coincidence, a national cult of Vladimir Putin has "spontaneously" emerged since 1999, including T-shirts decorated with his face, immortalization in children's books, sculptures, obsequious media coverage and speeches "in praise of the great leader," all reflecting the reality that Putin loyalists… now dominate the bureaucracy, parliament and state broadcasting."[468]

These political developments were all summed up by Yelena Bonner, widow of the Soviet dissident physicist Andrei Sakharov, when they first began: "Under Putin, a new stage in *the introduction of modernized Stalinism* has begun. Authoritarianism is growing harsher, society is

---

[464] Ibid.
[465] Ibid.
[466] "Russian youth: Stalin good, migrants must go: poll," Reuters (July 25, 2007).
[467] Richard Galpin, "Stalin's new status in Russia," loc. cit.
[468] *Electronic Telegraph*, May 8, 2001.

being militarized, the military budget is increasing."[469]

Given all these facts, to hold that there has been a "miraculous political conversion" of Russia since the "consecration" of 1984, and that this is what Our Lady of Fatima promised, is not only preposterous, but an insult to the Mother of God.

No "Martial Conversion" in Russia

Some Fatima revisionists even go so far as to propose a "conversion of Russia" amounting to nothing more than a supposed "turning away from war," a kind of "martial conversion," as if to suggest that Putin's Russia is beating its swords into plowshares, and that this "miracle" has resulted from the 1984 "consecration" ceremony. Yet again, the facts demolish the fantasy. Let us consider only a few of them:

- In August 2008 the Russian Army invaded neighboring Georgia and conducted bombing raids deep inside Georgia after South Ossetia proclaimed itself a republic and Georgian forces moved to prevent secession. Despite a peace agreement negotiated under EU auspices requiring total withdrawal from Georgia, Russia still maintains "buffer zones" on Georgian territory around South Ossetia that would serve as beachheads for a full-scale invasion of the country.

- Military analyst Pavel Felgenhauer warns that Russia plans to invade Georgia from these bases,[470] and in May of 2009 U.S. Ambassadors to Georgia William Courtney and Kenneth Yalowitz, and Denis Corboy, warned of a Russia military buildup in South Ossetia and Abkhazia.

- As the journal *Human Events* has observed: "The timing of Russia's invasion of Georgia signals an ominous new dawn for East-West relations. If Moscow defeats the democratic forces in Georgia and the West remains stymied on the sidelines, the rest of the former Soviet satellites could again become the Kremlin's puppets, and Moscow could become more provocative with its words and its armed forces."[471]

- Russia has stepped up the pace of its nuclear weapons development. In June 2007 globalsecurity.org, in a report entitled "Weapons of Mass Destruction," reported on a major and quite threatening "upgrade" of Russia's ballistic missile arsenal: The RS-24, a "new-generation intercontinental ballistic missile... equipped with a multiple independently targetable reentry vehicle (MIRV) warhead..." The new missile is "expected to greatly strengthen" Russia's *strike capability*, as well as that of its allies until the mid-21st century."[472]

---

[469] *Electronic Telegraph*, March 2, 2000.

[470] "Plan of Georgian Occupation Worked Out in the Kremlin," *Georgian Daily*, February 23, 2009.

[471] Robert Maginnis, "Russian Invasion of Georgia Is an East-West Tipping Point," August 11, 2008, at http://www.humanevents.com/article.php?id=27975.

[472] "Weapons of Mass Destruction", at http://www.globalsecurity.org/wmd/world/russia/rs-24.htm.

- Further, Russia has developed single-warhead RT-2UTTH Topol-M missiles, which Vladimir Putin boasted during a televised press conference "are hypersonic and capable of changing their flight path," and which, according to one military analyst, "act like a 'swarm of bees.'"[473]

- On August 4, 2009 Russia resumed nuclear attack sub patrols off the United States coast for the first time in fifteen years, "a rare mission that has raised concerns inside the Pentagon and intelligence agencies about a more assertive stance by the Russian military."[474]

As the Russians rattle their nuclear sabers, they are also ramping up their military alliance with China, which was kicked off in a big way with a massive joint Russian-Chinese military exercise in August 2007. "This new potent military alliance," writes Paul Craig Roberts, "is a real world response to neoconservative delusions about US hegemony."[475] Delusions they are.

The idea that Putin's nationalistic Russia no longer poses any threat to peace and stability in the world because of a 1984 ceremony at the Vatican which deliberately avoided any mention of Russia is itself a delusion. There has been no "martial conversion" of Russia.

No "Economic Conversion" in Russia

Clearly desperate to explain away the non-conversion of Russia since 1984, some Fatima revisionists even go so far as to redefine "conversion" to mean the supposed economic "transformation" of Russia after the "fall of communism." Here as well, fact dispels fantasy. Although Russia's Gross Domestic Product (GDP) has grown on account of the exploitation of its oil reserves, Russia today remains economically a Third World country. The World Health Organization ranks Russia's health care system at 130th out of the 190 countries of the United Nations. There is not even gas and running water in the many rural villages associated with the now-abandoned agricultural "collectives."

As for the wealth generated by Russia's "booming" oil-based economy, investigative reporter Jonathan Dimbleby explains that "a criminal system of government [has] taken shape under Putin in which the Kremlin has been selling state assets cheaply to Putin's cronies and buying other assets back from them at an exorbitant price." For example, Roman Abramovich, "one of Putin's closest allies," paid $100 million for Sifnet (the Russian state oil company) only to sell it back to the government ten years later, for $13.7 billion, "an astronomical sum and far above the going market rate."[476] As Dimbleby concludes:

---

[473] *USA Today*, "On Deadline", January 31, 2006.

[474] Marr Mazzetti and Thom Shanker, *New York Times*, August 5, 2009.

[475] Paul Craig Roberts, "US Hegemony Spawns Russian-Chinese Military Alliance," August 9, 2007, at http://antiwar.com/roberts/?articleid=11422.

[476] Daily Mail Online, May 17, 2008.

"You can forget any talk from the new President [Medvedev] about 'stamping out' corruption. This social and economic disease is insidious and rampant."[477] In fact, Putin himself has benefitted mightily from the plunder, and now has a personal worth of some $41 *billion*.[478]

What is more, on August 5, 2009 Associated Press noted that the global financial crisis of 2008-2009 has "revers[ed] eight years of solid economic growth under Putin's presidency..."[479] And on August 10, 2009 an AFP report quoted Russia's figurehead "President" Medvedev as admitting that "As soon as the crisis took place, (the economy) crumbled. And worse than in many other countries." And now the Russian government is forecasting "a contraction of up to 8.5 percent in GDP in 2009 as lower oil prices hit the energy sector and industry battles a sharp decline in orders from abroad."[480]

Thus, even the supposedly "vibrant" Russian economy under Putin, whose primary beneficiaries are his cronies, is collapsing some 25 years after the alleged "consecration" of Russia. Not even real and lasting temporal blessings have resulted from the 1984 ceremony. Despite growth in GDP for the benefit of a relative few, "In modern Russia two-thirds of the population are on the verge of poverty. The health care system is worse today than it was in the Fifties. Stalin murdered about 20 million, while in today's Russia the population is falling by a million people a year."[481]

Conclusion:
No "Conversion" of Any Kind in Russia

Again, there is no argument against a fact, and the facts will admit no contrary conclusion: Russia has not converted in *any* sense of the word—not to the Catholic Faith (which is the only correct signification of the word "convert" in this context), not to Russian Orthodoxy, not morally, not politically, not even economically. Furthermore, as the rampant practice of abortion in Russia today demonstrates, Russian society has not even converted to an adherence to the most basic requirements of the natural law.

The same is true, of course, of societies throughout the world, nearly a century after Russia began to spread her errors. As Pope Pius XII declared on February 11, 1949: "We are overwhelmed with sadness and anguish, seeing that the wickedness of perverse men has reached a degree of impiety that is *unbelievable and absolutely unknown*

---

[477] Ibid.
[478] See "No-One Has Ever Disputed Vladimir Putin's Secret Wealth", *Soviet Analyst*, Volume 31, No. 2 & 3, p. 20.
[479] Lynn Berry, "The Russian Bare: Putin Strips to Waist for Photographers," reported at http://www.canadaeast.com/news/article/751712
[480] Stuart Williams, "Russian economy hitting 'dead end': Medvedev," AFP report, August 10, 2009, at http://www.google.com/hostednews/afp/article/ALeqM5ipvpeAiu7MDwBWhAD420YzMRnmTQ
[481] Bonner, *Electronic Telegraph*, March 2, 2000.

in other times."[482] Two years later the Pope declared that "almost the whole human race is today allowing itself to be driven into two opposing camps, for Christ or against Christ. *The human race is involved today in a supreme crisis*, which will issue in its salvation by Christ, or in its destruction.[483] And Pius said these things even before Russia's "legalization" of abortion had spread to every nation, along with the rest of Russia's errors—precisely as Our Lady of Fatima predicted.

Those who insist there has been a "conversion of Russia" since 1984 and that the "Fatimists" are just "prophets of doom" remind us of those who scoffed at Noah as he labored obediently year after year on the building of his saving Ark, while it seemed to the scoffers that their comfortable world would go on forever.

No Peace in the World

Consider that as this, the second edition of this book, goes to press (December 2009), it has been fully a quarter-century since the supposed "consecration of Russia" on March 25, 1984. Since the Vatican apparatus refuses to allow Russia to be mentioned in any consecration ceremony, not only has Russia failed to convert, but the period of world peace promised by Our Lady has not been seen either. The wars in Iraq and Afghanistan speak for themselves, as does the never-ending crisis in the Middle East, not to mention massive ethnic genocides in such places as Darfur (in the Sudan) and Rwanda.

But there is another war that has gone on unceasingly all over the world since 1984: the war on the unborn child. Throughout the world the abortion holocaust burns ever higher in the sight of God. There have been at least 600 million victims of the war on the unborn since the "consecration" of 1984, the blood of every victim crying out to Heaven for vengeance. Clearly, the time is ripe for a divine chastisement of all humanity.

Yet it seems that nothing will deter the Vatican apparatus from its pursuit of the new "post-Fatima" orientation of the Church. Instead of the consecration of Russia, the Vatican staged another ceremony, this time called an "entrustment," during which John Paul II, in the presence of some 1,500 bishops during the Jubilee of Bishops, declared as follows:

> We entrust to you all people, beginning with the weakest: the babies yet unborn, and those born into poverty and suffering, the young in search of meaning, the unemployed, and those suffering hunger and disease. We entrust to you all troubled families, the elderly with no one to help them, and all who are alone and without hope.[484]

Noble words indeed, and no doubt those mentioned received a

---

[482] Letter of February 11, 1949.

[483] *Evangelii Praecones*, Acta Apostolicae Sedis, AAS 1951, p. 497.

[484] Act of Entrustment to Mary Most Holy, October 8, 2000.

spiritual benefit from that papal "entrustment." But Our Lady of Fatima did not request an "entrustment" to Her of the unemployed, youth in search of meaning, the sick and the hungry, or even families and the elderly, as laudable as those intentions are. She came to ask for one thing in particular: the *Consecration* of *Russia* to Her Immaculate Heart. But this is the one thing the Vatican apparatus simply refuses to give Her.

The search for humanly devised substitutes for what Our Lady requested continued with the World Day of Prayer for Peace at Assisi on January 24, 2002. Catholics, Orthodox, Protestants, Hindus, Muslims, Jews, African animists, Buddhists, Shintoists, Confucians, Tenrikyoists and Zoroastrians were shuttled from the Vatican to Assisi in what *L'Osservatore Romano* called "a peace train." The "representatives of the world's religions", including a witch doctor, all gave sermons on world peace from a large wooden pulpit set up in the lower plaza of the Basilica of Saint Francis. As part of the event, each non-Christian "religion" was given a room in the Sacred Convent of Saint Francis to perform pagan rituals and offer prayers for peace to various gods and spirits. At the end of this scandalous and even sacrilegious event— the "new orientation" at its worst—the "representatives of the world's religions" placed little burning oil lamps on a table to symbolize their supposed commitment to interreligious brotherhood and world peace, and then went home.

Afterwards there was, of course, no peace. On the very next day the Israelis began bombing Palestinian targets, as the Arab-Israeli conflict continued to hurtle toward all-out war, while India tested a nuclear missile. Over the next few weeks, the Hindus and Muslims whose "representatives" had gone to Assisi to deposit their oil lamps on the table began slaughtering each other in western India; the death toll in just three days of riots was nearly 300.[485] And the world has been at war ever since, with the victims, both born and unborn, piling up by the tens of millions.

In his landmark encyclical *Ubi Arcano Dei* (1922), Pope Pius XI proclaimed what belongs to the essence of the Fatima Message—that the only peace worthy of the name is the peace of Christ, and that only the Catholic Church can bring the peace of Christ to this troubled world. As the Pope declared only 40 years before the "new orientation" began to afflict the Church:

> The Church is the safe and sure guide to conscience, for to Her safe-keeping *alone* there has been confided the doctrines and the promise of the assistance of Christ, She is able not only to bring about at the present hour *a peace that is truly the peace of Christ*, but can, better than any other agency which We know of, contribute greatly to the securing of the same peace for the future, to the making of war impossible in the future. For the Church teaches (*She*

---

[485] *New York Times*, March 2, 2002.

alone has been given by God the mandate and the right to teach with authority) that not only our acts as individuals but also as groups and as nations must conform to the eternal law of God.[486]

In their relentless pursuit of the "new orientation," however, the Vatican bureaucracy of the present time disdains such clear preaching as "unecumenical" and "triumphalistic," preferring to continue a fallible human program of seeking "peace" through human institutions controlled by unbelievers and even positive enemies of God and the Church. Hence in July 2002 Catholic news organs reported with dismay that Cardinal Sodano actively supported the newly-created International Criminal Court (ICC), even to the extent of making a financial contribution to its coffers.[487] Catholic commentators, joined by secular political commentators, have long warned that the ICC is a direct threat to the rights of sovereign nations and their peoples because it will assert jurisdiction to conduct politically motivated trials—from which there will be no appeal—of the citizens of any nation, based on an ever-expanding list of prosecutable "offenses".[488] These trials would be conducted without any of the procedural safeguards on admission of evidence and the right to confront witnesses which are essential to due process of law.[489] And yet the Vatican Secretary of State, mingling incompetent politics with his high ecclesiastical office, is actively collaborating in the creation of this judicial monster, preparing yet another disaster for the Church.

No peace in Russia, no peace in the world. Instead, what Pope Benedict rightly calls "the dictatorship of relativism" is rising in every nation, and we are confronted, more than ever before, by what John Paul II described at Fatima in 1982: "almost apocalyptic menaces looming over the nations and mankind as a whole." This is the consequence of ignoring the warnings in that heavenly intelligence report conveyed to the world at Fatima.

No Peace in the Church

And what of peace within the Church? Here too the Virgin of Fatima gave us a warning, and here too the men who tell us that the Third Secret of Fatima "belongs to the past" have disregarded it. As the first edition of this book made its appearance, the corruption and collapse of the Church's human element over the past forty years was already erupting into full view for the entire world to chronicle daily and mock to scorn. This was happening because churchmen themselves have

---

[486] *Ubi Arcano Dei*, n. 44.

[487] "Vatican Contributes to International Criminal Court," Zenit news report, July 3, 2002.

[488] "World Court Now A Reality" by Mary Jo Anderson, April 11, 2002, *WorldNetDaily;* and "Stopping the International Criminal Court," by Mary Jo Anderson, at www.catholic education.org/articles/social_justice/sj0003.html

[489] "The International Criminal Court vs. the American People," by Lee A. Casey and David B. Rivkin, Jr., a Heritage Foundation Report dated February 5, 1999, which can be found at www.heritage.org/Research/InternationalOrganizations/BG1249.cfm

spurned the Fatima prophecies, which gave us the means to know in advance and take measures to avoid the homosexual infiltration of the priesthood that is now raging out of control.

As this book was first being composed in 2002 the press was exposing the massive pedophile scandal in the Archdiocese of Boston, where Cardinal Law had been hiding the activities of priestly predators for decades. Evidently in a panic over potential liability, diocese after diocese in North America had suddenly begun submitting lists of priests suspected of sexual abuse to law enforcement authorities, after years of hiding this information from the victims and their families and shifting the perpetrators from one place to another. The diocese-by-diocese review of priestly sexual abuse of little boys was provided in cover stories by *Newsweek* and *National Review* and in a host of other stories in national and local newspapers.

One can only imagine what lies beneath the tip of this iceberg, even today. And it is widely known that among the few men who do enter "mainstream" seminaries adhering to the post-conciliar "reforms", a very large percentage is homosexual. Father Donald Cozzens, head of Saint Mary's Seminary in Cleveland, Ohio, was only admitting what everyone can see when he observed in his book *The Changing Face of the Catholic Priesthood* that: "At issue at the beginning of the 21st century is the growing perception that the priesthood is, or is becoming, a gay profession ... Heterosexual seminarians are made uncomfortable by the number of gays around them. ... The straight seminarian feels out of place and may interpret his inner destabilization as a sign that he does not have a vocation for the priesthood. ... The sexual contacts and romantic unions among gay seminarians create intense and complicated webs of intrigue and jealousy."[490]

The plague of sexual abuse and perversion among the priesthood is hardly limited to North America. England, France and Spain have their own scandals involving homosexual and pedophile priests, and even a leading Polish Archbishop had been turned over to the Vatican by the fellow priests he had sexually extorted and abused. As recently as July of 2009, Pope Benedict suspended and then accepted the resignation of Uruguayan Bishop Francisco Domingo Barbosa Da Silveira of Minas after he was blackmailed by two convicts with whom he had had homosexual liaisons captured on cell phone photographs.[491]

Nor are the scandals confined to homosexual conduct. In Africa, a vast scandal involving the sexual abuse of nuns by African priests had been reported in the world press and admitted by the Vatican. Vatican spokesman Father Bernardo Cervellera (director of Fides, the Vatican's missionary news service) offered the outrageous defense that

---

[490] Donald Cozzens, *The Changing Face of the Catholic Priesthood,* (Liturgical Press, Collegeville, Minnesota, 2002) p. 135.

[491] "Pope accepts resignation of Uruguayan bishop accused of sexual misconduct," Catholic News Agency, July 1, 2009.

"the problem was limited to sub-Saharan Africa and related to negative cultural views there of women and of the value of celibacy ... These are not cases of 'psychopathic' violence against women, but instead a 'cultural way of living' that is common throughout the region ..." The abuse of nuns by African priests is "a cultural way of living" in Africa! African priests simply don't appreciate the "value" of celibacy! According to Reuters, the Vatican is "monitoring the situation ... but no direct action has been taken."[492]

And yet, while there has been no "direct action" by the Vatican against priests who sexually abuse nuns, Father Nicholas Gruner was declared "suspended" in the Congregation for the Clergy's *only public announcement* concerning the "discipline" of any of the Church's 260,000 diocesan priests in 2001—"suspended" for an offense that has never been specified, for none exists. "Suspended," in fact, for no other reason than that he has not desisted from promoting the authentic Message of Fatima. Such are the Vatican's priorities under the "new orientation" of the Catholic Church and the Secretary of State's Party Line on Fatima.

But as bad as the previously mentioned sexual scandals are, they are dwarfed by the even greater scandal of massive apostasy among the Catholic clergy and laity.[493] Only a year after this book's first edition, and only two years before his death, John Paul II declared in his apostolic exhortation *Ecclesia in Europa* that "European culture gives the impression of 'silent apostasy' on the part of people who have all that they need and who live as if God does not exist." And we have already seen that John Paul's successor, Benedict XVI, has since lamented that "in vast areas of the world the faith is in danger of dying out like a flame which no longer has fuel," that after the Second Vatican Council "certain fundamental truths of the faith, such as sin, grace, theological life, and the last things, were not mentioned anymore," and that the Church now suffers from a "secularized ecclesial environment" and even a "desert without God."

A desert without God, indeed. It has long been known that the majority of Catholics, victims of decades of senseless liturgical and ecumenical "reforms", no longer possess a faith in the Holy Eucharist and no longer regard their Church as any different in essence from a Protestant denomination; nor do they feel obliged to follow the Church's teaching on marriage and procreation. The seminaries and convents of North America and Europe are practically empty or closed, except for those operated by small "traditionalist" orders (like the SSPX and the Priestly Fraternity of Saint Peter) which follow "the old ways". There are not nearly enough vocations to replace the older priests who are dying or retiring in the "mainstream" Church.

This would explain why Pope Benedict is attempting to change the

---

[492] CNN, March 21, 2001.
[493] John Paul II, *Ecclesia in Europa*, n° 7 & 9, *DC* n° 2296, July 20, 2003, pp. 671-672.

Church's course of the forty years preceding his pontificate: "liberating" the traditional Latin Mass and declaring that every priest in the Church is free to offer it; refusing any longer to distribute Communion in the hand at papal Masses; calling for a "hermeneutic of continuity" between Vatican II and the Church's constant teaching before the Council; lifting the "excommunication" of the bishops of the Society of Saint Pius X; and initiating theological discussions with the Society's representatives precisely on the question of Vatican II's conformity with Catholic Tradition. Tellingly, the Pope has not simply demanded that the Society's adherents "obey Vatican II," whatever that might mean, but rather has launched *discussions* about the Council and what it really teaches—a sure sign that the Council has been an enormous and unprecedented problem for the Church.

As we suggested in Chapter 15, it is entirely likely that Benedict, who as Cardinal Ratzinger read the Third Secret in its entirety, has taken these steps as Pope *because he knows that the Secret warns of apostasy in the Church*, perhaps in connection with a problematical Council and the confusion it engendered. Even if the powerful anti-Fatima party in the Vatican apparatus has expediently deemed the missing part of the Secret to be "inauthentic," following John XXIII's dictate that he would "leave it to others to comment or decide" on the supernatural origin of what is contained in the "Capovilla envelope" we have yet to see, is it not clear that Benedict, out of prudence, is trying to cure the plague of apostasy foretold in the words of the Virgin that accompany that wordless vision of "the Bishop dressed in white"?

And what are we to make of what Antonio Socci has observed in his own examination of the Third Secret—that Pope Benedict has indicated "precisely *martyrdom* as his own 'pastoral program.'" In *Fourth Secret* Socci notes that during the Mass for his "installation" as Pope—the Church of the "new orientation" refuses to call it a coronation, as all of Tradition has done—the new Pope declared that "we are not alone in life nor in death," and then alluded to the danger of death that confronts the Pope himself:

> My dear friends—at this moment I can only say: Pray for me, that I may learn to love the Lord more and more. Pray for me, that I may learn to love His flock more and more—in other words, you, the holy Church, each one of you and all of you together. Pray for me, that I may not flee for fear of the wolves....

So, the Pope himself admits that he is surrounded by wolves! And this after more than forty years of useless "dialogue with the world" that was supposed to have made the Church better understood and more attractive to "contemporary man." As Socci writes, the Pope has consistently presented the theme that "one can only 'flee' or face martyrdom" and that "From its beginning, in sum, Benedict seems to have given to his pontificate the horizon of martyrdom." Socci further notes that during the consistory of March 24, 2006, at which he created numerous Cardinals, the Pope reminded the new Cardinals that the red they wear "will signify for you a more intense participation in the mystery of the Cross and in the sharing of the sufferings of Christ. And we are all really witnesses of the sufferings of today, in the world *and also in the Church*."

And two days later, on March 26, at the Angelus the Pope declared: "*The sacrifice of life* is a distinctive characteristic of Cardinals, as attested by their oath and by the symbolism of the crimson, which has the color of blood." And on May 7, 2006, Socci points out, the Pope attacked "careerism" in the Church during a Mass for the ordination of fifteen deacons for the diocese of Rome, reminding the ordinands that "the only legitimate assent toward the ministry of the pastor is the Cross… the pastor *gives his life for the sheep*… To give life, not to take it. It is in just this way that we can experience liberty."

Socci links Benedict's declarations concerning martyrdom to the words of John Paul II at Fulda in November 1980, six months before the assassination attempt, in which the late Pope, speaking of the Third Secret, warned that "We must prepare ourselves to suffer great trials at a time not long from now, which will require from us a willingness to part with our lives…" From all of which Socci reaches a conclusion with which we concur—that the Third Secret predicts, among other things, the unique event of a papal martyrdom in the midst of an apocalyptic scenario:

> Benedict XVI has not explained the reason for his continuous and grave meditation on martyrdom, on the necessity of being ready to give one's life, but objectively—rereading these interventions from the first year of his pontificate—one cannot avoid remembering the text of the most sensational public prophecy in the two thousand years of Christianity, officially recognized by the Church: the so-called Third Secret of Fatima, which contains precisely the vision of a pope who "at the foot of a great Cross is killed by a group of soldiers… and at the same time there were dying with him, one after the other, bishops, priests, religious and various members of the laity, men and women of different classes and stations."

> It is evident that the apocalyptic event prophesied here with such solemnity by the Madonna of Fatima has a gravity absolutely unique in the history of the world and of the Church, where there are not lacking persecutions, immense massacres, and even attempts on the life of the Pope.[494]

And yet, as Socci also concludes in the passages we have already cited, the Church and the world have been deprived of the very words of the Virgin which explain how the Pope depicted comes to be executed on a hill at the foot of a cross, outside a half-ruined city filled with

---

[494] *The Fourth Secret of Fatima*, English ed., p. 38; popular ed., p. 32; Italian ed., p. 46.

corpses. But the Pope has seen those words, even if it appears that he considers himself bound by the determination of his predecessors and their advisors that the words are to be kept hidden from the faithful. This would explain why the Pope would send Socci a note of thanks for having written a book that accuses the Vatican apparatus of having conspired to keep from the Church and the world the dire warnings of the Virgin Mother of God.

While doubtless motivated by his knowledge of the Secret and its warning of "dangers threatening the faith and the life of the Christian, and therefore (the life) of the world" (to recall Cardinal Ratzinger's revelation of 1984), Pope Benedict's gestures toward a restoration of the Church and his allusions to martyrdom have not sufficed to end the crisis the Church and the world now face. On the contrary, the situation grows worse by the day. Although the Church's new orientation is a disastrous failure in every respect, producing nothing but the bitterest of fruits, the members of the Vatican apparatus who hound Father Gruner persevere in it unswervingly. So far as they are concerned, there will be no return to the "model" of the Church represented by the Message of Fatima. There will be no "embarrassing" public Consecration of Russia. There will be no "outdated" conversion of Russia to the Catholic Faith. There will be no triumph of the Immaculate Heart, for this would be a setback to "ecumenical dialogue" with the Protestants and the Orthodox. For this all would be a setback to the Masonic plans for turning the Catholic Church into a tool for the Masons to manipulate the Church into changing its purpose from saving souls to promoting the New World Order (NWO) one world religion—with democracy being what justifies whatever the NWO masters want. And so Russia has not converted, and there is no peace in the world, and the Catholic Church remains in a state of near-chaos—just as predicted in the Third Secret.

Everywhere—in the Church, in Russia, in the world—the practitioners of the Vatican Secretary of State's Party Line on Fatima see the evidence of its failure. Yet Cardinal Sodano's successor, Cardinal Bertone, his collaborators and their Fatima revisionist dupes throughout the Church, continue to insist that Russia was consecrated to the Immaculate Heart 25 years ago, that recent events in Russia are "a miracle", that the Third Secret and the Message of Fatima as a whole "belong to the past" and need no longer concern us. It seems not even the Pope can rid the Vatican of the bureaucracy that continues to entrap the Church in diplomacy, "dialogue," and cooperation with worldly powers and their increasingly diabolical New World Order.

Meanwhile, unjustly derided Catholics like Father Nicholas Gruner, who continue to point out the obvious, are still subjected to the equivalent of a Stalinist purge for their lack of fidelity to the Party Line. They are denounced as "disobedient" and even "schismatic", and their "loyalty to the Pope" is questioned, even though neither John Paul II nor Benedict XVI has ever personally endorsed or imposed the Party Line on Fatima but rather both pontiffs have given compelling indications of its utter falsity, as we have already shown: John Paul II by making it clear that Our Lady is "still awaiting" the Consecration of Russia, and Benedict XVI by declaring on May 13, 2009, the anniversary of the first apparition at Fatima, that "You promised the three children of Fatima that 'in the end, My Immaculate Heart will triumph.' May it be so!" That it is not yet so must be admitted by any objective observer of the state of the Church and the world.

The Present and Future Cost

How does one count the cost of this foolhardy determination to do away with the prophecies of the Mother of God at Fatima? The cost in temporal suffering and harm to souls is already beyond all human calculation: the misery of the Russian people and the continuing State persecution of Russian Catholics; the abortion holocaust; a rising tide of violence throughout the world; a worldwide economic collapse; and, above all, the loss of innumerable souls through the undermining of the Catholic Faith and the corruption of the Catholic clergy now on display before the whole world. And yet all of this was predicted in that part of the Third Secret we have not been allowed to see; and *all of it could have been avoided if the men who rule the Church today had followed, rather than despised, the Virgin of Fatima's simple requests.*

But what will be the cost in the coming days, if the course established by the Vatican prelates we have mentioned is not corrected soon? Our Lady of Fatima has already answered that question: wars and persecution of the Church, the martyrdom of Catholics, the suffering of the Holy Father, the annihilation of nations, the loss of millions more souls, until we reach that scene in the vision of the "Bishop dressed in white," wherein a Pope (Benedict or a successor?) is executed outside a half-ruined city in a world that has clearly undergone a divine chastisement.

Those who have engineered the Church's new orientation and imposed the Party Line on Fatima insist that we ignore the divine warnings of the Third Secret, even though they were delivered by the Mother of God Herself and authenticated by a public miracle without precedent in human history. They insist that we obey them who have no jurisdiction or authority to command such obedience. They insist we obey them even though Sacred Scripture commands us: "Do not extinguish the spirit. Do not despise prophecies." (1 Thess. 5:19-20)

No, we cannot ignore the warnings. *The time has come to declare that it is not the Message of Fatima, but the all-too-fallible human advice of these men that we must ignore.* By their fruits ye shall know them, and the fruits of their policies and judgments are there for all to see: the Church is in the depths of Her worst crisis in 2,000 years, and the world is headed toward an apocalypse.

We have made our case as best we can; we have discharged our duty of conscience before the Church and the bar of history. Now, we submit, a duty descends upon you, the reader. God commands that you must seek the truth and serve it. You must consider the evidence we have presented. We ask you to render your verdict—a verdict that good cause exists to ask that the highest authority in the Church judge and correct the actions of these men, repairing the damage they have done and thus doing justice to the community of the faithful in the Church and to humanity at large.

But while we wait for justice to be rendered, we must do whatever is in our power to protect ourselves, our loved ones, our fellow Catholics, and the world from further harm.

This means, first of all, that we must reject the false counsel of those in authority who have tried to replace the words of the Blessed Virgin Mary with their own words, and Heaven's plan for peace with their own plan. We have seen the disastrous results of their fallible human wisdom, which they continue to try to impose upon the Church against the evidence of our senses, the dictates of our reason and the counsel of the Mother of God Herself, speaking in the name of Her divine Son. With all due respect to their offices in the Church, we must say of these men that, insofar as the Message of Fatima and its implications for the Church and the world are concerned, they have forfeited their own credibility. We should no longer follow them.

As we have seen in Cardinal Newman's apt description of the Arian crisis, the present crisis in the Church would not be the first time in Her history that the laity were left to carry on the Faith without the help of much of the upper hierarchy or even most bishops, relying instead on their own *sensus catholicus* and a few good priests and prelates who did not succumb to the reigning confusion. During the Arian crisis nearly the entire hierarchy lost sight of something as fundamental as the divinity of Christ, and the laity—for the safety of their own souls—had to cease following those in authority for at least 40 years. It is manifest that a comparable situation has arisen today. Can anyone looking objectively at the present condition of the Church seriously deny that She is undergoing a crisis of faith and discipline at least no less severe than that in the time of Arius?

In *The Reform of the Roman Liturgy*, the renowned liturgist Msgr. Klaus Gamber, lamenting the ecclesial destruction caused by the liturgical "reforms" of Pope Paul VI, observed as follows in a book *praised by Cardinal Ratzinger*, who is now our Pope:

> Great is the confusion! Who can still see clearly in this darkness? Where in our Church are the leaders who can show us the right path? Where are the bishops courageous enough to cut out the cancerous growth of the modernist theology that has implanted itself and is festering within the celebration of the most sacred mysteries, before the cancer spreads and causes even greater damage? What we need today is a new Athanasius, a new Basil, bishops like those who in the Fourth Century courageously fought

against the Arian heresy when almost the whole of Christendom had succumbed to the heresy.[495]

The Pope cannot act alone in dispelling this confusion and darkness. He needs a new Athanasius, or rather many such courageous prelates, if the Church is to be restored and the Fatima prophecies fulfilled by the collegial consecration of Russia. Until such leadership emerges in the Church, until the current crisis has ended and things are set right again, we must educate ourselves and others about the Faith, defending it as best we can. In our time, this task requires that we also defend the Message of Fatima; for as Saint Thomas teaches, in every age God sends prophets, not to give a new doctrine, but to remind the faithful of what they must do to save their souls. The great prophet of our age is Our Lady of Fatima. As Sister Lucy herself said in the famous interview with Father Fuentes in 1957:

> Father, the Most Holy Virgin is very sad because no one has paid any attention to Her Message, neither the good nor the bad. The good continue on their way, but without giving any importance to Her Message. ...

> Tell them Father, that many times, the Most Holy Virgin told my cousins Francisco and Jacinta, as well as myself, that *many nations will disappear from the face of the earth*. She said that Russia will be the instrument of chastisement chosen by Heaven to punish the whole world if we do not beforehand obtain the conversion of that poor nation.

Any believing Catholic should be able to see that the annihilation of nations surely *is* coming unless the men who govern the Church change course, abandon their destructive novelties, and simply do what the Mother of God told them to do at Fatima. Until then, we can no longer risk relying on the advice of those who are determined to ignore the true signs of the times, the signs of a gathering apocalypse foretold by the Virgin. Imploring the grace of God, we will have to advance the cause of true peace in the world and restoration in the Church without the help of our own superiors, so many of whom have been blinded in their pursuit of a new and alien vision.

In this undertaking we must gather together under the mantle of Our Lady of Fatima, praying incessantly for Her intercession in this time of confusion and darkness, never forgetting Her unbreakable promises to the Church and the world. Our Lady of Fatima, Pray for Us!

---

[495] Msgr. Klaus Gamber, *The Reform of the Roman Liturgy*, (Foundation For Christian Reform, Harrison, New York, 1993) p. 113.

The three seers of Fatima—Blessed Jacinta Marto, Blessed Francisco Marto and Lucia dos Santos—photographed in front of the Marto house several days before October 13, 1917, the date on which the Miracle of the Sun occurred.

A photograph of part of the 70,000 witnesses as they are actually observing the Miracle of the Sun at Fatima on October 13, 1917.

The first chapel of Our Lady of Fatima built on the exact spot where Our Lady appeared. It was dynamited by anti-Catholic forces in Portugal on March 6, 1922. The photograph above shows the hole in the roof from the explosion. Providentially, the original statue of Our Lady of Fatima, which was normally housed in this chapel and is pictured on page IV of this photo section, was not in the chapel at the time.

The window of the jail where the Mayor of Ourem imprisoned the three children.

Arturo de Oliveira Santos, the Mayor of Ourem, who personally kidnapped the Fatima seers and had them imprisoned in August 1917, threatening the children with execution if they did not reveal the Secret the Virgin Mary told them. They refused to give in to the threat and were finally released.

Millions of pilgrims continue to come to Fatima each year. Pictured above is an aerial view of the piazza in front of the Fatima Basilica. More than one million people were present there when Pope Paul VI (seen inside the white circle) visited Fatima on May 13, 1967, the 50th anniversary of the first apparition of Our Lady of Fatima. Similarly, large crowds of pilgrims came to Fatima when Pope John Paul II visited there on May 13 of 1982, 1991 and 2000.

The statue of Our Lady of Fatima, which was carved according to the descriptions of the three child seers, is carried in procession on May 13th to the delight and joy of hundreds of thousands of devoted pilgrims who fill the plaza. Seen below is another picture of the procession and, in the background, the Fatima Basilica.

Bishop da Silva was entrusted with the Third Secret of Fatima which contained the words of Our Lady. Her words followed the "etc" in the phrase "In Portugal the dogma of the faith will always be preserved etc." Sister Lucy put in the "etc" to hold the place for the rest of Our Lady's words. The words of Our Lady were written down by Sister Lucy under obedience to Bishop da Silva, placed in an envelope and delivered to the bishop on June 17, 1944. Bishop da Silva took Sister Lucy's envelope containing Our Lady's words in the Third Secret and placed that envelope into a larger envelope, on which he wrote:

Este envelope com o seu conteudo sera entregue a Sua Eminencia O Sr. Cardeal D. Manuel, Patriarca de Lisboa, depois da minha morte.
Leiria, 8 Dezembro de 1945
† Jose, Bispo de Leiria.

This envelope with its contents shall be entrusted to His Eminence, his Lordship Cardinal Don Manuel [Cerejeira], Patriarch of Lisbon, after my death.
Leiria, December 8, 1945
† Jose, Bishop of Leiria.

This photograph appeared in the January 3, 1949 edition of *Life* magazine.

Pope Pius XII revealed that in the Message of Fatima Our Lady warned the Church against "the suicide of altering the Faith, in Her liturgy, Her theology and Her soul." This is further explained on pages 36-37, 92-100, 104, 195 and 219-220.

In his widely-acclaimed, insightful book *Athanasius and the Church of Our Time* published in 1974, Bishop Rudolph Graber, of Regensburg, Germany, a Professor of Theology since 1941 and consecrated a bishop in 1962, recounts the avowed aims of the Church's enemies to destroy the Church through the means of an ecumenical Council. He quotes the excommunicated, revolutionary priest Canon Roca who foretold of a Council that would usher in a "new religion, new dogma, new ritual, new priesthood". Bishop Graber also quotes the Masonic Rosicrucian Dr. Rudolph Steiner who declared in 1910, "We need a council and a Pope to proclaim it." Bishop Graber, commenting on these predictions, remarks "A few years ago this was still inconceivable to us, but today...?"

Father Joaquin Alonso (above), who held doctorates in theology and philosophy from the Gregorian University in Rome and who was professor of theology in Rome, Madrid and Lisbon, was the official archivist at Fatima for 16 years, having been appointed by the Bishop of Fatima to prepare the critical and definitive study of Fatima. He is probably the foremost expert on Fatima of our time. Yet Father Edouard Dhanis, one of the authors of the infamous, notorious and scandalous *Dutch Catechism*, and who made a veritable career out of trying to debunk the Fatima message, was the only Fatima "expert" mentioned by the former Cardinal Ratzinger in the June 26, 2000 document, *The Message of Fatima*.

Father Alonso († 1981) had many interviews with Sister Lucy, the lone surviving seer of Fatima. (She died on February 13, 2005.) He tells us that according to Sister Lucy, "The conversion of Russia is not to be limited to the return of the Russian Peoples to the Orthodox Christian religion, rejecting the Marxist atheism of the Soviets, but rather, it refers purely, plainly and simply to the total, integral conversion of Russia to the one true Church of Christ, the Catholic Church."

Cardinal Alfredo Ottaviani was the head of the Vatican's Holy Office during the reigns of Popes Pius XII, John XXIII and Paul VI. He read the Third Secret, and confirmed that it was written on one sheet of paper.

He also interviewed Sister Lucy on behalf of Pope Pius XII. He confirmed that the Third Secret of Fatima is a true prophecy. He also confirmed that the *Neues Europa* report contained some of the substance of the Third Secret (see pages 216-217 and footnote 341). In that report we read, "Cardinal will oppose Cardinal and bishop will oppose bishop", obviously referring to a doctrinal crisis of Faith, causing a clash between those prelates who remain steadfast in the Faith and those prelates who do not.

It was Cardinal Ottaviani who, prior to Vatican II, rightly suppressed modernist theologians such as Father Karl Rahner. Yet Father Rahner, shown below at the Council with a young Father Joseph Ratzinger, was among the progressivist theologians who gave the decisive orientation to Vatican II. Rahner never changed his progressivist views.

Liberal theologians such as Karl Rahner (see previous page), Yves Congar (left) and Henri de Lubac (right) saw their writings suppressed during the reign of Pope Pius XII. In the 1960s, however, these same modernist "theologians'" opinions were given widespread influence at Vatican Council II.

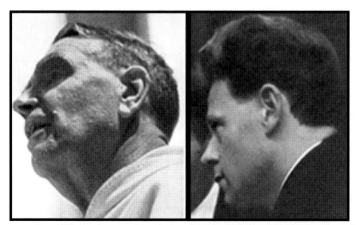

Two other liberal, modernist "theologians": Fathers Dominique Chenu (left) and Hans Küng (right) at the time of Vatican II.

X

Sister Maria Lucia of the Immaculate Heart (Sister Lucy), photographed at Fatima during the pilgrimage of Pope Paul VI on May 13, 1967. She entered the Carmel of Coimbra on Holy Thursday, 1948, and remained there until her death on February 13, 2005. It is around the time of this photo that Sister Lucy, in her private letters, speaks about the "diabolical disorientation" of certain persons in the Church who have great responsibility. She also speaks about the same persons as "blind and leaders of the blind" and those "doing evil under the guise of good." For more details about Sister Lucy's remarks about misguided members of the hierarchy, see pages 36 and 105.

Silvio Cardinal Oddi   Mario Luigi Cardinal Ciappi

Cardinal Oddi tells us that the Third Secret of Fatima "was alerting us against the apostasy in the Church." Cardinal Ciappi tells us that in the Third Secret "it is foretold, among other things, that the great apostasy in the Church will begin at the top." In other words, the apostasy will be spread from the Vatican to various parts of the Church (see page 198).

Pope John Paul II tells us that the Fatima Message is a warning against the Catholic Faith being undermined from within the Church and for us to be on our guard against the apostate "stars of Heaven" (Apoc. 12:4) in our time (see pages 198-200). John Paul II is also warning us against the apostasy in the Church today.

Pope John Paul II

Bishop Joao Venancio, the second Bishop of Leiria-Fatima, testifies as an eyewitness that the text of the Third Secret is on one sheet of paper with margins of 3/4 of a centimeter on both sides of the page with approximately 25 lines of text (see page 29). It is obviously not what was released by Cardinal Ratzinger and Archbishop Bertone on June 26, 2000, since their text was 62 lines with no margins.

Bishop Joao Venancio

XII

What follows are translations (and true copies—see pages XIII and XIV of this photo section) of the contemporaneous documentation of Archbishop Loris F. Capovilla, personal secretary to Pope John XXIII, confirming the existence of the "Capovilla envelope" pertaining to the Third Secret of Fatima, which was kept in the papal apartment. Cardinal Bertone has never produced this envelope, even though Capovilla's evidence has finally forced him to admit its existence.

FATIMA

A Reserved Note of L.F. Capovilla

17 May 1967

LORIS FRANCESCO CAPOVILLA
ARCIVESCOVO DI MESEMBRIA

Thursday the 27th of June 1963, I was on duty in the Anticamera in the Vatican [the outer office where the Pope meets various persons]. Paul VI in the early morning received among others, Cardinal Fernando Cento (who had been Papal Nuncio to Portugal) and shortly afterwards the Bishop of Leiria Monsignor Joao [John] Pereira Venancio. Upon leaving, the Bishop asked for "a special blessing for Sister Lucia".

It is evident that during the audience, they spoke about Fatima. In fact in the afternoon the Sostituto [the Substitute Secretary of State] Monsignor Angelo Dell'Acqua telephoned me on Via Casilina (I was a temporary guest of the Sisters of the "Poverelle"):

"I am looking for the package [plico] of Fatima. Do you know where it is kept?"

"It was in the drawer on the right hand side of the desk, named 'Barbarigo'[1], in the [papal] bedroom."

One hour later Dell'Acqua called me back: "Everything is okay. The envelope [plico] has been found."

Friday morning (28 June) between one meeting and another Paul VI asked me: "How come on the envelope there is your (Capovilla's) name?"
"John XXIII asked me to write a note regarding how the envelope arrived in his hands with the names of all those to whom he felt he should make it known."
"Did he make any comment?"
"No, nothing except what I wrote on the outer file [involucro]: 'I leave it to others to comment or decide.'"[2]
"Did he later ever return to the subject?"
"No, never. However the devotion of Fatima remained alive in him."

1. It is called thus because it belonged to St. Gregory Barbarigo. The Pope received it as a gift from Co. Gius. Dalla Torre (1960).

2. See the attached diary entry of John XXIII, 10 November 1959. **[See page XIII in this photo section.]**

From John XXIII's 1959 diary,
Entry for 10 November,
Feast of St. Andrew Avellino

Dalla Agenda 1959
di Giovanni XXIII , 10 novembre ,
S.Andrea Avellino

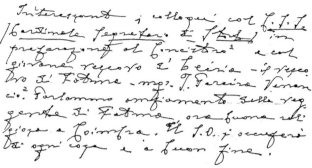

[handwritten entry of John XXIII]

1. Concistoro 14-17 dicembre con creazione di otto cardinali.

2. João Pereira Venâncio , nato 1904; vescovo tit. di Eurea di Spireo 1954 ; vescovo di Leiria 1958

Interessanti i colloqui col C.S.S (Cardinale Segretario di Stato) in preparazione al Concistoro, e col giovane vescovo di Leiria - il vescovo di Fatima - mgr J. Pereira Venancio. Parlammo ampiamente della veggente di Fatima,ora buona religiosa a Coimbra. Il S(anto) O(fficio) si occuperà di ogni cosa e a buon fine .

$\mathcal{L}.F.C.$

[Photographic reproduction of Archbishop Capovilla's typed transcription of Pope John XXIII's handwritten entry noted above. The text below is a translation of Capovilla's typewritten copy of John XXIII's handwritten original document shown above.]

Interesting conversations with C.S.S. (Cardinal Secretary of State) in preparation for the consistory[1] and with young Bishop of Leiria – the Bishop of Fatima – Monsignor J. Pereira Venancio.[2] We have spoken at length of the seer of Fatima, who is now a good religious at Coimbra. The Holy Office will take care of everything to a good end.

1. Consistory 14-17 December with the creation of eight Cardinals.

2. Joao Pereira Venancio, born 1904, titular Bishop of Eurea di Epireo 1954 | Bishop of Leiria 1958.

**Portion of Certified Confidential Note
of Archbishop Capovilla, 17 May 1969**

Also in this photo section, see the rest of this certified note in Italian on page XIV; see translation of that portion on page XII.

F A T I M A

Note riservate di L.F.Capovilla

17.v.1967

LORIS FRANCESCO CAPOVILLA
ARCIVESCOVO DI MESEMBRIA

Giovedì 27 giugno 1963 sono in servizio d'Anticamera in Vaticano. Paolo VI in mattinata riceve,tra gli altri,il card. Fernando Cento (che fu nunzio in Portogallo) e subito dopo il Vescovo
di Leiria mons. João Pereira Venancio. Nel congedarsi ,il Vescovo chiede "una speciale benedizione per Suor Lucia".

E' evidente che durante l'udienza hanno parlato di Fatima . Di-
fatti nel pomeriggio il Sostituto mons. Angelo Dell'Acqua mi tele-
fona in Via Casilina (sono ospite provvisorio delle Suore delle Poverelle) ;

" Cercano il plico di Fatima. Lei sa dov'è custodito ?

" Sta nel cassetto di destra della scrivania detta "Barbarigo",1

in stanza da letto .

Un'ora dopo, Dell' Acqua mi ritelefona : " Tutto a posto. Il
plico è stato rinvenuto ".

Venerdì mattina (28.VI) tra un'udienza e l'altra,Paolo VI mi
chiede :

" Come mai sul plico c'è il suo (di Capovilla) nome ?

" Giovanni XXIII mi chiese di stilare una nota circa le modalità
di arrivo del plico nelle sue mani con i nomi di tutti coloro ai
quali ritenne doveroso farlo conoscere .

" Fece qualche commento ?

" No niente,tranne quanto scrissi sull'involucro :,,Lascio ad altri
commentare o decidere".2

" In seguito tornò mai sull'argomento?

" No,mai. Tuttavia la devozione di Fatima rimase viva in lui "

1. Così detto, perché appartenuto a S.Gregorio Barbarigo. Il Papa l'ebbe in dono dal Co.Gius. Dalla Torre (1960

2. Vedere allegata nota di agenda Giovanni XXIII,10 novembre 1959 .

For the translation of this very important testimony of Archbishop Loris F. Capovilla, the still-living (as of December 2009) personal secretary to Pope John XXIII, see page XII of this photo section.

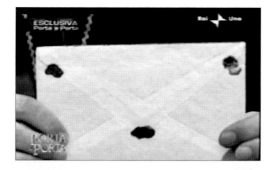

Figure 1

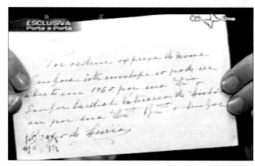

Figure 2

Figure 3

The two Third Secret envelopes.

Top and middle: **The front and back (showing wax seals) of the Third Secret envelope #1, bearing Sister Lucy's handwritten notation of the "express order of Our Lady" that this envelope can only be opened in 1960.**

Bottom: **Third Secret envelope #2, also bearing Sister Lucy's handwritten warning "by express order of Our Lady" that also this envelope can only be opened in 1960.**

Cardinal Bertone failed to mention the existence of these two envelopes, and the "express order of Our Lady" written on each, at any time from June 26, 2000 until he showed them on camera during the telecast of May 31, 2007. Bertone had always represented before May 31, 2007 that there was only one envelope and that Lucy had never received an order from the Blessed Virgin regarding 1960.

Note the differing lineation of the Portuguese words "Nossa Senhora" (Our Lady) in the first two lines of each envelope (see Figures 2 and 3).

L'OSSERVATORE ROMANO

Lunedì-Martedì 26-27 Marzo 1984

«Maria, aiutaci ad inaugurare un mondo nuovo perché il vecchio è ingiusto, ci opprime, ci fa paura»

«Oggi si sono volute affidare le sorti del mondo, degli uomini, dei popoli al Tuo Cuore Immacolato per arrivare al centro stesso del mistero ... in cui si può vincere il peccato». Con queste parole, il Papa ha ricordato il solenne atto di affidamento a Maria compiuto da tutti i Vescovi del mondo. Lo ha fatto nella Basilica Vaticana, dove è sceso ieri pomeriggio per rendere nuovamente omaggio alla statua della Madonna di Fatima, prima che fosse portata nella Basilica di San Giovanni in Laterano. Con il Santo Padre erano riuniti in preghiera dinanzi alla piccola effigie i Cardinali Pironio, Poletti e Baldie, numerosi Arcivescovi e Vescovi e una folta folla di fedeli. Salito all'altare della Confessione dove era stata collocata la statua Giovanni Paolo II ha pronunciato le seguenti parole:

Fratelli e sorelle,

prima che abbia termine questa sosta mariana nella Basilica di San Pietro, lasciatemi dire una parola di ringraziamento. Voglio ringraziare Te, Madre di Cristo, Nostra Signora di Fatima, che ci hai fatto questo onore, oggi, terza Domenica di Quaresima, giorno del Giubileo delle famiglie; che ci hai fatto questa visita in un giorno così pieno della nostra fede e della nostra speranza. Come Vescovo di Roma, voglio ringraziare Te, Madre di Cristo, Nostra Signora di Fatima per questa Tua visita nella Basilica di San Pietro, in un giorno in cui questa Basilica e questa piazza, riempita dai pellegrini dell'Anno Santo della Redenzione, hanno potuto assistere ad un solenne, atto di affidamento, atto rivolto al Tuo Cuore Immacolato e, nel Tuo Cuore Immacolato, rivolto al Tuo Figlio, Redentore del mondo, Redentore dell'uomo. Ci fidiamo di questo Tuo Cuore Immacolato, Cuore materno, perché in questo Tuo Cuore hai portato Lui come madre. Ci fidiamo di questo Tuo Cuore materno, perché con questo Cuore Tu abbracci tutti i Suoi discepoli, anzi tutti gli uomini.

Ecco, oggi si sono volute affidare le sorti del mondo, degli uomini, del popoli al Tuo Cuore Immacolato per arrivare al centro stesso del mistero della Redenzione, del mistero che è più forte di tutti i peccati dell'uomo e del mondo, del mistero in cui si può vincere il peccato nelle sue diverse forme, in cui si può incominciare, inaugurare un mondo nuovo perché sperimentiamo sempre più che il mondo vecchio, il mondo del peccato, ci opprime, ci fa paura, ci porta varie forme di ingiustizia; molte volte sotto il nome della giustizia, si porta ingiustizia.

Così, abbiamo voluto scogliere questa domenica, terza della Quaresima dell'anno 1984, ancora nell'arco dell'Anno Santo della Redenzione, per l'atto dell'affidamento, della consacrazione del mondo, della grande famiglia umana, di tutti i popoli, specialmente di quelli che hanno tanto bisogno di questa consacrazione, di questo affidamento, di quei popoli per i quali Tu stessa aspetti il nostro atto di consacrazione e di affidamento. Tutto questo abbiamo potuto fare secondo le nostre povere, umane possibilità, nella dimensione della nostra umana debolezza. Ma con una fiducia enorme nel Tuo materno amore, con una fiducia enorme nella Tua materna sollecitudine.

Nostra Signora di Fatima, a cui siamo tanto devoti e tanto riconoscenti, anche nel senso più intimo e personale. Tu hai voluto farci visita in questo giorno così importante qui a Roma. Come ne siamo grati! Come ne siamo riconoscenti. Quale grazia ci hai fatto con questa Tua presenza, direi personale. E la nostra riconoscenza si rivolge al custode del Tuo santuario a Fatima, il nostro amatissimo confratello nell'episcopato, il Vescovo di Leiria-Fatima. Gli siamo grati per averci portato l'immagine della Madonna di Fatima. Siamo grati tutti, tutti i romani, soprattutto il Vescovo di Roma. Fatima qui, nella Cappella Paolina del Vaticano, poi nella mia Cappella privata, poi in piazza San Pietro durante la grande celebrazione, infine in questa Basilica. Ora, si conclude in questa Basilica la visita della Madonna di Fatima che andrà, per essere presente ancora a Roma, nella Cattedrale del Vescovo di Roma, San Giovanni in Laterano e poi, secondo quello che ho saputo, anche nel santuario del Divino Amore. Scusaci, o Madonna, scusaci, Madre di Dio, se ti dobbiamo incontrarti in questa Roma, in diversi luoghi, in diversi posti. Dobbiamo aprire, vogliamo aprire la grazia della Tua presenza ai diversi ambienti di questa grande città e diocesi del Papa. Ringrazio per tutto e nel nome di tutti, specialmente nel nome del Cardinale Vicario di Roma, dei miei Confratelli nell'episcopato, di tutti i sacerdoti, di tutto il popolo di Dio di questa città e di questa Chiesa.

Bacio i Tuoi piedi per aver voluto indirizzare i Tuoi passi verso di noi.

E ti sia permesso, o Maria, Nostra Signora di Fatima, di dare alla Tua presenza, ancora una Benedizione a tutti i presenti e a tutta la Chiesa di Roma.

Thus we have willed to choose this Sunday, the third Sunday of Lent of the year 1984, still within the Holy Year of Redemption, for the act of entrustment, of consecration of the world, of the great human family, of all the peoples, especially of those who have such need of this consecration, of this entrustment, of those peoples for whom You Yourself await our act of consecration and of entrustment. All this we have been able to do according to our poor human possibilities, within the capacity of our human weakness. But with enormous confidence in Your maternal love, with enormous confidence in Your maternal solicitude.

This is the complete text of the prayer of thanksgiving addressed to Our Lady of Fatima spoken by Pope John Paul II at 4:00 p.m. on Sunday, March 25, 1984. The text reported here is a photographic reproduction of the article published in the *L'Osservatore Romano* on March 26-27, 1984. In the translated section, one can clearly read that Pope John Paul II knew that he had not fulfilled the request of Our Lady of Fatima for the Consecration of Russia.

Chapter 17

Framing a Grievance

Great is the calamity that now afflicts Holy Church and the world at large. In the previous chapter we noted that Pope Benedict XVI himself admits that "in vast areas of the world the faith is in danger of dying out like a flame which no longer has fuel," and that after Vatican II "certain fundamental truths of the faith, such as sin, grace, theological life, and the last things, were not mentioned anymore," so that the Church now suffers from "a secularized ecclesial environment" and even in many places seems to be a "desert without God."

This state of affairs did not arise by accident. The Pope's admissions are an implicit indictment of the members of the hierarchy who have presided over this catastrophe and are responsible for it. The Pope, who as Cardinal Ratzinger read the Third Secret in its entirety, is surely speaking in light of what the full Secret reveals.

In these extraordinary times, just as in the time of the Arian crisis, the laity must shoulder burdens that in ordinary times would not be theirs. As members of the Mystical Body of Christ, we have a duty to combat the current crisis according to our station in life. We must reject the advice of those who tell us to indulge in the gross presumption that "God is in charge of the Church", by which they mean that we must do nothing to oppose error and injustice perpetrated by members of the hierarchy, but rather blindly submit to every decision of authority, no matter how destructive its consequences.

Our Duty in Justice and Charity to Speak Out

That is not the Catholic way. That is not what the laity and faithful clergy did during the Arian crisis, and it is *not* what we should do today. Our silence and acquiescence in the face of this ongoing disaster would, first of all, be an injustice to the Church and a betrayal of our solemn duty in justice as confirmed Catholics, as soldiers of Christ.

Then, too, there is our obligation in charity toward our fellow Catholics, including our superiors in the hierarchy. *We have a duty in charity to our superiors to oppose what is happening in the Church, even if that means taking the extraordinary step of having to rebuke our own superiors in public.*

As Saint Thomas Aquinas taught: "if the faith were endangered, a subject *ought* to rebuke his prelate even publicly." Why is it both just and *charitable* for a subject to rebuke his prelate, even publicly, in such cases? St. Thomas here observes that the public rebuke of a prelate "would seem to savor of presumptuous pride; but *there is no presumption in thinking oneself better in some respect*, because, in this life, *no man is without some fault.* We must also remember that when a man reproves his prelate charitably, it does not follow that he thinks himself any better, but merely that he offers his help to one who, 'being in the higher position among you, *is therefore in greater danger,*' as Augustine observes in his Rule quoted above."[496] Of course, there is also danger to our fellow Catholics— the gravest possible danger—from the current course of destructive innovation being followed by certain members of the Vatican apparatus, who have turned their backs not only on the Message of Fatima but on the Church's salvific dogma and mission.

This disordered desire to bury the past in the name of Vatican II and a "new orientation" of the Church is what has provoked the currently reigning Pope to call for a "hermeneutic of continuity" concerning the Council, rather than a "hermeneutic of rupture" that treats the Council as a break with the past. That the Pope would have insisted that the Council is in continuity with the Church's past—Her traditional teaching, liturgy, practices and devotions—is itself a sign of the magnitude of the crisis that confronts us. And yet Pope Benedict's attempts at a restoration—his "liberation" of the Latin Mass, his "rehabilitation" of the Society of Saint Pius X, his refusal to administer Communion in the hand, and so forth—are either ignored, protested or met with outright resistance within the Church. And the Pope remains largely a captive of a Vatican bureaucracy, dominated by the Secretary of State, that seems to have a life of its own. And so it is necessary for the faithful to demand relief from the acts and omissions of their own superiors, who are either implicated in the crisis or have failed to act decisively against it.

The teaching of Saint Thomas on the duty to rebuke our superiors when their actions threaten harm to the faith reflects the unanimous teaching of the Saints and Doctors of the Church. As St. Robert Bellarmine, Doctor of the Church, taught in his work on the Roman Pontiff, *even the Pope* may be rebuked and resisted if he threatens harm to the Church:

> Just as it is licit to resist the Pontiff that aggresses the body, it is also licit to resist the one who aggresses souls or who disturbs civil order, or, above all, who attempts to destroy the Church. I say that it is licit *to resist him by not doing what he orders and by preventing his will from being executed*; it is not licit, however, to judge, punish or depose him, since these acts are proper to a superior.[497]

Likewise, the eminent Sixteenth Century theologian Francisco Suarez (whom Pope Paul V praised as *Doctor Eximius et Pius*, i.e. "Exceptional and Pious Doctor") taught as follows:

> And in this second way the Pope could be schismatic, if he were unwilling to be in normal union with the whole body of the Church, as would occur if he attempted to excommunicate the

---

[496] St. Thomas Aquinas, *Summa Theologiae*, Q. 33, Art. V, Pt. II-II.
[497] St. Robert Bellarmine, *De Romano Pontifice*, Book II, Chapter 29.

whole Church, or, as both Cajetan and Torquemada observe, if he wished to *overturn the rites of the Church based on Apostolic Tradition.* ... If [the Pope] gives an order contrary to right customs, he should not be obeyed; *if he attempts to do something manifestly opposed to justice and the common good, it will be lawful to resist him*; if he attacks by force, by force he can be repelled, with a moderation appropriate to a just defense.[498]

If even the Pope may legitimately be resisted when he takes actions that would harm the Church, all the more so the prelates mentioned in the preceding pages. Quite simply, as Pope St. Felix III declared: *"Not to oppose error is to approve it; and not to defend truth is to suppress it."* Members of the laity and lower-ranking clergy are not exempt from that injunction. All the members of the Church are subject to it.

We thus have a duty to speak out concerning what these prelates have done or failed to do. We have a duty to bring to the Pope's attention what we believe in conscience is a well-founded allegation that they have caused, and imminently will cause, grave harm to the Church and the world by a veritable conspiracy against the Message of Fatima, which conspiracy includes their goal to "revise" the Message in order to conform it to the fallible worldly wisdom of men who think they can "update" the Church and reconcile Her to "the modern world." We have a duty to petition the Holy Father for redress of this injustice against Our Lady of Fatima and Her Message to the Church and all mankind.

Indeed, this entire book is effectively a petition to the Holy Father, over and above the formal Petition set forth in Chapter 19. Likewise, Antonio Socci's book, *The Fourth Secret of Fatima*, which also accuses the Vatican Secretary of State of a cover-up of part of the Third Secret, and of thwarting the Consecration of Russia, served as a petition of sorts to the Holy Father, who not only has read Socci's book but, as he has reported (see Chapter 14), the Pope sent him a personal letter "concerning my book, *thanking me for 'the sentiments* which have suggested it.'"[499] Let no one say, therefore, that this book exceeds or abuses the right of the faithful to communicate to each other and to the members of the hierarchy, including the Sovereign Pontiff, their concerns about legitimate grievances in the Church—a natural right codified in the Church's Code of Canon Law.[500]

We are about to submit our case for your consideration as fellow members of the Holy Catholic Church in the hope that you will join us in petitioning the Holy Father for relief in the matter of Fatima. We will now summarize briefly what the evidence has shown. In general, the evidence presented in the preceding chapters has established five basic points.

---

[498] *De Fide*, Disp. X, Sec. VI, N. 16.
[499] Socci, "Dear Cardinal Bertone...", loc. cit.
[500] Cf. 1983 Code of Canon Law, can. 212.

I.

The Message of Fatima is contrary to, and warns against, the "new orientation" of the Church imposed after the Second Vatican Council.

The Message of Fatima is a true and authentic prophecy of vital importance for the Church and the world in this epoch of human history. The Message was delivered in person by the Mother of God; authenticated by indisputable public miracles witnessed by tens of thousands of people; has been pronounced worthy of belief by the Church; and has received the explicit endorsement of a series of seven Popes, including John Paul II and Benedict XVI. In short, *the Message of Fatima simply cannot be ignored.* As Pope John Paul II himself has said, the Message of Fatima imposes an obligation on the Church.

The Message calls for the establishment in the world of devotion to the Immaculate Heart of Mary—and thus *the Catholic Faith*—throughout the world. To that end, *God Himself* has decreed these things for our time: the solemn public Consecration of Russia—specifically and only Russia—to the Immaculate Heart by the Pope and the bishops together, the conversion of Russia to Catholicism, and the consequent Triumph of the Immaculate Heart in Russia and ultimately throughout the world.

The Third Secret of Fatima (in that portion yet to be revealed) predicts what Catholics see all around them today: a catastrophic loss of faith and discipline in the Church—heresy, scandal, apostasy reaching into nearly every corner of the Catholic world. Aside from the mountain of other evidence we have presented on this point, one piece of evidence standing alone proves this: the crucial phrase in the Message, which has been buried through the efforts of the Vatican Secretary of State in the hope that we will all forget it: "In Portugal the dogma of the Faith will always be preserved etc."—in Portugal, yes, but not in other countries, as we have seen. To recall once again Pope Pius XII's warning in light of the Fatima apparitions only 31 years before the Council:

> I am worried by the Blessed Virgin's messages to Lucy of Fatima. This persistence of Mary about *the dangers which menace the Church* is a divine warning against the suicide of altering the Faith, in Her *liturgy,* Her *theology,* and Her *soul.* ... I hear all around me innovators who wish to *dismantle* the Sacred Chapel, *destroy* the universal flame of the Church, *reject* Her ornaments and make Her feel remorse for Her historical past.

Sister Lucy insisted that the Third Secret be made public by 1960, because in that year it would be "much clearer." We know that by 1960 the Second Vatican Council had been called. The men who have governed the Church since 1960 have given the human element of the Church an entirely "new orientation." They have done this by means of an "opening to the world" through which "dialogue" with heretics, schismatics, Communists, atheists and other opponents of the one true

Church has *de facto* replaced the Church's once manifest great love for Her enemies by Her fierce opposition to error and Her faithfulness to Her obligation to pass on to all the following generations the Catholic Faith whole and inviolate, as Christ commanded the Church to do. Not content with ignoring their own solemn duty to keep and pass on the Faith, the Modernistic and anti-Fatima prelates also persecute those who seek to adhere to that duty.

As early as 1973 Pope Paul VI was forced to admit that "the opening to the world has become a veritable invasion of the Church by worldly thinking"—that is, by liberalism. This invasion of the Church by liberalism, and the consequent collapse of faith and discipline within the Church, represents the cherished goal of organized Masonry and Communism: not the complete overthrow of the Church, which they know is impossible, but the *adaptation* of the Church to liberal ideas. The present state of the Church is precisely what these forces boldly predicted they would achieve, and precisely what a long line of pre-conciliar Popes warned was the object of their conspiracies.

Instead of fighting against the new orientation that adapts the Church to liberal ideas, however, post-conciliar churchmen, including those we identify here, have unswervingly pursued the "new orientation" by taking and implementing decisions in the name of Vatican II, including (a) *Ostpolitik*, a policy by which many members of the Church are made to avoid any condemnation of or active opposition to Communist regimes; (b) the "ecumenical venture" and "interreligious dialogue", which *de facto* abandon both the conversion of non-Catholics to the one true religion and the dogma that the Catholic Church is the one true Church, outside of which there is no salvation; (c) the introduction of novel and ambiguous terminology in conciliar and post-conciliar documents which (like the formulas of the Arians in the 4th Century) undermine belief in the dogmas of the Faith; (d) a totally unprecedented "reform" of the liturgy by abandoning the traditional Latin Rite; (e) permission for or toleration of various forms of heteropraxis (practices which favor heretical beliefs) such as Communion in the hand, the altar not facing *ad orientem*, removal of the tabernacle from the main altar, etc., which undermine belief in the Catholic dogmas about the Holy Eucharist, the Holy Mass and the sacrificial priesthood.

The Message of Fatima, with its simple call for the public Consecration of Russia to the Immaculate Heart of Mary by the Pope and bishops, the conversion of Russia to Catholicism and the Triumph of the Immaculate Heart (and with it the miraculous growth of the Catholic Church) throughout the world, cannot be reconciled with the new orientation of the Church, in which *Ostpolitik*, "ecumenical dialogue" and "interreligious dialogue" prevent the Church from publicly declaring that Russia must be consecrated and converted to the true religion for the good of that nation and the world.

II.

The Vatican Secretary of State has adopted and enforced a "Party Line" on Fatima that seeks to "minimize," "place in the past," "revise," "interpret" and obscure the Message of Fatima, including the Third Secret and the Consecration of Russia to the Immaculate Heart, so that it poses no obstacle to the "new orientation" of the Church.

The leading churchmen who have implemented the new orientation have attempted to "revise" the Message of Fatima to make it conform to the new orientation by insisting upon an "interpretation" of the Message that

• eliminates the Consecration of Russia by name (which, in their anti-Fatima prejudices, they regard as an intolerable "ecumenical" offense or "provocation" to the Russian Orthodox),

• eliminates the conversion of Russia to the Catholic Faith (which they have expressly abandoned as "outdated" ecclesiology), and

• eliminates the Triumph of the Immaculate Heart throughout the world (which they ignorantly regard as "triumphalistic", embarrassing and "non-ecumenical").

Under Cardinal Angelo Sodano, the Vatican Secretariat of State, which had assumed *de facto* control of the daily governance of the Church since the reorganization of the Roman Curia by the Masonic Cardinal Jean Villot (Secretary of State of Pope Paul VI), has dictated this veritable "Party Line" on Fatima.

According to the Party Line, the Message of Fatima in general, and the Third Secret in particular, are to be "neutralized" by stripping the Message of its prophecies of future events, converting them into past events, and reducing its specifically Catholic content to mere generic "Christian" piety that will not "offend" the Russian Orthodox, the Protestants or other non-Catholics.

Sodano's Party Line on Fatima is in keeping with the Balamand Declaration (1993), negotiated by Sodano's representative, Cardinal Cassidy, which declares that the return of the Orthodox to Rome is "outdated ecclesiology"—as is, therefore, (according to Cardinal Sodano) the conversion of Russia to the Catholic Faith called for by Our Lady of Fatima.

Cardinal Sodano took control of the "interpretation" of the vision of the "Bishop dressed in white," published by the Vatican on June 26, 2000. While the vision depicts a Pope being executed by soldiers outside a half-ruined city filled with bodies, Sodano offered what Antonio Socci has called a "preventative interpretation" of the vision designed to prevent anyone from linking the vision to the crisis in the Church and a related coming chastisement of the world.

According to the "preventative interpretation," the clearly apocalyptic scenario in the vision signifies nothing more than the failed attempt on the life of Pope John Paul II by a lone assassin in 1981 and other events of the 20th Century, including World War II. This patently false "interpretation" of the vision—blatantly designed to consign Fatima to the past in keeping with the "new orientation" of the Church—was cited no less than four times in the commentary on the Message of Fatima and the Third Secret, *TMF*, composed by the former Cardinal Ratzinger and Monsignor (now Cardinal) Bertone, and published along with the vision in 2000.

In service of Sodano's Party Line, then-Archbishop Tarcisio Bertone perpetrated a demonstrable fraud by asserting in *TMF* that "Sister Lucia personally confirmed that this solemn and universal act of consecration [of the world in 1984] corresponded to what Our Lady wished ('*Sim, està feita, tal como Nossa Senhora a pediu, desde o dia 25 de Março de 1984*': 'Yes it has been done just as Our Lady asked, on 25 March 1984': Letter of 8 November 1989). Hence any further discussion or request [for the Consecration of Russia] is without basis."

The fraud is demonstrable since the cited "letter of 8 November 1989" was printed out by a computer that the aged Sister Lucy did not use (as Cardinal Bertone admitted in his book, *Last Visionary*, on page 89 of the English edition and page 101 of the Italian edition), and contains an error of fact that Sister Lucy would never have made: that Pope Paul VI performed a consecration of the world during his visit to Fatima in 1967, when Pope Paul never consecrated anything during his fleeting appearance there.

Yet Bertone deliberately relied solely upon the patently bogus "letter of 8 November 1989" even though he (and the rest of the Vatican apparatus) had complete access to Sister Lucy in April-May 2000 and could have asked her to confirm that the 1984 consecration of the world sufficed for a consecration of Russia—contrary to her consistent testimony for many decades.

Only one day after publication of the vision and *TMF*, Sodano pointedly demonstrated his adherence to the "new orientation" by inviting Mikhail Gorbachev, the pro-abortion, ex-Soviet dictator, to the Vatican for a bogus "press conference" (no questions allowed), during which Sodano, Gorbachev and Cardinal Silvestrini sat together to heap praise on a key element of the new orientation, developed by Sodano's predecessor, Cardinal Casaroli: namely, *Ostpolitik*, under which the Church "dialogues" with Communist regimes rather than opposing them, and observes diplomatic silence in the face of Communist persecution of the Church.

III.

The Vatican Secretary of State has overseen the concealment of a part of the Third Secret of Fatima: a text in which the Virgin, in Her own words, gives the solution to present-day problems in the Church while She explains the vision of the "Bishop dressed in white," which Secretaries of State Sodano and Bertone have "interpreted" falsely as a mere depiction of past events when, in fact, it predicts the present-day, ongoing and worsening apostasy in the Church and a divine chastisement of the world.

That portion of the Third Secret which contains the "words of the Virgin" referred to by the Vatican itself in 1960—the words which almost certainly follow the incomplete phrase "In Portugal the dogma of the Faith will always be preserved etc." and which explain the vision of the "Bishop dressed in white"—has been withheld from the faithful.

The Vatican commentary published in connection with the vision, *TMF*, falsely characterizes the precious words of the Virgin pertaining to the dogma of the Faith, recorded in Sister Lucy's Fourth Memoir, as merely "some annotations" by Sister Lucy, when in fact the words she recorded are clearly those of the Mother of God. To avoid those words, Sodano and his collaborators in *TMF* conspicuously avoided the Fourth Memoir in favor of the less complete Third Memoir.

In a vain attempt to quell legitimate doubts about the completeness of the disclosure on June 26, 2000, Sodano, dispatching then-Monsignor Bertone for the task, obtained a secret "interview" of Sister Lucy in November 2001, for which there is no transcript or other complete record. It appears that during this "interview" the seer was essentially induced to "agree" that she likely concocted those elements of the Fatima Message that contradict the Party Line, and was further induced to repudiate (without the slightest explanation) her unwavering testimony for 60 years that the Consecration of Russia requires explicit mention of Russia and the participation of both the Pope and the world's bishops in a joint public ceremony.

Although the "interview" is alleged to have lasted more than two hours, Msgr. Bertone offered only *forty-four words* from Sister Lucy related to the Consecration of Russia and the Third Secret, which words are presented without any surrounding context, so that it is impossible to tell exactly what Sister Lucy was asked, and how exactly she answered. Among other incredible things, we are asked to believe that during this two-hour interview, of which we are given only forty-four relevant words:

• Sister Lucy repudiated a lifetime of unwavering testimony that Our Lady asked for the Consecration of *Russia* by the Pope and all the world's bishops, not the consecration of the world by the Pope and a few bishops.

- Sister Lucy "confirms everything that is written" in *TMF*, including its suggestion that she concocted the Third Secret vision from things she had seen in books, and that Edouard Dhanis is an "eminent scholar" on Fatima, even though Dhanis asserted that Sister Lucy concocted virtually every prophetic element of the Fatima Message.

- Sister Lucy "confirms" that the Triumph of the Immaculate Heart has nothing to do with the consecration and conversion of Russia, but only the Virgin Mary's *fiat* 2,000 years ago.

Instead of a transcript or other record of the two-hour "interview," the Vatican provided only an Italian-language summary in *L'Osservatore Romano*, signed by Msgr. Bertone and (purportedly) by Sister Lucy, who did not even speak Italian. Sister Lucy's "signature" does not appear on the English translation of the "summary."

The absence of any independent record of the interview—audio, video or even a certified and complete transcript—only adds to the grounds for suspicion, and Antonio Socci rightly concluded that the few words attributed to the late seer "lack credibility."

Msgr. Bertone conducted this patently suspect "interview" even though he had a vested interest in coercing Sister Lucy to support the Party Line, and to defend his own preposterous claim in *TMF* that the press conference of June 26, 2000 "brings to an end a period of history marked by tragic human lust for power and evil ..."

As successor to Cardinal Sodano in the office of Secretary of State, Cardinal Bertone has continued the cover-up of the missing portion of the Third Secret in which he participated as Archbishop Bertone. Even as he has done so, however, his defense of the "official account" and the Sodano/Bertone "preventative interpretation" of the vision of the "Bishop dressed in white" has been demolished by the following explosive further revelations in 2006-2007:

- As revealed by Archbishop Loris F. Capovilla, the still-living personal secretary of Pope John XXIII, there are *two different envelopes and two different texts* comprising the Third Secret in its entirety: the "Bertone envelope," containing the vision of the "Bishop dressed in white," lodged in the Holy Office archives; and the "Capovilla envelope" and its contents, lodged in the papal apartment, on which the Archbishop wrote his name, the names of all those who had read the text inside, and the dictation of Pope John XXIII that "I leave it to others to comment or decide."

- Cardinal Bertone now admits the existence of the "Capovilla envelope" in the papal apartment, but has thus far failed to produce it.

- As Bertone himself revealed on television for the first time in 2007 (after having never mentioned it before), Sister Lucy prepared *two different sealed envelopes*—clearly for two different texts—pertaining to the Third Secret, with each envelope bearing her handwritten warning that "By *express order of Our Lady*, this envelope can only be opened in 1960 [only] by the Cardinal Patriarch of Lisbon or the Bishop of Leiria."

• Contrary to what the twin envelopes prepared by Sister Lucy confirm, Bertone had been claiming for seven years (2000-2007) that Sister Lucy "confessed" to him that she never received any communication from the Virgin linking the Third Secret to 1960. The envelopes expose Bertone's claim as a falsehood and thus destroy his credibility entirely, for it can hardly be the case that Sister Lucy, not he, was lying about what the Virgin had said to her concerning the Third Secret and its relation to 1960 and thus the already-announced Second Vatican Council.

• Three successive Popes have read texts of the Third Secret on two different occasions during their respective pontificates: John XXIII in 1959 and 1960, Paul VI in 1963 and 1965, and John Paul II in 1978 and 1981. Yet only *one* of the two readings by each Pope was mentioned in the "official account" promulgated by then-Archbishop Bertone and still defended by him to this day.

• There was, according to Archbishop Capovilla, an "attachment" to the vision of the "Bishop dressed in white," which attachment has never been produced.

In view of this and all the other evidence we have presented, Antonio Socci—a renowned and respected Catholic intellectual in Italy, and an acquaintance and collaborator of both Bertone and Pope Benedict XVI (when he was Cardinal Ratzinger)—has concluded (reversing his earlier opinion) that it "is certain" that the Vatican is concealing a text pertaining to the Third Secret, containing "the words of the Madonna [which] preannounce *an apocalyptic crisis of the faith in the Church* starting at the summit." This second text, he further concludes, is probably "also an explanation of the vision… (revealed on June 26, 2000)."

Despite the continuing cover-up, however, the Third Secret has in fact been revealed in its essence not only by the testimony of numerous witnesses, but by Pope John Paul II himself, who has twice (in sermons at Fatima) explicitly linked the Message of Fatima to the Book of the Apocalypse, and in particular to the fall of one-third of the stars of Heaven (the clergy) after they are dragged down by the "tail of the dragon" (Apoc. 12:3-4)—an event nowhere seen in the first two parts of the Message, and therefore undoubtedly to be found in the unpublished part of the Third Secret.

Socci hypothesizes that the revelations by John Paul II are a "compromise solution" devised by the Vatican under which the Pope would reveal the missing part of the Third Secret "indirectly" so that it could be said by the Vatican Secretary of State and others (with a mental reservation) that "all has been revealed."

IV.
The Vatican Secretary of State has overseen the persecution of Father Nicholas Gruner on account of his opposition to the Party Line on Fatima and his work in bringing to light the concealment of part of the Third Secret.

Because he has in conscience refused to adhere to the Party Line on Fatima and has raised compelling questions concerning the completeness of the disclosure of the Third Secret under the "management" of the Secretary of State, Father Nicholas Gruner, perhaps the Church's leading exponent of the authentic Fatima Message, has been subjected to persecution by the Vatican Secretary of State (following "worried signals" from Sodano's predecessor, Cardinal Casaroli, to Father Gruner's bishop in 1989). In particular:

- Sodano is the "higher authority" (the Vatican term for the Secretary of State) who announced a bogus "suspension" of Father Gruner on September 12, 2001.

- Documents falsely denouncing Father Gruner and pressuring priests and bishops to shun his apostolate's conferences have been circulated throughout the world over the years by apostolic nuncios, who are ecclesial "diplomats" attached to the Secretariat of State.

Further, Sodano dictated the actions of Cardinal Dario Castrillón Hoyos, formerly Prefect of the Congregation for the Clergy, respecting the persecution of Father Gruner, including the following:

- In the midst of the worst crisis of faith and discipline in Church history, and a clerical sexual scandal of monumental proportions, he issued public condemnations, notices of "suspension" and even a threat of excommunication regarding only one priest in the entire Catholic Church: Father Nicholas Gruner, who has committed no offense against faith or morals, has kept his vow of celibacy, has kept the faith, and has done absolutely nothing to warrant any punishment.

- In his letter to Father Gruner of June 5, 2000, Cardinal Castrillón Hoyos threatened him with excommunication—only days before the June 26, 2000 press conference called to "gently debunk" the Message of Fatima, under the direction of Cardinal Sodano.

- On February 16, 2001, Cardinal Castrillón Hoyos sent Father Gruner another letter, renewing the threat of "excommunication" and demanding that he "publicly retract" criticism of Cardinal Sodano, and other matters of free opinion in the Church, found in certain articles in *The Fatima Crusader*—an unprecedented demand, and one that is quite ludicrous considering the profusion of heretical literature promoted by unfaithful priests and even bishops during his tenure, about which Cardinal Castrillón Hoyos did nothing.

- In the same letter, Cardinal Castrillón Hoyos revealed his motive of furthering the Party Line on Fatima, dictated by Cardinal Sodano, when he castigated Father Gruner for not accepting the new version of Fatima: "the Blessed Mother appeared to the three little visionaries in the Cova da Iria at the beginning of the century, and *marked out a program for the New Evangelization* which the whole Church finds itself engaged in, which is even more urgent at the dawn of the third millennium." Of course, Our Lady of Fatima said nothing about any "New Evangelization", but only the Consecration of Russia, the conversion of Russia to Catholicism, and the triumph of Her Immaculate Heart—all of which Cardinal Castrillón Hoyos studiously ignored, along with the other Vatican prelates identified here.

- In a Church beset by widespread clerical corruption that he generally tolerated during his tenure, Cardinal Castrillón Hoyos attempted to destroy the good name and life's work of a lone faithful priest, Father Nicholas Gruner, simply and only because he would not accept a counterfeit of the Message of Fatima dictated by the Vatican Secretary of State.

- This persecution of Father Gruner and his Fatima apostolate continues under Cardinal Bertone, with the current Secretary of State attempting to prevent the attendance of bishops at the apostolate's Fatima conferences in Brazil and India, while circulating through private channels the false insinuations or accusations against Father Gruner (duly incardinated in the Archdiocese of Hyderabad, India) including the ludicrous suggestion that Father Gruner is "suspended."

V.

The Vatican Secretary of State's campaign to revise and conceal the authentic Fatima Message has had disastrous consequences for the Church and the world, with even worse consequences to come.

As the direct result of the concerted effort, orchestrated by the Vatican Secretary of State, to revise and conceal the authentic Message of Fatima in favor of the "new orientation" of the Church—

- Russia has not been consecrated to the Immaculate Heart of

Mary as the Mother of God requested.

- Russia has not converted to the Catholic Faith as Our Lady promised if Her requests were heeded, but rather has only further degenerated spiritually, morally, socially, politically, and even economically, while the Kremlin prepares for war in alliance with China and the Catholic Church suffers official restrictions and outright persecution in "that poor nation," as Sister Lucy called it.

- There is no peace in the world but only moral depravity, wars and genocides in many places, social unrest and decay, economic collapse and, worst of all, the holocaust of abortion which cries out to Heaven for divine retribution.

- The Church is in the depths of an unprecedented crisis, admitted by the currently reigning Pope himself, and many millions of souls are at risk.

But even worse consequences are to come, both for the Church and all of humanity. As the Virgin of Fatima declared: "If people do what I ask, many souls will be saved." And as She has warned the Church and the world: "Many souls go to hell because they have no one to pray and make sacrifices for them." Regarding her own mission, Sister Lucy said to Father Fuentes on December 26, 1957:

> [M]y mission is not to indicate to the world *the material punishments which are certain to come* if the world does not pray and do penance beforehand. No! My mission is to indicate to everyone *the imminent danger we are in of losing our souls for all eternity* if we remain obstinate in sin.

In sum, the evidence shows that in consequence of what can only be called a conspiracy against Our Lady of Fatima, the world is facing the eternal loss of many millions of souls and the annihilation of various nations which Our Lady of Fatima warned would be the consequences of spurning Her requests. The conspirators, acting according to the dictates of a mere Vatican bureaucrat who was given no divine commission by Our Lord—the Secretary of State—have attempted to hide the missing part of the Third Secret and do away with the Consecration of Russia at precisely that moment in history when the Church's correspondence to Our Lady's requests would avert what anyone can see is a coming global catastrophe.

The civil authorities of the world, armed with only the fallible intelligence reports of their human operatives, are wise enough to prepare for the worst. But Vatican prelates, in possession of a precious and infallible heavenly intelligence report clearly warning of dire coming events for the Church and humanity, dare to maintain that it "belongs to the past," is probably not reliable, and can in any event be safely disregarded.

A Summary of Falsehoods

The evidence shows that those who are determined to do away with the Fatima prophecies have perpetrated at least ten distinct falsehoods upon the Church and the world. These untruths have already caused grave harm to the Church and mankind at large, and they imminently threaten even graver harm to every man, woman and child on the face of the earth, as the Virgin of Fatima Herself has warned us. Let us review them:

Falsehood #1

> The vision of the "Bishop dressed in White" published on June 26, 2000 is all there is to the Third Secret of Fatima.

This falsehood deprives the Church and the world of the obvious prophetic warnings in the vision, which can only be explained by the missing words of the Blessed Virgin. The missing words would not only explain the vision but also tell us how to avoid the future catastrophe it depicts, which includes the execution of a Pope (or a bishop dressed in white) by a band of soldiers outside a half-ruined city.

We are told that the vision must be interpreted "figuratively" (as representing the persecution of the Church during the 20th Century), yet the same Vatican prelates who perpetrate this false reading, led by Cardinals Sodano and Bertone, then turn around and *interpret it literally themselves* as a depiction of the failed assassination attempt against the Pope in 1981. They simply ignore Sister Lucy's own explanation in the published text of the vision that "the Pope *is killed*". They also ignore Sister Lucy's purported letter of May 12, 1982—which they themselves offer as evidence in *TMF*! In that letter, supposedly written a year *after* the assassination attempt, Sister Lucy warned: "And if we have *not yet seen* the complete fulfillment of the final part of this prophecy, *we are going towards it with great strides.*"

By withholding the words of the Virgin which are clearly missing from the Third Secret, they have deprived us of precious heavenly guidance in this time of unprecedented crisis in the Church, while attempting to hide their own role in causing the crisis, which the Third Secret in its entirety no doubt reveals.

Falsehood #2

> The Third Secret depicts events that "belong to the past," including the failed attempt on the life of Pope John Paul II.

The effort to "interpret" the vision of a future disaster befalling the Pope and the hierarchy (including a public execution) as nothing more than a *failed* assassination attempt more than 25 years ago is a most blatant error. As we have shown abundantly, this falsehood is the most dangerous aspect of the Secretary of State's campaign against Fatima, since it leads the entire Church down the primrose path to ruin by counseling all the faithful to abandon any concern about vitally prophetic warnings—including the annihilation of various nations—which have clearly not yet come to pass.

This fraud is exposed by the former Cardinal Ratzinger's description of the contents of the Third Secret in 1984, standing alone and even without all of the other evidence we have presented. At that time the Cardinal said nothing of his 2000 "interpretation" that the Third Secret culminated in the 1981 assassination attempt. This "interpretation," foisted upon the Church by the Vatican Secretary of State, is obviously a recent fabrication designed to misdirect and mislead the faithful.

Recall here Cardinal Bertone's effort to persuade the world that Sister Lucy "confessed" to him that the Blessed Virgin had never told her that the Third Secret was linked to 1960 and could not be revealed before then, when in truth Sister Lucy had prepared two envelopes recording the Virgin's "express order" in that regard, as Bertone himself finally revealed on television in 2007. This is clear evidence of a deliberate attempt to mislead the faithful about the Third Secret's real meaning, which involves its connection to the era of the Second Vatican Council.

Falsehood #3

The Message of Fatima offers no specific prescription for the current crisis in the Church and the world beyond generic piety in the form of prayer and penance.

The conspirators against Fatima we have identified and their collaborators have endeavored to persuade the faithful that Our Lady of Fatima did not specifically request, *by the will of Almighty God Himself*: the Consecration of Russia to the Immaculate Heart of Mary by the Pope together with all the Catholic bishops of the world at the same time; and the Five First Saturdays devotions, including the Holy Communions of Reparation for man's sins against Our Lady's Immaculate Heart, numbered among which are all of man's blasphemies against the Immaculate Heart.

The evidence shows that these requests from Heaven have been buried and ignored by the identified Vatican prelates because such things are too explicitly Catholic for the new "ecumenical" and worldly orientation of the Church which they obstinately pursue and promote. Thus the very means God has ordained to obtain special graces in our time for the salvation of souls from hell are inexcusably removed from view.

Falsehood #4

All the requests of the Virgin of Fatima, including the Consecration of Russia, have been honored.

On the contrary, the Vatican prelates involved in the effort to do away with Fatima have spurned Her requests. They have substituted a consecration of the world, in which very few bishops participated, for the Consecration of Russia that must be done by the Pope together with all the world's Catholic bishops in a solemn public ceremony. They have "adjusted" what the Mother of God requested on the authority of Her divine Son in order to fit their failed and worthless human plans and initiatives, including an utterly fruitless "ecumenism" that has produced nothing but continued contempt for the Pope on the part of an unconverted, Kremlin-controlled, Russian Orthodox hierarchy.

Instead of seeking the conversion of Russia, the Triumph of the Immaculate Heart, and reparation for sins as God commanded them at Fatima, these prelates have participated in the fraudulent repackaging of the Message of Fatima as a bland and meaningless "program for the New Evangelization" (to recall Cardinal Castrillón Hoyos' ridiculous assertion in this regard). As we have shown, "the New Evangelization" abandons the constant teaching of the Church that not only the Russian Orthodox but also all schismatics and heretics must return to the Catholic Church, and that Moslems, Jews and pagans also need conversion, faith in Jesus Christ and Baptism to be saved from hell. "The New Evangelization"—much in the manner of Communist slogans—means the opposite of what it says. It means *no* evangelization—of anyone!—and thus no honoring of the Virgin's requests concerning the conversion of Russia.

Falsehood #5

The alarming state of the Church and the world is the best we can expect from the falsely claimed "obedience" to the Message of Fatima.

It is a very grave deception, with the most horrific consequences, to tell the faithful that the current state of Russia and the world at large represents in any way the fulfillment of the promises of the Mother of God at Fatima. The Church and the world are thus robbed of the untold temporal and spiritual benefits that God would bestow if the Message of Fatima were respected and obeyed.

We have been given a demonstration of those benefits in the case of Portugal, a nation miraculously transformed into a Catholic social order following its consecration to the Immaculate Heart in 1931—a result the head of the Portuguese hierarchy explicitly declared would occur throughout the world if Russia were likewise consecrated.

In fact, at the very least, it borders on blasphemy to attribute the horrendous spiritual and moral condition of Russia and the world today to the triumph of the Immaculate Heart.

Falsehood #6

We can do nothing to avoid the great chastisement foretold by Our Lady of Fatima, including the annihilation of various nations, besides offering individual prayer and penance.

This falsehood conceals from the Church and the world the two precise means that Heaven has ordained for protection from temporal harm and the obtainment of extraordinary graces in this epoch of Church history: namely, the Consecration of Russia and the widespread practice of the Five First Saturdays devotions.

The prelates involved in perpetrating this falsehood have placed the Church and civil society alike on the same path as that followed by the unfortunate kings of France, who failed to heed Our Lord's command that France be consecrated to His Sacred Heart in a solemn public ceremony. The execution of the King of France by French revolutionaries in 1793 mirrors the fate that awaits the Pope and many members of the hierarchy, as seen in the Third Secret vision: that is, the execution of the Pope and his ministers by soldiers, outside the half-ruined city.

Yet we are told that the apocalyptic scenario depicted in the vision represents nothing but a *failed* assassination attempt against the Pope alone more than 25 years ago! It is hard to imagine a more reprehensible falsification of the Message of Fatima, one that is designed precisely to put the Church and the world into slumber in the face of the gravest dangers.

Falsehood #7

The Message of Fatima is a mere "private revelation" that does not impose any obligation on the members of the Church to believe it or to follow it.

While paying lip service to the Message of Fatima, perhaps to humor the late John Paul II, who clearly believed in it, the Vatican Secretary of State and his collaborators have suggested that the Message of Fatima is nothing more or less than a help which is offered, but *which one is not obliged to use*. That is, they claim that the Church is not obliged to heed the requests of the Virgin of Fatima—including the Consecration of Russia and the widespread implementation of the Five First Saturdays devotions.

Yet while they tell us that no one need believe or heed the Message of Fatima, Pope John Paul II himself declared that the Message of Fatima "imposes an obligation on the Church." To demonstrate this, he had a Feast of the Virgin of Fatima inserted into the new Roman Missal, which the universal Church will celebrate on May 13 each year. Thus, according to the worldly wisdom of the Secretary of State and those who carry out his worldly policies, the Church celebrates a feast day in honor of an apparition in which no one has to believe!

To hold that a heavenly Message warning of the loss of many souls and a great chastisement in which "various nations will be annihilated" need not be given credence if we choose to disbelieve it—even though it was authenticated by an unprecedented public miracle witnessed by 70,000 people—is the height of human folly. The Second World War, the Korean War, the Vietnam War, the terrorist attacks of September 11, 2001, the worldwide economic collapse of 2008-2009—all these are but a foretaste of what the world will suffer as the consequence of this arrogant demotion of the counsels of the Mother of God at Fatima.

Falsehood #8

> The Fatima prophecies "belong to the past," and the Third Secret in particular contains "no great mystery," "no surprises," and no warnings about the future.

By this falsehood the faithful are illegitimately deprived of heavenly warnings and prescriptions of utmost importance for the Church in our time. Had the Message of Fatima been heeded, incalculable temporal and spiritual harm could have been avoided.

And, by continuing to perpetrate this falsehood, the Vatican prelates involved leave the Church and the world powerless to avoid a literal "annihilation" of "various nations," the enslavement of whole surviving populations of the world, and the loss of countless millions of souls in hell for all eternity—the ultimate consequences of failing to heed Our Lady's requests.

Falsehood #9

> The pretense of a pious belief in the Message of Fatima by the Vatican prelates arrayed against it.

While they hide behind a false appearance of belief in the Message of Fatima, the objective words and deeds of the Vatican prelates mentioned here reveal a systematic attempt to undercut and destroy all credence in the explicitly Catholic prophetic content of the Message. They revealed their true intention by citing Edouard Dhanis as an "eminent scholar" on Fatima in *TMF*, when Dhanis cast doubt on every prophetic aspect of the Message. By citing Dhanis as their great authority, the identified Vatican prelates signal their fellow "illuminated ones" (but not the uninformed general public) that they regard the Message of Fatima as essentially the pious concoction of Sister Lucy, whose claim to have spoken with the Virgin about the consecration and conversion of Russia, and so forth, cannot really be taken seriously by the "enlightened" men of the post-conciliar Church.

Their failure to admit openly that they really do not believe in the authentic Message of Fatima, even as they purport to "interpret" it for us, is an outrage upon the Church. Just as in a court of law, where judges and potential members of the jury must disclose any possible prejudices they may have regarding the case at hand, so too should the identified Vatican prelates have revealed their prejudices openly before they pretended to be unbiased judges of the Fatima Message.

Falsehood #10

Catholics who do not agree with the identified Vatican prelates concerning the Message of Fatima are "disobedient" to "the Magisterium".

By "Magisterium" the Vatican Secretary of State and his collaborators in the Fatima affair mean nothing more than their own opinions about the Message of Fatima, which opinions in fact contradict what Pope John Paul II himself has said and done to vouch for the authenticity of the Message—including his institution in 2002 of the Feast of the Virgin of Fatima in the Church's liturgical calendar.

Thus, ironically enough, it is the Vatican prelates who have orchestrated a campaign to nullify the Message, who are being disloyal to the Magisterium when they seek to demote it to the status of "private revelation" that may be disregarded by the entire Church with complete safety.

An Offense Beyond Calculation

How can one assess the magnitude of the offense committed by those who would bury, in misrepresentation and concealment, a precious Message from Heaven, delivered by the Mother of God Herself for the temporal and eternal welfare of Her children? The offense is beyond all human calculation because it involves not only temporal calamity but also the loss of countless millions of souls, which could be avoided by heeding the Virgin's request for the Consecration of Russia and Her other requests at Fatima (including the widespread promotion of the Five First Saturdays devotions, which "enlightened" Vatican prelates refuse to promote).

The Virgin of Fatima Herself promises the benefits we will receive if only Her requests were obeyed: "If My requests are granted, many souls will be saved and there will be peace." Her requests have not been granted, and those responsible (along with their collaborators) will be liable before God and His Blessed Mother for the consequences to the Church, to the world, and to countless millions of souls who have been robbed of the graces Our Lady of Fatima came to provide them in the name of Her Son.

A Mystery of Iniquity

Why are the Vatican prelates we have mentioned and those who labor with them in pursuit of the Church's new orientation so adamant in their refusal to reveal the entirety of the Third Secret and to allow the Pope and the bishops to perform the simple ceremony that Our Lady of Fatima requested? Why do they move mountains to prevent the utterance of one word—*Russia*—in a public consecration of "that poor nation"? What do they have to lose (besides their personal pride) by revealing the words of the Virgin which explain the vision of the "Bishop dressed in white" and by carrying out Her requests to the letter, without amendments imposed by Vatican diplomats and ecumenists? Nothing. And what do they, the Church and the world have to gain? Everything.

There is simply no legitimate explanation for such perverse resistance to the heavenly hand offered at Fatima. Something unnatural is at work here. Without judging the subjective motives of the persons involved, one is driven to the conclusion that their otherwise inexplicable and seemingly senseless refusal to heed the Message of Fatima is the result of diabolically insidious interventions resulting in a strategic, ongoing (and thus far successful) campaign against the minds, hearts and wills of numerous powerful Vatican prelates and other influential persons in the Vatican itself. By this we mean what Sister Lucy herself meant: an intervention by the Adversary himself, who, as Lucy declared, is "in the mood for engaging in a **final decisive battle** against the Blessed Virgin."

As we have shown, this "final battle" being waged by the devil—the very phrase from which the title of this book was derived—has involved the penetration into the Church of the organized forces that have long sought to bring Her to ruin. This is what Pope Paul VI was compelled to lament publicly when he declared that "the smoke of Satan has entered the temple of God." Whether they subjectively intend it or not, the prelates involved in this controversy have acted in a way that only serves the aims of the Church's worst enemy. And the results of their actions speak for themselves. "By their fruits ye shall know them." (Mt. 7:16) What are the fruits of their governance of the Church? Simply look at the condition of the Church today and you will know the answer.

Along with many others in high positions in the hierarchy, the Vatican prelates who have literally conspired against the Fatima Message have presided over the worst crisis of faith and morals in Church history. In their pursuit of the ruinous novelties that have brought on the crisis, they spurn a heavenly prescription that would restore the Church to health and bring peace to a warring world. Instead of listening to the advice of the Mother of God at Fatima, they press on with their utterly fruitless "ecumenism", "interreligious dialogue", and "dialogue with the world"; their hobnobbing with men of blood like Mikhail Gorbachev, whose presence desecrated the Vatican only one day after the Message of Fatima was "gently debunked" (to recall the words of the *Los Angeles Times*) by the very prelates who had a duty to cherish, promote and carry it out. As they and their collaborators continue to palaver endlessly with the forces of the world, countless souls in need of the light of Christ for their salvation in Russia and elsewhere are allowed to remain in darkness.

Over the years which have passed since that fateful year of 1960—the year when the Third Secret was to have been revealed—the enemies of the Church have delighted in seeing Her rendered almost powerless to oppose them, which is why they erupted in outrage when Pope Benedict made tentative attempts to restore the Church by "liberating" the Latin Mass and lifting the "excommunication" of the bishops of the Society of Saint Pius X. In 2009, as when this book first appeared seven years earlier, the Church continues to retreat as the forces of the world continue to advance against Her. Yet Cardinal Bertone persists in his suicidal attempt to embrace the world instead of truly loving all the persons today living in the world by allowing Our Lady's Immaculate Heart to sweetly conquer it spiritually for Christ the King. Cardinal Bertone, who controls the Vatican apparatus at this time, does not wish to offend the Russian Orthodox or anyone else with a show of Catholic militancy, which he views as embarrassing and "outdated"—to use one of the favorite words of the Modernists. The Church's abject retreat from battle warms the hearts of the Masons and the Communists, who labored for generations in the hope of seeing the Church reduced precisely to this pathetic condition.

And yet Cardinal Bertone, the Vatican apparatus he leads, and the other members of the hierarchy involved in this almost unimaginable debacle—the very debacle predicted in the Secret—are not without militancy of a sort. While they have done little or nothing to stop infiltrators of the Church from spreading heresy and moral corruption with virtual impunity, they pursue unswervingly their disastrous policies of "reform", "openness" and "renewal," while hounding, denouncing and ostracizing any Catholic who offers legitimate resistance. At the same time, they thumb their noses at the Pope and his effort to restore the Latin liturgy, which most bishops continue to quarantine as if it were a strain of anthrax.

Consider that in the entire Catholic world of one billion souls, only four people are deemed "schismatic" by "enlightened" opinion in the Church today: the four bishops of the Society of Saint Pius X. And this continues to be the case even *after* the Pope lifted their "excommunication." It seems that the only remaining "heresy," the only remaining "schism," consists of disagreement with a "new orientation" of the Church that has definitively excluded the Message of Fatima in its traditional Catholic sense—or so they think.

This is the "diabolical disorientation" of the Church that only obedience to the Message of Fatima will remedy. And since only the Pope can lead the Church, including the world's bishops, in that obedience, it is finally to the Pope that we, the faithful, must now turn.

The Remedies to Which the Faithful Are Entitled

What is it that we seek from the Holy Father as remedies for the acts and omissions of the men we have identified? We seek the following:

First,
The Consecration of Russia—
There Is Still Time

By this we mean precisely what Our Lady of Fatima requested: The immediate Consecration of Russia—*by name and without equivocation*—to the Immaculate Heart of Mary, in a solemn public ceremony by the Pope together with all the Catholic bishops of the world.

We must petition the Pope to command under pain of excommunication all the Catholic bishops (except those prevented by imprisonment or serious illness) to consecrate solemnly, publicly and specifically Russia, according to the requests of Our Lady of Fatima, together with the Pope on the same day and at the same hour specified by the Pope.

Some will say it is already too late to obtain the Consecration and that it is pointless to go on requesting it. That is simply not so. As Our Lord Himself revealed to Sister Lucy in the revelation at Rianjo in August of 1931:

> Make it known to My ministers that given they follow the example of the King of France in delaying the execution of My command, they will follow him into misfortune ... They [the ministers of the Catholic Church] did not want to heed My command. Like the King of France they will repent of it, *and they will do it*, but it will be late. Russia will already have spread her errors throughout the world, causing wars and persecutions of the Church. The Holy Father will have much to suffer.[501]

Further, as Our Lord also revealed to Sister Lucy on the same occasion: *"It will never be too late to have recourse to Jesus and Mary."* That is, even though we are now suffering the consequences of delay in the execution of Heaven's command, the worst of those consequences, including the annihilation of various nations, may yet be avoided if the command to consecrate Russia is heeded, however belatedly.

It is outrageous that human respect—fear of offending the Russian Orthodox—has been allowed until now to prevent the Church's fulfillment of Heaven's plan for peace in our time. As members of the Church Militant, we can no longer allow those who claim "to speak for the Pope" to declare that "the Pope" has pronounced unequivocally, authoritatively, and definitively the consecration to be accomplished. We have shown how Pope John Paul II himself had publicly said quite the opposite. We must implore His Holiness Pope Benedict XVI to reject

---

[501] *The Whole Truth About Fatima* - Vol. II: *The Secret and the Church,* pp. 543-544. See also *Toute la vérité sur Fatima* - Tome II: *Le Secret et L'Église,* pp. 344-345.

the manifestly bad advice he and his predecessor have been given, and to follow Heaven's advice instead.

With each passing day, our hindsight shows ever more clearly how badly advised were all the Popes since 1931 in rejecting the command to consecrate Russia. Seeing the disasters of World War II; the Soviet gulag; the war of abortion with over 800 million innocent victims; with ongoing wars in the Middle East, in Iraq, Afghanistan, etc.; what more disasters must be visited upon mankind before the Pope and his advisors finally accept the obvious truth?

Second,
Disclosure of the Full and Integral
Third Secret of Fatima

This disclosure would have to include what we now know for certain exists: the text of the words of the Blessed Virgin explaining the vision that was published on June 26, 2000. That such a text exists has been proven to a moral certainty by a mountain of direct and circumstantial evidence, every piece of which points to a missing text of one page of some 25 lines in letter form, containing the words of the Virgin Herself, and probably contained in the "Capovilla envelope" that was lodged in the papal apartment and which the Vatican Secretary of State has failed and refused to produce.

The Church and the world have the right to know the contents of the Third Secret, which obviously contains salutary warnings about the current crisis in the Church involving, as Cardinal Ratzinger revealed in 1984, "dangers threatening the faith and the life of the Christian, and therefore (the life) of the world." Pope John Paul II's clear indications that the Secret relates to the apostasy and fall of consecrated souls described in the Book of the Apocalypse tell us that he himself was constrained by his advisors not to reveal the Third Secret in its entirety, but rather to offer only hints of its contents. Meanwhile, those who actually control the daily affairs of the Church continue to bury what the Secret must reveal about their own failed governance of the Church.

Third,
A Call for Daily Recitation of the Rosary

Our Lady of Fatima exhorted us to remember what the Church has long known: that the Rosary is infinitely more powerful than any weapon devised by man. There is no difficulty that cannot be overcome, no battle that cannot be won, with the aid of the Holy Rosary. If enough Catholics pray the Rosary with the correct intention, the enemies of the Church will be routed from their strongholds within Her and driven out. As Fatima itself shows us, by the will of God the Virgin Mary is our refuge and our strength in times of crisis. In this gravest of crises, the whole Church must seek recourse to Her through daily recitation of the Rosary.

While we need not, and should not, wait to institute a perpetual

Rosary Crusade at all levels in the Church where we can, we should also petition the Pope to inspire such a campaign throughout the Church by writing encyclicals on the Rosary every year in the manner of Pope Leo XIII and appointing a dicastery headed by a Cardinal to promote the Rosary by various initiatives through the network of Catholic shrines and Marian priests (both religious and diocesan). Such initiatives, of course, must be entirely in keeping with authentic Catholic doctrine and practices promoting all the great privileges of Our Lady.

The Rosary should, of course, include the prayer prescribed by Our Lady of Fatima as an addition to the Rosary: "O my Jesus, forgive us our sins, save us from the fires of hell. Lead all souls to Heaven, especially those most in need." It is most telling about our situation that during the "entrustment" of the world to the Immaculate Heart in October of 2000 the public recitation of the Rosary at the Vatican *conspicuously omitted this prayer*, even though Sister Lucy said the prayer in her convent on that very occasion. This is yet another sign of the "new orientation," which abhors any reference to hell and damnation.

It is crucial to recall here Pope Benedict's own admission that after Vatican II a tendency arose in the Church according to which "certain *fundamental truths of the faith*, such as sin, grace, theological life, and the last things, *were not mentioned anymore*." That is exactly what we are dealing with when it comes to Fatima and the "new orientation" of the Church—an orientation that has produced what the Pope himself calls "a secularized ecclesial environment."

Fourth,
Promotion of the First Saturdays Devotions

Those who have undertaken to "revise" the Message of Fatima have attempted to bury in silence this part of the Message, along with all its other explicitly Catholic elements. Indeed, the whole concept of man making reparation to God and the Blessed Virgin Mary for blasphemies and other sins has been gravely diminished in the Church's new orientation. (One of the key elements obscured in the new liturgy is that the Mass is a *propitiatory* sacrifice to make reparation to God for sin, not merely a "sacrifice of praise.")

The widespread promotion of the Five First Saturdays devotions is one of Heaven's chosen means to restore in our time a sense of the need for reparation for sin by the members of the Church. Who can doubt that now, more than ever before, the Church must renew Her effort to offer reparation to God and to the Immaculate Virgin Mother of God, thus staying the execution of God's wrath? Yet the wrath of God is another thing of which we hear nothing from modern churchmen. By promoting the Five First Saturdays devotions, the Holy Father will marshal the Church's power to offer reparation for sin at this critical time in world history.

Fifth,
Reestablishment Throughout the Church of Devotion to *the* Immaculate Heart of Mary

The shameful attempt in *TMF* to equate the one and only Immaculate Heart to the heart of anyone who repents of his sins is only typical of the new orientation, which abhors the concept of Original Sin as much as it does hell and damnation. As Pope, the former Cardinal Ratzinger has evidently repudiated the theological revisionism of *TMF*, having declared, as we have shown in Chapter 9, that

> The heart that resembles that of Christ more than any other is without a doubt the Heart of Mary, His Immaculate Mother, and for this very reason the liturgy holds Them up together for our veneration.

Among all human persons, only the Immaculate Heart of Mary was preserved free from all stain of Original Sin and was never under the dominion of Satan. In contemplating the one and only sinless Immaculate Heart of Mary, we are drawn by the beautiful sweetness of our heavenly Mother. At Rianjo it is Jesus Himself who urges us to often pray "Sweet Heart of Mary ..." Reflecting on Her goodness, holiness and kindness inspires us with hope in Her merits and intercession as we become ever more aware of our own wretchedness. In all this we see the need of all men for Baptism and the other sacraments of the Church to preserve each of us in a state of grace.

The uniquely Catholic devotion to the Immaculate Heart of Mary is a rebuke of the new orientation of the Church, whose "ecumenism" downplays the dogma of the Immaculate Conception (and the Assumption) out of human respect for the sensibilities (which are based on prejudices and ignorance) of non-Catholics. That is precisely why, as Our Lady of Fatima told us, God wishes to establish *in the world* devotion to Her Immaculate Heart. God wishes the world to see that devotion to Mary is necessary for salvation, as St. Alphonsus proved in his book *The Glories of Mary*. And also to see that it is the Catholic Church, and none other, which is the ark of salvation. Pope Benedict's own words show that he will be sympathetic to our petition in this regard.

Sixth,
The Removal of Prelates from Office as Necessary to Secure Obedience to the Message of Fatima

As we have proven, the identified Vatican prelates—first and foremost, Cardinal Bertone—have combined and conspired to do away with the full Message of Fatima in its traditional Catholic sense. They have tampered with the meaning of the very words of the Mother of God, buried in silence and obscuration much, if not all, of the explicitly Catholic and prophetic elements of the Message, and persecuted those who have offered a principled opposition to their revisionist program, their Party Line on Fatima. By so doing, they have already caused untold damage to the Church and have exposed both the Church and the world to the gravest possible dangers, including the loss of millions of souls and the annihilation of various nations foretold by Our Lady of Fatima as the consequence of failing to heed Her requests. Her dire warning bears repeating yet again: "*If* My requests are not granted, Russia will spread her errors throughout the world raising up wars and persecutions against the Church, the good will be martyred, the Holy Father will have much to suffer, and various nations will be annihilated." She also promised: "*If* My requests are granted, many souls will be saved and there will be peace."

The continuing course of conduct we have traced in this book, in which Cardinal Bertone and his collaborators obstinately persist, imminently threatens the Church and the world with incalculable harm. We have every right to petition the Pope for the removal from office of the prelates responsible for "revising" the Message of Fatima and concealing a portion of the Third Secret of Fatima, not excluding the Vatican Secretary of State himself. Some will object, however, that it is the height of arrogance for mere members of the laity to petition the Pope for the removal of any high-ranking prelate. On the contrary, *it is our duty as Catholics* to do so, no matter what the rank of the prelates in question.

Further, even though the offending prelates identified by name in this book have, with the exception of Cardinal Bertone, moved on to retirement or other offices in the Church and no longer appear to have an active role in the course of conduct at issue, what we have shown here applies with equal force to any member of the Vatican apparatus now collaborating with the Secretary of State, or indeed any member of the hierarchy at all who continues to serve the Secretary of State's Party Line on Fatima.

The Example of St. John Gualberto

No less than a canonized saint of the Catholic Church gives us the example to follow when the faithful are confronted with a wayward prelate who is harming the Church.[502]

St. John Gualberto lived in the 11th Century. He is not only a saint but founder of the Val Ambrosian Benedictines. His feast day is July 12 in the old calendar. St. John's heroic Christian virtue is demonstrated by his having forgiven the murderer of his own brother. Encountering the weaponless and defenseless killer in a blind alley, St. John (who was not yet a monk) was moved to forgiveness when the man put up his arms in the form of a cross and asked for mercy for the sake of Christ crucified. St. John forgave the man even though he had been searching for him with a band of soldiers in order to exact vengeance. That very day, which was Good Friday, St. John saw the image of Christ

---

[502] See Coralie Graham, "Divine Intervention", *The Fatima Crusader*, Issue 70, Spring 2002, pp. 8ff.

on a crucifix come alive and nod His head toward St. John. At this moment, Our Lord imparted to St. John an absolutely extraordinary special grace, because he had forgiven his own brother's murderer. It was that moment of grace which led St. John to become a monk.

Now, as we can see, St. John Gualberto was the very model of Christian forgiveness. If he could forgive his brother's own murderer, he could forgive any offense. He was also a man of considerable importance in the hierarchy of the Church, having gone on to found a monastery and an order of monks that still exists to this day. The order had—and still has—charge of a church in Rome, the Church of St. Praxedes, wherein nothing less than the column at which Christ was scourged is to be found. The church, literally just around the corner from St. Mary Major, also contains a painting of St. John Gualberto forgiving his brother's murderer—clearly, a very significant event in Church history.

Yet despite his exemplary Christian mercy and forgiveness and his great stature in the Church, St. John Gualberto did not hesitate to seek the removal of a corrupt prelate of his own day. St. John went to the Lateran (where the Pope resided in those days before the creation of the Vatican enclave) to ask that the Archbishop of Florence be removed because he was unworthy of his office. The grounds for St. John's petition were that the Archbishop had paid money to certain persons of influence in order to have himself appointed Archbishop. That is, he had purchased his ecclesiastical office, which constitutes a grave sin of simony.

After the Pope's officials in the Lateran—including no less than St. Peter Damian—would take no action to remove the Archbishop, citing a supposed lack of proof, God gave St. John a special inspiration: In order to demonstrate that St. John was telling the truth about the Archbishop, God would give a sign. One of the brothers in St. John's order, Blessed Brother Peter, surnamed Igneus, would walk through a bonfire from which he would emerge miraculously unscathed, to testify to the truth of St. John's accusation against the Archbishop. St. John called all the townspeople together and told them to construct a huge bonfire with a narrow passage in the middle. He explained to them what was about to happen and why. Then Brother Peter, under holy obedience, walked through the narrow, fiery passage and emerged at the other end without injury. For his own great faith, Brother Peter was beatified (his feast day is on February 8 in the Roman Martyrology). When the lay faithful saw this miraculous sign, they arose as one and literally drove the Archbishop out of Florence. The Archbishop had to flee for his life, and the Pope had to appoint an honest replacement.

The Removal of Wayward Prelates in Our Own Time

What does this event in Church history tell us about our own situation today? It teaches us that the laity have the right and the duty to protect themselves from wayward prelates who are harming the Church and souls by their misconduct. And in this time of unparalleled crisis in the Church, we are hardly alone in seeking this extraordinary remedy from the Pope.

Consider that in March of 2002 Pope John Paul II received a canonical petition from various members of the faithful in the Archdiocese of San Antonio, seeking the removal of Archbishop Flores from his office on grounds that he had covered up criminal acts of sexual abuse by homosexual priests under his charge and paid millions of dollars in "hush money" to silence the victims of these predators. The petition to the Pope charged that Archbishop Flores had "been grossly negligent in the exercise of his episcopal office, has failed to protect the temporal goods of the archdiocese, and has *endangered the faith of* the people entrusted to his care by allowing sexual predators within the clergy free rein."[503]

In like manner, thousands of members of the faithful called for the resignation of Cardinal Law of the Archdiocese of Boston because of his complicity in shielding dozens of homosexual predators from exposure and punishment.[504] *And he did resign.* Would anyone accuse the faithful of the Archdiocese of San Antonio or the Archdiocese of Boston of arrogance for exercising their canonical and God-given right to seek the removal of prelates whose acts and omissions have caused so much damage to the Church and to countless innocent victims?

By what peculiar standard of justice, then, are prelates who happen to work in the Vatican apparatus exempt from accountability to the Pope for their actions? Clearly, they are not exempt. And while the sexual abuse of members of the flock by their very pastors is among the gravest of scandals—justifying a movement of the laity against the priests who commit these unspeakable acts and the bishops, and even Cardinals, who shield the offenders—there is a scandal even greater than this. We mean the scandal of spurning the very prescriptions which the Mother of God Herself gave to the Church at Fatima—prescriptions which, had they been followed, would have prevented not only the sexual scandal now racking the Church but indeed the entire ecclesial and world crisis we now see. We mean also the scandal of a Vatican apparatus that does nothing to combat the true enemies of the Church in Her very midst, while it persecutes faithful traditional clergy for the "offense" of being too staunchly Catholic for the "ecclesial reality of today"—to recall once again the telltale phrase of Cardinal Castrillón Hoyos. For no other reason than to prevent the collapse of faith and discipline which we now witness did Our Lady come to Fatima. Yet it is precisely the

---

[503] "Abuse Victims File Petition Seeking Removal of Archbishop", *The Wanderer*, April 4, 2002.

[504] "Internal church documents showed that from the mid-1980's and into the 90's Cardinal Law and his top aides were aware of the problems of Father Geoghan, who was eventually accused of molesting more than 130 children over 30 years. In February, he was sentenced to 9 to 10 years in prison for fondling a 10-year-old boy. After the Church's role [that is, the Boston Archdiocese officials' role] in protecting Father Geoghan became known, the Cardinal gave local prosecutors the names of more than 80 priests accused of sexual abuse over decades." Quoted from "As Scandal Keeps Growing, Church and Its Faithful Reel", *New York Times*, March 17, 2002.

Message of Fatima which the opponents of Our Lady have devoted so much time and effort to burying, while they do virtually nothing about the ecclesial crisis that is raging all around them.

The example of St. John Gualberto teaches us also that when God gives a sign through a chosen messenger, the laity are entitled to rely upon that sign, even if the highest prelates in the Church choose to ignore it. Such is the case with the Message of Fatima, for there could be no greater sign from Heaven than the Miracle of the Sun. The Message of Fatima clearly involves a warning of apostasy and malfeasance among the members of the upper hierarchy, as well as the fall of many consecrated souls from their stations. We are witnessing the fulfillment of that prophecy at this very moment. We are entitled to rely upon the sign of Heaven that authenticates that prophecy beyond all reasonable doubt, no matter what the Message of Fatima's "debunkers" in the Vatican may claim.

Knowing what Heaven has told us at Fatima, it is our duty as members of the Church to try to convince the Pope to remove the errant advisors who surround him and to follow instead the advice of the Mother of God at Fatima. We must plead with the Pope to perform the Consecration of Russia to the Immaculate Heart exactly in the manner She requested, *without alteration by any worldly-wise member of the Vatican apparatus*. Further, we should ask the Pope to remove from office, if necessary, any prelate in the Vatican who attempts to prevent the Pope from carrying out the Virgin's requests.

Likewise, we must petition the Pope to remove from office those who have conspired to prevent full disclosure of the Third Secret of Fatima. The Third Secret is obviously of the utmost importance in understanding and combating the crisis in the Church, while protecting ourselves from its devastating spiritual effects—of which the unspeakable crimes committed by so many priests are but one manifestation. *The faithful are entitled to know what Heaven itself wishes them to know for their own spiritual safety.* The coordinated actions of those who prevent full disclosure of the Third Secret are grave offenses against the Church and the Blessed Virgin Mary and thus are crimes against Almighty God Himself.

The Church's Urgent Need for Militant Prelates

Today the Church needs more than ever true soldiers of the Church—men possessed of an unabashed Catholic militancy, who are not afraid of a confrontation with the forces of the world which invaded the Church while those who should have been the Church's guardians, including prelates in the Vatican itself, did (and do) nothing or even encouraged the invasion. The Church needs men who will act decisively to root out the pandemic heresy and scandal in the Church, instead of hounding and oppressing traditional Catholic clergy who decline to be "inserted" into what Cardinal Castrillón Hoyos called "the ecclesial reality of today." The Church needs men to stand up for the truth and the rights of God and of the Church in all charity and zeal; in short, the Church needs spiritual warriors, not practitioners of "dialogue", "ecumenism" and *Ostpolitik*.

The Message of Fatima itself is a call to spiritual warfare—to a battle that is to culminate in the consecration and conversion of Russia and the *triumph* of the Immaculate Heart of Mary. The identified Vatican prelates regard such things with the squeamishness of those who seem to think themselves more enlightened than all the generations of Catholic Saints, Doctors, martyrs and Popes whose militancy down through the centuries is a living testament to the very words of Christ Himself:

> "If the world hate you, know ye, that it has hated Me before you. If you had been of the world, the world would love its own: but because you are not of the world, but I have chosen you out of the world, therefore the world hates you." (Jn. 15:18-19)

> "Do not think that I came to send peace upon earth: I came not to send peace, but the sword. For I came to set a man at variance against his father, and the daughter against her mother, and the daughter-in-law against her mother-in-law. And a man's enemies shall be they of his own household." (Mt. 10:34-36)

For far too long the Church has suffered under the governance of those who would have us believe that there is no spiritual combat between Christ and His Church on the one hand, and the world on the other. For far too long these men have been allowed to pursue and promote a false "vision" of a Church reconciled to the world, rather than a world reconciled to the Church. For far too long these men have yoked the Church to the utopian notion of worldly peace among men of all religions or no religion at all, rather than the true peace that can come only when the souls of men are conquered by the grace of Christ the King, which He deigns to mediate to men through the Immaculate Heart of Mary and through the Holy Roman Catholic Church.

Fatima shows us the way to true peace in the world, "the peace of Christ in the Kingdom of Christ," as Pope Pius XI put it in his encyclical *Quas Primas*. Yet the men we name and many other contributors to the crisis in the Church have blocked our progress along that way, exposing the Church and the world to the risk of an ultimate calamity. If the victims of the scandal of sexual abuse by clergy have the right to seek the removal of the prelates whose negligence brought about the scandal, all the more are we entitled to seek that same remedy as to the prelates who have presided over the scandalous campaign to nullify the Message of Fatima. It is the men who have thwarted fulfillment of the Fatima Message, not ordinary Catholics, who are lacking in vision. It is they, not we, who are narrow-minded. It is they, not we, who are being unrealistic. They must step aside for the good of all humanity.

Chapter 18

What Can Be Done in the Meantime?

The Petition to the Pope set forth in the next and final chapter of this book is an important step in a program for obtaining the Church's obedience to the Message of Fatima and ending the crisis in the Church. But, of course, unless there be raised up a groundswell of many people, maybe even millions of people, speaking out as well as writing against the anti-Fatima forces in the Vatican, there is no guarantee that the men who surround the Pope will allow him to read any petition from the faithful. Nevertheless, in the meantime we must still deal with the crisis on our own. Until the Pope takes definitive actions to carry out the imperatives of the Fatima Message, we must deal with the crisis as best we can according to our stations in life. We recall here Cardinal Newman's description of the state of the Church during the Arian crisis:

> The body of bishops failed in their confession of the Faith. ... They spoke variously, one against another; there was nothing, after [the Council of] Nicea [325 A.D.], of firm, unvarying, consistent testimony, for nearly sixty years. There were untrustworthy Councils, unfaithful bishops; there was weakness, fear of consequences, misguidance, delusion, hallucination, *endless, hopeless, extending into nearly every corner of the Catholic Church.* The comparatively few who remained faithful were discredited and driven into exile; the rest were either *deceivers or deceived.*[505]

What, specifically, can Catholics do in this time of darkness for the Church, as we wait for those who lead Her to put Her back on the proper course? We must do whatever it is in our power to do, which includes at least the following:

Above All, Prayer

First and foremost, there is the power of prayer—and particularly the most efficacious prayer of the Holy Rosary. The importance of the Rosary and other forms of Catholic prayer in this struggle cannot be overemphasized. We are dealing with forces and circumstances that, humanly speaking, seem impossible to overcome. The Pope is surrounded by powerful men who have thus far successfully impeded fulfillment of the Message of Fatima. The Pope still has to contend with these men or like-minded successors in office, for the internal enemies of the Church are now legion.

How can we, simple members of the rank-and-file laity or clergy, hope to reverse the current course of events in the Church and the

---

[505] John Henry Newman, *On Consulting the Faithful in Matters of Doctrine*, p. 77.

world? How can we secure the Consecration of Russia when so many of the high and powerful are so opposed to it? Humanly speaking, we cannot. But with the power of the Holy Rosary, we can. Is this not indeed why Our Lady of Fatima, with our present circumstances clearly in view, called for daily recitation of the Rosary? As Our Lady, speaking of Herself in the third person, declared: "Only Our Lady of the Rosary can help you!"

First of all, then, *pray the Rosary* for the intention of Our Lady's final triumph over the crisis in the Church and the world through fulfillment of Her requests at Fatima, and urge your friends, relatives and neighbors to pray for the same intention. If ten percent of the world's Catholics prayed the Rosary daily for this precise intention, the battle would be won. History records that ten percent of the population of Austria, by mounting a Rosary Crusade, brought about the miraculous and otherwise inexplicable withdrawal of an invading Soviet army after the end of World War II. Therefore, begin right now to organize a Rosary Crusade among your friends and relatives and in your parish—a Rosary Crusade for the Consecration of Russia and the Triumph of the Immaculate Heart of Mary.

In addition to the powerful prayer of the Rosary, Catholics must perform other spiritual works, including the Sacred Heart devotions (the Nine First Fridays, having sacred images of Jesus in our homes, and making frequent visits to the Blessed Sacrament) and, of course, the Five First Saturdays devotions prescribed by Our Lady of Fatima Herself. By these means we address spiritually the many sacrileges and outrages committed against Our Lord, particularly Our Lord in the Blessed Sacrament, Who has been abused innumerable times by the sacrilege of Communion in the hand which is a part of the current crisis of faith and discipline in the Church. By making reparation in this way, we will hasten the coming of the Triumph of the Immaculate Heart.

Catholics must also have recourse to the sacramentals of the Church by which we can gain spiritual favors for ourselves and others. These include the Brown and Green Scapulars, bestowed by Heaven itself, which are all but forgotten in this time of diabolical disorientation in the Church.

Finally, of course, each of us must strive to live a holy life with prayer, penance, sacrifices and through frequent reception of the great Sacraments of the Holy Catholic Church, whose grace arms us for the battles ahead and keeps us from the pitfalls which have claimed so many others in this crisis.

In short, through prayer (especially the Rosary) and the sacramental life, we must do everything we can to become more fervent in the faith and to make others more fervent as well. For this struggle is, first and foremost, a spiritual combat in which every soul is needed, and every soul is at risk.

We Must Also Work (*Ora et Labora*)

Naturally, Catholics must back up their prayer with good works. As St. Ignatius said, we must pray as though everything depends on God and work as though everything depends on us. What are some of the things Catholics can do in their respective stations in life?

As simple members of the laity, we can—

- arm ourselves against the crisis by knowing our faith, and by informing ourselves about the Message of Fatima and what it really means;

- tell our fellow Catholics, and everyone else we meet, about the relation of the Message of Fatima to the crisis in the Church and the crisis in the world;

- provide by our lives an example of Christian faith and good morals;

- respectfully insist that local bishops and pastors of parishes provide sound Catholic doctrine and a sound liturgy, particularly the traditional Latin Mass in obedience to Pope Benedict XVI's *motu proprio Summorum Pontificum* of July 7, 2007, declaring that every priest in the Church is free to celebrate the traditional Latin liturgy, and that the faithful who request it have a right to it, no matter what a given bishop may think;

- *withhold financial support* from parishes and dioceses where doctrinal and moral corruption and liturgical abuse are allowed to fester—an action that many Catholics have already taken in response to the sexual scandals now afflicting the priesthood;

- *call for the removal* of morally and doctrinally corrupt priests and bishops, in keeping with our God-given right to petition Church authorities, including the Pope, for redress of grievances in the Church;

- pray and get others to pray—especially the Rosary, which can conquer all heresies and other threats to the Church;

- pray and offer sacrifices for the Holy Father, as Jesus urged Sister Lucy to do, that the Pope might be moved to vanquish the enemies of the Church and to fulfill the requests of Our Lady of Fatima.

As priests and religious, we can—

- preach and defend the traditional Roman Catholic Faith;

- make known to everyone the Message of Fatima and what it requires of the Church;

- provide by our lives an example of Christian faith and good morals;

- call upon our superiors, including the Pope, to honor the Message of

Fatima and take other actions to end the moral and doctrinal crisis in the Church, including the rooting out of morally and spiritually corrupt leaders of whatever rank who are wolves among the sheep.

As Catholic journalists, authors and publishers, we can—

- write the truth about Fatima and make it as widely known as possible;

- write the truth about the current crisis in the Church, and its doctrinal, liturgical, disciplinary and practical causes, as we have discussed in this book;

- investigate, expose and condemn the conspiracy against Fatima;

- publish the truth about Fatima in whatever forums are available to us—as we have done with this book and as Antonio Socci has done with his book, for which (as we have seen) Pope Benedict himself expressed an appreciation to the author that confirms the right of the faithful to publish on the matter.

As Catholic lay people; political leaders; captains of industry, commerce and finance; diplomats; and military leaders, we can—

- implore the Pope to pursue *Heaven*'s plan for peace as given to us at Fatima, rather than the failed diplomacy and treaties of mere men, including Vatican bureaucrats such as Cardinal Sodano, former Secretary of State, and Cardinal Bertone, the current Secretary of State;

- support with our financial means those apostolates and apostolic initiatives which promote, advance and defend the authentic and complete Fatima Message;

- use our influence to prevail upon members of the hierarchy to cooperate in carrying out the imperatives of the Fatima Message for the good of the whole world.

There is Still Time to Avert Disaster

No less than Pope Saint Gregory the Great declared:

> "It is better that scandal arise than that the truth be suppressed."

Whatever our station in life, each of us is a member of the Church militant, a soldier of Christ. As such, each of us has a duty to defend the Church according to his ability. As Pope Saint Felix III declared:

> "Not to oppose error is to approve it, and not to defend truth is to suppress it, and indeed to neglect to confound evil men, when we can do it, is no less a sin than to encourage them."

It should be obvious to any Catholic that time is fast running out for much of the present generation of leaders and laypeople in the Church and for civilization at large. As Saint Paul warned us, God will not be mocked. If salvation history teaches us anything, it teaches that when men rebel against God on the massive scale such as we are now witnessing, then the world will be swiftly and terribly punished with a divine chastisement. The Message of Fatima is nothing if not a warning that such a chastisement is imminent in our time if man does not turn away from sin.

The Virgin of Fatima offered us the means to avoid that chastisement, yet we find that many men of the Church—both clergy and laypeople—have spurned the heavenly offer. Even bishops and Cardinals do so. Like the Kings of France, who spurned Our Lord's simple command for the consecration of that nation to His Sacred Heart, the men who control the Vatican apparatus today have charted a course toward disaster—a disaster vastly greater than the one that befell France.

But there is still time to change course. It is the supreme urgency of our situation that has moved us to write this book and to describe the partisans against Fatima, their tactics, their errors and what you can do, *what you must do* to oppose their schemes. We have presented our case to you, not to engage in provocation for its own sake, and not merely for the justice of this cause, but also as *an act of mercy*—mercy not only for the victims of the great crime against Fatima but also for those who are owed in charity an opportunity to be confronted with the magnitude of what they have done so that they might change their course and begin to make amends before it is too late for them—and for us. To recall the teaching of Saint Thomas mentioned in the previous chapter, "when a man reproves his prelate charitably, it does not follow that he thinks himself any better, but merely that he offers his help to one who, 'being in the higher position among you, *is therefore in greater danger*' as Saint Augustine observes..."

The acts and omissions of Vatican prelates and their collaborators have jeopardized the temporal safety of the Church and the world, and the eternal safety of countless souls. How can we remain silent in the face of this danger? To remain silent is to cooperate in objective sins against the Church and humanity, whatever the intentions of the persons responsible.

We Ask For Your Verdict

We believe the evidence we have presented imposes a duty that cannot be ignored by Catholics of good will. It is no longer possible to remain neutral at this critical point in the battle for the Church and the world. We have shown you the evidence, and it is overwhelming. Having seen the evidence, you must make a decision. As Sister Lucy said:

> [F]rom now on we must choose sides. Either we are for God or
> we are for the devil. There is no other possibility.

We pray that your decision will be to join us in this effort, however humble, to set right what has gone so terribly wrong. Over the seven years which have passed since the first edition of this book, you can see that tremendous progress—even a "breakthrough for Fatima"—has occurred. But we are still a long way from our goals: (1) full disclosure of the Third Secret and the vital warnings and other counsels it no doubt contains; and (2) the collegial Consecration of Russia, and the Triumph of the Immaculate Heart, which Socci rightly describes as a titanic victory over evil. He calls it "a radical change in the world, an overthrow of the mentality dominating modernity, probably following dramatic events for humanity," as prophesied in the Third Secret.[506]

What we said seven years ago remains true today: We ourselves are of little importance in the great drama of Fatima, but we labor in the cause of the One Who, by the will of God, stands at its very center. She cannot fail in what She promised, if only Her children, freed from the designs of erring men, will do what little She asked of them: "If My requests are granted, many souls will be saved and there will be peace. … In the end, My Immaculate Heart will triumph."

---

[506] Socci, *The Fourth Secret of Fatima*, English ed., p. 217; popular ed., p. 146; Italian ed., p. 227.

Chapter 19

Petition to the Supreme Pontiff

To His Holiness Pope Benedict XVI (and, if necessary, his successor):

We, being faithful members of the Holy Catholic Church, are compelled in conscience to submit this Petition to Your Holiness, who is the final judge of matters in controversy in the Church.

This Petition is an extraordinary action by Catholics who have no representative to intercede for them before Your Holiness in the midst of the unprecedented crisis of faith and discipline that has followed the Second Vatican Council.

This Petition is an exercise of our God-given right as baptized Catholics to make direct recourse to the Supreme Pontiff, without any intervening canonical procedures. (First Vatican Council - 1870 A.D., Dz. 1830, D.S. 3063; Second Council of Lyons - 1274 A.D., Dz. 466; 1983 Code of Canon Law, can. 212, can. 1417 § 1.)

The grounds for this Petition are contained in the study entitled *The Devil's Final Battle* (*DFB*). They are also to be found in the work by Antonio Socci, *The Fourth Secret of Fatima*, whose conclusions correspond to those of *DFB*. Your Holiness (who is acquainted with Mr. Socci, a renowned and respected Catholic) has personally thanked him for his book and "the sentiments which motivated it."

Having considered the evidence, we are persuaded to a moral certainty of the following things:

First, the Message of Fatima is a vital prophecy for our time, whose veracity has been placed beyond all doubt by the absolutely extraordinary circumstances of its revelation (including a public miracle witnessed by 70,000 people), its approval as authentic by competent Church authorities, its acceptance by and incorporation into the life of the Church, and by the very statements and actions of Pope John Paul II, including the institution of the Feast of Our Lady of Fatima on May 13 in the Church's liturgical calendar. As Pope, you yourself have vouched for the authenticity of the Fatima apparitions by declaring on the anniversary of the first apparition:

> "You promised the three children of Fatima that 'in the end, My Immaculate Heart will triumph.' May it be so!" (Prayer addressed to Our Lady by Benedict XVI in Bethlehem, May 13, 2009)

You have also declared, Holy Father, that the Message of Fatima is "the most prophetic message of the 20th Century" (at the National Shrine of Our Lady of Aparecida in Brazil, May 13, 2007).

Second, the Vatican Secretary of State and those who have collaborated with him have attempted to impose upon the Church an expedient "revision" of the Message of Fatima in order to adapt it to a supposed "new orientation" of the Church following the Second Vatican Council, a break with the past that contradicts Your Holiness's own call for a "hermeneutic of continuity" between the Council and all of Catholic Tradition. This "new orientation," which incessantly pursues "ecumenism," "dialogue" and Vatican diplomacy with worldly powers, would negate the specifically Catholic prophetic content of the Fatima apparitions: their warnings of imminent grave consequences for the lives and souls of many millions of people, for the Church and, in fact, for the whole world if the heavenly counsels, warnings and commands of the Message are not heeded.

The version of Fatima promoted by Cardinal Sodano *et al.* is incomplete, inexact and falsified. This "revised" Message of Fatima, with its specious "interpretation" of the Third Secret and Mary's call for the specific Consecration of Russia to Her Immaculate Heart, would bury the entire Fatima event in obscurantism and leave its intended recipients—every Catholic and indeed every member of the human race—in ignorance of its true meaning and thus in grave peril of the consequences it foretells with all the infallibility of the Virgin Mother of God. In particular, this "revision" of the Message of Fatima:

(a) Dispenses with the Consecration of Russia requested by Our Lady of Fatima and arbitrarily replaces it with a consecration of the world, from which any mention of Russia has been deliberately omitted for shallow political reasons.

(b) Erroneously represents—contrary to what Your Holiness himself declared on May 13, 2009—that the Triumph of the Immaculate Heart has already occurred with a mere regime change in Russia around 1991; even more offensively, that it means nothing more than the Virgin's *fiat* in agreeing to become the Mother of God 2,000 years ago.

(c) Asserts that the visional aspect of the Third Secret, which depicts the Pope and numerous members of the hierarchy being executed by a band of soldiers outside a half-ruined city, signifies nothing more than Pope John Paul II *escaping* death at the hands of a lone assassin in 1981, thereby lulling the faithful into a false sense of security in the face of the clearly apocalyptic scenario depicted in the vision, for which we have not been provided the words of the Virgin which undoubtedly explain the vision precisely to avoid such false interpretations.

(d) Concludes (based on these false interpretations) that the events depicted in the Third Secret, and thus the Message of Fatima as a whole, "belong to the past."

Third, the "new orientation" represents the substantial attainment of the openly professed goal of the Church's worst enemies, as various Popes and prelates warned before the Council. That goal is to liberalize and "instrumentalize" the Church so that She will not only cease to resist effectively, but actually lend Herself to, the process of universal secularization and apostasy that has destroyed much of former Christendom and now threatens to subjugate the whole world to a universal secular collective, in which the Church will cease to openly promote the Gospel of Jesus Christ, to have any effective public authority or influence for God's rights.

Fourth, the new orientation is partly the result of "the demolition of bastions" that Hans Urs von Balthasar promoted. Not surprisingly, this "demolition of bastions" has produced only confusion, loss of faith and discipline, and ruin to the commonwealth of the Church, of which the current worldwide sexual scandal among priests and bishops is only one of innumerable manifestations. As even Pope Paul VI was forced to admit shortly after the Council:

> The smoke of satan has entered into the Church. ... The opening to the world has become a veritable invasion of the Church by worldly thinking. We have perhaps been too weak and imprudent.

Fifth, lamenting the current condition of the Church, your predecessor, Pope John Paul II, spoke of a "silent apostasy" in his *Ecclesia in Europa*, while Your Holiness himself has declared that "in vast areas of the world the faith is in danger of dying out like a flame which no longer has fuel," and that after the Second Vatican Council "certain fundamental truths of the faith, such as sin, grace, theological life, and the last things, were not mentioned anymore," and that the Church now suffers from "a secularized ecclesial environment" and even what seems in many places to be a "desert without God."

Sixth, Cardinal Bertone and his collaborators, whose actions and omissions have been documented in *DFB* and in Antonio Socci's work, have sacrificed the Message of Fatima, with its explicitly Catholic prophetic content, to a new worldly, liberalized, ecumenical, pan-religious orientation for the Church, which they promote in the name of Vatican II. In keeping with the said "new orientation," Cardinal Bertone and his associates mentioned in *DFB* and in Socci's work have systematically prevented the Consecration of Russia to the Immaculate Heart of Mary, which they falsely portray as a needless "provocation" of the Russian Orthodox "Church".

Seventh, in an effort to maintain their false interpretation of the Message of Fatima, the identified Vatican prelates imposed an unjust regime of silence and secrecy upon the late Sister Lucy, while attempting to pressure her into embracing their interpretation. No objective party was allowed access to Sister Lucy in order to investigate alleged sudden "changes" in her unwavering testimony, for more than 60 years, that the Virgin of Fatima requested the Consecration of Russia *only*, not the world, precisely because God wished the world to know that it was the power of His grace, mediated through the Blessed Virgin, which had miraculously converted Russia to the Catholic Faith.

Further, nearly all of the 24 volumes of Fatima documents compiled by Father Alonso, which undoubtedly answer many questions about the Third Secret and the Message of Fatima as a whole, remain under lock and key 35 years after their being made ready for publication.

Eighth, in pursuit of their "management" of the Message of Fatima, the prelates in question, their collaborators and successors in office, acting under the auspices of the Secretary of State, have persecuted and attempted to ostracize from the community of the faithful Father Nicholas Gruner, who represents legitimate opposition to their attempt to do away with the Message of Fatima in its traditional Catholic sense. At the same time, very little, if anything, has been done to impose effective discipline upon the true enemies of the Church within Her structure, who (to recall the lamentations of Pope Paul VI) have opened the Church to the "smoke of satan" and the "invasion of the Church by worldly thinking."

Ninth, in an attempt to cover up their complicity in the ecclesial debacle that the "new orientation" and all its novelties have produced, the Vatican prelates who are identified in this book have fraudulently withheld from the Church and the world a text which appertains to the vision of the Third Secret. That text, as *DFB* and Socci's work conclude, in all likelihood contains the missing words of the Virgin following Her incomplete statement in the Fourth Memoir of Sister Lucy: "In Portugal the dogma of the faith will always be preserved etc."—words which we are convinced predict the current crisis in the Church and provide the means to avoid or end it.

Indeed, Holy Father, in 1931 the future Pope Pius XII predicted precisely the current situation in the Church in light of the Message of Fatima:

> I am worried by the Blessed Virgin's messages to Lucy of Fatima. This persistence of Mary about the dangers which menace the Church is a divine warning against the suicide of altering the Faith, in Her liturgy, Her theology and Her soul. ... A day will come when the civilized world will deny its God, when the Church will doubt as Peter doubted. She will be tempted to believe that man has become God. In our churches, Christians will search in vain for the red lamp where God awaits them. Like Mary Magdalene, weeping before the empty tomb, they will ask, "Where have they taken Him?"

Holy Father, what Pope Pius XII foresaw has happened! And given that Pius XII foresaw these developments in light of Fatima, they can only have been mentioned in the Third Secret since those portions of the Message of Fatima thus far disclosed say nothing about such events in the Church.

We also know, Holy Father, that Pope John Paul II alluded to the Third Secret in his sermon at Fatima on May 13, 2000, which warns the Church to beware of the tail of the dragon that drags down one-third of the stars of Heaven (commonly interpreted as one-third of the Cardinals, bishops and priests). As Socci concludes, and as we agree, it appears that John Paul II was constrained by his advisors to confine himself to this veiled reference to a hitherto undisclosed portion of the Third Secret, whose full disclosure his advisors had prevented him from making since he was so enfeebled by illness.

Tenth, following the publication of Socci's book in late 2006, the Catholic world has learned, through the widely publicized testimony of Archbishop Loris F. Capovilla, the still-living personal secretary of Pope John XXIII, that there was (and possibly still is) an envelope lodged in the papal apartments. This envelope he called the "Capovilla envelope," that contains a text pertaining to the Third Secret, and that on the outside of this envelope was written the Archbishop's name, the names of all those who had read its contents, and the dictation of Pope John expressing his demurral from any judgment on the text. When asked by a Fatima scholar if this meant that there are two different texts and two different envelopes comprising the entirety of the Third Secret, the Archbishop replied "Exactly so." This envelope has never been produced, even though the Secretary of State, who has led efforts to persuade the faithful that nothing has been hidden, now admits its existence.

Further, Holy Father, the Secretary of State, in an effort to defend his position, has appeared on Italian television in 2007 to reveal that Sister Lucy prepared two different envelopes pertaining to the Third Secret, and that she wrote on the outside of each of the envelopes an identical "express order of the Virgin" that the contents were not to be revealed before 1960. Yet, the Secretary of State had previously assured the public that Sister Lucy told him she never received any such order from the Virgin.

For this and many other reasons which would lengthen this Petition unduly, Holy Father, we are deeply grieved and saddened because so many of the faithful no longer trust the Vatican Secretary of State. This is because they are convinced that Cardinal Bertone personally, with others, is hiding a text of the Third Secret that contradicts his clearly untenable "interpretation" of the vision. We must agree with the conclusion of Antonio Socci, whose reputation, Catholic fidelity, and veracity are well known to Your Holiness:

> [T]hat there is a part of the Secret not revealed and considered unspeakable *is certain*. And today—having decided to deny its existence—the Vatican runs the risk of exposing itself to very heavy pressure and blackmail.

We also agree with Socci's conclusion that this suppressed text contains "the words of the Madonna [which] preannounce an apocalyptic crisis of the faith in the Church starting at the summit," and that it is probably "also an explanation of the vision... (revealed on June 26, 2000)."

Eleventh, a veritable conspiracy against the Message of Fatima has deprived the Church of the benefits of this authentic Message and prevented the Church from accomplishing what the Virgin of Fatima requested: the Consecration of Russia—by name—to the Immaculate Heart of Mary, the consequent conversion of Russia, the Triumph of the Immaculate Heart, the salvation of many souls, and peace in the world. ("If My requests are granted, many souls will be saved and there will be peace. … In the end, My Immaculate Heart will triumph. The Holy Father will consecrate Russia to Me, which will be converted, and a certain period of peace will be granted to the world.")

The direct result of the acts and omissions of the Secretary of State and the prelates collaborating with him is that the Church and the entire world have suffered the loss of untold temporal and spiritual benefits. These benefits are only faintly suggested by the miraculous transformation of Portugal following the public consecration of that nation to the Immaculate Heart of Mary in 1931. It was the Cardinal Patriarch of Portugal himself, together with Sister Lucy, who declared at that time that the benefits experienced by Portugal would spread throughout the world if only Russia were similarly consecrated.

Twelfth, whatever their subjective intentions may be, the prelates involved have committed what is, objectively speaking, an incalculable crime against the Church and humanity. Their subversion of the Message of Fatima exposes us all to the imminent threat of wars, famine, further persecutions of the Church, further suffering for Your Holiness and your successors, the annihilation of various nations, and the loss of countless souls—all of which Our Lady of Fatima warned would follow from a refusal to honor Her requests.

Therefore, we most respectfully but most urgently petition Your Holiness for the following relief:

> First, the immediate consecration of Russia, by name, to the Immaculate Heart of Mary, by Your Holiness together with all the world's bishops in a solemn public ceremony.

> Second, full disclosure of the Third Secret of Fatima, including the words of the Virgin that describe the vision published on June 26, 2000.

> Third, a lifting of the seal of secrecy imposed upon Sister Lucy's messages, letters, documents and recorded conversations, and the publication in their entirety of Father Alonso's 24 volumes of documents pertaining to the Message of Fatima, which have been suppressed since 1975.

> Fourth, an end to the persecution of Father Nicholas Gruner, a faithful priest who has followed his conscience in promoting the cause of Our Lady of Fatima.

Fifth, immediate Vatican intervention, through apostolic visitations, investigations, and prompt disciplinary measures, to (a) punish the guilty, rather than the innocent; (b) restore sound orthodoxy in the seminaries; (c) remove sexually deviant persons from the seminaries, monasteries, diocesan clergy and episcopacy; and (d) restore the many elements of Catholic tradition (including traditional seminary life and priestly formation) that have been abandoned in the pursuit of the "new orientation" of the Church since Vatican II, including the traditional Latin liturgy wherever the historic *motu proprio* issued by Your Holiness on July 7, 2007, *Summorum Pontificum*, is being ignored or defied.

Sixth, declare once and for all, with an exercise of your infallible Magisterium where necessary, that neither Vatican II nor any subsequent papal pronouncement has altered in any way what Catholics must believe and practice to keep the perennial and Apostolic Catholic Faith as affirmed by all the Popes and Councils before Vatican II.

Seventh, the widespread promotion by Your Holiness himself of the Five First Saturdays devotions and daily worldwide recitation of the Rosary for an end to the crisis in the Church and the world.

This is our Petition to Your Holiness from your spiritual children. As your children, we are asking you for bread, not a stone or a scorpion. (Luke 11:11-12) We petition Your Holiness with all the respect and reverence owed to your exalted office as Vicar of Christ, but with all the insistence our perilous situation demands. For the present suffering of the Church and the world are as nothing compared to what will ensue if there is no correction of the course charted by those who have despised the prophecies of Our Lady of Fatima.

Yours most respectfully and reverently,

Please send your signed petitions to the publisher at the address provided on page xxvi. The publisher will forward them to the Pope in Rome. You may also write the Pope directly, at benedictxvi@vatican.va. For extra copies of this petition, photocopy it or download it from our web site (http://www. devilsfinalbattle.com) or write the publisher.

Appendix I

Pope John Paul II Acknowledges Russia NOT Consecrated

On December 8th, 1983, Pope John Paul II wrote to all the bishops of the world, inviting them to join in with him on March 25, 1984, in consecrating the world to the Immaculate Heart of Mary. He included with his letter his prepared text of consecration. On March 25, 1984, the Pope, making the consecration before the statue of Our Lady of Fatima, departed from his prepared text to add the words highlighted above and translated below. As you can see they were reported in *L'Osservatore Romano*. The words he added at this point indicate clearly, that the Pope knew then that the consecration of the world done that day did not fulfill the requests of Our Lady of Fatima. After performing the consecration of the world proper, a few paragraphs above, the Pope added the highlighted words which translate: "Enlighten especially the peoples of which You Yourself are awaiting our consecration and confiding." This clearly shows he knew Our Lady is awaiting the Pope and bishops to consecrate certain peoples to Her, that is the peoples of Russia.

Reproduction of the March 26-27, 1984 issue of *L'Osservatore Romano*, with translation, enlarged, of Pope John Paul II's words. Opponents of the Consecration of Russia have, conveniently, from 1984 until this day, omitted to report that the Pope actually said, in effect, that he had not done the Consecration of Russia as requested by Our Lady of Fatima.

Appendix II

A Chronology of the Fatima Cover-up

A brief history of the interventions of Our Lady of Fatima to bring real peace to all mankind and the ongoing campaign to thwart, silence, falsify and obstruct Her message of peace, hope, joy and salvation.

The unprecedented terrorist attack on America on September 11, 2001, and the credible reports that Islamic terrorists have acquired nuclear bombs as well as biological and chemical weapons, brings immediately to mind Our Lady of Fatima's warning: (see insert about Fatima on pages 342-343) If Russia is not consecrated to Her Immaculate Heart "various nations will be annihilated," and that only by means of the Consecration of Russia can the world achieve true peace in our time.

More than ninety years after Our Lady of Fatima first appeared, Her request for the Consecration of Russia remains unfulfilled, and Her warning unheeded.

And yet, as the world moves ever closer to a final apocalyptic event, certain elements in the Vatican seem more determined than ever to consign the Message of Fatima to the past, while persecuting those who continue to proclaim it.

Only one day after the terrorist attack of September 11, 2001 claimed more than 3,000 lives and stunned the entire world—only one day!—the Vatican press office released a statement condemning Father Nicholas Gruner and his Fatima apostolate and declaring that no one should attend the apostolate's conference (scheduled for October 7-13, 2001) on *world peace* through the Fatima Message!

Are these Vatican officials more afraid of Fatima than world terrorism? Are they more concerned about a conference on Fatima in Rome than they are about the heresy and scandal which are wounding the Church throughout the world—on their watch? Clearly, these Vatican officials have lost all sense of proportion about the state of the world, and the state of the Church over which they preside.

Here we present key events in the long history of a great and terrible paradox: the efforts of a few men, acting within the Catholic Church itself, to suppress, revise and thwart the fulfillment of Heaven's plan for true peace in our time.

1925 - 1965

December 10, 1925 - The Blessed Virgin Mary fulfills Her promise to Lucy and returns in an apparition to Lucy in her convent cell and requested the Communion of Reparation of the Five First Saturdays. Our Lady said:

...announce in My name that I promise to assist at the moment of death, with all the graces necessary for salvation, all those who, on the First Saturday of five consecutive months shall confess, receive Holy Communion, recite five decades of the Rosary, and keep Me company for fifteen minutes while meditating on the fifteen mysteries of the Rosary, with the intention of making Reparation to Me.

At the same time, the Child Jesus accompanies the Blessed Virgin and pleads for us to make reparation to the Immaculate Heart of Mary. **June 13, 1929 -** Twelve years after Her original appearances at Fatima, and in fulfillment of Her promise at Fatima on July 13, 1917, Our Lady of Fatima appears most solemnly to Sister Lucy at Tuy, Spain. Our Lady stands on a cloud in the presence of God the Father and the Holy Ghost beside Her Divine Son Jesus, on the Cross, and says:

> The moment has come in which God asks the Holy Father to make, and to order that in union with him and at the same time, all the bishops of the world make the consecration of Russia to My Immaculate Heart, promising to convert it because of this day of prayer and worldwide reparation.

August 1931 - Our Lord Himself speaks to Sister Lucy. Concerning the Consecration of Russia, He tells her:

> Make it known to My ministers given that they follow the example of the King of France in delaying the execution of My command, like him they will follow him into misfortune.

January 21, 1935 - Sister Lucy writes to her confessor, Father Goncalves, in answer to his questions: "Regarding the matter of Russia, I think that it would please Our Lord very much if you worked to make the Holy Father comply with His wishes ... [You ask] if I think that you should insist with the bishop? I think that it would please Our Lord very much. If you should modify anything? I think that it should be exactly as Our Lord asked it ..."

May 1936 - Our Lord speaks again to Sister Lucy and tells her that the conversion of Russia will occur only when that nation is solemnly and publicly consecrated to the Immaculate Heart by the Pope together with all the bishops. As Sister Lucy reported in her letter of May 18, 1936:

> Intimately I have spoken to Our Lord about the subject, and not too long ago I asked Him why He would not convert Russia without the Holy Father making that consecration?

Then Our Lord said to her:

> *Because I want My whole Church to recognize that consecration as a triumph of the Immaculate Heart of Mary, so that it may extend its cult later on, and put the devotion to this Immaculate Heart beside the devotion to My Sacred Heart.*

On other occasions, Our Lady tells Sister Lucy that Russia was to be the instrument of world chastisement, unless beforehand the conversion of "that poor nation" was obtained. (See entry for December 26, 1957.)

October 31 and December 8, 1942 - Pope Pius XII, acting alone, consecrates the world, but not Russia, to the Immaculate Heart. A few weeks later Winston Churchill observes that "the hinges of fate" have turned, and the Allies begin winning most of their battles against Hitler's armies. In the spring of 1943, Our Lord tells Sister Lucy that world peace will not result from this consecration. He said that the war will be shortened because of the consecration of the world. World War II continues for another two years.

September 1943 - Sister Lucy is very ill. The Bishop of Fatima fears that she will die and take the Third Secret of Fatima (see insert on pages 342-343) with her to the grave. He suggests that she write it down and put it in a sealed envelope. She replies that such an initiative would be too much for her—but if the bishop would take responsibility by formally commanding her, then she would willingly obey.

October 1943 - After one month of prayer and reflection, the Bishop of Fatima, His Excellency José da Silva, gives Sister Lucy a formal, written order to write down the Third Secret. Sister Lucy tries to obey immediately, but for over two months is mysteriously unable to commit the Third Secret to paper.

January 2, 1944 - Our Lady again appears to Sister Lucy and bids her to write down the third part of the Secret entrusted to her at Fatima in July 1917, which will become known as simply the Third Secret of Fatima. The Virgin requests that the Third Secret be revealed to the world not later than 1960. When later asked why the Third Secret had to be revealed by 1960, Sister Lucy states: "Because the Blessed Virgin wishes it so," and "It [the Third Secret] will be clearer then."

January 9, 1944 - Sister Lucy writes to tell the Bishop of Fatima that after months of being unable to do so, and causing the bishop to wait so long, she was finally able to obey his command that she write down the Third Secret. The Bishop of Fatima is allowed to read the Secret immediately, but chooses not to.

June 17, 1944 - Sister Lucy will not allow anyone but a bishop to deliver to her bishop the one-page letter containing the words of Our Lady in the Third Secret. Up to this date it has not been given to the Bishop of Fatima. On this day a bishop visits near the Portuguese/Spanish border and Sister Lucy leaves her convent in Tuy, Spain to entrust the Secret to him. He in turn delivers it to Bishop José da Silva of Fatima on that same day.

July 15, 1946 - In answer to a question from Professor William T. Walsh, Sister Lucy points out that Our Lady *did not ask for the consecration of the world* (as was done by Pope Pius XII in 1942), but only and specifically RUSSIA. "If this is done," says Sister Lucy, Our Lady promises to "convert Russia and there will be peace."

May 1952 - Our Lady appears to Sister Lucy and says: "Make it known to the Holy Father that I am always awaiting the Consecration of Russia to My Immaculate Heart. Without the Consecration, Russia will not be able to convert, nor will the world have peace."

July 7, 1952 - Pope Pius XII consecrates Russia specifically, but he is not joined by all the Catholic bishops of the world because he did not ask them to participate, not having been advised that this was necessary. The war in Korea continues, and other wars follow.

September 2, 1952 - Father Schweigl interrogates Sister Lucy about the Third Secret at her convent in Coimbra, Portugal. He had been sent there by Pius XII on a special mission. On his return to the Russicum in Rome, Father Schweigl confides this to one of his colleagues: "I cannot reveal anything of what I learned at Fatima concerning the Third Secret, but I can say that it has two parts: *one concerns the Pope*. The other, logically— although I must say nothing—would have to be the continuation of the words: *In Portugal the dogma of the Faith will always be preserved.*"

The Message of Fatima
Our Only Hope Against Terrorism and War

The appearance and message of Our Lady of Fatima is a beacon of hope, joy and peace for our troubled world. Our obedience to the message is our only hope for world peace and freedom from terrorism as you will see below.

God worked the great Miracle of the Sun on October 13, 1917 as a certain proof that the entire message indeed is guaranteed authentic as coming from Him.

This prophetic message started during World War I when Pope Benedict XV—after three years of terrible suffering in the greatest war up to then—pleaded in great anguish with the Blessed Virgin in a very public prayer of May 5, 1917 to ask Her to show him and all humanity the way to peace. He knew and acknowledged that human efforts alone were not enough.

The most gracious Virgin replied eight days later by giving a message at Fatima which is "addressed to every human being", as Pope John Paul II said.

She gave this message through three shepherd children, Lucy, Jacinta and Francisco. Our Lady appeared once each month from May 13 to October 13. She returned to Sister Lucy—the sole surviving seer—on December 10, 1925 and June 13, 1929 to further explain and complete the requests for world peace (see the 1929 event in the chronology above).

Also on July 13, 1917 Our Lady confided a secret to Sister Lucy which was to be revealed later to the Pope and to all the faithful. This Secret contains the key to world peace. The Secret is divided into three parts. The first two parts were revealed by Sister Lucy in 1941. The third part was to be released later, as we shall see in this appendix.

Our Lady promised "If My requests are granted, many souls will be saved and there will be peace". But She pointed out the folly of ignoring Her message. She said, "If My requests are not granted … the good will be martyred, the Holy Father will have much to suffer and various nations will be annihilated."

Because God has been publicly insulted by the 1917 Russian revolution—that, as its most cherished public policy, sought to exclude God from Russia and conspired to use God's children in Russia to fight God and His followers everywhere—God, in the Fatima Message, insisted on a public act of reparation for this most grave crime against God Himself. On June 13, 1929 Our Lady of Fatima, in the presence of the Most Blessed Trinity, explained that God asked for the Consecration of Russia to the Immaculate Heart of Mary. (See June 13, 1929 and then the 1931, 1935 and 1936 events noted in the chronology above.)

It is this act which God insists upon as an Act of Reparation for the crime of state-imposed atheism, otherwise our sins will reap the consequences of the terrible apostasy, heresy, vices and sins engulfing the world. This act of obedience is our only hope of being delivered from war and terrorism and is our only hope for world peace—not because this act is so difficult but because it is so easy, and thus people will see that the resulting peace is entirely due to God and the intercession of the Blessed Virgin Mary.

God insists in the Fatima Message that it is only "by this means" that we will have peace and freedom from terrorism and war because God wants to establish in the world devotion to the Immaculate Heart of Mary in order to save many sinners from going to hell.

May 17, 1955 - Cardinal Ottaviani, head of the Vatican's Holy Office, is sent by Pius XII to the Convent in Coimbra to interrogate Sister Lucy concerning the contents of the Secret. Cardinal Ottaviani's interrogation will be followed by an order that the text of the Third Secret be transferred to the Vatican.

March 1957 - Just before its transfer to the Vatican, Bishop John Venancio holds up to a strong light the outer envelope of Bishop da Silva containing **one** inner envelope (sealed with wax) of Sister Lucy inside of which he sees the single page upon which is written the Third Secret. He carefully notes that the Secret is about 25 lines long and is written on *a single sheet of paper* with *3/4 centimeter margins* on both sides.

April 16, 1957 - The text of the Third Secret, sealed with wax in the original envelope and the outer envelope, is transferred to the Vatican. The text is placed in a safe in the papal apartments, as shown in a photograph in *Paris-Match* magazine.

December 26, 1957 - Father Fuentes interviews Sister Lucy. She tells him of many nations disappearing from the face of the earth and of many souls going to hell as a result of ignoring Our Lady's Fatima Message. As

Sister Lucy told Father Fuentes:

> Tell them, Father, that many times, the Most Holy Virgin told my cousins Francisco and Jacinta, as well as myself, that many nations will disappear from the face of the earth. She said that Russia will be the instrument of chastisement chosen by Heaven to punish the whole world if we do not beforehand obtain the conversion of that poor nation.

1958 - Father Fuentes publishes the interview with Sister Lucy with the Imprimatur of the Bishop of Fatima. It is read widely and no one questions its authenticity.

October 9, 1958 - Pope Pius XII dies.

July 2, 1959 - Father Fuentes' interview with Sister Lucy is suddenly denounced as fraudulent in an *anonymous* report from the bishop's chancery office in Coimbra. To this day, more than fifty years later, no official will take responsibility for this report.

August 17, 1959 - First text of the Third Secret is read by Pope John XXIII, who then instructs Archbishop Capovilla, his personal secretary, to write on the envelope "I leave it to others to comment or decide." This is known as the Capovilla envelope. This text contained difficult Portuguese dialect expressions, thus requiring that an Italian translation be prepared by a native Portuguese priest before the Pope could comprehend it. This Capovilla envelope is still hidden by Bertone.

November 10, 1959 - Meeting of Pope John XXIII with Bishop Venancio and Cardinal Cento (the former Vatican nuncio who brought the Secret to Rome in 1957). In a handwritten note John XXIII refers to Sister Lucy "who is now a good religious at Coimbra. The Holy Office will take care of everything to a good end." (See Ferrara, *The Secret Still Hidden*, p. 219.) Shortly after this, Sister Lucy is placed under an order of complete silence and not allowed to speak with almost any visitors.

February 8, 1960 - Despite Our Lady's express request to Sister Lucy, and repeated promises from the Bishop of Fatima and the Cardinal Patriarch of Lisbon, unknown persons in the Vatican *anonymously* announce that the Third Secret will not be revealed and will probably "remain, forever, under absolute seal." The announcement (through A.N.I. news agency) describes the text of the Third Secret as follows:

> It has just been stated, in very reliable Vatican circles, that it is most likely that *the letter* will never be opened, in which Sister Lucy wrote down *the words which Our Lady confided* as a secret to the three little shepherds in the Cova da Iria.

1960 - Sister Lucy is officially forbidden to speak about the Third Secret and can receive no visitors except close relatives and people she has known for a long time. Her own confessor of many years, Father Aparicio, returns from Brazil and is not allowed to see her.

1960 - Pope John XXIII reads a second text of the Third Secret, contained in another sealed envelope. Unlike the first text, which the Pope removed from its envelope on August 17, 1959 but could not read without the aid of a translator because of its difficult Portuguese, this text posed no difficulty for the Pope and he was able to comprehend it completely on his own reading. (Over the years since John XXIII's reading of the two texts, Archbishop Capovilla, the Pope's secretary, repeatedly affirmed, both orally and in writing, that the text read in 1959 contained difficult Portuguese dialect expressions for which the Pope required a translation.)

1961 - Despite being defended by the Cardinal Primate of Mexico and his own Archbishop, Pio Lopez, Father Fuentes is dismissed as Postulator of the Cause for Beatification of Jacinta and Francisco Marto on the basis of the anonymous July 2, 1959 Coimbra report.

October 1962 - Just before the opening of the Second Vatican Council, the Vatican agrees with Moscow that the Council will not condemn Soviet Russia or Communism in general, in exchange for which two Russian Orthodox observers would attend the Council, as desired by Pope John XXIII. This agreement launches the policy of *Ostpolitik*, which constrains the Vatican from opposing Communism by name as well as prevents it from condemning communist regimes which persecute Catholics. The new Vatican policy is in favor of "dialogue" and negotiations with the communists. This policy departs from the teaching of Popes Pius XII, Pius XI, Saint Pius X, Leo XIII and Blessed Pius IX on the duty of the Church to condemn and openly oppose Communism and to refrain from any collaboration with communists, who always exploit such collaboration to advance their war against Christ and His Church.

June 20, 1963 - Paul VI is elected Pope, within days he asks to see the Third Secret.

June 27, 1963 - In the afternoon, the Substitute Secretary of State telephones Archbishop Capovilla, personal secretary to Pope John XXIII, anxious to know where the Third Secret is kept. Capovilla tells him exactly where to find it in the papal apartment. Capovilla testifies to this fact in his certified note of May 17, 1967 (see pages XII-XIV in the photo section). He further testifies to this to Solideo Paolini in 2006 (see the July 2006 entry later in this Chronology). A text of the Third Secret is found and then read by Pope Paul VI.

June 28, 1963 - In the morning, Paul VI asks Archbishop Capovilla in person why Capovilla's name is on the envelope containing the Third Secret. He responds that John XXIII asked him to write a note regarding how the envelope arrived in John XXIII's hands with the names of all those to whom the Pope felt he should make it known. Paul VI then asks if John XXIII said anything else regarding the Third Secret. Capovilla responds, "No, nothing except what I wrote on the outer envelope: 'I leave it to others to comment or decide.'"

November 21, 1964 - Pope Paul VI, during the closing ceremonies of the third session of the Second Vatican Council, consecrates the world again. In keeping with *Ostpolitik*, there is no mention of Russia, lest the communists be offended. World peace remains elusive. The Vietnam War continues into the 1970's.

March 27, 1965 - Pope Paul VI reads the other text of the Third Secret. According to the official account (in *TMF*), Cardinal Bertone claims that Paul VI read the Third Secret for the first time on this date. However, Archbishop Capovilla testified in July 2006 to Solideo Paolini, as reported in *The Fourth Secret of Fatima* by Socci as well as in Capovilla's certified note of May 1967, that Paul VI read the Third Secret for the first time on June 27, 1963 (see above).

December 8, 1965 - The Second Vatican Council closes.

1966 - 1983

1966 - In the aftermath of Vatican II, the Bishop of Fatima, Bishop John Venancio, comes to understand the necessity and urgency of defending the authentic message of Our Lady against the perfidious attacks of the progressivists—all disciples of the modernist Jesuit, Father Dhanis. To defend the Message of Fatima against revisionists, in 1966 the bishop commissions a learned Claretian priest, Father Joaquin Alonso, to establish a complete critical history of the revelations of Fatima. Ten years later, Father Alonso will complete his work, entitled *Fatima Texts and Critical Studies*. The massive work presents at least 5,396 documents, ranging from the beginnings of the Fatima apparitions until 12 November 1974. His manuscripts were "very well prepared," according to the Abbé René Laurentin, who consults them himself.

November 15, 1966 - New revisions in the Code of Canon Law permit anyone in the Church to publish on Marian apparitions, including those at Fatima, without need of an imprimatur. Out of the one billion Catholics in the world, only Sister Lucy—the very person who received the Message of Fatima—was still forbidden to reveal the Fatima secret, even though Our Lady had expressed Her will that the Secret be revealed to the Church and the world no later than 1960. Sister Lucy remained under an order of silence until her death on February 13, 2005, unable to speak freely about Fatima without special permission from the Vatican, specifically from then Cardinal Ratzinger or Pope John Paul II.

1967 - Sister Lucy's Memoirs are published, in which she reveals Our Lady's 1929 request for the Consecration of Russia. A huge public campaign begins with the collection of thousands of signatures asking the Pope to consecrate Russia.

February 11, 1967 - At a press conference, Cardinal Ottaviani, who has read the Third Secret, reveals that the Secret is written on *a single sheet of paper*.

May 13, 1967 - Sister Lucy meets Paul VI in the open public square of Fatima during his visit there. In the presence of 1,000,000 pilgrims, she pleads to speak with the Pope. She weeps when the Pope rebuffs her and tells her "speak to your bishop." According to at least one Fatima expert, Sister Lucy pleaded with Pope Paul VI to release the Third Secret, but he refused.

1975 - After 10 years of studying the Fatima archives, Father Alonso declares, in public, that Father Fuentes' published 1957 interview of Sister Lucy was a true and accurate report of her statements concerning the content of the Message of Fatima.

1975 - Father Alonso's 24 volumes of 800 pages each are ready for publication. This monumental work on the Message of Fatima includes at least 5,396 documents. The presses are literally stopped by the new Bishop of Fatima, Monsignor do Amaral, preventing Father Alonso's ten years of research from reaching the public. Two of the twenty-four volumes will eventually be published (in 1992 and 1999, respectively), but only in a heavily-edited form.

October 16, 1978 - Pope John Paul II is elected. He reads the Third Secret within days of his election, according to a statement to Associated Press (in May 2000) by the Pope's spokesman, Joaquin Navarro-Valls. The statement by Navarro-Valls will be contradicted by Msgr. Bertone of the Congregation for the Doctrine of the Faith, who will claim in June 2000 that the Pope read the Third Secret on July 18, 1981 for the first time. John Paul II read the same text of the Secret which was placed in the safe in the papal apartments in 1957. The statements in which two different dates are provided for when three different Popes—John XXIII, Paul VI, and John Paul II—each read the Third Secret for the first time (as noted here and on pages 344-346 and in Chapter 14) clearly indicate the existence of two distinct texts comprising the Third Secret *in toto*.

1980 - In only three years, in an expanded campaign sponsored by Cardinal Josyf Slipyj, public petitions for the Consecration of Russia garner over 3 million signatures, which are received at the Vatican.

May 13, 1981 - Pope John Paul II is shot on the very anniversary of the first apparition of Our Lady of Fatima. The shots are fired at the same instant the Pope turns to look at a picture of Our Lady of Fatima pinned to a little girl's sweater. The bullets miss their mark. The Pope recognizes that Our Lady of Fatima intervened to save his life.

June 7, 1981 - The Pope consecrates the world, but not Russia, while still recovering from his wounds.

July 18, 1981 - According to Msgr. Bertone (who, as just noted, is contradicted by the Pope's spokesman, Joaquin Navarro-Valls, on this point), Pope John Paul II reads the Third Secret for the first time.

December 12, 1981 - Father Alonso dies. But before his death, he was able to publish a number of articles and short books on Fatima. Here are some of the most important conclusions of his research on the Third Secret:

> "In the period preceding the great triumph of the Immaculate Heart of Mary, terrible things are to happen. These form the content of the third part of the Secret. What are they? If 'in Portugal the dogma of the Faith will always be preserved,'... *it can be clearly deduced from this that in other parts of the Church these dogmas are going to become obscure or even lost altogether*" ...

"Thus it is quite possible that in this intermediate period which is in question [after 1960 and before the triumph of the Immaculate Heart of Mary], *the text [of the Third Secret] makes concrete references to the crisis of the Faith of the Church and to the negligence of the pastors themselves.*" Father Alonso speaks further of "internal struggles in the very bosom of the Church and of *grave pastoral negligence by the upper hierarchy,*" of "*deficiencies of the upper hierarchy of the Church*" ...

"Does the unpublished text speak of concrete circumstances? It is very possible that it speaks not only of a real crisis of the faith in the Church during this in-between period, but like the secret of La Salette, for example, there are more concrete references to the internal struggles of Catholics or to the fall of priests and religious. *Perhaps it even refers to the failures of the upper hierarchy of the Church*". "For that matter, none of this is foreign to other communications Sister Lucy has had on this subject."

Significantly, Sister Lucy never corrects these conclusions of Father Alonso, even though—within the limits posed by obedience—she had never hesitated to correct other statements by clerics and various authors concerning Fatima when they were in error. Father Alonso has access to the documents and to Sister Lucy herself. Thus, his testimony is of capital importance.

March 21, 1982 - Sister Lucy meets with the Papal Nuncio, another bishop and Dr. Lacerda and informs them of the requirements for a valid Consecration of Russia according to the request of Our Lady of Fatima. Sister Lucy's full message *is not transmitted to the Pope* by the Nuncio, who is told by the bishop who accompanied him not to mention the requirement that the world's bishops participate in the Consecration.

May 12, 1982 - On the eve of Pope John Paul II's visit to Fatima, *L'Osservatore Romano*—the Pope's own newspaper—publishes an article by Father Umberto Maria Pasquale, S.D.B. about one of his conversations with Sister Lucy and her subsequent letter to him on the subject of the Consecration of Russia. In this interview, Father Pasquale reveals to the world that Sister Lucy clearly and emphatically told him that Our Lady of Fatima *never asked for the consecration of the world* but only the consecration of Russia. Father Pasquale also publishes a photographically-reproduced copy of a handwritten note by Sister Lucy attesting to their conversation on this point.

Father Pasquale, a well-known Salesian priest, has known Sister Lucy since 1939. Up to 1982 he has received 157 letters from her. Here is his own testimony, as published in *L'Osservatore Romano*:

I wanted to clarify the question of the Consecration of Russia, in having recourse to the source. On August 5, 1978, in the Carmel of Coimbra, I had a lengthy interview with the seer of Fatima, Sister Lucy. At a certain moment I said to her: "Sister, I should like to ask you a question. If you cannot answer me, let it be! But if you can answer it, I would be most grateful to you, for you to clear up a point for me which does not appear clear to many people ... Has Our Lady ever spoken to you about the consecration of the world to Her Immaculate Heart?" - "No, Father Umberto! Never! At the Cova da Iria in 1917, Our Lady had promised: *I shall come to ask for the consecration of Russia ... to prevent the spreading of her errors throughout the world, wars among several nations, persecutions against the Church ...* In 1929, at Tuy, as She had promised, Our Lady came back to tell me that the moment had come to ask the Holy Father for the consecration of that country (Russia)"...

After this conversation, Father Pasquale, wishing to have a written declaration from Sister Lucy, had addressed this request to her: "Has Our Lady ever spoken to you about the consecration of the world to Her Immaculate Heart?" Father Pasquale then received a written response from Sister Lucy, dated April 13, 1980. A copy is reproduced below.

Here is the translation of Sister Lucy's handwritten note:

"Reverend Father Umberto,

"In replying to your question, I will clarify: Our Lady of Fatima, in Her request, referred only to the Consecration of Russia.

"In the letter which I wrote to the Holy Father Pius XII—at the direction of my confessor—I asked for the consecration of the world with explicit mention of Russia.

"Yours devotedly and in union of prayers. Coimbra, April 13, 1980 (signed) Sister Lucia"

May 12, 1982 - Sister Lucy writes a letter, allegedly "to the Holy Father". The Vatican document of June 26, 2000 will present a photographic reproduction of part of this handwritten letter and will claim that it was addressed to Pope John Paul II. However, a close comparison of the handwritten Portuguese text (a lesser portion is photographically reproduced below) with versions provided by the Vatican (English, Spanish, Italian, French and Portuguese) reveals that a crucial phrase, which proves that this letter could not have been written to the Pope, has been omitted from all 5 versions.

The corresponding text in the English version provided by the Vatican is photographically reproduced on the following page.

> *The third part of the secret is a symbolic revelation, referring to this part of the Message, conditioned by whether we accept or not what the Message itself asks of us: 'If my requests are heeded, Russia will be converted, and there will be peace; if not, she will spread her errors throughout the world, etc.'.*

In the above statement taken from Sister Lucy's letter, just referred to, the underlined text has been deliberately omitted from the Vatican's printed versions: "A terceira parte do segredo, **que tanto ansiais por conhecer**, e uma revelação simbolica ..." which translates to "The third part of the secret, **that you are so anxious to know**, is a symbolic revelation ..."

This omitted phrase (in bold text in the previous paragraph) states that the recipient is "so anxious to know [the Secret]" even though Pope John Paul II had already read the Third Secret—either in 1978, within days of becoming Pope (according to the papal press secretary, Dr. Joaquin Navarro-Valls) or on July 18, 1981 (according to then Msgr. Bertone). Since the Pope had already read the Third Secret by 1981, why would he be "so anxious to know" what it contained in 1982? Furthermore, how could Sister Lucy possibly state that the Pope was so anxious to know the Third Secret, when he could have obtained one text from the Holy Office building archives and the other more important text of the Third Secret from the desk in the papal apartment any time he wished?

The same letter states: "And if we have not yet seen the complete fulfillment of the final part of this prophecy, we are going towards it with great strides." Why would Sister Lucy tell Pope John Paul II in 1982 that the prophecy of the Third Secret was not yet fulfilled if the prophecy had already been fulfilled with the failed attempt on the Pope's life on May 13, 1981 (as the then-Cardinal Ratzinger and Msgr. [now Cardinal] Bertone will later claim on June 26, 2000)?

May 13, 1982 - John Paul II consecrates the world, but not Russia, at Fatima. The bishops of the world do not participate.

May 19, 1982 - In *L'Osservatore Romano*, the Holy Father explains why he did not specifically consecrate Russia, declaring that he had "tried to do everything possible in the concrete circumstances."

July/August 1982 - The Blue Army's *Soul Magazine* publishes an alleged interview with Sister Lucy in which she supposedly claims that the Consecration of Russia has been accomplished by the ceremony of May 13, 1982.

1982-83 - In private comments to friends and relatives, Sister Lucy repeatedly denies that the consecration has been done. When asked to say so publicly in early 1983, Sister Lucy tells Father Joseph de Sainte Marie that she must have "official permission from the Vatican" before she can make such a statement.

March 19, 1983 - At the Holy Father's request, Sister Lucy meets again with the Papal Nuncio, Archbishop Portalupi; Dr. Lacerda; and this time also with Father Messias Coelho. During this meeting Sister Lucy confirms that the Consecration of Russia was *not* done because Russia did not appear clearly as the object of consecration and the world's bishops did not participate. She explains that she could not say so publicly before because *she did not have the permission of the Vatican.*

May-October 1983 - Father Caillon and Father Gruner publish several articles exposing the July/August 1982 *Soul Magazine* interview as false.

1984

March 25, 1984 - The Holy Father at Rome, before 250,000 people, again consecrates the **world** to the Immaculate Heart of Mary. Immediately afterwards, Pope John Paul II departs from his prepared text and prays "Enlighten especially the peoples of which You Yourself are awaiting our consecration and confiding." The Pope thus publicly acknowledges that Our Lady of Fatima is *still awaiting* the Consecration of Russia (see photo of *L'Osservatore Romano* in Appendix I, page 338).

March 26, 1984 - The Pope's own newspaper, *L'Osservatore Romano*, reports the words set forth above, exactly as the Holy Father spoke them.

March 27, 1984 - The Italian Catholic bishops' newspaper *Avvenire* reports that the Holy Father, on March 25 at 4:00 in the afternoon, *three hours after* he consecrated the world, prays at St. Peter's, asking Our Lady to bless "those peoples for whom You Yourself *are awaiting* our act of consecration and entrusting," and thus again admits that the Consecration of Russia remains unfulfilled.

May 1984 - Fatima expert Father Messias Coelho, under a pen name, insists that the Consecration still has not been done (*Mensagem de Fatima*, Issue 158, May 1984). He will consistently maintain this position until the summer of 1989.

September 10, 1984 - Bishop Alberto Cosme do Amaral, the Bishop of Fatima, declares during a question and answer session in the *aula magna* of the Technical University of Vienna, Austria: "Its [the Third Secret's] content concerns only our faith ... The loss of faith of a continent is worse than the annihilation of a nation; and it is true that faith is continually diminishing in Europe". His remarks are published in the February 1985 issue of *Mensagem de Fatima* published by Father Messias Coelho.

November 11, 1984 - Cardinal Ratzinger gives an interview in *Jesus* magazine, a publication of the Pauline Sisters. The interview is entitled "Here is Why the Faith is in Crisis," and is published with the Cardinal's explicit permission. In the interview Cardinal Ratzinger states that the crisis of Faith is affecting the Church around the world. In this context, he reveals that he has read the Third Secret and that the Secret refers to **"dangers threatening the faith and the life of the Christian and therefore of the world."**

The Cardinal thus confirms Father Alonso's thesis that the Secret pertains to widespread apostasy in the Church. Cardinal Ratzinger says in the same interview that the Secret also refers to "the importance of the *Novissimi* [the Last Times / the Last Things]",[507] "the absolute importance of history", and that "If it is not made public—at least for the time being—it is in order to prevent religious prophecy from being mistaken for a quest for the sensational ..." The Cardinal further reveals that "the things contained in this 'Third Secret' correspond to what has been announced in Scripture and has been said again and again in many other Marian apparitions, first of all that of Fatima ..."

In the portion of the text of the interview shown in the photo below, the Cardinal says that the Third Secret contains "religious prophecy" which cannot be revealed "to prevent [its] being mistaken for a quest for the sensational". Yet on June 26, 2000, the same Cardinal Ratzinger says that the Third Secret refers only to events which had already happened

Photo of Original Italian Extract from *Jesus* Magazine

La Madonna come difesa della fede

«Perché occorre tornare a Maria»

Diamo qui, dunque, l'intervista come è stata approvata da S.E. Ratzinger ai primi di ottobre. [1984]

...*A una delle quattro sezioni della Congregazione spetta l'occuparsi di apparizioni mariane.* «Cardinal Ratzinger, lei ha letto il cosiddetto "terzo segreto di Fatima", quello inviato da suor Lucia a papa Giovanni che non volle rivelarlo e ordinò di depositarlo negli archivi?». «Sì, l'ho letto». «Perché non viene rivelato?». «Perché, stando al giudizio dei pontefici, non aggiunge nulla di diverso a quanto un cristiano deve sapere dalla rivelazione: una chiamata radicale alla conversione, l'assoluta serietà della storia, i pericoli che incombono sulla fede e la vita del cristiano e dunque del mondo. E poi, l'importanza dei Novissimi. Se non lo si pubblica – almeno per ora – è per evitare di far scambiare la profezia religiosa con il sensazionalismo. Ma i contenuti di quel "terzo segreto" corrispondono all'annuncio della Scrittura e sono ribaditi da molte altre apparizioni mariane, a cominciare da quella stessa di Fatima, nei suoi contenuti noti. Conversione, penitenza, sono condizioni essenziali alla salvezza»...

We give here a photographic reproduction of the actual typeset of the key part of Cardinal Ratzinger's interview as it has been approved by His Eminence in the first days of October and published in the November 11, 1984 issue of *Jesus* magazine, concerning the Third Secret. The original Italian text reported at left was photographically reproduced and published in *The Fatima Crusader*, Issue 37, Summer 1991. The English translation (appearing on the following page) together with a photographic reproduction of the original Italian text were published in *The Fatima Crusader*, Issue 18, October-December 1985 and in *The Fatima Crusader*, Issue 37, Summer 1991 (with a circulation of 500,000). *The Fatima Crusader*'s translation of Cardinal Ratzinger's warning that the Secret contains "the dangers threatening the faith and the life of the Christian, and therefore of the world", which is the heart of the Secret, has never been challenged by anyone.

---

[507] See footnote 89 in Chapter 4.

(culminating in the attempted assassination of the Pope in 1981) and contains no prophecy concerning the future. What has happened to make Cardinal Ratzinger change his prior testimony? Why does he suggest on June 26, 2000 that the Third Secret could be the result of Sister Lucy's imagination alone? Does he really believe in the Message of Fatima? If not, can his personal interpretation of the Message of Fatima be trusted?

1985 - 1988

June 1985 - The November 1984 interview in *Jesus* magazine is published in a book entitled *The Ratzinger Report*. Key references in the interview concerning the contents of the Third Secret have been mysteriously deleted from the book. The book is published in English, French, German and Italian and reaches over 1,000,000 copies in print. Although the revelations concerning the Third Secret have been censored, the book admits that the crisis of Faith which Father Alonso tells us is predicted in the Third Secret is already upon us, and that it encompasses the whole world.

September 1985 - In an interview in *Sol de Fatima* magazine (a publication of friends of the Spanish Blue Army), Sister Lucy affirms that the Consecration of Russia still has *not* been done because, yet again,

---

We give here, therefore, the interview as it has been approved by His Eminence Cardinal Ratzinger in the first days of October.

One of the four sections of the Congregation (for the Doctrine of the Faith) concerns itself with Marian apparitions;

"Cardinal Ratzinger, have you read what is called the Third Secret of Fatima: i.e., the one that Sister Lucia had sent to Pope John XXIII and which the latter did not wish to make known and consigned to the Vatican archives?" (In reply, Cardinal Ratzinger said:)

"Yes, I have read it," (which frank response provoked a further question:)

"Why has it not been revealed?" (To this the Cardinal gave the following most instructive reply:) "Because, according to the judgment of the Popes, it adds nothing (literally: 'nothing different') to what a Christian must know concerning what derives from Revelation: i.e., a radical call for conversion; the absolute importance of history; the dangers threatening the faith and the life of the Christian, and therefore (the life) of the world. And then the importance of the 'novissimi' (the last events at the end of time). If it is not made public – at least for the time being – it is in order to prevent religious prophecy from being mistaken for a quest for the sensational (literally: 'for sensationalism'). But the things contained in this 'Third Secret' correspond to what has been announced in Scripture and has been said again and again in many other Marian apparitions, first of all that of Fatima in what is already known of what its message contains. Conversion and penitence are the essential conditions for salvation."

Russia was not the clear object of the 1984 consecration and the world's episcopate did not participate.

1985 - Cardinal Gagnon, in an interview with Father Caillon, acknowledges the Consecration of Russia has still not been done.

1986 - Maria do Fetal publicly quotes Sister Lucy (her cousin) as saying that the Consecration of Russia still has not been done. Maria do Fetal will consistently maintain that Sister Lucy told her this until July 1989.

1986 - 1987 - Father Paul Leonard Kramer writes "The Plot to Silence Our Lady" (June 1986) and a sequel entitled "The (USA) Blue Army Leadership Has Followed a Deliberate Policy of Falsifying the Fatima Message" (April 1987). Both articles expose the bogus 1982 *Soul Magazine* interview and the USA Blue Army's subsequent disinformation about the Consecration requested by Our Lady.

July 20, 1987 - Interviewed quickly outside her convent while voting, Sister Lucy confirms to journalist Enrico Romero that the Consecration of Russia has not been done.

October 25, 1987 - In an audience with a dozen Catholic leaders, Cardinal Mayer publicly acknowledges that the Consecration has not been done according to Our Lady's specific request.

November 26, 1987 - In a private meeting, Cardinal Stickler confirms that the Consecration has not been done because the Pope lacks the support of the bishops. "They do not obey him," says Cardinal Stickler.

1988 - Cardinal Gagnon attacks Father Gruner for publishing the Caillon report of his 1985 statement that the Consecration has not yet been done. Cardinal Gagnon admits speaking to Father Caillon, and does not deny the truth of his report, but says it was not meant for publication.

1989 - 1990

1989 - More than 350 Roman Catholic bishops respond to a letter from Father Gruner, confirming their willingness to consecrate Russia with the Pope as requested by Our Lady at Fatima.

1989 - Since 1980, by conservative estimates, an additional 1,000,000 signatures have been received by the Vatican on petitions calling for the Pope and the bishops to consecrate *Russia* to the Immaculate Heart of Mary.

July 1989 - In the presence of three witnesses at the Hotel Solar da Marta in Fatima, Father Messias Coelho reveals that Sister Lucy has just received an anonymous "instruction" from unidentified persons in the Vatican bureaucracy. The "instruction" states that Sister Lucy and her fellow religious must now say that the Consecration of Russia was accomplished in the ceremony of March 25, 1984, even though Russia was never mentioned and the world's bishops did not participate.

After this development, various witnesses—including, it is claimed, Sister Lucy herself—begin to repudiate their own prior statements that the Consecration has not been done. These witnesses previously clearly stated that Russia could not possibly have been consecrated as requested in the Fatima Message because of the failure to mention Russia and the failure to obtain the participation of the world's bishops. Thus begins a process of "revising" Our Lady's request from the Consecration of Russia to the consecration of the world. At the same time, powerful forces from within the Vatican apparatus begin to target Father Gruner and his apostolate for suppression.

July 1989 - The Papal Nuncio to Portugal is replaced. In keeping with the anonymous "instruction" from within the Vatican bureaucracy, shortly afterwards Maria do Fetal suddenly reverses herself, contradicting all her prior statements to the effect that her cousin, Sister Lucy, did not think the Consecration had been accomplished; Maria do Fetal now claims that Sister Lucy believes the 1984 consecration of the world satisfied Our Lady of Fatima's request.

July 10, 1989 - Father Gruner respectfully replies to the new Bishop of Avellino's letter dated May 29, 1989 and points out that he has written permission to be in Canada from Bishop Pasquale Venezia, the previous Bishop of Avellino.

There is no explanation for why the letter has taken a month to reach Father Gruner. The letter reveals that the Cardinal Secretary of State has sent "worried signals" about Father Gruner's work in promoting the Message of Fatima, which work includes especially promoting the proper Consecration of Russia as requested by Our Lady of Fatima and requesting the full disclosure of the Third Secret.

The new bishop appears to be unaware that his predecessor gave Father Gruner permission to live outside the Diocese of Avellino while engaging in his Fatima Apostolate.

July 24, 1989 - Cardinal Innocenti writes to Father Gruner rebuking him for refusing an "invitation" to visit with the Papal Nuncio in Canada. The Nuncio has never issued any order that Father Gruner see him. Cardinal Innocenti threatens Father Gruner with possible suspension unless he is either incardinated in a Canadian diocese or returns to Avellino by September 30, 1989.

August 9, 1989 - An unsolicited offer of incardination is suddenly issued to Father Gruner by Bishop Fulton in Canada, but only on condition that Father Gruner cease his work in promoting the Message of Fatima. This offer to incardinate is apparently due to pressure applied to the Bishop of Avellino by the Cardinal Secretary of State, prompting the Bishop of Avellino to turn the matter over to Bishop Fulton.

August 21, 1989 - Father Gruner replies to Cardinal Innocenti's letter dated July 24, 1989 (which he did not receive until after August 14), pointing out that the Cardinal has no right to interfere since the Bishop of Avellino has given no orders of his own in the matter. Father Gruner points out that he is acting within the law of the Church. Father Gruner then appeals to the Pope against Cardinal Innocenti's abuse of authority. Thereafter, the Cardinal never replies or writes again to Father Gruner. The Cardinal orders everyone in his office never to mention Father

Gruner's name to him again.

September 1, 1989 - *The Fatima Crusader* points out the right of every priest to publish the truth about the Message of Fatima. Accordingly, Father Gruner's 10-page reply to Cardinal Innocenti is published in this issue of *The Fatima Crusader*.

Late August - Early September 1989 - The so-called "coup d'etat" in Moscow occurs, in which the Communist regime follows a script intended to deceive the West. This plan was partly written in 1958 and published in 1984 by KGB defector Anatoliy Golitsyn, who was at the planning session of 1958. His book *New Lies for Old* makes 148 predictions concerning the Russian Communists' plan for strategic deception of the West. By 1993, 139 of his predictions will have come true.

The plan revealed by Golitsyn would be well served by deceiving people who believe in Our Lady of Fatima into thinking that the merely political changes of 1989 are part of the triumph of the Immaculate Heart predicted by Our Lady. In fact the changes in Russia during the period 1989-2001 will demonstrate only a further perversion of Russian society, not Russia's conversion.

It is no mere coincidence that in 1989, the very year Russia's strategic deception begins, there also begins a coordinated campaign to suppress or revise the Message of Fatima, including moves to silence Father Gruner and his apostolate and the sudden appearance of computer-generated letters from Sister Lucy who does not type, nor does she use a computer, declaring that the Consecration of Russia has been accomplished by ceremonies which did not even *mention* Russia.

August 1989 - November 1989 - Computer-generated and typewritten notes and letters supposedly signed by Sister Lucy suddenly appear, flatly contradicting all prior statements she has made for more than 60 years about the Consecration. These notes contain factual errors Sister Lucy could not have made (e.g. the false statement that Pope Paul VI consecrated the world to the Immaculate Heart during his 1967 visit to Fatima) and phraseology she had never used before. Until now, "Sister Lucy" has never conducted correspondence with typewriters or word processors, and she still continues to write everything else, including her lengthy memoirs, by hand.

January 29, 1990 - At about 8:30 a.m., Maria do Fetal, at Fatima, states to Father Pierre Caillon that she "was inventing" when she earlier reported Sister Lucy's statement that the 1984 consecration of the world was not in conformity with Our Lady's request for the consecration of Russia.

October 11, 1990 - Sister Lucy's own blood sister, Carolina, tells Father Gruner, in Fatima, that little or no trust can be put in any typewritten letter from Sister Lucy, *as she does not even know how to type.*

October 22, 1990 - In a written report, a highly regarded forensic expert indicates that Sister Lucy's purported signature on a November 1989 computer-generated letter is a forgery. Excerpts from this letter, published by an Italian Catholic magazine in March 1990, are being circulated widely and cited as "proof" that the Consecration has been done. Several wire services carry that story from the Italian magazine and spread the fraudulent claim worldwide.

November 1990 - Father Gruner and The International Fatima Rosary Crusade launch a worldwide campaign to free Sister Lucy from her 30-year ordeal of silence and to encourage the Holy Father to release the Third Secret of Fatima.

1991 - 2002

May 13, 1991 - Sister Lucy declines to go to Fatima during the Pope's visit but is commanded to do so under holy obedience. Pope John Paul II visits Fatima for the second time, and has a half-hour meeting with Sister Lucy. After this meeting neither the Pope nor Sister Lucy make any announcement concerning the Consecration of Russia having been done—an announcement that would have been forthcoming had the "letters of Sister Lucy" from 1989-90 been genuine.

The silence of the Pope and Sister Lucy concerning the Consecration of Russia is most revealing. There is an obvious disagreement between Sister Lucy and a certain part of the Vatican apparatus, which has been trying to suggest that the consecration of Russia is over and done with. Although Sister Lucy is alleged to agree that the Consecration has been accomplished, she continues to be bound by the order to be silent, imposed upon her in 1960, and she does not defend herself publicly against this rumor because her enforced silence continues. Father Alonso's 24 volumes of at least 5,396 original Fatima documents are still banned from publication.

October 8, 1992 - *The Fatima Crusader's* Peace Conference is held in Fatima. False and misleading declarations are published in *L'Osservatore Romano* by Cardinal Sanchez and Archbishop Sepe, suggesting that ecclesiastical permission is required for the Conference when it is clearly not necessary under Church law. Similar falsehoods are published in the Portuguese press on October 7-9. Nevertheless, more than 100 bishops accept the invitation and payment of expenses for their trip to Fatima for the Conference. While 65 bishops ultimately attend, 35 others are "persuaded"—by the anti-Fatima establishment in Fatima itself as well as by certain officials of the Vatican Secretary of State—to not attend the Fatima Crusader conference. Some of the bishops are literally hijacked upon their arrival at the Lisbon airport. The Fatima Crusader apostolate displays a large welcoming kiosk in the arrival zone to receive the bishops and escort them to their hotel paid for by donors of the Fatima Crusader apostolate. But the anti-Fatima group whisks a number of the bishops, whose travel arrangements *The Fatima Crusader* had paid for, off to the shrine, falsely telling them that the Fatima Crusader conference had been cancelled.

October 10, 1992 - Father Gruner is beaten up by Fatima Shrine workers, one of whom later admits he was acting under orders of the Rector of the Shrine, Msgr. Guerra. Bishop Amaral, the Bishop of Fatima, is retired from office four months later, but Msgr. Guerra remains Rector of the Shrine until his retirement in 2008.

October 11, 1992 - A questionable interview of Sister Lucy is conducted by Father Pacheco, Cardinal Padiyara, Bishop Michaelappa and a chauffeur, Carlos Evaristo. Evaristo later publishes a doctored version of the interview, which he admits was "reconstructed." Among other falsehoods, the "interview" contains a statement by "Sister Lucy" that Mikhail Gorbachev knelt in front of the Holy Father and asked pardon for his sins. This claim is denounced as a total fabrication by papal spokesman Joaquin Navarro-Valls. Father Pacheco publishes a repudiation of the bogus "interview" within six months. Fatima scholar Frère François concludes that this "interview" was put together by the Rector of the Shrine in order to stop petitions for the Consecration of Russia. Today, Evaristo's totally discredited interview is no longer mentioned as "proof" of Sister Lucy's alleged affirmation that the Consecration has been done.

1992 - The first heavily-edited volume of Father Alonso's critical documents on Fatima is published, leaving 23 other volumes under lock and key.

July 31, 1993 - A prominent bishop in India gives written assurances that he is willing to incardinate Father Gruner, thus apparently ending any effort by the anti-Fatima establishment officials in the Vatican to force Father Gruner's return to Avellino, Italy.

November 3, 1993 - The Bishop of Avellino, Antonio Forte, admits to Father Gruner that he is being prevented from approving Father Gruner's transfer out of the Diocese of Avellino because Cardinal Sanchez and Archbishop Sepe, at the Vatican's Congregation for the Clergy, will not allow it. Cardinal Sanchez and Archbishop Sepe are working with the Secretariat of State to silence Father Gruner and his apostolate. Their actions violate the jurisdiction of the Bishop of Avellino and have no basis in canon law. No other priest in the entire Catholic Church is being subjected to such interference in transferring from one diocese to another.

January 13, 1994 - Bishop Forte tells Father Gruner that he has nothing against him, and when Father Gruner asks him what he should do, the bishop tells him to return to Canada.

January 14 - 31, 1994 - Cardinal Sanchez, Archbishop Sepe and Bishop Forte begin making the final moves in "the incardination game" they are playing against Father Gruner. They command him to find another bishop, then obstruct incardination by other bishops, while refusing him excardination from Avellino. The "checkmate" is to declare that since Father Gruner has "failed" to be incardinated elsewhere, he must now return to Avellino or else be suspended from the priesthood.

January 31, 1994 - Bishop Forte sends Father Gruner a letter accusing him of being a *vagus* (wandering) priest because he has not returned to Avellino from Canada—even though Bishop Forte himself *had just told Father Gruner to go back to Canada only 18 days earlier*. This incredible behavior is explained in *Fatima Priest*. It continues today, and is still being appealed in the Vatican tribunals and before the Pope.

October 1994 - The Secretary of State and the Papal Nuncios write to bishops around the world, directing them not to attend the second Fatima Crusader Peace Conference to be held in Mexico. Visas are denied and other obstacles put in the way of more than 100 Catholic bishops who accept invitations to the conference.

1995 - In a personal communication to a Professor Baumgartner in Salzburg, Austria, Cardinal Mario Luigi Ciappi, no less than the personal theologian of John Paul II (and of his predecessors since 1955), reveals that: "In the Third Secret it is foretold, among other things, that the great apostasy in the Church will begin at the top."

July 12, 1995 - The first *Open Letter* to the Pope is published in a leading daily Roman newspaper, *Il Messaggero*. It covers 2 full pages, publicly protesting the gross abuse of position, prestige and power by anti-Fatima Vatican bureaucrats during the period 1992-1994. It is signed by two bishops and thousands of priests and lay people. The Pope does not act (or is prevented from acting), although privately word is received that His Holiness did read the *Open Letter*.

November 1996 - The third Fatima Crusader Peace Conference is held in Rome. Again, all bishops are invited to attend, with all expenses paid. Despite the constant repetition of the same falsehoods circulated by certain members of the anti-Fatima establishment in the Vatican apparatus in 1992 and 1994—combined with pressure not to attend the conference applied by Cardinal Gantin, various Papal Nuncios and other Vatican bureaucrats—more than 200 bishops, priests and lay people do in fact attend.

November 20, 1996 - Father Gruner's Canonical Complaint against Cardinal Sanchez and Archbishop Sepe and their accomplices is placed in the Pope's own hands, as shown in a photograph reproduced in *Fatima Priest* and published April 2, 1998 in *Il Messaggero*.

February 26, 1997 - Coralie Graham, Editor of *The Fatima Crusader*, sends Cardinal Gantin a registered letter containing seven pertinent questions concerning his illegal actions in trying to prevent bishops and priests from attending the Peace Conference. More than ten years later her entirely respectful letter still has not been answered.

April 2, 1998 - The second two-page *Open Letter* is published. This time the *Open Letter* garners the signatures of 27 bishops and Archbishops, as well as 1,900 priests and religious and more than 15,000 lay people. It is published in Italian in *Il Messaggero*. Thousands of posters of the *Open Letter* are posted around the Vatican during 1998.

Meanwhile, Father Gruner's canonical case continues to wend its way through the Vatican court system. Details of the "rigged" and absurdly unjust proceedings are provided in *Fatima Priest*. During the process, Archbishop Grochelewski, now chief judge in the case (after Cardinal Agustoni is forced to recuse himself due to the appearance of prejudice), admits that the case is not about Father Gruner's incardination, but what he says (concerning Fatima). This is the real reason for the numerous unprecedented and illicit actions against Father Gruner, even though it is nowhere admitted in the written acts of the proceedings. A cardinal principle of natural justice is that the accused must be informed of the precise charges against him so that he can defend himself. To put Father Gruner on trial for an alleged "offense" concerning his incardination, when the real issue is what he says about Fatima, flies in the face of this principle.

October 1998 - The various lies, innuendoes and accusations against Father Gruner are summarized in a lengthy accusatory document prepared and issued by the Promoter of Justice, appointed by the Vatican apparatus to prepare a supposedly "impartial" summary of the canonical positions of the parties. Father Gruner is told he may not even have a copy of this "impartial" document unless he takes an oath to keep it secret. This bizarre request is issued by the Tribunal itself. **(A copy of the tribunal's demand for secrecy is available to any bishop who requests it.)** Father Gruner refuses to take this oath of secrecy. He is forced to review the Promoter's document in the presence of his canon lawyer, who must travel to Canada from Rome and then take the document back to Rome without leaving a copy.

October 10, 1998 - The Promoter's document reveals, for the first time, the existence of some 20 letters secretly circulating against Father Gruner and his apostolate. The letters are replete with misrepresentations and outright falsehoods by certain members of the Congregation for the Clergy, the Secretariat of State and even the Congregation for the Doctrine of the Faith, going back to the early 1980s.

December 10, 1998 - Despite the almost impossible obstacles and very limited time allowed for his reply, Father Gruner submits an 80-page canonical response to the Promoter's document, conclusively refuting its every allegation. The Promoter's document is never again mentioned by the Tribunal.

December 1998 - Father Gruner, by registered mail, requests copies of the approximately 20 letters against him from the Congregation for the Clergy and from the tribunal. The letters are never provided. Falsehoods continue to circulate behind Father Gruner's back, greatly hindering his efforts to persuade bishops that the Consecration of Russia must be done in the proper manner in order to avoid the annihilation of nations, of which Our Lady of Fatima warns.

August 1999 - Father Gruner provides a new document to the Bishop of Avellino that demonstrates that Father Gruner is incardinated elsewhere.

September 3, 1999 - The Apostolic Signatura issues a decision (not even noting the new document of August 1999), backdated to July 10, 1999. The manifest groundlessness of the decision is demonstrated in "A Law for One Man" (a chapter in *Fatima Priest*), and by documents attached to Father Gruner's rebuttal, dated October 14, 1999 (also reproduced in *Fatima Priest*, 2000 A.D. edition), to which the Apostolic Signatura offers no reply. Meanwhile, Father Gruner's third canon lawyer comes under pressure to turn against him. (The misconduct of the first two canonists is detailed in *Fatima Priest*.) Only 16 canonists are allowed to defend 400,000 Catholic priests in the Signatura, making it easy to pressure these lawyers with threats of the termination of their admission to the Tribunal.

October 12-18, 1999 - The apostolate's Peace Conference in Hamilton, Ontario is subjected to the same pattern of harassment, abuse of authority and calculated untruths **which have hindered the apostolate's previous Fatima conferences.** Bishops and priests attend, but in reduced numbers. It has become increasingly difficult to reach the priests and bishops because of the Vatican's campaign of blackening the reputation of Father Gruner and his apostolate. Over 300 people attend, most of them lay people.

November 22, 1999 - A second Canonical Complaint by Father Gruner is sent by registered mail to the Pope from the Vatican post office. This complaint names Cardinals Agustoni, Innocenti, and Sanchez, Archbishop Sepe, Archbishop Grochelewski and Bishop Forte.

December 1999 - The second volume of Father Alonso's manuscripts is finally published, but with extremely heavy editing. The other 22 volumes are still unpublished after 35 years (as of December 2009), even though they were fully prepared for the press in 1975.

April 20, 2000 - Father Gruner invokes Canon 1506, which requires the Pope to accept both canonical complaints against the named Cardinals and bishops. The complaints are deemed accepted under canon law, once the May 2000 deadline has passed. Pope John Paul II did not respond, although he was bound to do so by the law he himself promulgated. Even the Pope is bound by the prevailing law of the Church until such time as he promulgates a new law.

May 13, 2000 - During the ceremonies for the beatification of Jacinta and Francisco, Cardinal Sodano announces that the Third Secret of Fatima will be revealed. (The Secretariat of State had previously tried to divert the beatification ceremonies from Fatima to a group beatification ceremony at the Vatican, involving other beati unrelated to Fatima.)

Cardinal Sodano, however, gives a misleading description of the Third Secret, claiming that it consists of a vision in which "the Pope apparently falls dead". The actual text of the vision (to be revealed in the following month) states that the Pope is *killed*. Cardinal Sodano is clearly paving the way for a bogus "interpretation" of the Secret which will claim that the Third Secret culminated with the failed attempt on the Pope's life in 1981, and that all the events prophesied in the Secret, to use his words, "now belong to the past."

June 5, 2000 - A letter threatening Father Gruner with a totally groundless "excommunication" is signed by Cardinal Castrillón Hoyos. The letter is delivered to Father Gruner's home by a Vatican emissary on June 21 at 10:00 p.m. The emissary lies his way into Father Gruner's living room by claiming he has good news from "the Holy Father."

June 26, 2000 - At a press conference, the Vatican publishes a text it claims is the entire Third Secret. The text describes a vision in which the Pope (a "Bishop dressed in white") is *killed* by a band of soldiers who shoot him down while he is kneeling at the foot of a large wooden cross atop a hill, after having traversed a half-ruined city filled with corpses. The execution of the Pope is followed by the execution of many bishops, priests and laity.

Questions abound. (See Chapter 13 and the article by Andrew Cesanek in *The Fatima Crusader*, Issue No. 64.) Among these questions is why the published vision contains no words of Our Lady, even though, when it announced suppression of the Secret in 1960, the Vatican itself referred to "the words which Our Lady confided to the children as a secret." The vision fails to mention the words which clearly follow "In Portugal the dogma of the Faith will always be preserved etc."—the phrase Sister Lucy included in her fourth memoir as part of the integral text of the Third Secret of Fatima. The phrase concerning the dogma of the Faith in Portugal is mysteriously demoted to a footnote in the Vatican commentary on the Secret, where it is ignored by both Cardinal Ratzinger and Msgr. Bertone, the co-authors of the commentary.

Cardinal Ratzinger's portion of the commentary specifically states that he and Msgr. Bertone are following the "interpretation" given by Cardinal Sodano: i.e., that the Message of Fatima, and the Third Secret in particular, relates entirely to events which now belong to the past. Accordingly, Cardinal Ratzinger claims that the Pope's escape from death in 1981 is what is depicted in the vision of the Pope being *killed*. Even *the secular media recognize that this interpretation is obviously wrong.*

The published text of the vision contains *none* of the elements described by Cardinal Ratzinger in his mysteriously censored 1984 interview in *Jesus* magazine. The published vision says nothing about "dangers threatening the faith and the life of the Christian and therefore (the life) of the world", nothing about "the importance of the end times", nothing about what is contained "in many other Marian apparitions" approved by the Church and nothing about prophecies "announced in Scripture". Further, while Cardinal Ratzinger said in 1984 that the Third Secret contains "religious prophecy"—a statement he made three years *after* the attempt on the Pope's life—he now says there is no prophecy, but only a description of past events, culminating in the 1981 assassination attempt.

Further, the *TMF* commentary disturbs, disorients and divides the faithful by claiming that the triumph of the Immaculate Heart of Mary is nothing more than love conquering bombs and guns, and that devotion to the Immaculate Heart means nothing more than each person doing God's will and thus acquiring an 'immaculate heart' of his or her own. The conversion of Russia to Catholicism and the spreading of devotion to the one unique Immaculate Heart of Mary throughout the world are not even mentioned in the *TMF* commentary.

The only Fatima "authority" Cardinal Ratzinger cites is Father Edouard Dhanis, S.J., a modernist Jesuit who spent years casting doubt on the prophetic elements of the Message of Fatima concerning Russia. Father Dhanis claimed these elements of the Message were pious inventions of Sister Lucy. Father Dhanis refused to study the official Fatima archives or consult other unpublished documents made available to him in order not to have to withdraw his false thesis. In keeping with Father Dhanis' errors, which reduce Fatima to generic piety with no prophecy of future events, Cardinal Ratzinger's portion of the commentary concludes by asserting that all that remains of the Message of Fatima is prayer and penance.

> The decision of His Holiness Pope John Paul II to make public the third part of the "secret" of Fatima brings to an end a period of history marked by tragic human lust for power and evil,

The astounding statement by Monsignor Bertone, Cardinal Ratzinger's assistant, in the commentary (photographically reproduced [in part] in the box immediately above, from the Vatican's booklet *The Message of Fatima [TMF]*) shows how deeply into error and revisionism Msgr. Bertone and the rest of the anti-Fatima establishment have fallen. Msgr. Bertone says here, in effect, that Our Lady's promise of a period of peace was dependent on the revelation of the Third Secret, when, in fact, Our Lady said that a period of peace will be granted to the world **only when Russia has been consecrated to Her Immaculate Heart and thereby converted.** If one had not seen Msgr. Bertone's words in print, one would have doubted that any sensible Catholic theologian or Church official could have presented such a gross misrepresentation of the Message of Fatima. In view of the current state of the world, Msgr. Bertone's proclamation of the end of an era "marked by tragic human lust for power and evil" is so false, so obviously wrong that who in their right mind could ever believe it? What does he think we have today—an era of peace and tranquility?

Msgr. Bertone's portion of the commentary also claims that any further request for the Consecration of Russia "is without basis." He cites as his only evidence for this claim an alleged "letter from Sister Lucy" in 1989, addressed to an unidentified party. The "letter from Sister Lucy" demolishes itself by falsely stating that during his visit to Fatima in 1967 Pope Paul VI consecrated the whole world to the Immaculate Heart— an event which never occurred. Sister Lucy could not have made such a blunder since she attended the whole of Pope Paul VI's brief visit to Fatima.

Incredibly, the only person not to participate in the "revelation" of the Third Secret on June 26, 2000 was Sister Lucy herself. She was still not allowed to speak, even though the public was now being told that the Message of Fatima has been fully revealed and that nothing else remains hidden. Her crucial testimony concerning the Consecration of

Russia was not elicited, even though Cardinals Sodano and Ratzinger and Msgr. Bertone and other members of the Vatican apparatus were in Fatima only weeks before and could have spoken to her about the matter. The obviously discredited 1989 letter is the only evidence on which these Vatican officials expressly rely for their claim that the Consecration has been done. Curiously, Sister Lucy was not even asked to authenticate this letter.

At the conclusion of the June 26 press conference, Cardinal Ratzinger mentions Father Gruner by name, claiming that he must be submissive to "the Magisterium" concerning Fatima and the Consecration of Russia. *There is no claim, however, that the Pope himself has proclaimed the Consecration to be over and done with.* Pope John Paul II plays no role in the June 26 press conference or the Ratzinger/Bertone commentary, which is not a document of the Church's Magisterium (the authentic teaching office of the Pope or the Pope together with all the bishops in union with him) and therefore binds no one to believe what it claims. Even Cardinal Ratzinger himself admits that his and Msgr. Bertone's interpretation is not binding.

July 11/12, 2000 - Father Gruner continues to resist the groundless threat of excommunication from Cardinal Castrillón Hoyos, publishing his reply to the Cardinal. Father Gruner is the only priest being exposed to such a direct, public threat from a Vatican official. Yet, at the same time, the Vatican turns a blind eye toward innumerable priests who are spreading heresy and engaging in unspeakably scandalous behavior in every nation.

July 14, 2000 - Father Gruner learns that Cardinal Castrillón Hoyos is commanding various Nuncios of the world to continue to plague Father Gruner **with false accusations**. For example, the Nuncio to the Philippines circulates the lie that Father Gruner is guilty of forging Vatican Secretariat of State documents to imply Vatican endorsement of his apostolate—a manifest absurdity. These lies are refuted by the apostolate's published declaration. (See *Fatima Priest*.) Cardinal Castrillón Hoyos ignores Father Gruner's repeated requests that he retract the false allegation of forgery. Instead, Cardinal Castrillón Hoyos simply revises the accusation to alleged "inappropriate use" of *genuine* documents, refusing to admit that his original accusation was a lie. All of Cardinal Castrillón Hoyos' accusations are refuted in the apostolate's reply but he refuses to retract any and all of his false allegations.

July 15, 2000 - Issue 64 of *The Fatima Crusader* is published by Father Gruner. This issue demonstrates that the text of the Third Secret released on June 26 is incomplete. (See, especially, in this magazine the article by Andrew Cesanek about the existence of two texts. Copies are available in English, Italian, Portuguese, Spanish and French on the Fatima website, www.fatima.org. See also Chapter 13 of this book.)

August 8 - October 16, 2000 - Cardinal Castrillón Hoyos refuses to withdraw his threat of excommunication. In mid-October he says he is referring the matter to "higher authority." He refuses to identify this "higher authority," although it is clearly the Vatican Secretary of State.

August 31, 2000 - Father Gruner files with the Holy Father a second reminder concerning his canonical complaint and recourse to Pope John Paul II against Cardinals Innocenti, Sanchez and Agustoni, Archbishop Sepe, Archbishop Grochelewski and Bishop Forte, under Canon 1506. The grounds for the complaint are abuse of power and violation of canonical due process. The complaint notes that (unless and until the Pope promulgates a new law) the Pope is bound by the laws he has already promulgated to hear the case.

October 8, 2000 - Yet another consecration of the world, but not Russia, is performed in a Vatican ceremony. This ceremony is called an "entrustment." Although anti-Fatima propagandists say the Consecration of Russia is impossible, some 1,400 bishops and 76 Cardinals are gathered in the Vatican on this date and can easily mention Russia during the "entrustment." In fact, a number of bishops think this is exactly what they are going to do. The text of the entrustment is not made public until October 7, the day before the ceremony. The text makes no mention of Russia, but does mention an "entrustment" of the world, "the unemployed," "youth in search of meaning" and other objects of "entrustment"—anything and anybody but Russia.

November 30, 2000 - *Inside the Vatican* magazine reveals that a Cardinal described as "one of the Pope's closest advisors" admits that His Holiness has been counseled *not to make mention of Russia* in any consecration ceremony because this would offend the Russian Orthodox. That *Ostpolitik* and Vatican diplomacy have prevented the specific Consecration of Russia is here confirmed by a Vatican prelate.

December 20, 2000 - Father Gruner finishes writing a canonical complaint to His Holiness Pope John Paul II against Cardinal Castrillón Hoyos for crimes against Church law and formally requests, in due canonical form, the Cardinal's removal from office. Canons 1405, 1406 and 1452 §1 are invoked, under which the only competent judge in such cases is the Pope, and that the Pope is bound to decide the complaint.

May 16, 2001 - Reflecting the growing skepticism of millions of Catholics, Mother Angelica states on her live televison show on this date that she does not believe the Vatican has revealed the entirety of the Third Secret:

> As for the Secret, well *I happen to be one of those individuals who thinks we didn't get the whole thing*. I told ya! I mean, you have the right to your own opinion, don't you, Father? There, you know, that's my opinion. *Because I think it's scary*.

August 30, 2001 - The Fatima Center sends a letter to thousands of the press and world leaders containing the following warning in the light of the Fatima Message:

> There will come a day, sooner than you think, when bombs will

start exploding even in the "peaceful" parts of the world.

September 11, 2001 - Terrorists hijack two airliners and crash them into the twin towers of the World Trade Center in New York City, causing them to collapse. Another hijacked airliner crashes into the Pentagon. More than 3,000 people are killed in the bloodiest terrorist episode the world has ever seen. This act of war is definitive proof that the Consecration of Russia, which Our Lady promised will bring world peace, has not been done. Yet the anti-Fatima establishment insists that the Message of Fatima was gloriously fulfilled with the consecration of the world in 1984 and that the triumph of the Immaculate Heart of Mary is upon us.

September 12, 2001 - Revealing their bizarre obsession with Father Gruner and his Fatima apostolate, only *one day* after the worst terrorist attack in world history, Vatican officials cause the Vatican press office to publish a "Declaration" to the world alleging that Father Gruner has been "suspended" from the priesthood, and that no one should attend a Fatima-related *peace conference* being sponsored by the apostolate in Rome from October 7-13, 2001. The "Declaration" states that it has been issued upon "the mandate from a higher authority". The carefully inserted article in the phrase "*a* higher authority" clearly indicates that the "authority" in question is not the highest authority in the Church—namely, the Pope. The expression "a higher authority" is Vaticanspeak for the Secretary of State—at that time, Cardinal Sodano. In any case, under Church law a "mandate" by a nameless person is null and void.

The "Declaration" gives no grounds for the "suspension," there being no grounds beyond the bogus accusation that Father Gruner "failed" to find another bishop to incardinate him and must therefore "return" to Avellino after 23 years. This is the same "failure" which the Vatican bureaucracy had engineered through its unprecedented interference in offers of incardination by a series of friendly bishops over the years, all of whom wished to foster Father Gruner's work.

The Vatican announcement claims that the conference in Rome does not "enjoy the approval of ecclesiastical authority." The statement is evidently calculated to mislead, since these Vatican officials are well aware that no approval whatsoever is required under Church law (canons 212, 215, 278, 299), which guarantees the natural right of clergy and laity to associate and discuss matters of concern in the Church. Incredibly, Vatican officials have never taken such dramatic measures, or indeed any measures at all, to prevent innumerable conferences and other gatherings constantly being held throughout the Church by priests, nuns and lay people who openly dissent from Catholic doctrine. These same Vatican officials seem to view the Message of Fatima as the greatest threat to the Church today.

That the Vatican should step up its persecution of Father Gruner only hours after thousands of Americans were slaughtered in an unprecedented terrorist attack, demonstrates beyond doubt the utter perversity of the opposition to the Message of Fatima from within certain elements of the Vatican bureaucracy. Neither the spread of heresy nor innumerable sexual scandals among the clergy over the past forty years has ever prompted such action from these same Vatican elements, who are duty-bound to protect the Church from her real enemies. It is a mystery of iniquity that the prime imperative of these Vatican officials, even in the midst of worldwide bloodshed and apostasy, has become suppression of the Message of Fatima—the very means by which bloodshed and apostasy can be averted.

September 13, 2001 - The Fatima Center responds to the "Declaration" published by the Vatican Press Office, noting, among other things, that Father Gruner appears to be the only priest in the living memory of the Church who has been publicly denounced to the world for an "offense" that is not even specified, by "a higher authority" who is not even named.

September 21, 2001 - After receiving what she privately admitted was an "ecclesiastical telephone call" from someone in the Vatican bureaucracy, an agent of the Catholic University of the Sacred Heart in Rome sends a letter advising that the apostolate's contract for their facilities for the October 7-13, 2001 Conference on World Peace will not be kept—and that they refuse to keep their written contract. All this less than three weeks before the Conference begins, and after the apostolate has expended more than $100,000 on advertising and other arrangements. When pressed for an explanation for this breach of contract, the Catholic University of the Sacred Heart claims that it suddenly had to schedule a "structural inspection" of its facilities—during the very week the apostolate's conference is to be held!

September 28, 2001 - Father Gruner receives a letter directly from Bishop Dziwisz, the Pope's personal secretary, dated August 24, 2001, which is photographically reproduced along with the English translation on the following page. In the letter, Bishop Dziwisz warmly wishes Father Gruner well with his upcoming conference on Fatima and world peace in Rome and expresses his regrets that he could not attend the conference due to the Synod of Bishops taking place at the same time. Bishop Dziwisz has been Pope John Paul II's personal secretary for some 35 years, and is like a son to the Holy Father. Bishop Dziwisz's expression of support and good wishes to Father Gruner demonstrates that the worthless denunciation of Father Gruner published by "mandate of a higher authority" on September 12, 2001 could not have emanated from the papal household, leaving Cardinal Sodano as the only other "higher authority" who could have instigated the groundless denunciation.

October 25, 2001 - Cardinal Ratzinger admits to a "*destabilizing [of] the internal equilibrium of the Roman Curia*" due to reports (following the September 11th terrorist attack on New York) of a letter from Sister Lucy to the Pope concerning the Third Secret and dangers to the world and the person of the Pope. Ratzinger does not explicitly deny the existence of

Castel Gandolfo, 24 agosto 2001.

Reverendo Padre,

Con lettera in data 10 luglio scorso, mi ha rivolto l'invito a partecipare alla quinta Conferenza per la Pace nel Mondo, che sarà tenuta a Roma dal 7 al 13 ottobre scorso.

La ringrazio vivamente e fin d'ora auspico che quest'incontro su un tema tanto importante come la Pace nel Mondo, sia coronato da grande successo.

Non potrò essere presente alla manifestazione perché in quel periodo è in corso, qui in Vaticano, il Sinodo dei Vescovi.

Con cordiale saluto e con l'auspicio che il Signore, per intercessione di Nostra Signora di Fatima, doni a tutti ogni desiderato bene.

+ Stanislaw Dziwisz

Rev.do
Padre Nicolas GRUNER
Fatima Center
452 Kraft Rd
FORT ERIE ON L2A 4M7
Canadà

Castel Gandolfo, 24 August 2001

"Reverend Father,

"In your letter of last July 10 you have invited me to participate in the fifth Conference for World Peace which will take place in Rome from the 7th to the 13th of October.

"I thank you warmly and up to now I have hopes that this meeting dealing with such an important topic as World Peace will be crowned with great success.

"I will not be able to be present at the event because at that time the Synod of Bishops will be in progress here in the Vatican.

"With cordial greetings and the wish that the Lord, through the intercession of Our Lady of Fatima, grant to all every desired good."

Signed By   (Bishop) + Stanislaw Dziwisz

---

this letter. This admission indicates that widespread skepticism over the Vatican's Fatima disclosures apparently extends even into the Curia itself.

December 2001 - Father Gruner gives an interview with the editor of *The Fatima Crusader* in an article entitled "Don't Shoot the Messenger". It is summarized by the following statement: "God's law and the law of the Catholic Church (Canon Law) itself states clearly (see Canons 221, 1321, 1323) that no priest in the Catholic Church can be penalized with any ecclesiastical penalty whatsoever, if the priest has not committed a criminal act or transgression of Church Law or precept. Since no such crime or transgression has ever been committed by Father Gruner, it is absolutely clear and certain that Father Gruner is not suspended *a divinis*. Anyone, even a Cardinal, who says Father Gruner is suspended is either misinformed or malicious."

December 20, 2001 - In response to mounting public skepticism about the completeness of the Vatican's disclosure of the Third Secret, the Vatican apparatus suddenly publishes a secret "interview" of Sister Lucy, purportedly conducted by Archbishop Bertone more than a month earlier (November 17) at the convent at Coimbra. The "interview" consists of nothing more than Bertone's Italian language report of what Sister Lucy is supposed to have said in Portuguese. According to Bertone, Sister Lucy said that the consecration of the world in 1984 has been "accepted by heaven" (for what purpose she did not say), and that "everything has been published."

The "interview", which Bertone claims went on for two hours, contains *only 44 words* alleged to be from the mouth of Sister Lucy concerning the matters in controversy (the consecration of Russia and the Third Secret). No transcript or other independent record of the "interview" is provided, making it impossible to determine what exactly Sister Lucy was asked during the closeted two-hour interrogation, or the context of the 44 words she is alleged to have uttered during those unrecorded two hours. [The numerous suspicious circumstances of this secret "interview" are analyzed in the article entitled "Let Us Hear the Witness, for Heaven's Sake", by Christopher A. Ferrara, Esq. in Issue 70 (Spring 2002) of *The Fatima Crusader*. See also Chapter 11 of this book.]

January 2002 - Despite the Vatican's claim that the entire Third Secret has been released, Sister Lucy remained under orders not to speak in public about the Message of Fatima without permission from Cardinal Ratzinger or Pope John Paul II himself. And, as the world spirals downward into violence and the loss of God, the Consecration of Russia remains undone. The annihilation of nations hangs in the balance as the world prepares for war. When this book originally went to press in December 2002 and the threat of war loomed even greater, Sister Lucy was still bound to silence.

2005 - 2007

February 13, 2005 - Sister Lucy of Fatima dies at the age of 97.
April 2, 2005 - Pope John Paul II dies.
April 19, 2005 - The former Cardinal Ratzinger is elected to the papacy, taking the name of Benedict XVI.
June 5, 2005 (First Saturday) - Pope Benedict XVI states that the heart closest to Christ is the Immaculate Heart of Mary, reversing some of his remarks published in *TMF* on June 26, 2000.
June 22, 2006 - Benedict XVI appoints Cardinal (formerly Archbishop) Tarcisio Bertone to replace Cardinal Sodano as Vatican Secretary of State, with Bertone assuming the office on September 15, 2006.
July 18, 2006 - Archbishop Capovilla, personal secretary to Pope John

XXIII, admits to Solideo Paolini that there are two texts of the Third Secret, one yet to be published. Capovilla also informs Paolini that each text is contained in its own distinct envelope.

November 2006 - Antonio Socci, a renowned Catholic intellectual and commentator, acquaintance and collaborator of both the former Cardinal Ratzinger and Cardinal Bertone, publishes *The Fourth Secret of Fatima*. In his book Socci levels the accusation that the Vatican is hiding a text pertaining to the Third Secret which contains the words of the Virgin predicting an apocalyptic crisis of faith in the Church and dramatic events for humanity, and explaining the vision published in 2000. The Virgin's words, Socci further concludes, probably follow Her declaration, recorded in Sister Lucy's Fourth Memoir, that "In Portugal the dogma of faith will always be preserved etc."—the "etc" having been added by Lucy to reflect a continuing discourse pertaining to the contents of the Third Secret.

Pope Benedict sends Socci a note thanking him for the book "and the sentiments which motivated it." The book cites the testimony of Archbishop Loris F. Capovilla in July 2006, to Catholic scholar Solideo Paolini, that there are two different texts and two different envelopes pertaining to the Third Secret, that one of the envelopes and its contents—the "Capovilla envelope"—was kept in the papal apartment, not in the archives of the former Holy Office where the text of the vision was lodged, and that Paul VI read its contents on June 27, 1963, two years before the Bertone "official account" claims the Pope first read the text of the vision. The "Capovilla envelope" and text have never been produced.

May 10, 2007 - Cardinal Bertone publishes and attacks Socci in his own book, *The Last Visionary of Fatima*, written in the form of an interview by a fawning Vatican affairs reporter, Giuseppe De Carli, who poses no challenging questions but rather avoids all of the issues, including Capovilla's explosive testimony. In response, Socci proclaims publicly that his own book has been vindicated by the Cardinal's complete failure to answer it, which Socci calls a disturbing development as it means that there is indeed an ongoing cover-up on the part of the Vatican regarding the Third Secret.

May 31, 2007 - Cardinal Bertone appears by remote live feed on the Italian TV talk show *Porta a Porta* to attack Socci's book again. During this telecast Bertone displays not only the text of the vision but also two separate sealed envelopes prepared by Sister Lucy, each bearing the warning in Sister Lucy's own handwriting that "By express order of Our Lady, this envelope can only be opened in 1960 [only] by the Cardinal Patriarch of Lisbon or the Bishop of Leiria."

The two sealed envelopes, and other revelations by Cardinal Bertone during the telecast, further confirm the existence of two texts comprising the Third Secret in its entirety. Further, the "express order of Our Lady" noted on the envelopes flatly contradicts Cardinal Bertone's earlier repeated representations that Sister Lucy "confessed" to him in private, unrecorded conversations that the Virgin has never given any such order (see page 254).

Following the telecast, from which Socci has been excluded, Socci declares that Bertone has not only failed to "give even one answer" to Socci's book, but "On the contrary, he did more: He offered the proof that I am right" and "that it is a matter of fact the explosive part of the 'Third Secret of Fatima' exists yet is well hidden...."

September 21, 2007 - Bertone stages a second television appearance for himself, this time on the Telepace network, to attack Socci's book for a third time. The press are invited to attend. Socci, who appears at the telecast location to question Cardinal Bertone, is forcibly ejected from the premises by security guards. During the telecast Bertone once again avoids any discussion of the issues. Instead, he presents a heavily-edited videotape of an interview of Archbishop Capovilla conducted by Giuseppe De Carli, a partisan of Cardinal Bertone, in which the Archbishop not only fails to deny the testimony he gave to Paolini (whose name is never mentioned) about the "Capovilla envelope," but rather fully confirms its existence and location in the papal apartment, and the reading of its contents by Paul VI in 1963, not 1965 as the Bertone "official account" had claimed.

Contrary to what he said in 1960 (see entry on pages 344-345), Archbishop Capovilla will appear to suddenly reverse himself, claiming that since he never knew the Portuguese language he was incorrect for all these years to say that the Third Secret contained passages written in difficult Portuguese dialect. Of course his lack of Portuguese was always known and never stopped him before from telling the world something he obviously learned from the Portuguese translator of that text.

September 22, 2007 - The Italian newspaper *Il Giornale* reports that before the guards threw Socci out on the street at the location of the telecast of September 21, he was able to play for the assembled journalists an audiotape of Capovilla's statements to Paolini during a meeting on June 21, 2007. On the tape Capovilla is heard to state: "Besides the four pages [of the vision of the bishop dressed in white] there was also something else, an attachment, yes." As the reporter from *Il Giornale* concludes, Capovilla's statement "would confirm the thesis of the existence of a second sheet with the interpretation of the Secret"— namely, the words of the Virgin following the "etc."

September 2007 to December 2009 - The Holy See continues to observe an official silence concerning Socci's accusations.

See page xxvi to order extra copies of this
Chronology of the Fatima Cover-up.

Appendix III

Dear Cardinal Bertone:

Who Between ⇐ You and Me ⇒ is Deliberately Lying?

Cardinal Bertone

Antonio Socci

by Antonio Socci

On the 90th anniversary of the Fatima apparitions (May 13, 1917), the time has come to say the whole truth and to lend an ear to Our Lady...

What a mistake! Who knows why Cardinal Bertone got himself into such trouble, getting the Vatican into a mess too! Personally, I should be more than happy that the Secretary of State (hence number two in the Church's hierarchy) published a book, *The Last Seer of Fatima*, to refute mine, *The Fourth Secret of Fatima*. It is something unprecedented. Not even Dan Brown [Translator's Note: author of the blasphemous *The Da Vinci Code*] had such an honor!

Evidently, my book must be really hot. The prelate lost complete control of the situation because—with many salutations to Christian charity—he claims my theses are "pure fabrications", and states my inquiry would help "the ancient plots of Masonry to discredit the Church". And the Cardinal menacingly continues "It astonishes me that journalists and writers who claim to be Catholic lend themselves to this game". Eventually, he says that I'm a "liar", and "someone who consciously lies."

But unfortunately he doesn't show how and when I actually lied. I only asked him to explain—to give just one example—why in his commentary on the Third Secret published by the Vatican he quotes a letter by Sister Lucy, but (without saying it) he omits a decisive phrase which would debunk his entire interpretation. By reporting this "oddity" (one of the many) in my book, I tried to save the good faith of the prelate by any possible means. But in his book, Cardinal Bertone not only doesn't give any explanation for it, but he again quotes that "modified" letter in the same way. We're dumbstruck. It's simply not possible to use the documents that way! You are only scoring points against yourself!

The Core of the Dispute

But what is the core of our dispute? It resides in this question: the famous "Third Secret" of Fatima—which contains the prophecy regarding what is going to happen to the Church and to the world in the very near future—was it entirely published in 2000? When I started to conduct my inquiry, I was convinced that the Vatican had in fact published it all. But then I realized that the facts told me the contrary. As a matter of fairness, I had to take note of these facts, and decided to speak up and point out the incredible amount of "holes" and contradictions contained in the official version. Since the Third Secret is a mystery which for decades has caused a true psychosis within the mass media (and even within governments and the secret services), a prophetical text of the greatest importance for Christians (and for our future), a text which the Church gave credence to, after recognizing the most important Marian apparition of its [the Catholic Church's] history, I pointed out the necessity that the Vatican either clarify all the enormous "mess" ("pasticci") contained in the official version, or publish the hidden text (as a recent Petition to the Holy Father written by Solideo Paolini asks for). During my inquiry, I had asked for a personal meeting with Cardinal Bertone, who, as an Archbishop, had a leading role in the publication of the Secret on June 26, 2000. Even though he knows me well, he denied me an interview and yet [Translator's Note: after Socci published his book on November 22, 2006] he immediately activated himself to publish a book in reply to mine, which he accomplished during these past few days, in time for the 90th anniversary of Fatima.

No Straight Answers

The problem is that this book doesn't give even one single answer to the questions I raised. On the contrary it causes further problems. I felt totally embarrassed while reading such a messed-up and self-injuring response. For any author, being personally attacked by the Vatican Secretary of State without a scrap of evidence would be a notable success. But for me it is a disaster, because I consider myself first of all a Catholic before being a journalist. I would have preferred to be terribly wrong and to be confuted. Or I hoped that the Holy See would finally decide to reveal the entire truth about the Third Secret of Fatima, by publishing—as Our Lady requested— the still concealed part. Otherwise, I would have preferred to be ignored, snubbed, boycotted. But the only mistake, the only thing to avoid, is exactly what Bertone did: exposing himself publicly, without answering anything and, rather, adding new items which are disastrous for himself and for the Vatican.

What Are They Afraid Of?

First of all, there is the problem of the "handling" of the Fatima witness, Sister Lucy: for years, everybody has been able to openly talk about Fatima except her, who, since 1960, was ordered to keep silent by the Vatican. What were they afraid of? Before the publication of the text, in 2000, the Pope sends Bertone to Sister Lucy in Coimbra. He will send him again in November 2001. Eventually, the prelate will come back to her in December 2003. These three personal meetings were the great opportunity to allow the last living seer, almost 100 years old, to leave to Christendom and to the whole human race her complete and most precious testimony about the most important Marian apparition in history: It was an epochal opportunity.

Not only to silence the many rumors and legends but also to protect the Vatican from charges of manipulation, Bertone should have recorded (or even better, to have filmed) these exceptional interviews, so as to leave them to posterity. Or, at least, he should have arranged a complete transcription of the questions and answers, which the seer would sign in order to avoid any future and foreseeable contestations.

But, incredibly enough, these three interviews, which lasted "at least 10 hours"—as the prelate says—were not recorded, nor filmed, nor transcribed. Today the prelate explains that he "took notes". So, in the official documents of Fatima, only a few short phrases attributed to Sister Lucy are reported, phrases of uncertain credibility and not at all satisfactory, because he didn't ask her the decisive questions, the ones which could be used for clarifying any doubt—or at least they are not reported by Bertone. In my book, I've asked him: why out of 10 hours of interviews, do you report just a few phrases of the Sister, which at the maximum last 4 minutes? What else did she say during all those hours? Why didn't you ask Sister Lucy the fundamental questions, or why didn't you report her answers? In his book, Bertone does not give any clarification about all this. And the worst thing is that he attributes to the Sister—who died in the meantime and cannot deny anything—some phrases which were never reported in the official document of the year 2000.

According to Bertone, regarding the text of the year 2000 the Sister said that "this is the Third Secret", "the only text", and "I never wrote anything else". Why did Bertone never report such an important phrase in his official publication? And why didn't the prelate ask the seer if she ever wrote the sequel to those mysterious words pronounced by Our Lady and indicated by that "etc." ("In Portugal, the dogma of the faith will always be preserved, etc.") which has always been considered by the Fatima scholars as the beginning of the Third Secret? It is really odd. It's like the other new statement that now—and only now that the seer is already dead—the prelate attributes to her.

According to this new statement Sister Lucy, when informed of the attempt on the Pope's (John Paul II) life in 1981, "immediately thought that the prophecy of the Third Secret was fulfilled". Why on earth was such a crucial confirmation never reported in the official document? Why in the commentary by the Vatican which contained the text of the vision (with the "Bishop dressed in white who is killed"), did nobody—neither Sister Lucy, nor Cardinals Sodano and Ratzinger, not even Bertone himself—explicitly write that the attempt on the Pope's (John Paul II) life in 1981 was the fulfilment of the Third Secret?

No "Official" Interpretation

And why did Ratzinger say that such interpretation was just a mere hypothesis and there were no "official interpretations" by the Church, whereas today Bertone pretends to impose it as the official version? And in the letter to the Pope which was attached to the Vatican commentary and was written in 1982, one year after the assassination attempt, why did Sister Lucy explain that "we have not seen yet the final fulfilment of this prophecy" (of the Third Secret), but that "we are going there little by little with big steps"? Why, in that letter to the Pope, did not Sister Lucy even mention the attempt on the Pope's life that had just taken place if in fact that assassination attempt was the fulfilment of the Secret?

Some people had claimed that Bertone neither recorded nor transcribed the interviews with the seer because this would have shown the psychological pressures applied against the cloistered Sister, in order to persuade her to endorse certain theses. These thoughts came back to my mind while I was reading a passage of Bertone's book, in which the Cardinal remembers that at one point the seer was "irritated", and she told him "I'm not going to confession!".

What kind of question could Sister Lucy answer to so strongly? Maybe someone was reminding the old Sister of the ecclesiastical power, and hinting that she would "not get absolution"? We don't know, because the prelate—who knows and remembers the Sister's (quite tough) answer very well—says he literally "forgot" what his question was.

The Fourth Secret Exists

It is evident that the "Fourth Secret" of Fatima (the hidden part of the Third Secret) exists and I think I've proven it in my book. There is not only the resounding revelation of an exceptional witness, Archbishop Capovilla, secretary of Pope John XXIII (and who was present with the Pope at the opening of the Third Secret), whose words were gathered by Solideo Paolini and about which—incredibly—Cardinal Bertone doesn't say anything in his book. But there's also the rest of my book.[508] As regards that "censored" part, we know that it is written on a single sheet of paper, and not on four sheets like the text of the vision disclosed in 2000 (this fact was revealed by Cardinal Ottaviani, the right-hand man of Pope Pius XII and John XXIII, and today Bertone copes with it this way: "I don't know what Cardinal Ottaviani's words refer to"). But we even know the dimensions of that sheet of paper (9 x 14 cm), we know that it is contained in an envelope measuring 12 x 18 cm, we know that there are 20-25 lines of text, we know the dates (different from the text regarding the vision) on which the envelope was received in the Vatican and was read by the various Popes. And we know that—starting with Pius XII—it was not stored in the Holy Office (as the text of the vision revealed in 2000) but in the Pope's apartment. There is the photographic evidence, published on October 18, 1958 in the magazine *Paris-Match* by Robert Serrou; there is the testimony of the most confidential collaborator of Pius XII, Sister Pasqualina ("inside there, there is the Third Secret of Fatima"); and there is the testimony of Archbishop Capovilla (I published the document from the archive), who was sought out by Pope Paul VI on June 27, 1963, because the Pope wanted to know from him where the "Fatima package" was. Msgr. Capovilla answered: "It was in the drawer on the right hand side of the desk, named 'Barbarigo', in the bedroom." And, in

---

[508] Much of the facts and reasons given by Socci—to demonstrate there is a second text of the Third Secret—in the rest of this paragraph were first published in the first edition of *The Devil's Final Battle*.

fact, it was found there.

To all of these testimonies, Bertone gives not one answer in his book, but in an interview: (he says) "The cinematographic reconstructions of the envelope hidden in the night table of the Pope are pure fantasies". And why? He doesn't explain it. In his book he adds an attack on me, because I would have suggested that the Secret foresees the "apostasy of the Church of Rome", and of the upper hierarchy. First of all: Bertone should carefully read again what Jesus said to Sister Lucy in His apparition in August 1931. Furthermore, it's not me who talked about apostasy, but Cardinal Ottaviani and Cardinal Ciappi ("In the Third Secret, it is foretold, among the other things, that the great apostasy in the Church will begin *at the top*"). An analogous concept appears in Sister Lucy's words to Father Fuentes and in two statements by Cardinal Ratzinger. I only did my part as a journalist, explaining that many people interpret this apostasy in relationship to the effects of Vatican II.

Numerous Falsehoods

Of course I can't enumerate all the gaffes of this book because there isn't enough space here. But there is room to report some of them. Bertone informs us that "Sister Lucy never used a computer", for instance. It's a valuable piece of information, because in an interview to *Repubblica* dated February 17, 2005, he had declared that Lucy "used, in the end, even the computer". At the time, it had the purpose to give credence to certain letters by Sister Lucy dated 1989, which were not written in her own hand and which contradicted what she had previously declared about the "Consecration of Russia".

Curiously, in his book the Secretary of State gives credence even to the rumors that, during the historical visit to Pope Wojtyla on December 1, 1989, Gorbachev pronounced a "mea culpa" in front of the Pope, whereas this allegation was officially denied by the Vatican Press Office (*Sala Stampa*) on March 2, 1998. On the other hand, today Bertone holds out as absolutely authentic even the explosive statements about the Third Secret which were attributed to John Paul II in Fulda, in November 1980, whereas the Vatican Press Office and even Cardinal Ratzinger denied them ("this meeting in Fulda is false, it never happened and the Pope didn't say those things").

Furthermore, Bertone takes care to say that "the interpretation by Cardinal Ratzinger" of the Third Secret "was not a dogma of faith". But he lets his interviewer introduce Bertone's thought this way: "his words, after so many interpretations of the Message of Our Lady ..., are the imprimatur of a definitive version."

Absolutely superior to Ratzinger. Obviously, the letter of the Pope to the prelate is used in the book as an introduction, even if the Pope only writes about things in general. For my part, I keep for myself the letter regarding my book which Benedict XVI wrote thanking me for the "sentiments that inspired it". These words bring comfort to me, while I'm insulted by crude accusations of doing "the game of Masonry".

A Glossary of Ecclesiastical Terms, Organizations and Persons
Ecclesiastical Terms, Organizations

Anathema: A condemnation placed on anyone who rejects any dogma of the Catholic Faith, thereby expelling oneself from the Catholic Church.

Apostasy: Complete abandonment of the Catholic Faith.

Apostolate: An organized activity, lay or clerical, for promoting some aspect of the Catholic Faith.

Apostolic Nuncio: An ambassador of the Vatican State, attached to the Vatican Secretariat of State.

Apostolic See: The Holy See, consisting of the papal office and various immediate subordinates of the Pope in the Vatican, to whom certain tasks have been delegated.

Arianism: A Fourth Century heresy in which the dogma that Christ is consubstantial with God the Father was denied.

Canon: A law of the Catholic Church.

Canonical: Of or pertaining to the canons, or laws, of the Catholic Church.

Communion of Reparation: The worthy reception of Holy Communion with the intention of making reparation to God for sacrileges and offenses against Him and blasphemies against the Virgin Mary, as prescribed by the Virgin Mary in Her Fatima apparitions.

Conciliar: Of or pertaining to a general council of the Catholic Church, authorized by the Pope and attended by the bishops of the world, and, more recently, of or pertaining to the Second Vatican Council (1962-65).

Congregation for the Clergy: Office within the Roman Curia which oversees that the activities of diocesan or secular Catholic priests worldwide adhere to the faith and morals of the Catholic Church.

Congregation for the Doctrine of the Faith (CDF): Prior to the reorganization of the Roman Curia in 1967, this office (which oversaw all the other congregations within the Roman Curia) was known as the Holy Office, whose head was the Pope. Since 1967, the head of the CDF is a Cardinal Prefect and is of lesser rank than the Secretary of State.

Consecrate: In general, to set apart a thing or a person from a common and profane use to a sacred use, or to dedicate a specific person(s) or thing(s) to the service of God or of the Blessed Virgin Mary by prayers, rites and ceremonies.

Doctor of the Church: A Catholic saint considered so preeminent in his or her knowledge of the Faith as to be considered a worthy teacher for all Catholics and explicitly named a Doctor by decree of the Pope.

Dogma: Doctrine that has been infallibly defined by the Church; it is what Catholics must believe in order to be Catholic. The dogmas of the Faith are what is contained in the solemn, infallible definitions of the Magisterium—given by the Pope alone, or the Pope together with a Sacred Council.

Ecclesia Dei Commission: A Vatican commission established with the ostensible purpose of serving the needs of those "attached" to the traditional Latin Mass, and which is supposed to help carry out the wishes of Pope John Paul II, expressed in his letter *Ecclesia Dei*, that all Catholics who wish to worship at the traditional Mass be given access to it.

Excardinate: To officially detach a priest or deacon from the jurisdiction of his ordinary, such as the bishop. The Catholic Church has always maintained the principle that excardination cannot be denied to a priest or deacon who seeks incardination in another jurisdiction of the Church unless there exists a just reason.

Heresy: The denial or obstinate doubt of any one or more dogmas of the Catholic Faith.

Imprimatur: A seal or statement of approval by a bishop or other competent Church authority, certifying that a Catholic writing contains no errors against the faith or morals.

Incardinate: To officially attach a priest or deacon to a specific diocese of the Catholic Church or to a recognized religious community, making that priest or deacon subject to the lawful commands of the bishop of that diocese or the superior of that religious community.

Indult: A privilege or permission granted under Church law, as an exception from or relaxation of the law, given under specific conditions.

Latae sententiae: The Latin phrase referring to a penalty under Church law that operates automatically, without need of any further declaration by Church authority (e.g., the excommunication of any Catholic who materially assists in procuring an abortion).

Magisterium: From the Latin, *magister*, meaning "teacher". The teaching office of the Church, and especially the teaching office as exercised by the Pope alone, speaking in a way that clearly binds the Universal Church to believe in what he is pronouncing, or by the Pope together with all the Catholic bishops in an ecumenical council issuing such binding pronouncements.

Mary's *fiat*: The agreement of the Virgin Mary to be the Mother of God, which She expressed during the apparition of the Archangel Gabriel when She said: "Let it be done unto Me according to thy word."

Motu proprio: From the Latin, meaning "by his own act." Refers to papal letters issued over the Pope's personal signature and containing some specific advice or directive. This is to be distinguished from encyclicals, which have more general teaching purposes.

Ostpolitik: The policy propagated by the Vatican Secretary of State in 1962, and followed by all his successors, under which the Church has ceased all condemnation and opposition to Communist regimes in favor of "dialogue" and "quiet diplomacy".

Prefect: The head of a Vatican congregation.

Roman Curia: The central administration in the Vatican assisting in the governance of the Church, subject to the authority of the Pope.

Roman Pontiff: The Pope.

Sanctuary: That part of the church near the high altar, which is reserved to the clergy.

Schismatic: One who is cut off from communion with the Holy Catholic Church—e.g. members of the various Orthodox Churches which reject the papal primacy of jurisdiction over all bishops (i.e. the authority to command bishops and their subjects in their own dioceses).

Secretary of State: The Cardinal who presides over the Vatican Secretariat of State, which oversees the affairs of the Vatican State and all the congregations within the Roman Curia.

Useful Idiot: A person who promotes the agenda of a second party while denouncing anyone who questions it, not realizing that this agenda is also detrimental to himself as well. Lenin coined this term to describe all non-communists and even anti-communists who, through their being gullible and/or lacking diligence, actually advance the communist cause.

Persons

Alonso, C.M.F., Father Joaquin Maria: (R.I.P.) Commissioned by Bishop Joao Venancio in 1966 to establish a complete critical history of the revelations of Fatima, he spent the next 10 years studying the Fatima archives. In 1975 his monumental work, consisting of 24 volumes of about 800 pages each and including at least 5,396 original documents, was ready for publication. 22 volumes have been suppressed from publication ever since; the first two were published in heavily edited form in the 1990's. Died December 12, 1981.

Bertone, S.D.B., Cardinal Tarcisio: Born on December 2, 1934 in Romano Canavese, Italy; consecrated bishop on August 1, 1991; appointed as Secretary of the Congregation for the Doctrine of the Faith by Pope John Paul II in 1995. He was created Cardinal in October 2003, appointed as Secretary of State by Pope Benedict XVI and took the reins of this office in September 2006.

Bianchi, Father Luigi: Italian diocesan priest who claims to have met and interviewed Sister Lucy many times and talked about, among other things, the Third Secret at her cloistered Carmelite convent in Coimbra, Portugal. He met her as recently as October 2001.

Capovilla, Archbishop Loris Francesco: Born on October 14, 1915 in Pontelongo, Italy; served as personal secretary to Pope John XXIII; and was consecrated bishop on July 16, 1967.

Castrillón Hoyos, Cardinal Dario: Born on July 4, 1929 in Medellin, Colombia; consecrated bishop on July 18, 1971; appointed Prefect of the Congregation for the Clergy by authority of Pope John Paul II on October 1, 1996 (in October 2006 he retired from this position). He was created Cardinal on February 21, 1998. See entries in "Appendix II: A Chronology of the Fatima Cover-up" for June 5, July 11/12, July 14, August 8, October 16, and December 20, 2000 for further information on Cardinal Castrillón Hoyos.

Ciappi, O.P., Cardinal Mario Luigi: (R.I.P.) Born on October 6, 1909 in Florence, Italy; consecrated bishop on June 18, 1977; created Cardinal by Pope Paul VI on June 27, 1977; and died in 1996. Also served as papal theologian to Pius XII, John XXIII, Paul VI, John Paul I, and John Paul II.

da Silva, Bishop José Alves Correia: (R.I.P.) First Bishop of Leiria-Fatima; received envelope containing the Third Secret from Sister Lucy in 1944. Retained possession of the Third Secret until March 1957. Died in 1957.

do Amaral, Bishop Alberto Cosme: (R.I.P.) Born on October 12, 1916 in Touro, Portugal; consecrated bishop on August 23, 1964; appointed as the third Bishop of Leiria-Fatima on July 1, 1972; and retired on February 2, 1993.

Forte, O.F.M., Bishop Antonio: (R.I.P.) Born on July 9, 1928 in Polla, Italy; consecrated bishop on September 10, 1988; and appointed Bishop of Avellino on February 20, 1993.

Francisco Marto, Blessed: (R.I.P.) One of the three seers (1909 – 1919) of the Fatima apparitions, brother of Blessed Jacinta Marto, and cousin of Lucia dos Santos (Sister Lucy). Francisco was beatified on May 13, 2000.

François de Marie des Anges, Frère: Author of *Fatima: Intimate Joy, World Event*, a one-book summary of Frère Michel de la Sainte Trinité's 3-volume monumental work *The Whole Truth About Fatima*. In English Frère François' one volume is published as four small books.

Fuentes, Father Agustín: Was in 1957 the Vice Postulator of the Cause for the Beatification of Jacinta and Francisco. Interviewed Sister Lucy on December 26, 1957 in which she made many important statements which touched on the Third Secret. Published this interview in 1958 with an imprimatur of Archbishop Sanchez of Veracruz, Mexico and the approbation of the Bishop of Fatima.

Galamba de Oliviera, Canon José: (R.I.P.) Convinced Bishop da Silva in September 1943 to suggest to Sister Lucy that she write down the Third Secret. At that time Sister Lucy was stricken with pleurisy, and the Bishop of Fatima feared that Lucy would die without revealing the Secret.

Jacinta Marto, Blessed: (R.I.P.) The youngest of the three seers (1910 – 1920) of the Fatima apparitions, sister of Blessed Francisco Marto, and cousin of Lucia dos Santos (Sister Lucy). Jacinta was beatified on May 13, 2000.

Levada, Cardinal William: Born on June 15, 1936 in Long Beach, California; consecrated bishop on May 12, 1983; appointed as Prefect of the Congregation for the Doctrine of the Faith on May 13, 2005; and created Cardinal by Pope Benedict XVI on March 24, 2006.

Lucia dos Santos, O.C.D., Sister: (R.I.P.) The eldest of the three child seers of the Fatima apparitions in 1916 and 1917. Born March 28, 1907, Sister Lucy was a Carmelite nun at the cloistered convent in Coimbra, Portugal. She died at the age of almost 98 years old on February 13, 2005.

Magee, Bishop John: Born on September 24, 1936 in Newry, Ireland; consecrated bishop on March 17, 1987; and served as Secretary to Popes Paul VI, John Paul I and John Paul II.

Michel de la Sainte Trinité, Frère: Fatima expert and author of the monumental work *The Whole Truth About Fatima* (3 volumes, about 800 pages each). Volume III, focusing on the Third Secret, contains over 1,150 footnotes, citing numerous documents, witnesses and testimonies.

Oddi, Cardinal Silvio: (R.I.P.) Born on November 14, 1910 in the Diocese of Piazenza in Italy; consecrated bishop on September 27, 1953; created Cardinal by Pope Paul VI on April 28, 1969; appointed as Prefect of the Congregation for the Clergy by Pope John Paul II on September 28, 1979; retired in 1987; and died in 2001.

Ottaviani, Cardinal Alfredo: (R.I.P.) Prefect of the Holy Office during the pontificates of Popes Pius XII, John XXIII and Paul VI. On February 11, 1967 he testified during a press conference at the Pontifical Marian Academy in Rome that he had read the Third Secret and that it was written on a single sheet of paper. Also encouraged the publication of the *Neues Europa* version of the Third Secret and, together with Cardinal Bacci, wrote a Preface to *A Short and Critical Study of the New Order of Mass*, and presented it to Paul VI.

Pasquale, S.D.B., Father Umberto Maria: A well-known Salesian priest who knew Sister Lucy since 1939 and who received 157 letters from her, up to 1982. He interviewed Sister Lucy concerning the Consecration of Russia in 1978 and published the contents of that interview on May 12, 1982 in the *L'Osservatore Romano* in Vatican City.

Pierro, Bishop Gerardo: Born on April 26, 1935 in Mercato, San

Severino in Italy; consecrated bishop on August 2, 1981; and served as Bishop of Avellino from February 28, 1987 until May 25, 1992, when he was promoted to Archbishop of Salerno.

Ratzinger, Cardinal Joseph; now Pope Benedict XVI: Born on April 16, 1927 in the Diocese of Passau, the town of Marktl am Inn, Germany; consecrated bishop on May 28, 1977; created Cardinal by Pope Paul VI on June 27, 1977; and appointed as Prefect of the Congregation for the Doctrine of the Faith by Pope John Paul II on November 25, 1981. He held this position until April 2, 2005 when Pope John Paul II died. He was elected Pope (Benedict XVI) about two weeks later.

Schweigl, S.J., Father Joseph: Entrusted by Pope Pius XII with a secret mission in 1952 to interrogate Sister Lucy about the Third Secret.

Sodano, Cardinal Angelo: Born on November 23, 1927 in Isola d'Asti, Italy; consecrated bishop on January 15, 1978; appointed as Vatican Secretary of State on December 1, 1990; and created Cardinal by Pope John Paul II on June 28, 1991. Even though he was already beyond the normal retirement age of 75, he still held this position until September 2006. Sodano praised the arch-heretic Hans Küng on March 25, 1998; promoted the International Criminal Court (ICC); and hosted a press conference with Mikhail Gorbachev in the Vatican on June 27, 2000.

Valinho, S.D.B., Father Jose dos Santos: Sister Lucy's nephew.

Venancio, Bishop Joao Pereira: (R.I.P.) Born on February 8, 1904 in Monte Redondo, Portugal; consecrated bishop (and appointed Auxiliary Bishop of Leiria-Fatima) on December 8, 1954; appointed second Bishop of Leiria-Fatima on September 13, 1958; retired on July 1, 1972; and died in the mid-1980s. In March 1957, he held the envelope containing the Third Secret up to a strong light and carefully noted that the Secret is about 25 lines long and is written on a single sheet of paper with 3/4 centimeter margins on both sides.

Venezia, Bishop: (R.I.P.) Born on June 4, 1911; consecrated bishop on April 15, 1951; and served as Bishop of Avellino, Italy from June 1967 until February 28, 1987.

Selected Bibliography
Videos/DVDs

Heaven's Key to Peace. Fort Erie: The Fatima Center, 2006.

The Secret Still Silenced. Fort Erie: The Fatima Center, 2009.

Books

Alban, Francis (and Christopher Ferrara), *Fatima Priest*, Editions 1 through 4. Pound Ridge: Good Counsel Publications, 1997-2000. Italian Edition, *Il Sacerdote di Fatima*, Pound Ridge: Good Counsel Publications, 2000.

Alonso, Father Joaquin, *La verdad sobre el Secreto de Fatima*. Madrid: Centro Mariano, 1976.

Benedictine Sisters of Clyde, Missouri, *Saint Gertrude the Great*. Rockford: TAN Books and Publishers, Inc., 1979.

Bertone, Cardinal Tarcisio, *L'Ultima Veggente di Fatima*. Milan: Rai and Eri Rizzoli, 2007.

————, *The Last Secret of Fatima*. Milan: Rai and Eri Rizzoli, 2007.

Bougard, Bishop Emile, *The Life of Saint Margaret Mary Alacoque*. New York: Benzinger, 1890. (Republished by TAN, 1990).

Cahill, S.J., Rev. E., *Freemasonry and the Anti-Christian Movement*. Dublin: Gill, 1959.

Catholic Encyclopedia, New York: Encyclopedia Press, 1913.

Congregation for the Doctrine of the Faith, *The Message of Fatima* (English edition). Vatican City: Libreria Editrice Vaticana, 2000.

Council Daybook, Washington: National Catholic Welfare Conference.

Cozzens, Donald, *The Changing Face of the Catholic Priesthood*. Collegeville: Liturgical Press, 2001.

Davies, Michael, *Pope John's Council*. Kansas City: Angelus Press, 1992.

————, *Pope Paul's New Mass*, Kansas City: Angelus Press, 1980; second printing, 1988.

De Poncins, Vicomte Leon, *Freemasonry and the Vatican*. Palmdale: Christian Book Club, 1968.

Denzinger: The Sources of Catholic Dogma. Translated by Roy J. Deferrari. London: Herder, 1957.

De Marchi, I.M.C, Father John, *Fatima from the Beginning*. Fatima: Missoes Consolata, 1981, third edition. (First published in 1950).

Dillon, D.D., Msgr. George E., *Grand Orient Freemasonry Unmasked*. Palmdale: Christian Book Club. (Originally published by M. H. Gill in Dublin, 1885).

The "Divine Impatience". (Speeches from the 1992 Fatima Conference.) Buffalo: Immaculate Heart Publications, 2000.

Documents of Vatican II, edited by Walter M. Abbot, SJ. New York: American Press, 1966.

Fahey, C.S.Sp., Father Denis, *The Mystical Body of Christ in the Modern World*.

Dublin: Regina Publications, 1939.

Fellows, Mark, *Fatima in Twilight*. Niagara Falls, Ontario: Marmion Publications, 2003.

————, *Sister Lucia: Apostle of Mary's Immaculate Heart*. Buffalo: Immaculate Heart Publications, 2007.

Ferrara, Christopher A., *EWTN: A Network Gone Wrong*. Pound Ridge: Good Counsel Publications, 2006.

————, *The Secret Still Hidden*. Pound Ridge: Good Counsel Publications, 2008.

Fisher, Paul, *Their God is the Devil*. Washington: American Research Foundation, 1990.

François de Marie des Anges, (Frère) *Fatima: Intimate Joy World Event*, Book I, *Fatima: The Astonishing Truth*. Buffalo: Immaculate Heart Publications, 1993.

————, *Fatima: Intimate Joy World Event*, Book II, *Mary's Immaculate Heart and Your Salvation*. Buffalo: Immaculate Heart Publications, 1993.

————, *Fatima: Intimate Joy World Event*, Book III, *The Only Way to World Peace*. Buffalo: Immaculate Heart Publications, 1993.

————, *Fatima: Intimate Joy World Event*, Book IV, *Fatima: Tragedy and Triumph*. Buffalo: Immaculate Heart Publications, 1994.

Frère Michel, see Michel de la Sainte Trinité, (Frère).

Frère François, see François de Marie des Anges, (Frère).

Gamber, Msgr. Klaus, *The Reform of the Roman Liturgy*. Harrison: Foundation for Christian Reform, 1993.

God's Endorsement of Fatima. Fort Erie: The Fatima Center, 2001.

Goodier, SJ, Archbishop Alban, *The Public Life of Our Lord Jesus Christ*, Vol. I. London: Burns Oates and Washborne Ltd., 1932.

Graber, Bishop Rudolph, *Athanasius and the Church of Our Time*. Palmdale: Christian Book Club, 1974.

Gruner, Father Nicholas, *World Enslavement or Peace ... It's up to the Pope*. Fort Erie: The Fatima Crusader, 1988.

Guimarães, Atila Sinke, *Animus Delendi - I (The Desire to Destroy)*. Los Angeles: Tradition in Action, 2001.

————, *Animus Delendi - II (The Desire to Destroy)*. Los Angeles: Tradition in Action, 2002.

————, *In the Murky Waters of Vatican II*. Metairie: Maeta, 1997.

Haffert, John M., *Meet the Witnesses*. Fatima: AMI International Press, 1961.

Kelly, Msgr. George, *The Battle for the American Church*. Garden City: Image Books, 1981.

Kramer, Father Herman Bernard, *The Book of Destiny*. Rockford: TAN, 1975.

Kramer, Father Paul, *The Suicide of Altering the Faith in the Liturgy*. Terryville: The Missionary Association, 2006.

Le Roux, Father Daniel, *Peter Lovest Thou Me?*. (English Edition) Yarra Junction: Instauratio Press, 1989.

Lefebvre, Archbishop Marcel, *Open Letter to Confused Catholics*. Kansas City: Angelus Press, 1992.

———, *They Have Uncrowned Him*. Kansas City: Angelus Press, 1988.

Leo XIII, Encyclical *Humanum Genus*, 1884.

Lucia dos Santos, Sister, *Fatima in Lucia's Own Words*. Fatima: Postulation Centre, 1976.

———, *Memorias e Cartas da Irma Lucia*, edited by Father Antonio Maria Martins. Porto, Portugal: Missoes Consolata, 1973, 1976.

Manifold, Deirdre, *Fatima and the Great Conspiracy*. Galway, Ireland: Firinne Publications, Seventh Edition, 1992.

Miceli, SJ, Father Vincent, *The Antichrist*. Harrison: Roman Catholic Books, 1981.

Michel de la Sainte Trinité, (Frère) *The Secret of Fatima ... Revealed*. Buffalo: Immaculate Heart Publications, 1986.

———, *The Whole Truth About Fatima*, Volume I, *Science and the Facts*. Buffalo: Immaculate Heart Publications, 1989.

———, *The Whole Truth About Fatima*, Volume II, *The Secret and the Church*. Buffalo: Immaculate Heart Publications, 1990.

———, *The Whole Truth About Fatima*, Volume III, *The Third Secret*. Buffalo: Immaculate Heart Publications, 1990 and 2001.

Muller, C.SS.R., Father Michael, *The Catholic Dogma*. New York: Benzinger, 1888.

Newman, Cardinal John Henry, *On Consulting the Faithful in Matters of Doctrine*. Kansas City: Sheed and Ward, 1961.

Novos Documentos de Fatima. Sao Paulo: Loyola editions, 1984.

Our Lady's Urgent Appeal. Fort Erie: Fatima Center, 2006.

Pelletier, A.A., Father Joseph A., *The Sun Danced at Fatima*. New York: Doubleday, 1983.

Pius IX, Pope, Encyclical *Quanta Cura,* 1864.

Pius X, Pope, Encyclical *Pascendi Dominici Gregis*, 1907.

Pius XI, Pope, Encyclical *Ubi Arcano Dei*, 1922.

———, Encyclical *Quas Primas*, 1925.

———, Encyclical *Divini Redemptoris*, 1937.

Pius XII, Pope, Encyclical *Mystici Corporis*, 1943.

———, Encyclical *Humani Generis*, 1950.

The Popes Against Modern Errors, 16 Papal Encyclicals. Rockford: TAN, 1999.

Popian, Father Linus Dragu, *I 24 Giorni Della Fuga*. Udine: Edizioni Segno, 1998.

Ratzinger, Joseph, *Theological Highlights of Vatican II*. New York: Paulist Press, 1966.

———, *Principles of Catholic Theology*. San Francisco: Ignatius Press, 1987.

Roche, Msgr. Georges, *Pie XII Devant L'Histoire*. Paris: Editions Robert Laffont, 1972.

Sister Lucia, See Lucia dos Santos, Sister.

Socci, Antonio, *Il Quarto Segreto di Fatima* (Fourth Secret). Milan: Rizzoli, 2006.

————, *The Fourth Secret of Fatima*. Fitzwilliam: Loreto Publications, 2009.

Talantov, Boris, *Patriarchate and Sergianism*. Platina: St. Herman of Alaska Press, 1982.

Tosatti, Marco, *Il Segreto Non Svelato*. Casale Monferrato: Edizioni Piemme Spa, May 2002.

Tracy, David, Editor, (with Hans Küng and Johann Metz) *Vatican II, the Work that Needs to be Done*. New York: Seabury Press, 1978.

Trinchard, Father Paul, *The Awesome Fatima Consecrations*. Metairie: Maeta, 1992.

Vennari, John, *The Permanant Instruction of the Alta Vendita, A Blueprint for the Subversion of the Catholic Church*. Rockford: TAN, 1999.

Walsh, William Thomas, *Our Lady of Fatima*. New York: Doubleday, 1947.

Wiltgen, Father Ralph, *The Rhine Flows into the Tiber*. New York: Hawthorne, 1967. (TAN, 1985)

Wycislo, Most Reverend Aloysius, *Vatican II Revisited, Reflections by One Who Was There*. Staten Island: Alba House, 1987.

Articles

"A World View Based on Fatima", John Vennari, *The Fatima Crusader*, Issue 64, Summer 2000.

"Abuse Victims File Petition Seeking Removal of Archbishop", *The Wanderer*, April 4, 2002.

"Activist Says Child Porn Prosecutions Will be Difficult in Indonesia, Russia", Christine Brummitt, *Associated Press*, August 9, 2001.

"Analysis: Persons Who Have Studied the Apparitions Say That the Third Secret Could Concern the Destruction of the Faith. A Crisis in the Interior of the Church Would be the Third Secret", *Euronoticias*, March 24, 2000.

"The Apparitions of Our Lady of Fatima, 1917", Father Nicholas Gruner. (Transcript of speech from Fatima Conference in Rome, October 2001).

"The Apparitions of Pontevedra/Rianjo/Tuy: The Consecration of Russia and the Five First Saturdays", Father Nicholas Gruner. (Transcript of speech from Fatima Conference in Rome, October 2001).

"Are There Two Original Manuscripts on the Third Secret?", Andrew M. Cesanek, *The Fatima Crusader*, Issue 64, Summer 2000.

"As Scandal Keeps Growing, Church and Its Faithful Reel", *New York Times*, March 17, 2002.

"Barbarism Then and Now", Thomas Woods, Ph.D. (Transcript of speech from Fatima Conference in Rome, October 2001).

"The Beatification of the Little Shepherds Definitely Will Be at Rome", *Voz da Verdade*, October 31, 1999.

"The Blessed Mother and the Return to Holiness", Cornelia Ferreira. (Transcript of speech from Fatima Conference in Rome, October 2001).

"Big Brother Goes too far for Staid Russians", Mark Franchetti, *Sunday Times (London)*, November 25, 2001.

"Bishop of Leiria-Fatima, March 21 press conference"; *Euronoticias*, March 24, 2000.

"Cardinal Ratzinger's Third Secret", Rev. Canon Gregorius D. Hesse, S.T.D., J.C.D. (Cand.), *The Fatima Crusader*, Issue 66, Winter 2001.

"Catholic Church Unveils 'Third Secret of Fatima'; The Vatican's Top Theologian Gently Debunks a Nun's Account of Her 1917 Vision That Fueled Decades of Speculation", Richard Boudreaux, *Los Angeles Times*, June 27, 2000.

"Catholic Clergy in Siberia Face Growing Difficulties", *Catholic World News*, November 19, 1997.

"Catholicism Dissolved, the New Evangelization" (Four-part series), John Vennari, *Catholic Family News*, October 1998 to January 1999.

"Chronology of a Cover-up", Father Paul Kramer, *Catholic Family News* Special Supplement, April 2002. Also at www.fatima.org.

"Chronology of a Cover-up – Parts I, III and IV", Father Nicholas Gruner. (Transcripts of speeches from Fatima Conference in Rome, October 2001).

"Chronology of a Cover-up – Part II: The Vatican Commentary, 'The Message of Fatima'," Christopher Ferrara. (Transcript of speech from Fatima Conference in Rome, October 2001).

"The Consecration of Russia: Our Lady of Fatima vs. the Culture of Death", Father Nicholas Gruner. (Transcript of speech from Fatima Conference in Rome, October 2001).

"Crisis: The Bishop of Leiria-Fatima Creates A Mystery Around the Visit of the Pope Without Telling the Patriarch What It Concerns, Will the Pope Reveal the Third Secret?", *Euronoticias*, March 24, 2000.

"The Coming Cashless Society" (Parts I & II), John Vennari. (Transcript of speech from Fatima Conference in Rome, October 2001).

"Defense of Father Gruner: The Right to Hold the Conference", Christopher Ferrara. (Transcript of speech from Fatima Conference in Rome, October 2001).

"Divine Intervention", Coralie Graham, *The Fatima Crusader*, Issue 70, Spring 2002.

"Fatima in Twilight", Mark Fellows. Series run in *The Remnant*, 1995 and *Catholic Family News*, 1995.

"Fatima Inquest", David Boyce, *The Fatima Crusader*, Issue 35, Winter 1990-1991.

"Fatima Snapshot of Martyr's Past Century", *The Irish Times*, June 27, 2000.

"Fatima: Why Isn't the Mother of God Being Obeyed as She Should Be?", Father Fabrice Delestre, *Angelus*, June 2000.

"Father Pierre De Smet, SJ: Missionary Hero of the 19th Century", John Vennari. (Transcript of speech from Fatima Conference in Rome, October 2001).

"Final Secret of Vatican Published by Vatican", *Boston Herald*, June 27, 2000.

"Foreign Priests Spark Controversy", Sarah Karush, *Associated Press*, February 12, 2002.

"Fundamentalism and Integralism: Christians Confronting Ecumenism", Pierre Lathuiliere, *Service International de Documentation Judeo-Chretienne (SIDIC)*, Vol. XXXII, No. 3 - 1999, English Edition.

"Gorbachev Helps Introduce Casaroli Memoirs", *Catholic World News*, June 27, 2000.

"The Greatest Conspiracy", *Christian Order*, November 2000.

"Heaven's Request for Reparation to the Holy Face of Jesus" (Part III), John Vennari, *Catholic Family News*, August 2001.

"The International Criminal Court", William Jasper. (Transcript of speech from Fatima Conference in Rome, October 2001).

"It Doesn't Add Up", John Vennari, *Catholic Family News*, February 2002 and *The Fatima Crusader*, Issue 70, Spring 2002.

"Jeremiah & Jude vs. Juvenile Naivety", Gerry Matatics. (Transcript of speech from Fatima Conference in Rome, October 2001).

"Joint Catholic-Lutheran Vespers at Vatican", CWNews.com, November 13, 1999.

"June 26, 2000: Revelation of the Third Secret of Fatima or a Curtailed Revelation?", Father Fabrice Delestre, *SSPX Asia Newsletter*, July-August 2000.

"Let Us Hear the Witness, For Heaven's Sake", Christopher Ferrara, *The Fatima Crusader*, Issue 70, Spring 2002.

"Lucy and the Pirates", Mark Fellows, *Catholic Family News*, February 2002 and *The Fatima Crusader*, Issue 70, Spring 2002.

"The Lying Press Conference of June 26, 2000", Father Paul Kramer. (Transcript of speech from Fatima Conference in Rome, October 2001).

"The Magnificent Promise for the Five First Saturdays", Brother Michael of the Most Holy Trinity. *The Fatima Crusader*, Issue 49, Summer 1995.

"The Metz Pact", Atila Sinke Guimarães, *Catholic Family News*, September 2001.

"The Myth of a Converted Russia", Marian T. Horvat, Ph.D., *Catholic Family News*, March 2001.

"New Visa System Seen Choking Russia's Catholic Parishes", *Russia Reform Monitor*, No. 485, July 28, 1998.

"Non-Catholics Join Pope in Rite", *Los Angeles Times*, January 19, 2000.

"Now Is the Time: Consecrating Russia Will Help, Not Harm, Catholic-Orthodox Dialogue," Cathy Pearson, *Inside the Vatican*, August/September 2008; also in *The Fatima Crusader*, Issue 91, February 2009.

"Open Letter to the Vatican", Cardinal Kung Foundation, March 28, 2000.

"Our Lady, Conqueror of All Heresies: The Consecration of Portugal, 1931", John Vennari. (Transcript of speech from Fatima Conference in Rome, October 2001).

"Our Lady of Fatima vs. the Desire to Destroy our Catholic Heritage", John Vennari. (Transcript of speech, Fatima Rally Against Terrorism, New York, Nov. 2001).

"The 'Party Line' in Relation to Fatima", Father Paul Kramer, *The Fatima Crusader*, Issue 69, Winter 2002.

"Pope John Paul II Gives us the Key to the Real Third Secret", (Three-part series) Father Nicholas Gruner, *The Fatima Crusader*, Issues 67-69. Summer 2001, Autumn 2001, Winter 2002.

"The Pope Will Return to Portugal; Fatima is the Place of the Beatification", *Voz da Verdade*, December 5, 1999.

"Previous Attempts at the Consecration", Father Nicholas Gruner. (Transcript of speech from Fatima Conference in Rome, October 2001).

"The Prophecy of Bella Dodd", Christopher Ferrara, Fatima Perspectives (www. fatima.org).

"Russia Legalizes Homosexuality", *United Press International*, May 28, 1993.

"Satanism on the Rise in Russia!", John Vennari, Fatima News and Views (www. fatima.org).

"Satan's War Against Innocents", Michael Matt. (Transcript of speech, Fatima Rally Against Terrorism, New York, Nov. 2001).

"The Secret Red Plan to Take Over the Church", *The Fatima Crusader*, Issue 19, February-April 1986.

"The Stalinization of the Catholic Church", Christopher Ferrara. (Transcript of speech from Fatima Conference in Rome, October 2001).

"The Suicide of Altering the Faith in the Liturgy", Father Paul Kramer. (Transcript of speech from Fatima Conference in Rome, October 2001).

"The Tail of the Dragon", Gerry Matatics. (Transcript of speech from Fatima Conference in Rome, October 2001).

"There is No Such Thing as the 'Global Community'", Thomas Woods, Ph.D. (Transcript of speech from Fatima Conference in Rome, October 2001).

"The Third Secret", Father Nicholas Gruner (Transcript of speech from Fatima Conference in Rome, October 2001).

"The Third Secret Handwritten Text Essential: An Interview with Fr. Paul Kramer", Fatima News and Views (www.fatima.org).

"The Third Secret of Fatima: Has it been Revealed?", Father Gerard Mura, *Catholic*, March 2002.

"Third Secret Spurs More Questions; Fatima Interpretation Departs from Vision", Bill Broadway and Sarah Delancy, *The Washington Post*, July 1, 2000.

"This Present Darkness" (Four-part series), Mark Fellows, *Catholic Family News*, August-November 2000.

"Thomism and the New Theology", Father David Greenstock, *The Thomist*, 1950.

"The Threat of U.N. Globalization – Panel", Cornelia Ferreira, William Jasper, John Vennari. (Transcript from Fatima Conference in Rome, October 2001)

"To Whom Shall We Go? – Concerning an Appeal to Pope John Paul II", Father Nicholas Gruner, *The Fatima Crusader*, Issue 66, Winter 2001.

"The United Nations: Chief Instrument of Russia's Errors", Cornelia Ferreira. (Transcript of speech from Fatima Conference in Rome, October 2001).

"The United Nations Exposed", William Jasper. (Transcript of speech from Fatima Conference in Rome, October 2001).

"Update on the Perestroika Deception", Cornelia Ferreira. (Transcript of speech from Fatima Conference in Rome, October 2001).

"Vatican's Ostpolitik and Ecumenism Tried to Block My Conversion to Catholicism", Father Linus Dragu Popian. (Transcript of speech, Fatima Rally Against Terrorism, New York, Nov. 2001).

"Vatican Praises Purveyor of Heresy While it Hounds Apostle of Fatima", John

Vennari, *The Fatima Crusader*, Issue 57, Spring/Summer 1998.

"Vatican Secret is Out", *The Express*, June 27, 2000.

"Vatican II vs. the Unity Willed by Christ", John Vennari, *Catholic Family News*, December 2000.

"Vatican Unease as it Reveals the Full Third Secret of Fatima", *Financial Times (London)*, June 27, 2000.

"Vatican Says, You Must Not Become Catholic", John Vennari, *Catholic Family News*, December 2001 and *The Fatima Crusader*, Issue 69, Winter 2001.

"The Vatican-Moscow Agreement", Jean Madiran, *The Fatima Crusader*, Issue 16, September-October 1985.

"We are a Sign of Contradiction", interview with Bishop Bernard Fellay, SSPX, *Latin Mass Magazine*, Fall 2001.

"Where Have They Hidden the Body?", Christopher Ferrara, *The Remnant*, June 30, 2001.

"Where is the New Theology Taking Us?", Father Reginald Garrigou-Lagrange, O.P. First published in the *Angelicum*, 1946. English translation, *Catholic Family News*, August 1997.

"The Woman Clothed with the Sun: Fatima and Sacred Scripture", Gerry Matatics. (Transcript of speech from Fatima Conference in Rome, October 2001).

"World's Elite Gather to Talk Depopulation", John Henry Western, *The Interim*, April 1996.